Societies and Political Orders in Transition

This book series presents scientific and scholarly studies focusing on societies and political orders in transition, for example in Central and Eastern Europe but also elsewhere in the world. By comparing established societies, characterized by well-established market economies and well-functioning democracies, with post-socialist societies, often characterized by emerging markets and fragile political systems, the series identifies and analyzes factors influencing change and continuity in societies and political orders. These factors include state capacity to establish formal and informal rules, democratic institutions, forms of social structuration, political regimes, levels of corruption, specificity of political cultures, as well as types and orientation of political and economic elites.

This series welcomes monographs and edited volumes from a variety of disciplines and approaches, such as political and social sciences and economics, which are accessible to both academics and interested general readers.

Topics may include, but are not limited to, democratization, regime change, changing social norms, migration, etc.

More information about this series at http://www.springer.com/series/15626

Sergey Smirnov • Ataman Ozyildirim •
Paulo Picchetti
Editors

Business Cycles in BRICS

Springer

Editors
Sergey Smirnov
Higher School of Economics
National Research University
Moscow, Russia

Ataman Ozyildirim
The Conference Board Inc.
New York, NY, USA

Paulo Picchetti
Fundação Getulio Vargas, Brazil/IBRE/
São Paulo School of Economics
São Paulo, Brazil

ISSN 2511-2201 ISSN 2511-221X (electronic)
Societies and Political Orders in Transition
ISBN 978-3-030-07915-4 ISBN 978-3-319-90017-9 (eBook)
https://doi.org/10.1007/978-3-319-90017-9

This Springer imprint is published by the registered company Springer Nature Switzerland AG
The registered company address is: Gewerbestrasse 11, 6330 Cham, Switzerland

Foreword

At the latest after the outbreak of the Great Financial Crisis, the benefits of having reliable but especially timely data to analyse the current stand of the economy have generally been recognized. How else can policymakers react adequately to shocks or cyclical movements if they cannot analyse their magnitude and impact in statistical data first? Many official time series, e.g. those that are published as part of the System of National Accounts, are however published with a delay often not allowing politicians to introduce countervailing measures timely enough. For that reason, more and more countries around the world are nowadays publishing so-called business tendency surveys, qualitative survey results on firms that are released shortly after collection and thereby do deliver timely information on the state of the respective economy.

This volume centres on such surveys conducted in the so-called BRICS countries, while also looking into the measurement and forecasting of cyclical development using composite indicators. Whereas particularly in Europe there has been a long tradition in this field, for these swiftly emerging BRICS that has not yet been the case. This volume takes stock of what has been achieved so far and stimulates further developments in this field. It thereby helps closing the gaps across countries, including but not only restricted to these BRICS economies. I am sure that also researchers in other parts of the world will greatly benefit from the knowledge brought together in this volume.

At CIRET (Centre for International Research on Economic Tendency Surveys), the only truly global network of researchers and institutions interested in and working on or with surveys related to economic tendencies, we are therefore thrilled to see this volume emerge out of the conferences, workshops and meetings that we have organized over the years. This is an excellent example of what we hope to achieve with our networking activities: create a platform on research related to economic tendencies that allows experiences to be exchanged by participants all around the world and that results in further improvements in the creation and use of economic tendency surveys.

Congratulations to the editors on creating this milestone.

KOF Swiss Economic Institute, Zurich, Switzerland Jan-Egbert Sturm
CIRET, Zurich, Switzerland
March 2018

Preface

This volume is a collaborative effort of authors affiliated with prominent think tanks, universities and statistical offices from Brazil, Russia, India, China and South Africa—a group of countries with emerging economies collectively called BRICS. This group has recently attracted great attention because of their large and growing economic and political power both in their regions and globally. For now, BRICS is a new "centre of gravity" which aspires to compete with that of the post-WWII era composed of the group of large mature economies (the G-7).

The idea for this book first appeared during a number of meetings and workshops of the Center for International Research on Economic Tendency Surveys (CIRET), where the editors and many of the authors of the contained chapters first met and gained access to the very active research being done on business cycles and tendency surveys on the BRICS, among other countries. The initial aim of our project was quite narrow: to harmonize national business tendency surveys (BTSs) in the BRICS countries. But very soon it expanded to encompass the wider themes of business cycles being researched by its editors and authors: the interdependence of BRICS with and within the global economy, the measurement of business cycles (including the construction of composite cyclical indicators and the dating of turning points), their driving forces, the detection of early warning signals and the identification and forecasting of recessions in real time.

While the harmonization of national BTSs or systems of cyclical indicators remains an ongoing project, significant progress has been made in identifying and understanding the peculiarities of business cycles in BRICS as well as the possibilities and limitations of using various indicators for monitoring and forecasting fluctuations in national economic activity. The BRICS experience may prove useful for other emerging countries and countries in transition—potentially as useful as the extensive experience of the most developed countries (such as the USA and the largest European economies), which have different economic structures and more advanced national statistical systems.

We are grateful to National Research University Higher School of Economics (HSE); Instituto Brasileiro de Economia (IBRE) and São Paulo School of Economics

(EESP) at Fundação Getulio Vargas (FGV); and The Conference Board (TCB) for their continuous support during the preparation of this book. We would like to express our appreciation to the contributing authors for sharing their expertise. A special acknowledgement goes to our colleagues from the Center for International Research on Economic Tendency Surveys (CIRET) and among the CIRET membership. Over the course of several years, a significant part of the topics covered in this volume has been presented and discussed at CIRET conferences and workshops.

Moscow, Russia	Sergey Smirnov
New York, USA	Ataman Ozyildirim
São Paulo, Brazil	Paulo Picchetti

Contents

Introduction

Sergey Smirnov, Ataman Ozyildirim, and Paulo Picchetti

1 What Is a Business Cycle (in the BRICS)?

The most quoted definition of business cycles, which is invaluable for all empirical research, was provided by Arthur F. Burns and Wesley C. Mitchell 70 years ago:

> Business cycles are a type of fluctuation found in the aggregate economic activity of nations that organize their work mainly in business enterprises: a cycle consists of expansions occurring at about the same time in many economic activities, followed by similarly general recessions, contractions, and revivals which merge into the expansion phase of the next cycle; this sequence of changes is recurrent but not periodic; in duration business cycles vary from more than one year to ten or twelve years; they are not divisible into shorter cycles of similar character with amplitudes approximating their own. (Burns and Mitchell 1946: 3)

We believe this definition is also appropriate for many emerging economies, including the BRICS economies. When applying this definition to the BRICS, the main "theoretical" difficulty relates to the assumption that we are dealing with market economies in which the principal role is played by "business enterprises." Clearly, not all BRICS countries can be considered ideal open-market economies, either now or historically. Is it possible to apply the Burns-Mitchell definition to such economies? Theoretically, the answer is not clear. But pragmatically, the answer is clearly yes: medium-term fluctuations are inherent to *any* national economy, and it is

---

Support from the Basic Research Program of the National Research University Higher School of Economics is gratefully acknowledged by Sergey Smirnov.

S. Smirnov (✉)
National Research University Higher School of Economics, Moscow, Russia
e-mail: svsmirnov@hse.ru

A. Ozyildirim
The Conference Board Inc., New York, NY, USA

P. Picchetti
Fundação Getulio Vargas, Brazil/IBRE/São Paulo School of Economics, São Paulo, Brazil

S. Smirnov et al. (eds.), *Business Cycles in BRICS*, Societies and Political Orders in Transition, https://doi.org/10.1007/978-3-319-90017-9_1

appropriate to use all relevant empirical tools to study them. The practical experience that BRICS countries have accumulated, and the diversity of empirical applications, confirms this thesis.

When considering economies with long-running growth trends, the idea that business cycles consist of alternating sequences of expansions and contractions has been amended to state that a cycle consists of a sequence of positive and negative deviations from the trend. This approach, called the growth cycle approach, is usually attributed to Ilse Mintz, who wrote almost 50 years ago:

> The widened [introduced by Mintz—Eds.] concept requires only a minor amendment of the Burns and Mitchell definition of business cycles… The definition speaks of "expansions occurring at about the same time in many economic activities followed by similarly general ... contractions..." Here the words "adjusted for their long-run trends," have to be inserted. When long-run trends are horizontal, there will, of course, be no difference between the two versions of the concept. (Mintz 1969: 3)

The reason for Mintz's amendment is obvious. Her research was focused on the long postwar recovery in Germany (1950–1967), during which there were several periods of acceleration and deceleration in economic growth but no contraction. This was in stark contrast to the economic context of the American Great Depression, which saw a decline in GDP of 25% and in industrial production of 46%. The narrower definition proposed by Burns and Mitchell simply could not be applied to this new reality of sustained growth based on reconstruction and catching up. As Mintz argued that the speed of growth—not only its direction—was important, she proposed this modified definition, which was broadly accepted by the expert community, especially in Europe (in the USA, the Burns and Mitchell's vision of business cycles has remained more popular).

Since the 1970s, these two empirical concepts of economic cycles coexist: in the USA, The Conference Board (TCB) and the Economic Cycle Research Institute (ECRI) continue to follow the approach taken by the National Bureau of Economic Research (NBER) based on the work of Arthur F. Burns, Wesley C. Mitchell, Geoffrey H. Moore, and later by Julius Shiskin, Phillip A. Klein, and Victor Zarnowitz. By contrast, the Organisation for Economic Co-operation and Development (OECD) currently takes an approach that is closer to Ilse Mintz's definition (for details, see Ozyildirim 2017; Gyomai et al. 2017).

Sometimes, "business cycle" is also used as a catch-all term for any medium-term fluctuations in economic activity. However, it is important to agree on common definitions and notations because they have different implications for the meaning of economic recessions. In modern literature, economic fluctuations described by Burns and Mitchell's definition are usually termed "classical business cycles"; those described by Mintz's definition are named "growth cycles"; and fluctuations of growth rates (which are also a common subject of research, especially when applied to annual or year-on-year data) are named "acceleration cycles" or "growth rate cycles" (Mazzi and Ozyildirim 2017: 50–54). In the case of classical business cycles, recessions occur when the level of economic activity contracts. In contrast, in the case of growth cycles, recessions (or rather slowdowns) occur when the economy moves from its maximum distance above its long-term trend to its maximum distance below this trend.

A word of caution for the reader: in different BRICS countries, the term "business cycle" is understood in different ways. We have not attempted to harmonize the definitions in the book: each country has its own tradition regarding the definition of economic cycles. To harmonize these definitions would create an unreasonable break with the national traditions in favor of "formal" uniformity and could cause further confusion. However, we hope that it is always clear what the authors mean by the words "business cycle," "recession," etc. and that the readers will draw the correct inferences from the economic cycles under discussion.

2 Social and Political Ins and Outs of Economic Cyclicity

Whatever definition of "business cycle" is used, it is clear that economic fluctuations have social and political preconditions and social and political consequences. Although this generally holds true, these effects tend to be mitigated in relatively more mature economies, where the political system is well established, the division of authorities is commonly recognized, and the societal conditions are stable. Under these conditions, self-correcting economic mechanisms and institutions are designed to offset political influences, and this explains why the social and political aspects of business cycles are not the focus of research into American or European cycles.[1]

BRICS economies provide very different examples of the interaction between business cycles and social and political spheres. Here, political decisions (sometimes, it is proper to call them political shocks or even political cycles) have led to the relocation of industrial facilities, moved millions of people from towns to villages or vice versa, opened the national economy to the world or led to international sanctions and autarky, and encouraged or stifled the spirit of enterprise. In other words, in BRICS, it is not just the monetary and fiscal authorities that affect the organization and resource allocation in the economy. The political authorities also inordinately influence the economy and national business cycle through much more direct channels. On the other hand, in BRICS, economic and social troubles have sometimes changed political regimes and led to radical reforms. In this regard, emerging countries and countries in transition are more similar to the BRICS than the mature economies of the West. This should be kept in mind by any researcher of business cycles in emerging economies. In these cases, shocks to trend are often the primary source of economic fluctuations (Aguiar and Gopinath 2007).

[1]See Mazzi and Ozyildirim (2017: 56) for a short survey.

3 Cyclical Indicators in Emerging Countries: Using BRICS as a Template

The recently published *Handbook on Cyclical Composite Indicators* (European Union and the United Nations 2017) thoroughly considers all issues related to the construction and use of cyclical indicators. However, it is primarily based on the long tradition and best practices of the most developed countries. These principles and practices cannot be applied to emerging countries or countries in transition without significant simplification and modification. In some senses, the experience of the BRICS is more applicable to the "real world" of emerging economies than the sophisticated methodologies more applicable to the data in rich statistical environment of the mature economies.

Three distinctive features of national statistics in emerging economies or countries in transition should be mentioned here. They are as follows: (a) the relatively short monthly historical time series (business cycles are best analyzed using monthly data); (b) official seasonally adjusted indices are often lacking (seasonally adjusted data are needed to distinguish between cyclical and seasonal fluctuations); and (c) unexpected (for researchers accustomed to studying Western economies) systematic flaws in statistics which make difficult to construct continuous and comparable time series (e.g., in China, there is no official data on industrial production for the month of January; in Russia, month-on-month and year-on-year monthly growth rates are not strictly comparable at a regional level, etc.). The BRICS experience shows how these problems may be managed in a situation of incomplete and imperfect statistical information.[2]

4 Structure of the Book

Our book consists of five parts, which in most cases include "national" chapters devoted to one or several of the BRICS economies.

- Part I deals with the BRICS countries as a whole: their role in the global economy, internal coherence of the BRICS group, the connectedness of business cycles between BRICS and with other countries, etc.
- Part II contains a historical overview of economic cycles in each BRICS country and describes the driving forces of those cycles. The role of social and political shocks as a cause of fluctuations in economic activity (as well as the inverse relationship) is illustrated in these chapters. They are written by insiders in very different styles but are essential reading for anyone studying BRICS countries who believes that analyzing business cycles means investigating live economic

[2]For more on business cycle indicators in an environment of poor data availability, see Abberger and Nierhaus (2011).

processes, not pure academic research using sophisticated methods on static historical data.

- Part III describes Business Tendency Surveys (BTSs) in BRICS. Such surveys are an indispensable tool for macroeconomic monitoring and forecasting and in particular for predicting business cycles. In the BRICS countries, they differ in a number of important ways, such as periodicity, types of questions, and sampling schemes. These aspects are examined in detail in this volume, in most cases by experts who manage the national BTSs. This allows for their better understanding, comparison, and usage.
- Part IV is devoted to monitoring and forecasting business cycles with cyclical indicators. Procedures for dating cyclical turning points; criteria in selecting cyclical indicators and classifying them as leading, coincident, and lagging; and methods of aggregating components into a composite index—all these traditional issues are examined in the context of the specificities of the national economy and the peculiar national statistical system in each BRICS country. Several original instruments for monitoring and forecasting cycles are proposed.
- Finally, Part V consists of a single chapter, which examines how the experience of BRICS countries can be used for the analyses of business cycles in other emerging countries. These issues include the applicability of different business cycle definitions for a given national economy; the role of political and social factors as driving forces of economic cycles and vice versa; possible options for dating cyclical turning points; the quality of national BTSs and potential for their harmonization; possible approaches to combining the high international standards of business cycle analysis and insufficient national statistics; the role of expert judgments in forecasting business cycles, especially recessions; the role of National Statistical Offices (NSOs) and independent think tanks (TTs) in the production of leading, composite, and sentiment indicators.

References

Abberger K, Nierhaus W (2011) Construction of composite business cycle indicators in a sparse data environment. CESifo working paper series no 3557

Aguiar M, Gopinath G (2007) Emerging market business cycles: the cycle is the trend. J Polit Econ 115(1):69–102

Burns AF, Mitchell WC (1946) Measuring business cycles. NBER

European Union and the United Nations (2017) In: Mazzi GL, Ozyildirim A (eds) Handbook on cyclical composite indicators for business cycle analysis. Publications Office of the European Union, Luxembourg

Gyomai G, Ahmad N, Astolfi R (2017) The OECD system of composite leading indicators. In: Mazzi GL, Ozyildirim A (eds) Handbook on cyclical composite indicators for business cycle analysis. Publications Office of the European Union, Luxembourg, pp 273–291

Mazzi GL, Ozyildirim A (2017) Business cycles theories: an historical overview. In: Mazzi GL, Ozyildirim A (eds) Handbook on cyclical composite indicators for business cycle analysis. Publications Office of the European Union, Luxembourg, pp 27–71

Mintz I (1969) Dating postwar business cycles: methods and their application to Western Germany, 1950–67. Occasional paper 107. National Bureau of Economic Research, New York
Ozyildirim A (2017) Business cycle indicator approach at The Conference Board. In: Mazzi GL, Ozyildirim A (eds) Handbook on cyclical composite indicators for business cycle analysis. Publications Office of the European Union, Luxembourg, pp 225–240

Part I
The Global Economy and BRICS

BRICS in the Global Economy

Sergey V. Smirnov and Daria A. Avdeeva

1 Who Is BRICS?

It was Jim O'Neill at Goldman Sachs who first grouped Brazil, Russia, India and China together under the term BRICs (O'Neill 2001). This term recognised the dramatic growth of these emerging economies, in the expectation that they would not only increase their weight in the global economy but would take their place among the world's leading economies and would be able to compete and even outstrip the 'old world' global economic leaders—the G-7 countries. In October 2003, other Goldman Sachs employees continued this line of analysis, additionally stressing the potential significance of the African continent as a whole and South Africa—its largest economy—in particular (Wilson and Purushothaman 2003).

Five years after the acronym BRIC was coined, it ceased to be merely an analytical concept, as the member countries started to build political links between themselves. On 20 September 2006, in New York, during the 61st UN General Assembly, the first meeting of BRIC countries' foreign ministers took place. The first joint meeting of leaders of the four states took place on 9 July 2008 in Toyako Onsen (Japan) during the G-8 summit. The first full summit of BRIC countries took place in 2009, and they have been held annually since then.

In November 2010, at the G20 summit in South Korea, South African president Jacob Zuma announced that his country wished to join the BRICs club, and by the end of the year, South Africa had received an official invitation to the summit in Spring 2011. South Africa's inclusion in what was henceforth known as the BRICS

Support from the Basic Research Program of the National Research University Higher School of Economics is gratefully acknowledged.

S. V. Smirnov (✉) · D. A. Avdeeva
National Research University Higher School of Economics, Moscow, Russia
e-mail: svsmirnov@hse.ru

S. Smirnov et al. (eds.), *Business Cycles in BRICS*, Societies and Political Orders in Transition, https://doi.org/10.1007/978-3-319-90017-9_2

group was less related to ideas expounded by experts but was more a result of the political will and ambitions of the governments of all these five countries.[1]

That was essentially when the lengthy and gradual development of financial infrastructure within the BRICS framework began. In 2012, the idea of creating a joint bank was proposed, and it was approved a year later by the leaders of BRICS countries; a year after that, at the sixth summit in Fortaleza (Brazil), the Agreement on the New Development Bank (NDB) was signed, containing the legal groundwork for its operation. The following year it came into force, and the NDB has been operational since 2016, with its headquarter in Shanghai (China). In 2016, the Bank's Board of Directors approved a significant proportion of the principles and procedures governing its operation, as well as seven projects with a total value of about 1.56 billion USD, involving all five countries. In 2017, projects worth 2.5–3 billion USD were set to be endorsed.

In addition to the NDB, the financial architecture of BRICS includes a reserve currency pool to provide short-term support to the balance of payments. The overall capital of this pool amounts to 100 billion USD, comprising contributions ranging from 5 billion USD from South Africa to 41 billion USD from China. If needed, Brazil, India and Russia can ask the pool for a maximum of 18 billion USD; China, a maximum of 21 billion USD; and South Africa, 10 billion USD. The pool has been operational and able to carry out transactions since October 2016.

Over the past 15 years, we have seen that the BRICS group, which was initially chiefly of interest to experts and investors, has turned into an international 'club' with its own agenda, regular high-level meetings and its own financial infrastructure. It is likely that potential political and geopolitical benefits were one of the main motivations for member states to participate in the BRICS initiative. These included the opportunity to increase the countries' international profile and independence from external influence, without direct confrontation with the United States. At the same time, there were also expectations that the initiative would deliver economic benefits from the strengthening of trade partnerships, the expansion of export markets and the encouragement of investment. In addition, the BRICS format was intended to encourage the international community to accept the potential for parallel structures in the global financial architecture.[2] However, the formation of the BRICS group has been a gradual process and its scale remains modest. To date, member countries seem to prefer to retain a significant degree of autonomy in their actions.

Nonetheless, the BRICS countries should not only be considered independently but also as a group. Despite the diversity of economic models, economic structures and national characteristics and traditions, and although bilateral trade ties are not well developed, the BRICS group as a whole is a flagship for the developing world,

[1]Some analysts preferred not to include South Africa in the BRIC economic analysis, based on the relatively small scale of its economy (e.g. O'Neill 2012).

[2]For more detail on BRIC countries' motivation to participate in the group, see Vasiliev et al. (2015).

not only as it forms a kind of counterweight to the G-7 countries but also as an example of the wide range of alternatives for many developing countries that are looking for economic models to adopt.

2 BRICS in the Global Economy: Macro-indicators

The five BRICS countries (Brazil, Russia, India, China and South Africa) in 2016 accounted for 29.5% of the global landmass, 41.8% of the global population and 31.1% of world GDP by parity purchasing power (PPP). There are, of course, differences within the group. In terms of territory, the undoubted leader is Russia; it is almost double the size of China and Brazil, which alongside the United States and Canada are the top five largest countries in the world (see Fig. 1). However, even India, which is not a leading BRICS nation in this regard, is larger than the entire Eurozone, while South Africa is 2.2 times larger than France, the largest country in Western Europe.

While the territorial balance between the countries over the past decade was essentially stable, BRICS countries' share in the world population fell (see Fig. 2). From 1990 to 2016, it contracted from 44.3% to 41.8%. The main drivers of this were slowing population growth in China as a result of the 'one-child' policy (over this period its population grew by 243 million, but its share of global population fell by 3.0 percentage points) and population decline in Russia (an overall reduction of 4 million people, reducing its share by 0.9 percentage points). The only BRICS country boasting population growth that outstripped the world average is India, where the population increased by 454 million (1.5 times). As a result, its share of the global population grew by 1.3 percentage points; the populations of China and India are now almost equal (there are just 54 million more people in China). Combined, China and India accounted for 36.3% of the global population in 2016.

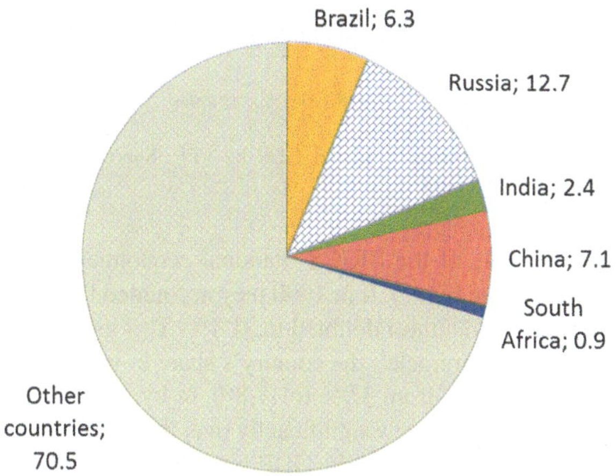

Fig. 1 BRICS share in global surface area, 2016. Source: World Development Indicators (WDI), author's calculations

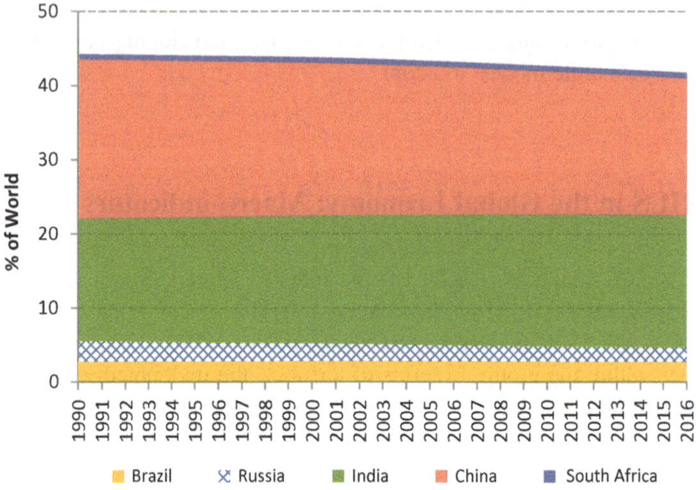

Fig. 2 BRICS share in global population. Source: World Development Indicators (WDI), author's calculations

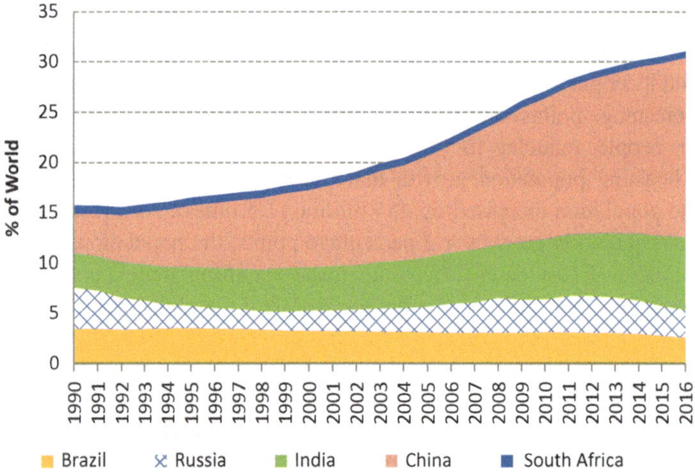

Fig. 3 BRICS share in global GDP by PPP. Source: World Development Indicators (WDI), author's calculations

The scale of the BRICS' national economies is also impressive and relatively dynamic (see Fig. 3). If in 1990 they accounted for 15.7% of world GDP by PPP, by 2016 this had almost doubled to 31.1%. This growth was overwhelmingly linked to the 'Chinese miracle': the country's share in world GDP by PPP rose by a factor of 4.6 in 26 years, from 3.9% to 17.8%, or by 13.9 percentage points. India's share in global GDP also grew significantly over these years: it more than doubled from 3.4% in 1990 to 7.2% of world GDP by PPP in 2016. Over this period, the remaining

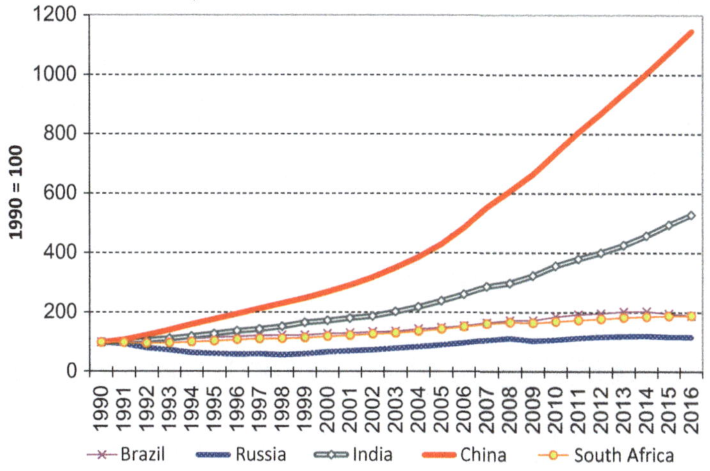

Fig. 4 GDP in comparable prices, indices 1990 = 100. Source: World Development Indicators (WDI), author's calculations

BRICS countries ceded ground somewhat for various reasons: Brazil, by 0.9 percentage points to 2.6%; Russia, by 1.3 percentage points to 2.8%; and South Africa, by 0.2 percentage points to 0.6%.

The most important, but not the only, factor driving growth in GDP by PPP is growth in GDP in comparable prices (see Fig. 4). China is the absolute leader by this indicator (increasing 11.5 times between 1990 and 2016), followed by India (5.3 times). The results of other BRICS countries are more modest: Brazil and South Africa rose 1.9 times and Russia by 17% over 26 years (here the main reason was the so-called transformational fall in 1990–1996; during the transition from a planned economy to a market economy, Russian real GDP fell by 40%).[3]

The rapid growth of Chinese and Indian economies over such a prolonged period is largely due to the low starting level in terms of economic development. In 1990, the average per capita GDP by PPP in these countries was about 1000 USD (in current values); both countries were in the second decile in terms of this indicator, i.e. they were among the poorest countries in the world. In Brazil, Russia and South Africa, the average per capita GDP by PPP was 6400–8000 USD, and they were in the seventh decile, i.e. they were wealthier countries. By 2016, average per capita GDP by PPP had significantly grown (see Fig. 5), especially in China (due to the rise in production volumes) and Russia (due to the combination of stable currency exchange rate and high inflation). China significantly improved its position in relation to other countries (moving from the second to the sixth decile), as did India (moving from the second to the third) and Russia (from the seventh to the

[3]If 1996 is taken as the starting point, then in the subsequent period Russian growth was actually slightly faster than that seen in Brazil and South Africa, but still two to three times slower than in India and China.

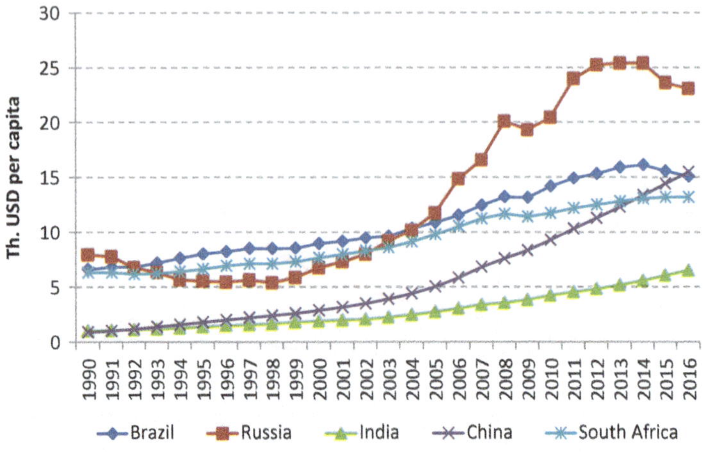

Fig. 5 Average per capita GDP by PPP, in current international USD. Source: World Development Indicators (WDI), author's calculations

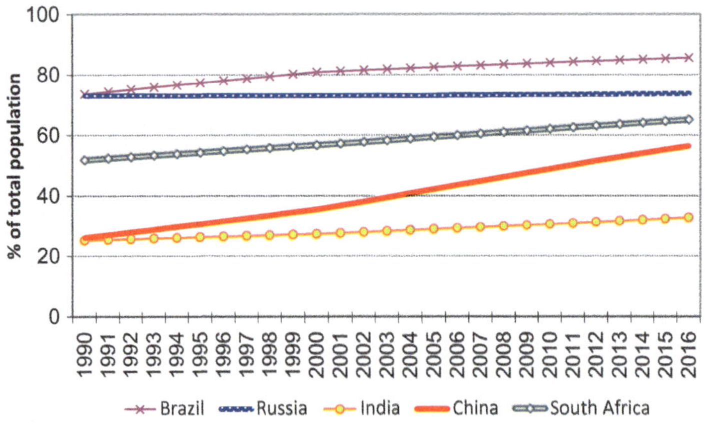

Fig. 6 Share of urban population in BRICS. Source: World Development Indicators (WDI), author's calculations

eighth). Brazil and South Africa, however, lost some ground—falling from the seventh to the sixth decile. While in 2016 per capita GDP by PPP in all the BRICS countries apart from Russia was lower than the world average, now all these countries excluding India have achieved a level of development such that the low starting point can no longer be relied on to boost growth rates.

Another factor that helped to facilitate the rapid growth in China over the preceding quarter century was intensive migration from the countryside to the cities (see Fig. 6). Urbanisation engaged people in a different type of production, one that delivered added value, and also created substantial consumer demand, leading to significant growth of the domestic consumer market. From 1990 to 2016, the urban population in China grew from 26.4% to 56.8%. The potential for the further urbanisation of China remains, but it is unlikely that this process will be as intensive as it has been. Today, encouraging the movement of the rural population to cities and involving it in the market economy is an important driver of growth only in India (the share of the urban population in India in 2016 was 33.1%).

3 The Role of BRICS in Global Goods Production

The position of the BRICS countries (and in particular China) in many markets is even more impressive than measured by macroeconomic indicators. For example, BRICS produce up to 49% of the world's usable iron ore and 67% of primary aluminium, of which 16% and 54%, respectively, are produced by China; 18% of the world's usable iron ore are produced by Brazil (see Fig. 7).

BRICS also plays a smaller but still very important role in the refined copper and gold markets (see Fig. 8). In 2015,[4] China produced 34.6% of the world's copper supply; followed by (among the BRICS countries) Russia, at 3.7%; and India, at 3.4%, while the others' share was significantly smaller. In terms of gold extraction, China also outperforms the other countries; its market share has been growing consistently and in 2016 amounted to 14.7% of global supply (in 1990 it was 4.6%). Russia's share was half of that (8.1%), about the same as in 1990 (it then fell to 4.6% after the crisis of 1998 but has now returned to its initial level). The South African gold mining crisis is also noteworthy: in 1990 South Africa accounted for 28% of the world's supply; in 2016, this had fallen to 4.5% (in physical terms the volume of South African gold production fell 4.3 times over these years).

BRICS' share of the oil and gas markets is also significant; here it is Russia, not China, that takes the lead (see Fig. 9). However, Russia's share in global gas production has contracted significantly: in 1990 it stood at 30%, but by 2016 it had almost halved to 16.3% (China's share grew from 0.8% to 3.9% over this period).

China does not have its own oil and gas reserves but compensates for this with intensive coal production (see Fig. 10). It accounted for 45.7% of coal produced worldwide in 2016 (in 1990 this was 22.6%, which is also a sizable share). The remaining BRICS countries' share in global coal production amounted to 17.9% in 2016, virtually unchanged from 1990.

BRICS' share of global cereal production fluctuates around a more or less constant level of about 38% of the world's harvest (see Fig. 10).[5] The share of all countries apart from India in cereal production is 1–3 percentage points higher than their share of global population. Only India has a share of global cereal production

[4]Data for 2016 are still unavailable.

[5]Data for 2015–2016 are still unavailable.

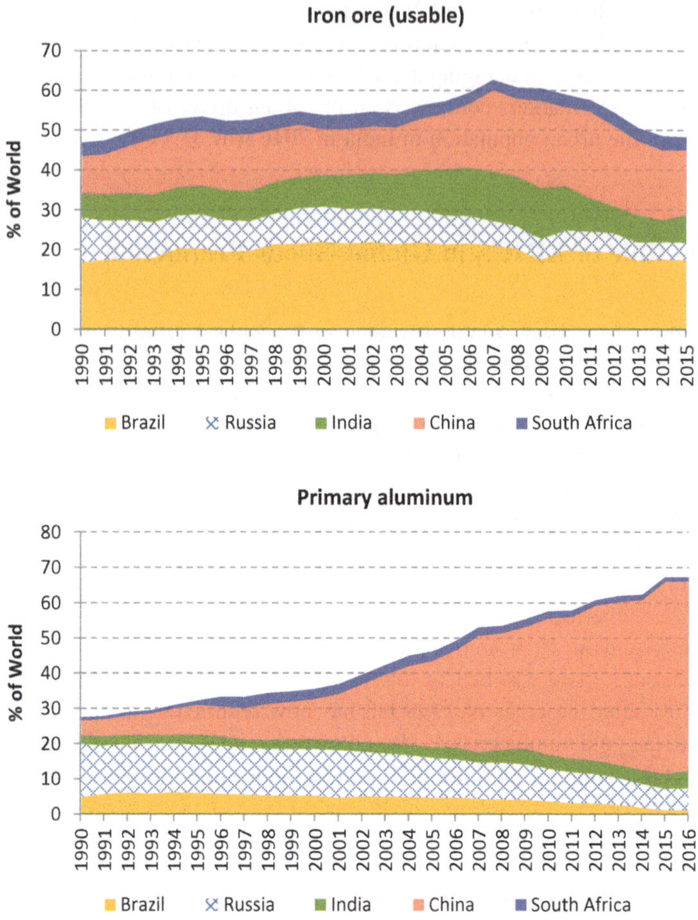

Fig. 7 BRICS share in the production of usable iron ore and primary aluminium. Source: US Geological Survey, author's calculations

that is significantly lower than its share of the world population (10–11% and 17–18%, respectively).

BRICS countries play a key role not only on the global resource market but also in the production of industrial goods, including technologically complex ones. In 2016, BRICS countries accounted for 43.5% of global production of passenger cars; 33.9% were produced in China—which back in 1997 (the first year for which the data is available) accounted for just 1.3% (see Fig. 11). BRICS also plays an important role in commercial automobile production, although a much less significant one than for passenger cars. Until 2009, BRICS' share of the commercial and passenger car market had been growing at similar rates, but in 2010 commercial automobile production in the United States (and therefore, in the world) grew

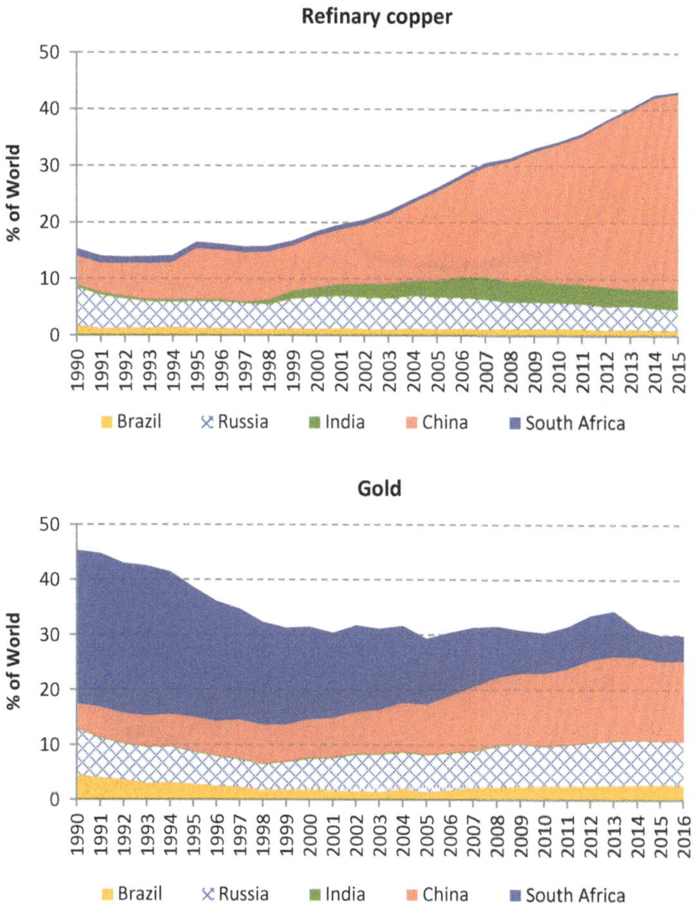

Fig. 8 BRICS share in the production of refined copper and gold. Source: US Geological Survey, Indian Bureau of Mines, author's calculations

significantly, and from 2011 a contraction started in China. In 2016, BRICS produced 23.3% of commercial automobiles, with 16.2% of that produced in China.

BRICS role in the production of other important goods and services is also significant. For example, in 2016 the BRICS as a whole produced 67% of the world's hydraulic cement (indicative of high activity in the construction sector); and in 2013 BRICS' production hit a peak of 70% (see Fig. 12). The production of hydraulic cement is largely concentrated in China. In 2016, it accounted for 57.4% of global production (in 2013–2014 this figure stood at 59%). Global construction is largely concentrated in China.

The number of Internet users provides an indication of how receptive a country is to the latest advances in the IT sector. In all BRICS countries apart from India, the share of the world Internet users exceeds these countries' share of global population.

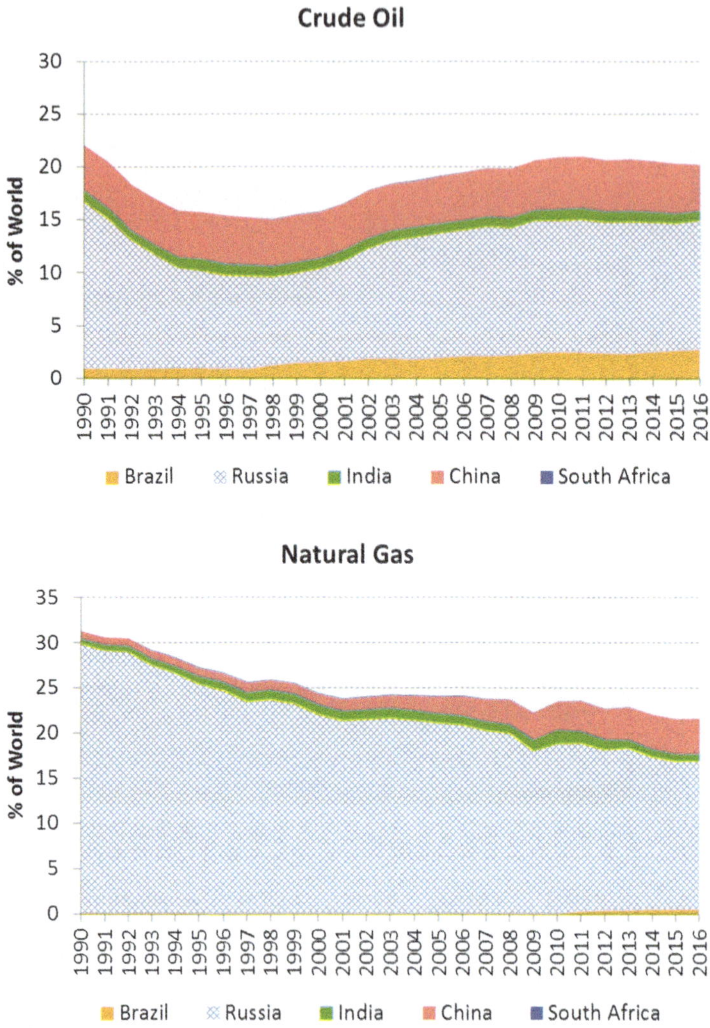

Fig. 9 BRICS share in oil and natural gas production. Source: BP Statistical Review of World Energy (June 2017), author's calculations

Russia is the most 'advanced' in this regard: on average, 76% of people use the Internet (the same level as in the United States). In Brazil, China and South Africa, 50–60% of people use the Internet. In India the figure is just 30%, indicating that India lags significantly behind the other countries on this index (taking into account its overwhelmingly rural population, this is not a surprise).

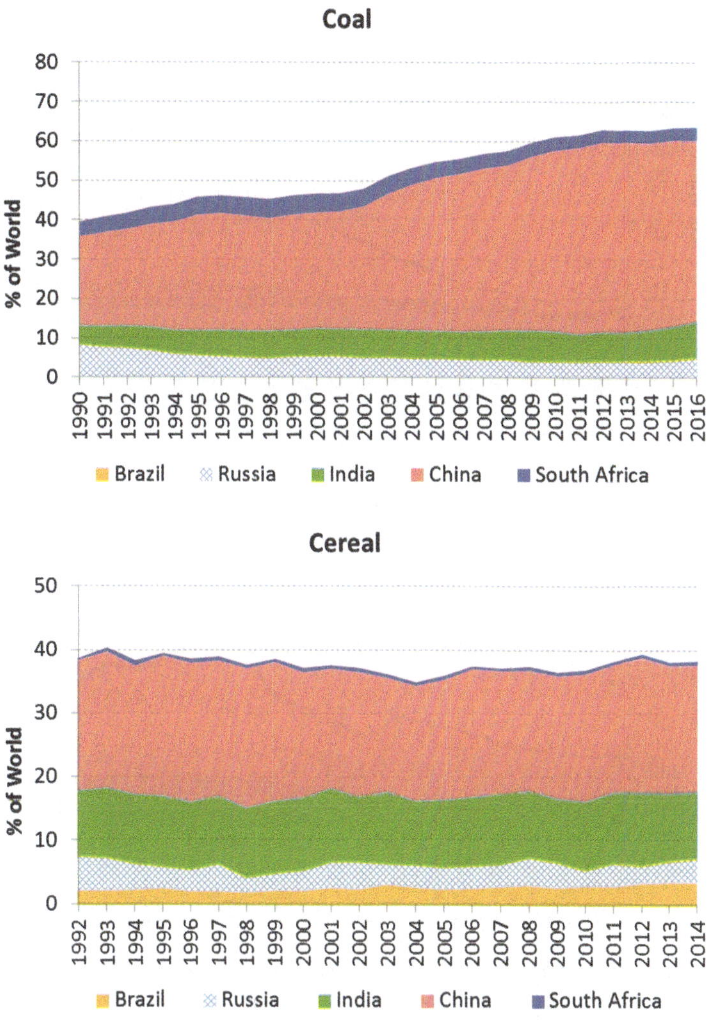

Fig. 10 BRICS share in coal and grain production. Source: BP Statistical Review of World Energy (June 2017), World Development Indicators (WDI), author's calculations

4 BRICS in Global Commodities and Capital Markets

BRICS countries are not only leaders in the production of a variety of key goods but also play a vital (while more modest) role in world trade.[6] In 2016, they accounted for 18.1% (19.0% in 2015) of global merchandise exports and 14.6% (15.2% in 2015) of global imports—with China (13.1% and 9.8%, respectively) playing the

[6]For more detail, see Evenett (2015), Keeler (2012) and Purugganan et al. (2014).

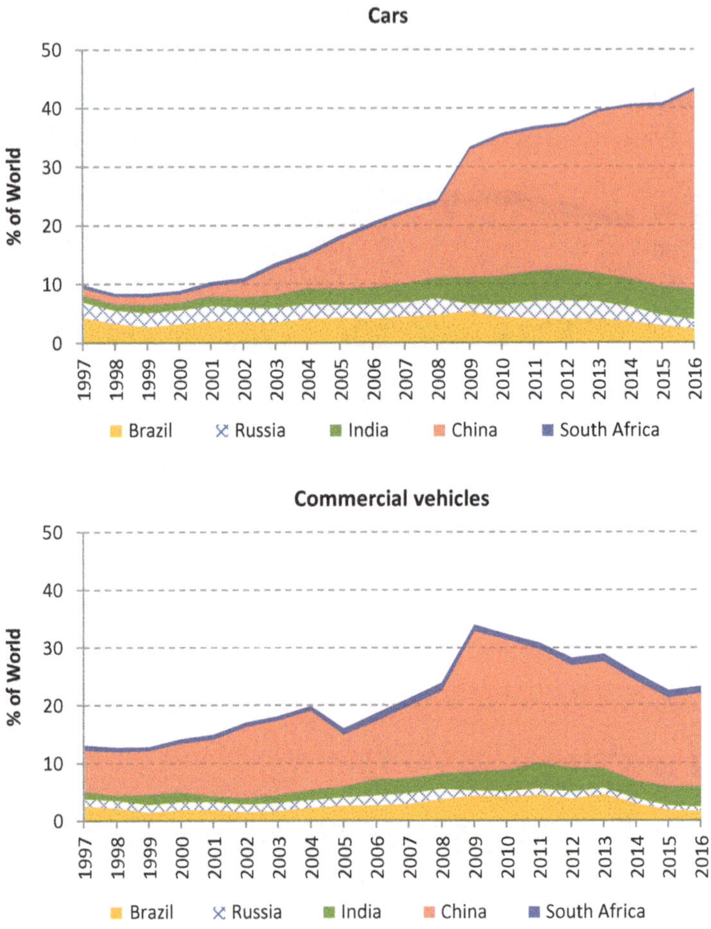

Fig. 11 BRICS share in the production of cars and commercial vehicles. Source: Organisation Internationale des Constructeurs d'Automobiles (OICA), author's calculations

key role in each (see Figs. 13 and 14). China's trade surplus is almost equivalent to the trade surplus of the BRICS as a whole; for Brazil and South Africa, this indicator is close to zero. Russia has a significant positive trade surplus, while India has a significant negative one. At a BRICS-wide level, they balance each other out.

The expansion in Chinese exports deserves particular attention. In 1990, its share in global exports was just 1.8%, less than that of Russia in the same year (2.3%). However, over the past 26 years, China's share grew 7.3 times, while India's share grew 3.2 times, Brazil's 1.3 times and Russia's and South Africa's shares contracted by 24% and 31%, respectively. China's exports grew particularly rapidly from 2000; in 2007, it exceeded US exports (the Eurozone still remains the world's largest exporter, exporting twice as much as China). China even expanded its share in global exports in 2015, when the share of other BRICS countries fell because of falling

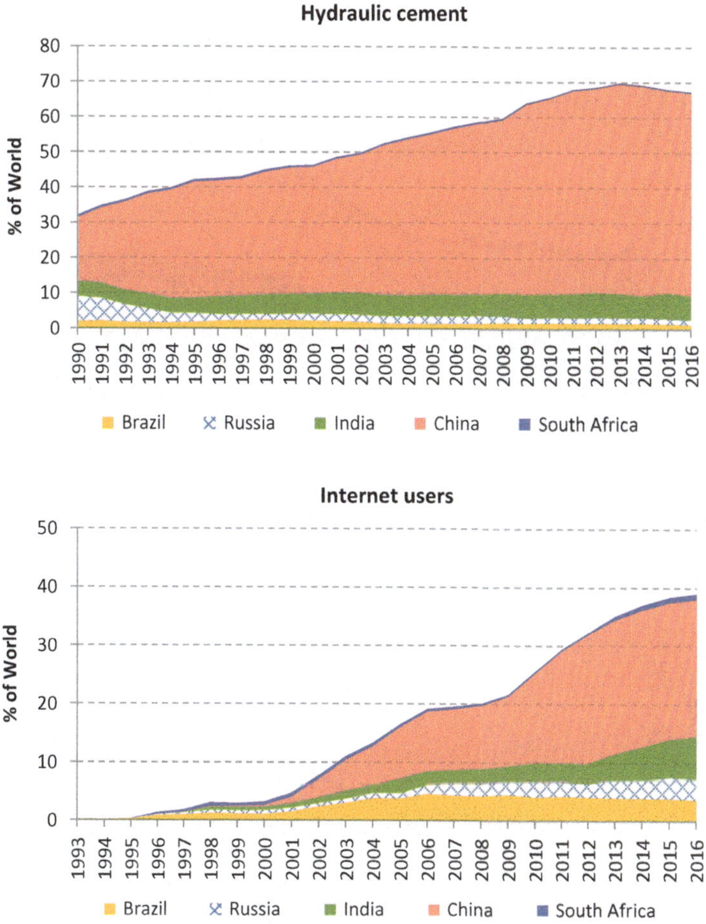

Fig. 12 BRICS share in the production of cement and the number of Internet users. Source: US Geological Survey, World Development Indicators (WDI), author's calculations

prices for oil and other resources and the appreciation of the US dollar in relation to most national currencies (as a result of which, the same physical volume delivered a smaller value in USD).

The BRICS' share in global merchandise imports has been falling since 2013. In 2014–2016, it contracted by 1.8 percentage points (see Fig. 14). The most significant contraction took place in Russia (by 0.6 percentage points). This was a result of a number of factors: reduced domestic demand during the recession, reduced foreign currency inflows due to falling oil prices (hence reduced resources for acquiring imported goods), the devaluation of the Russian rouble and the sanctions and counter-sanctions introduced between Russia and other countries. The total share of all remaining BRICS countries fell 1.2 percentage points, of which 0.9 percentage points are accounted for by China and Brazil.

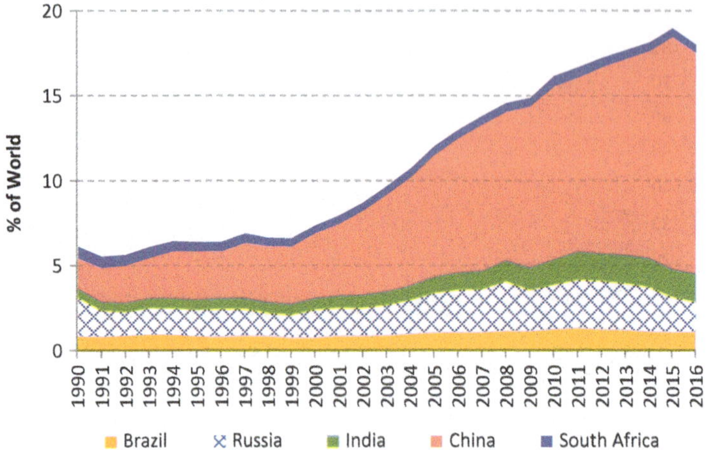

Fig. 13 BRICS share in merchandise exports. Source: World Development Indicators (WDI), author's calculations

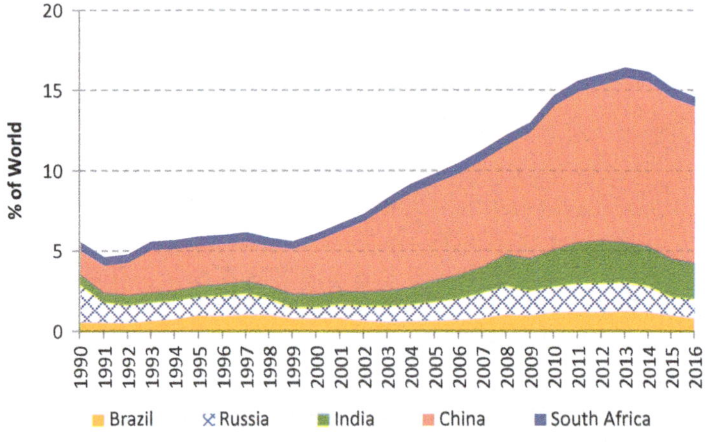

Fig. 14 BRICS share in merchandise imports. Source: World Development Indicators (WDI), author's calculations

Chinese imports fell the most over the 2014–2016 period (down by 362 billion USD), followed by Russian imports (150 billion USD); imports of other BRICS countries declined by 247 billion USD (in total). Due to reduced demand from BRICS, global imports fell by 4.0%. The overall fall in 2014–2016 was 14.7%; one may conclude that during 2014–2016 the BRICS had a de-stimulating impact on the global economy, with China and then Russia delivering the greatest negative contribution.

BRICS countries are not only important participants in global merchandise trade, they account for significant volumes of foreign direct investment (FDI) (see Fig. 15).

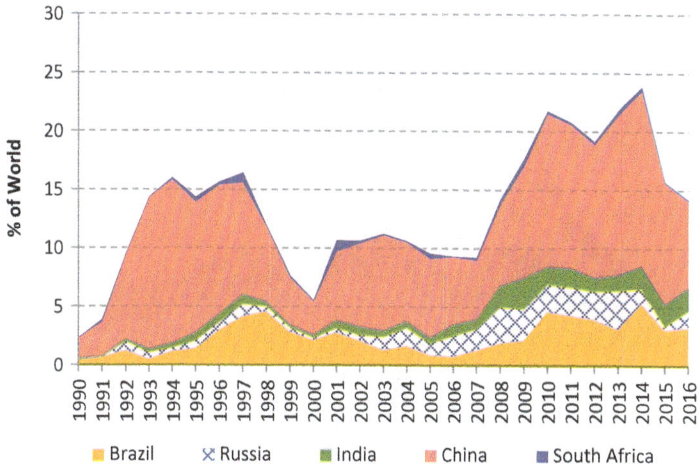

Fig. 15 BRICS share in global FDI inflow. Source: World Development Indicators (WDI), author's calculations

The main recipients of FDI are mature economies (chiefly the Eurozone and the United States), but the BRICS countries are clear leaders among developing economies.[7] China is quite a long way ahead of the others, as 2.7 trillion USD of FDI was invested over 2001–2016 (about 9% of total global volume). Brazil comes in second at 826 billion USD, followed by Russia at 529 billion and India at 390 billion. India is clearly not yet very involved in the process of attracting FDI (for an economy of that size the investment level is small), while in Russia the inflow of FDI was significant from the second half of the 2000s to 2013 (about 53 billion USD per year). The reduction in the trade balance due to falling oil prices and sanctions meant that the inflow of FDI into Russia has all but dried up (it dwindled to 6.9 billion USD in 2015 and partially recovered to 32.5 billion USD in 2016). South Africa only attracts several billion USD in FDI per year; from 2001 to 2016, it attracted a total of 72 billion USD—or on average 4.5 billion per annum.

The relative appeal of BRICS countries to international investors is also indicated by the market capitalisation of companies (see Fig. 16). Here again, China is the undisputed leader. In 2005, its share in global company market capitalisation (1.0%) was lower than that of Brazil, India and South Africa (1.2–1.3%) and only a little bit higher than that of Russia (0.8%). However, 2 years later, at the beginning of the global financial crisis, China's share had grown to 7.3%, which meant that China's stock market was one of the world leaders in the second tier (the United States' share of the global stock market at that point was 32%; the EU, 16%; and Japan, 7%). China's position didn't change much in the following 6 years, but in 2015 it expanded to 13%, while the US share was 41% (during times of heightened

[7]For more details, see Collins (2013), EDIP Research Team (2013), Fratzscher (2011), Holtbrugge and Kreppel (2012), Labes (2015) and Vijayakumar et al. (2010).

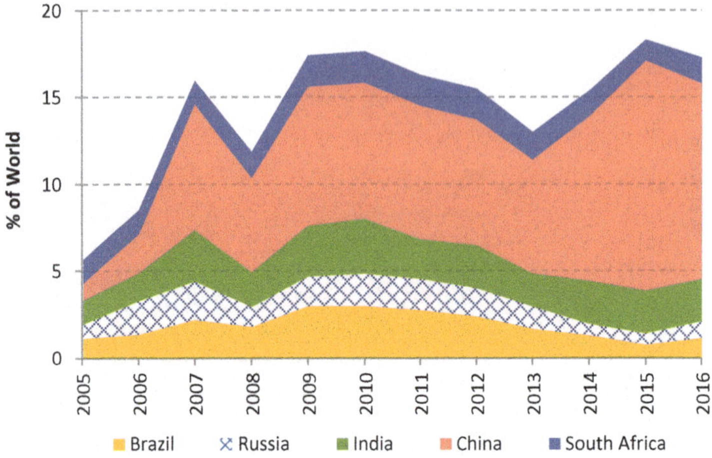

Fig. 16 BRICS share in global capitalisation of stock markets. Source: World Development Indicators (WDI), NAUFOR, author's calculations

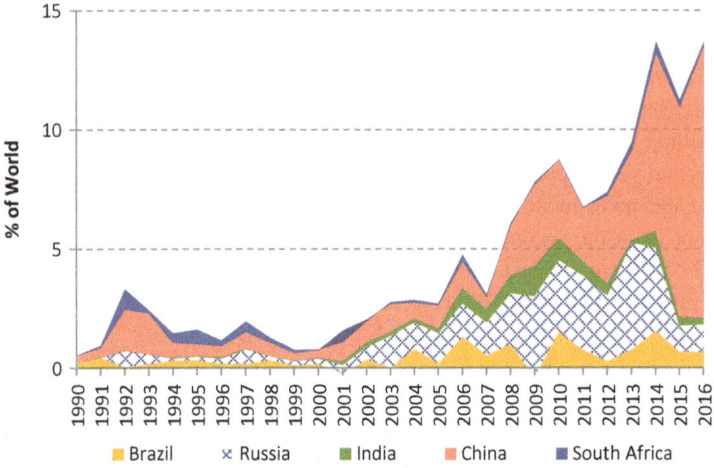

Fig. 17 BRICS share in global FDI outflow. Source: World Development Indicators (WDI), author's calculations

uncertainty, investors tend to invest in the United States) and that of the Eurozone was 10%; of Japan, 8%; and of all other BRICS countries, 5%.

As for capital outflows, China's share was only significant after the 2008–2009 recession and Russia's from the early 2000s to 2014 (see Fig. 17). In 2015, capital outflows from Russia significantly contracted, which is not surprising given the reduced current account balance and the Bank of Russia's free-floating exchange rate policy (essentially, there is almost nothing to take out of the country).

The expansion of Chinese capital has become a reality: in 2016 China accounted for 11.4% of global outbound FDI. In the case of Russia, it is harder to determine the

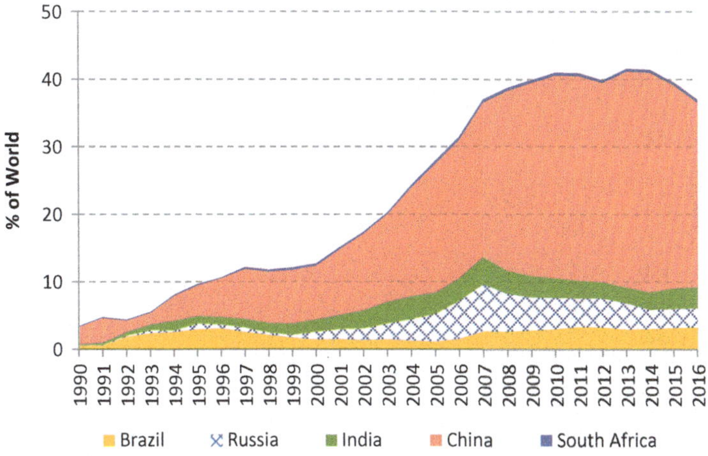

Fig. 18 BRICS share in the global foreign currency reserves. Source: International Financial Statistics (IFS), author's calculations

reason for the outflow in 2014: international expansion or capital flight due to the unfavourable investment climate (a combination of these factors is the most likely explanation).

Another important channel for capital outflows from developing economies with significant current account surpluses (of the BRICS countries this chiefly means China and Russia)—when a central bank is not ensuring a free-floating currency—is growing foreign currency reserves (see Fig. 18). China and Russia accumulated their reserves most actively before the 2008–2009 crisis, as they experienced inflows not only to their current account but also to their financial account and sought to avoid further strengthening of their national currency. At the end of 2007, Russia had accumulated 467 billion USD and China 1530 billion USD. During the global economic recession, Russia spent a significant part of its reserves but then restored them and in 2012 achieved a new record (487 billion USD).[8] However, since the beginning of the period of stagnation and new recession, Russia's foreign currency reserves have started to contract. By the end of 2016, they had fallen by over a third, to 318 billion, and were smaller than those of Brazil and India.

Meanwhile, reserves in China grew over this period, and by 2014 they had reached 3860 billion USD (about ten times greater than in Russia, a third of all currency reserves in the world). However, in 2015 they fell by 514 billion USD (a massive amount for any country other than China), prompted by China's desire to reduce its dependence on the United States and to cut investments in US Treasury bonds. Currently, China's currency reserves are continuing to fall, albeit more slowly—at the end of 2016, they were 3030 billion USD.

[8]This is the year-end record. By 1 August 2008, reserves amounted to 583 billion USD.

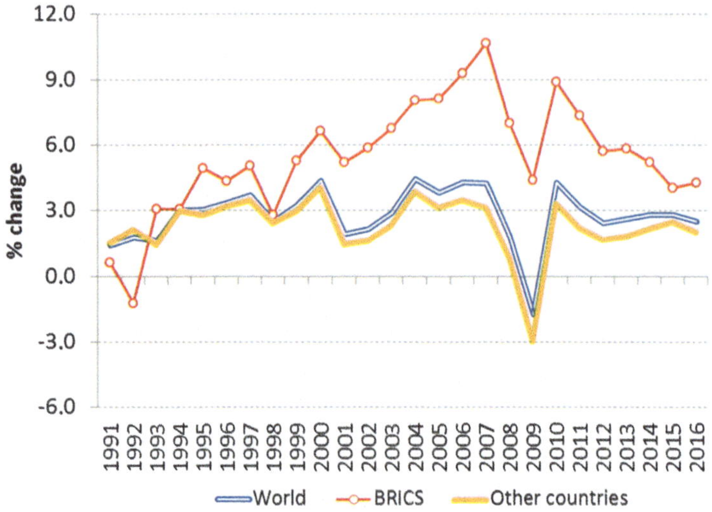

Fig. 19 Annual real GDP growth rates, BRICS and non-BRICS averages. Source: World Development Indicators (WDI), author's calculations

5 BRICS' Contribution to Global Growth

Given the factors outlined above, it should not be surprising that BRICS make a significant and stabilising contribution to global GDP growth (see Fig. 19). For example, during the 2008–2009 global financial crisis, the average rate of GDP growth among BRICS countries, although falling by almost half compared to previous years, remained positive and amounted to 4.3% (for 2009).[9] The average growth rate across all non-BRICS countries fell to −2.9%.

For a quantitative evaluation of the contributions of individual countries to the growth in global GDP, it is vital to take into account not only their GDP growth rates in comparable prices but also the relative sizes of their national economies. Figure 20 shows the contribution to global GDP growth made annually by each BRICS country. It is the role of China that really stands out. The contributions of other BRICS countries (even India to an extent) are more modest.

China's role has been particularly significant since the early 2000s (see Fig. 20). On average, over the period of 2001–2016, China accounted for 0.7 percentage points of the 2.8% annual growth in global GDP (see Fig. 21).[10] The total

[9]According to the World Bank methodology, to calculate the GDP growth rate for an aggregate (such as the world economy as a whole), GDP growth rates in comparable prices are weighed against nominal GDP volumes calculated in USD by the 2010 exchange rate. We used this methodology to calculate average growth rates for BRICS as a group. With the use of GDP by PPP as weights, the role of BRICS would be significantly greater.

[10]The average rate of growth in global GDP was 2.8% both for 1991–2000 and for 2001–2016. It is shown in Fig. 21 by a horizontal broken line.

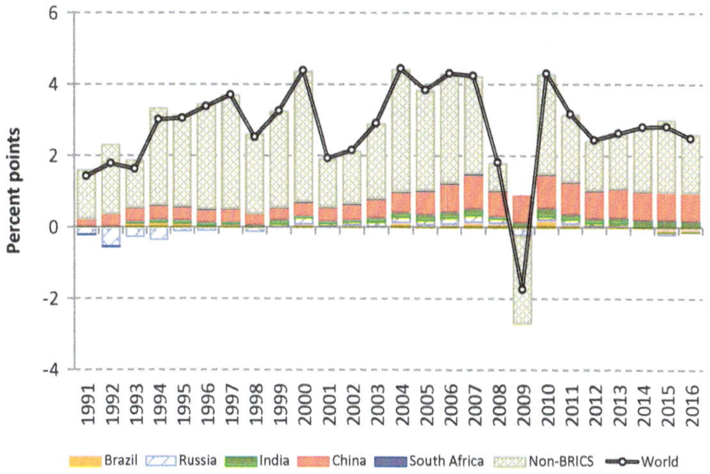

Fig. 20 Annual contributions to global GDP growth rates. Source: World Development Indicators (WDI), author's calculations

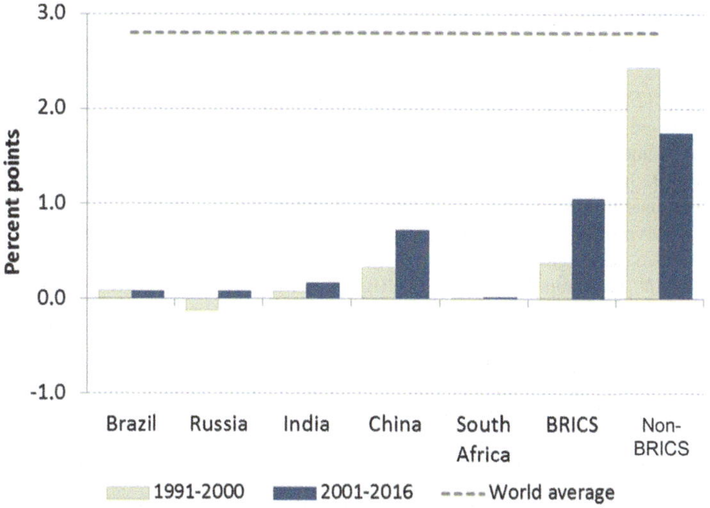

Fig. 21 Average contributions to global GDP growth, by periods. Source: World Development Indicators (WDI), author's calculations

contribution of all other BRICS countries was about half that made by China alone, and the BRICS as a whole accounted for just under 40% of global GDP growth. In 2001–2016, China's contribution to global GDP growth was roughly equal to the contribution made by the United States, Eurozone and Japan taken together, and the total BRICS contribution was 1.4 times greater. This indicates the significant redistribution of the 'centre of gravity' of the global economy, as during the period

1991–2000, China's contribution (0.3 percentage points) and that of all BRICS countries combined (0.4 percentage points) were 4–4.5 times less than the contributions made by the traditional global economic leaders named above (1.5 percentage points, out of which 0.8 percentage points were due to the United States).

References

Collins D (2013) The BRIC states and outward foreign direct investment. Oxford University Press, Oxford

EDIP Research Team (2013) BRICS FDI: a preliminary view. Economic Diplomacy Programme Policy Briefing 63

Evenett S (2015) Global trade alert—BRICS trade strategy: time for a rethink. Centre for Economic Policy Research Report, London

Fratzscher M (2011) Capital flows, push versus pull factors and the global financial crisis. ECB working paper 1364

Holtbrugge D, Kreppel H (2012) Determinants of outward foreign direct investment from BRIC countries: an explorative study. Int J Emerg Mark 7(1):4–30

Keeler D (2012) Special report: BRICS—shifting trade flows and the new consumer. Global Financ. gfmag.com/archives/147-february-2012/11604-special-report-brics

Labes S-A (2015) FDI determinants in BRICS. CES Work Pap 7(2):296–308

O'Neill J (2001) Building better global economic BRICs. Goldman Sachs, Global Economics paper no 66

O'Neill J (2012) Building BRICS: from conceptual category to rising reality. In: Larionova M, Kirton JJ (eds) BRICS New Delhi Summit 2012: stability, security and prosperity. Newsdesk Media, London, pp 24–25

Purugganan J, Jafri A, Solon P (2014) BRICS: a global trade power in a multi-polar world. Transnational Institute Shifting Power Working Paper

Vasiliev S, Movchan A, Topychkanov P, Gabuev A (2015) Why do Brazil, Russia, India, and China need BRICS? Carnegie Moscow Center. carnegie.ru/commentary/60636

Vijayakumar N, Sridharan P, Rao KCS (2010) Determinants of FDI in BRICS countries: a panel analysis. Int J Bus Sci Appl Manag 5(3):1–13

Wilson D, Purushothaman R (2003) Dreaming with BRICs: the path to 2050. Goldman Sachs, Global Economics paper no 99

Institutions, Productivity Change, and Growth

Andrei Akhremenko, Alexander Petrov, and Egor Yureskul

1 Introduction

The topics of economic performance, economic growth, and their determinants have been the subject of intense academic debate and rigorous empirical research for several decades now, both in economics and political science. Due to their share in the world's economy, their rapidly changing political systems, and high growth rates in the 1990s and early 2000s, countries of the BRICS bloc (Brazil, Russia, India, China, South Africa) attracted considerable attention as subjects for empirical research into economic growth, productivity, and institutional development.

From a traditional neoclassic economic perspective, it has been shown that factors such as technology transfer, foreign direct investment, and restructuring the economy play a key role in providing sustainable economic development. However, even in the context of international globalization and rapid technological progress, few countries have achieved high enough rates of growth to reach the welfare level of the so-called developed countries, which is also evident on the case of BRICS.

While many studies in political science proposed democratic transition as the main engine of sustainable economic growth, empirical evidence remains inconclusive: countries with stable, long-standing democratic traditions retain stable levels of

---

This chapter is an output of a research project implemented by Laboratory for Qualitative and Quantitative Analysis of Political Regimes within the Annual Thematic Plan for basic and applied research at the National Research University—Higher School of Economics. Project title: "Economic Efficiency and the Evolution of Political Regimes: A Theoretical Model of Interdependence, Cross-Country, and Dynamical Analysis."

A. Akhremenko (✉) · E. Yureskul
National Research University Higher School of Economics, Moscow, Russia
e-mail: aakhremenko@hse.ru

A. Petrov
Keldysh Institute of Applied Mathematics, Moscow, Russia

S. Smirnov et al. (eds.), *Business Cycles in BRICS*, Societies and Political Orders in Transition, https://doi.org/10.1007/978-3-319-90017-9_3

growth; many newly democratized countries still fall behind in economic progress; lastly, there are multiple cases of authoritarian governments capable of providing economic development on a par with most democratic ones. Again, some BRICS countries have exhibited increasing rates of growth despite their lack of democratic institutions.

Scientific inquiry into business cycles remains a distinct branch of economic literature. Some of the key topics include attempts to build a theoretical model which explains business cycles as a phenomenon (Burnside and Eichenbaum 1996; García-Cicco et al. 2010) and inquiries into business cycle determinants (Berger 2012). While the relative shares of demand shocks and technological innovation in business cycle propagation remain a topic of discussion (Dufourt 2005), a consensus on the interdependence between business cycles and changes in total factor productivity does seem to exist. TFP was widely believed to be procyclical by RBC adepts (Field 2010; Mayer et al. 2016), but recent studies have shown significant variation in the cyclicality of TFP across different countries and institutional settings (Fernald and Wang 2016; Lazear et al. 2016; Cavalcanti 2007). A pronounced strand of literature considers the possible institutional determinants for business cycle heterogeneity and disparities in TFP cyclicality (Kawaguchi and Murao 2012; Cavalcanti 2007; Iversen and Soskice 2006). However, due to the nature of business cycle research, most studies focus primarily on fiscal and labor market institutions, as well as variation in macroeconomic policy. To our knowledge, very few studies consider political institutions such as governance and property rights protection as the link between economic development in general (including economic growth, TFP change, and business cycles) [see Altug and Canova (2014) for a literature review]. We believe that the connection between TFP, political institutions, and economic growth is worthy of investigation in order to provide a contextual foundation for future research into business cycles in developing countries.

In this paper, we aim to consider empirical evidence from BRICS countries in comparison with the rest of the world. Brazil, Russia, India, China, and South Africa account for a considerable share of the world's GDP, as well as natural and labor resources. Rapid economic growth rates in the 1990s and 2000s, as well as accompanying political changes, make the BRICS a natural subject of research into both economic and political transitions.

Our contribution to the existing body of literature is twofold. Firstly, we propose an aggregate measure of accounting for productivity levels and change based on existing economic databases. We assume a neoclassical two-factor production function and use nonparametric methods (a variant of data envelopment analysis) to obtain a measure of total factor productivity (TFP) across a large sample of countries in the period between the years of 1990 and 2013. This approach allows us to create a dataset containing productivity measures that are comparable both dynamically and in a cross section. Our utilization of DEA allows us to construct trajectories of TFP change for BRICS countries against the backdrop of the world's economies and link relative factor shares to growth rates and institutional differences.

Secondly, we conduct a comprehensive analysis of the relationship between both levels and dynamics of TFP, on the one hand, and varied indicators of institutional and political development, on the other hand. In contrast to many existing studies in both economics and political science, we aim to construct complex measures of political variables using a wide array of existing datasets.

Our analysis shows that in the general country-year sample, the theoretical assumptions are supported by empirics: institutions remain a factor of productivity levels and economic growth. However, BRICS countries demonstrate considerable deviations from the general rule, exhibiting high levels of growth in the early twenty-first century despite vast differences in institutional development. Still, our study into TFP change shows that institutional factors indeed explain reduced BRICS growth rates in recent years.

We also employ panel regressions to test our empirical observations regarding the relationship between institutions and TFP, controlling for several macroeconomic variables.

The rest of the paper is organized as follows. In Sect. 2, we review existing literature concerned with topics of economic growth and political development. Section 3 details our approach to measuring total factor productivity. In Sect. 4, we provide the results of our empirical study. Section 5 serves as a conclusion.

2 Literature Review

BRICS countries, being a group of largest developing economies with highly diverse political systems, are natural subjects of research into institutional determinants of growth. However, empirical studies into the development of BRICS countries are relatively few in number. There are several works considering economic growth from a purely economic standpoint (Samargandi and Kutan 2016; Samake and Yang 2014; Kurt and Kurt 2015), as well as multiple qualitative case studies for both individual countries and the BRICS as a bloc (Bojnec et al. 2014; WTO 2013). Still, several studies consider institutional and policy implications for growth. For example, a popular review of the BRICS economies by the Goldman Sachs Group explicitly states that "Institutions affect the 'efficiency' of an economy much in the same way as technology does: more efficient institutions allow an economy to produce the same output with fewer inputs" (Wilson 2003). A more recent informational bulletin by the World Bank considers that "bouts of policy uncertainty" have, among external economic factors, contributed to a decline in growth since 2010 (Davis 2017).

It should be noted that many contemporary studies are more concerned with policy than institutions, namely, competition policy (Gancia and Zilibotti 2009), national macroeconomic strategy and business culture (Yao et al. 2009), strategic public investment (Aghion and Roulet 2014), labor market regulation, and state-encouraged extraction of management techniques (Malesky and London 2014). Several authors suggest their own conceptual models for the role of policy in efficiency differences across countries (Parente and Prescott 2005; Restuccia and Rogerson 2008). While many of the mentioned studies reveal the crucial role of policy in economic growth and efficiency, none of them focus predominantly on institutional factors. Moreover, it has previously been shown that institutions remain a more fundamental factor of growth than policy, and the influence of policy disappears once one controls for institutions (Easterly 2005).

In this chapter, we adopt a different approach to analyzing economic growth in BRICS countries. First, we focus entirely on institutional determinants of growth and their relationships with total factor productivity, in contrast with many studies considering policy as a factor of growth. We chose to focus on institutions as their function is to provide a fundamental impact on the economy and, as Douglass North aptly put it, "define and enforce the economic rules of the game" (North and Thomas 1973). Moreover, there is plenty of valid cross-country data on institutions, while policy remains the subject of small-N qualitative research, thus lending very few indicators fit for statistical empirical analysis. Second, we look at BRICS in comparison with the rest of the world, not limiting our country sample to "BRICS and the world's leading economies." Generally, we explore the dynamical triad "productivity, institutions, and economic growth" in BRICS countries against the world trends' background. Total factor productivity is considered to be the key element of the triad in our framework.

Below, we consider several main strands of theoretical and empirical research concerning TFP and economic development. Studies in economic growth date back as far as the early twentieth century. Initial advances in growth accounting allowed researchers to isolate growth that wasn't explained by mere factor accumulation (Copeland and Martin 1938). In his notable contribution, Robert Solow demonstrated how changes in total factor productivity (TFP), the residual growth rate of output not explained by input increases, could be accounted for in a standard neoclassical two-factor production function (Solow 1956). From that point on, total factor productivity became a constant consideration in economic growth research.

TFP has also been a constant subject of inquiry in business cycle research. Most studies look into the cyclical nature of TFP (Field 2010; Fernald and Wang 2016), while others consider alternate directions of causality between TFP and cycles (Mayer et al. 2016).

Empirical literature on the TFP-growth nexus is extremely vast and typically considers the mutual relationships between relative technological advancement, economic productivity, production factor efficiency, and growth trajectories of countries. Works in this field are usually concerned with convergence to steady-state production levels (Barro 1991) and attempt to explain differences in output levels and output growth through differences in TFP (Azariadis and Kaas 2010; Gourinchas and Jeanne 2013; Caselli et al. 1996). As an explanatory variable in growth regressions, total factor productivity is generally synonymous with allocative efficiency (i.e., the allocation of resources between firms that allows for most efficient output levels) and was proven to be a factor of economic development

(Storesletten and Zilibotti 2014; Inklaar and Timmer 2009; Caselli and Feyrer 2007). Other studies consider the effect of sector-level variables on TFP and, by extension, aggregate growth: examples include resource reallocation (Hsieh and Klenow 2009) and energy efficiency (Tugcu and Tiwari 2016).

A different set of theoretical and empirical works focuses on the technological component in TFP while adopting a distinct conceptual model: while total factor productivity is a driver for growth, high TFP levels are driven by innovation, which in turn requires both knowledge and a skilled workforce (Dávila 2016). Recent studies show that knowledge accumulation is a significant factor of economic growth due to high human capital having positive externalities for firms (Inglesi-Lotz et al. 2013). Influential works by Lucas (1990) and Acemoglu and Zilibotti (2001) demonstrate the importance of human capital in the process of technology adoption: while imitation may be equally available to everyone in the modern world, developing countries often lack complementary factor endowment to properly implement new and improved capital assets. This strand of literature lays the theoretical foundation for interdisciplinary studies in economic growth, bordering on political science.

The key research question in the third (and the most important for this study) strand of literature is not whether productivity leads to sustainable growth (or vice versa) but which factors are fundamental in ensuring high productivity levels. In other words, which social and political institutions drive technological innovation and capital investment? In the spirit of North's groundbreaking paper (North and Thomas 1973), most researchers agree that the protection of property rights is the basic determinant of market efficiency. Hall and Jones (1999) point out that certain political and social institutions may incentivize productive activity either through fair allocation of market resources to efficient firms (i.e., economic policy) or through suppression of both private and state diversions (i.e., reducing corruption and theft). Government effectiveness has also been viewed as a determinant of economic productivity in many studies, particularly by economic organizations. In our empirical work, we investigate all the major institutional components—property rights protection, anticorruption, and government effectiveness—in the context of TFP and growth.

In this chapter, we aim to expand upon the existing literature in a number of ways. Firstly, we base our research on existing theoretical frameworks. Therefore, we follow the developments in both political science and new institutional economics in order to examine the relationships between TFP, growth, and institutions. Secondly, we construct our own TFP estimates for a large country-year sample using nonparametric frontier methods and a two-factor neoclassical production function (see Sect. 3). This allows us to draw TFP estimates that are comparable both over time and in a cross section of countries. Moreover, due to the nature of the method, we are able to assess relative factor efficiency and obtain trajectories for individual countries that represent different stages of economic development. More precisely, we characterize and classify the trajectories of the BRICS on the "labor-capital" productivity plane. Next, we use a large number of political variables to construct valid indicators of institutional development. Since we focus on the relationship between growth, institutions, and TFP, we perform multiple validity checks on all constructed variables before conducting any statistical tests. Finally, we aim to add to the literature by choosing a topical subject of research: while many studies consider BRICS countries as a natural example of economic growth driven by institutional development, few have looked at their position within a large country sample.

3 Measuring TFP

In this section, we detail our approach to measuring TFP. By using nonparametric methods, we are able to forego the necessity for disaggregated price data yet retain the discriminative power required for in-depth analysis of TFP trajectories and factors of growth.

Our reliance on nonparametric methods is due to a number of reasons. Traditional measures of productivity such as Tornqvist quantity indices (or any other econometric index) and perpetual inventory methods require highly disaggregated price data, which would limit our country sample and the ability to compare BRICS productivity against the countries of the world. Moreover, index measures of productivity allow either cross-sectional or time-series comparisons, but not both. By using data envelopment analysis with a production possibility metafrontier, we are able to construct panel data on productivity changes across the countries of the world and across a relatively large period of time. While DEA was initially conceived as a firm-level productivity estimation method, there have been successful attempts at implementing DEA efficiency scores at regional and national level (Boyle 2006; Afonso and St. Aubyn 2006, 2010).

In addition, the DEA approach allows us to incorporate various productivity components into a single productivity measure. Generally, TFP (aside from being "a measure of our ignorance") is believed to be a composite measure incorporating technological progress, managerial efficiency, and allocative efficiency. We forego the decomposition of TFP estimates in favor of a generalized look at institutional and economic factors related to TFP. A detailed look at our estimation methodology is provided below.

We assume a neoclassical two-factor production function: a country's output Y (i.e., its GDP) is produced through a combination of capital K and labor L. It is worth noting that we don't specify the form of the production function $Y = F(K, L)$, which is typical for nonparametric approaches to measuring productivity. We only assume constant returns to scale, so $F(\lambda K, \lambda L) = \lambda F(K, L)$.

We use World Bank data to obtain values for key indicators:

- Y: General government capital stock, PPP, constant 2005 dollars.
- K_g (public capital): calculated from general government capital stock, percentage of GDP.
- K_p (private capital): calculated from private capital stock, percentage of GDP.

Fig. 1 Constructing the best-practice frontier

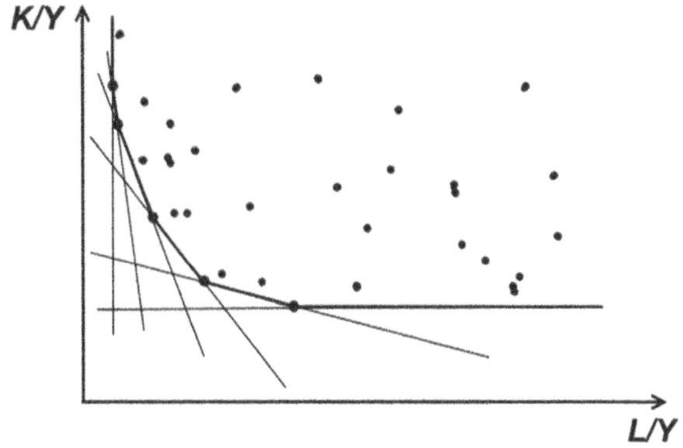

Total capital is measured as a sum of public and private capital: $K = K_g + K_p$.

To measure labor stock L, we use the World Bank indicator, labor force, and total.

To obtain cross-country TFP estimates, we use data envelopment analysis (DEA), which takes a particularly simple form under these assumptions (Farrell 1957).

Taking the data for a certain year, we consider each country as a point on the (L/Y, K/Y) plane.

The frontier is piecewise linear and wraps around the most productive points (see Fig. 1) on the plane, therefore satisfying the following conditions:

1. No point lies between frontier lines and the origin.
2. The slope of each frontier line is negative (except for two frontier pieces that form its top-left and bottom-right parts).

From a theoretical point of view, this means that the frontier is formed by the best practices achieved by countries in the sample, for which we assume TFP = 1. This allows us to normalize TFP values for all other countries in the $0 < \text{TFP} < 1$ range: the closer a country is to the frontier, the higher its TFP.

Note that the frontier set contains both countries with high capital-labor ratio (K/L), such as Qatar, and the so-called third world countries with low capital-labor ratios (e.g., Equatorial Guinea).

Over time, countries change their position on the (L/Y, K/Y) plane. To account for these changes, we use several variants of DEA. The first is Long-Memory DEA (LMDEA), introduced by Forstner and Issaksson (2002): over time, the frontier can't move further from the origin (there is no technological regress); in this variant, a country that is part of the frontier is always considered for frontier estimation in the following years. The second variant, plain DEA (PLDEA), assumes that the frontier may shift in any direction. Therefore, each year is considered a separate sample for the purposes of frontier estimation. Finally, the meta-DEA variant assumes that the frontier remains the same for the whole country-year sample: that is, we use the best-practice countries from the whole period to form the frontier. This means that the best technology levels remain the same, and productivity increases consist of "catching up" toward the contemporary technology. For most countries in the

Fig. 2 Best-practice frontiers in 1998: plain DEA, LMDEA, meta-DEA. World Bank's ISO codes are used to denote Equatorial Guinea, Qatar, Kuwait, and Barbados. The figure is not to scale

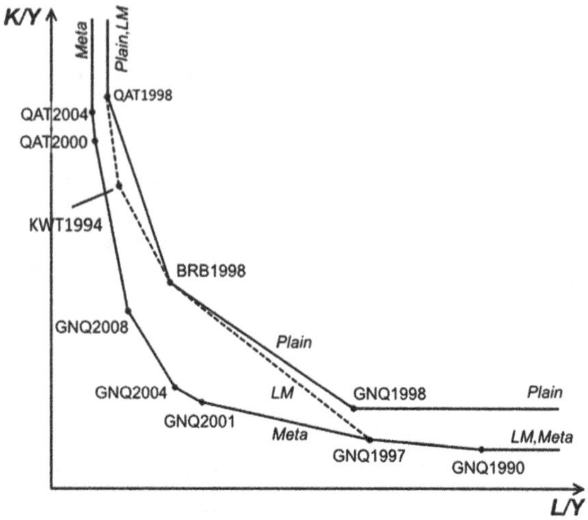

sample, meta-DEA estimates show increasing TFP in the period between 1990 and 2013.

We illustrate the differences between estimation methods in Fig. 2.

In 1998, productivity levels for some countries were lower than in the preceding years. For instance, TFP levels in Equatorial Guinea were lower in 1998 than in the previous year: this was due to a decrease in capital productivity (*K*/*Y*) which led to the country's point moving away from the origin.

If we assume that it is possible for the technological frontier to move backward, we only use current year data (PLDEA). If we assume that technological progress is strictly nonnegative, then for each year we add data points that formed the frontier in the previous years, thus acquiring LMDEA estimates. Therefore, certain countries appear in the sample more than once: e.g., Equatorial Guinea is represented on Fig. 3 by its results in 1998 but also by its results in 1990 and 1997, when it formed a part of the frontier. Equatorial Guinea is, in a way, a corner case: between 1990 and 2013, it experienced capital growth proportional to GDP growth and therefore formed the southern part of the frontier in this period (Figs. 2 and 3). Finally, when using meta-DEA, we first find all the best-practice results for the whole period and then measure the TFP.

Using the three DEA variants, we obtain TFP estimates for 149 countries of the world in the period between 1990 and 2013.

For comparison, we provide trends in average TFP levels for BRICS and OECD countries, as well as 46 African countries (see Fig. 4). TFP estimates show that BRICS countries demonstrate relatively low levels of productivity, comparable to those of African countries. The TFP dynamics for Russia look the most impressive and demonstrate a visible comeback from the 1990s economic collapse. Compared to other BRICS countries, barriers for growth in Russia seem to stem more from a lack of investment than from low productivity.

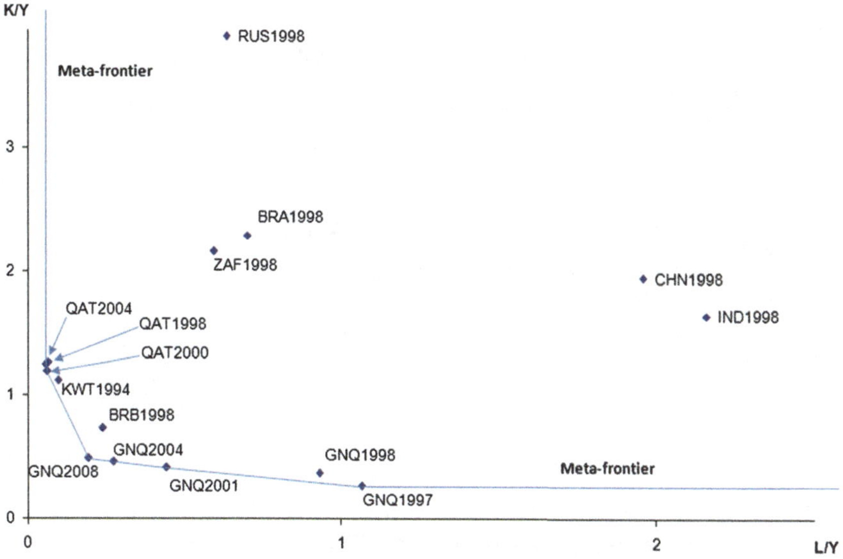

Fig. 3 Positions of BRICS relative to frontier countries

While some estimates of productivity we provide may seem counterintuitive at first glance (such as certain African countries having productivity levels higher than the BRICS and China having lower productivity than India), they do not contradict our approach to understanding and measuring TFP. Since DEA provides a complex measure of productivity (due to economies being ranked against similar economies and not the whole country sample) and relies on frontier estimation instead of market share estimation, there are bound to be certain discrepancies between our estimates and existing country-level TFP estimates (such as those provided by Penn World Tables). Still, the correlation between DEA estimates and PWT estimates remains consistently high for each year in the sample.

Below we show how the dynamics of factor productivity and balance between factors (productivity trajectories) affect economic development within the BRICS.

Productivity Trajectories

Changes in factor productivity for a given country may be represented by productivity trajectories, i.e., $(L(t)/Y(t),\ K(t)/Y(t))$ lines for the whole sample period. Figure 5 shows productivity trajectories for BRICS.

In general, movement toward the origin means increasing productivity, while movement away from the origin means a decrease in productivity. Figure 5 shows that the BRICS may be divided into two distinct groups.

The first group consists of countries with high reciprocal labor productivity (i.e., low capital-labor ratios) in 1990, namely, China and India. Both countries were far behind the rest of the bloc in terms of labor productivity, with low GDPs and enormous labor forces. Over time, they exhibited almost horizontal movement

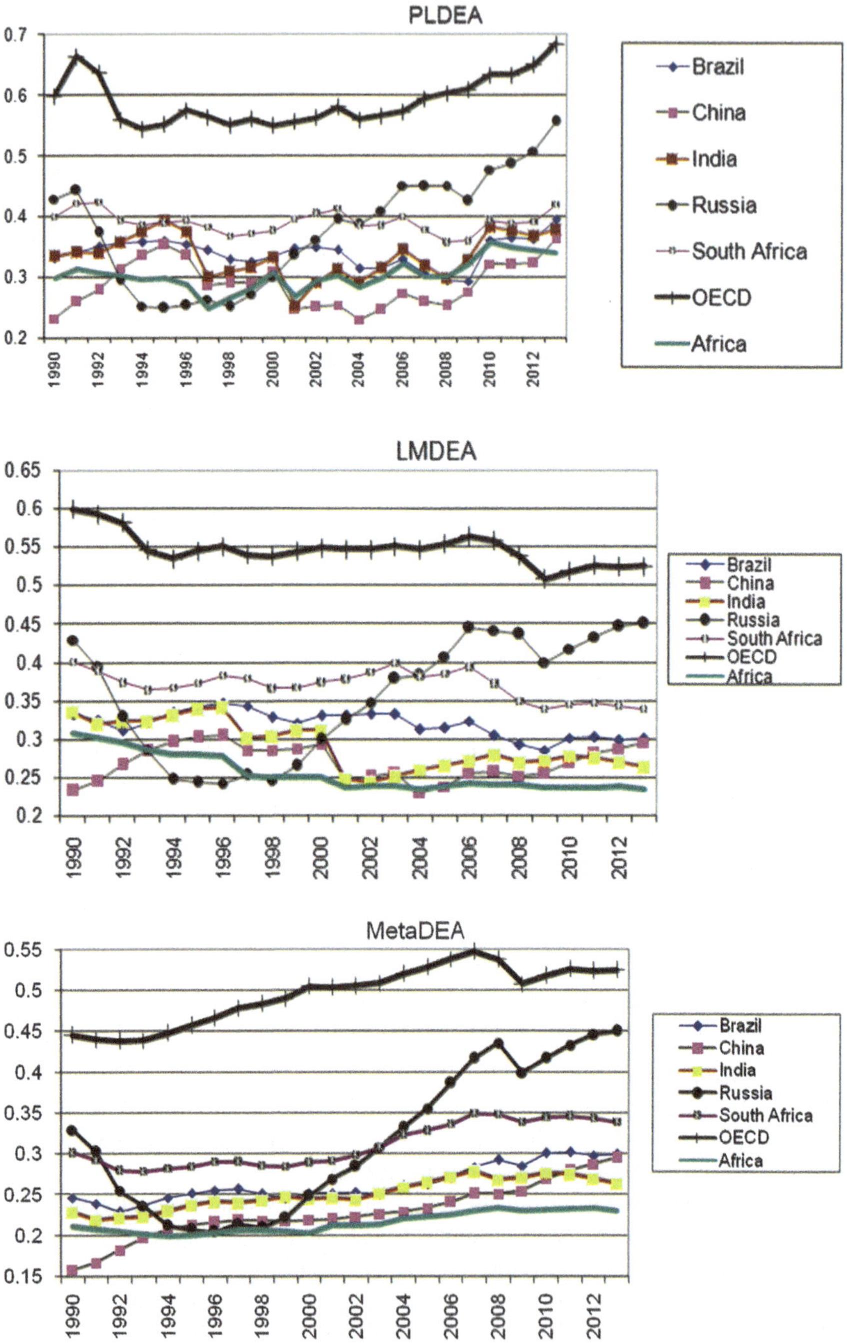

Fig. 4 TFP estimate dynamics for BRICS, OECD, and African countries

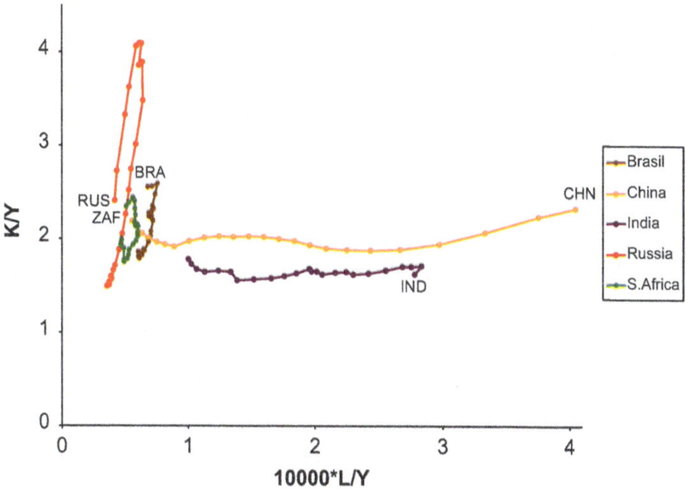

Fig. 5 Productivity trajectories for BRICS between 1990 and 2013. Country ISO codes denote starting points

Table 1 Relative variation in factor productivity within the BRICS

	(L/Y) *10,000		$V_L = (\max - \min)/\min$	*K/Y*		$V_K = (\max - \min)/\min$	V_K/V_L
	Min	Max		Min	Max		
China	0.55	4.04	6.35	1.89	2.35	0.24	0.04
India	1	2.83	1.83	1.56	1.73	0.11	0.06
Brazil	0.6	0.75	0.25	1.8	2.6	0.44	1.76
Russia	0.35	0.63	0.8	1.5	4.1	1.73	2.16
South Africa	0.46	0.6	0.3	1.76	2.45	0.39	1.30

toward the origin: their capital productivity remained virtually the same, while their labor productivity grew significantly. Let us call this a labor-driven path.

The second group (Brazil, Russia, and RSA) exhibits diagonal trajectories, with overtime changes attributed mostly to capital productivity shifts. Let us call this a capital-driven path. This qualitative observation coincides with calculations in Table 1, which shows relative variation in L/Y and K/Y for the BRICS: both China and India exhibit significantly higher variation in labor productivity, while the rest of the BRICS exhibit higher variation in capital productivity over the 23-year period.

In addition, analyzing the shape of TFP trajectories over time allows us to make intuitive assumptions into mechanisms of growth within the BRICS. First, it is important to note that balanced growth (based on increasing the productivity of both factors, i.e., TFP-driven growth) trajectories result in diagonal movement toward the origin. It is evident from Fig. 5 that none of the BRICS exhibit balanced growth, with India and China moving horizontally and the rest of the bloc moving vertically. TFP trajectories for the BRICS suggest that these countries employ extensive mechanisms of growth due to initial imbalances in factor endowment. Moreover, Russia and Brazil demonstrate drastically reduced growth rates in the recent years, while RSA, China, and India show signs of approaching TFP decline (i.e., movement away from the world's best-practice frontier).

4 TFP, Institutions, and Growth

In this section, we show how general empirical trends in institutional development, productivity, and economic growth are represented in BRICS countries. The study is based on a sample of 149 countries. We produced TFP estimates for the period between 1990 and 2013; however, most institutional indicator databases (such as World Bank's WGI indices) begin in 1996. Therefore, we use the 1996–2013 period as a base for comparison (since it provides more data).

We consider the relationships between levels of institutional development, economic welfare, and productivity. We also consider the mutual dynamics of these measures: our results show that these two specifications (levels and change) provide drastically different research outcomes.

We use GDP per capita in constant 2011 prices as our welfare indicator. For productivity, we employ our own measures of TFP (including measures of labor and capital productivity). We use the metafrontier DEA model for our productivity measures (see Sect. 3; results for other frontier types are not shown below but are qualitatively the same for all types of TFP estimates).

In terms of institutional variables, we define three groups of indicators related to productivity and economic growth:

(a) Transparency and absence of corruption (*anticorruption and transparency*)
(b) Property rights protection
(c) Government effectiveness

For transparency and absence of corruption, we use the following data: Bayesian Corruption Index,[1] Andrew Williams Transparency Index,[2] Index of Political Corruption[3] from the "Varieties of Democracy" Project, TI's Corruption Perceptions Index,[4] as well as WGI's Control of Corruption Index.[5] We conduct a principal component analysis on the five variables and use the first component as a proxy, since it explains 87.1% of the variation in data. However, all the results are valid for individual variables as well. For the sake of simplicity, we present most results for

[1]http://www.sherppa.ugent.be/BCI/BCI.html

[2]https://andrewwilliamsecon.wordpress.com/datasets

[3]https://www.v-dem.net/en/data/data-version-6-2

[4]http://www.transparency.org/research/cpi/overview

[5]http://info.worldbank.org/governance/wgi/index.aspx#home

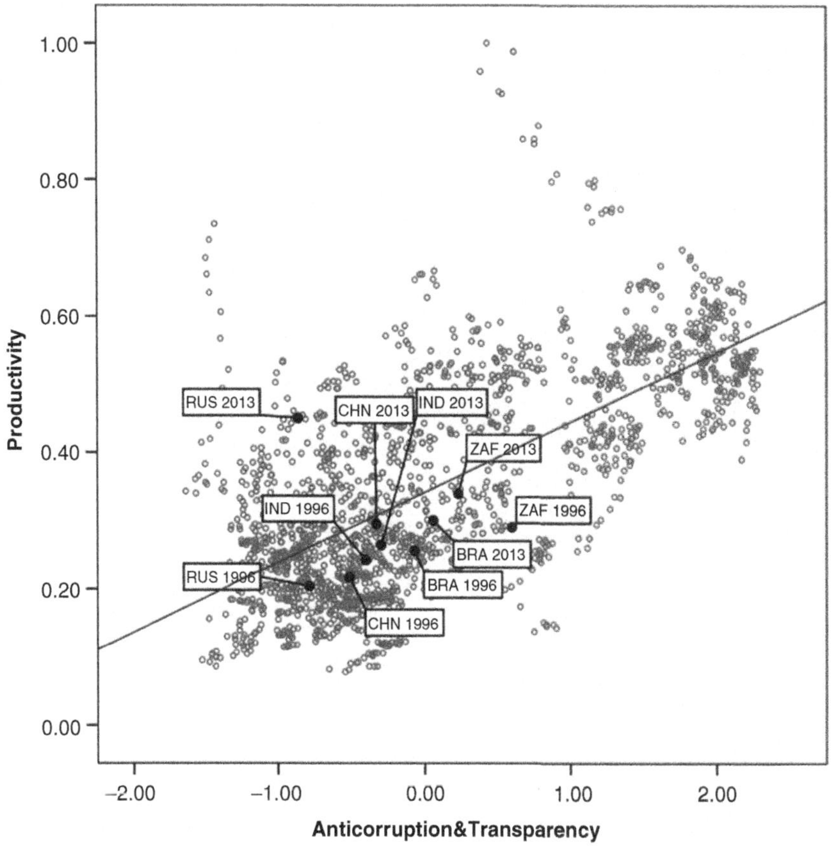

Fig. 6 Anticorruption and transparency in BRICS countries against productivity levels

the whole country sample, while all the calculations have been checked for individual countries.

Figures 6 and 7 plot *anticorruption and transparency* in BRICS countries against productivity levels and logged per capita GDP levels.

Firstly, we note the positive mutual relationship between anticorruption and transparency, as well as between productivity and economic welfare. Spearman correlations between these indicators are significant and measure at 0.64 and 0.77, respectively. These results are completely in accord with current theory.

Secondly, institutional development in the fields of transparency and anticorruption in BRICS countries may be characterized as average with a slight skew toward the negative side: the values for BRICS range from −0.85 (Russia 2013) to 0.55 (RSA 1996) and are within 1.4 standard deviations.[6] Over time, the gap is closing.

[6]Since we are using principal components, these are normalized data.

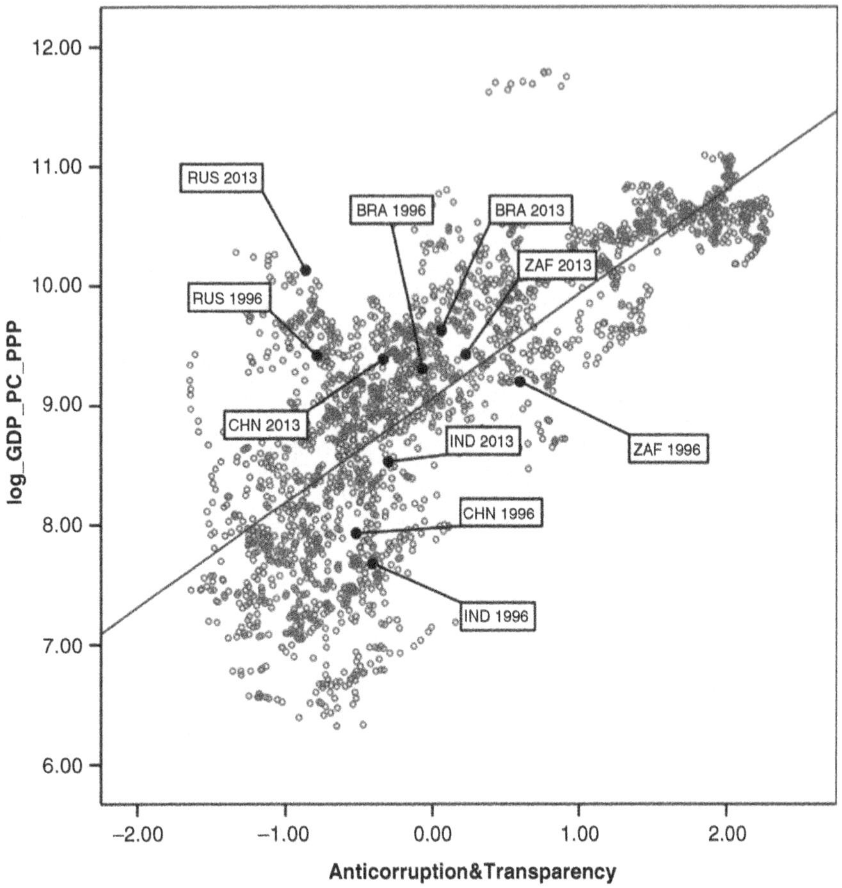

Fig. 7 Anticorruption and transparency in BRICS countries against logged per capita GDP levels

Finally, we do not observe any significant changes on the transparency axis. India, China, and Brazil demonstrate a slight increase, RSA—a slight decrease—while Russia remains the same. The results of K-means clustering support this kind of dynamics: upon dividing our whole country sample into four clusters, BRICS countries never change their membership. Russia remains in the cluster with the worst institutions; India, Brazil, and China belong to the "worse than average" cluster, while RSA stays in the "better than average" group.

We measure property rights protection using three variables: the Fraser Institute's Legal Structure and Security of Property Rights Index,[7] the Heritage Foundation's Property Rights Index,[8] and the WGI Rule of Law Index. The first principal

[7]https://www.fraserinstitute.org/economic-freedomdatasets_efw.html

[8]http://www.heritage.org/index/explore

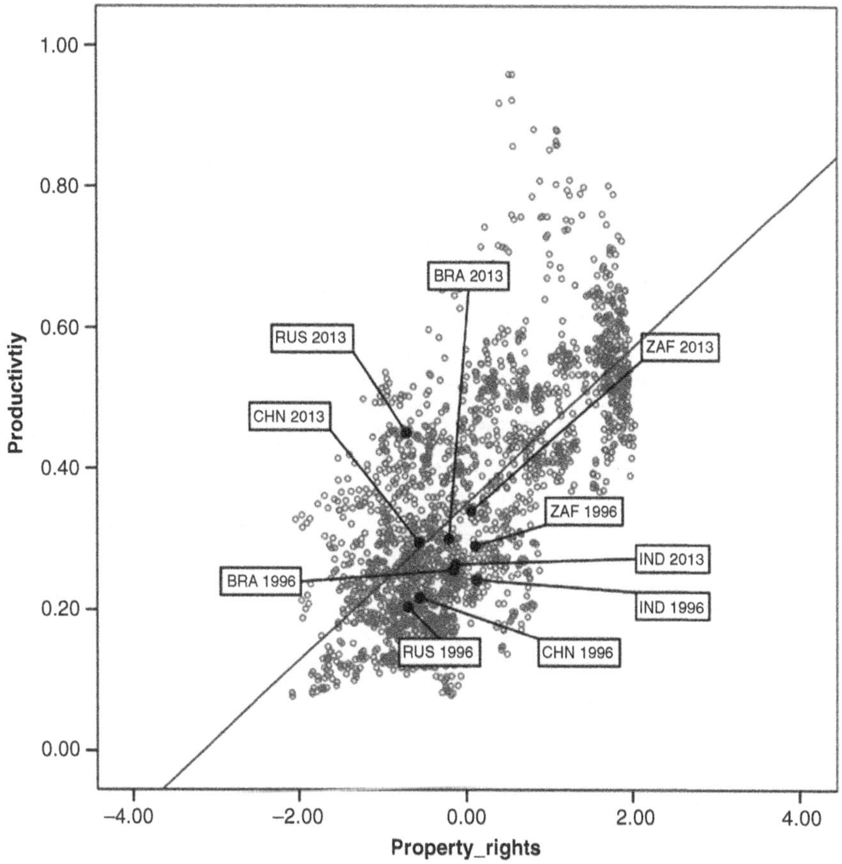

Fig. 8 Property rights protection in BRICS countries against productivity levels

component explains 90.8% of overall variation, so we'll be using it in our descriptions (*property rights*).

At a glance, the scatter plot in Fig. 8 remains very similar to the one regarding transparency. Again, for the whole country sample, we observe a positive relationship between property rights and both productivity and wealth levels. Spearman's coefficients measure at 0.67 and 0.79, respectively, and are significant at $p < 0.01$.

BRICS countries are even closer to each other on the property rights axis: they place within one standard deviation. Here, the negative trend is more prominent: BRICS lie between −0.7 and 0.16 (Fig. 9).

The changes in property rights in BRICS are mostly slow and negative: in the period between 1996 and 2013, there are no registered increases in any country of the bloc. Things remain the same in Russia and China; Brazil, India, and RSA experience a slight negative dynamic. These observations are further supported by the cluster analysis results.

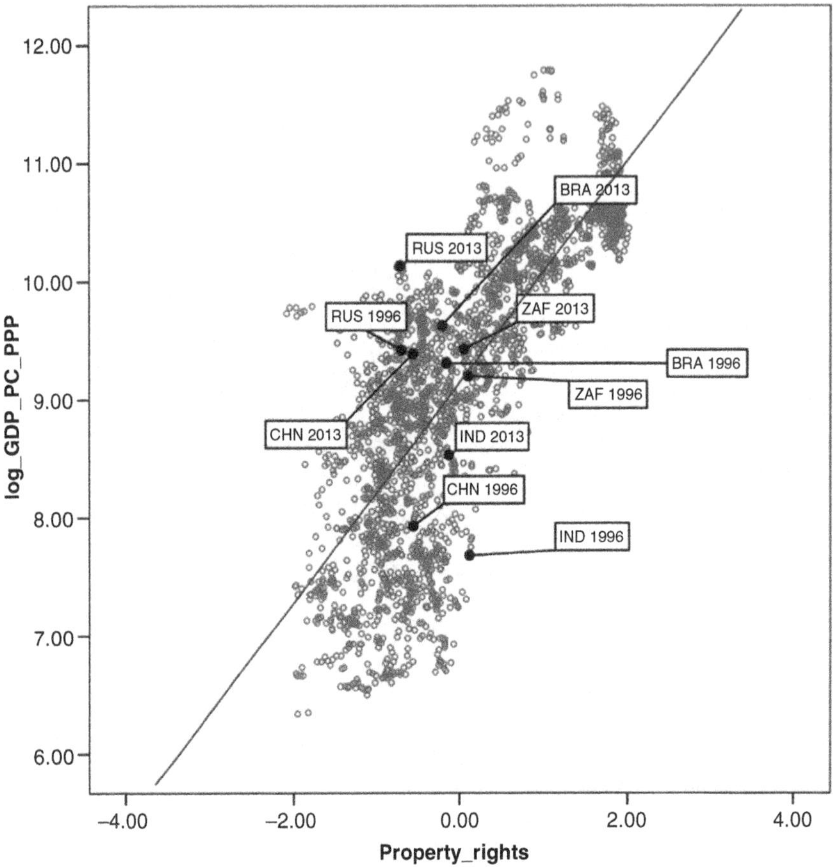

Fig. 9 Property rights protection in BRICS countries against logged per capita GDP levels

To measure the quality of governance, we use three indicators: ICRG's quality of government indicator and both government effectiveness and regulatory quality indices from the WGI. The first principal component explains 93.8% of the overall variation; therefore we use it instead of raw indicators.

Qualitatively, the picture remains the same as with transparency and property rights protection (Figs. 10 and 11). We observe a significant correlation between quality of governance and both TFP and wealth levels (Spearman's rho is 0.72 and 0.79, respectively). The variation within BRICS lies within 1.35 standard deviations.

In other words, the quality of governance in BRICS measures slightly better against other countries of the world than transparency and property rights protection. However, this indicator demonstrates the most negative trend out of all three: all the BRICS countries exhibit a slight decrease in quality of governance between 1996 and 2013. K-means clustering shows that only Brazil has moved from the third cluster into the second, which is mostly due to Brazil being in a transitional state already.

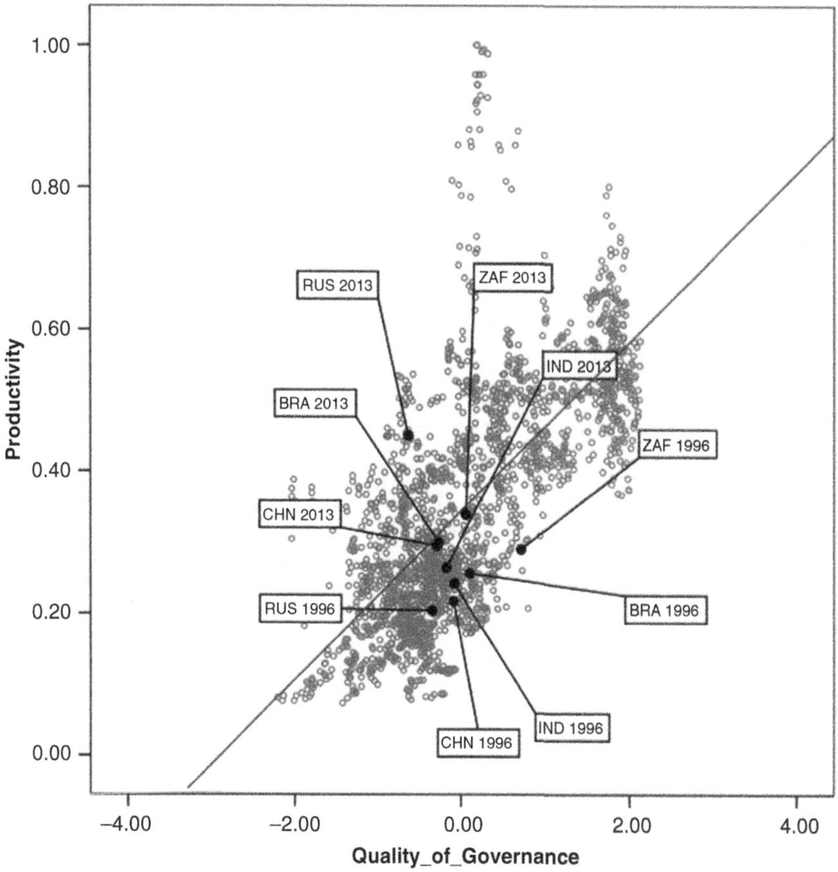

Fig. 10 Quality of governance in BRICS countries against productivity levels

Overall, BRICS countries demonstrate significant similarities in values and dynamics of different institutional indicators. These indicators also correlate with each other within our country sample (see Table 2).

We therefore construct a single first principal component (more than 90% variation explained) out of all the institutional indicators and use it to draw a picture of BRICS institutional development against the countries of the world (Figs. 12 and 13).

We use panel regressions to further test these observations (see Table 3). We use TFP levels as a dependent variable and macroeconomic indicators (inflation and unemployment levels) as control variables. Model (1) utilizes fixed country effects and robust standard errors and shows that when accounting for in-sample heterogeneity there is no significant connection between TFP and institutions. Model (2) is a panel regression without fixed effects and shows that our observations hold: institutional development remains a significant and positive predictor for TFP levels

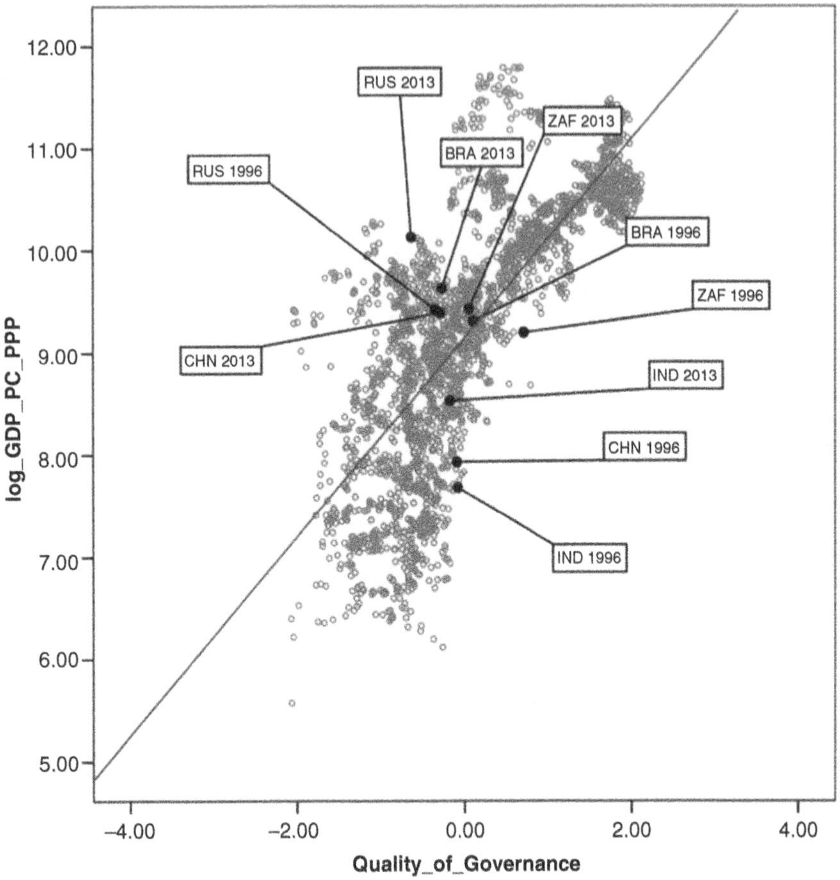

Fig. 11 Quality of governance in BRICS countries against logged per capita GDP levels

when no additional measure of country heterogeneity is introduced. In Model (3) we take TFP first differences as a dependent variable and use lagged institutional development and control variable levels (Table 3 shows results for 1-year lags, but the results remain the same for bigger lags as well): institutions, like in Model (1), become a negative and insignificant predictor for TFP. Finally, we compare TFP change to institutional change (Model (4)): institutions again become a positive and significant predictor. Models with fixed effects and robustness measures exhibit results qualitatively similar to Model (4).

Dynamical analysis further illustrates our observations. We also analyzed cross-correlations between institutional, productivity, and GDP per capita time series for each of the BRICS countries. All the conclusions made above hold: we observe no significant relationship between institutions and productivity at any reasonable lag value, while GDP per capita and TFP are correlated strongly (with mean $r = 0.8$, zero lag) and significantly.

Table 2 Correlations between institutions, TFP, and per capita GDP

		Anticorruption and transparency	Property rights	Quality of governance	GDP PC PPP
Property rights	Spearman's rho	0.93**			
	N	1860			
Quality of governance	Spearman's rho	0.95**	0.95**		
	N	1866	2234		
GDP PC PPP	Spearman's rho	0.77**	0.79**	0.79**	
	N	2085	2450	2475	
TFP	Spearman's rho	0.64**	0.67**	0.72**	0.8**
	N	1856	2092	2055	3403

**Significant at $p < 0.01$

This allows us to make the following conclusions:

- For the overall country sample, institutional development is a good predictor for productivity and wealth: in accordance with theory, these indicators exhibit a positive relationship.
- For a limited sample of BRICS countries between 1996 and 2013, the above statement does not hold. For instance, Russia's TFP and per capita GDP levels were the highest among BRICS in 2013, yet its institutional development level was the worst in the bloc. China's institutions are worse than India's, yet it demonstrates better growth dynamics. However, the BRICS case doesn't contradict the theory in general.
- Despite vast differences in institutional structure between BRICS countries, their development levels aren't drastically different. The variation within the BRICS comprises a relatively small interval (about 25%) of the overall variation in institutional quality between countries of the world. The BRICS tend toward the "average/slightly below average" group of countries in terms of institutions.
- From a dynamics perspective, the development trend for institutions in the BRICS is moderately negative. Crudely put, there isn't very much happening to institutions within the bloc. At the same time, China is one of the leading countries in the world in terms of per capita GDP growth, while the rest of the BRICS are at least no worse than average. In terms of TFP growth, China and Russia are considerably above average compared to the rest of the country sample.

This does not mean that BRICS countries are unique: when it comes to the interdependence between institutional and economic dynamics, they tend to exhibit average results. At the national level, we observe significant relationships between levels of wealth, productivity, and institutions, while dynamics are more complicated. Below, we show that there is no direct relationship between institutional development and the dynamics of both wealth and productivity.

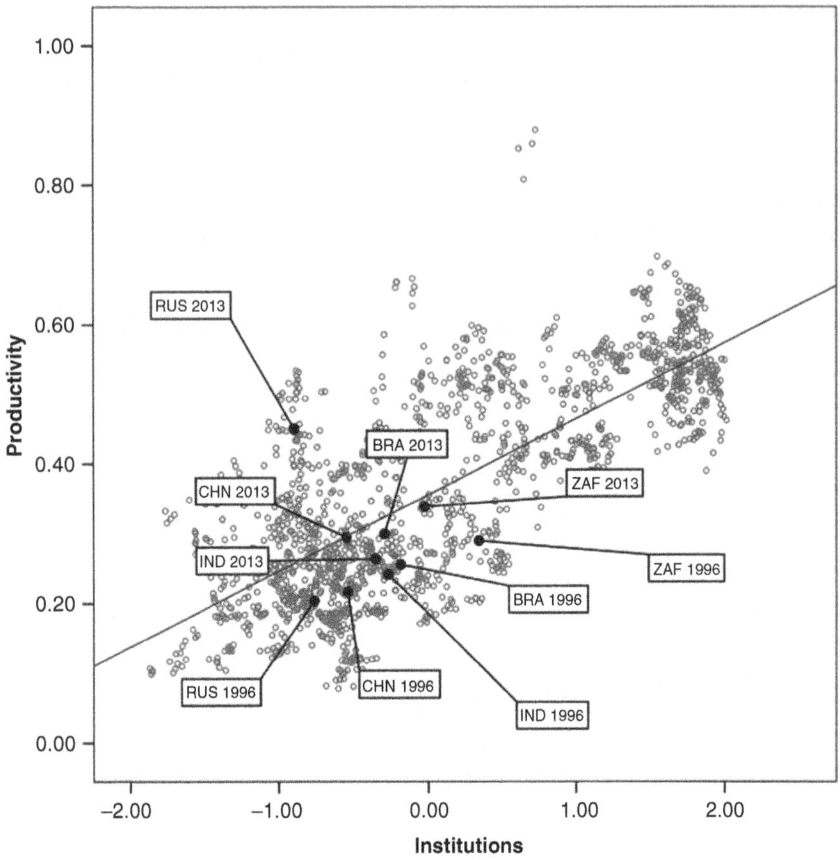

Fig. 12 Institutional development in BRICS countries against productivity levels

For all the variables in the analysis, we calculate growth rates in percentage points $\left(\frac{y_t}{y_{t-1}} - 1\right) \times 100\%$, as well as differences between the first and last years $\frac{y_{2013} - y_{1996}}{y_{1996}}$. In addition, we account for possible development delays by using lagged variables with lags between 1 and 6.

The analysis shows no strong correlation between economic development and institutional development. The coefficients retain significance only for the whole country-year sample; when analyzing separate years (which drastically reduces N), the correlations become insignificant or even change their sign. The same tendency applies when using initial indicators instead of principal components, as well as when using lags and differences between initial and ending points (Table 4).

Meanwhile, we observe the expected strong positive relationships between TFP dynamics and economic growth (Table 5). This tendency is also evident for the BRICS sample (Fig. 14).

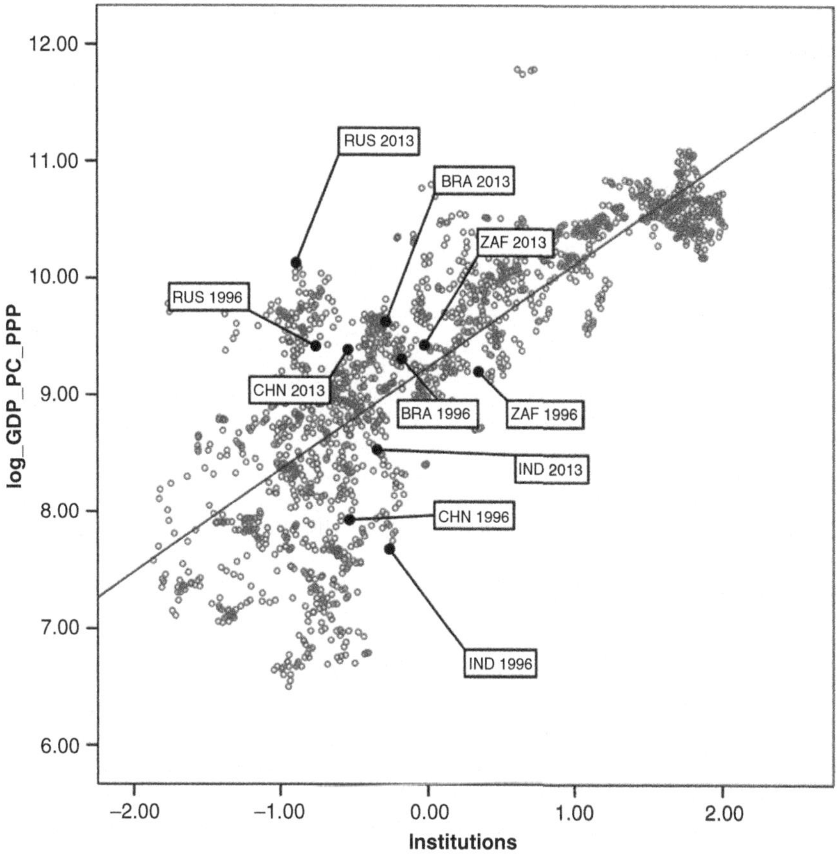

Fig. 13 Institutional development in BRICS countries against logged per capita GDP levels

BRICS countries aren't unique in terms of institutional dynamics: other countries and regions don't demonstrate drastic changes in institutional quality in the recent decades. K-means clustering into four groups shows that, for institutional principal components, none of the 150 countries in our sample has changed its cluster membership twice (i.e., from cluster 1 to cluster 3 or from cluster 2 to cluster 4) since 1996. For the 1990–2013 sample (which inevitably reduces the number of variables due to data constraints), the cluster analysis reveals three such countries: Albania, Panama, and Tunisia. However, the dynamics for the aforementioned countries don't show any consistent trends. Only a single country (Chile) has joined the "high institutional levels" cluster, but its economic wealth and productivity levels remain wanting.

Table 3 Effects of institutional quality on total factor productivity

Dependent variable: total factor productivity					
	(1)		(2)	(3)	(4)
Institutions	−0.01706		0.10376***	−0.0002	0.0362***
	(0.0243)		(0.0031)	(0.0004)	(0.0077)
Unemployment	−0.00713***		−0.0014**	0.0003***	0.0004***
	(0.001)		(0.0005)	(0.0001)	(0.0001)
Inflation	−0.00111***		0.00002	−0.00006	−0.00004
	(0.0002)		(0.0003)	(0.0000)	(0.00004)
Constant	0.469***		0.380***	0.0015	0.0013
	(0.0131)		(0.0062)	(0.0008)	(0.0008)
N	1157		1157	1097	1062
R-squared			0.53	0.02	0.044
	Within	0.3097			
	Between	0.0092			
	Overall	0.0095			

*Significant at $p < 0.1$. **Significant at $p < 0.01$. ***Significant at $p < 0.001$

5 Conclusion and Discussion

In this chapter, we analyze the mutual relationships between total factor productivity, economic welfare, and political institutions. To do so, we construct our own TFP estimates using nonparametric techniques (a variant of data envelopment analysis) for 149 countries of the world. We then use the data obtained to compare the economic growth and performance of BRICS countries relative to each other and the rest of the world, as well as in conjunction with institutional development. We use statistical methods to validate our findings. We show that levels of institutional development are a significant predictor for both growth rates and per capita GDP levels, as well as TFP levels. Our tests for differences in TFP and growth remain inconclusive.

In this study we were limited by the available data, so we only considered the period between 1990 and 2013, for which we could calculate TFP estimates. However, valid economic growth statistics are available from the World Bank database (World Bank[9]) and don't appear to be inspiring for BRICS countries. For Brazil, Russia, and RSA, we observe negative growth rates in 2015 (−4.7%, −3.9%, −0.39% correspondingly). China maintains its positive growth trend but at decelerating rates: 7.3% in 2013, 7.8% in 2014, and 6.14% in 2015. Preliminary 2016 estimates and forecasts for 2017 are also not very positive. The only BRICS country to maintain its growth momentum is India: 5.3% in 2013, 5.9% in 2014, and 6.3% in 2015.

[9]http://data.worldbank.org/indicator/NY.GDP.PCAP.KD.ZG

Table 4 Correlations between dynamics of institutions, GDP, per capita GDP, TFP, and labor and capital productivity

		GDP PC PPP growth, %	GDP PPP growth, %	TFP growth, %	Labor productivity growth, %	Capital productivity Growth, %
Anticorruption and transparency change, %	Spearman's rho	0.08**	0.09**	0.09**	0.1**	0.07**
	N	1904	1904	1701	1687	1687
Property rights change, %	Spearman's rho	0.14**	0.13**	0.14**	0.11**	0.12**
	N	2305	2305	1952	1933	1933
Quality of governance change, %	Spearman's rho	0.15**	0.14**	0.15**	0.13**	0.13**
	N	2352	2352	1939	1920	1920
Institutional change, %	Spearman's rho	−0.021	−0.006	−0.039	0.031	0.036
	N	1525	1525	1430	1416	1416

**Significant at $p < 0.01$

Table 5 Correlations between TFP dynamics and economic growth

		TFP growth, %	Labor productivity growth, %	Capital productivity growth, %
GDP PC PPP growth, %	Spearman's rho	0.71**	0.87**	0.58**
	N	3275	3252	3252
GDP PPP growth, %	Spearman's rho	0.66**	0.79**	0.55**
	N	3278	3255	3255

**Significant at $p < 0.01$

Can the results of our study shed any light on the current growth dynamics in BRICS? We hope it can explain at least some of the trends and even make a few predictions.

The analysis of productivity trajectories (Fig. 5) basically shows that the existing drivers of economic growth in BRICS countries are close to exhaustion. China and India have been moving along the labor-driven path for many years. These countries with initial shortages of capital and excess labor resources (i.e., low capital-labor ratio) managed to attract enough investment thanks to stability and FDI rights protection. However, with growing labor costs leading to lower investment flows and lack of alternative resources, these opportunities for growth may not be available for a long time. This is already true for China and seems like a real future possibility for India in the coming years.

Russia, growing along the capital-driven path, has exhausted a different resource of growth: its low initial position due to an economic collapse in the 1990s. In

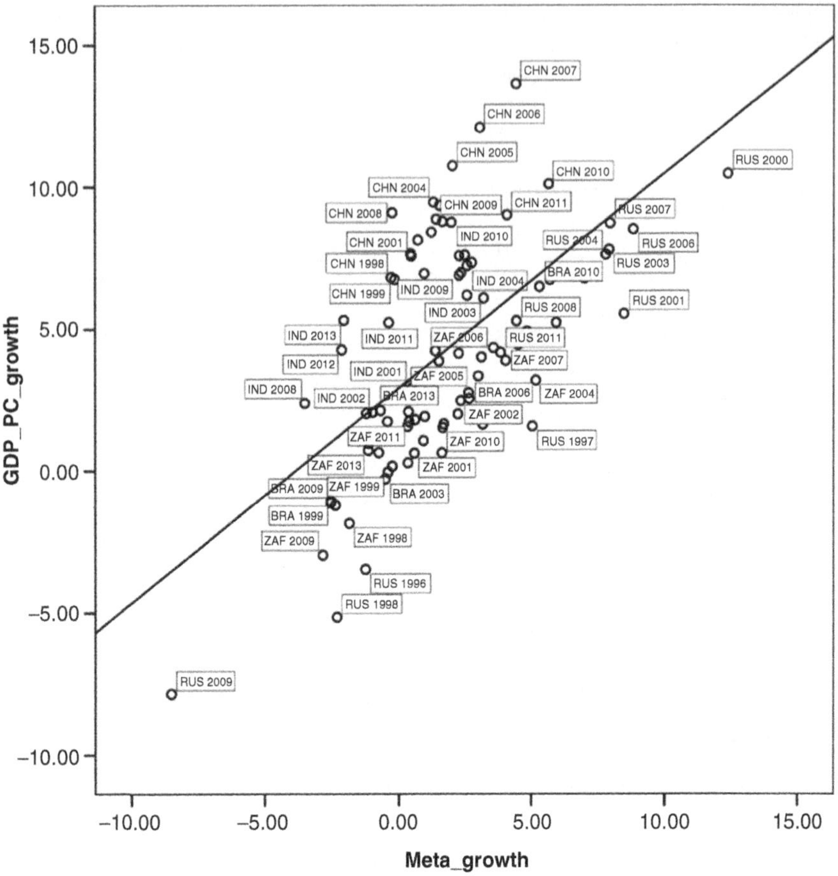

Fig. 14 GDP growth against productivity growth in BRICS countries

conjunction with high oil prices, this effect provided for quick progress in GDP accumulation (more precisely—GDP restoration).

We suggest that the only practical opportunity for the countries facing the exhaustion of "traditional" growth sources—the "extensive" ones—is switching to TFP-driven growth. In terms of Fig. 5, it means shifting to the diagonal trajectory directed toward the origin. But for now, this option doesn't seem very realistic for BRICS countries in general and for China and India specifically, taking into consideration the existing growth trajectories and inevitable inertia in the choice of growth determinants. This is why we predict a reduction in growth rates for China and India.

What can cause a shift to TFP-driven growth? While our analysis didn't allow us to obtain inference from empirical data, we can offer an intuitive assumption: the impetus toward TFP-driven growth is only possible with noticeable progress in institutional quality.

Whether any of the BRICS countries can manage an "institutional breakthrough" should be the subject of separate research involving a detailed case study of political systems and regimes within the BRICS. Our initial empirical results show that this might not be an easy task.

References

Acemoglu D, Zilibotti F (2001) Productivity differences. Q J Econ 116(2):563–606

Afonso A, St. Aubyn M (2006) Relative efficiency of health provision: a DEA approach with non-discretionary inputs. Working papers Department of Economics 2006/33. ISEG—School of Economics and Management, Department of Economics, University of Lisbon

Afonso A, St. Aubyn M (2010) Public and private inputs in aggregate production and growth: a cross-country efficiency approach. Working paper series 1154. European Central Bank

Aghion P, Roulet A (2014) Growth and the smart state. Annu Rev Econom 6:913–926

Altug S, Canova F (2014) Do institutions and culture matter for business cycles? Open Econ Rev 25:93–122

Azariadis C, Kaas L (2010) Capital misallocation and aggregate factor productivity. Working Paper series 39_10, Rimini Centre for Economic Analysis

Barro RJ (1991) Economic growth in a cross section of countries. Q J Econ 106(2):407

Berger D (2012) Countercyclical restructuring and jobless recoveries. No 1179, Meeting papers, Society for Economic Dynamics

Bojnec Š, Fertő I, Fogarasi J (2014) Quality of institutions and the BRIC countries agro-food exports. China Agric Econ Rev 6(3):379–394

Boyle R (2006) Measuring public sector productivity: lessons from international experience. CPMR discussion paper #35

Burnside C, Eichenbaum M (1996) Factor-hoarding and the propagation of business-cycle shocks. Am Econ Rev 86(5):1154–1174

Caselli F, Feyrer J (2007) The marginal product of capital. Q J Econ 122(2):535–568

Caselli F, Esquivel G, Lefort F (1996) Reopening the convergence debate: a new look at cross-country growth empirics. J Econ Growth 1(3):363–389. https://doi.org/10.1007/BF00141044

Cavalcanti TV (2007) Business cycle and level accounting: the case of Portugal port. Econ J 6:47

Centre for WTO Studies (2013) BRICS trade policies. Institutions and Areas for Deepening Cooperation

Copeland MA, Martin EM (1938) The correction of wealth and income estimates for price changes. Studies in income and wealth, vol 2. National Bureau of Economic Research, New York, pp 85–135

Dávila J (2016) Output externalities on total factor productivity. Macroecon Dyn:1–37

Davis SJ (2017) Regulatory complexity and policy uncertainty: headwinds of our own making. SSRN Electronic Journal

Dufourt F (2005) Demand and productivity components of business cycles: estimates and implications. J Monet Econ 52(6):1089–1105

Easterly W (2005) National policies and economic growth: a reappraisal. In: Aghion P, Durlauf S (eds) Handbook of economic growth, vol 1. North-Holland, Amsterdam, pp 1015–1059

Farrell MJ (1957) The measurement of productive efficiency. J R Stat Soc Ser A Gen 120 (3):253–290

Fernald JG, Wang JC (2016) Why has the cyclicality of productivity changed? What does it mean? Annu Rev Econ 8:465–496

Field AJ (2010) The procyclical behavior of total factor productivity in the United States, 1890–2004. J Econ Hist 70(2):326–350

Forstner H, Isaksson A (2002) Productivity, technology, and efficiency: an analysis of the world technology Frontier; when memory is infinite. Statistics and Information Networks Branch of UNIDO
Gancia G, Zilibotti F (2009) Technological change and the wealth of nations. Annu Rev Econ 1 (1):93–120
García-Cicco J, Pancrazi R, Uribe M (2010) Real business cycles in emerging countries? Am Econ Rev 100(5):2510–2531
Gourinchas PO, Jeanne O (2013) Capital flows to developing countries: the allocation puzzle. Rev Econ Stud 80(4):1484–1515. https://doi.org/10.1093/restud/rdt004
Hall RE, Jones CI (1999) Why do some countries produce so much more output per worker than others? Q J Econ 114(1):83–116
Hsieh CT, Klenow PJ (2009) Misallocation and manufacturing TFP in China and India. Q J Econ 124(4):1403–1448
Inglesi-Lotz R, Chang T, Gupta R (2013) Causality between research output and economic growth in BRICS. Working papers 201337. University of Pretoria, Department of Economics
Inklaar R, Timmer MP (2009) Productivity convergence across industries and countries: the importance of theory-based measurement. Macroecon Dyn 13(S2):218–240
Iversen T, Soskice D (2006) New macroeconomics and political science. Annu Rev Polit Sci 9:425–453
Kawaguchi D, Murao T (2012) Who bears the cost of the business cycle? Labor-market institutions and volatility of the youth unemployment rate. IZA J Labor Policy 1:10
Kurt S, Kurt U (2015) Innovation and labour productivity in BRICS countries: panel causality and co-integration. Procedia Soc Behav Sci 195:1295–1302
Lazear E, Shaw K, Stanton C (2016) Making do with less: working harder during recessions. J Labor Econ 34(S1):S333–S360
Lucas R (1990) Why Doesn't capital flow from rich to poor countries? Am Econ Rev 80(2):92–96
Malesky E, London J (2014) The political economy of development in China and Vietnam. Annu Rev Polit Sci 17:395–419
Mayer E, Rüth S, Scharler J (2016) Total factor productivity and the propagation of shocks: empirical evidence and implications for the business cycle. J Macroecon 50:335–346
North DC, Thomas RP (1973) The rise of the western world: a new economic history. Cambridge University Press, New York, p viii + 171
Parente SL, Prescott EC (2005) A unified theory of the evolution of international income levels, handbook of economic growth, chapter 21. In: Aghion P, Durlauf S (eds) Handbook of economic growth, vol 1, 1st edn, pp 1371–1416
Restuccia D, Rogerson R (2008) Policy distortions and aggregate productivity with heterogeneous establishments. Rev Econ Dyn 11(4):707–720
Samake I, Yang Y (2014) Low-income countries' linkages to BRICS: are there growth spillovers? J Asian Econ 30:1–14
Samargandi N, Kutan AM (2016) Private credit spillovers and economic growth: evidence from BRICS countries. J Int Financ Mark Inst Money 44:56–84
Solow RM (1956) A contribution to the theory of economic growth. Q J Econ 70(1):65–94
Storesletten K, Zilibotti F (2014) China's great convergence and beyond. Annu Rev Econ 6 (1):333–362
Tugcu CT, Tiwari AK (2016) Does renewable and/or non-renewable energy consumption matter for total factor productivity (TFP) growth? Evidence from the BRICS. Renew Sust Energ Rev 65:610–616
Wilson D (2003) Dreaming with BRICs: the path to 2050. Goldman Sachs Archives http://www.goldmansachs.com/ourthinking/archive/brics-dream.html
Yao X, Watanabe C, Li Y (2009) Institutional structure of sustainable development in BRICs: focusing on ICT utilization. Technol Soc 31(1):9–28

The Connectedness of Business Cycles Between the BRICS

Paulo Picchetti

1 Introduction

Business cycle analysis has received a lot of attention for some time now. The growth of world trade and financial linkage has created an additional interest in the co-movements of cycles between nations. Important contributions to this area of research include Arouba et al. (2011), Canova et al. (2007), Kose et al. (2003, 2008), and Stock and Watson (2005).

Particular groups of countries that are somehow linked receive special interest. Kose et al. (2008) employ a hierarchical factor model, where business cycles are derived as factors representing the common dynamics of a number of series related to economic activity and can be calculated for different levels of aggregation of individual countries. Each country in this analysis has a business cycle resulting from factors related to the world economy as a whole, factors associated with particular groups of countries, and finally their own individual fundamentals.

While the greater part of the results analyzes countries in the G-7 group, here we focus on a measure of business cycle relationships between members of the BRICS (Brazil, Russia, India, China, and South Africa), based on the methodology of "connectedness."

P. Picchetti (✉)
Fundação Getulio Vargas, Brazil/IBRE/São Paulo School of Economics, São Paulo, Brazil
e-mail: paulo.picchetti@fgv.br

S. Smirnov et al. (eds.), *Business Cycles in BRICS*, Societies and Political Orders in Transition, https://doi.org/10.1007/978-3-319-90017-9_4

2 Connectedness Theory

The connectedness theory approach is developed by Diebold and Yilmaz in a series of papers (Diebold and Yilmaz 2009, 2012, 2014). The main idea is to measure the influence of developments in other economies to the "innovations" of economic activity measures in each country. These innovations are taken as the forecast errors from models which take into account the information contained in the present and lagged values of each series. In principle, any model generating the forecasts conditional on these information sets can be used. Here, we employ the vector auto-correction (VEC) model methodology, whose details are explained in Sect. 3.2.

The variance decompositions of the forecasts produced by the Vector Auto-Correction model for each series represent the percentage of these errors attributed to shocks in each series. As explained in Sect. 2.3, these decompositions will be interpreted as the proposed connectedness measures.

In Table 1, each entry denoted as d_{ij} represents the percentage of the forecast error decomposition in each series x_i due to shocks of their own and of the others series.

The margins of Table 1 contain formulas that will be fully interpreted in Sect. 3.3 but can be thought of as the contribution of shocks in each series to the variance decomposition of the error in forecasts for each other series (rows) and the contribution of shocks in every other series to the decomposition of the forecast error for each series (columns).

3 Business Cycle Connectedness Across the BRICS

3.1 Data

The analysis is based on a common sample for industrial production indices for the BRICS, which spans monthly values from January 1988 through December 2015. All series are seasonally adjusted, and unit-root tests are performed in each one of them controlling for a break around the end of 2008. These tests do not reject the presence of stochastic trends for the cases of the seasonally adjusted series of Brazil, India, Russia, and South Africa. In the case of China, the seemingly exponential growth pattern during the sample period does not seem to be adequately represented by a deterministic trend—even allowing for polynomial trends of high orders in time; the resulting detrended series are still nonstationary. Differencing the seasonally adjusted series once still produces a stochastically trended series, as indicated by a unit-root test. Montasser and Gupta (2014) find similar results but also point out the existence of a unit root at the seasonal frequency for the Chinese series of industrial production. Here, we work with the seasonally adjusted series and prefer to control for breaks which are probably responsible for the changing behavior of the seasonal patterns during the VAR modeling below.

Table 1 Theoretical connectedness

	x_1	x_2	x_3	x_4	x_5	From others
x_1	d_{11}	d_{12}	d_{13}	d_{14}	d_{15}	$\sum_{j=1}^{5} d_{1j}{}^{j=1}{}_{j=1}, j \neq 1$
x_2	d_{21}	d_{22}	d_{23}	d_{24}	d_{25}	$\sum_{j=1}^{5} d_{2j}{}^{j=1}{}_{j=1}, j \neq 2$
x_3	d_{31}	d_{32}	d_{33}	d_{34}	d_{35}	$\sum_{j=1}^{5} d_{3j}{}^{j=1}{}_{j=1}, j \neq 3$
x_4	d_{41}	d_{42}	d_{43}	d_{44}	d_{45}	$\sum_{j=1}^{5} d_{4j}{}^{j=1}{}_{j=1}, j \neq 4$
x_5	d_{15}	d_{52}	d_{53}	d_{55}	d_{55}	$\sum_{j=1}^{5} d_{5j}{}^{j=1}{}_{j=1}, j \neq 5$
To others	$\sum_{J=1}^{5} d_{i1}{}^{J=1}{}_{J=1}$ $i \neq 1$	$\sum_{J=1}^{5} d_{i2}{}^{J=1}{}_{J=1}$ $i \neq 2$	$\sum_{J=1}^{5} d_{i3}{}^{J=1}{}_{J=1}$ $i \neq 3$	$\sum_{J=1}^{5} d_{i4}{}^{J=1}{}_{J=1}$ $i \neq 4$	$\sum_{J=1}^{5} d_{i5}{}^{J=1}{}_{J=1}$ $i \neq 5$	$\frac{1}{5} \sum_{i,J=1}^{5} d_{ij}{}^{i,J=1}{}_{i,J=1}$ $i \neq j$

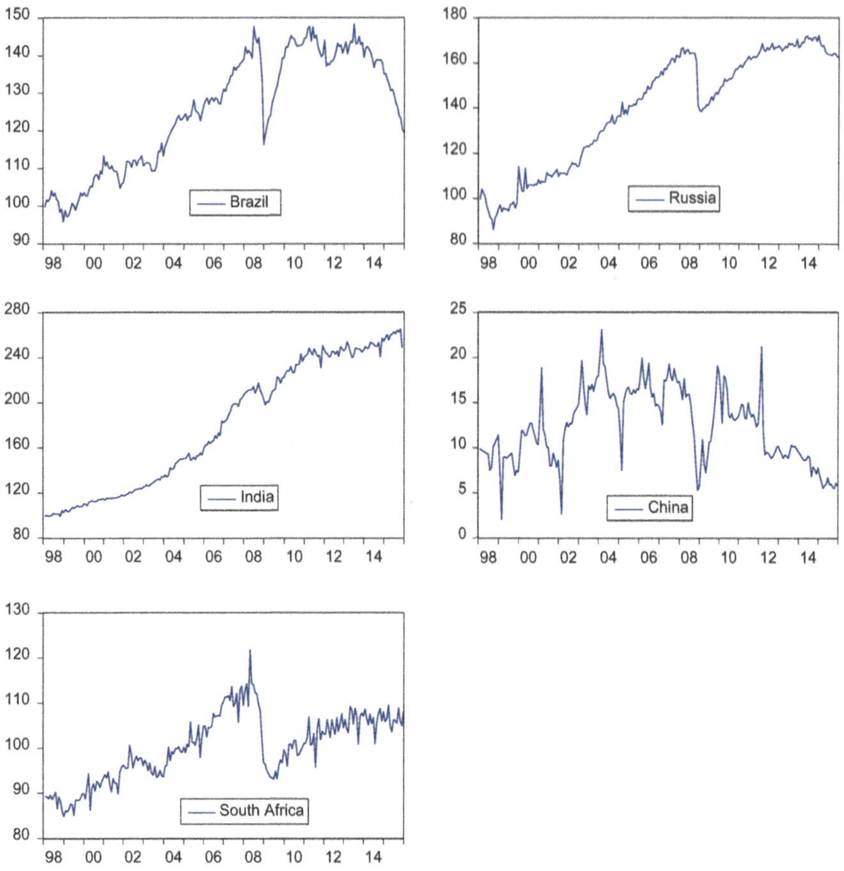

Graph 1 Monthly industrial production (seasonally adjusted)

Graph 1 depicts the seasonally adjusted series for each country, where China's series is first differenced.

3.2 *Econometric Model*

Given that the methodology for obtaining the connectedness measure is essentially based on the estimation of variance decompositions for the forecast errors, the specification of the VAR representing the dynamics of our series is of course of fundamental importance. The first step was to model the VAR in first differences, including dummies for the obvious breaks in the sample, mainly the ones that appear as additive outliers toward the end of 2008. A specification search based on the Schwarz Information Criteria pointed to a simple dynamics specified by a VAR

(1) representation. The next step involved applying this specification to testing the presence of cointegration between the series in their original levels, which all included stochastic trends. Since in the case of the Chinese series the stochastic trend is present in the first difference, we are actually testing for multicointegration following the procedure suggested by Granger and Lee (1989). The test results imply the presence of a cointegration relationship, meaning that the dynamics between the series has a fundamental dimension in terms of a long-run equilibrium relationship. The forecast error decompositions used to calculate the connectedness measures are obtained from the corresponding VEC specification.

3.3 *Results*

3.3.1 Static Connectedness

The variance decompositions for each entry in Table 1 are interpreted as measuring *pairwise directional connectedness.* Changing the notation for a more clear representation, the variance decomposition of a shock in series, e.g., 3 to the forecast error in series 1, depicted in Table 1 as d_{13}, will be from now on shown as $C_{1 \leftarrow 3}$, making the direction of shock to forecast error explicit. The notation can be made still more clear, using subscripts B for Brazil, R for Russia, I for India, C for China, and S for South Africa, so that, for instance, $C_{S \leftarrow R}$ now represents the pairwise connectedness of shocks in the Russian industrial production to the variance decomposition of forecast errors in the South African industrial production series. The entries in the connectedness matrix are of course not symmetric, since the variance decompositions of the forecast errors are not (in general) symmetric. Therefore, in general we have $C_{i \leftarrow j} \neq C_{j \leftarrow i}$ when $i \neq j$.

Table 2 presents the pairwise connectedness measures calculated from the information in the whole sample, which we will call *static.*

The connectedness from shocks, e.g., in India to South Africa, is 6.9, while the one from shocks in South Africa to India is 11.1. The margins in Table 2 present, as shown explicit in Table 1, the sums for the "to" and "from" measures for each country. The effects of shocks in the Brazilian series to the other members of the

Table 2 Estimated connectedness

	B	R	I	C	S	From others
B	82.4	1.0	0.0	13.2	3.4	17.6
R	0.5	67.5	0.9	30.5	0.7	32.5
I	2.7	4.9	68.4	13.0	11.1	31.6
C	0.3	4.5	1.3	87.0	6.8	13.0
S	1.1	28.5	6.9	1.8	61.6	38.4
To others	4.6	38.8	9.3	58.5	22.0	**26.6**
NET	−13.0	6.3	−22.4	45.4	−16.4	

group are 4.6, while the one relative to the shocks in the Chinese series is much larger (58.5). China, on the other hand, experiences the smallest effects from the other countries in the group (13.0), while South Africa experiences the largest (38.4). The average measure of static connectedness representative for the BRICS group as a whole is 26.6. This is not far from the one Diebold and Yilmaz (2014) obtain for the countries in the G-7 group (28.8).

The final row in Table 2 captures the net effects of connectedness, as simply the differences for each country between the contribution of their shocks to the others and the contributions of others' shocks to the forecast errors. China and Russia are the net "exporters" of shocks affecting other countries, while Brazil, India, and South Africa are the net "importers."

3.3.2 Dynamic Connectedness

The connectedness measures presented in Table 2 are directly computed from the variance decompositions of the forecast errors obtained from the estimated VEC model, using information from the whole available sample (January 1998 through December 2015). During these 17 years, important structural changes and business cycle turning points characterized the world economy as a whole and the countries within the BRICS group in particular. From an econometric perspective, this implies a strong potential for parameter variation in any class of models. This is of course true for our estimated VEC, meaning that our connectedness measures will be accordingly affected.

Following Diebold and Yilmaz (2014), we compute a dynamic measure of connectedness from a rolling estimation of the parameters and variance decompositions of the specified VEC. The window for this rolling estimation is fixed in 5 years, and the VEC is re-estimated sequentially using the information from samples discarding one observation from the beginning and adding one observation to the end of the resulting subsample. For each of these estimated VECs in the sequence, we compute the variance decompositions for the 12-month-ahead forecast errors and each of the connectedness measures accordingly.

The evolution of the total connectedness measure can be seen in Graph 2.

The dynamic total connectedness series begins in 2003, since it results from estimation using sequential fixed windows of 60 months, starting in 1998. There is no overall clear trend in total connectedness in this period; instead, we can think about three distinct phases. From 2003 to 2008, the index fluctuates around a stationary mean around 35%. The international financial crises, starting in mid-2008, considerably augment total connectedness indicating that even though the crises had its origins much more associated with developments of countries in the G-7 group, the transmission of its effects through members of the BRICS also played an important role. A third phase marks a continuous decline in connectedness from 2012 onward. It can be argued that each particular country within the BRICS group faced different challenges and chose different sets of policies in the aftermath of the

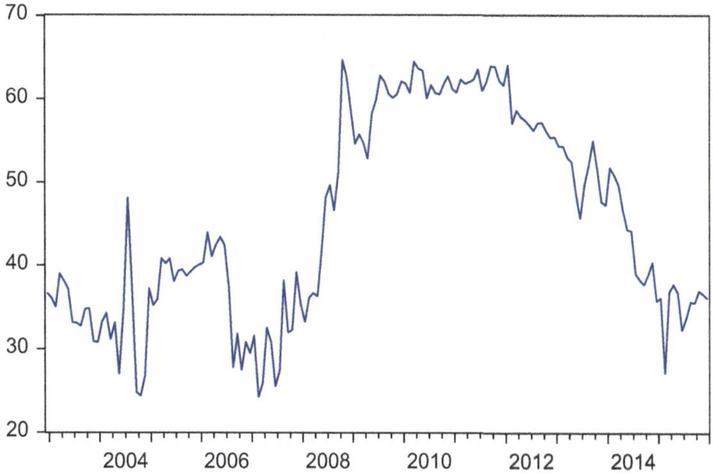

Graph 2 Dynamic total connectedness

global financial crisis, rendering the relative importance of the shocks transmitted by other economies in the group smaller.

This analysis is far from homogenous across the different members of the BRICS. In Graph 3, we can see the dynamic effects of shocks in every country to the rest of the members in the group.

Shocks in the industrial production series of China and Russia display the largest effects to the forecast errors of all countries in the group in absolute terms, and their rise is clearly associated with the global financial crisis. Brazil, India, and South Africa affect the groups' forecast errors of industrial production in an increasing manner after 2013.

Graph 4 depicts the evolution of the influence in each country of the shocks of the industrial production series of the BRICS members (excluding themselves in each particular case).

China's industrial production is the least affected in absolute terms and even so only significantly after 2013. Brazil, Russia, and South Africa increasingly face the effects after 2008 until 2013, after when their own internal shocks gain in relative importance. India, on the other hand, has a peak of transmission of the shocks from the other members around 2008, but the participation of these external factors falls rapidly shortly after that.

Finally, the dynamics of the net effects can be seen in Graph 5.

Throughout the period analyzed, China is by far the greater "exporter" of shocks affecting the forecast errors of the other countries. It is only after 2013 that the relative importance of shocks in other members' industrial output renders China more susceptible to the external shocks. While Brazil, Russia, and India oscillate through time as net importers or exporters of forecast errors, South Africa is a net importer of forecast error shocks for practically the whole period.

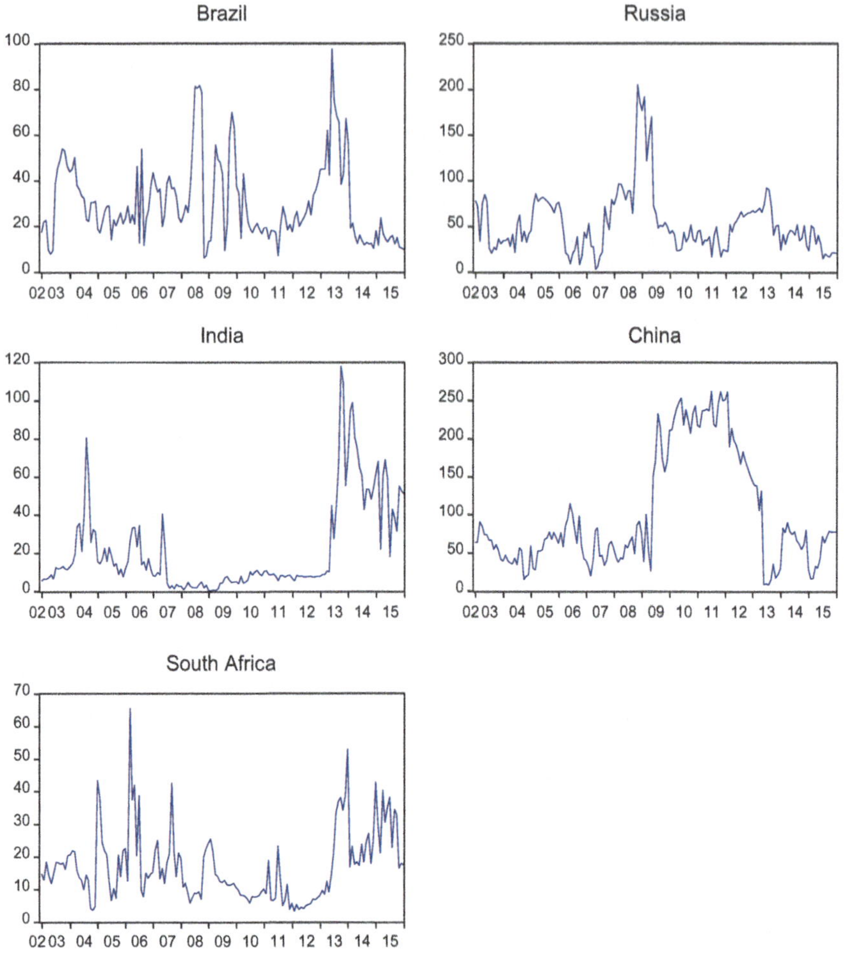

Graph 3 Dynamic connectedness: to others

4 Conclusions

The BRICS acronym became popular among international finance analysts in the beginning of the twenty-first century, as a result of a number of similarities between the growth potential and challenges of the five emerging economies. Yet, a number of fundamental institutional and demographic differences, along with geographic distances, call into question the extent to which these economies are indeed related.

The analysis of connectedness conducted here, applying a methodology originally proposed by Diebold and Yilmaz (2014), complements the traditional approach to co-movements in business cycles across countries with a number of advantages and important results.

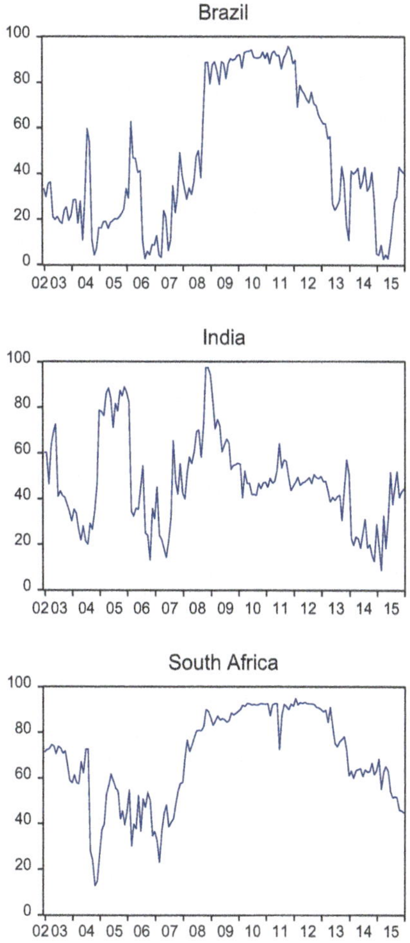

Graph 4 Dynamic connectedness: from others

First, there is a considerable relationship between the members of the BRICS, as measured by the transmission of the effects of shocks in one country to the others. In the overall measure, this relationship is not significantly different from the one observed for countries in the G-7 group.

Second, these relationships have been show to evolve considerably through time, as the dynamic analysis presented in Sect. 3.3.2 makes clear. This captures the rapidly changing nature of the relationships between the economies in the BRICS. These findings make particularly important the affirmation following the similar findings by Diebold and Yilmaz (2014): "The quick and large increase in cross-country connectedness suggest that recovery from 'the great global recession' may require coordinated policy actions among the major industrial and emerging market economies."

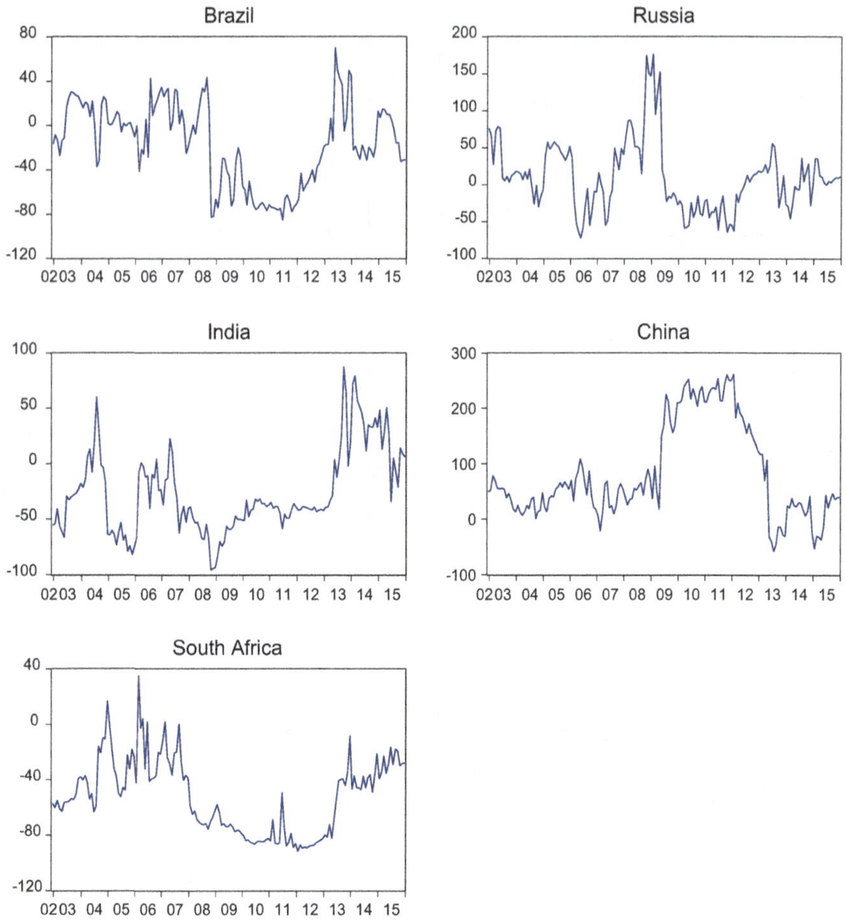

Graph 5 Dynamic connectedness: NET

Third, the approach based on the analysis of industrial production series provides a relatively high frequency and rapid set of results, compared to traditional analyses based on more comprehensive measures of economic activity such as GDP. The approach (Kose et al. 2003, 2008) is very promising in that it efficiently aims to circumvent these limitations by analyzing the greatest possible number of series for each country, even allowing for mixed frequencies. However, the availability of this kind of information for sufficiently long periods is not warranted in the BRICS case.

A fundamental dimension to complement the analysis conducted here is to consider results of trade balances between the countries along with the effects of shocks directly linked to measures of economic activity. This is a promising topic for further research.

References

Arouba SB, Diebold FX, Kose M, Terrones M (2011) Globalization, the business cycle, and macroeconomic monitoring. In: Clarida R, Giavazzi F (eds) NBER international seminar on macroeconomics 2010. University of Chicago Press, Cambridge, pp 245–301

Canova F, Ciccarellu M, Ortega E (2007) Similarities and convergence in G-7 cycles. J Monet Econ 53:850–878

Diebold FX, Yilmaz K (2009) Measuring financial asset returns and volatility spillovers, with application to global equity markets. Econ J 119:158–171

Diebold FX, Yilmaz K (2012) Better to give than to receive: predictive measurement of volatility Spillovers (with discussion). Int J Forecast 28:57–66

Diebold FX, Yilmaz K (2014) On the network topology of variance decompositions: measuring the connectedness of financial firms. J Econ 182(1):119–134

Granger RF, Lee T (1989) Investigation of production, sales and inventory relations using multicointegration and non-symmetric error-correction models. J Appl Econ 4(Suppl):S145–S159

Kose M, Otrok C, Whiteman C (2003) International business cycles: world, region, and country-specific factors. Am Econ Rev 93:1216–1239

Kose M, Otrok C, Whiteman C (2008) Understanding the evolution of world business cycles. J Monet Econ 75:110–130

Montasser G, Gupta R (2014) An application of a new seasonal unit root test for trending and breaking series in industrial production of the BRICS. http://econpapers.repec.org/RePEc:pre:wpaper:201435

Stock J, Watson M (2005) Understanding changes in international business cycle dynamics. J Eur Econ Assoc 3:968–1006

Part II
History and Driving Forces of Economic Cycles in BRICS

Economic Cycles in Brazil

Leonardo Weller

1 Introduction

Volatility and stagnation characterized economic cycles in Brazil from 1981 to 2017. The country went through nine recessions during these 36 years. Recessions were longer and more severe in the 1980s and the early 1990s, when inflation was very high, but they still happened in the following decades. Overall growth was mediocre, and the economy failed to transpose the mid-income trap. Brazilian economists often compare this stop-and-go process to a "chicken flight." These dismal results contrast with the dynamism of the postwar, when a state-led and inward-looking industrialization process made Brazil one of the world's fastest-growing economies.

This chapter provides a brief historical narrative that helps to explain why economic activity was so erratic. It contextualizes the analysis of the Brazilian economic cycles provided in this book, summarizing key events that conditioned the recessions that occurred in 1981–1983, 1987–1988, 1989–1992, 1995, 1998–1999, 2001, 2003, 2008–2009, and 2014–2016.[1] The chapter does not address the complex question of why Brazil failed to catch up with the developed world. Yet it shows that business cycles were a weak force in determining the timing and pace of economic growth. This is in line with Burgarin et al. (2010), according to whom "behavior of technological progress can fairly describe the dynamism of the Brazilian economy."

The chapter is divided into six sections besides this introduction and conclusion. Section 2 highlights that Brazilians do not save and invest enough to achieve rapid

[1]These recessions are dated by CODACE, which does not follow the rule of "two quarters of negative real GDP growth" [see Picchetti (2018) for details]. At annual level GDP, growth rates may be (and in some instances are) positive in the years indicated above as recessions.

L. Weller (✉)
EESP-FGV, São Paulo, Brazil
e-mail: leonardo.weller@fgv.br

S. Smirnov et al. (eds.), *Business Cycles in BRICS*, Societies and Political Orders in Transition, https://doi.org/10.1007/978-3-319-90017-9_5

sustainable growth. It argues that demand-driven policies and exogenous shocks rather than supply-side growth have been the main drivers of fluctuation in economic activity. The remaining of the chapter analyzes how specific policies and shocks have caused cycles of expansion and recession since the 1980s. Section 3 is on the inflationary period, from 1981 to 1993, when stabilization plans caused three recessions. Section 4 explains how the combination of unsound fiscal accounts and the 1994 Real Plan made the economy vulnerable to external shocks, which triggered two recessions. Section 5 is on the relatively prosperous decennial that started in 2004. Price stability and favorable external conditions promoted growth and social inclusion, which was only interrupted by a short recession during the world crisis of 2008–2009. The public finance problem persisted, however, as became evident in the severe recession of 2014–2016, which is addressed in Sect. 6. Section 7 concludes.

2 Stagnant Productivity and Unsustainable Growth

Brazilians save and invest a smaller share of their income than most other peoples in the developing world. The investment rate has been fluctuating below 20% since the 1980s.[2] Infrastructure is a major bottleneck for growth: investment in that sector fell from 3.6% of GDP in the 1980s to 2.3% in the 1990s and to only 2.1% in the 2000s—against 5.6% in India and 7.3% in China in 2007.[3] A low investment rate reduces the scope for growth not only because of lack of capital but also, indirectly, through productivity. Besides low capital formation, rigid labor laws dating back from the 1940s also prevent productivity from rising. Firing workers is expensive and companies may be sued if they require their employees to perform tasks that are not specified in contracts.

Figure 1 shows that GDP per capita grew more rapidly than total factor productivity (TFP) for most of the period analyzed in this chapter. The opposite did happen briefly a few times, but most often during recessions. The only exception was the mid-1990s, when GDP per capita grew below TFP growth. That was a peculiar period, during which the government liberalized trade and capital flows, privatized unproductive state-owned companies, and launched a monetary reform that controlled inflation. TFP growth accelerated between 2004 and 2013, but the pattern persisted and GDP per capita grew even more, except for the anomalous and recessive year of 2009.[4]

Similarly to productivity, factors of production can hardly explain per capita growth: the low invest rate depresses capital formation, and the average number of

[2]See Bonelli and Bacha (2013) for new reconstructed series.

[3]Frischtak (2008, 2013).

[4]Barbosa Filho and Pessôa (2014, p. 164).

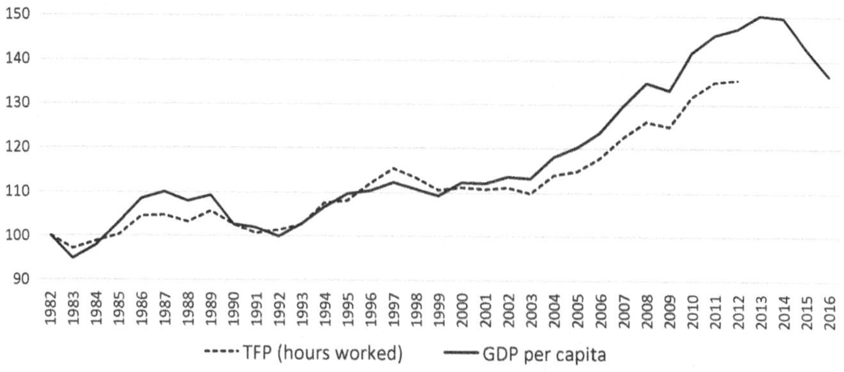

Fig. 1 GDP per capita and TFP growth (1982 = 100). Sources: IBGE, Barbosa Filho and Pessôa 2014, p. 164)

hours worked per week fell by 10% from 1982 to 2013.[5] Brazil has been recurrently growing above its potential GDP growth, and the economy has occasionally (and painfully) bounced back to its potential GDP during recessions. There is yet no data on TFP for the period that followed 2013, but given the severity of the last recession, it seems that, once again, the economy has approached its potential GDP per capita in a crisis—now more dramatically than before.

Instead of productivity gains related to business cycles, abrupt changes in economic policy, terms of trade, and world liquidity have determined economic cycles. Brazil is subject to balance of payment crises because it is a commodity exporter and capital importer. World commodity and financial markets became increasingly more volatile since the 1970s, and a succession of external shocks have contributed to the outbreak of recessive cycles. Nevertheless, Brazil is not alone in this category, and thus factors specific to that country must tell why its economic cycles are so singularly erratic.

Public finance is the main reason why economic growth has been so mediocre and inconsistent. State-led industrialization increased the size of the state since the 1930s. Brazil stopped industrializing in the 1980s, but the state continued to grow. In real terms, the primary spending of the central government expanded three times from 1980 to 1994 and more than doubled from that year until 2009. The primary federal budget grew from less than 10% to over 20% of GDP from the 1980s to the 2010s.[6] The state as a whole, including regional and municipal governments, accounts for more than a third of GDP. This ratio is comparable to developed economies but is significantly higher than other mid-income countries, particularly those that have been growing consistently. Brazil is in an adverse situation: it lacks the public services of developed and the economic dynamism of developing economies.

[5]Ibid, p. 162.

[6]Brazilian National Treasury.

The remaining of this chapter shows that fiscal deficits caused inflation in the 1980s and external vulnerability in the 1990s. All these decades' recessions were, in one way or another, linked to unsound public finance. The recession that started in 2014, which turned out to be the most severe of all, was also the consequence of fiscal deterioration.

3 Inflation and Failed Stabilization Plans: 1981–1993

Brazil had one of the world's most persistent processes of high inflation. Table 1 shows that inflation was above 100% for most of the 1980s and reached the thousands in the turn of the 1990s. Economic policy was the primary driver of inflation. The government depreciated the national currency in real terms to boost exports. It also printed money to finance unsound fiscal accounts, which increased demand but did not generate sustainable growth.[7] In a few occasions, policymakers attempted to control inflation by implementing tight fiscal and monetary policies. Nevertheless, the inflationary process was particularly persistent, and these orthodox policies only caused recessions—rather than price stability.[8]

Inflation accelerated during the early 1980s debt crisis, which was a Latin American phenomenon. Brazil was the largest debtor in the continent. State-owned companies borrowed abroad to finance massive investment projects in heavy industry. The spike in world interests in 1979 and the fall in terms of trade that followed the second oil shock, also in that year, deteriorated the balance of payments. The government devalued the *cruzeiro* (the Brazilian currency of the time) to boost exports and to run a trade surplus, with which the economy generated the foreign exchange the government needed to service the external debt. Table 1 shows the rise in reserves, which allowed Brazil to service the debt for longer than its neighbors—the debt only went into default in 1987. However, the exchange rate depreciation came with a cost: together with expensive oil, the weak cruzeiro boosted inflation.[9]

João Figueiredo's administration (1979–1985), the last of Brazil's two-decades-long dictatorship, tightened fiscal and monetary policies and reduced real wages to control inflation and keep imports at low levels. Launched in 1981, Figueiredo's package caused the first recession addressed in this chapter, which was almost as intense as the recent recession that started in 2014. GDP fell by 8.5% in nine quarters, resulting in 2 years of negative growth and a year of stagnation, as shown in Table 1. Yet these policies failed to control inflation. Strong cartelization

[7]See Bacha (1994) on the relation between unsound fiscal policy and inflation.

[8]See Arida and Resende (1985) for a contemporary criticism to the orthodox policies of the 1980s. The article highlights the indexation problem and proposes a reform that would become the fundamental idea of the Real Plan, which stabilized the economy in 1994.

[9]Carneiro and Modiano (2014).

Table 1 Macroeconomic indicators, 1981–1993 (This Table does not include fiscal data as that was unreliable during the inflationary period)

	GDP growth (%)	Inflation CPI (%)	Exports (US$ billion)	Imports (US$ billion)	Foreign exchange reserves (US$ billion)
1981	−4.25	95.62	23.29	22.09	7.51
1982	0.83	104.79	20.18	19.39	3.99
1983	−2.93	164.01	21.90	15.43	4.56
1984	5.40	215.26	27.01	13.92	12.00
1985	7.85	242.23	25.64	13.15	11.61
1986	7.49	79.66	22.35	14.04	6.76
1987	3.53	363.41	26.22	15.05	7.46
1988	−0.06	980.21	33.79	14.61	9.14
1989	3.16	1972.91	34.38	18.26	9.68
1990	−4.35	1620.97	31.41	20.66	9.97
1991	1.03	472.70	31.62	21.04	9.41
1992	−0.47	1119.10	35.79	20.55	23.75
1993	4.67	2477.15	38.55	25.26	32.21

Source: IBGE, IPEA, Central Bank of Brazil

prevented competition from squeezing markups, which would have caused disinflation due to falling real wages.[10] Peculiar laws established that wages and yields on the public debt were to increase automatically according to previous inflation. In addition to that, the rise in interests increased the cost of sterilizing the interventions in the foreign exchange market, and the government relied on monetary emission to purchase dollars and service the foreign debt.[11]

This recession lasted until the first quarter of 1983, which marked the beginning of democratization. Opposition parties won most state-level elections, defeating the politicians who had supported the military regime. A campaign for direct presidential election failed to prevent an electoral college from choosing the new president in 1984, but helped the opposition candidate Tancredo Neves to win the content. Neves died shortly thereafter, and Vice-President José Sarney (1985–1990) took office. Voters elected a Congress that was in charge of writing a new Constitution, which was promulgated in 1988.

Sarney formed a coalition administration that ran lose economic policies. It attempted to control inflation by implementing a series of price freeze programs. Launched in 1986, the Cruzado Plan (named after a new currency that featured the plan) was the first of these initiatives. The plan increased wages before freezing prices, which made the president popular but caused shortages of goods. The spread of black markets forced the government to lift the price freeze later that year.[12]

[10]Bresser Pereira and Nakano (1984).

[11]Carneiro and Modiano (2014).

[12]Modiano (1986).

The government launched a new plan in 1987. It combined a new price freeze with exchange rate depreciation, falling real wages, and some initiatives to retrench expenditure. The recession of 1987–1988 was a consequence of those policies. The weaker currency and low domestic demand produced a trade surplus, but the government's accounts remained unsound.[13] The combination of fiscal deficit and exchange rate depreciation was behind that year's moratoria on the external debt, which reduced investments and also contributed to the recession of 1987–1988.

The economy was on the edge of hyperinflation by the end of Sarney's presidency. Yet the monetary system never collapsed: The public continued to operate most transactions in Brazilian currency rather than in dollars, even though inflation nearly reached 2000% in 1989.[14] Another recession started in that year and lasted until December 1991. The threat of hyperinflation made markets unstable and abrupt policy changes were expected to follow the 1989 presidential elections, the first since 1960. Lula da Silva, then a left-wing union leader, disputed the second round against Fernando Collor (1990–1992), who was elected based on a liberalizing platform.

Collor's administration froze savings accounts, imposed a short-term price freeze, and cut expenditure. Inflation did fall but continued at rather high levels, around 20% per month.[15] The cost of those policies was noteworthy: GDP declined by 4.35% in 1990.[16] Collor was in the center of a corruption scandal that escalated into a political crisis. Under intense pressure from popular movements and street demonstrations, Congress impeached the president in 1992. Economic and political instability prevented the economy from recovering from the crisis that had started in 1989. It explains why this was—together with the 2014–2016 recession—the longest in our period of analysis, lasting for 11 quarters.

4 Economic Stabilization and Adverse Shocks: 1993–2003

The Real Plan stabilized the Brazilian economy in 1994, during the presidency of Itamar Franco (1992–1994), the vice-president who took office after Collor's impeachment. A team under the command of the future president Fernando Henrique Cardoso (1995–2002), then the finance minister in Itamar's administration, introduced the new currency *real*. Capital inflow appreciated the *real* right after its launching. Together with trade liberalization, the strong exchange rate deflated

---

[13]Modiano (1987).

[14]To a great extent, indexation—the main cause of the inflation's persistency—preserved the demand for national currency and held the monetary system together. Franco (2005) presents a somehow different interpretation when he argues that the very high inflation of the period characterizes hyperinflation. The main point, however, is that the acceleration of inflation caused a crisis between late 1989 and early 1990.

[15]Faro (1991).

[16]IBGE.

Table 2 Domestic macroeconomic indicators, 1994–2003

	GDP growth (%)	Unemployment (%)	Inflation CPI (%)	Primary surplus (% GDP)	Net total public debt (% GDP)	SELIC rate (% annual)
1994	5.33	–	916.46	5.64	43.9	52.7
1995	4.42	6.7	22.41	0.26	29.5	43.4
1996	2.15	7.6	9.56	−0.10	31.9	24.5
1997	3.38	8.5	5.22	−0.96	32.8	22.4
1998	0.04	9.7	1.65	0.02	39.4	25.7
1999	0.25	10.4	8.94	3.23	48.5	23.0
2000	4.31	–	5.97	3.47	47.0	16.2
2001	1.39	10.1	7.67	3.38	51.5	16.1
2002	3.05	9.9	12.53	3.21	59.9	17.7
2003	1.14	10.5	9.30	3.34	54.3	21.2

Source: IBGE, IPEA, Central Bank of Brazil

the tradable sector and finally reduced inflation. The monthly CPI rate fell from 46.6% to 0.6% in the second half of 1994.

The end of high inflation conditioned a consumption boom, for it prevented real wages from falling and enabled the appearance of a credit market directed to consumers. The economists who designed the plan had anticipated this spike in demand and suggested fiscal retrenchment to maintain prices stable. The government cut expenditure in the months that preceded the plan, but the reform was short-lived and fiscal accounts worsened subsequently.[17] Table 2 shows that the primary surplus turned into a deficit and the public debt started to increase vis-à-vis GDP in 1996.

The end of high inflation contributed to this fiscal deterioration. A law dating from the 1960s pegged the nominal value of taxes to inflation but did not introduce any mechanism of readjustment to expenditure. While inflation was high, the government made cash by postponing payments, a source of revenue that disappeared with stability. Moreover, 1994 was a general election year. Cardoso won the race for office in the first round. His party alliance formed a majority in Congress and elected governors in main states. This political success would have been less pronounced had the government cut expenditure as the *real* team had advised. Finally, the 1988 Constitution granted stability to civil servants and stipulated minimum levels for the health and education budgets, reducing the scope for measures designed to slow the pace of growth of the state's budget.[18] Once in office, Cardoso failed to pass a comprehensive fiscal reform in Congress and the government ran primary deficits.[19] The nominal deficit fluctuated around 3%, which was a

[17]Bacha (1995) and Franco (1995).

[18]See Rezende et al. (1989) for a contemporary view on the fiscal impact of the 1988 Constitution and Mendes (2014) for a recent work on its long-term consequences.

[19]Giambiagi (2002).

Table 3 External macroeconomic indicators, 1994–2003

	Exports (US$ billion)	Imports (US$ billion)	Foreign exchange reserves (US$ billion)	Nominal exchange rate (RS/US$)	Real exchange rate (1995 = 100)
1994	43.55	33.08	38.81	0.87	107.69
1995	46.42	50.99	51.84	0.92	100.00
1996	47.71	54.35	60.11	1.01	95.35
1997	52.82	60.80	52.17	1.08	95.21
1998	51.11	58.84	44.56	1.16	97.12
1999	48.26	50.38	36.34	1.85	143.66
2000	55.31	56.94	33.01	1.83	136.38
2001	58.26	56.73	35.87	2.35	161.52
2002	60.43	48.38	37.82	3.00	157.61
2003	73.11	49.36	49.30	3.06	156.69

Source: IBGE, IPEA, Central Bank of Brazil

problem because interest rates were high and economic growth was low. The result was the rapid rise of public debt in proportion to GDP, as shown in Table 2.

Given the lack of fiscal consolidation, the Central Bank raised the interests on the public debt (the SELIC rate) to high levels in an attempt to limit demand. Such tight monetary policy maintained the investment rate low, but the consumers' demand for credit was inelastic, a consequence of decades of financial repression. The economy grew strongly in 1994, particularly in sectors such as durable consumer goods, which benefited from the credit boom.

Although consumption was growing in spite of the tight monetary policy, high interest rates crucially contributed to the anti-inflationary plan through the external front. The government had arranged a settlement on the foreign-denominated sovereign debt, which enabled the Brazilian economy to access foreign savings. The high SELIC rate attracted capital and appreciated the *real* to the record rate of 84 cents to the dollar in the second half of 1994—the new currency had been launched at a 1:1 parity in July. The strong currency conditioned a spike in imports that accommodated the rising consumption, allowing inflation to fall. Table 3 shows that the trade balance became negative. Brazil was running twin deficits (both trade and fiscal), which was sustainable as long as capital flew in. That was going to change as two adverse external shocks hit the economy in the second half of the 1990s.[20]

The first shock happened in early 1995.[21] A run on the Mexican peso depreciated that currency and Mexico nearly defaulted on its external debt. The Tequila Crisis, as it became known, triggered capital outflow from the rest of Latin America, including Brazil. The *real* weakened, approaching the initial parity with the dollar.[22] An

[20]Figueiras (2000).

[21]CODACE recognized 1995Q2 and 1995Q3 as recessionary quarters, but at annual level, the real GDP growth rate was 4.4% in 1995.

[22]Bacha (1997).

eventual sharp depreciation would have threatened price stability right at the beginning of Cardoso's first term.

The Central Bank reacted to the crisis on two fronts. The monetary policy became even tighter, with the SELIC rate reaching 51% in March (inflation was still high at 17%, but way lower than the SELIC). Besides, the Central Bank started to intervene in the foreign exchange market to maintain the exchange rate into preestablished limits. This sudden policy change safeguarded the Real Plan but created instability in Brazil's financial market. Along with the tightening of monetary policy and the end of the previous year's consumption boom, uncertainty related to the Tequila Crisis conditioned the first recession of the post-stabilization period, which lasted for most of 1995.

A second shock hit Brazil in 1997–1998: the Asian and Russian crises reduced capital inflow, forcing the Central Bank to implement a second round of monetary tightening.[23] Once again, external vulnerability slowed economic activity, causing the subsequent recession in 1998. The Central Bank protected the exchange rate stability until it lacked enough foreign exchange to do so.[24] The *real* finally weakened in January 1999, the first month of Cardoso's second term. The Central Bank maintained the SELIC rate high to limit the pass-through effect on inflation. The economy resumed growing already in the second trimester of that year. With inflation under control, the exchange rate depreciated in real terms, starting a decade-long export boom that was subsequently amplified by rising commodity prices.

Cardoso's second administration established a new macroeconomic framework that included flexible exchange rate, primary surplus, and inflation target. The first two items allowed Brazil to depart from the twin deficits, reducing its reliance on external savings and vulnerability to external shocks. The central government increased taxation to run a primary balance and a new fiscal code prevented local authorities from overspending.[25] Given the large and expensive public debt, though, the government still ran a nominal deficit. The Central Bank maintained the SELIC rate high to converge the inflation to the target, which was consolidated at 4.5% in 2003.[26]

An energy crisis hit Brazil in 2001. Hydroelectric power responds for most of the nation's electrical matrix, which increases the risk of power shortages during droughts. Different rainfall regimes mitigate this problem, for heavy rains usually fill up reservoirs in the South during winter, which is the driest season in the populous Southeast. However, the government attempted but failed to attract private capital to develop the high-voltage cable system that unites both regions. Given the fiscal deterioration of the 1990s, the public sector lacked the resources needed to launch such infrastructure projects. The result of underinvestment in the energy

[23]Kaltenbrunner (2010) and Baig and Goldfajn (2001).

[24]See Table 1.

[25]Giambiagi (2002).

[26]Zilberman and Barboza (2017) and Barbosa-Filho (2008).

sector was a series of power cuts in the dry winter of 2001, which caused one more recession.[27]

The last recession of the economic stabilization period happened in 2003, Lula's first year in office. Low growth rates under Cardoso raised unemployment to two digits, which contributed to Lula's popularity as the opposition candidate. His imminent victory in the 2002 election raised Brazilian risk and caused a run against the *real*, even though Lula had abandoned his previous radical left-wing platform. The Enron Crisis in the United States completed that year's adverse shocks. The currency depreciated by 65% in the 5 months that preceded elections. The weak exchange rate pressured inflation, but the Central Bank failed to raise the SELIC rate in mid-2002. A tightening monetary policy would have reduced the already slim chances of Cardoso's candidate José Serra of beating Lula. The Central Bank is not independent in Brazil, which explains why it only raised interest rates after elections were already over in November. Inflation was nearly out of control by then: the annualized CPI rate reached 27% in January 2003, when Lula took office.[28]

The next recession would have started in 2002 had the Central Bank acted consistently to the inflation target regime. Inaction imposed a heavy burden on Lula's first administration. The problem was particularly severe as about a quarter of the domestically denominated public debt was pegged to the dollar, and thus the weakening *real* raised the cost of servicing the debt.[29] Consistently to his new approach to macroeconomic policy, President Lula appointed a team of economists committed to the inflation target and sound fiscal accounts. The Central Bank increased the SELIC rate and inflation reached the target in 2005. The Finance Ministry raised taxes and cut expenditure to run a primary surplus above 3.75% of GDP, a previously established target for the federal government. The Treasury reduced the fiscal exposure to the exchange rate by swapping the debt pegged to the dollar for long-term SELIC bonds. These policies prevented inflation from rising and maintained fiscal policy sound, but they caused a recession in 2003. Although unpopular, such measures were crucial for political stability—Lula would not have been able to govern as he did had inflation accelerated during his first presidency.

5 Growth, Unsustainable Policies, and Recession: 2004–2014

The recession that happened in Lula's first year in office was short, and Brazil was already growing by the end of 2003. That was the beginning of the longest period of expansion analyzed in this chapter. Fundamentals became strong and policymakers

[27] Pinguelli Rosa (2001).

[28] See Fig. 1.

[29] Banco Central do Brasil. https://www.bcb.gov.br/fis/Consorcios/port/consorcio_banco_de_dados.asp?idpai=consorcio

Table 4 External macroeconomic indicators, 2004–2017

	Exports (US$ billion)	Imports (US$ billion)	Foreign exchange reserves (US$ billion)	Nominal exchange rate (RS/US$)	Real exchange rate (1995 = 100)
2004	96.44	63.90	52.93	2.92	153.14
2005	118.25	74.82	53.80	2.41	129.93
2006	137.81	92.69	85.84	2.17	118.51
2007	160.67	122.18	180.33	1.93	112.01
2008	198.38	174.58	206.81	1.83	117.51
2009	153.61	128.65	239.05	1.99	117.87
2010	201.32	182.83	288.57	1.76	105.56
2011	255.51	227.88	352.01	1.67	114.92
2012	242.28	224.86	378.61	1.96	145.42
2013	241.58	241.19	375.79	2.17	109.60
2014	224.10	230.73	374.00	2.36	111.31
2015	190.09	172.42	370.23	3.39	135.64
2016	184.45	139.42	372.22	3.45	125.41
2017	194.78	144.43	378.38	3.20	–

Source: IBGE, IPEA, Central Bank of Brazil
Note: Data projected for 2017

counted with enough reputation to achieve sustainable growth and low inflation. The investment rate increased to above 20%, and GDP growth started to converge to TFP growth, although slightly above it, as has been shown in Fig. 1. The government could have set the basis for sustainable growth had sound economic policy persisted, which did not happen—policies became unsound after the 2008–2009 world crisis.[30]

The rise in world commodity prices and a trade boom with China had profound impacts in the Brazilian economy during the 2000s. Table 4 shows that the growth in exports resulted in a large trade surplus. Strong capital inflow completed this favorable external front. The *real* appreciated sharply, which helped the Central Bank to manage the inflation target regime but also made national companies less competitive in the tradable sectors. The government intervened in the exchange rate market to slow down the pace of exchange rate appreciation, which explains the rise in reserves. The state became a net external creditor, an entirely new event in Brazilian history.

Brazil's inflation target (4.5%) is significantly above the inflation rate of its main trade partners, and thus the nominal exchange rate appreciation resulted in a strong appreciation in real terms. Imports increased rapidly, speeding up a deindustrialization process that had started in the inflationary and recessive 1980s and gained momentum with the trade liberalization of the 1990s. Dynamism in the primary and tertiary sectors compensated for the underperforming secondary sector. The primary sector was responsible for most productivity gains of the period, while

[30]This conclusion is in line with a contemporary paper by Giambiagi and Montero (2005).

Table 5 Domestic macroeconomic indicators, 2014–2017

	GDP growth (%)	Unemployment (%)	Inflation CPI (%)	Primary surplus (% GDP)	Net total public debt (% GDP)	SELIC rate (% annual)
2004	5.76	9.7	7.60	3.69	50.2	15.1
2005	3.20	10.2	5.69	3.74	47.9	17.6
2006	3.96	9.2	3.14	3.15	46.5	14.1
2007	6.07	8.9	4.46	3.24	44.5	11.3
2008	5.09	7.8	5.90	3.33	37.6	11.8
2009	−0.13	9.1	4.31	1.94	40.9	9.5
2010	7.53	7.5	5.91	2.62	38.0	9.3
2011	3.97	7.3	6.50	2.94	34.5	11.0
2012	1.92	6.7	5.84	2.18	32.2	8.2
2013	3.00	7.1	5.91	1.71	30.5	7.9
2014	0.50	7.5	6.41	−0.56	32.6	10.4
2015	−3.77	9.0	10.67	−1.85	35.6	13.0
2016	−3.60	11.9	6.29	−2.47	45.9	14.3
2017	0.73	12.1	3.09	−2.46	53.6	7.0

Source: IBGE, IPEA, Central Bank of Brazil
Note: Data projected for 2017

labor-intensive services reduced unemployment and increased income among low-wage workers.[31] Economic growth was sustainable as long as the primary sector continued to grow, which depended on China's purchases of Brazilian commodities. Without this external demand, the primary sector would have had less scope for rising productivity. Commodity exports were vital for the prosperity of the 2000s.

Economic growth increased tax revenue and strengthened fiscal account, as shown in Table 5. Price stability allowed the Central Bank to cut the SELIC rate, which reduced the pressure on the Treasury. The government nearly reached a nominal fiscal balance, which was an informal target for the orthodox economists who ran macroeconomic policy. However, fiscal consolidation encountered resistance among the government's heterodox economists, who were inspired by an interventionist interpretation of Keynesianism and the theories of trade protection developed under the influence of the Economic Commission for Latin America (ECLAC) in the postwar. These policymakers defended the rise in expenditure to boost demand, which they believed would stimulate investment and deliver sustainable growth according to a high multiplier effect.

The heterodox group had limited influence over the national budget and the Central Bank during Lula's first term, but it dominated industrial policy through bodies such as the Social and Economic National Development Bank (BNDES). The most eminent heterodox economist was the future president Dilma Rousseff (2011–2016), who served as mining and energy minister and Lula's chief of staff before

[31]Bonelli and Pinheiro (2013).

running for office in 2010. Rousseff pushed for the expansion of social programs, the launching of large public investment projects, and the distribution of subsidies.[32]

The 2008–2009 crisis shifted the balance in favor of these heterodox policymakers. The government used the BNDES to provide the short-term finance exporters needed, which mitigate the effects of the global credit crunch in the external sector. The exchange rate depreciated but quickly bounced back. The government implemented a countercyclical fiscal policy to stimulate the economy. It momentarily suspended the primary surplus target, running an expansionist fiscal policy that largely explains why this recession lasted for only two quarters, a noteworthy result given the proportions of that year's international crisis.

Countercyclical policies in China increased exports sharply in the following-up of the recession, and the economy grew at the record rate of 7.5% in 2010 (see Tables 4 and 5, respectively). Loose monetary policies in developed countries caused an inflow of capital that strengthened the national currency. The real exchange rate reached its most appreciated level since the 1990s. Imports grew rapidly, maintaining price stability in spite of the high rate of growth and low unemployment.

It was in that benign environment that Rousseff took office in 2011. In contrast with Lula, who delegated economic decisions, the new president centralized policies. The Rousseff administration expanded expenditure and failed to meet the targets for primary surplus. In a highly controversial and nebulous series of episodes, the Finance Ministry manipulated data to improve official fiscal accounts. The maneuver included the postponement of transfers related to social programs carried out through the state-owned banks Banco do Brasil and Caixa Econômica Federal. These banks paid the final beneficiaries without receiving the funds due from the Treasury, which included these unpaid values in the primary surplus. The government was in practice borrowing from its banks—which is illegal—in an attempt to meet fiscal targets. That had terrible consequences, not only because the Treasury had to pay the banks back at some point, which it did after Rousseff's reelection, but also (and mainly) due to detrimental reputational effects.

Rising demand pushed inflation to about 6.5%, the highest bound of the 4% interval around the 4.5% target. The Central Bank departed from the inflation target regime, reducing the SELIC rate in mid-2011 even though inflation was rising above 4.5%. In practice, the monetary authority was pursuing an informal exchange rate target to protect the tradable sector. The strong *real*, a consequence of the period's great capital inflow, speeded up the deindustrialization process. By reducing the SELIC rate, the Central Bank made Brazil a less attractive destination for foreign capital and allowed the *real* to deppreciate.

As this expansionist monetary policy put extra pressure on inflation, the government forced the state-owned energy companies Petrobrás and Eletrobrás to freeze prices, which deteriorated their books and compromised even more the quality of official macroeconomic data. Maintaining inflation under control was politically important—the opposition strongly criticized Rousseff's inflationary policies. In a

[32]Werneck (2014).

striking inversion of roles, the Central Bank became an instrument for industrial policy, while state-owned companies helped the government to achieve macroeconomic targets.

The Chinese economic growth slowed down to one digit in the mid-2010s, reducing the rate of growth of Brazil's exports and hence the scope for productivity gains in the primary sector. Rousseff's expansionist policies aimed to foster investment in the secondary sector to compensate for the end of the commodity boom. The economy grew during most of her first administration, although less than when Lula was in office. Yet the investment rate fell from about 19% to 17% from 2010 to 2014.[33]

There is no consensus on why investment decreased in spite of the government's stimulus, but institutions seem to have been determinant. Lack of fiscal transparency and the government's interference in state-owned companies worsened the institutional environment. Moreover, a public investigation on Petrobras' contracts known as Car Wash (named after a company involved in a money-laundry scheme) turned out to become Brazil's largest corruption scandal ever. The Justice imposed heavy fines on companies involved in wrongdoing, such as the construction giant Odebrecht,[34] which cut investment projects to deal with the adverse financial consequences of the Car Wash investigations.

6 Fiscal Abyss and Deep Recession: 2014–2017

The recession that started in mid-2014 became Brazil's longest and most severe ever recorded. The causes of the crisis are complex and there is still no consensus on how they interacted. Political instability, the Car Wash investigation, and falling commodity prices played a role, but fiscal deterioration was also important. To a great extent, the crisis was self-inflicted. Early signs of recovery such as growth in sales and falling inventories indicate that the recession was over by the end of 2016, but there is no way one can predict whether a new expansion cycle will end what is likely become Brazil's second lost decade—after the terrible 1980s.

The economic slowdown in China in the early 2010s left the public sector as the sole source of growth in Brazil. The government expanded spending sharply before the 2014 election, launching a myriad of tax breaks, cash transfer programs, and subsidies. Primary surplus converted into deficit and the ratio between public debt and GDP, which had fallen for most of Lula's years, assumed a sharp upward trend after 2013. Commodity prices began to fall in 2014, finishing a decade-long

[33]Ibidem.

[34]One of the most recurrent corruption schemes consisted of rigged bidding rounds in which Odebrecht and other "competing" construction companies such OAS and Andrade Gutierrez offered overpriced contracts to Petrobrás. These companies took turns in winning bidding rounds. The wrongdoers shared the inflated profits with the politicians and officials who ran Petrobrás, which therefore became a stable source of rent.

expansion. Salaries were still rising in 2014, even though productivity had stagnated and the retailed sector started to shrink. Profit squeeze resulted in a sharp rise in unemployment, which is shown in Table 5. Unemployed reached 13.7% in mid-2017, an unfortunate all-times record.[35]

Rousseff refused to acknowledge the early signs of recession and fiscal deterioration while running for reelection in 2014. Agents feared that her victory would trigger a steep rise in inflation and an eventual default on the public debt, and the *real* started a long and intense depreciation cycle. Once in office in 2015, however, the president appointed an orthodox economic team to reduce the fiscal deficit. Yet the recession heavily compromised tax revenue and fiscal results worsened even though the government was cutting expenditure.

Rousseff lost grip of the political game in Congress, where her administration failed to pass reforms that would have broadened its scope for fiscal consolidation. The most notorious defeat happened when the government sent a bill to raise the retirement age. Opposition congressmen from centrist and center-right parties—including Cardoso's party PSDB—who had always defended the reform of the pension system joined left-wing members of the Rousseff's parliamentary base and voted against the reform. A generous pension system created in the 1988 Constitution has pressured public finance as Brazil's population ages. The pension fund responded to 19% of the federal budget and its deficit was the equivalent of 2.4% of GDP in 2017.[36] That is high considering that Brazil's population is still relatively young.

The government lifted price controls in the energy sector, which together with the exchange rate depreciation raised inflation to two digits in 2015. Dovish in the previous years, the Central Bank responded by lifting the SELIC rate, which contributed to the deepening of the recession and put extra pressure on the already unsound fiscal accounts. Brazil lost the investment grade rate, a symbol of the prosperous Lula's years. High risk intensified the depreciation of the real, maintaining inflation high in spite of the recession. Rising inflation and unemployment compressed real wages. A by-product of the boom of credit that took place in the previous decade, nonperforming loans reached record highs, reducing sales. Inventories increased, pressuring companies to delay investment projects and fire even more workers. Brazil was all of a sudden in a terrible vicious cycle that explains why the 2014–2016 recession was so severe.

The economic crisis reduced Rousseff approval rate to about 10% and fueled the social unrest that by and large explains why the president was impeached on rather weak legal basis in 2016.[37] Like her predecessor, President Michel Temer (2016–

[35]IBGE.

[36]Brazilian National Treasury.

[37]Datafolha.

2018) lacks the political support to push for the fiscal reforms needed to create conditions for sustainable growth. Temer has been implicated in corruption scandals, which has drastically reduced his leverage over Congress and his approval rate (only 5% according to the recent polls, which makes him the world's most unpopular head of state).[38]

The deep recession reduced inflation, but volatile politics and uncertainty related to the sustainability of fiscal accounts make a vigorous economic recovery unprovable. The general election of 2018 is likely to be a watershed. Brazil's rapid aging population leaves little time for a fiscal reform before a collapse in the pensions system ruins public finance as a whole. If the next government postpones the fiscal reforms the country needs, Brazil will likely face another severe crisis in the 2020s, but this time with probably worst consequences that could include rising inflation and the collapse of state capacity.

7 Conclusion

Brazil went through nine recessive cycles between 1981 and 2017, a period during which economic growth was feeble and volatile. Rather than supply-side business cycles, policy change and external shocks conditioned economic activity. Unsound public finance is the ultimate cause of such poor results.

Falling terms of trade, the debt crisis of the 1980s, and orthodox monetary and fiscal policies designed to control inflation caused recessions in 1981–1983 and 1987–1988. Inflation not only persisted but accelerated, for successive anti-inflationary plans did not reduce the economy's high degree of indexation. Orthodox policies were not consistent, and the government relied on monetary printing to finance the fiscal deficit. Inflation assumed an exponential trend in 1989, when the 1989–1992 recession begun. The economy was experiencing the negative consequences of hyperinflation, which did not fully materialize because President Collor implemented an extremely tight policy package that included the freezing of saving accounts. Collor was impeached in a political crisis. Unstable politics and a disastrous economic plan explain why this recession was, together with the 2014–2016 recession, the longest among all addressed in this chapter—although the latter was the most severe.

Recessions were shorter and lighter in the two decades that followed the Real Plan, which stabilized the economy in 1994. Based on an appreciated currency peg, the government controlled inflation but increased the country's vulnerability to external shocks. That was not what the team of economists in charge of the plan had envisaged. They intended to launch a fiscal reform to control inflation without a fixed exchange rate regime. In spite of some initiatives to cut expenditure, fiscal

[38]Ibidem.

accounts deteriorated in the second half of the 1990s, during Cardoso's first presidency. Two external shocks—the Tequila and Asian/Russian crises—caused recessions in 1995 and 1998–1999.

Cardoso's second term improved fiscal accounts and established an inflation target regime, which maintained price stability in spite of exchange rate depreciation. The currency weakened in real terms, which together with rising commodity process, a result of China's spectacular growth, conditioned an export boom in the 2000s. Yet Brazil faced three recessions in that decade. An energy crisis caused a recession in 2001, a consequence of Brazil's persistently low investment in infrastructure. The recession of 2003 was the outcome of Lula's presidential election. A former left-wing union leader, Lula adopted a conservative economic agenda while campaigning for office. Yet his eminent victory caused a run on the *real*, which depreciated sharply, pressuring inflation. As a response to the crisis, the Central Bank raised interest rates and the Finance Ministry cut expenditure and increase taxation during Lula's first year in office, which maintained price stability but reduced economic activity.

A period of growth was only interrupted during the world credit crunch crisis. The recession of 2008–2009 was relatively minor in Brazil, for the government reduced the primary surplus and expanded public credit in a countercyclical package. Economic orientation changed after that event, especially during the Rousseff presidency. The government increased expenditure and distributed subsidies and tax breaks in an attempt to foster investment. The plan backfired. Unsound policies raised inflation, deteriorated fiscal accounts, and, together with the fall in commodity prices, caused the 2014–2016 recession, the worst in the country's recorded history.

Economic policy and external shocks conditioned the cycles of growth and recession in Brazil since the 1980s. The deep recessions that happened in 1981–1983 and 2014–2016 were the combination of falling export prices and fiscal tightening after cycles of unsound expansionist policies. The booming 2004–2008 happened when export prices were growing due to China, which allowed the government to implement fiscally sustainable policies without compromising growth. The high rate of growth in 2010 (Lula's last year) was the combination of rising spending and high export prices.

Besides trade, international liquidity was another important source of fluctuation in economic activity. Rising world interest rates and capital outflow generated recessions in 1995, 1998–1999, and 2009, besides playing a role in the 1981–1983 recession. The shock was particularly intense in 2009 (the world financial system collapsed), but the recession was relatively mild because the government ran countercyclical expansionist fiscal policy. Matters were different during the other recessions, when the government did not have the financial leverage to stimulate the economy as it had done in 2009. External shocks did not play a relevant role in the 1987–1988 and 1989–1992 recessions, which were due to policies designed to control inflation. Since overspending was the main cause of inflation, it follows that these recessions were also related to public finance.

While policy has driven cycles, cycles have driven politics. Brazil had seven presidents since the 1980s, four of whom were directly elected. Two out of these four presidents were impeached—Collor and Rousseff. Both impeachments happened at the end of the two longest recessions, in 1992 and 2016. The government-backed candidate Cardoso was elected president at the end of an expansion period in 1994. The opposition leader Lula won the 2003 election partially because the 1998–1999 and 2001 recessions made Cardoso's government unpopular. Lula was reelected during the booming 2000s, and Rousseff won an election in 2010, when the country was growing at record rates. Rousseff won by a tight margin in 2014, the beginning of Brazil's worst recession. Her government overspent to mitigate the early signs of the crisis. Brazilian economic cycles are so closely connected to economic policy, public finance, and politics that business cycles have played a relatively minor role. As a consequence, the economic activity is volatile and growth is not sustainable.

References

Data Sources

Banco Central do Brasil, https://dadosabertos.bcb.gov.br

Brazilian National Treasury, http://www.tesouro.fazenda.gov.br/pt_PT/dados-e-estatisticas

Datafolha, http://datafolha.folha.uol.com.br

Instituto Brasileiro de Geografia e Estatística (IBGE), https://www.ibge.gov.br/estatisticas-novoportal/economicas/

Instituto de Pesquisa Econômica Aplicada (IPEA), http://www.ipeadata.gov.br

Secondary Sources

Arida P, Resende AL (1985) Inertial inflation and monetary reform in Brazil. In: Williamson J (org) Inflation and indexation: Argentina, Brazil and Israel. MIT Press, Boston

Bacha EL (1994) O fisco e a inflação: uma interpretação do caso brasileiro. Revista de Economia Política 14(1):5–27

Bacha EL (1995) Plano Real: uma avaliação preliminar. Revista do BNDES 3:3–26

Bacha EL (1997) Plano Real: uma segunda avaliação. In: O Plano Real e outras experiências internacionais de estabilização. CEPAL/IPEA, Brasília

Baig T, Goldfajn I (2001) The Russian default and the contagion to Brazil. In: Claessens S, Forbes KJ (eds) International financial Contagion. Springer, Boston

Barbosa Filho FH, Pessôa SA (2014) Pessoal ocupado e jornada de trabalho: uma releitura da evolução da produtividade no Brasil. Revista Brasileira de Econometria 68(2):149–169

Barbosa-Filho N (2008) Inflation targeting in Brazil: 1999–2006. Int Rev Appl Econ 22(2):187–200

Bonelli R, Bacha E (2013) Crescimento brasileiro revisitado. In: Veloso F, Ferrira PC, Giambiagi F, Pessôa S (org) Desenvolvimento econômico: uma perspectiva brasileira. Campus, Rio de Janeiro

Bonelli R, Pinheiro AC (2013) Competitividade e desempenho industrial: além do câmbio. In: Reis Velloso JP (org) Rumo ao Brasil Desenvolvido. Campus, Rio de Janeiro

Bresser Pereira LC, Nakano Y (1984) Inflação e recessão. Brasiliense, São Paulo
Burgarin MNS, Ellery R Jr, Gomes V, Teixeira A (2010) From a miracle to a disaster: the Brazilian economy in the past 3 decades. Braz Rev Econometrics 30(1):3–22
Carneiro DD, Modiano EM (2014) Ajuste externo e desequilíbrio interno, 1980-1984. In: Abreu MP (org) A ordem do progresso: dois séculos de política econômica no Brasil. Campus, Rio de Janeiro
Faro C (1991) Plano Collor: os primeiros nove meses. Texto de Discussão no 170. IPGE-FGV
Figueiras LAM (2000) A história do Plano Real: fundamentos, impactos e contradições. São Paulo, Boitempo Editora
Franco G (1995) O Plano Real e outros ensaios. Francisco Alves, Rio de Janeiro
Franco G (2005) Auge e declínio do inflacionismo no Brasil. In: Giambiagi F, Villela A, Barros de Castro L, Hermann J (eds) Economia brasileira contemporânea (1945–2004). Campus, Rio de Janeiro
Frischtak C (2008) O Investimento em infraestrutura no Brasil: histórico recente e perspectivas. Pesquisa e Planejamento Econômico 38(2):307–348
Frischtak C (2013) Infraestrutura e desenvolvimento no Brasil. In: Veloso F, Ferreira PC, Giambiagi F, Pessôa SA (orgs) Desenvolvimento econômico: uma perspectiva brasileira. Elsevier, São Paulo
Giambiagi F (2002) Do déficit de metas às metas de déficit: a política fiscal do período 1995-2002. Pesquisa e Planejamento Econômico 32(1):1–48
Giambiagi F, Montero F (2005) O ajuste da poupança doméstica no Brasil, 1999-2004. Pesquisa de Planejamento Econômico 35(2):131–187
Instituto Brasiliero de Geografia e Estatística (IBGE), https://seriesestatisticas.ibge.gov.br/
Instituto de Pesquisa Econômica Aplicada (IPEA), http://www.ipeadata.gov.br/Default.aspx
Kaltenbrunner A (2010) International financialization and depreciation: the Brazilian real in the international financial crisis. Compet Chang 14(3–4):296–323
Mendes M (2014) Por que o Brasil cresce pouco: desigualdade, democracia e baixo crescimento no país do futuro. Campus, Rio de Janeiro
Modiano EM (1986) Da inflação ao cruzado: a política econômica no primeiro ano da Nova República. Campus, Rio de Janeiro
Modiano EM (1987) Novo cruzado e velhos conflitos: o programa brasileiro de estabilização de 12 de junho de 1987. Texto para Discussão 183. PUC-Rio, Departamento de Economia
Picchetti P (2018) Brazilian business cycles as characterized by CODACE. In: Smirnov S, Ozyildirim A, Picchetti P (eds) Business cycles in BRICS. Springer, Heidelberg
Pinguelli Rosa L (2001) O apagão: por que veio? Como sair dele? Revan, Rio de Janeiro
Rezende F, Afonso JRR, Villela R, Varsano R (1989) A questão fiscal. In: Perspectiva da economia brasileira, 1989. Ipea, Rio de Janeiro
Werneck RLF (2014) Alternância política, redistribuição e crescimento, 2003–2010. In Abreu MP (org) A Ordem do progresso: dois séculos de política econômica no Brasil. Campus, Rio de Janeiro
World Bank, https://data.worldbank.org/
Zilberman E, Barboza RM (2017) O regime de metas: anotações para o futuro. In: Giambiagi F, Almeida MF Jr (eds) Retomada do crescimento: diagnósticos e propostas. Elsevier, Rio de Janeiro

Economic Fluctuations and Their Drivers in Russia

Sergey V. Smirnov

1 Introduction

What does one mean by the word "Russia?" Several medieval principalities? The prerevolution Russian Empire? The Union of Soviet Socialist Republics (the USSR)? The post-Soviet Russian Federation (the RF)? In fact, it can mean all of these things in the proper context. But, as modern Russia in its current borders is the only economic and political reality, the economic history of just this territory is of special interest. Paradoxically, we know more about the historical macroeconomic trajectories of the Russian Empire (Gerchuk 1926; Varzar 1928; Kafengauz 1930; Goldsmith 1961; Gregory 2003a; Bokarev 2006; Suhara 2006; Markevich and Harrison 2011) or the USSR (Bergson 1961; CIA 1963, 1971, 1990; JEC 1962, 1973, 1976, 1982, 1990, 1993; Moorsteen and Powell 1966; Davies et al. 1994; Harrison 2002 and others)[1] than we do about the contemporary RF. In fact, Russia is a country with a nearly unknown economic history.

One of the main reasons for this lack of knowledge of the economic history of Russia is that systematic and comparable historical time-series are unavailable. This situation was caused by some inherent features of the Soviet statistical system, in particular its focus on data for the whole USSR, the ubiquity of indicators important to Marxist economic theory and communist propaganda but not for conventional

This chapter is an updated version of the earlier article: Smirnov S. V. Economic Fluctuations in Russia (from the late 1920s to 2015). Russian Journal of Economics. 2015. Vol. 1. No. 2. P. 130-153. The author is grateful for nonprofit partnership "Redaktsiya zhurnala 'Voprosy Ekonomiki'" for permission to republish it. Support from the Basic Research Program of the National Research University Higher School of Economics is also gratefully acknowledged.

[1]See Smirnov (2012) for a survey.

S. V. Smirnov (✉)
National Research University Higher School of Economics, Moscow, Russia
e-mail: svsmirnov@hse.ru

S. Smirnov et al. (eds.), *Business Cycles in BRICS*, Societies and Political Orders in Transition, https://doi.org/10.1007/978-3-319-90017-9_6

economic analysis (e.g., on the Marxist "theoretical basis," the service sector was almost fully ignored), very poor information on prices and deflators, a small number of regularly published indicators (because of a comprehensive regime of secrecy), etc. Of course, there was a long Western tradition of high-quality research into the Soviet economy. As a result, the most important methodological aspects for a more-or-less reliable recalculation of Soviet statistics into conventional Western standards were clarified, and a solid statistical foundation for empirical investigation of the USSR was built. The trouble is the inadequacy of using historical time-series for the whole Soviet Union as an undoubted proxy for the Russian Soviet Federative Socialist Republic (the RSFSR), which had the same borders as the RF for decades (the RSFSR was a part of the USSR from 1922 until 1991).[2]

There are also several interrelated publications by Ponomarenko, Kuboniwa, and Rosefielde that introduced a set of historical time-series for the RSFSR, including real GDP growth rates for 1961–1990 (see in particular Kuboniwa 1997; Ponomarenko 2002; Rosefielde and Kuboniwa 2003). Their estimations are in line with the Bergson-CIA's methodological approaches and use a lot of internal (unpublished) information by Rosstat (Federal State Statistics Service). Not a single academic researcher could even dream of improving on or repeating their recalculations of Soviet statistical data for the RSFSR into the now commonly used SNA format. But this data set also has two serious shortcomings: first, it depends heavily on the official Soviet volume indices for agriculture, retail trade, and some other sectors, and these indices are most likely overstated because of the underestimation of official deflators [see Rosefielde (2003) for a keen criticism of the initial Soviet statistics and Western estimates computed from them]. And, second, this data set tells us nothing about the many intriguing periods of Russian economic history, e.g., collectivization, industrialization, WW2, and the immediate post-war years.

Hence, our first aim was to construct statistical time-series that might be useful to describe the long-run trajectory of the Russian economy (the RSFSR's and the RF's economies successively).[3] It was not an easy task to pick out historical information for Russia in its present-day borders. But the real trouble was the fact that during the entire Soviet period, a lot of detailed economic information was collected through centralized Soviet ministries, and not all important statistical indicators were published (or even calculated) at a regional level.[4] Hence, it's an arduous task to estimate an indicator like historical GDP (many specially designed statistical sources that didn't exist in the Soviet Union are needed), and it may be fully impossible to construct historical high-frequency (monthly and quarterly) time-series. In this

[2]In the West, the word "Russia" is often applied to the USSR. Strictly speaking, it's no more justified than it is to use the word "England" for "Great Britain" or to use "Great Britain" and "the United Kingdom" as full synonyms.

[3]Hereinafter, we shall use "Russia" as a synonym for the Russian Federation (the RF) and/or the Russian Soviet Federative Socialist Republic (the RSFSR).

[4]It's especially true for the defense and military statistics. One has no real foundation for splitting this kind of data into time-series for the RSFSR and for "all other" regions of the USSR.

paper, we tried to meet a less ambitious challenge, namely to construct long-run *annual* time-series for several of the *most important* sectors of the Russian economy. We tried to trace them back as far as possible; in fact, most of them began in the late 1920s.

Our second goal was to trace the continuous historical macroeconomic trajectory of Russia (the RSFSR *and* the RF), to denote periods of growth and contraction in the Russian economy and to reveal the economic factors that caused changes in the trajectory. Periods of contraction during the era of the planned economy were of special interest for us because even now many think that economic recessions caused by economic reasons are impossible in a planned or command economy. We checked this idea against the long-run statistics.

2 The Data

2.1 Official Data in Natural (Physical) Units for the RF and the RSFSR

There was an ideological dogma in the USSR that inflation simply could not exist in a planned economy. Since all prices in the Soviet Union were under strict government control and were very seldom raised officially, one might even believe this dogma. Now, the methodological trick is well-known: the Soviet Central Statistical Administration (CSA) compared prices only for strictly unchanged products and services. Since price increases were prohibited without explicit government permission, the official statistics usually showed no or very low price increases. But if a producer modified (even slightly) its product, then the government considered this product to be completely new; the State Price Committee permitted a new (usually higher) price, while the CSA never compared it with the price of the old (unmodified) product. Hence, there was some inflation in reality, but none in statistics.[5]

It doesn't mean that all of the Soviet "volume indices" are completely useless (much of the research mentioned above has used them successfully), but here we—arbitrarily to some extent—decided to limit ourselves to indicators in natural ("physical") units. This decision meant an absence of long time-series for trade (retail and wholesale) and for fixed investments in our set of indicators. The only exclusion from this rule was the Y-o-Y rate for industry; for this sector, we used indices calculated from data with physical units and from official data in "fixed-year list-prices" as well (we provide arguments for this below).

More specifically, we compiled the following time-series, most of them from the late 1920s (see Table 1).

[5]See Harrison (1998) for interesting analyses.

Table 1 Main official Russian macroeconomic indicators, by sector

Sectors of economy	Units	Initial year[a]
Industry		
Index of industrial production, official	1960 = 100	1929
Agriculture		
Livestock inventory	Millions of heads	1927
Grain production[b]	Millions of tons	1928
Grain area planted	Millions of hectares	1925
Transportation		
Railroad freight transportation	Millions of tons	1928
Residential construction		
New completions, state organizations, and establishments	Millions m^2	1946
New completions, population[c]	Millions m^2	1980

Sources: See Appendix 2 for details
[a]All time-series end with preliminary estimates for 2017
[b]The method of estimation radically changed in 1953
[c]Workers and employees for 1946–1980

One must keep in mind that several changes occurred in the territory of the RSFSR/RF during these decades. The most important are[6]:

- The exclusion of Kazakhstan and Kyrgyzstan from the RSFSR in 1936 (they got the highest possible status of a "Union Republic" in the regional structure of the USSR). Therefore, we *excluded* the data for these territories from the official data for the RSFSR for the years through 1936.
- The transfer of Crimea from the RSFSR to the Ukrainian Soviet Socialist Republic in 1954. Therefore, we *excluded* the data for Crimea from the official data for the RSFSR for the years through 1954. In 2014, Crimea was returned to the RF, but official statistics for previous years still doesn't include it.
- During 1940–1956, the Karelo-Finnish Soviet Socialist Republic had the highest status of a "Union Republic". Before 1940 and after 1956, it had the status of an "Autonomous Republic" in the regional structure of the RSFSR. Therefore, we *added* the data for the Karelo-Finnish Soviet Socialist Republic to the official data for the RSFSR for 1940–1956 period.[7]
- In 1945 (as a result of WW2), the Kaliningrad Region in the west and South Sakhalin (with several Kuril Islands) in the east were allied to the RSFSR. The economic role of these territories is not negligible (according to Rosstat, it may be up to 1% of GDP). Unfortunately, any correction is impossible because there

[6]There were also several minor changes of the borders between the RSFSR and other Union Republics. Their macroeconomic outcomes are close to zero.

[7]In 1940 as a result of the 1939–1940 Winter War, the area of the Karelo-Finnish Soviet Republic slightly expanded as some territories (Vyborg and several others) were ceded from Finland to the USSR. There is no necessary statistical information to make this amendment, but it is definitely negligible for macroeconomic indicators.

Table 2 Alternative annual indices of industrial production for Russia

Source	Period	Number of products
Suhara (2000)	1961–1997	100
Ponomarenko (2002)	1961–1990	117
Alekseev (1994) and Alekseev et al. (1996)	1976–1994	222
Smirnov (2013a)	1981–1992	108
Baranov and Bessonov (1999)[a]	1990–2006	126
Baranov and Bessonov (1999)[a]	1995–2010	236

[a]Time-series were kindly supplied for our research by the authors

is no information on the economic situation in these regions prior to their accession to the USSR. Thus, we can only suppose that the growth rates for some macroeconomic indicators were overstated for 1945, but not to a great extent.

Our main sources of official data were:

- Databases from Rosstat's website (www.gks.ru).
- Annual statistical yearbooks for the USSR and the RSFSR; other (nonperiodic) official statistical handbooks.[8]
- Never-published documents by the Soviet Central Statistical Administration (CSA) and by other branches of the Soviet government; those documents are now stored in the Russian State Economical Archive (RSEA).

For all compiled time-series and their detailed sources, see Appendices 1 and 2.

2.2 *Alternative Index of Industrial Production for the RSFSR and the RF, Post-1960*

The alternative index of industrial production (1960 = 100) is calculated using the geometric means of Y-o-Y percent changes which, in turn, were calculated from base indices published by several independent (non-government) researchers (see Table 2). All of them estimated their indices as a weighted average of technical base indices, one index per one industrial product (its output is in physical units). The authors used various weights and various sets of goods. The total number of products varied from 100 to over 200, but all of them were nonmilitary. Therefore, strictly

[8]Scanned copies of most of them can be found on the private website http://istmat.info/statistics

speaking, the aggregated indices are not for "total industry" but only nonmilitary or civilian. The role of military production for the official index of industrial production is unknown.[9]

3 Economic Dynamics in Russia, from the Late 1920s to 2017

3.1 Main Annual Indicators Trajectories

The long-run trajectories for the main Russian macroeconomic indicators are shown in Fig. 1.[10] Of course, a few brief comments are needed.

Industrial Production The official index of industrial output begins in 1929 and ends in 2017; the alternative index begins in 1960 and ends in 2010. As the official Y-o-Y % changes are quite close to the alternative estimates in recent years, there is little interest in any alternative figures now (that is why our mean alternative index ends in 2010). But this was not the case prior to 1991. At that time, the official Y-o-Y rates were calculated using the list prices from some fixed year (initially, the 1926/1927 fiscal year, then the 1953 calendar year, etc.). As in reality there was some permanent (unknown) inflation, the official industrial rates were too high. A comparison with the mean alternative index for the 30 years from 1961 to 1990 indicates an average overshoot of 2.0–2.5 percentage points. On the whole, the official index rose five times during this period, while the mean alternative index rose 2.5 times.[11] On the other hand, the two time-series of rates moved in a more or less synchronized manner during this period (the correlation coefficient is 0.94). It means that for the past periods, one may use not only alternative indices but also the official index to date decelerations and accelerations of industrial trends.

The most definitive declines in industrial production took place in 1942, 1945–1946, 1979, 1989–1996, 1998, 2009, and 2015.

---

[9]Needless to say, this is a very intriguing issue, but it's also very special and highly complex. We do doubt that enough information has ever existed to split—in a meaningful manner—the historical data on military expenses and military production in the USSR between the RSFSR and all other regions of the Soviet Union. On the role of the defense or military sector in the USSR, see Simonov (1996) and Gregory (2003b). The current situation in the RF is described in Balashov and Martianova (2015).

[10]We also tried a semilog scale and charts for Y-o-Y % changes, but charts for absolute levels are more distinct. Other types of diagrams are available from the author upon request.

[11]If one views the Soviet statistics as an "instrument of propaganda," one would agree that its effectiveness was quite high: for each "unit" of output produced by industrial establishments during 1961–1990, the statistical system created just another "unit." As a result, in 1990 the total "official" index was twice the (more realistic) "unofficial."

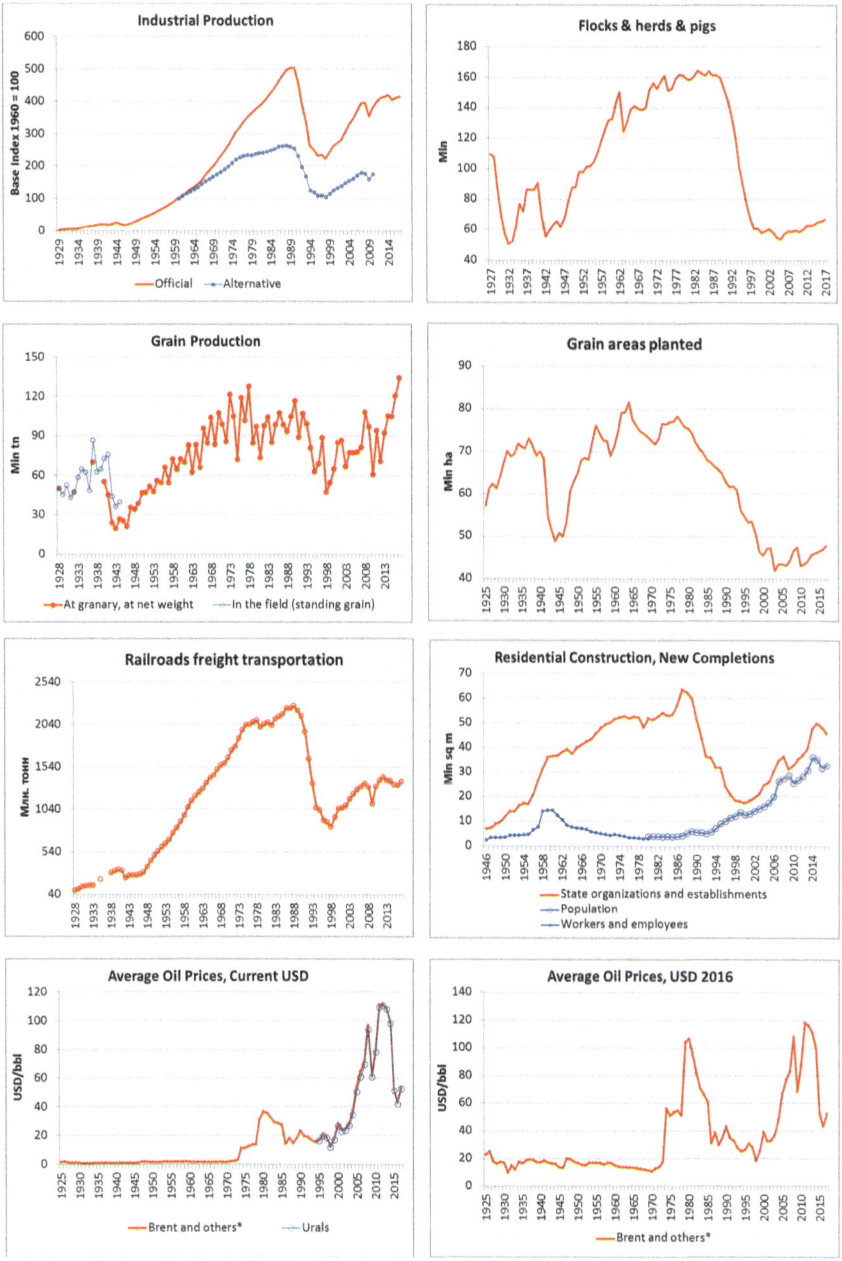

Fig. 1 Main annual indicators for the RF and the RSFSR. (Asterisk) Brent since 1984; US average through 1944; Arabian light for 1945–1983. Sources: Appendix 1; BP Statistical Review of World Energy 2017; Reuters

Agriculture We used livestock inventory as a main indicator to characterize the total activity in the Russian agricultural sector.[12] Large declines in this inventory are clearly connected to the periods of "hard times" in the Russian economic history. The most significant reductions (more than 5% in a year) in livestock inventory took place in:

- 1928–1932: Collectivization.[13] The rural population slaughtered more than half of their private livestock. It's well known from a lot of "nonstatistical" sources (including memories and witnesses) that the main driver of this drop was a strong unwillingness to present their private livestock to "collective farmers."[14,15] Another major reason was a shortage of feed for horses and cattle.
- 1941–1942: The first two years of the war between the USSR and Nazi Germany: a lot of Russian territory was temporarily lost.
- 1936, 1946, 1963, and 1975: The years of crop failures[16]; the number of pigs was the most volatile since their owners preferred to eat them in lieu of feeding them.
- 1987–2000: A prolonged transition period in the animal industry; the appearance of a high volume of meat imports which had never previously occurred.
- 2003–2005: High exports of grain against the backdrop of low crop yields brought high fodder prices; low-producing livestock were slaughtered.

Residential Construction In 1950, the average per capita urban floor space in the RSFSR was only 6.4 m^2. Evidently, there was a great need for housing. However, in a planned economy, since limits to production were set by supply rather than by demand, residential construction was at a very low level for years until the special enactment No 931 was approved by the Central Committee of the Communist Party and the Soviet Government on July 31, 1957. It had an immediate effect: by 1958, the Y-o-Y increase in new residential completions made by workers and employees exceeded 80%. In the following years, new completions made by state organizations and new completions made by the total population (workers and employees up to

[12] As supplementary indicators for agriculture, we also used time-series on grain production and on grain area planted. It is worth noting that the average harvest after 2000 (slightly more than 80 million tons) is roughly equal to the average harvests of the 1960s, while the area planted is 1.7 times less. One could argue that an increase in agricultural productivity occurred across the world and was related to the use of fertilizers, better seeds, and new harvesting machines. But the following facts are very revealing: from 1970 to 1991 (the last year of the USSR), the global average cereal yield grew 57%, while in Russia it declined 3%; on the contrary, from 1991 to 2014 (more recent global data are unavailable), the global average cereal yield grew 37% which is much less than in Russia (58%). Does anyone need any other proof as to the ineffectiveness of the Soviet planned economic system?

[13] See Davies and Wheatcroft (2009) for excellent research of this period.

[14] See, for example, Lopatin and Lopatina (2009, pp. 22, 30, 84), and others.

[15] According to www.merriam-webster.com, a collective farm (or "kolkhoz" in Russian) is "a farm... formed from many small holdings collected into a single unit for joint operation under governmental (and the Communist Party's—S.S.) supervision." The collectivization in the USSR was a highly forced process.

[16] The 1963 crop failure was the first time grain was imported to the USSR for many decades.

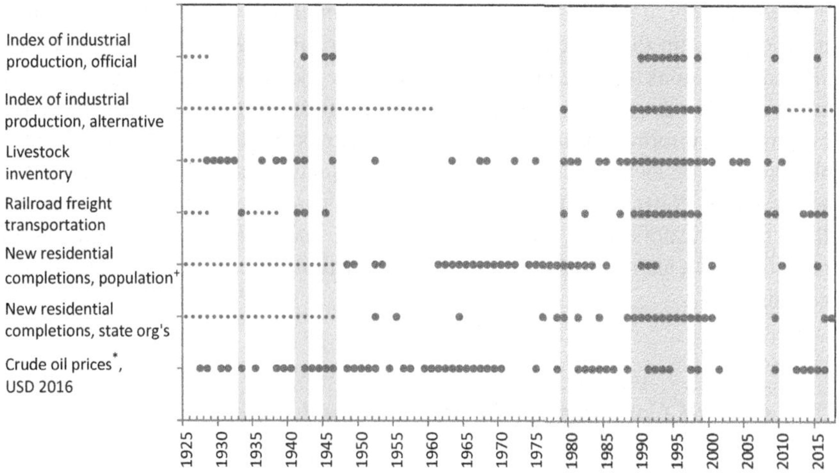

Fig. 2 Main Russian macroeconomic indicators: years of contraction. Gray columns, the years of overall economic recessions; dark gray circles, the years of negative or zero growth rate of a particular indicator; small circles, data not available; (plus) workers and employees for 1946–1980; (times) Brent since 1984; Arabian light for 1945–1983; US average through 1944. Sources: Appendices 1 and 2

1980) usually moved in opposite directions. They became more or less synchronized only after 2000.

Railroad Freight Transportation The volume of railroad freight transportation is an indicator which is definitely well synchronized with the level of economic activity in Russia.[17] Ordinarily its growth is highly monotonic; a decline in railroad freight transportation always indicates serious problems in the Russian economy.

Crude Oil Prices Many believe that the Russian economy is highly dependent on the international oil market (as was the Soviet economy prior to 1991).[18] The annual time-series of international prices for Russian oil ("Urals") began just recently in 1995, but the trajectory of the Russian oil market is very close to the trajectories for other types of oil, even in small details. It means that we may use historical prices for international oil types as a proxy for the Urals price. One may assume that high or rising oil prices were positive for the Russian economy, while low or declining prices were negative.

For all considered indicators, the years of decline in absolute terms are highlighted in Fig. 2 with dark grey circles.

[17]It may even be a leading one because the transportation of raw materials—not other goods—has been the main specialization of Russian railroads. Surely, the leading effect may not be observable with annual data but can be seen by examining more frequent data (e.g., monthly). See Smirnov (2013b) and Macheret (2015).

[18]See Kuboniwa (2014) and the references herein for the most important details.

Unfortunately, it's impossible to reasonably combine all of these indicators into a single composite: (a) the indices are available for different time periods and have different omissions (usually in the 1930s); (b) some indices are flows (e.g., industrial output), while others are stocks (e.g., livestock inventory); and, most importantly, (c) there is no information about potential "weightings" for the components; the only thing we may be aware of is that these weightings have changed significantly since the end of the 1920s. Therefore, all we can do is to carefully trace the trajectories for all of the indicators, look for their contractions, and then—based on qualitative analysis—try to identify years with overall contractions, or contractions of the whole economy.

3.2 *Overall Contractions in the Russian Economy*

In the late 1920s and the early 1930s, Russia was shaken with the controversial processes of collectivization and industrialization. As mentioned above, these years were very destructive for the Russian animal industries: livestock inventory in 1932 was only 46% of the 1927 level. On the other hand, the crop output from the Russian agricultural sector was not so bad. The total grain area planted in 1932 was 12% higher than in 1928, and grain production was only 5% lower. Despite this, there was a great famine in Russia in 1932 and 1933, with up to several million victims.[19] Since total grain production was not too low in 1931 and 1932, the source of the famine could only be found in the Soviet government's decisions. The most popular idea (almost an "official" one) connects the requisition of crops from individual rural households with the needs of rapid industrialization (supposedly, the grain was exported, and the earnings were spent for industrial equipment).[20] Indeed, the growth rates for industry in the RSFSR were very high during the first and the second economic plans (1929–1937): always double-digit and sometimes around 20% or more per year. Of course, the official figures were based on list prices from fiscal year 1926/1927 and may be overstated because of unknown inflation to an unknown extent. In any event, they were usually high, with one important exception: the growth rate was only 5% in 1933. This is in stark contrast with the preceding and subsequent years; it is also near the level of the differences between the official and the alternative industrial indices caused by inaccurate deflators in the official statistics and may be observed in the 1960s and later years.

Therefore, it's quite plausible that real industrial growth was close to zero or even negative in 1933. Russia's railroad freight transportation volume also fell in 1933

[19]The famine was not less serious in the current territories of Kazakhstan and especially Ukraine, but here we focus on Russia only.

[20]Some other researchers emphasize great losses while gathering the harvest due to the low level of agricultural technologies and the high level of irresponsibility on the part of newly established collective farmers. See Zhuravlev (2012).

(it had been a very rare event before WW2). So, we hypothesize that the total level of economic activity in the RSFSR declined during 1933, and the first crisis in the planned economy took place sometime that year. The famine in rural areas, the very low (or even negative) growth in industry, and declining railroad freight transportation, all of these can be considered arguments for this proposition.[21] The roots of this crisis were in the Soviet government's economic policy concerning the agricultural sector, as well as low world prices on grain exports by the USSR.[22]

The next economic contraction occurred in 1941 and 1942. Obviously, it was related to the destruction caused by the war and temporary losses of territory (the Soviet statistics didn't account for economic output in the territories occupied by Germany). The agricultural sector was most heavily damaged: the livestock inventory dropped by 25% in 1941 and by 19% in 1942; grain production decreased 18% in 1941 and by 47% in 1942.[23] Railroad freight transportation fell 3% in 1941 and 27% in 1942. Lastly, according to official data, industrial production grew by only 4% in 1941 and declined by 9% in 1942.[24] So, there is strong evidence that the total output of the Russian economy did contract in 1941 and especially in 1942.

During the next 2 years (1943–1944), strong economic growth was observed as the territories previously occupied by Germany were returned to Soviet control and the production of military goods expanded greatly. But by the end of the war and shortly after, a more or less ordinary post-war recession began. A lot of military goods and ammunition became unnecessary, and their excessive production had to be cut. Therefore, industrial production dropped by 16% in 1945 and by 22% in 1946.[25] The drought of 1946 dealt another negative blow to the Russian economy. Grain production declined by 17% in 1946 (after a 6% decline in 1945); livestock

[21]Detailed analyses in Davies (1996) don't contradict this thesis.

[22]These low prices were the main channel of influence of the Great Depression in the USA and some other industrialized countries on the Soviet economy. By that time, the USSR had departed from the world economy to a great extent. All other economic interconnections were weak, except "imports of brains" [see Korneychuk (2015) for interesting details].

[23]And by an additional 18% in 1943. Total grain production in 1943 was only 36% of 1940 production.

[24]The growth of 1941 may be overestimated because of incorrect deflators. On the other hand, this disturbance is probably less than usual because price control was evidently stricter during the war years. In any case, the industrial production of the RSFSR was much more dynamic than in the USSR as a whole (a drop by 2% in 1941, and by 21% in 1942). There are two reasons for this: (a) the loss of territories (in percent) for the USSR was much greater than for the RSFSR, as all the Soviet republics in the west of the USSR (Ukraine, Belarus, Moldova, the Baltic States) were totally occupied, and their contribution to the total output of the USSR was equal to zero (a decline of 100%); (b) a number of large industrial plants were moved from the Western regions of the USSR to the Eastern regions of the RSFSR during the first months of the war. Their output in the new locations expanded the industrial production of the RSFSR.

[25]It's impossible to split the official index of industrial production into military and civilian parts. Hence, from the point of view of common sense, one may be sure that a significant decrease of military production took place, but several hypotheses about civil production are possible.

inventory declined by 6%. Railroad freight transportation grew by 5% in 1946, but there had been a decline of 1% in 1945.

The post-war expansion which started in 1947 was long and pronounced. Growth rates were very high in the late 1940s and through the first half of the 1950s (often around 15–20% annually for industrial production and railroad freight transportation). Then they began to slow down and 25 years later dropped to a level of 2–3%. It's possible that they could have slowed further, and quite quickly, but in 1974 the world price for crude oil (Russia's main export item) was increased 3.5 times by OPEC, from USD3.3 to USD11.6 per barrel. This price hike granted the Russian economy a respite, but only until the end of the 1970s.[26]

In 1979, there was the second post-war crisis: industrial production fell by 0.4%,[27] livestock inventory by 0.2%, grain production by 33%, railroad freight transportation by 4%, and new residential completions by 6–7%. It may be noted that the crisis of 1979 was that of the planned Russian economy as a system. First, some constraints had appeared on the supply side: up to this moment, the main resources of the Russian economy had ceased growing rapidly (e.g., the ratio of the urban population to the total population had almost reached its "saturation point" and the growth of this—more-productive-than-rural—labor force had dramatically slowed down; grain area planted was nearing its maximum potential, etc.). Second, there were no major incentives on the demand side. While a lot of relatively modern plants for chemicals, electronics, automobiles, and other industries had been introduced during the previous two decades, there was no large additional demand for these products.[28] And third, there was little incentive to have an active business position for either individuals or organizations. Career advancement for individuals was very slow. For organizations, the largest part of their profits (not just taxes!) was withheld from them by the state. The Kosygin-Liberman reforms implemented in 1965 to encourage private initiative and responsibility had been exhausted by the early 1970s. By the late 1970s, all previous discussions about them were completely forgotten.

[26]The factors for the long retardation of Russian growth were discussed by Easterly and Fischer (1995) and Rosefielde and Kuboniwa (2003).

[27]Measured by the average alternative index. The official data gives +3% (the minimum for all years since 1947).

[28]Of course, one must keep in mind that there is some specificity in the concept of "demand" under the planned economy. For example, in 1971 the first conveyor line at the largest Soviet automobile plant was implemented; at the end of 1973, the whole plant was completed. Total production of autos in 1974 (1 million autos) turned to be roughly four times larger than in 1970 (0.26 million). Does it mean that the demand for autos was fulfilled? Of course not. The number of autos per capita in Russia was many times lower than in the US or European countries; those who wanted to buy an auto had to wait for permission for 2 or 3 years or to buy one immediately at the black market. But there was no "demand" for production of more autos from those in the USSR who were responsible for investment decisions; they thought they had done "enough" for the population. The output of autos in the planned Russian economy never exceeded 1 million by more than 16%, while there were zero auto imports.

The crisis of 1979 was quite acute, but it wasn't too deep or too long. OPEC raised oil prices 2.3 times (up to USD31.4 per barrel) and saved the Soviet planned economy at that time, but it never returned to rapid growth. As the price of oil was going down, military expenses for the war in Afghanistan were going up, and no structural problems of the planned economy were solved, the Russian economy was experiencing a long stagnation. From 1980 to 1988, the growth rate in the alternative index of industrial production was never higher than 1.5–1.7%[29]; the average annual growth rate for railroad freight transportation was only 1.3%; and the livestock inventory stopped increasing at all. After oil prices were halved in 1986 (to USD14.4 per barrel), the situation became much worse and perspectives much more pessimistic. There was a burst of enthusiasm after the accession of Mikhail Gorbachev in 1985, but his reforms were poorly thought out and inconsequential; in some aspects, they unsettled the Soviet financial system. An excessive amount of money emerged, and the deficit of consumer goods worsened.

From 1989 to 1991, the first wave of the Great Russian Depression came. Industrial production decreased by 12% during these 3 years,[30] railroad freight transportation dropped by 13%, livestock inventory was down by 10%, new residential completions made by the state organizations declined by 30%, etc. Monetary reform was unsuccessful in 1991; the financial system became unbalanced, and there was an overall deficit of consumer goods.

At the very end of 1991, the USSR collapsed as a unified whole, and the Soviet planned economic system crashed. Russia began to exist as an independent state within the boundaries of the RSFSR. The new government initiated serious pro-market economic reforms. These reforms were based on ideas proposed by the IMF and included liberalization of prices, liberalization of foreign trade, privatization of state enterprises, and several structural reforms. The reforms were neither very consistent nor easily accepted; there was a strong lobby against them.

The second wave of the Great Russian Depression (the so called "transition crisis" or the regeneration of a market economy) lasted from 1992 to 1996. For these 5 years, industrial production contracted by 50%,[31] livestock inventory shrank by 48%, railroad freight transportation declined by 47%, and new residential completions made by state organizations were down by 45%. Taken together, the two waves of the Great Russian Depression were much more damaging than the American Great Depression of the 1930s. For example, in the USA, the maximum decrease in industrial output (using annual statistics) was 47% (from 1929 to 1932); in Russia, this indicator was 56% (from 1988 to 1996).

There were three main reasons for this drop. The first was the distorted structure of the Russian economy. Since it had been mutilated by the planning system, the

[29]With only one exception: in 1986 it was equal to 2.8%.

[30]If measured by the alternative index. The official industrial index began to decrease in 1990; it fell by 8.1% during 1990–1991.

[31]Official statistics became much more reliable after the USSR; there is no need for alternative estimates after 1991.

output of military goods and certain low-quality products was too high. In a market economy, without the only decision-making (planning) center, there would be no reason to produce these goods in the same quantities. Therefore, the production volumes for large numbers of goods had to be reduced. The second reason for the sharp decline was the low competitiveness of most sectors of the Russian economy; strong competition from imported goods and services rooted out large numbers of Russian goods (import competition was quite new to Russian producers). The third reason was that Russian owners and managers had no experience in seeking consumers and suppliers, exporting, receiving bank credit, setting prices for their own production, etc. In the planned economy, every establishment had all of these parameters fixed by the Central Planning Agency. During the transition period, Russians learned all these market wisdoms, but this learning was really very costly. The absence of market experience was probably the most important factor in the transition crisis. For this reason, output of nonmilitary and highly competitive Russian goods also declined (e.g., oil production declined 49%, from 1988 to 1996).

During the transition period, a large number of state plants were privatized, market laws were adopted, a new budget system and banking sector were built, economic agents accumulated initial market experience, and the risk of reestablishing communism diminished.[32] The Russian economy had hit rock bottom, and there was nowhere to go but up. Therefore, in 1997, after 8 years of continuous decrease where the output of the Russian economy had been cut in half, there was a short recovery.

This first recovery of the Russian post-planning era was fully disrupted in November 1997. First, the world crisis, which began at the end of 1997 in Southeast Asia, caused foreign capital outflows from all emerging markets, and Russia was no exception. Second, as the world economy slowed down and global demand for crude oil lessened, oil prices declined to USD10–11 per barrel (much less than was needed to fulfill the Russian budget). Therefore, the international exchange reserves of the Russian Central bank were exhausted, and the federal budget couldn't service the government's debt. Under these circumstances, there were two important decisions: the Russian Government declared a default on its bills and bonds, and the Russian Central Bank stopped adhering to a fixed exchange rate regime.[33] As a result, several of the largest Russian commercial banks went into bankruptcy, a lot of individuals and nonfinancial companies lost their money, and the Russian ruble was devalued four times over a period of just months. In 1998, real GDP fell by 5.3%, industrial production by 4.8%, railroad freight transportation by 5.9%, etc. As the base level wasn't very high, there wasn't very far to fall, and the contraction in 1998 was much less than during the transition period. In any case, at its lowest point, the total output of the Russian economy was thrown back to levels from the early 1960s.

The strong devaluation of the ruble generated the process of substituting imports with domestic goods and services. This factor became the most important driver for

[32]The political risk of restoring communism and returning to a planned economy existed until the presidential election in the middle of 1996. Then Boris Yeltsin won a new 4-year term.

[33]To the "crawling peg" regime, according to the IMF's classification, to be precise.

the recovery in 1999 and 2000. Later, the output of the Russian economy was driven by rapidly rising oil prices and increasing oil exports. Since 2004, the main "locomotive" for the Russian economy has been a rise in household expenditures backed by fast-growing personal incomes and a large expansion of personal credit. In 2007, oil prices were slightly under USD80–90 per barrel, and domestic demand grew by 10–12% per year. The high dependency of the Russian economic growth on skyrocketing oil prices and unsecured consumer loans gave rise to the hypothesis of overheating. The drastic decline in inventories during the Russian crisis of 2008–2009 proved this hypothesis to be true.

The 2008–2009 recession came to Russia through the world financial markets, which were shaken up by the Lehman Brothers' bankruptcy. From the end of 2007 to September 2008, there was an illusion that the Russian economy—with its enormous (more than half a trillion dollars) and still growing foreign exchange reserves, federal budget surplus, and oil prices at more than USD100 per barrel—might be a haven of stability for the stormy world economy. Oil prices cut to one-third of their prior level (to USD38 per barrel in December, 2008), massive capital outflow, and pulling Russian banks and companies off the world financial markets (therefore, leading to major problems for getting credit) crashed this naive dream. The overheating of pre-crisis domestic demand and a lack of skill in managing inventories resulted in a significant decline in production. In 2009, real GDP declined by 7.8%, industrial production by 10.7%, new residential completions made by state organizations declined by 14.4%, and railroad freight transportation sank 15% (after a 3% decline in 2008).[34]

After the recovery in 2010–2011, it became clear that the old pattern of Russian growth, which was based on high and continually increasing oil prices, had become inappropriate. With nearly stable domestic oil production and nearly stable (and still very high!) world oil prices, no other driver for the Russian economy had appeared. Capital outflow remained high; the competitiveness of goods (except for crude oil and certain other raw materials) remained low; most regional budgets fell into deep deficits; the ratio of bad debts to banks' assets increased; (ineffective) government companies obtained an unreasonably swollen role; inflation continued to be significant (6–8% per year), which prevented the Central Bank from lowering the high interest rates; the investment climate for private businesses (foreign as well as domestic) became worse; etc. As a result, a dismal stagnation occurred in 2012 and 2013.

Since the spring of 2014, Western financial sanctions connected with the Ukrainian crisis, related Russian countersanctions on food imports and—several months later—a deep drop in oil prices pushed the Russian economy into a new recession (or rather stagflation, because inflation rose to double-digit levels in the beginning of 2015). Real Russian GDP fell by 2.5% in 2015 and an additional 0.2% in 2016. This recession was not deep as large inventories were not accumulated

[34]As the deep crisis in Russia began only in the end of the third quarter of 2008 and there had been previous overheating, there was not enough time to make the 2008 annual growth rates negative for most other indicators.

Table 3 Russian recessions and their causes, 1928–2017

Years of contraction	Causes of contractions
1933	Destruction of the agricultural sector caused by the "overall collectivization" policy. Low world prices on raw Russian exports
1941–1942	Destruction of assets due to the war. Temporary loss of territories
1945–1946	Cuts of no longer required military production. The drought of 1946
1979	Exhaustion of extensive factors, including the conversion of the population from rural to (the more productive) urban. Huge implementations of modern industrial equipment during the two previous decades; no drive belts between final demand and investment decisions. Weak incentives to grow and to develop for individuals and organizations
1989–1991	The first wave of the great Russian depression (the death throes of the planned economic system). All structural problems of the late soviet planned economic system were aggravated by vague reforms and decreasing oil prices. Unbalanced financial system and overall deficit of consumer goods
1992–1996	The second wave of the great Russian depression (the transition from a planned to a market economy). The complete absence of "market experience," distorted structure of the economy, low competitiveness of Russian goods and services, and incompleteness of market reforms resulted in roughly halving the output of the Russian economy
1998	The Russian economy was infected with the southeast Asian financial crisis. Intensive foreign capital outflow and a decline of Russian oil prices to USD10–11 per barrel forced default on treasury bills and bonds, bankruptcy of several of the largest commercial banks, loss of money by many economic agents, contraction in total output by roughly 5%, and four times devaluation of the ruble
2008–2009	After the Lehman brothers' bankruptcy in September 2008, Russian banks and companies were nearly cut off from the world financial markets, massive capital outflow began from Russia and other emerging markets, and oil prices fell to one-third of their pre-crisis levels. Overheating of pre-crisis domestic demand and a lack of skill in managing inventories resulted in a significant decline in production
2015–2016	Consistent quelling of entrepreneurial spirit and excessive administrative pressure on business paved the way for the recession triggered by the mutual sanctions from the west and especially by the major drop in oil prices. At the moment, any positive drivers for economic growth are not obvious

during the stagnation of 2012–2013; however, Russia may now experience a prolonged period without steady economic growth. Most forecasts of Russian GDP growth rates over the next 5–7 years are well below 2% per annum. This is too slow for an emerging economy.[35]

In Table 3 all nine recessions for the Russian economy over the past 90 years (1928–2017) are shown.[36]

[35]See Akindinova et al. (2017) for a deeper analysis of the economic and institutional reasons for this.

[36]Here we count two waves of the Great Russian Depression as separate ones.

4 Conclusions

In this chapter, we compiled several important annual time-series for the RSFSR and the RF in physical units and corrected them for territorial changes. This allowed us to trace the trajectory of the Russian economy (the economy of the RSFSR and the RF) from the late 1920s up to the current time. And although we didn't estimate historical GDP for Russia (Russian data on internal trade and services are extremely incomplete and unreliable for the Soviet period, and the data on foreign trade are completely unavailable), we could discern the periods of economic expansion and the years of contraction using information previously stored in archives.

In total, there were nine recessions in the Russian economy (two of them merged as two successive "waves" of the Great Russian Depression—the first just before the crash of the USSR and the second immediately after). Four contractions took place during the 63-year period of the planned economy; one was a transitional crisis (it lasted for 5 years), and the last four occurred during the modern—more or less ordinary—market Russian economy during its 26-year history.

Evidently, contractions of output under the planned Soviet economy were rarer events than under market conditions. Up to the very end, they were also less profound. We think this is because in a market economy, any economic agent will pay for his own (or someone else's) errors in the near future; mistaken actions will soon have consequences. On the contrary, in a planned economy, the consequences of erroneous decisions may be contained through additional commands and directives, but there will be an inevitable "default" in the end. If one does not correct one's errors regularly, then one will hardly be successful in a difficult new situation.[37] We strongly believe that the main reason for the depth and endurance of the transitional crisis in the first half of the 1990s was just an "ossification" of the Soviet planning system with all of its mechanisms and proportions: since there was never the political will to adjust it gradually, it finally broke off completely. Therefore, in our judgment, the deep drop during the two waves of the Great Russian Depression is totally on the "conscience" of the Soviet command system. We consider the risk of a sharp decline after a long period of stable growth as a special risk for planned economies.

Of course, good or bad decisions made by monetary and nonmonetary authorities are significant not only for Russia. For example, one may argue that too many years of low interest rates in the mid- 2000s caused the American Great Recession of 2008; one may even blame the Federal Reserve for this expensive misstep. But for the command Soviet economy, the centralized decision-making process was of critical importance. In this context, one may remember not only the collectivization but also the industrialization in the 1930s, or the campaign for developing virgin lands initiated by Nikita Khrushchev (the Soviet leader in 1953–1964), or the construction of the Baikal-Amur Railroad (a 30-year project begun in 1972), and so on. Mega-projects were always the focus of the Central Planning Agency, and the

[37]There is a huge amount of economic literature dedicated to the transition period of Russian economy [e.g., see Åslund (2013) for its description].

track of the Soviet economy was determined by their success or failure to a much greater extent than in any market economy with its millions of "decision-making centers." Highly centralized decision-making, an aspiration to concentrate the production of any good at only a few giant establishments, and sometimes politically or ideologically (not purely economically) motivated decisions protected the Soviet economy from remarkable contractions for decades. But wasn't its far lower ability to self-adjust simply the other side of the same coin?

The role of internal imbalances and external shocks (especially from world oil markets) were also significant, especially as Russia became more open to the world, not only through markets for goods and services but also through financial markets. The crises of 1998 and 2008–2009 were definitely triggered by external processes (as well as both recessions connected with WW2). The crises of 1933, 1989–1991, 1992–1996, and 2015–2016 were deepened by low oil prices (grain prices in 1933), and the crisis of 1979 was softened and even reversed by rising oil prices. But the roots of all five of these recessions were inside Russia, not outside.

Does this mean that Russia has experienced more or less standard business cycles over the past 90 years? The answer depends on how we interpret the classical definition of business cycles provided by Burns and Mitchell (1946, p. 3). If we follow Burns and Mitchell in their belief that business cycles are confined to "nations that organize their work mainly in business enterprises," the answer is clearly negative: "business enterprises" seeking profits and setting prices for their production certainly did not exist during the Soviet period. But if we emphasize the existence of medium-term nonperiodic fluctuations in aggregate economic activity while disregarding the nonmarket nature of the planned Soviet economy, the answer is positive: the Russian economy evidently has had several sequences of expansions and contractions since the end of 1920s. We might elect not to label them "business cycles" and to use the term "economic cycles" to avoid terminological debates (although there is some literature on business cycles in planned economies).[38] From a practical point of view, it is important to note that the methods of monitoring, forecasting, and empirical analysis of drivers of fluctuations in general economic activity are roughly the same for economies with very different mixes of market and nonmarket elements.

[38]See Ickes (1986) for a survey.

Appendix 1

Main Russian Macroeconomic Indicators (1928–2017[a])

Years	Index of industrial output		Agriculture				Residential construction, new completions			Railroad
	Official	Alternative	Livestock inventory	Grain production, at granary	Grain production, in the field	Grain area planted	State organizations and establishments	Total population	Workers and employees	Freight transportation
	Y-o-Y % change		Millions of heads	Millions of tons		Millions of hectares	Millions of m^2			Millions of tons
1928	Na	Na	108.0	50.0	50.0	61.4	Na	Na	Na	88.6
1929	20.0	Na	87.0	Na	45.5	64.0	Na	Na	Na	107.1
1930	22.0	Na	68.0	Na	52.5	67.2	Na	Na	Na	133.7
1931	18.0	Na	57.0	Na	43.4	70.2	Na	Na	Na	144.9
1932	15.0	Na	50.7	47.5	47.5	69.0	Na	Na	Na	151.2
1933	5.2	Na	52.5	Na	58.8	69.5	Na	Na	Na	150.2
1934	19.2	Na	62.1	Na	65.1	71.9	Na	Na	Na	Na
1935	22.7	Na	77.2	Na	62.5	71.2	Na	Na	Na	219.9
1936	28.7	Na	72.2	Na	48.9	70.8	Na	Na	Na	Na
1937	11.2	Na	86.6	70.4	86.4	73.1	Na	Na	Na	299.3
1938	12.1	Na	86.6	Na	63.0	71.4	Na	Na	Na	295.3
1939	17.2	Na	86.5	Na	64.9	69.2	Na	Na	Na	317.5
1940	10.5	Na	91.1	55.6	73.0	70.1	Na	Na	Na	333.9
1941	3.8	Na	68.5	45.5	75.9	68.5	Na	Na	Na	322.7
1942	−8.9	Na	55.7	24.0	44.0	54.6	Na	Na	Na	236.8
1943	17.5	Na	59.5	19.8	36.3	51.4	Na	Na	Na	265.7
1944	13.2	Na	63.4	26.9	39.8	48.9	Na	Na	Na	271.0

(continued)

Years	Index of industrial output		Agriculture				Residential construction, new completions			Railroad
	Official	Alternative	Livestock inventory	Grain production, at granary	Grain production, in the field	Grain area planted	State organizations and establishments	Total population	Workers and employees	Freight transportation
	Y-o-Y % change		Millions of heads	Millions of tons		Millions of hectares	Millions of m^2			Millions of tons
1945	−15.6	Na	65.8	25.4	Na	50.9	Na	Na	Na	268.3
1946	−21.7	Na	62.0	21.2	Na	50.0	7.0	Na	2.5	282.9
1947	19.3	Na	67.6	35.7	Na	53.3	7.3	Na	3.3	302.1
1948	24.2	Na	77.9	34.2	Na	61.0	9.0	Na	3.3	370.9
1949	18.7	Na	87.9	38.9	Na	63.2	9.8	Na	3.3	439.3
1950	19.9	Na	88.3	46.8	Na	64.9	11.9	Na	3.6	498.2
1951	15.4	Na	98.3	47.5	Na	68.2	14.1	Na	4.3	547.9
1952	10.9	Na	97.9	51.9	Na	68.6	14.1	Na	4.3	597.6
1953	11.2	Na	101.5	48.2	Na	68.2	16.5	Na	4.3	638.7
1954	12.9	Na	102.1	56.3	Na	72.5	17.5	Na	4.5	677.7
1955	11.7	Na	105.1	54.7	Na	76.2	17.1	Na	4.7	761.7
1956	9.6	Na	110.6	66.5	Na	74.4	20.9	Na	6.6	819.9
1957	9.0	Na	117.9	54.9	Na	72.7	26.6	Na	7.7	891.5
1958	9.1	Na	125.6	72.9	Na	72.5	31.6	Na	14.2	970.3
1959	11.0	Na	132.2	64.9	Na	69.1	36.3	Na	14.5	1061.3
1960	8.8	Na	133.1	72.6	Na	71.4	36.7	Na	14.6	1140.7
1961	8.1	8.2	143.3	70.3	Na	74.5	36.9	Na	12.4	1193.8
1962	9.0	6.3	150.6	83.1	Na	79.2	38.4	Na	10.6	1236.7

1963	8.1	5.3	124.9	62.8	Na	79.4	39.4	Na	8.4	1285.0
1964	6.0	5.6	130.8	83.2	Na	81.6	37.7	Na	7.7	1350.0
1965	7.2	5.2	139.1	66.3	Na	77.6	40.2	Na	7.3	1415.8
1966	8.4	6.7	141.5	95.6	Na	76.1	41.3	Na	7.1	1441.3
1967	9.9	6.2	139.6	84.8	Na	74.9	42.6	Na	6.8	1514.9
1968	8.1	5.1	138.7	103.8	Na	74.3	43.6	Na	5.9	1558.9
1969	6.9	4.2	140.2	83.9	Na	73.5	45.9	Na	5.4	1585.3
1970	8.0	4.4	151.8	107.4	Na	72.7	48.1	Na	5.0	1648.2
1971	7.6	4.2	156.5	98.8	Na	71.8	49.5	Na	4.6	1736.6
1972	6.4	4.3	152.7	86.0	Na	73.1	50.3	Na	4.4	1782.6
1973	7.3	4.9	157.0	121.5	Na	76.6	51.9	Na	4.6	1879.0
1974	7.8	5.7	161.7	105.1	Na	76.5	52.5	Na	4.3	1979.8
1975	7.2	4.5	151.5	72.4	Na	77.0	52.9	Na	4.0	2039.8
1976	4.9	3.2	152.9	119.0	Na	77.2	52.0	Na	3.3	2041.5
1977	5.4	1.8	159.5	101.6	Na	78.4	52.7	Na	3.3	2072.2
1978	4.5	1.4	162.2	127.4	Na	77.0	52.4	Na	3.1	2090.6
1979	3.0	−0.4	161.9	84.8	Na	75.9	48.4	Na	2.9	2010.2
1980	3.0	1.7	159.1	97.2	Na	75.5	52.1	4.0	2.9	2047.9
1981	2.9	0.8	158.6	73.8	Na	74.1	51.5	3.9	Na	2065.3
1982	2.7	0.7	161.4	98.0	Na	72.0	52.7	3.9	Na	2032.9
1983	3.8	1.6	165.0	104.3	Na	70.7	54.3	3.8	Na	2110.5
1984	3.8	1.6	163.2	85.1	Na	69.7	53.2	3.9	Na	2134.8
1985	3.7	1.5	162.0	98.6	Na	68.1	53.6	3.7	Na	2165.0
1986	4.8	2.8	164.8	107.5	Na	67.5	57.4	3.9	Na	2236.0
1987	3.6	0.8	161.9	98.6	Na	66.7	63.8	4.2	Na	2228.0
1988	3.8	0.6	161.8	93.7	Na	66.0	62.6	5.2	Na	2261.0

(continued)

Years	Index of industrial output		Agriculture				Residential construction, new completions			Railroad
	Official	Alternative	Livestock inventory	Grain production, at granary	Grain production, in the field	Grain area planted	State organizations and establishments	Total population	Workers and employees	Freight transportation
Years	Y-o-Y % change		Millions of heads	Millions of tons		Millions of hectares	Millions of m^2			Millions of tons
1989	1.4	−1.4	160.1	104.8	Na	64.9	60.3	5.9	Na	2205.0
1990	−0.1	−2.2	153.6	116.7	Na	63.1	51.6	5.5	Na	2140.0
1991	−8.0	−8.9	145.3	89.1	Na	61.8	44.0	5.4	Na	1957.3
1992	−16.0	−14.9	135.1	106.9	Na	61.9	36.6	4.9	Na	1640.1
1993	−13.7	−14.4	121.2	99.1	Na	60.9	36.2	5.6	Na	1347.8
1994	−21.6	−26.1	102.7	81.3	Na	56.3	32.1	7.1	Na	1058.2
1995	−4.6	−5.2	90.4	63.4	Na	54.7	32.0	9.0	Na	1028.0
1996	−7.6	−8.6	77.0	69.2	Na	53.4	24.3	10.0	Na	911.5
1997	1.0	0.1	67.6	88.5	Na	53.6	21.2	11.5	Na	887.2
1998	−4.8	−4.2	61.3	47.8	Na	50.7	18.6	12.1	Na	834.8
1999	8.9	9.2	61.2	54.6	Na	46.5	18.3	13.7	Na	947.4
2000	8.7	8.1	58.3	65.4	Na	45.6	17.7	12.6	Na	1046.8
2001	2.9	4.5	59.2	85.1	Na	47.2	18.6	13.1	Na	1057.5
2002	3.1	3.4	60.8	86.5	Na	47.4	19.7	14.2	Na	1083.7
2003	8.9	6.2	58.6	67.0	Na	42.1	21.3	15.2	Na	1160.9
2004	8.0	5.5	54.9	77.8	Na	43.6	24.9	16.1	Na	1221.2
2005	5.1	3.2	54.0	77.8	Na	43.6	26.0	17.5	Na	1273.3
2006	6.3	5.0	57.9	78.2	Na	43.2	30.6	20.0	Na	1311.6

2007	6.8	5.4	59.4	81.5	Na	44.3	34.9	26.3	Na	1344.6
2008	0.6	−0.8	59.0	108.2	Na	46.7	36.7	27.4	Na	1304.4
2009	−10.7	−9.9	59.9	97.1	Na	47.6	31.3	28.5	Na	1108.8
2010	7.3	9.5	59.0	61.0	Na	43.2	32.9	25.5	Na	1312.0
2011	5.0	Na	60.3	94.2	Na	43.6	35.5	26.8	Na	1381.7
2012	3.4	Na	62.9	70.9	Na	44.4	37.3	28.4	Na	1421.1
2013	0.4	Na	63.0	92.4	Na	45.8	39.8	30.7	Na	1381.2
2014	1.7	Na	63.5	105.3	Na	46.2	48.0	36.2	Na	1375.4
2015	−3.4	Na	65.4	104.8	Na	46.6	50.1	35.2	Na	1329.0
2016	1.3	Na	65.6	120.7	Na	47.1	48.4	31.8	Na	1325.2
2017[a]	1.0	Na	66.4	134.1	Na	47.9	45.9	32.7	Na	1362.3

Sources: See Appendix 2

Note: *Na* not available

[a]Preliminary

Appendix 2: Statistical Sources for the Main Russian Macroeconomic Indicators

Below we use the following translations from Russian to English:

- Динамика и география грузового движения на путях сообщения СССР—Dynamics and Geographical Distribution of Freight Transportation in the USSR
- Народное хозяйство РСФСР (или СССР)—National Economy of the RSFSR (or the USSR);
- Посевные площади СССР (Статистический сборник)—USSR: Areas Planted. Statistical Digest
- Российский статистический ежегодник—Russian Statistical Yearbook
- Сельское хозяйство, охота и охотничье хозяйство, лесоводство в России—Agriculture, Hunting, and Forestry in Russia
- Сельское хозяйство СССР. Ежегодник—Agriculture in the USSR. Yearbook
- Социалистическое строительство СССР. Статистический ежегодник—Socialist Construction of the USSR. Statistical yearbook
- Социально-экономические показатели Российской Федерации в 1991–2016 гг. Приложение к «Российскому статистическому ежегоднику (РСЕ)»—Socioeconomic indicators of the Russian Federation: 1991–2016. Supplement to "Russian Statistical Yearbook (RSY)"
- СССР—страна социализма. Статистический сборник—The USSR is a Country of Socialism. Statistical Digest
- Транспорт и связь СССР (Статистический сборник)—Transportation and Communication in the USSR. Statistical Digest
- Центральная база статистических данных (ЦБСД)—Centralized Base of Statistical Data (CBSD)
- Российский государственный архив экономики (РГАЭ)—The Russian State Economical Archive (RSEA)

The sources for each indicator are placed in a table—one table per indicator; there are also some methodological comments, if necessary. The information stored in the RSEA was initially "secret" or "top-secret," but since 1956, the same indicators have been published in official statistical yearbooks.

Index of Industrial Production, Official

The official index of industrial production (1960 = 100) is in fact not fully official. We calculated it using official Y-o-Y percent changes (if available) or Y-o-Y percent changes that, in turn, were calculated using official base indices (with various bases) or values of industrial production in list prices (also with various bases). We took 1960 as a base to have a time-series comparable with the alternative index of industrial production.

Years	Source: title/archive and code	Page(s)
1929–1932, 1946–1965	National Economy of the RSFSR in 1965. Moscow: Statistika, 1966	46–47
1933–1936[a]	National Economy of the USSR in 1963. Moscow: Statistika, 1965	110
1938–1945, ex. 1941	RSEA 1562-33-2903	59–60, 64
1941	RSEA 1562-329-1488	18–19
1966–1975	National Economy of the RSFSR in 1975. Moscow: Statistika,1976	45
1976–1980	National Economy of the RSFSR in 1980. Moscow: Finansy i Statistika,1981	50
1981	National Economy of the RSFSR in 1985. Moscow: Finansy i Statistika,1986	55
1982–1985	Rosstat, CBSD	–
1986–1991	Russian statistical yearbook. 1994. Moscow: Goskomstat Rossii, 1994	296
1992–2016	Rosstat, supplement to RSY	–

[a]As a rough estimate we used data for the whole USSR for these years

Livestock Inventory

We added together the total number of cattle, sheep, goats, and pigs. Almost continuous time-series, beginning with 1927, are published in only one source; more recent and fully comparable data may be taken from the CBSD held by Rosstat. The "holes" for almost 90 years are 1928 and 1938. We succeeded in patching the hole in 1928 and substituted the average of 1937 and 1939 for 1938.

Years	Source: title/archive and code	Page(s)
1927–1989, e.g., 1928 and 1938	Agriculture, hunting and forestry in Russia. 2013. Moscow: Rosstat, 2013	90–91
1928[a]	RSEA 1562-41-66	297
1938[b]	Not available	–
1990	Rosstat, CBSD	–
1991–2016	Rosstat, supplement to RSY	–

[a]Incl. Crimea and excl. The Karelo-Finnish Soviet Socialist Republic
[b]We used the average for 1937 and 1939

Grain Production

According to the present methodology (in use since 1953), the garnered grain is counted (at the granary at net weight). According to the "old" methodology, the harvest is estimated in the field (standing grain). It's not a surprise that the "old" methodology gave higher numbers than the "present"; it's a surprise that, according to Rosstat, for 1928 and 1932, both methodologies gave equal volumes. Therefore, one may doubt if Rosstat's re-estimations for the 1920s and the 1930s were made in a proper way; in practice, it also means that one can't use "old" data to interpolate the "new." For this reason, we preferred to use both time-series in parallel (one for the "present" methodology, another for the "old" one).

Years	Source: title/archive and code	Page(s)
In the field (old methodology)		
1928, 1932–1944	RSEA 1562-329-1409	1–2, 8
1929–1931	Agriculture in the USSR. Yearbook. 1935. Moscow: Selhozgiz, 1936	270–271
At granary (new methodology)		
1928, 1932, 1937, 1940–1990	Agriculture, hunting, and forestry in Russia. 2013. Moscow: Rosstat, 2013	74
1991–2016	Rosstat, supplement to RSY	–

Grain Area Planted

The grain area planted was counted by the Soviet statistical system beginning in 1925. This indicator is more or less comparable through time. Some minor problems were connected with two factors: (a) the changes of the RSFSR's borders (as a rule, these problems were easily solved, as the relevant regional information was usually available); and (b) with corn grain of milky-wax ripeness, which was included in total grain for several years in the second part of 1950s, and excluded for all other years. To handle with this bug we had to make our own estimates of this factor for 1956–1957 using information for the USSR as a whole; the correction was around 1.5% of the total area planted in the RSFSR.

Years	Source: title/archive and code	Page(s)
1925–1926[a]	Agriculture in the USSR. 1925–1928. Moscow: Stat. Izd-vo TsSU SSSR, 1929	220
1927	Socialist construction of the USSR. Statistical yearbook. 1934. Moscow, Soyuzorguchet, 1934	178, 190
1928, 1932, 1945, 1950–1956[b]	USSR: Areas planted. Statistical digest. 1957. Vol. 1. Moscow: Gosstatizdat, 1957	20–21
1929–1931	Agriculture in the USSR. Yearbook. 1935. Moscow: Selhozgiz, 1936	245–247
1933–1940	RSEA 1562-329-1409	1–2, 8
1941–1944	RSEA 1562-329-1490	157–158
1946–1949[c]	RSEA 1562-329-3871	90, 316
1957[b]	National Economy of the RSFSR in 1958. Moscow: Gosstatizdat, 1959	223
1958–1965	National Economy of the RSFSR in 1965. Moscow: Statistika, 1966	190–191

(continued)

Years	Source: title/archive and code	Page(s)
1966–1969	National Economy of the RSFSR in 1969. Moscow: Statistika, 1970	152–153
1970–1974	National Economy of the RSFSR in 1975. Moscow: Statistika, 1976	164–165
1975–1980	National Economy of the RSFSR in 1980. Moscow: Finansy i Statistika, 1981	134–135
1981–1984	National Economy of the RSFSR in 1985. Moscow: Finansy i Statistika, 1986	116
1985–1989	National Economy of the RSFSR in 1990. Moscow: Resp. inf.-izd. Centr., 1991	418
1990	Rosstat, CBSD	–
1991–2016	Rosstat, supplement to RSY	–

[a]Data are lowered 1.5% to be comparable with information from latter sources
[b]1955–1957 data are corrected for corn grain of milky-wax ripeness
[c]Areas planted in Crimea are estimated as 0.5 million of hectares (average for 1945 and 1950)

New Residential Completions

Historical information on residential construction is less available than on other sectors of the Russian economy, at least those considered here. Publication of the RSFSR's data on new residential completions began in 1946; we couldn't find any older information, even in unpublished documents stored in archives. Our hypothesis relates this to the fact that the main goal of economic policy during the Soviet period was the creation of large-scale industrial establishments, especially those which were specialized in producing machines and equipment (capital goods). The Communist and Soviet authorities paid far less attention to the production of consumer goods and to residential construction (it even seems that for years, the Soviet statistics simply didn't count the new houses built by collective farmers, which were the majority of the houses in rural areas). As the official figures for total new residential construction consist of different components for different years, we decided not to use them at all. Instead, we chose three time-series: one for state organizations and establishments (it's roughly comparable for all years) and two for the population, for workers and employees up to 1980, and for the total population beginning in 1980 (we hope that the trajectories of the latter two are similar).

Years	Source: title/archive and code	Page (s)
State organizations and establishments[a] and/or population[b]		
1946–1956	National Economy of the RSFSR in 1958. Moscow: Gosstatizdat, 1959	344
1957–1960	National Economy of the RSFSR in 1965. Moscow: Statistika, 1966	381
1961–1967	National Economy of the RSFSR in 1967. Moscow: Statistika, 1968	366
1968–1969	National Economy of the RSFSR in 1970. Moscow: Statistika, 1971	327
1970–1974	National Economy of the RSFSR in 1975. Moscow: Statistika, 1976	339

(continued)

Years	Source: title/archive and code	Page (s)
1975–1979	National Economy of the RSFSR in 1980. Moscow: Finansy i Statistika, 1981	230
1980–1984	National Economy of the RSFSR in 1985. Moscow: Finansy i Statistika,1986	246
1985–1990	National Economy of the RSFSR in 1990. Moscow: Resp. inf.-izd. Centr., 1991	203
1991–2016	Rosstat, supplement to RSY	–

[a]Including nonagricultural cooperatives
[b]Workers and employees up to 1980

Railroad Freight Transportation

Railroad statistics for the RSFSR was openly published up to the mid-1930s and after 1958 with the more than a 20-year gap in between. We found almost all of the necessary information in unpublished documents stored in archives. Unfortunately, at the moment we still have three holes: 1934 and 1936–1937. It makes it impossible to say anything reasonable about the dynamics of railroad freight transportation during the second 5-year plan (1933–1937), but it's enough to detect the contraction in 1933.

Years	Source: title/archive and code	Page(s)
1928–1931	Dynamic and geographical distribution of freight transportation in the USSR. 1928–1931. Moscow, TsUNHU SSSR, 1932	12–13
1932	Socialist construction of the USSR. Statistical yearbook. 1934. Moscow, Soyuzorguchet, 1934	263–264
1933	Socialist construction of the USSR. Statistical yearbook. 1935. Moscow, Soyuzorguchet, 1935	400–401
1934	Not available	
1935	The USSR is a country of socialism. Statistical digest. 1936. Moscow, v/o Soyuzorguchet, 1936	188–189
1936–1937	Not available	
1938–1939	RSEA 1884-61-82	37, 124
1940, 1945–1955	RSEA 1562-33-2515	31
1941–1944	RSEA 1562-33-3445	380
1956–1957	National Economy of the RSFSR in 1958. Moscow: Gosstatizdat, 1959	355
1958–1962	National Economy of the RSFSR in 1962. Moscow: Gosstatizdat, 1963	369
1963–1964	National Economy of the RSFSR in 1964. Moscow: Statistika, 1965	321
1965–1970	Transportation and communication in the USSR. Statistical digest. 1972	113

(continued)

Years	Source: title/archive and code	Page(s)
1971–1975	National Economy of the RSFSR in 1975. Moscow: Statistika, 1976	309
1976–1980	National Economy of the RSFSR in 1980. Moscow: Finansy i Statistika, 1981	193
1981–1985	National Economy of the RSFSR in 1985. Moscow: Finansy i Statistika, 1986	202
1986–1989	National Economy of the RSFSR in 1989. Moscow: Resp. inf.-izd. Centr., 1990	618
1990	Rosstat, CBSD	–
1991–2016	Rosstat, supplement to RSY	–

References

Akindinova N, Chernyavskiy A, Kondrashov N, Yakovlev A (2017) Political response to the crisis: the case of Russia. In: Havlik P, Iwasaki I (eds) Economics of European crises and emerging markets. Palgrave Macmillan, New York, pp 239–262

Alekseev AV (1994) Alternative estimates of Russian economic growth. ECO no 11, pp 94–108 (in Russian) [Алексеев АВ (1994) Альтернативные оценки российского экономического роста. ЭКО. No. 11, C 94–108]

Alekseev AV, Kiselyov AV, Kuznetsova NN (1996) Long-run tendencies in Russian economic growth. ECO no 1, pp 108–126 (in Russian) [Алексеев АВ, Киселев АВ, Кузнецова НН (1996) Долгосрочные тенденции российского экономического роста. ЭКО. No. 1, C 108–126]

Åslund A (2013) How capitalism was built: the transformation of Central and Eastern Europe, Russia, the Caucasus, and Central Asia, 2nd edn. Cambridge University Press, New York

Balashov A, Martianova Y (2015) Re-industrialization of the Russian economy and the development of military-industrial complex. Voprosy Ekonomiki 9:31–44 [Балашов А, Мартьянова Я (2015) Реиндустриализация российской экономики и развитие оборонн-о-промышленного комплекса. Вопросы экономики 9:31–44]

Baranov EF, Bessonov VA (1999) Indexes of industrial production (Jan 1990–Dec 1998). Promyshlennost Rossii 3:4–12 (in Russian) [Баранов ЭФ, Бессонов ВА (1999) Индексы интенсивности промышленного производства (январь 1990 г. — декабрь 1998 г.). Промышленность России 3:4–12]

Bergson A (1961) The real national income of Soviet Russia since 1928. Harvard University Press, Cambridge

Bokarev YP (2006) Growth rates of industrial output in Russia from the late XIX to the early XX century. Econ J 1:158–190 (in Russian) [Бокарев ЮП (2006) Темпы роста промышленного производства в России в конце XIX–начале XX в. Экономический журнал 1:158–190]

BP (2017) Statistical review of world energy – underpinning data, 1965–2016. https://www.bp.com/en/global/corporate/energy-economics/statistical-review-of-world-energy.htm

Burns AF, Mitchell WC (1946) Measuring business cycles. NBER

CIA (1963) Index of civilian industrial production in the USSR, 1950–1961. CIA RR ER 63–29. US GPO, Washington

CIA (1971) Indexes of Soviet industrial production, 1950–70. CIA intelligence report RR IR 71–11. US GPO, Washington

CIA (1990) Measuring Soviet GNP: problems and solutions. A conference report, vol 3. US GPO, Washington

Davies RW (1996) Crisis and progress in the Soviet economy, 1931–1933. Palgrave School, Houndmills

Davies RW, Wheatcroft SG (2009) The years of hunger: soviet agriculture, 1931–1933. Revised edition. Palgrave Macmillan, New York [Russian edition: Дэвис, Роберт и Стивен Уиткрофт (2011) Годы голода. Сельское хозяйство СССР 1931–1933 гг. Росспэн, М]

Davies RW, Harrison M, Wheatcroft SG (eds) (1994) The economic transformation of the Soviet Union, 1913–1945. Cambridge University Press, Cambridge

Easterly W, Fischer S (1995) The Soviet economic decline. World Bank Econ Rev 9(3):341–371

Gerchuk YP (1926) Index numbers of the physical volume of industrial production computed by Conj. Inst. Economic Bulletin of the Conjuncture Institute 2:12–20 [Герчук ЯП (1926) Индексы физического объема промышленного производства, исчисленные Конъюнктурным институтом. Экономический бюллетень Конъюнктурного института 2:12–20]

Goldsmith RW (1961) The economic growth of tsarist Russia 1860–1913. Essays in the quantitative study of economic growth. Presented to Simon Kuznets on the occasion of his sixtieth birthday, April 30, 1961, by his students and friends. Econ Dev Cult Chang 9(3):441–475

Gregory P (2003a) Economic growth of the Russian empire (late XIX—early XX century). New estimates and calculations. Moscow: ROSSPEN (in Russian) [Грегори П (2003a) Экономический рост Российской империи (конец XIX - начало XX в.). Новые подсчеты и оценки. РОССПЭН, М]

Gregory P (2003b) Soviet defence puzzles: archives, strategy and underfulfilment. Eur Asia Stud 55 (6):923–937

Harrison M (1998) Prices, planners, and producers: an agency problem in Soviet industry, 1928–1950. J Econ Hist 58(4):1032–1062

Harrison M (2002) Accounting for war: Soviet production, employment, and the defence burden, 1940–1945, 2nd edn. Cambridge University Press, Cambridge

Ickes BW (1986) Cyclical fluctuations in centrally planned economies: a critique of the literature. Sov Stud 38(1):36–52

JEC (1962) Dimensions of Soviet economic power. Part II. The measure of production. US GPO, Washington

JEC (1973) Soviet economic prospects for the seventies. US GPO, Washington

JEC (1976) Soviet economy in a new perspective. US GPO, Washington

JEC (1982) USSR: measures of economic growth and development, 1950–80. US GPO, Washington

JEC (1990) Measures of Soviet gross national product in 1982 prices. US GPO, Washington

JEC (1993) The former Soviet Union in transition. M.E. Sharpe, New York

Kafengauz LB (1930) Evolution of industrial output of Russia (from the last third of the XIX century to the 1930s). Publishing House 'Epiphany', Moscow, 1994 [Кафенгауз ЛБ (1930) Эволюция промышленного производства России (последняя треть XIX в.—30-е годы XX в.). М.: Эпифания,1994]

Korneychuk B (2015) The role of foreign participation in Soviet industrialization: an institutional view. Voprosy Ekonomiki 9:109–123 (in Russian) [Корнейчук Б (2015) Роль иностранного участия в советской индустриализации: институциональный аспект. Вопросы экономики 9:109–123]

Kuboniwa M (1997) Economic growth in post-war Russia: estimating GDP. Hitotsubashi J Econ 38 (1):21–32

Kuboniwa M (2014) The impact of oil prices, total factor productivity and institutional weakness on Russia's declining growth. RRC working paper series no 49. Hitotsubashi University, Tokyo

Lopatin LN, Lopatina NL (2009) The collectivization and dispossession: testimony of witnesses and documents. Publishing House 'Axiom', Kemerovo (in Russian) [Лопатин ЛН, Лопатина НЛ (2009) Коллективизация и раскулачивание (очевидцы и документы свидетельствуют). Кемерово, Изд-во Аксиома]

Macheret D (2015) The dynamics of railway cargo transportation as a macroeconomic indicator. Econ Policy 10(2):133–150 (in Russian) [Мачерет Д (2015) Динамика железнодорожных перевозок грузов как макроэкономический индикатор. Экономическая политика 10 (2):133–150]

Markevich A, Harrison M (2011) Great war, civil war, and recovery: Russia's national income, 1913 to 1928. J Econ Hist 71(3):672–703

Moorsteen R, Powell R (1966) The Soviet capital stock, 1928–62. RD Irwin, Homewood

Ponomarenko AN (2002) Russia's national accounts in retrospect, 1961–1990. Financy i Statistika, Moscow (in Russian) [Пономаренко АН (2002) Ретроспективные национальные счета России: 1961–1990. М., Финансы и статистика]

Rosefielde S (2003) The riddle of post-war Russian economic growth: statistics lied and were misconstrued. Eur Asia Stud 55(3):469–481

Rosefielde S, Kuboniwa M (2003) Russian growth retardation then and now. Eurasian Geogr Econ 44(2):87–101

Simonov NS (1996) The military-industrial complex of the USSR from the 1920s to the 1950s. ROSSPEN, Moscow (in Russian) [Симонов НС (1996) Военно-промышленный комплекс СССР в 1920–1950-е годы: темпы экономического роста, структура, организация производства и управление. Росспэн, М]

Smirnov SV (2012) Industrial output and economic cycles in the USSR and Russia, 1861–2012. National Research University 'Higher School of Economics'. Publishing House of the Higher School of Economics, Moscow (in Russian) [Смирнов СВ (2012) Динамика промышленного производства и экономический цикл в СССР и России, 1861–2012: Нац. исслед. ун-т «Высшая школа экономики». Изд. дом Высшей школы экономики, М]

Smirnov SV (2013a) Cyclical mechanisms in the US and Russia: why are they different? Working paper WP2/2013/01. National Research University 'Higher School of Economics', Moscow

Smirnov SV (2013b) Cyclical patterns of railroad freight transportation (RFT) in Russia. CIRET/KOF workshop on sectoral dimensions in economic cycles, Zurich, 4–5 Oct 2013

Suhara M (2000) An estimate of Russian industrial production: 1960–90. Voprosy Statistiki 2:55–63 (in Russian) [Сухара М (2000) Оценка промышленного производства России: 1960–1990 годы. Вопросы статистики 2:55–63]

Suhara M (2006) Russian industrial growth: an estimate of a production index, 1860–1913. Research Institute of Economic Science, College of Economics, Nihon University. Working paper series, no 05-03

Varzar V (1928) Index of physical volume of consumption of the USSR for forty years (manuscript). Russian State Historical Archive (RSHA) F. 1607. Op. 1. D. 59 [Варзар ВЕ (1928) Индекс физического объема потребления СССР за сорок лет (рукопись). Российский государственный исторический архив (РГИА) Ф.1607. Оп. 1. Д. 59]

Zhuravlev S (2012) The 1932–33 Famine: false and real causes. Expert no 1 (26 Dec 2011–15 Jan 2012) (in Russian) [Журавлев С (2012) Голод 1932–1933 годов: причины реальные и мнимые. «Эксперт» 1 (26 дек. 2011–15 янв. 2012)]

Business Cycle Measurement in India

Radhika Pandey, Ila Patnaik, and Ajay Shah

1 Introduction

In India, the interest in business cycle research is relatively new, though industrialised economies and some emerging economies have a fairly long history of business cycle measurement. Two distinct periods emerge in the analysis of business cycles in India: the pre-1991 period and the post-1991 period. In this chapter we present an overview of the methods used for arriving at the business cycle chronology in the two periods and the macroeconomic conditions that shaped the cyclical fluctuations in the two periods.

The next section presents an overview of literature on business cycle turning points in the pre-1991 period. The next section describes the Indian business cycles from 1991 onwards. This section first begins with a description of the balance of payments crisis in 1990–1991 that served as a trigger event for a series of reform measures introduced to address the structural imbalances in the economy. Subsequently the section presents an overview of cyclical turning points in the post-1991 period. The subsequent section presents our work on cyclical chronology using official quarterly GDP numbers. Finally the chapter presents a description of the current cyclical conditions in the economy in the post-2012 period before concluding.

R. Pandey (✉) · I. Patnaik · A. Shah
National Institute of Public Finance and Policy (NIPFP), New Delhi, India
e-mail: radhesp@gmail.com

S. Smirnov et al. (eds.), *Business Cycles in BRICS*, Societies and Political Orders in Transition, https://doi.org/10.1007/978-3-319-90017-9_7

2 Indian Business Cycles: 1950–1991

In the India of old, business cycle, downturns in the pre-liberalisation period were associated with drought or oil price hike and saw sharp declines in GDP. There were no investment-inventory cycles or periods of expansion followed by periods of contraction that are typically seen in industrialised countries. Few studies have attempted to establish the cyclical fluctuations in the prereform period at varying frequencies. The studies apply the three approaches of business cycle measurement: classical, growth and growth rate cycle.

Table 1 shows the dates of peaks and troughs identified in the Indian business cycle literature using the different approaches to business cycle measurement.

Patnaik and Sharma (2002) examined annual GDP data[1] for the period 1950–1951 to 1999–2000 (base = 1993–1994) from the National Accounts Statistics to identify cycles.[2] The authors used a simple rule of thumb to identify cycles. The authors identified periods of contraction as those when growth rate fell by 4 or more percentage points and to around 1%. Following this rule of thumb, the authors identified four episodes of contraction: 1957–1958, 1965–1966, 1979–1980 and 1991–1992. Even if we apply the traditional definition of contraction (period of negative growth rate), we broadly identify the same periods with the exclusion of 1991–1992 and the addition of 1972–1973 when the growth in annual GDP contracted to −0.3%. The notable point is that in each of these years, there was a sharp decline in agricultural output. While 1957–1958 also saw a sharp decline in growth in manufacturing which turned to negative, in 1965–1966 it was mainly the drought that caused GDP (agriculture) to decline by over 11%. 1979–1980 saw a sharp fall in GDP (agriculture) by over 12%. GDP (manufacturing) also declined, and its growth was −3.2%. In 1991–1992 there was a balance of payment crisis, a fall in agricultural and manufacturing growth and a decline in GDP growth.[3]

Table 2 shows the GDP growth rate and the sector-wise breakdown of growth rates.

Dua and Banerji (2012) identified business cycle monthly chronology for India using the classical approach. The authors identified periods of expansion and contraction based on the consensus of cyclical co-movements in the broad measures of output, income, employment and domestic trade measures. The authors constructed a coincident indicator using gross domestic product, general index of monthly industrial production, wages to workers in factory sector, monthly registered unemployement and industrial production of consumer goods. The periods of contraction identified are December 1964 to November 1965, May 1966 to April 1967, July 1972 to May 1973, December 1973 to February 1975, May 1979 to

[1]Annual data in Indian statistics follow the "financial year" convention, i.e. from April to March. As an example, the year 1951–1952 would cover the period from April 1951 to March 1952.

[2]Quarterly data for GDP is available only since 1996–1997.

[3]Note: Meanwhile the GDP growth rate was positive. For a discussion of this phenomenon, see Sect. 3.2.

Table 1 Trough and peak dates in literature: the pre-1991 period

Trough	Peak
Patnaik and Sharma (2002), Classical approach (annual)	
	1956–1957
1957–1958	1963–1964
1965–1966	1978–1979
1979–1980	1990–1991
1991–1992	
Dua and Banerji (2012), Classical approach (monthly)	
	November 1964
November 1965	April 1966
April 1967	June 1972
May 1973	November 1973
February 1975	April 1979
March 1980	March 1991
Dua and Banerji (2012), Growth rate cycle approach (monthly)	
	September 1960
July 1961	February 1962
November 1962	May 1964
November 1965	April 1966
March 1967	April 1969
February 1974	February 1976
September 1977	May 1978
December 1979	October 1980
February 1983	August 1984
September 1985	October 1986
December 1987	June 1988
May 1989	March 1990
September 1991	
Mall (1999), Growth cycle approach (quarterly)	
	1951–1952
1953–1954	1956–1957
1959–1960	1964–1965
1967–1968	1969–1970
1974–1975	1978–1979
1980–1981	1989–1990
Mohanty et al. (2003), Growth cycle (monthly)	
November 1971	December 1972
October 1973	July 1974
January 1976	August 1976
March 1978	March 1979
September 1980	May 1982
September 1983	September 1984
December 1986	July 1987

(continued)

Table 1 (continued)

Trough	Peak
April 1988	January 1989
November 1989	September 1990
Chitre (2004), Growth cycle (monthly)	
	January 1952
November 1953	June 1956
June 1958	March 1961
February 1962	March 1965
January 1968	April 1970
November 1970	February 1972
January 1975	November 1976
October 1977	May 1978
April 1980	

This table captures the dates of troughs and peaks identified in the literature on Indian business cycle using different approaches to business cycle measurement

March 1980 and April 1991 to September 1991. The chronology of turning points by Dua and Banerji (2012) is also part of the Economic Cycle Research Institute (ECRI) chronology for India.

Mall (1999) used the growth cycle approach to examine the cyclical behaviour of the Indian economy since 1950. The author identified six sets of turning points in index of industrial production [IIP (manufacturing)] as the peaks and troughs of the cycle in the period.

Mohanty et al. (2003) identified 13 growth cycles of varying durations during the period 1970–1971 to 2001–2002 using monthly index of industrial production (IIP) series. The computation of cycles is based on the dates identified using the Bry-Boschan algorithm.

Chitre (2004) identified turning points in an index based on 94 monthly series for the period 1951–1982. After considerable experimentation, 11 monthly economic indicators are selected to determine the reference dates in India's overall economic activity. The author identified 8 peaks and 8 troughs using this index of 11 series.

The literature identified some common periods of contraction[4] and deceleration[5] for the period 1950–1991:

1. 1957–1958 is identified as a year of contraction by Patnaik and Sharma (2002) and as a period of deceleration by Mall (1999) and Chitre (2004).
2. 1965–1966 is identified as a year of contraction by Patnaik and Sharma (2002) and as a period of deceleration by Mall (1999) and Chitre (2004).

[4]Periods of contraction (decline in the level of output) are identified from studies using the classical approach.

[5]Periods of deceleration (slowdown in the rate of growth) are identified from studies using the growth or growth rate cycle approach.

Table 2 Growth of GDP and its components

Year	GDP (at factor cost)	GDP (manufacturing)	GDP (agriculture)
1951–1952	2.3	3.1	1.4
1952–1953	2.8	3.4	3.1
1953–1954	6.1	7.7	7.7
1954–1955	4.2	7.0	2.9
1955–1956	2.6	7.8	−0.8
1956–1957	5.7	7.5	5.4
1957–1958	−1.2	3.8	−4.5
1958–1959	7.5	4.9	10.1
1959–1960	2.2	6.7	−1.0
1960–1961	7.1	8.3	6.7
1961–1962	3.1	8.5	0.1
1962–1963	2.1	7.3	−1.9
1963–1964	5.1	9.4	2.3
1964–1965	7.6	6.9	9.2
1965–1966	−3.6	0.9	−11.0
1966–1967	1.0	0.7	−1.4
1967–1968	8.1	0.4	14.9
1968–1969	2.6	5.5	−0.1
1969–1970	6.5	10.7	6.4
1970–1971	5.0	2.3	7.1
1971–1972	1.0	3.2	−1.8
1972–1973	−0.3	3.9	−5.0
1973–1974	4.5	4.4	7.2
1974–1975	1.1	2.9	−1.5
1975–1976	9	2.1	12.9
1976–1977	1.2	8.7	−5.7
1977–1978	7.4	6.2	10.0
1978–1979	5.5	12.3	2.3
1979–1980	−5.2	−3.2	−12.7
1980–1981	7.2	0.19	12.8
1981–1982	5.9	8.0	5.3
1982–1983	3.0	6.6	−0.6
1983–1984	7.7	10.1	9.5
1984–1985	4.3	6.5	1.4
1985–1986	4.4	3.9	0.7
1986–1987	4.3	6.9	−0.6
1987–1988	3.8	7.3	−1.3
1988–1989	10.4	8.8	15.4
1989–1990	6.7	11.7	1.4
1990–1991	5.5	6.0	4.1
1991–1992	1.3	−3.6	−1.5

Source: Central Statistical Organisation (CSO)

Table 3 Changing composition of GDP[a]

	Agriculture	Industry	Services
1951–1952	53.1	16.5	30.2
1992–1993	28.8	27.4	43.8
2009–2010	14.6	28.4	57.0

[a]1951–1952 represents the period from April 1951 to March 1952 and similarly for other years

3. 1972–1973 is identified as a period of contraction by Dua and Banerji (2012) and as a period of deceleration by Mohanty et al. (2003).
4. 1979–1980 is identified as a year of contraction by Patnaik and Sharma (2002) and as a period of deceleration by Mall (1999), Mohanty et al. (2003) and Chitre (2004).
5. 1991–1992 is identified as a period of contraction by Patnaik and Sharma (2002) and Dua and Banerji (2012).

The major drivers of fluctuations in the pre-1990s period were:

Agricultural Growth In the pre-1990s period, a good year was one with a good monsoon, and a downturn was generally about a bad monsoon. These developments played out over a short horizon of 1 or 2 years. Output fluctuations were an outcome of uncorrelated monsoon shocks (Shah 2008). India did not have a conventional business cycle. Table 3 shows the composition of GDP. The table shows that in 1951, agriculture contributed a sizeable proportion of GDP. Till the end of 1970s, agriculture accounted for up to 40% of output. Thus the fluctuations in GDP in the pre-1990s period were primarily driven by monsoon shocks. (Ghate et al. 2013)

Restrictive Economic Policy The economic policy landscape was characterised by an array of licences and quotas that constrained output growth and expansion. These restrictions restricted the scope for private sector participation in business and prevented the interplay of investment-inventory fluctuations that is the basis of business cycle fluctuations.

1. Tariff and non-tariff barriers on imports: Import duties were amongst the highest in the world, with duty rates above 200% being fairly common. The restrictive approach towards imports is evident from the fact that in 1990–1991, the import-weighted average rate of tariff for all imports was as high as 87% (Kotwal et al. 2011). In addition to tariff barriers, a system of import licences restricted the amount that could be imported.
2. Restrictions on private investments: Private investments were restricted through an investment licensing regime under which central government permission was needed for investment by incumbents as well as by prospective entrants. In addition, industrial groups that were designated as "large" could not expand without permissions that had to be obtained under the Monopolies and Restrictive Trade Practices (MRTP) Act. Some industry segments were "reserved" for production by small-scale units to protect them from competition from large-

scale units. Price and distribution controls were often applied to industries such as steel, cement, fertilisers, petroleum and pharmaceuticals (Kotwal et al. 2011).

While there were restrictions on imports and private sector investment, the prominent source of investment was public sector investment in the form of plan expenditure, which did not show any cyclical fluctuations. There were controls on capacity creation.

3. Restrictions on foreign investment: Until 1991 India followed a restrictive regime towards foreign direct investment. FDI was perceived as a means of acquiring industrial technology. Further, there were restrictions on the rate of royalty payments and technical fees. The erstwhile foreign investment law stipulated foreign firms to have equity holding only up to 40 percent with exemptions granted at the government's discretion (Nagaraj 2003).

3 Indian Business Cycles: 1991 Onwards

3.1 Radical Changes at the Turn of the 1990s

The period from 1989 onwards was marked with a series of developments that shocked the economy further.

1. The break up of the Soviet Union: Soviet Union was India's significant trading partner in the 1980s. In fact, it emerged as the largest trading partner and the biggest destination of India's exports in the first half of the 1980s decade. A significant proportion of capital goods imports from the erstwhile USSR was financed through long-term trade credits. These arrangements came to a halt, resulting in an increase in the repayment burden.
2. Iraq-Kuwait war: India depended on Kuwait and Iraq for its crude oil supplies. The invasion of Kuwait by Iraq at the beginning of August 1990 resulted in an increase in crude oil prices. India's oil import bill increased by about 60% in 1990–1991.
3. Political uncertainty: The political uncertainty caused by frequent changes in government during this period hampered the implementation of effective policy response.

   The immediate cause was the Gulf War in 1990–1991 which led to a surge in oil prices and India's import bill (Acharya 2002).

3.2 The Balance of Payments Crisis in 1990–1991

India faced a severe balance of payments crisis in the early 1990s. While the crisis hit India in 1990–1991, it had been building for half a decade prior to the crisis year.

The fiscal deficit was rising, and exchange rate rigidity[6] led to a rise in current account deficit. The restrictive framework governing foreign investments resulted in current account deficit translating into rising levels of external debt. A quick snapshot of the key macroeconomic indicators revealed that the situation was acute[7]:

1. The year 1990–1991 ended with a fiscal deficit of 8.4% of GDP.
2. As a consequence of the increase in the import bill for crude oil and petroleum, imports in rupee terms rose by 21.9% as against an increase of 17.5% in the case of exports in 1990–1991.
3. The trade deficit widened substantially. Combined with loss of remittance from West Asia in particular Iraq and Kuwait and a decline in non-resident deposits, the foreign exchange reserves got depleted from Rs. 50.5 billion at the beginning of August 1990 to Rs. 43.8 billion at the end of March 1991. The decline in reserves would have been much greater if the government had not resorted to borrowing from the IMF.[8]
4. Inflation surged to double digit in 1990–1991.

Most of the major industries recorded a lower growth in 1991 as compared to 1990. Three categories of industries, capital goods, consumer goods and export-oriented industries, were particularly affected. Capital goods industries suffered due to a decline in government investment, consumer durables suffered owing to high cost of imported inputs, and export-oriented sectors suffered owing to collapse of demand in the market in erstwhile Soviet Union. However the infrastructure sector particularly the railways and coal production witnessed a respectable growth. Financial and transport services did well; as a result, we see a decline in GDP growth but not a steep contraction in the crisis that hit in the year of 1991–1992 (Ministry of Finance, Government of India 1992). Clearly there was a need for effective reforms to address the problems that led to the emergence of chronic balance of payments crisis.

3.3 Reforms to Address the Crisis

To address the crisis-like situation, a series of reforms towards a market-oriented economy were introduced. The government recognised that correcting the macroeconomic imbalances and replacing the myriad system of controls with the discipline of deregulation and competition could help in overcoming the crisis. The political

[6]India followed a fixed exchange rate regime administered by the Central Bank.

[7]Source: see Ministry of Finance, Government of India (1991).

[8]The first recourse was made during July–September when India drew Rs 11.7 billion which constituted 22% of India's quota and could be drawn upon without any obligations. This was followed by another recourse when Rs 33.3 billion were borrowed under the compensatory and contingency financing facility.

establishment recognised that the balance of payments could be put on a sustained path through liberalisation of trade and investment flows. Some of the key reforms introduced in the early 1990s were:

1. Devaluation and transition to a market determined exchange rate: This was achieved through a phased approach: (a) a dual exchange rate system in the initial 2 years and (b) a move to an integrated, market-based exchange rate system in 1993–1994.
2. Phased reduction of peak import duties: The peak rate of import duties was as high as 300% in 1990–1991. In addition a vast array of general, specific and end-use exemptions were built in as part of the trade policy regime. The subsequent years were marked by a progressive reduction in peak custom duties to 40% in 1997–1998 and further to 10% by 2007–2008 and gradual elimination of exemptions.
3. Policies to encourage foreign direct and portfolio investment: The approach favoured liberalisation of external flows towards foreign direct investment (FDI) and foreign portfolio investment (FPI), while restricting debt, particularly the short-term debt, flows. The foreign direct investment up to 51% foreign equity was allowed under the automatic route for a number of sectors. In parallel, a liberalised regime governing foreign portfolio investment was put in place. It was thought that the flow of foreign equity would help in developing the domestic equity market, by stimulating competition. Foreign portfolio investments were allowed up to 24% of the total equity of any company.
4. Abolition of industrial licensing and greater role for private sector participation: The licensing regime was considerably liberalised. Under the New Industrial Policy of 1991, no licences were required for setting up new industrial units or for substantial expansion in the capacity of the existing units, except for a short list of industries relating to country's security and strategic concerns, hazardous industries and industries causing environmental degradation. The New Industrial Policy also stressed on greater role for private sector participation through reduced reservation for public sector.
5. Gradual liberalisation of interest rates: In the pre-liberalisation period, the interest rate structure in India was highly regulated and controlled by the government. The government propounded the philosophy of subsidised credit to certain sectors. Further government directed banks to invest a mandated proportion of their deposits in government securities. Referred to as the statutory liquidity ratio (SLR), it was as high as 40% in the pre-liberalisation period. Expert committees set up to propose reforms to the financial sector recommended that banks should be given greater freedom to determine the interest rates. Further financial repression through SLR and directed priority sector lending should be progressively reduced. In the post-liberalisation period, we have seen phased reduction of SLR and a move towards market-based determination of interest rates.
6. Setting up of Securities and Exchange Board of India (SEBI) as capital market regulator and decontrol of government over raising of capital by companies. Prior to 1992, the pricing of capital issues was controlled by Controller of Capital

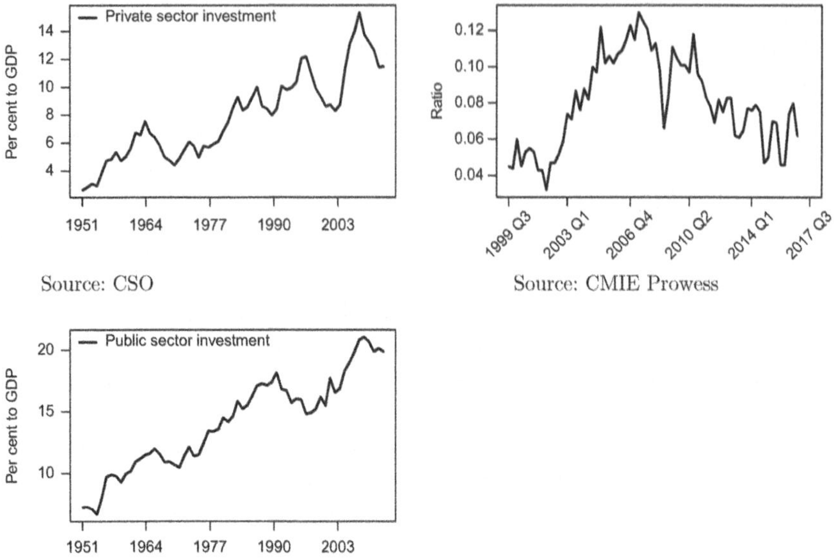

Source: CSO

Source: CMIE Prowess

Source: CSO

Fig. 1 Gross fixed capital formation (private and public) and net profit margin of firms

Issues (CCI). The CCI granted approval for issue of securities and also determined the amount, type and price of the issue.

The CCI was abolished with the introduction of Securities and Exchange Board of India (SEBI) with the prime objective of protecting the interests of investors in securities, promoting the development of, and regulating, the securities market. Under the liberalised regime, the companies could issue securities directly in the market provided they followed guidelines related to disclosure and investor protection.

With eased controls on capacity creation and dismantling of trade barriers, private sector investment as a share of GDP has shown a significant rise. With reduced barriers, competition has increased. Profits are uncertain, and expectations about profit drive investment decisions, as is the case with firms in market economies. Since 1991, while India has seen a sharp increase in private corporate sector investment as a share of GDP, this share has shown sharp upswings and downswings. The first plot in Fig. 1 shows the time series of private corporate gross fixed capital formation (GFCF) expressed as a percent to GDP. In the mid-1990s, private corporate GFCF rose from 5% of GDP in 1991–1992 to 9% of GDP. This fell dramatically in the business cycle downturn of 2000–2003 and hovered around 5% of GDP. It again surged to 12–14% of GDP in the period 2005–2007 before moderating in the recent years. Investment-inventory fluctuations are today central to understanding the emergence of business cycles in India. This is also reflected in the performance of firms. The second plot in Fig. 1 shows the quarterly net profit margin of nonfinancial firms. The series exhibits business cycle fluctuations as opposed to short-lived shocks associated with monsoons (Shah 2008). In contrast, the third plot shows the public sector capital formation (investment) as a percent to GDP. It was the dominant source of investment in the pre-1990s period.

3.4 *Turning Points*

Table 4 shows the chronology of turning points using classical, growth and growth rate cycle approach at monthly frequency. In these studies either a coincident index of monthly series or the monthly index of industrial production (IIP) is used to arrive at the chronology of dates.

Dua and Banerji (2012) present monthly classical and growth rate cycle chronology for India. As far as the classical approach is concerned, we see an expansion in the first half of the 1990s. A brief episode of contraction is seen from June 1996 to November 1996. The growth rate cycle approach identifies the periods of deceleration: May 1992 to April 1993, May 1995 to November 1996, and October 1997 to October 1998, April 2000 to July 2001, May 2004 to October 2004, November 2005 to March 2006 and February 2007 to January 2009.

Mohanty et al. (2003) present a growth cycle chronology using the monthly index of industrial production (IIP) series. The periods of deceleration identified are: December 1993 to September 1994, June 1995 to September 1995, September 1996 to March 1998 and December 2000 to September 2001.

Table 4 Peak and trough dates in literature: 1991 onwards

Trough	Peak
Dua and Banerji (2012), Classical approach	
September 1991	May 1996
November 1996	
Dua and Banerji (2012), Growth rate cycle approach	
September 1991	April 1992
April 1993	April 1995
November 1996	September 1997
October 1998	March 2000
July 2001	April 2004
October 2004	October 2005
March 2006	January 2007
January 2009	March 2011
Mohanty et al. (2003), growth cycle approach	
March 1993	November 1993
September 1994	May 1995
December 1995	August 1996
March 1998	November 2000
September 2001	

The classical approach identifies the first half of the 1990s decade as a period of expansion. The growth rate cycle approach also identifies the period from 1993 to 1995 as a period of accelerated growth. The second half of the 1990s see a combination of some brief spells of acceleration and deceleration in growth.

3.5 Methodology to Identify Turning Points from 1996 Onwards Using GDP

In our analysis we use the quarterly GDP series to identify the chronology of turning points (Pandey et al. 2017). We believe that the quarterly real GDP series is a better measure of the business cycle conditions since it is an aggregate of agriculture, industry and services.

The Indian GDP series at quarterly frequency is available from April to June 1996 onwards. In the Indian data, we do not see an absolute decline in levels of our proxy series: quarterly GDP. We use the growth cycle approach for establishing the turning points chronology. A brief description of methodology is presented below:

1. Seasonal adjustment: The first step is to adjust the series for seasonal fluctuations. In India, the official statistics do not feature seasonal adjustment. We seasonally adjust the series using the X-13-ARIMA-SEATS seasonal adjustment program using the steps developed in Bhattacharya et al. (2016).
2. Extraction of cycles: The next step is the extraction of the cyclical component. The seasonally adjusted series is filtered to extract the cyclical component.

   One tool that is widely used for this purpose is the Hodrick-Prescott filter. In recent years, it has become increasingly clear that this filter, while elegant and readily implemented, has important shortcomings. The business cycle facts that emerge from HP-filtered data are sensitive to the different values of the smoothing parameter (Bjornland 2000). Alp et al. (2011) find that the choice of the smoothing parameter (λ) in the HP filter has important implications for the volatility of the trend term and average business cycle length observed in the data. Hamilton (2016) shows that the HP-filtered series produces spurious dynamic relations that have no relation with the underlying data-generating process. The literature has increasingly come to rely on alternatives to the HP filter.

   The workhorses of the literature are the band-pass filters proposed by Baxter and King (1999) and Christiano and Fitzgerald (2003). Band-pass filters eliminate slow moving trend components and high-frequency components while retaining the intermediate business cycle fluctuations. These filters approach the de-trending and smoothing problem in the frequency domain.

   In a recent advance, Hamilton (2016) proposes a simple and robust estimator of the cyclical component. This is based on an estimate of an OLS regression of y_{t+h} on a constant and the four most recent values of y as of date t. Hamilton (2016) shows that the residual from this regression provides a reasonable

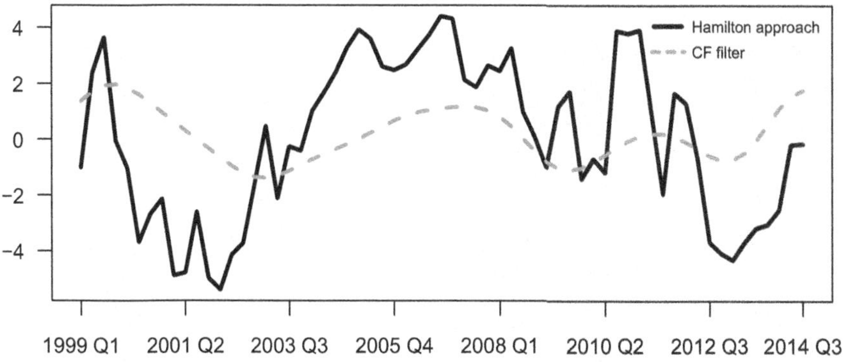

Fig. 2 GDP cyclical component: CF filter and Hamilton method. (a) Some observations are lost since we do lagged regression to extract the cyclical component using the Hamilton procedure. (b) The quarter designation is based on calendar year convention. As an example Q1 refers to January to March, and Q2 refers to April to June

de-trended approximation for a broad class of underlying processes. The residuals from the following OLS regressions

$$y_{t+h} = \beta_0 + \beta_1 y_t + \beta_2 y_{t-1} + \beta_3 y_{t-2} + \beta_4 y_{t-3} + v_{t+h}$$

are the cyclical component of the series:

$$\widehat{v}_{t+h} = y_{t+h} - \widehat{\beta}_0 - \widehat{\beta}_1 y_t - \widehat{\beta}_2 y_{t-1} - \widehat{\beta}_3 y_{t-2} - \widehat{\beta}_4 y_{t-3}$$

In our work, we use the asymmetric Christiano-Fitzgerald filter (CF) to isolate the trend and cyclical component. The cyclical component is standardised before the application of the dating algorithm.

In addition, we also use the methods of Hamilton (2016). Figure 2 superposes the cycles extracted from the CF filter and the Hamilton (2016) methodology. We get broadly similar turning points through the cycles extracted by the two methods.

3. The dating algorithm: The standardised cyclical component forms the input series for the application of the dating algorithm by Bry and Boschan (1971). The procedure was subsequently improved by Harding and Pagan (2002). The application of the dating algorithm gives us dates of peaks and troughs along with some summary statistics about the cycles.[9]

[9]See Appendix 1 for a description of the procedure used by the dating algorithm.

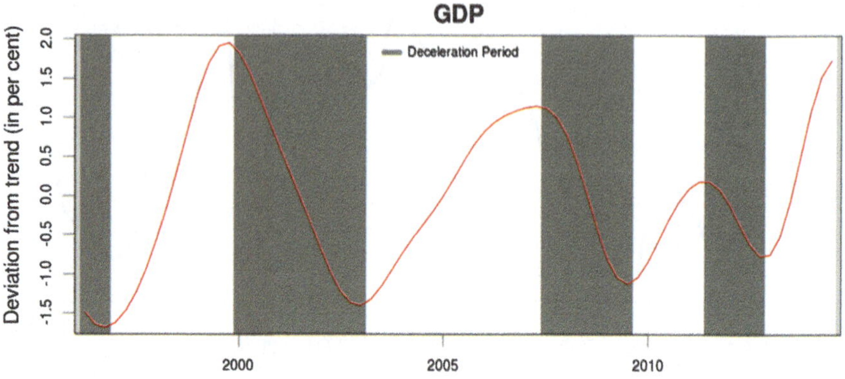

Source: CSO and Authors' computation

Fig. 3 Turning points in GDP

3.5.1 Quarterly Growth Cycle Turning Points

We use the quarterly GDP series (base year 2004–2005) to identify the chronology of business cycle turning points.[10] With chain-linking, this series is available from 1996-Q2 (April–June) to 2014-Q3 (July–September).

First, we extract the cyclical component of GDP using business cycle periodicity of 2–8 years as the typical duration of business cycles identified by the NBER is 2–8 years or 8 to 32 quarters (King and Watson 1996).[11] We then apply the dating algorithm by Harding and Pagan (2002).

Figure 3 and Table 5 show three episodes of deceleration in the economy during the period 1996–2014. Using GDP as the reference series, the first episode of deceleration was in the period 1999-Q4 to 2003-Q1, the second deceleration was in the period 2007-Q2 to 2009-Q3, and the third deceleration was in the period 2011-Q2 to 2012-Q4.[12]

The table also shows the average amplitude and duration of phases of acceleration and deceleration extracted from these dates. The average duration of acceleration is 12 quarters, and the average duration of deceleration is 9 quarters. The average amplitude of acceleration is seen to be 2.5%, while the average amplitude of deceleration is 2.2%.

[10]The Central Statistical Organisation revised the GDP series with a new base year of 2011–2012. The revised series is available only from 2011-Q2. Hence, we stick to the series with the old base year for our analysis.

[11]Some papers tweak the upper or lower bound of the length of the cycle. For example, Agresti and Mojon (2001) allow the upper bound on the length of the business cycle to be 40 quarters (10 years) instead of 32 quarters (8 years) depending on the observed length of the business cycle in European countries.

[12]Since the series begins from 1996 onwards, we do not include the first phase, i.e. from 1996-Q4 to 1999-Q3 in our formal analysis.

Table 5 Dates of turning points in GDP and their summary statistics

Phase			Duration (in quarters)	Amplitude (in percent)
Acceleration	1996-Q4	1999-Q3	12	3.6
Deceleration	1999-Q4	2003-Q1	13	3.3
Acceleration	2003-Q2	2007-Q2	17	2.5
Deceleration	2007-Q3	2009-Q3	9	2.3
Acceleration	2009-Q4	2011-Q2	7	1.3
Deceleration	2011-Q3	2012-Q4	6	0.9
			Average duration (in quarters)	Average amplitude (in percent)
Acceleration			12	2.5
Deceleration			9.3	2.2

This table shows the chronology of turning points using GDP as the reference series. It also shows the summary statistics of the turning points

Here Q1, Q2, Q3 and Q4 follow the calendar year convention. Q1 refers to January–March, Q2 refers to April–June, Q3 refers to July–September, and Q4 refers to October–December

4 Description of Acceleration and Deceleration Phases

4.1 The Decade of the 1990s

Against the backdrop of the reforms (discussed in Sect. 3.3), the external and real sector witnessed a sharp turnround. Table 6 shows a spurt in growth in GDP and its components in the initial postcrisis years. Figure 4 shows a sharp growth in industrial production and exports during the initial years of the 1990s. The initial postcrisis years saw a sharp growth in IIP with growth peaking at 13.7% in mid-1995. Export growth surged to 20% in 1993–1994.

The external debt indicators also witnessed an improvement (Table 7). The external debt stock to GDP ratio improved from 38.7% in 1991–1992 to 30.8% in 1994–1995 and further to 22% in 1999–2000. The ratio of short-term debt to total debt declined from 8.3% in 1991–1992 to 4.3% in 1994–1995 to 4% in 1999–2000. The ratio of foreign exchange reserves to total debt and the ratio of short-term debt to foreign exchange reserves also witness an improvement in the 1990s.

Aggregate savings and investments were also buoyant during the first half of the 1990s. Gross domestic savings as a percent to GDP rose from 21.3 in 1991–1992 to 24.2% in 1997–1998. Similarly gross domestic capital formation rose from 22.5% in 1991–1992 to reach a peak of 26.1% in 1995–1996 before slowing down to 22% in 1996–1997.

The year 1997 saw a moderation in India's growth (Acharya 2012).[13] GDP growth moderated to 4.3% in 1997–1998 from 8% in 1996–1997. Agriculture and

[13]Table 5 shows slowdown from 1999-Q4 through the growth cycle approach. Since the data is available from 1996-Q2, the growth cycle algorithm identifies the initial quarters as a period of upswing, and from 1999-Q4 we see a deceleration. However in the annual data of GDP growth, we see a moderation starting from 1997 to 1998 compared to the preceding years (see Table 6).

Table 6 Growth rate in GDP and its sectors

Year	GDP	Agriculture	Industry	Services
1991–1992	1.4	−2.0	0.3	4.7
1992–1993	5.4	6.7	3.2	5.7
1993–1994	5.7	3.3	5.5	7.4
1994–1995	6.4	4.7	9.2	5.9
1995–1996	7.3	−0.7	11.3	10.1
1996–1997	8.0	9.9	6.4	7.5
1997–1998	4.3	−2.6	4.0	8.9
1998–1999	6.7	6.3	4.2	8.3
1999–2000	7.6	2.7	6.0	11.2

This table shows the growth rate in GDP and its sectors in the 1990s. The table shows a pickup in growth rate during the initial postcrisis years from 1992 to 1996. Since 1997 a broad-based moderation is seen in growth rates for overall GDP, agriculture and industrial GDP

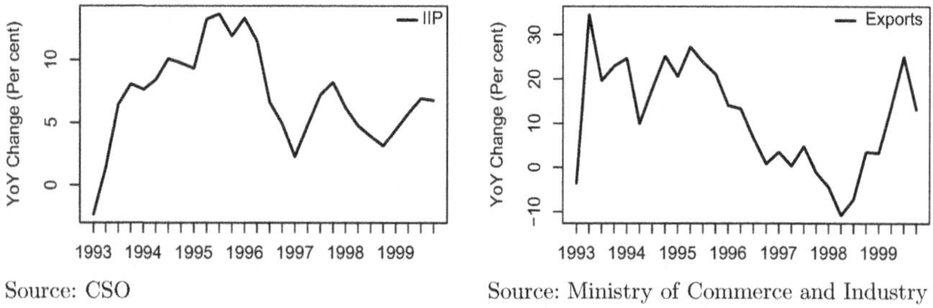

Fig. 4 Industrial production and exports (in nominal terms) in the 1990s

Table 7 External debt indicators in the 1990s

Year	External debt to GDP (%)	Ratio of short-term debt to total debt	Ratio of foreign exchange reserves to total debt	Ratio of short-term debt to foreign exchange reserves
1991–1992	38.7	8.3	10.8	76.7
1992–1993	37.5	7.0	10.9	64.5
1993–1994	33.8	3.9	20.8	18.8
1994–1995	30.8	4.3	25.4	16.9
1995–1996	27.0	5.4	23.1	23.2
1996–1997	24.6	7.2	28.3	25.5
1997–1998	24.3	5.4	31.4	17.2
1998–1999	23.6	4.4	33.5	13.2
1999–2000	22.0	4.0	38.7	10.3

Source: India's external debt: A status report 2014–15, Ministry of Finance. Government of India
This table shows the key external debt indicators in the 1990s. One of the outcomes of the reform measures introduced in the 1990s was the improvement in the external debt indicators

industrial growth also slowed down in 1997–1998. The growth in industry fell to 4% in 1997–1998 from 6.7% in the previous year. Figure 4 shows a slump in industrial production and exports in 1997. The moderation seen from 1997 to 1998 onwards could be attributed to the investment boom of the previous years that had built up large capacities, which discouraged further expansion. Another reason could be the advent of coalition governance that dampened business confidence. The massive depreciation of the Thai baht in July 1997 which triggered the Southeast Asian financial crisis also had a limited impact on the economy. India faced some fall in exports to the Southeast Asian economies, but given that these countries share in India's exports and imports was around 2–3%, the impact was not substantial. Another transmission channel was through exchange rate. There were periods of exchange rate depreciation and rise in volatility towards the end of 1997 and the beginning of 1998. However the Reserve Bank of India (RBI) intervened to arrest the excessive volatility of the rupee-dollar exchange rate. In addition a series of monetary tightening measures were introduced to stabilise the rupee.[14]

4.2 *The Phases of Acceleration and Deceleration from 1999 Onwards*

Figure 5 shows the performance of key macroeconomic variables during the three identified periods of deceleration. The shaded portions show the period of deceleration identified in the cyclical component of GDP. The first figure in the first row shows the year-on-year change in GDP growth. The year-on-year growth shows sharp moderation during the three-shaded periods of deceleration from 1999-Q4 to 2003-Q1, from 2007-Q2 to 2009-Q3 and from 2011-Q2 to 2012-Q4. The second figure in the first row shows the year-on-year growth in IIP. The growth in IIP also shows a decline during the shaded periods of deceleration. Similar trend is seen in credit growth and investment growth. Both the series show considerable decline during the shaded periods of deceleration. The above analysis shows that the trends in standard indicators conform to the chronology of deceleration.

1999-Q4 to 2003-Q1 Deceleration Table 8 shows the performance of key macroeconomic indicators during the period 2000–2003. GDP growth slowed down from 7.6% in 1999–2000 to 4.3% in 2000–2001. The ratio of gross fixed investment to GDP was lower than the ratio of savings to GDP. With low private investment demand, foreign investment was sought to improve the investment climate. However in the aftermath of the Asian financial crisis, FDI inflows did not gain momentum.

[14]Indian economy was largely unaffected by the onslaught of the crisis because (a) the short-term external debt was under tight control, (b) resident firms and individuals were subject to strict capital controls and (c) a series of financial sector reforms were undertaken in the period 1992 to 1997 which had helped to strengthen the financial sector. (d) Prudential limits on exposure of financial intermediaries to stocks and real estates helped reduce systemic risk concerns (Acharya 2012).

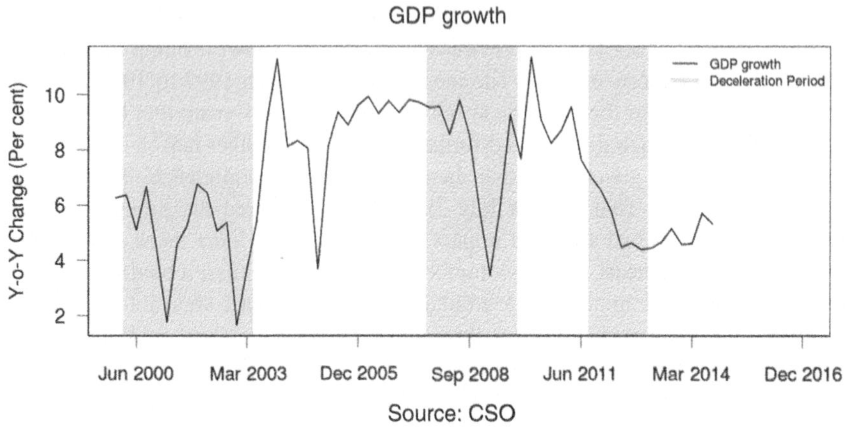

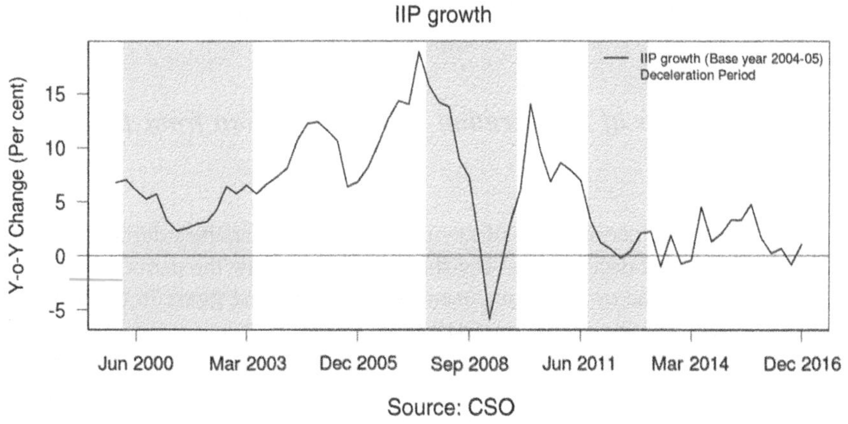

Fig. 5 Slowdown in macroeconomic variables during the identified periods of deceleration

The bursting of the dot-com bubble and the brief decline in software export growth after the "Y2K"[15] problem also contributed to the slowdown (Nagaraj 2013). On the whole, the macroeconomic conditions were largely moderate. But conditions began to look positive from 2003 onwards.

2003-Q2 to 2007-Q2 Acceleration The economy witnessed an upswing in the cycle, primarily led by high credit growth during this period when firms borrowed and initiated a number of projects. What triggered this boom? From 2001 to 2004, Reserve Bank of India (RBI) engaged in sterilised intervention. In early 2004, it ran out of bonds. This period was marked by currency trading that was not backed by sterilisation. Without sterilisation dollar purchases resulted in injection of rupee in

[15]Y2K was identified as a computer bug because of the practice of representing a year as two digit number by programmers, so years like 2019 and 1919 were hard to distinguish. It causes some date bugs in computer programs.

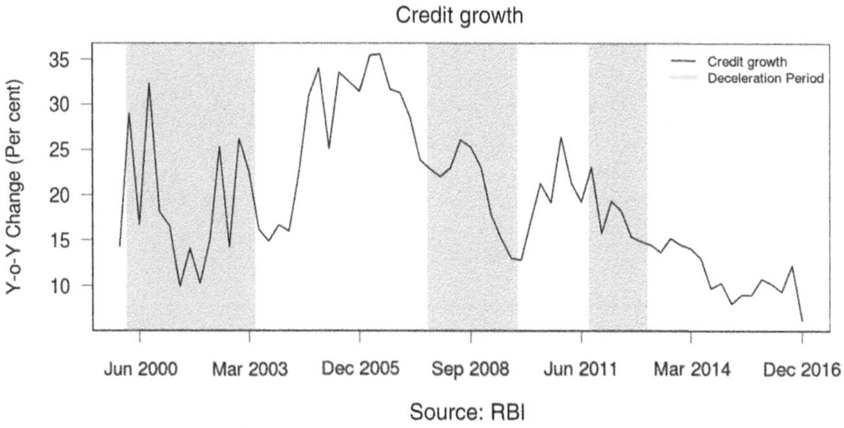

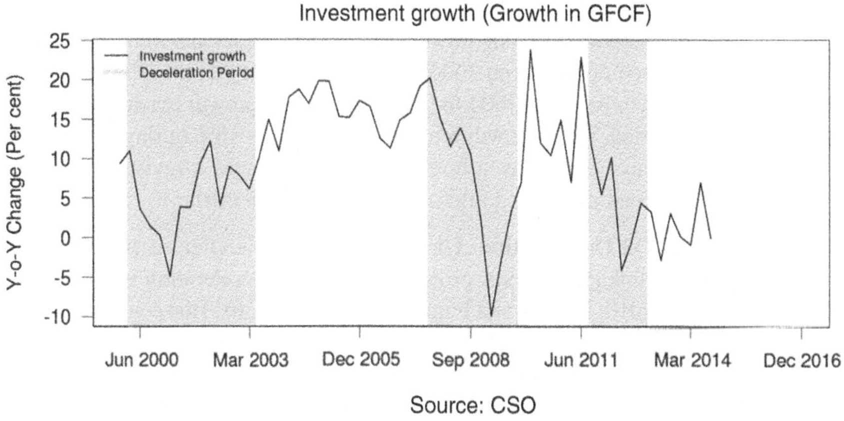

Fig. 5 (continued)

Table 8 Key macroeconomic conditions in 2000–2003

	1999–2000	2000–2001	2001–2002	2002–2003
Annual GDP growth rate	7.6	4.3	5.5	4.0
Gross fixed investment (GFCF) (as % to GDP)	24.1	22.8	25.1	23.7
Savings (% to GDP)	25.7	23.8	24.9	25.93

This table shows the growth rate in GDP, gross fixed investment as a ratio to GDP and savings as a ratio to GDP during 2000–2003 period. We see a moderation in GDP growth rate. Broadly, the savings rate exceeded the investment rate in this period

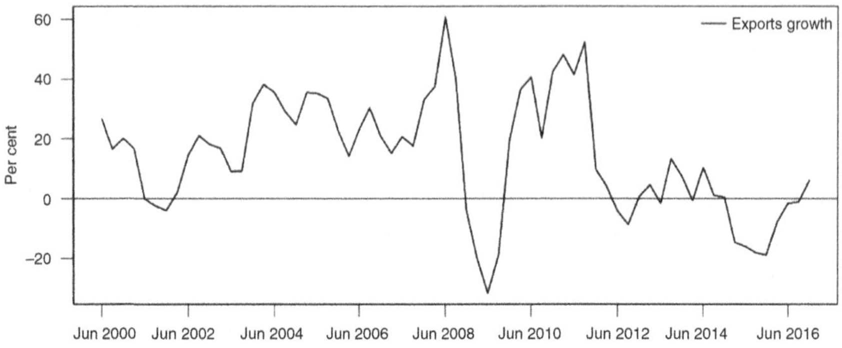

Source: Ministry of Commerce & Industry

Fig. 6 Slowdown seen in merchandise exports (Y-o-Y growth rate) in 2008–2009

the economy. The economy became flush with funds; interest rates went down. This kicked off a bank credit boom from 2004 to 2007. The third graph of Fig. 5 shows a surge in credit growth between 2004 to 2007. The credit growth reached a peak of 40% during this period. GDP growth remained strong at 8–10% during this period. The upswing was also driven by a boom in investment and a revival of foreign capital inflows that had moderated after the Asian financial crisis.

2007-Q3 to 2009-Q3 Deceleration Global financial crisis affected India through trade and financial linkages. Export growth saw a sharp deceleration in this period (Patnaik and Shah 2010; Patnaik and Pundit 2014) (see Fig. 6). This could have been the result of greater synchronisation of domestic cycles with global cycles (Jayaram et al. 2009). The immediate transmission of the financial crisis to India was through a slowdown of credit flows which was reflected in the spiking of overnight call money rates that rose to nearly 20 percent in October and early November 2008. Investment growth also slowed down in 2008–2009 (see the fourth graph of Fig. 5).

2009-Q4 to 2011-Q2 Acceleration We saw a business cycle upswing in 2009. GDP growth recovered to 8.6% in 2009–2010 from 6.72% in 2008–2009. The growth further strengthened to 8.9% in 2010–2011. The acceleration was an outcome of a coordinated monetary and fiscal policy stimulus package announced in 2008–2009. For example, the government introduced fiscal stimulus in the form of tax cuts and increased expenditure to boost consumer demand and production in key sectors.

The Fiscal Responsibility and Budget Management (FRBM) Act, 2003 (according to which, the government is required to follow fiscal prudence to reduce its deficits to a target rate), was suspended in 2009 in order to accommodate the stimulus policies. On the monetary side, the Reserve Bank of India introduced measures, such as rate cuts, to boost liquidity and ease credit in order to boost investment. The rate cut cycle began in October 2008 and continued till March 2010. Guidelines for External Commercial Borrowing were also liberalised to ease firms' access to external finance (Patnaik and Pundit 2014).

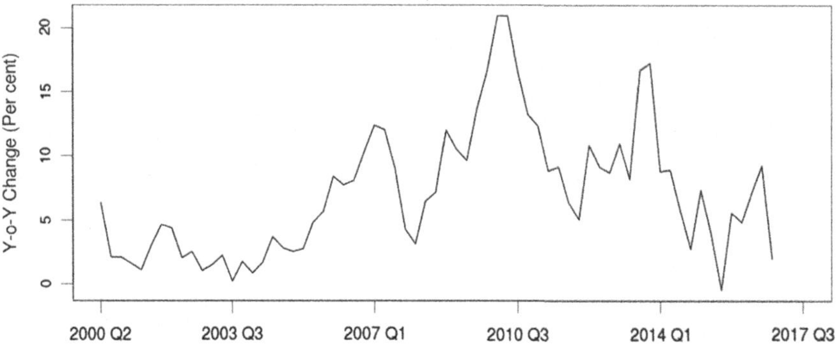

Fig. 7 Rise in food prices in 2011–2012

2011-Q3 to 2012-Q4 Deceleration Since 2011, again, we saw a business cycle slowdown. GDP growth plummeted to 6.7% in 2011–2012 and further to 4.5% in 2012–2013. This was a culmination of a number of factors. The macroeconomic policy stimulus intended to cushion the fallout of crisis, culminated in high inflation and current account pressures. The quality of the fiscal stimulus, which focused on tax cuts and increased revenue expenditure, added to demand pressures, resulting in high inflation. The efficacy of monetary policy in dealing with inflation was blunted by persistent rise in food prices (Bhattacharya and Sen Gupta 2015). Figure 7 shows the year-on-year growth in food prices. The Indian Central Bank followed a tight monetary policy during this period. From March 2011 to October 2011, the policy rate (the repo rate) was raised by 175 basis points from 6.75% to 8.5%.[16]

The inability to achieve fiscal consolidation coupled with surging current account deficit contributed to slowdown in the economy. The fiscal deficit as a ratio to GDP rose from 4.8% in the year ending March 2011 to 5.7% in the year ending March 2012. The current account as a percent to GDP also rose beyond comfort levels to 4.2% for the year ending March 2012 (see Fig. 8). High domestic inflation (see Fig. 9) and negative real interest rates on deposits encouraged gold imports, thus adding to current account deficit pressures.

A key manifestation of the growth slowdown was the weakness of the manufacturing sector during this time (see second graph of Fig. 5). An explanation for the weakness in industrial activity can be traced to the emergence of policy bottlenecks like obtaining environmental clearances, hurdles in land acquisition, etc. which resulted in stalling of a large number of projects (Mohan and Kapur 2015).

[16]See the RBI's monetary policy statements in 2011–2012 at https://www.rbi.org.in/scripts/Annualpolicy.aspx

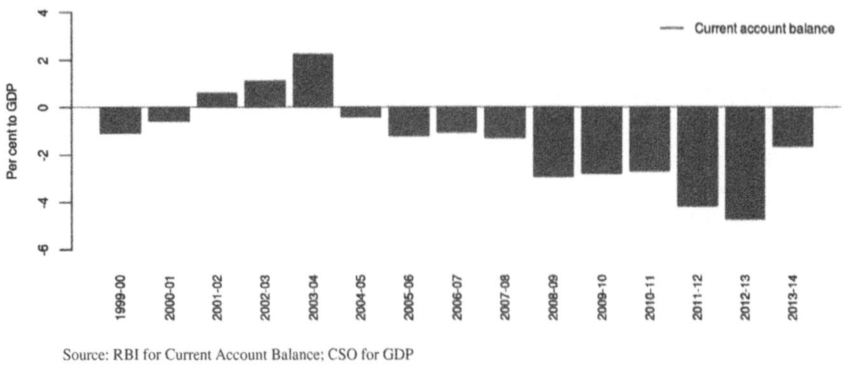

Fig. 8 Surge in current account deficit as a ratio to GDP during 2011–2012

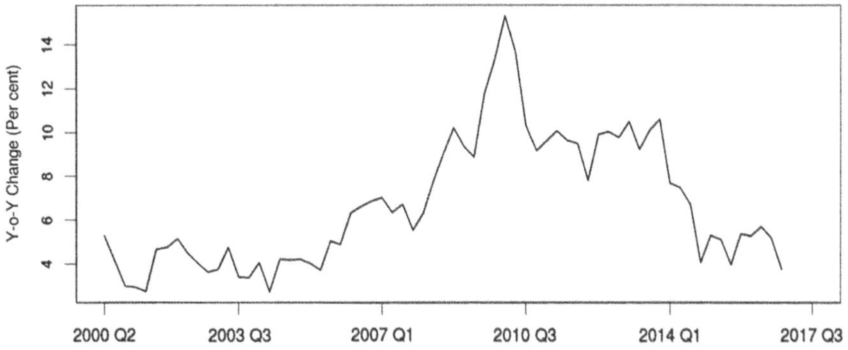

Fig. 9 High domestic inflation from 2011 onwards averaging around 9%

5 Current Cyclical Conditions: Post-2012-Q4

The growth cycle chronology presented in the preceding section is based on the GDP series with base year 2004–2005. In 2015, the Indian Central Statistical Office (CSO) introduced a new series of GDP with base year 2011–2012, replacing the earlier series with 2004–2005 as the base year.[17] As a result, the GDP series with base year 2004–2005 got discontinued since September 2014. Our analysis using the old GDP series identifies a slowdown in the Indian economy till 2012-Q4. How has the economy fared since 2012? Has the deceleration phase identified till 2012-Q4 ended? Do we see signs of a pickup in growth in the last 3 years? While a systematic analysis of growth cycle turning points is not feasible as the span of the new GDP series is too short, we try to derive inferences by looking at some of the macroeconomic series. The analysis is based on variables expressed at quarterly frequency.

[17]The new series has generated considerable debate amongst policy-makers, academicians and other stakeholders. For a discussion of the sources of debate, please see Appendix 2.

Table 9 Investment and exports as a percent to GDP

	GFCF	Exports
2011–2012	34.3	24.5
2012–2013	33.4	24.5
2013–2014	31.3	25.4
2014–2015	30.4	23.0
2015–2016	29.3	19.9
2016–2017	27.1	19.2

Source: CSO

1. *Investment slump*: Two important components of demand in india are from investment and exports. Table 9 Shows investment and exports as a percent to GDP. The table shows a consistent decline in the share of investment (as measured by gross fixed capital formation-GFCF) to GDP. The fourth plot of Fig. 5 shows the year-on-year growth in quarterly gross fixed capital formation. The graph indicated slowing of investment growth.
2. *Slowing credit off-take*: Another measure to gauge the performance of the economy is the credit demand. Since 2012, we have seen tepid growth in credit off-take from banks (see the third graph of Fig. 5). The credit growth as measured through year-on-year growth slowed down to 13–14% in 2013 and 2014. Since the beginning of 2015, credit growth has plummeted further.
3. *Slowdown visible in corporate performance*: Signs of slowdown are also visible in corporate performance. An analysis of firms excluding those in finance and oil sectors shows that their sales growth has been moderating since the mid of 2012. Figure 10 shows the year-on-year growth in the net sales of non-oil, nonfinance listed companies.[18] The profit margins of firms tell a similar story. The second plot of Fig. 1 shows a slide in profit margins of firms in this period. Here profit margin is computed as the ratio of profit-after-tax (PAT) to net sales of firms.
4. *Subdued exports*: Fig. 6 shows the year-on-year growth in merchandise exports. The graph shows a tepid growth in merchandise exports. Since the second half of 2016, we do see a recovery in exports. However given the subdued global demand conditions, it needs to be seen how far the recovery is sustainable.

   As a percentage to GDP, exports have been falling. The second column of Table 9 shows that the share of exports in GDP has fallen from 24.5% in 2012–2013 to 19.2% in 2016–2017. The fall in exports is not limited to goods. India's services exports have also been falling primarily due to a slide in its software exports.

[18]Finance companies have very different concepts underlying their accounting data and are hence excluded. Oil companies sometimes experience very large jumps in their revenues owing to decisions by the government about administered prices. These fluctuations are not a feature of underlying business cycle conditions. Hence, oil companies are excluded.

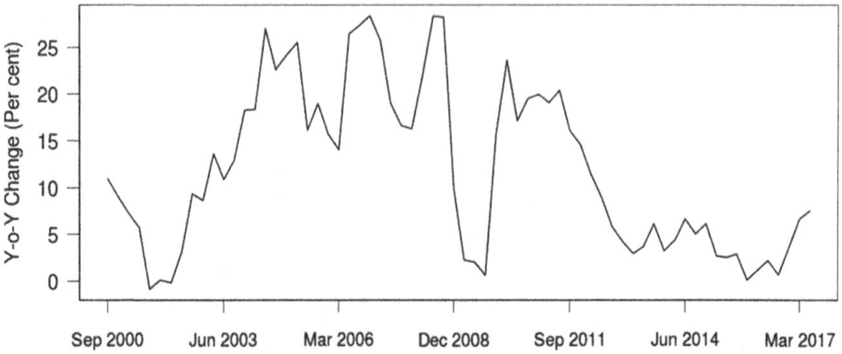

Source: CMIE Prowess database

Fig. 10 Deceleration visible in firms performance

5.1 Drivers of Deceleration Post-2012

The decelerating conditions are an outcome of both domestic and external conditions.

On the domestic front, an important dimension of this deceleration is the leverage of firms. From 2003 to 2008, a lot of debt was taken on by firms. This is evident in the high credit growth seen in the third plot of Fig. 5. It is likely that some of this credit was misallocated by banks who gave loans to firms without adequate due diligence. Some of these firms' profitability might have been adversely affected by the global financial crisis, and since 2011–2012, the economy was hit by a deceleration. Deceleration hampered profitability of firms due to weakness in demand. For many firms, the combination of low profits and high debt has generated credit stress. A key measure of credit stress is the interest cover ratio (ICR). ICR is defined as the ratio of operating profits (PBDIT) to interest expenses. Credit-stressed firms are defined as those whose ICR is less than 1, i.e. those firms whose interest expenses exceed their operating profits.

Our analysis of nonfinancial, non-oil listed firms shows that since 2012, the proportion of assets under credit stress has seen an increase as shown in Fig. 11. The time period of the study is from September 1999 to March 2015.[19] For each quarter we compute the ICR from the operating profits and interest expenses. Based on this, the firms with ICR greater than 1 are termed as *good companies*, and those with less than 1 are termed as *stressed companies*. For each firm (good and stressed), we collate the data on their corresponding annual assets. This helps in understanding the distribution of total assets amongst good and stressed firms. We find that the proportion of assets owned by stressed firms has increased since 2012.

[19]We show this analysis till 2015 because the sample of firms who report their financial results drops dramatically in the recent quarters.

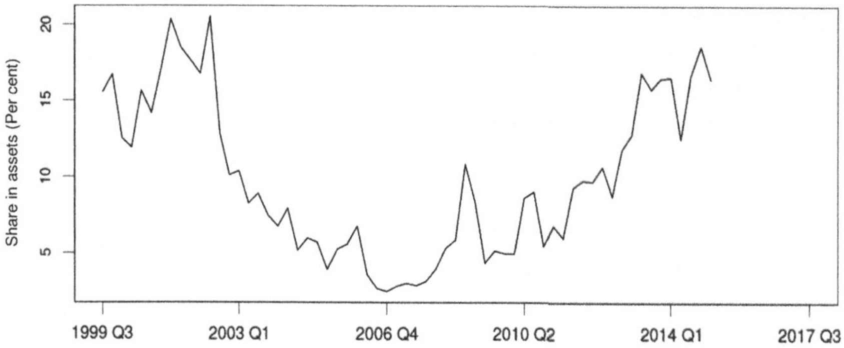

Fig. 11 Proportion of assets held by credit stressed firms

This implies that the credit-stressed firms constitute a significant part of the total universe of nonfinancial, non-oil listed firms.

Firms with credit distress are likely to have impaired investment activity which would result in lower capacity utilisation. To gauge the pulse of the Indian manufacturing sector, the RBI conducts *Order Books, Inventories and Capacity Utilisation Survey (OBICUS)*. A key variable measured through this survey is the capacity-utilisation of the manufacturing companies. Table 10 shows that the capacity utilisation rates have seen a decline since 2012 signalling presence of excess capacity in the manufacturing sector.

Stressed firms are likely to face difficulties in repaying loans to banks. On the supply side, an increase in the exposure of banks to stressed firms leads to surge in their nonperforming assets. Surge in nonperforming assets hampers their ability to advance loans to productive sectors, which leads to a further decline in investments.

On the external front, the slow and uneven recovery in advanced economies post by the global financial crisis has weakened demand for emerging economy exports including those of India. The World Bank database[20] shows a moderation in world exports of goods and services as a percent to GDP since 2012. One of the key reasons for the slowdown in global trade has been the sharp decline in prices of crude oil and commodities such as base metals.

6 Conclusion

India's analysis of business cycle measurement can be analysed into time periods, from 1950 to 1991 and from 1991 onwards. The nature of cyclical pattern is shaped by the economic structure and the policy environment in the two periods.

[20]http://data.worldbank.org/indicator/NE.EXP.GNFS.ZS

Table 10 Capacity utilisation in the manufacturing sector

Quarter	CU (%)
2012-Q1	78.4
2012-Q2	73.1
2012-Q3	73.3
2012-Q4	74.6
2013-Q1	78.0
2013-Q2	71.6
2013-Q3	72.8
2013-Q4	73.5
2014-Q1	76.1
2014-Q2	70.2
2014-Q3	73.6
2014-Q4	71.7
2015-Q1	74.0
2015-Q2	72.0
2015-Q3	71.1
2015-Q4	72.3
2016-Q1	74.4
2016-Q2	71.5
2016-Q3	71.0
2016-Q4	72.1
2017-Q1	74.1

Source: RBI

In the first period, the economic fluctuations were driven by agricultural fluctuations and oil price shocks. The policy environment was characterised by restrictions to private sector growth and expansion. Foreign investment was also limited. As an outcome, we did not witness business cycle fluctuations in the conventional sense of the term.

In the early 1990s, in response to the balance of payments crisis, a series of reforms were taken to make the economy more open and market oriented. The policy environment became more amenable to private sector participation, import duties were reduced in a phased manner, and foreign investment was allowed in a number of sectors. As a consequence of the changed policy environment, we saw the emergence of conventional business cycles.

We use quarterly GDP series for identifying the chronology of turning points. Since we do not see a decline in levels, we use the growth cycle approach. The cyclical component of GDP is the input series for identifying the turning points. We identify three periods of deceleration: 1999-Q4 to 2003-Q1, 2007-Q3 to 2009-Q3 and 2011-Q3 to 2012-Q4. The Indian Statistical Office revised the GDP series in January 2015. The old GDP series used as the reference series for this analysis got discontinued since 2014-Q3. We find that the deceleration identified till 2012-Q4 is still visible in a number of key indicators such as investment, credit growth, exports and firm performance indicators.

Appendix 1: Detection of Turning Points Using the Dating Algorithm

The Bry-Boschan (BB) and Harding Pagan (H-P) algorithms find the turning points as follows:

- The data is smoothed after outlier adjustment by constructing short-term moving averages.
- The preliminary set of turning points is selected for the smoothed series subject to the criterion described later.
- In the next stage, turning points in the raw series are identified taking results from smoothed series as the reference.

The identification of turning point dates is done subject to the following rules:

- The first rule states that the peaks and troughs must alternate.
- The second step involves the identification of local minima (troughs) and local maxima (peaks) in a single time series or in y_t after a log transformation.
- Peaks are found where y_s is larger than k values of y_t in both directions.
- Troughs are identified where y_s is smaller than k values of y_t in both directions.
- Bry and Boschan (1971) suggested the value of k as five for monthly frequency which Harding and Pagan (2002) transformed to two for quarterly series.
- Censoring rules are put in place for minimum duration of phase (from peak to trough or trough to peak) and for a complete cycle (from peak to peak or from trough to trough).
- Harding and Pagan identify minimum duration of a phase to be two quarters and the minimum duration of a complete cycle to be five quarters.
- For monthly data, the minimum duration is 5 months and 15 months for phase and cycle, respectively.
- The identification of turning points is avoided at extreme points.

Appendix 2: Recent Changes in the Indian GDP Measurement

The business cycle chronology presented in the preceding section is based on the GDP series with base year 2004–2005. In 2015, the Indian Central Statistical Office (CSO) introduced the new series of National Accounts Statistics with the base year 2011–2012, replacing the earlier series with 2004–2005 as the base year. In contrast to the earlier episodes of base year changes, this update was marked by changes to the methodology and data sources. The methodological changes were implemented to align the Indian National Accounts Statistics with international standards recommended by the System of National Accounts (SNA) 2008. The state of the economy is measured using gross value added (GVA) at basic prices, in place of the earlier practise of measuring it using GDP at factor cost.

Table 11 GDP and subsectors' growth rate

	Base year 2004–2005		Base year 2011–2012	
	2012–2013	2013–2014	2012–2013	2013–2014
GDP	4.4	4.7	4.9	6.6
Agriculture, forestry and fishing	1.4	4.7	1.7	3.8
Mining and quarrying	−2.1	−1.3	0.5	5.5
Manufacturing	1.1	−0.7	6.1	5.2
Electricity, gas and water supply	2.2	5.9	2.2	2.9
Construction	1.1	1.6	−4.3	2.5
Trade, hotels, transport, storage, communication	5.1	3.0	9.2	10.9
Financing, insurance, real estate and business services	10.9	12.8	8.9	7.9
Community, social and personal services	5.3	5.5	4.7	8.0

The key methodological refinement is seen in the manufacturing sector where the gross value addition is computed using comprehensive data sources such as the MCA-21.[21] Despite methodological improvements, the revised series has attracted considerable debate amongst academicians, policy-makers and other stakeholders (Sapre and Sinha 2016; EPW 2015; Nagaraj 2015a, b). In this section we discuss some concerns with the new series.

Changes in the Sub-sectors' Growth Table 11 shows that there are striking changes in the subsectors' growth rate for the two intermittent periods when we have data from both the series. For instance, the growth rate of the gross domestic product (GDP) for 2013–2014 according to the new series was 6.6%, compared to 4.7% in the earlier series. The greatest discrepancy is seen in the growth rates of manufacturing sector. According to the new series with base year 2011–2012, the growth rate of manufacturing was 5.3% in 2013–2014, while the old series shows a contraction in the manufacturing sector for the same year.

Disconnect Between the High Frequency Indicators and the Sectoral GVAs Due to changes in the methodology, the high-frequency indicators which conventionally mapped the trends in GDP subsectors no longer seem to be in sync with the new subsectors' GVA. Figure 12 shows the discordant trends in the high-frequency indicators and the related subsectors of GVA. Figure 12 shows that IIP is at odds with the movement of GVA in the manufacturing sector. Similarly bank credit data does not seem to be in sync with the new GVA of finance, insurance and real estate.

Choice of Deflator The estimates of real GVA in most advanced economies are arrived at using *double deflation*. In this method, nominal outputs are deflated using

[21]The MCA-21 is an electronic platform of the Ministry of Company Affairs created for companies to file their annual financial statements.

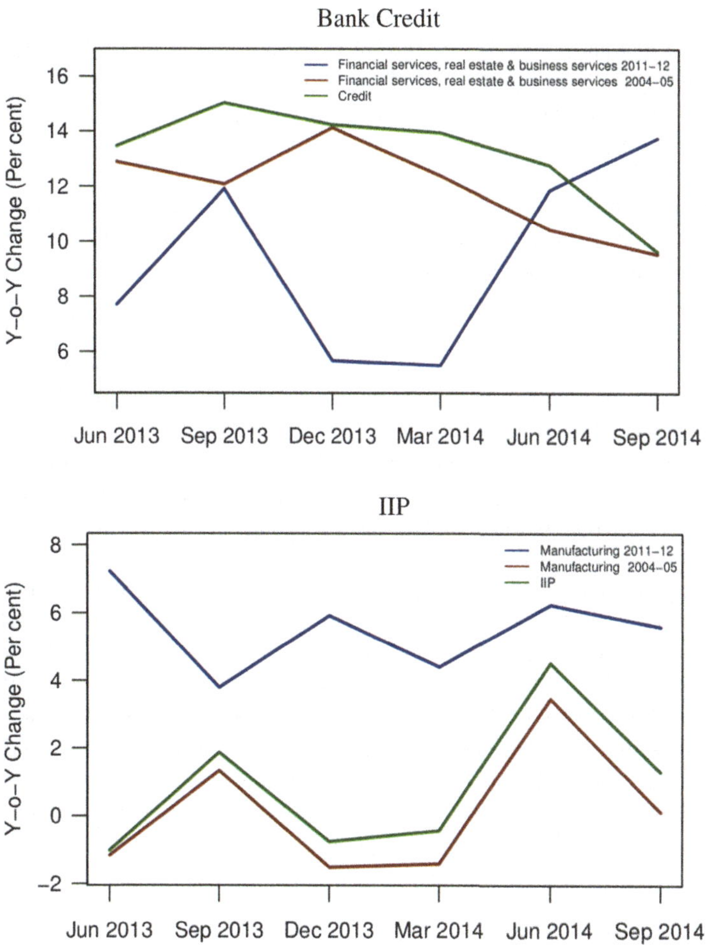

Fig. 12 Comparison with high-frequency indicators

an output deflator, while inputs are deflated using a separate input deflator. Then, the real inputs are subtracted from real outputs to derive real GVA. But in India things are done differently. Here, we compute the nominal GVA and then deflate this number using a *single deflator*.

If input and output prices are synchronous, both approaches will give similar results. But if the two price series diverge—as they have for the past few years in India—single deflation can overstate growth by a big margin (Sengupta 2015).

Issues with Manufacturing Gross Value-Added The manufacturing sector has been at the centre stage of the GDP debate.

1. Enterprise vs establishment approach: In a major change in methodology, the data collection for GVA computation shifted from *establishment* or factories to *enterprise* or firms. Conceptualising value addition at the enterprises level without

clarity on measures of costs and output could lead to misleading estimates of GVA (Sapre and Sinha 2016). The activities of *firms* can be much more diverse than those of *factories*, and if all these go into the calculation of GVA, it could inflate the estimate of output.

2. Blowing up of GVA: GVA calculation involves identifying a set of "active companies" that have filed their annual returns at least once in past 3 years. The problem is that for any given year, information from several active companies remains unavailable till a cut-off date of data extraction. In such a case, the GVA of available companies needs to be "blown-up" to account for the unavailable companies. Literature has commented on a number of issues with the blowing-up method.

   The year-wise number of available and active set of companies in the manufacturing sector is not publicly available, so the extent of blowing up is not known. Some experts have criticised the methodology of blowing-up. The critical input is the "blowing-up factor" which is the inverse of the ratio between the paid-up capital (PUC) for the available companies and that for the active set as a whole. Nagaraj (2015a, b) argues that this is inappropriate since a number of the companies in the "active set" could be shell companies existing only on paper. This could overestimate gross value added of the manufacturing sector.
3. Discrepancies in the underlying data sources: For the manufacturing sector, the GVA is derived from a combination of MCA-21 numbers, index of industrial production (IIP) estimates and estimates of the unorganised sector from the Annual Survey of Industries (ASI). While the MCA-21 is a new database, the base year for the IIP data is still 2004–2005. Also the data obtained from MCA-21 follows an "enterprise" approach as mentioned earlier, but the data obtained from ASI follows the old "establishment" approach. This could lead to misleading estimates of the GVA numbers (Sengupta 2015).

References

Acharya S (2002) India: crisis, reforms and growth in the nineties. Working paper 139. Stanford Center for Research on Economic Development and Policy Reform

Acharya S (2012) India: crisis, reforms and growth in the nineties. Working papers 139. Stanford Center for International Development. http://scid.stanford.edu/publications/india-crisis-reforms-and-growth-nineties

Agresti AM, Mojon B (2001) Some stylised facts on the euro area business cycle. Working paper series 0095. European Central Bank. https://ideas.repec.org/p/ecb/ecbwps/20010095.html

Alp H, Baskaya Y, Kilinc M, Yuksel C (2011) Estimating optimal Hodrick-Prescott filter smoothing parameter for Turkey. Iktisat Isletme ve Finans 26(306):09–23. http://EconPapers.repec.org/RePEc:iif:iifjrn:v:26:y:2011:i:306:p:09-23

Baxter M, King RG (1999) Measuring business cycles: approximate band-pass filters for economic time series. Rev Econ Statist 81(4):575–593

Bhattacharya R, Pandey R, Patnaik I, Shah A (2016) Seasonal adjustment of Indian macroeconomic time-series. Working papers 16/160. National Institute of Public Finance and Policy. https://ideas.repec.org/p/npf/wpaper/16-160.html

Bhattacharya R, Sen Gupta A (2015) Food inflation in India: causes and consequences. Working papers 15/151. National Institute of Public Finance and Policy. https://ideas.repec.org/p/npf/wpaper/15-151.html

Bjornland H (2000) Detrending methods and stylized facts of business cycles in Norway - an international comparison. Empir Econ 25:369–392

Bry G, Boschan C (1971) Cyclical analysis of time series: selected procedures and computer programs. National Bureau of Economic Research. http://www.nber.org/chapters/c2145

Chitre VS (2004) Indicators of business recessions and revivals in India 1951–82. Oxford University Press, Delhi, pp 258–287

Christiano L, Fitzgerald T (2003) The band pass filter. Int Econ Rev 44(2):435–465

Dua P, Banerji A (2012) Business and growth rate cycles in India. Working papers 210. Centre for Development Economics, Delhi School of Economics. https://ideas.repec.org/p/cde/cdewps/210.html

EPW (2015) New series of national accounts: a review. Econ Polit Wkly 50(7)

Ghate C, Pandey R, Patnaik I (2013) Has India emerged? Business cycle stylized facts from a transitioning economy. Struct Chang Econ Dyn 24(C):157–172. https://ideas.repec.org/a/eee/streco/v24y2013icp157-172.html

Hamilton J (2016) Why you should never use the Hodrick-Prescott filter. Working paper. University of California

Harding D, Pagan A (2002) Dissecting the cycle: a methodological investigation. J Monet Econ 49 (2):365–381. ISSN 0304-3932

Jayaram S, Patnaik I, Shah A (2009) Examining the decoupling hypothesis for India. Economic and Political Weekly 44(44): 109–116. ISSN 00129976, 23498846. http://www.jstor.org/stable/25663740

King RG, Watson MW (1996) Money, prices, interest rates and the business cycle. Rev Econ Stat 78(1):35–53. https://ideas.repec.org/a/tpr/restat/v78y1996i1p35-53.html

Kotwal A, Ramaswami B, Wadhwa W (2011) Economic liberalization and Indian economic growth: what's the evidence? J Econ Lit 49(4):1152–1199

Mall O (1999) Composite index of leading indicators for business cycles in India. RBI Occ Papers 20(3):373–414

Ministry of Finance, Government of India (1991) Economic Survey 1990–91. Technical report, Ministry of Finance, Government of India. http://indiabudget.nic.in/es1990-91/0

Ministry of Finance, Government of India (1992) Economic survey 1991–92. Technical report. Ministry of Finance, Government of India. http://indiabudget.nic.in/es1991-92_A/1

Mohan R, Kapur M (2015) Pressing the Indian growth accelerator: policy imperatives. IMF working papers 15/53. International Monetary Fund. https://ideas.repec.org/p/imf/imfwpa/15-53.html

Mohanty J, Singh B, Jain R (2003) Business cycles and leading indicators of industrial activity in India. MPRA paper. University Library of Munich, Germany. http://EconPapers.repec.org/RePEc:pra:mprapa:12149

Nagaraj R (2003) Foreign direct investment in India in the 1990s: trends and issues. Economic and Political Weekly 38(17):1701–1712

Nagaraj R (2013) India's dream run, 2003-08. Economic and Political Weekly 48(20)

Nagaraj R (2015a) Seeds of doubt on new GDP numbers. Economic and Political Weekly 50(13)

Nagaraj R (2015b) Seeds of doubt on new GDP numbers: Private Corporate sector overestimated?, Economic and Political Weekly, 50(13)

Pandey R, Patnaik I, Shah A (2017) Dating business cycles in India. Indian Growth Develop Rev 10 (1):32–61. https://ideas.repec.org/a/eme/igdrpp/igdr-02-2017-0013.html

Patnaik I, Pundit M (2014) Is India's long-term trend growth declining? ADB economics working paper series 424. Asian Development Bank. http://EconPapers.repec.org/RePEc:ris:adbewp:0424

Patnaik I, Shah A (2010) Why India choked when Lehman broke. Finance working papers 22974. East Asian Bureau of Economic Research. https://ideas.repec.org/p/eab/financ/22974.html

Patnaik I, Sharma R (2002) Business cycles in the Indian economy. Margin-New Delhi 35:71–80. ISSN 0025-2921

Sapre A, Sinha P (2016) Some areas of concern about Indian Manufacturing Sector GDP estimation, Working Papers 16/172, National Institute of Public Finance and Policy.

Sengupta R (2015) The great Indian GDP measurement controversy. https://ajayshahblog.blogspot.in/2016/09/the-great-indian-gdp-measurement.html

Shah A (2008) New issues in macroeconomic policy. Business Standard India:26–54

World Bank (1991) World Bank, policies for adjustment with growth. Technical report, World Bank. http://documents.worldbank.org/curated/en/962181468033534646/Policies-for-adjustment-with-growth

Economic Cycles and Crises in New China

Tiejun Wen, Kin Chi Lau, Erebus Wong, and Tsui Sit

1 Introduction

China's economic growth has been generally presented as a miracle, yet China's pursuit of industrialization has been, like many developing countries, fraught with fluctuations and crises.

In this chapter, we analyze ten economic cycles and crises in the People's Republic of China. By an economic cycle and crisis, we mean a period of economic decline or slowdown together with problems and instabilities such as fiscal deficit, inflation, and unemployment, among others. Particularly, international political economy, history of policy changes, and urban–rural relations are further discussed. In the next several sections, we describe—step by step—ten main periods of cycles and crises in the economic history of New China. In the end, we conclude that China

T. Wen
Institute of Advanced Studies for Sustainability, Renmin University of China, Beijing, China

Institute of Rural Reconstruction of China, Southwest University, Chongqing, China

Institute of Rural Reconstruction of the Straits, Fujian Agriculture and Forestry University, Fuzhou, China

K. C. Lau
World Forum for Alternatives, Dakar, Senegal

Global University for Sustainability, Hong Kong, China

Department of Cultural Studies, Lingnan University, Hong Kong, China

E. Wong
Kwan Fong Cultural Research and Development Program, Lingnan University, Hong Kong, China

T. Sit (✉)
Institute of Rural Reconstruction of China, Southwest University, Chongqing, China

S. Smirnov et al. (eds.), *Business Cycles in BRICS*, Societies and Political Orders in Transition, https://doi.org/10.1007/978-3-319-90017-9_8

can endure the cycles of economic decline, depending mainly on the development of rural society.

2 The Birth of New China

The point of departure for New China was a continuation of the long-term economic crisis lasting since the time of the previous regime.

In 1949, the gross production of agriculture was merely 105 billion kg, 75% of prewar average level, a decrease of more than 7.5 billion kg. The famine victims amounted to 40 million. The volume of goods turnover by modern transportation was only 229.6 ton-km, 52.7% of 1936, the year of currency reform. The total number of unemployed workers and intellectuals was about 1.5 million, not to mention the large number of semi-unemployed in the population. In October 1949, the war was going on. The new government doubled the money supply to pay 4.5 million soldiers as well as 1.5 million officials and staff working in enterprises. In that year, the national government's fiscal deficit amounted to 46.4% of the revenues.

The Kuomintang regime took all the gold reserve when retreating to Taiwan while the new government issued a huge amount of paper money. Consequently, there was a hyperinflation of around 500–600% at the very beginning of New China. And even though the government put a large amount of staple food onto the market, the estimated food price was expected to at least double in 1950 (Shen 2001).

The peasants who comprised 88% of the population remained loyal to the new regime under the leadership of the ruling party. This was in accordance with a historical regularity in ancient China where the dynasty practicing an equitable distribution of arable land and tax exemption would earn the loyalty of peasants. However, what this historical instance amounted to was an exercise of mass mobilization for the nation-building of New China via a land revolution.

3 The Korean War and "Sovietization" of the Chinese Economy

At the beginning of the new regime in 1949, China had failed to get any economic aid from the USSR despite adopting a one-sided pro-Soviet diplomatic strategy. However, it was given a precious chance because of the Korean War, which marked a major change in the geostrategic structure taking shape after WWII. In October 1950, China's People's Volunteer Army marched into Korea. In the next 3 years, China had mobilized 1.34 million soldiers to confront the 1.11 million allied troops from 17 countries. Out of these million-plus soldiers deployed, 140,000 died, and 250,000 were wounded or imprisoned or went missing. But because of this heavy human loss, China managed to build a strategic alliance with the USSR and therefore received aid worth USD5.4 billion (including the military expenditure of the Korean War) during 1950–1959 in the form of industrial facilities and technology transfer.[1] With the strong pull of external investment accompanying the Korean War, China rapidly got out of the economic slump after 1950 and began the process of rapid primitive accumulation for industrialization.

The Korean War afforded New China with the opportunity to introduce foreign capital for the first time. When introducing production facilities, China had to reconstruct its legal, economic, and social institutions (or "superstructure" in terms of Marxist theory) according to the Soviet model to accommodate the latter's mode of production. Industrialization was accelerated, while China paid a great price transforming itself. However, China could not repay its debts in the form of urban industrial products which were usually older models and not demanded in the USSR. The repayment was mainly in the form of products and minerals that were scarce in China.

Fully embracing the tutelage of the USSR and introducing from it heavy and military industries, China rapidly constructed an industrial system mainly concentrated in large and medium cities. Afterward, private industry, commerce, and peasant economy were transformed in line with the Soviet model. By the end of January 1956, all capitalist industry and commerce in the large cities and more than 50 medium cities had become joint state-private ventures. The centralized one-party system that had taken shape during the revolution had now turned into a system of state ownership of the three major factors of production: land, labor, and capital.

The private ownership of basic factors of production had existed in New China for less than 7 years before state ownership succeeded it according to the requirements of primitive accumulation for national industrialization. The outcome was a form of "government corporatism" with Chinese characteristics, an economic system embedded in the government. In practice, this system proved to be quite effective in shortening the period of primitive accumulation and accelerating the expansion of urban industrial capital under conditions of extreme capital scarcity. Nevertheless, it was also a system that transferred its enormous costs and risks directly onto peasants.

National industrialization as advocated in the New Democracy[2] took place merely for a short period before 1953. Afterward, as the state received large-scale foreign investment, it rapidly completed the institutional change from national capitalism to state capitalism, which would correspond to a centralized authoritarian system within western market ideological discourse. The crisis of the system eventually broke out in 1960 in the forms of foreign debt and fiscal deficit crisis. The

[1]Approximately USD538 billion in current prices.

[2]New Democracy or the New Democratic Revolution is a concept based on Mao Zedong's *Bloc of Four Social Classes* theory in post-revolutionary China which argued originally that democracy in China would take a decisively distinct path, much different from that of the liberal capitalist and parliamentary democratic systems in the western world as well as Soviet-style communism in Eastern Europe. See https://en.wikipedia.org/wiki/New_Democracy

introduction of foreign production facilities and technology translated into national debt. The central government had to extract agricultural surplus from the tripartite agrarian sector through large-scale collectivization at village and township levels.

The crisis of 1952–1960 is the second cyclical crisis incurred by domestic industrialization, a process initiated by the introduction of Soviet capital. The trigger was China's insistence on its territorial integrity and sovereignty. According to the treaty, the USSR had to return the Zhongchang railway and the "Dalian Special Zone" to China and withdraw its military bases in northeast China in 1956. In retaliation, the Soviet Union stopped its aid to and investment in China in 1957. The following year the USSR proposed a new military alliance requiring that China's military infrastructure be synchronized with Russia's military strategy in the Far East, including the establishment of a united command headquarters for the air force and navy and a common military radio communications system. Mao rejected the proposal.

During 1957–1958 when the Soviet investment dropped remarkably, the central government decentralized the power of fiscal revenues, planning, and enterprise management to call on local governments to build five "small-scale industries." In 1958, the central government advocated "mobilizing initiative in two aspects." It was an attempt to involve local governments in national industrialization hitherto monopolized by the central government. By mobilizing domestic and especially local public finance, China was barely able to keep the heavy industry-oriented national economy going. In that year, the weight of local fiscal expenditure in the total national expenditure jumped to 55.7%, up from 29.0% in the previous year of 1957.

The local governments that for the first time had autonomy in fiscal revenues, economic planning, and enterprise management received an initiation into the processes of industrialization. Their only available reference was the heavy industry model the central government had built with the Soviet investment. That is the reason the local governments' initiative at industrialization would eventuate in ridiculous practices such as the "Great Steel-making" and the "Great Leap Forward."

In 1958 when sharing only 20% of the national revenues, the central government made use of an increasing money supply as the means to accelerate accumulation. This caused the market price of scarce agricultural products to fluctuate. However, as the real purchasing power of the currency was limited by the coupon system, official price levels remained largely unaffected. Since the purchase and marketing of commodities was controlled by the state, the amount of goods available in the market was limited. It was therefore difficult to calculate a simple price index. The increased money supply generally returned to the banking system as deposits and served as the funding for the accumulation and reproduction of the national economy. Hence, even though fiscal revenues and investment declined during 1958–1960, the absolute numbers stayed at a high level. However, the fiscal deficit increased remarkably. The crisis of the system eventually broke out in 1960 in the forms of foreign debt and fiscal deficit crisis.

The central government mobilized local governments for autonomous industrialization, and investment and growth were maintained at a high level in 1958. However, as the flow of Soviet investments stopped and Soviet technical experts were withdrawn, GDP dropped from 9% in 1959 to 0% in 1960 and then −27.3% in 1961. The government strove to maintain a growth of fiscal budget for 3 more years till 1961, which marked the beginning of a recession in the name of "recuperation." If taking out the "balancing" through the means of public debt, the fiscal revenues deteriorated since 1957 and hit the bottom in 1961.

In 1960, the fiscal revenues were recorded to be at a historical high of RMB 57.229 billion since the founding of New China. However, it was not possible to maintain a growing revenue thereafter. The overexpansion of infrastructure construction resulted in enormous budget deficits. The expenditure was not enough for the normal operation of the state. After the deficit crisis, under a government corporatist system, the urban economy was mired in a recession. Due to the interruption of investment, urban employment crumbled from the peak number of 130 million to 45.37 million, a reduction of over 84 million in 2 years.

Since 1961, the government was forced to take up a "recuperation" policy. Tens of millions of people were mobilized to the rural areas to release the pressure of large-scale unemployment in the cities. Through the exclusion of labor, this became how the state's industrial capital could achieve a "soft landing" in the cities.

During the recession of 1961–1962, national fiscal revenues declined further from RMB 57.23 to 31.36 billion, back to the level of 1957. Meanwhile, China had to pay off its debt to the USSR, equivalent to USD 5.4 billion which had accumulated since 1950. It did this in the form of precious minerals and agricultural products, which were severely scarce. The shortage of agricultural products was therefore further aggravated leading to disastrous consequences.

According to revised statistics published in 1982, the normal trend of population growth turned downward during 1960–1962. Some researchers estimated that the number of population which did not materialize according to the trend of natural demographic growth was about 20 million. This was caused mainly by a decrease in the fertility rate and an increase of infant mortality rate because of malnutrition. A part of adult mortality was attributed to starvation. In the official wording of the time, the period of economic crisis and subsequent recession was known as the "3 years of natural disaster."

The recovery of 1962–1963 was not due to urban industrial growth and increase in employment as supposed. It was instead attributable to the fact that peasants could "retreat." Under crisis, the government had to adjust the policy of collectivization. Traditional peasant economy was partly allowed to retreat from the highly collectivized economy serving the state's industrial capital.

First, the overarching people's commune system was transformed into a production brigade-based village economy. Production brigades were formed with the natural village as the basic unit of accounting. This meant that traditional natural village economies could partly retreat from the collectivized economy at the county level.

Second, peasants could involve themselves in autonomous production within a production brigade (natural village). That implied traditional peasant household economy was partly allowed to retreat from the strictly controlled collectivized economy. In practice, the state relaxed its total control over the peasants since the "all-round Sovietization" in the 1950s. Peasants took back about 15% of the arable land at their disposal in the form of "reserved land," "marginal plot," and "courtyard." Since then, agricultural production resumed, and agricultural output increased in consecutive years. The weight of agricultural tax in national fiscal revenues rose from 8% to 22% in the 1950s during the first phase of national industrialization. The fiscal situation was ameliorated (Wen 2001).

4 "Self-Reliance" and the Third Front

In the late 1960s, during a period known as the "ultra-leftist age," the third cyclical crisis since the primitive accumulation for industrialization took place. Apart from being caused by general economic factors, the origins of this crisis lay in the reaction of the superstructure to the economic base, in terms of Marxism.

China was operating under a complete blockade, but the administrative structure built during the 1950s to fit the Soviet management model of heavy industry was not compatible with the guiding principle of "self-reliance and recalcitrant struggle," which relied on the laboring masses. When China needed to adjust its economy from one formerly based on USSR investment toward one of national autonomy, the external geopolitical situation and internal bureaucratism proved to be barriers. Under this complication and after paying off an enormous foreign debt, the urban economy suffered from the third crisis in the form of "fiscal deficit plus unemployment."

After the abortion of the Second Five-Year Plan due to the interruption of Soviet investment, the discussion about the Third Five-Year Plan took place in the early 1960s. Some leaders responsible for economic policy suggested that the guiding principle of the Third Five-Year Plan should be about balancing the weight of agriculture and light and heavy industries in economic development, which were supposed to be an adjustment to the industrial structure that was military-heavy industry-oriented.

Bearing in mind the necessity of economic reconstruction, this strategy was entirely understandable. However, the most pressing problem China faced at that time was geopolitical. During the Cold War, China was up against a series of regional "hot" confrontations: the plan of counterattack by the Kuomintang regime in Taiwan, the Sino-Indian War, the repetitive transgression of US battleships and aircrafts into the territorial waters of China (more than 800 times according to official record), and the threat of "nuclear attack on China" by the USA and the USSR. China was on the verge of "hot" war with the USSR and the West.

For this reason, the policy decision was oriented toward Mao's idea even though the opinions about China's economic construction in the 1960s were diverse. Mao felt that all technological power of China should focus on building a nuclear bomb. Meanwhile, basic industrial facilities along the coastal regions were transferred to the hinterland to minimize the consequences of military attack, even at the expense of economic loss. The result was an economic mode in preparation for war. The overall layout of the national industry was the construction of "Third Front," referring to three major layers of frontlines, whereas regional industry comprised three layers of minor frontlines.

Meanwhile, the National Planning Committee responsible for the Third Five-Year Plan was replaced. The idea of transplanting a foreign system according to the planned economy model as proposed by the officials and experts who had studied in the USSR was aborted. The economic divisions established in the time of Soviet investment were now totally blocked. Without any foreign investment or the availability of any external markets, the Soviet system was difficult to maintain in line with the new principle of "self-reliance and recalcitrant struggle." This urgently called for a reconstruction of the Chinese economy along different lines.

During 1968–1970, millions of young intellectuals were sent to the countryside. New employment was limited to military industry and construction of the three-layer structure. The industrial economy in the coastal regions was maintained in a mode of simple reproduction. In sum, the third urban crisis caused by fiscal deficits had achieved a "soft landing" once again through transferring their costs to rural communities.

5 Turn to the West

According to the cost-efficiency analysis, the construction of "Third Front" was extremely expensive yet with little economic benefits. During 1965–1975 (including the Fourth Five-Year Plan period), half of the domestic infrastructure expenditures was put into the construction of the strategic hinterland. It is estimated that from 1964 to the 1980s, investment into the Third Front economic structure costs about RMB 205.2 billion (Li and Jiang 2005). The Third Front structure was merely a spatial reallocation of national industrial investments without adjustment of the economic structure. Out of military considerations, new industrial facilities were transferred deep into the hinterland or to the mountain regions. It was therefore difficult to form a comprehensive industrial chain in any one region. The cost of infrastructure during the 1960s increased dramatically. The cost of the reconstruction of national industry was enormous and resulted in higher fiscal deficits, the accumulation of which would lead to economic crisis. Their cost, after all, had to be transferred to the rural sector.

From the late 1960s to the mid-1970s, China's military confrontation with the USSR along the border had reshaped the international geopolitical equations. Mao took advantage of the increasingly sharp contradictions between the two superpowers to resume diplomatic relationship with the West in 1972. Along with geopolitical adjustments and political concessions, China could take part in an international division of labor as well as exchange and transform its economic structure. By introducing a large amount of production facilities from the USA, Europe, and Japan, China started to adjust its hitherto heavy industry-oriented economic structure and endeavored to establish a complete national industrial system with different sectors.

China turned to western investment for economic reconstruction. Premier Zhou Enlai proposed the 43 Plans introducing production facilities worth USD 4.3 billion from the West to adjust China's industrial structure.[3] It was to be paid by the foreign exchange reserves in the People's Bank of China (Shi 1989). China instantly faced the same problem as in the 1950s when "opening up" to the USSR: lack of investment to enlarge production. Since 1974, the fiscal deficit exceeded the level of RMB 10 billion when the fiscal revenues at that time were less than 80 billion. The principle of economic structural adjustment of the second introduction of foreign facilities, technology, and management model since 1972 was congruent with the Third Five-Year Plan, which in 1963 had to be aborted to construct the Third Front.

China adjusted its economic structure by increasing the weight of light industry. Large-scale introduction of fertilizer manufacturing facilities from the West doubled the agricultural output during 1972–1974. For the first time, the urban population enjoyed Dacron clothing, nylon stockings, and washing powder. Then we had televisions, washing machines, and refrigerators.

The main difference between the first and second occasions of introducing foreign capital lays in the preferential conditions. During the 1950s, China had established a strategic alliance with the USSR. Soviet experts and technicians taught the Chinese the skills and techniques scrupulously. This had saved China a lot of technology and management costs. However, since the mid-1970s, China had to pay high prices to get services from Japan and the West.

Furthermore, government officials were obliged to painstakingly transform their practices. They had to abandon the old mentality (along with the whole institutions) transplanted from the USSR. Otherwise, it would have been impossible to adapt themselves to the institutional requirements necessitated by the production lines transplanted from the West. Reforms in economic and political systems were gradually proposed by these government officials in charge of the economy. In a sense, it is a passive form of institutional evolution.

However, because of introducing even more expensive facilities and services to adjust the domestic industrial structure, China instantly faced the problem like the First Five-Year Plan, and the fourth economic crisis of national industrialization broke out.

The measures the government took to deal with the crisis followed a certain path dependence. During 1974–1976, the government had to rely on Mao Zedong's remaining prestige to mobilize millions of unemployed urban labors once again to

[3]Approximately USD26.75 billion in current prices. See Shi (1989) for details about the "43 Plans" program.

the rural areas to secure their basic subsistence under the conditions of a rural collectivized ownership system.

This was the third occasion of urban industrial capital transferring the crisis to the rural sector and the last phase of the "young intellectuals going to countryside" movement. Under the dichotomous urban–rural system, China could once again achieve a "soft landing" in the economic crisis caused by the urban economy. In this case, it stemmed from the introduction of western production facilities and technology for the structural adjustment of industrial capital.

During Mao's reign, the state made use of an incomplete rural land ownership to force a collectivized rural economy. It was not out of the necessity of agricultural development according to productivity considerations at that time, nor was it beneficial to the interests of peasants. However, in practice, it provided an unexpected boom to the primitive accumulation of national industrialization. What was formed in the rural areas was a so-called peasant socialism with Chinese characteristics. Its main feature was equal and even distribution without an incentive mechanism. It contained the characteristics of traditional village community peasant system in which external risks could be resolved through internalization. This system had accepted 40 million young intellectuals going to the countryside in three installments over 20 years. During these repeated social movements, China's tripartite agrarian sector had silently shouldered at least three times the enormous costs of cyclical economic crises caused by the state capitalist system concentrated in cities.

After the death of Mao (1976), none of his successors could again send millions of the urban unemployed to the countryside as he had done when facing urban economic crises (Shi 1989). Subsequent urban economic crises would take a "hard landing" in the cities, except for the two crises of 1979–1980 and 2008–2009.

6 After Chairman Mao

In the late 1970s, China reinitiated the introduction of large-scale foreign investment. As a result, national debt and deficit skyrocketed. The year 1978 is generally regarded as the start of China's reform for it disclosed a major crisis resulting from unprecedented increases in investment. In response, the government took austere deflationary measures, plunging the economy into a crisis and recession. In 1979, the fiscal deficit was RMB 13.54 billion. In 1980, the fiscal deficit was RMB 6.89 billion. What is now considered to be the reform was in fact institutional change in response to the economic crisis.

Faced with a serious fiscal deficit, the new leadership under Hua Guofeng and Deng Xiaoping, who lacked experience in economic regulation policy, came up with a plan of introducing foreign capital at a scale larger than the former premier Zhou Enlai's 43 Plans. In 1978 alone, China signed agreements to 22 large projects with

Japan and the West, with a total value of USD7.8 billion,[4] and letters of intent regarding investments totaling another USD5 billion, while in 1978, the total fiscal revenues were not more than RMB 113.2 billion.

Mao's successors introduced massive inflows of foreign capital for the structural adjustment of domestic industry. In 1979 and 1980, the fiscal deficit had accumulated to RMB 20 billion. China's economic growth crumbled from 11.7% in 1978 to 5.1% in 1981. The state-owned fixed assets investment growth rate fluctuated violently, from 22% in 1978 to 4.6% in 1979 and then 6.6% in 1980. In 1981, it became −10.5%.

Another source of fiscal pressure came from the fact that after 1978, the government in transition embraced an expansionary policy. The expenditure in welfare and subsidies expanded very quickly. Under fiscal constraints, the government enlarged investment and at the same time attempted to improve people's living standards. However, for a society without external resource infusion, it was impossible to be highly accumulative and consumptive at the same time. In 1979–1980, the state witnessed serious fiscal deficits. In the meantime, excessive monetary expansion led to general inflation.

When the state withdrew from the function of fiscal expenditure, the right to the rural surplus together with the right to resource capitalization of factors like arable land and labor was returned to the peasants. In the early 1980s, the primitive accumulation of rural industry and commerce mainly depended on the mechanism of internalization within the rural community and peasant households. It was a process of intensive accumulation through labor force self-exploitation, making use of labor in substitution of capital. This was unlike the state-owned industrial sector which required national revenue and loans to support it. In the 1980s, the demand for consumer goods in China's market was generally greater than supply, which provided rural enterprise with enough space for development. The comprehensive development of the rural economy increased peasant incomes which stimulate the national economy to allow for a rapid recovery. In 1981, there was no fiscal deficit but a revenue surplus of RMB 3.74 billion.

After Mao, the government in transition could no longer directly transfer the cost to the agrarian sectors. The crisis took a hard landing in the urban sector. In 1980, the unemployment rate was almost 5%. Faced with rising crime rates, the government launched several national "strike-hard" campaigns in 1983–1986. It led to the so-called rural reform which in fact involved the state retreating from agriculture that was no longer profitable with the old system.

During this institutional transition of the state's withdrawal, the institutional cost was mainly taken up by agricultural sectors with collective organizations as the vehicles. Major institutional benefits therefore remained in villages. Peasant households resumed a household mixed operation model which was beneficial to them. At the same time, villages enjoyed an unprecedented chance to enter industry, commerce, and finance. The Chinese economy rapidly recovered and took off again.

[4]Approximately USD30.32 billion in current prices. See Shi (1989) for details.

7 Price Reform and High Inflation

The origin of the next crisis was high inflation. The consumer price index (CPI) had been rising since the second half of 1987. As the central government accepted the policy suggestion to implement price reform, the inflation rate rocketed in 1988. During the rampant inflation, however, the investment of money by national banks expanded to RMB 67.95 billion, compared with 23.61 billion in 1987 and merely 1.66 in 1978 at the beginning of the reform. In 1988, the new monetary supply increase was mostly in cash form. The amount invested into the circulation of production was relatively small (NBSC 2017).

Not only was the incremental rate of money supply higher than the general economic growth rate, fiscal expansion was also rapid. In 1988, the deficit was RMB 13.4 billion. In 1989, it was RMB 15.89 billion. If deficits in the fiscal system itself were also counted (including domestic loans, foreign loans, and fiscal deficits on the books), the total deficit value was up to 25.1% of fiscal revenue. In terms of fiscal deficits, the crisis and reform in 1988–1989 was like that which had occurred on the eve of the 1978 Reform.

To shrug away the invisible institutional cost of a dual price system (a form of price regulation), the government attempted to impose a radical price reform. What was exposed were two types of institutional costs covered up by the internalization of the dual price system: first, the cost of rent-seeking by nepotistic companies colluding with official departments to seek speculative profits and, second, the market cost of speculation under conditions of artificially induced commodity scarcity. Both led to high inflation.

To fight inflation, the government implemented stringent measures that in turn caused deflation. As the interest rate rose, the marketization which had intensified the conflicts between interest blocs further led to a concatenation of enterprise indebtedness. The national economy was ensnared in serious indebtedness.

As national finance was still controlled by local governments at various levels, the central government was not equipped with other financial means to regulate local economies except by directly decreasing monetary supply and raising the interest rate. After the Tax Revenue Partition Reform in 1994, the central government no longer had substantial means to regulate local governments. Therefore, just like in the last crisis, all the central government could do was to cut investment in state-owned enterprises. What followed was a recession. GDP crumbled from 11.7% in 1987 to 4.2% in 1989 and then down to 3.9% in 1990.

The government's counter-crisis measures relied once again on the path dependency of transferring institutional costs to rural society. In the name of coastal economic development strategy, township–village enterprises were requested to import raw materials from overseas and orient themselves toward exporting to the overseas market. They were forced to recede from domestic raw materials and product markets. Through this, the mainly state-owned and debt-ridden urban enterprises managed to eschew competition with the emerging rural enterprises not burdened by social cost. However, it was devastating to township–village enterprises still at an initial stage of development. Furthermore, fiscal investment into public goods such as education, medical care, and local governments and party organizations was cut.

From 1989, peasants' per capita cash income declined for three consecutive years. A huge number of rural laborers had no choice but to go to cities to seek employment. It was the origin of the wave of "migrant workers" in the 1990s. By 1993, the outflow of rural labor had rocketed to 40 million. At the same time, local governments and grassroots organizations transferred the costs to peasants by impositions of taxes and levies. As a result, social conflicts in rural regions increased greatly, and tensions were intensified.

A dramatic consequence of this regulation oriented toward urban interests was that the rural economy and consumption by peasants who comprised a majority of the population were suppressed. As a result, national domestic demand declined. The internal contradictions of the economic structure were exacerbated. The thrust of growth in the national economy was forced to turn from domestic demand to an export-led economy. Such a change explains why China in the 1990s was so eager to embrace globalization and to be integrated into the global capitalist economy.

8 Transformation into an Export-Oriented Economy

Unlike the previous two economic crises which were caused by inflating domestic demand for consumer goods, the seventh economic crisis was caused by a speculatively overheated economy which appeared for the first time after the reform. It was also a continuation of the last crisis as the government attempted to get out of the last recession.

After 1992, the central policy had confirmed the market economy as the goal of reform and intensified investments including speculative markets (stocks, futures, and real estate), which led to a huge demand of capital for speculative purposes. An overheated economy together with chaotic finance pushed up the interest rates to a high level. To keep the financial system functioning, the central government increased its supply of currency. Despite a large-scale monetary expansion, financial institutions all over the country were in extreme shortage of cash.

Fiscal deficits and abnormal monetary expansion led to hyperinflation. In 1994, the CPI reached 24.1%, the highest on record since the reform.

In 1993, China recorded deficits simultaneously in three vital sectors. Apart from a fiscal deficit, there was also a serious balance of payment deficit which threatened the normal functioning of China's foreign exchange reserve system. At the end of 1993, China's foreign exchange reserve was USD21.199 billion. Reduced by the short-term payable liability of USD13.546 billion, the remaining USD7.653 billion was not even enough for paying the trade deficit of USD12.22 billion in 1993, not to mention the accumulated trade deficit (up to USD38.46 billion at the end of 1993) and long-term debt of USD70.027 billion. At the end of 1993, foreign debts accounted for 13.9% of the GDP, compared with the fiscal revenue which represented only 12.6% of the GDP (NBSC 2017).

Since the 1980s, local governments had been permitted to accept foreign investments on a large scale. At the end of 1993, the central government therefore had to take up national foreign debts at the highest record since 1949. The third deficit was recorded in the financial sector. State-owned financial institutions generally recorded an unfavorable balance in total capital. In this dire situation, the central government was forced to accelerate marketization and push a series of major reforms, the profoundest since 1978.

In 1994, RMB's nominal exchange rate depreciated in one shot by 57% to promote exports to resolve the highly unfavorable international balance of payment. This reform greatly increased the Chinese economy's dependency on foreign trade and made it more susceptible to global economic fluctuation. Consecutive national budget deficits, from RMB 23.71 billion in 1991 to RMB 58.15 billion in 1995, exhausted all the capital money in the state-owned financial institutions and even resulted in the overdrawing of a part of the People's Bank of China's reserves. In addition to inflating demand by investment, public debts and monetary supply expanded simultaneously.

To release the central government from its fiscal predicament, the reform drastically changed the distributive weight of revenue between the central and local governments. In the past, local governments shared over 70% of the total fiscal revenue. From then on it went down to around 50%, while the central government took 50%. As a result, to compensate for budget deficits, local governments depended mostly on large-scale land enclosures as a source of revenue. After the tax reform during 1994–1998, despite declining economic growth rates and suppression by the central government, the average annual decrease of arable land was up to 215,000 hectares. The reform implied transferring the institutional cost to the peasants via land enclosure.

As the total revenue by the central and local governments as a weight of GDP dropped to 11–13%, the lowest in history, local governments forced the auctioning of state-owned enterprises. Tens of millions of workers were laid off, most of them without social security and medical insurance. During 1991–1995, China recorded unprecedented high growth rates in GDP and investment but also the lowest employment growth rate since the 1950s, as low as 1.3%.

Unlike in previous crises, there no longer existed any possibility of transferring urban unemployed labors to the rural sector. Furthermore, faced with serious budget deficits, the government withdrew substantially from the responsibility of providing public goods such as medical care and education. With the lack of basic social security, urban labor had to painfully bid farewell to the old system which had provided full welfare, thus losing their greatest privileged institutional position over their rural counterpart.

During this crisis, the interest groups in the urban sector directly bore most of the costs of the economic crisis caused by the expansion of national industrial capital and the recession to local governments to attract investments. From then on, the urban interest groups became fundamentally diversified. One may say that from 1994 onward in China, capital had enjoyed an absolute dominance over labor.

In 1993, the government cut the investment in medical care and education and totally withdrew its support from public services in rural regions. Urban citizens and peasants were forced to pay more for social services. At the same time, governmental departments depended increasingly on off-budget revenue for basic operations. Government-run businesses were common. Government departments which were supposed to deliver social provisions are charged for all kinds of services they offered. During 1994–1996, a booming economy had stimulated staple-crop production.

In 1996, the government announced a soft landing. In summary, the seventh crisis marked a dividing line. China began to transform into a dominantly export-oriented economy, increasingly susceptible to international economic fluctuations. At the same time, China's industrial capital had been gradually moving into a stage of overcapacity and excess. Financial capital had been expanding rapidly and becoming increasingly alienated from industrial capital.

9 Asian Financial Crisis and Its Aftermath

During the regulation in 1994–1997, a great structural transformation had taken place. Domestic demand declined and China became increasingly dependent on exports. China was eager to accelerate its integration into the global economy but was immediately hit hard by the risks of globalization and found itself in a difficult situation.

During 1995–2000, employment in state-owned and township collective enterprises decreased by 48 million (Wang et al. 2002: 26–33). In 1998, China shifted away from a capital-scarce economy toward industrial overcapacity (Ma and Lu 1999). Now exports had replaced investment as the greatest driving force of economic growth. It relied heavily on external markets to absorb its overcapacity. This fundamental structural change made China's economy highly susceptible to international economic fluctuations.

After the Asian Financial Crisis in 1997, China's exports contracted drastically. Just a few years previously, it was inflation that got on people's nerves. Now an unfamiliar term replaced it: deflation. During 1998–2002, China suffered deflationary depression. Meanwhile, the fiscal deficit went from RMB 92.22 billion in 1998 to RMB 314.96 billion in 2002.

The central government adopted several counter-crisis measures such as an enforcement of risk management reform in financial sectors and large-scale investment into infrastructure by expanding public debt to increase domestic demand. The government had turned the fiscal policy around from a restrictive policy since 1993 to a positively expansionary policy. During 1998–2000, long-term national debt had accumulated to RMB 360 billion. Most of this debt was invested in large-scale urban infrastructure. Simultaneous reforms were carried out in the commercialization of social services like housing, education, and medical care, to expand public goods consumption by means of deepening monetization. Furthermore, the government raised the export rebate rate to make Chinese products more competitive. These measures had successfully saved the economy from falling. However, it came at great cost to Chinese society.

Under an urban–rural dual structure, the rural sector once again served as a regulatory labor pool. Urban unemployment did not lead to social crisis. After the crisis, employment in the rural areas rose. However, a falling demand pushed down staple prices. Agricultural efficiency was also declining, and the rural economy slid into depression after the late 1990s.

Under conditions of industrial overcapacity and stringent financial measures, township enterprises faced a hostile business environment. Loans that were earmarked for rural enterprise production were appropriated by local governmental expenditures. Township–village enterprises sank deeper into indebtedness. To shrug off the financial burden, grassroots governmental bodies promoted the privatization of township–village enterprises. Detached from community, township–village enterprises no longer aimed at their original function of rural community employment maximization but instead turned to profit maximization. The process of capital intensification excluded employment growth. Township–village enterprises no longer shared the rural community welfare expenditure.

Since the 1990s, a series of reforms oriented toward resolving the urban crisis were implemented, including the rural financial reform beginning in 1998 which was aimed at lowering the risk to state-owned banks and the commercialization of social services to stimulate domestic demand. All these measures pumped capital out of the rural sector which was already facing a shortage of capital.

The expansionary fiscal policy was oriented toward urban infrastructure construction. However, the wherewithal was precious land resource which was already scarce. In the late 1990s, accelerated urbanization propelled through large-scale investment took place at the expense of massive rural land expropriation. The rapid enclosure of land from the agrarian sectors by the nonagricultural sector had exacerbated the scarcity of arable land resources in a nation already facing extreme shortages of per capita arable land.

As land was appropriated from the rural sector at a relatively low cost, it was often not used efficiently. During 1998–2002, urban areas in 660 cities annually expanded by 5%, whereas the urban population increased by merely 1.3%. As of 2005, the urban average area per capita was up to 133 m^2, 33 m^2 higher than the limit allowed by national urban planning, much higher than the average 82.4 m^2 in many developed countries. China's urban residential plot ratio[5] was merely 0.33, whereas in some foreign cities, it was up to 2.0 (Jiang et al. 2007: 1–9).

With deteriorating rural governance, the capitalization of land resources often led to distributive conflicts that further exacerbated social tension.

[5]Plot ratio is defined as the ratio between the gross floor area of a building and the area of the site on which it is erected.

10 The *Sannong* New Deal

In the late 1990s, macroeconomic fluctuation had led to the deterioration of, and crisis in, rural governance (Dong and Wen 2008: 67–75). Since 2003, the ruling party had reiterated the importance of the *sannong* (three irreducible agrarian sectors: peasants, rural society, and agriculture) highlighting it as the most important among all problems. In 2005, the policy of New Socialist Countryside was listed as the first major strategy in China's future development.

A series of pro-rural policies had since then been implemented, the rural sector was given a chance to rehabilitate, and the regulatory function of its labor pool was partly restored. Furthermore, the function of the county economy, as the second capital pool besides the urban sector, had been strengthened. It had played a positive role in rectifying the long-lasting structural imbalance of the national economy (industrial overcapacity, capital excess, labor surplus, disparities between coastal regions and hinterland, rural–urban polarization, as well as income inequality) and enhancing the sustainability of development.

First, during 2003–2008, the investment into the rural sector accounted for over RMB 1473.1 billion. The fiscal investment into the three agrarian sectors during 2003–2009 accumulated to RMB 3096.752 billion, RMB 15,000 per household on average. It substantially increased the capital stock in the rural capital pool. Infrastructure investment had provided a great number of local nonagricultural employment opportunities. The once heavily debilitated regulatory function of the rural labor pool had thus been restored.

Second, pro-rural investment had stimulated rural consumption demand. During 2000–2003, the annual increase of retail sales volume in rural consumer goods market below county level was only about RMB 100 billion. In 2004, the number doubled to RMB 231.2 billion. It was estimated that the big push by the New Rural Reconstruction would increase the rural retail sales volume of social consumer goods by RMB 400 billion annually, amounting to an increase of over 2% in GDP (Huang 2005).

Third, as significant resources were flowing back into the rural sector, the tension between the peasants and grassroots governments was mitigated. Now the tension was over the general distribution of benefits within rural communities. The rural sector at large had become more stable, which was necessary as it formed the social base of the *sannong*. These were the vital conditions affording China ample leeway to deal with the 2008 global crisis.

11 Global Financial Crisis of 2007–2008 and Its Aftershocks

From 2003 to 2007, China maintained a high GDP annual growth rate. However, the national economy became increasingly dependent on the international market. In 2006, it was estimated that China's dependency on foreign trade was up to 66%.

During 1980–2001, the dependency on trade in economies like the USA, Japan, India, and Germany was within 14–20%. Obviously, China's dependency on foreign trade was much higher than these major developed and developing economies (Shen 2004). Under the condition of general overcapacity, China could only "use the future overcapacity to digest the present overcapacity" (Lang 2010: 38–9).

The global credit crunch in 2008 instantly hit China's unbalanced economy. Export-dependent sectors were hit hard. The contribution of exports to GDP growth dropped from 2.6% in 2007 to 0.8% in 2008. International capital swept into commodities futures markets after the subprime crisis pushed up primary product prices. China suffered a serious imported inflation (Wang 2008: 11–3). The PPI rose up from 5.4% in 2007 to 8.1% in 2008. In 2008, the monthly CPI reached 8.7%. Long-lasting insufficient domestic demand and overdependency on export and investment had made China's economy highly susceptible to external crises. In 2008, the GDP growth rate declined to 9.7%. This was still considered a respectable growth figure, but compared with previous years, it was just a step to recession.

Just like in the last crisis, the central government's response was to stimulate domestic demand by positive fiscal investment. The planned scale was up to RMB 4 trillion by the end of 2010. However, there was a major difference. In the last crisis in 1998, the new public debt was mostly spent on infrastructure, whereas in 2008, of the RMB 120 billion, 10 billion was invested in public housing; 34 billion in rural livelihood and rural infrastructure; 25 billion in railway, highway, and airport; 13 billion in medical care, education, and culture; 12 billion in energy efficiency and environmental and ecological preservation; and 6 billion in supporting entrepreneurship initiatives and industrial structure adjustment. It is obvious that most of the new fund had been used in livelihood-related projects and over one third on rural projects. Only 25 billion was spent on infrastructure (Wen 2012).

Large-scale investment in the rural sector since the implementation of the policy of New Socialist Countryside, along with construction projects in the underdeveloped mid-west regions, had created tens of millions of nonagricultural employment posts for rural laborers. As a result, unemployment caused by the global crisis was absorbed. Otherwise it would have incurred serious social problems. It was estimated that in 2009 up to 25 million migrant workers lost their jobs in coastal regions that were oriented toward external markets. To the new rural generation no longer entitled to the right to arable land distribution, the opportunity for alternative employment became of paramount importance. *Sannong* has once again served as the vehicle for soft landing. However, thanks to consecutive rural investments and pro-rural policies, this stood in contrast to the brutal straightforward cost-transferring practices of the previous crises.

12 Global Financialization and Stock Market Crashes

In the summer of 2015, simultaneous assaults by domestic and foreign financial interests led to multiple stock market crashes. The renminbi exchange rate fluctuated wildly, and China's foreign currency reserves sharply declined. This most recent crisis was clearly not the result of isolated domestic factors, but was instead symptomatic of a globalization that had largely erased any distinction between domestic and foreign financial capital.

In the years since the 2008–2009 crisis, central banks in core countries have, through enormous amounts of quantitative easing (QE), provided capital at effectively zero-interest rates to institutional investors, allowing them to reap high returns from capital markets, resource privatization, raw material and food commodity markets, as well as derivatives, similar to those that precipitated the most recent financial collapse. Further, the zero-interest US dollar had spurred overseas investment and strategic acquisitions in the physical economies of developing countries. With basic commodity prices pushed up by international trade, domestic inflation has inevitably risen, which in turn had increased the cost of business transactions. Countering inflation would induce higher domestic capital costs, making it even more uncompetitive in the global investment market relative to the low-cost overseas investment (Wen et al. 2015).

In contrast, the US Federal Reserve's plan to "taper" QE and gradually raise interest rates had rattled global financial markets, especially in emerging countries whose physical economies were most dependent on foreign investment. Losing the "long-short" battle manipulated by this outside investment was one of the external factors that led to the recent slowdown of growth in developing countries, notably China.

It was reported that the Chinese government raised an amount of RMB 1.7 trillion (around USD258 billion) effectively to bail out the stock market.[6] Goldman Sachs estimated that the Chinese government had spent close to USD 140 billion to avert a stock market meltdown. Other industry analysts estimated that including social security, the China Securities Finance Corporation, and other institutional investors, the total fund for bailing out the market amounted to RMB 2–3 trillion (USD303–455 billion). Yet China's instability caused only a brief dip in US stocks, which quickly recovered. The decisive factor was the new currency swap agreement of October 2013, set up among the USA and other core countries of financial capital, that was able to smooth market fluctuations.

The multiple stock market destabilizations that had occurred since 2015 undoubtedly required the close collaboration of foreign investors and Chinese domestic capital. Yet this is not to say that China's vulnerable markets were the result of a conspiracy by the global financial elite. Rather, it accorded with larger objective trends in the global political economy. Representatives of China's financial capital and their allies had only to stress the guiding principle of the "market," implicitly rejecting the countercyclical measures that had long characterized Chinese macroeconomic policy, and, further, demand the government's adoption of so-called deepened reform. After the subsequent launch of derivatives trading products able to absorb large amount of excess currency, the interests of domestic and foreign financial capital would merge in the form of a Western-style virtualized financial capitalism. Viewed this way, no conspiracy theory would be needed to explain the

[6]"Amid Different Opinions, Premier Li Keqiang Outragedly Ordered to Bail Out the Stock Market by *Force*", *Hong Kong Economic Times*. http://china.hket.com/article/641873

weakening of China's physical economy and the volatility of its financial markets, only the fluttering of butterfly wings in Shanghai or New York—i.e., the cumulative consequences of every individual short-selling transaction (Tsui et al. 2017).

13 Concluding Remarks

China's industrialization had involved the internal extraction of surplus from the agricultural sector to support industrial accumulation. Nevertheless, the dominant dynamics of China's industrialization had been subject to the shifting parameters of global geopolitics and the international economic landscape.

There were two waves of industrialization in New China, both of which could be attributed to catching up with the unprecedented historical opportunities of industry transfer from developed to developing countries after WWII. The first occasion was the Korean War in the 1950s. On condition of getting involved in the war, China was offered the opportunity to transplant military-heavy industry from the Soviet Union.

At the end of the 1950s, the Soviet Union withdrew investment from China. During the subsequent crisis which lasted from the late 1950s to the early 1960s, China eventually achieved "delinking," unlike many developing countries under similar circumstances. It undertook primitive accumulation for industrialization while paying back its foreign debts to the Soviet Union, thus breaking its economic and political dependency.

The second wave of industrialization took place after the 1970s when China restored a rapprochement with Japan and the West. To an extent China had taken advantage of its rising geopolitical importance in the Asia-Pacific region when the USA and the Soviet Union struggled for supremacy there. It could therefore structurally adjust, shifting from a lopsided military-heavy industry to consumer goods production before the reform.

Since the early twentieth century in China, economic crises endemic to industrial civilization had tended to break out in the cities. Its impact on the urban sector and, hence, on industrialization and social progress in general depended on the extent the cost of the crisis could be transferred to the rural sector and peasants. Unlike the USA, China could not transfer institutional costs and the price of crises abroad.

In terms of social stabilization at large, Rural China had played an important role in absorbing the shocks to the cyclical economic crises that were caused by urban industrial capital in the last 68 years.[7] The agrarian sector was likely to be forged as a vehicle of soft landing in case of crisis.

[7]Wen Tiejun analyses the ten cyclical economic crises that China experienced since 1949 till now. Retrieved from http://our-global-u.org/oguorg/en/series-no-5-chinas-real-experiences-professor-wen-tiejun-on-ten-cyclicaleconomic-crises-in-china-1949-2016/

It is apparent in China's case that an unbalanced domestic economy that was increasingly integrated into the global economic system would once again have to bear risks associated with its overdependency on overseas markets. This would bring much uncertainty, increased by direct foreign investment which had accounted for 40% of China's domestic economy. The capricious flows of capital in and out of the country would have repercussions for its domestic economy and politics. These would pose a formidable challenge to the sustainable development of China's economy and society.

From China's experiences in dealing with crises, it is evident that *sannong* had been the primary bearers of the economic and social pressures caused by macroeconomic cyclical fluctuations. It also served as a shock absorber to regulate economic uncertainty. The importance of *sannong* to human security and sustainable development in China is without question. However, in the stage of late industrialization, the socioeconomic structure of Rural China, which had served as the stabilizing foundation and regulator of economic development, had been undergoing drastic and fundamental change.

Acknowledgments This chapter is an outcome of the subproject on "International Comparative Studies on National Security in the Process of Globalization," led by Dr. SIT Tsui, Southwest University, which is under the Major Project on "A Study of the Structure and Mechanism of Rural Governance Basic to the Comprehensive National Security" led by Professor WEN Tiejun, Renmin University of China. The major project is funded by the National Social Science Foundation of China (No. 14ZDA064).

Appendix: Main Macroeconomic Indicators of China, 1950–2017

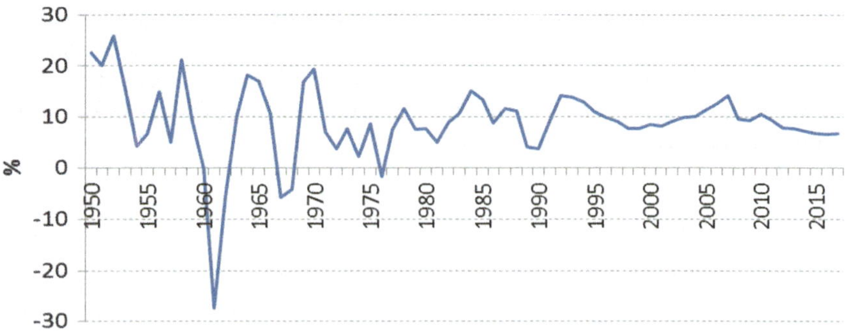

Fig. 1 Real GDP growth rate

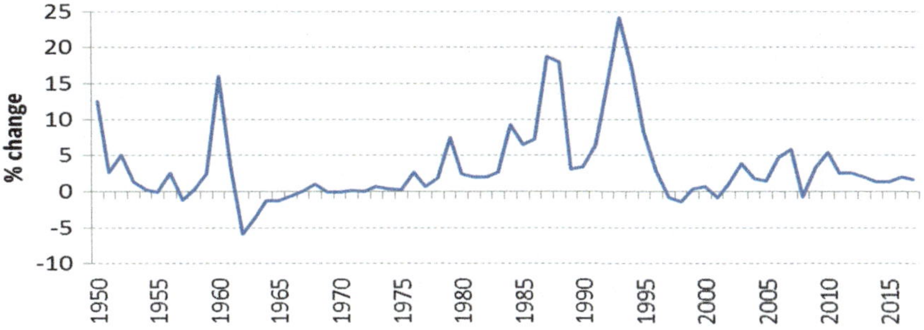

Fig. 2 CPI

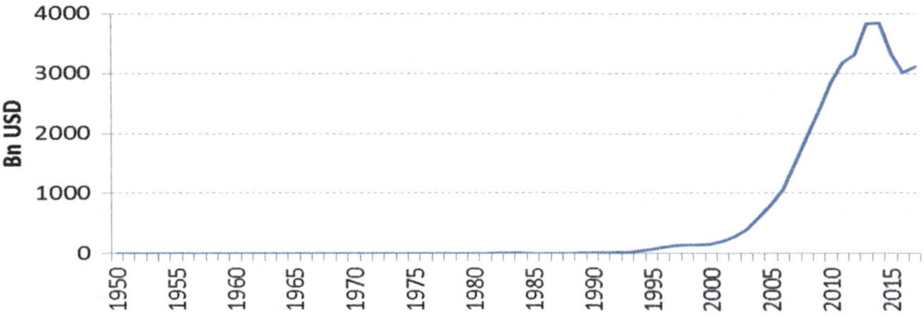

Fig. 3 Foreign exchange reserves

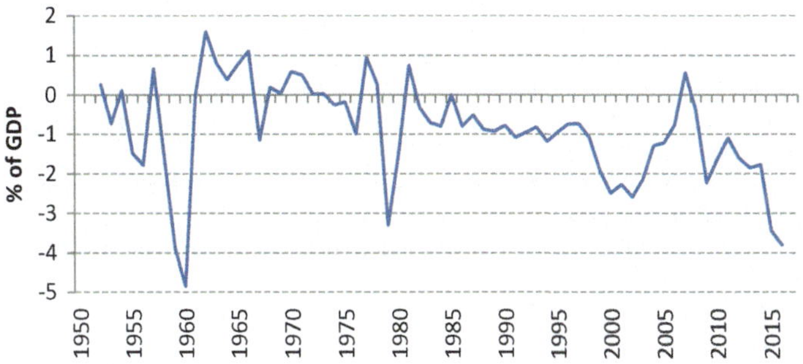

Fig. 4 Budget balance of general government

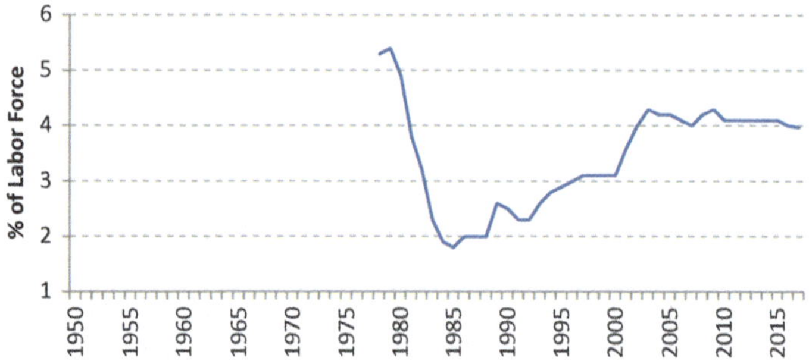

Fig. 5 Unemployment rate. Sources: National Bureau of Statistics of China (NBSC); State Administration of Foreign Exchange (SAFE)

References

Dong X, Wen T (2008) Macro economic fluctuations and crisis of rural governance. Manag World 9:67–75. http://cppcc.people.com.cn/GB/34961/50294/50298/3533378.html. Accessed 11 Jul 2005 (in Chinese)

Huang H (2005) Building a new socialist countryside—the countryside is a neglected dynamic element of domestic consumption. Outlook Weekly. Online. http://www.agri.gov.cn/jjps/t20051123_500588.htm. Accessed 23 Nov 2005 (in Chinese)

Jiang S, Liu S, Li Q (2007) Land system reform and national economic growth. Manag World 9:1–9 (in Chinese)

Lang X (2010) US is copy China as the second Japan. China Logist Purchas 12:38–39 (in Chinese)

Li C, Jiang D (2005) Historical experiences and lessons of the policy of "construction of third front". Northeast Normal Univ (Philos Soc Sci Ed) 4:89 (in Chinese)

Ma H, Lu B (1999) *China's* macro economics policy report. China Financial Economics, Beijing (in Chinese)

National Bureau of Statistics of China (NBSC) (2017) On-line. http://www.stats.gov.cn/english/statisticaldata/AnnualData/

Shen Z (2001) The soviet economic aid to China during the early period of new China—based on the archives from China and Russia. Russ Stud (1) (in Chinese)

Shen J (2004) On China's foreign trade dependence. Merchants Weekly 41:21 (in Chinese)

Shi L (1989) Overseas economic cooperation of contemporary China. Chinese Academy of Social Sciences Press, p 320 [quoted in Cui X (2008) China' s 30 years of taking advantage of foreign investment. China Finance and Economics Press, p. 6] (in Chinese)

Tsui S, Wong E, Chi LK, Tiejun W (2017) The tyranny of monopoly-finance capital: a Chinese perspective. Mon Rev:29–42

Wang J (2008) Concern about the turning point of situation of growth and inflation. Macroecon Manag 8:11–13 (in Chinese)

Wang S, Hu A, Ding Y (2002) Social instability hidden behind economics prosperity. J Strat Manag 3:26–33 (in Chinese)

Wen T (2001) An analysis of cyclical economic crisis and its responsive polices. http://www.macrochina.com.cn/zhtg/20010608007807.shtml (in Chinese)

Wen T (2012) Eight crises: lessons from China (1949–2009). Dongfang, Beijing (in Chinese)

Wen T, Gao J, Zhang J (2015) Double export by China to the US and its new changes. Econ Theory Bus Manag 7 (in Chinese)

China's Economic Cycles: Characteristics and Determinant Factors

Junli Zhao, Degang Jia, and Wei Chang

1 Introduction

Economic cycles, also called business cycles, refer to the economic fluctuations between periods of expansion and contraction without regularity. A cycle generally has four phases: prosperity, recession, depression, and recovery. The Chinese academy and the government have been paying close attention to the fluctuations of macroeconomic activities. A reasonable identification of China's economic cycles and an insight investigation of the occurrence are conductive to precisely understanding the cyclical regularity of the Chinese economy. This enables the government to use counter-cyclical measures to smooth out economic fluctuations and to promote steady and robust growth.

Since the People's Republic of China was founded in 1949, China has made remarkable achievements in economic development. Over six decades, China transformed from infancy to implementing a centrally planned economy until 1978, which was followed by 30 years of reform and opening-up and gradually turned into a socialist market economy.

This chapter firstly identifies China's economic cycles over the period of 1953–2016 and then outlines the principal characteristics of the cycles. The chapter then explains the drivers that cause the fluctuations.

J. Zhao · D. Jia · W. Chang (✉)
China Economic Monitoring and Analysis Center, National Bureau of Statistics of People's Republic of China, Beijing, People's Republic of China
e-mail: changwei@stats.gov.cn

S. Smirnov et al. (eds.), *Business Cycles in BRICS*, Societies and Political Orders in Transition, https://doi.org/10.1007/978-3-319-90017-9_9

Table 1 China real GDP growth (1950–2016)

Year	Growth (%)	Year	Growth (%)	Year	Growth (%)	Year	Growth (%)
1950	22.6	1967	−5.7	1984	15.2	2001	8.3
1951	20.1	1968	−4.1	1985	13.4	2002	9.1
1952	25.9	1969	16.9	1986	8.9	2003	10.0
1953	15.6	1970	19.3	1987	11.7	2004	10.1
1954	4.3	1971	7.1	1988	11.2	2005	11.4
1955	6.9	1972	3.8	1989	4.2	2006	12.7
1956	15.0	1973	7.8	1990	3.9	2007	14.2
1957	5.1	1974	2.3	1991	9.3	2008	9.7
1958	21.3	1975	8.7	1992	14.2	2009	9.4
1959	9.0	1976	−1.6	1993	13.9	2010	10.6
1960	0.0	1977	7.6	1994	13.0	2011	9.5
1961	−27.3	1978	11.7	1995	11.0	2012	7.9
1962	−5.6	1979	7.6	1996	9.9	2013	7.8
1963	10.3	1980	7.8	1997	9.2	2014	7.3
1964	18.2	1981	5.1	1998	7.8	2015	6.9
1965	17.0	1982	9.0	1999	7.7	2016	6.7
1966	10.7	1983	10.8	2000	8.5		

Source: http://www.stats.gov.cn/tjsj/zxfb/201607/t20160705_1373924.html

2 Identifying Cycles

This article uses the growth rate of gross domestic product (GDP), which is internationally accepted as a means to measure cyclical fluctuations, to investigate the characteristics of China's economic cycles (Xu 2009). GDP growth rates for the period of 1953–2016 are listed in Table 1. We only investigate the period of 1953–2016 and exclude 1950, 1951, and 1952 because China was restoring its economy after the civil war to normal working order during these 3 years. From 1953, when the First Five-Year Plan was implemented, China embarked on intensive programs of industrial growth.

In this chapter, we use the "trough-to-trough method" to identify the turning points of China's economic cycles. We believe that the Chinese economy experienced ten cyclical fluctuations between 1953 and 2016 (see Fig. 1 and Table 2), with five cycles taking place before the reform and opening-up in 1978 and four after 1978.

3 Characteristics of Cycles

The Chinese economy was in deep cycles with low average positions before the reform, but post-reform it evolved to fluctuate shallowly at high levels. The high positions signal the increment of growth potentials, and the shallow fluctuation

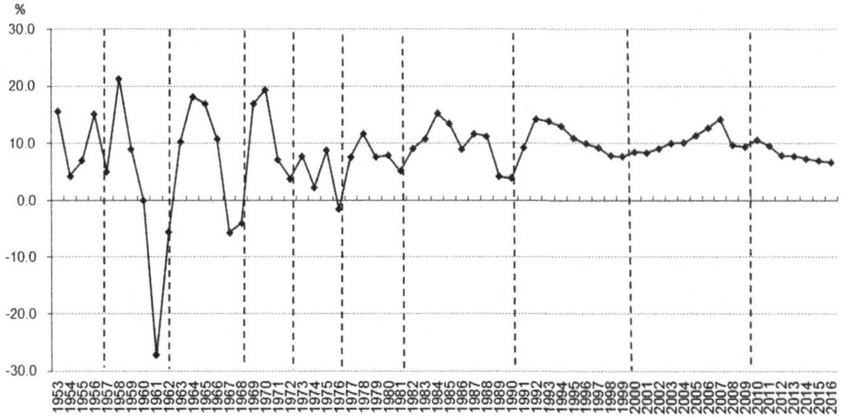

Fig. 1 China GDP growth (1953–2016)

Table 2 Typical characteristics of Chinese economic cycles

	Duration (years)	Average (%)	Standard deviation (%)	Peak (%)	Trough (%)	Amplitude (%)	Length of expansion (years)	Length of contraction (years)
1953–1957	5	9.3	5.49	15.6	4.3	11.3	3	2
1958–1962[a]	5	−1.9	18.10	21.3	−27.3	48.6	1	4
1963–1968	6	7.3	10.31	18.2	−5.7	23.9	2	4
1969–1972	4	11.6	7.49	19.3	3.8	15.5	2	2
1973–1976	4	4.2	4.84	8.7	−1.6	10.3	3	1
1977–1981	5	7.9	2.37	11.7	5.1	6.6	2	3
1982–1990	9	9.8	3.81	15.2	3.9	11.3	3	6
1991–1999	9	10.6	2.50	14.2	7.7	6.5	2	7
2000–2009	10	10.3	1.89	14.2	8.3	5.9	8	2
2009–present	7	8.1	1.44	10.6	6.7	3.9	1	6

[a]1962 is classified to the contraction period because the growth rate of 1962 is still negative even if it stands in the higher level than that of 1961

evidences the growth of Chinese economy becomes more stable (Liu 2011). In short, economic fluctuations tend to narrow down. Table 2 lists all the cyclical periods and the characteristics involved in each period.

1. From Classical Cycles to Growth Rate Cycles

   Before the reform and opening-up, China exhibited classical cycles. The real levels of GDP declined during the economic downturns and growth alternated between positive and negative. However, after the reform, GDP began increasing, and growth turned to be consistently positive, whatever higher or lower, exhibiting growth-driven cycles.
2. Duration Increased Throughout Time

   The duration of each of China's ten economic cycles differed greatly: the longest cycle was 10 years; the shortest was only 4 years. On average, the cycles lasted 6.4 years. Furthermore, the average duration of the first five cycles before the reform and opening-up was 4.8 years. Then after the reform, 1982–1990 cycle and 1991–1999 cycle both lasted for 9 years, and the 2000–2009 cycle lasted for 10 years, making it the longest cycle in the history. China exhibited longer cycles throughout time, entering into Juglar cycle periods.
3. Average Position Lifted Up

   The average position of an economic cycle is the geometric mean of GDP growth rates over the cyclical period, measuring the strength of economic growth. Looking at China's ten cycles, the 1969–1972 period positioned at the peak level of 11.6%, while 1958–1962 period reaches the bottom of −1.9%. Furthermore, the average position of the five cycles before the reform and opening-up is 5.9%, and the last four cycles as ended by 2016 positioned at an average of 9.8%. The elevating position witnesses the growing of Chinese economy.
4. Nonperiodical Fluctuations Became Less Volatile

   The cycle amplitude measures the extent that economic activity changes during the phase. The larger the amplitude is, the more volatility the economy endures. Overall, China's economic volatility dramatically declined over the ten cyclical periods, with the amplitude falling from 48.6% in 1958–1962 periods to 3.9% in the tenth period and the standard deviation going down from 18.1% to 1.9% accordingly. In more detail, before the reform and opening-up, China's economic volatility was noticeably greater with an amplitude of 48.6% and a standard deviation of 10.7%, while after the reform (Huang 2011), the amplitude and the standard deviation decreased by 37.3 and 8.0 percentage points to just 11.3% and 2.7%, respectively. In the twenty-first century, there was less volatility of cyclical fluctuation, and the stability of economic growth is greatly strengthened.
5. Period of Expansion Obviously Extended

   The symmetry of economic cycle is also a key feature revealing the relative duration of expansion and contraction. A shorter period of expansion with a longer period of contraction indicates that the economy can easily become "overheated" and is hard to cool down. There is evidence that among China's ten economic cycles, five are all with a shorter period of expansion. Before the reform and opening-up, economic acceleration and slowdown lasted for 2.2 years and 2.6 years, respectively, while in the after, the durations extended to 3.5 years and 5.25 years. Especially in the ninth period, expansion lasted for 8 years, suggesting that China's economic growth became more and more sustainable.

4 Determinant Factors of the Cycles

It is both internal dynamics and external shocks that evolve China's cycles from "swinging up and down" to "fluctuating at highs with little variation." Chinese economic fluctuations are correlated with economic growth and the improvement of economic structure in terms of stability and in part affected by macro regulations and the changes of international economic environment. To be specific, the fluctuations appeared to be determined by the following seven factors:

1. Economic System Reform

   Chinese economic system reform is a critical factor that causes economic cycles and also differentiates China's current cycle from the pre-reform ones or cycles of other countries (Wen et al. 2013). Since the reform and opening-up, China has experienced extraordinary institutional change which has gradually transformed China from a centrally planned economy to a socialist market economy. Under the planned economy, enterprises had little autonomy to do business, and production, supply, sales, and investment activities followed national planned quotas. While under the socialist market economy, economic entities are granted greater autonomy, and market mechanism such as prices, competition, and factor markets are introduced. This allowed the market to play a fundamental role in resource allocation, which brings unprecedented vigor and vitality to economic development. In conclusion, the structural reform warrants an important systematic basis for the high-speed growth with less variation.
2. Economic Structure Improvement

   Structure improvement is an endogenous dynamics highly correlated with growth and economic development. China's economic structure has changed significantly throughout time. The proportion of primary industry declined from 50.5% in 1952 to 27.7% in 1978 and leveled off to 8.6% in 2016. The secondary industry took a proportion of 20.8% in 1952, rose to 47.7% in 1978, and then became relatively flat after the reform, reaching 39.8% in 2016. The proportion of tertiary industry firstly dropped a bit from 28.7% in 1952 to 24.6% in 1978 but turned around after the reform to finally reach 51.6% in 2016 (see Fig. 2). Analyzing the interaction of structure improvement and economic fluctuations reveals that the primary sector's influence was declining, while secondary sectors became steadier and tertiary sectors increased. Tertiary sectors grow quickly with less volatility and are seldom constrained by natural resources. A bigger tertiary sector will help to enhance the stability of the economy, thus yielding an optimized industry structure that attenuates the influence of economic fluctuations.
3. Investment Fluctuations

   Investment is an intrinsic driving force of aggregate demand and is the allocation of economic resources. The fluctuation of investment growth has always been a key factor that causes or even decides China's economic cycle, though the extension of influence varies in different periods of time (Yao and Zhou 2013). Before the reform, China had a low savings rate, and investment was

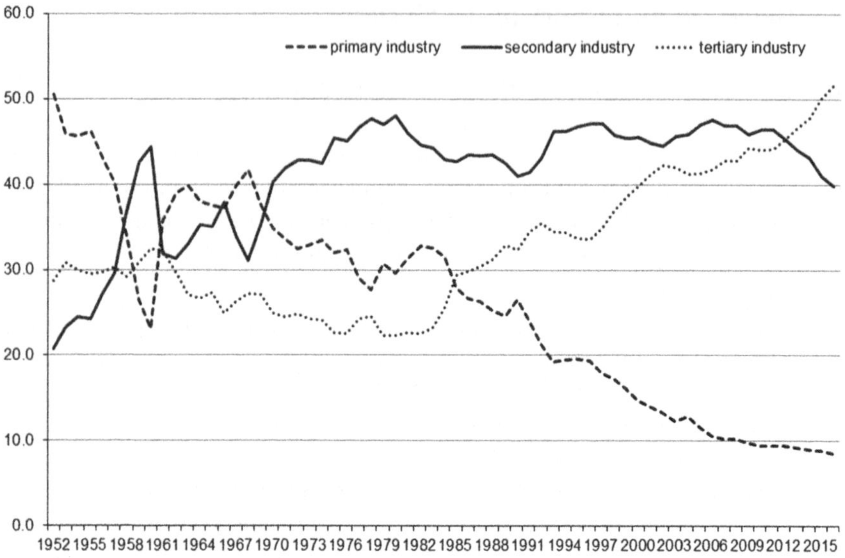

Fig. 2 Share of the three sectors of Chinese economy

not strong enough to boost growth. However, after the reform, as industrialization, urbanization, and modernization accelerated, the investment rate kept on rising resulting in a typical investment-driven economy. The accumulation rate calculated by national income utilization was 21.4% in 1952 and increased to 36.5% by 1978. The investment rate calculated by expenditure approach increased from 38.9% in 1978 to 44.9% in 2015 (see Fig. 3). Since it was founded, China experienced a series of investment booms such as introducing Soviet heavy industry investment, third lines construction,[1] western light industry investment, the rise of countryside and township enterprises, export-oriented investment, and real estate investment. The third plenary session of the 18th central committee of the Communist Party of China took place in November 2013 and demonstrated that China is stepping into a new era of deepening reform by transforming the growth pattern. Within the current cycle period, export-led investment will continue to slow down, the real estate sector will see overcapacity, and investment growth will turn weak. That being said, investment remains central to economic growth.

[1]In the early 1960s, China faced a serious situation in the international community. A sharp deterioration in relations between the Soviet Union and China, Chiang Kai-shek's counteroffensive, the nuclear war exercise in Taiwan Strait, these kinds of affairs threatened the safety of China directly. Chairman Mao decided to divide the country into three lines to get maximum development in that serious time and to develop large-scale industry.

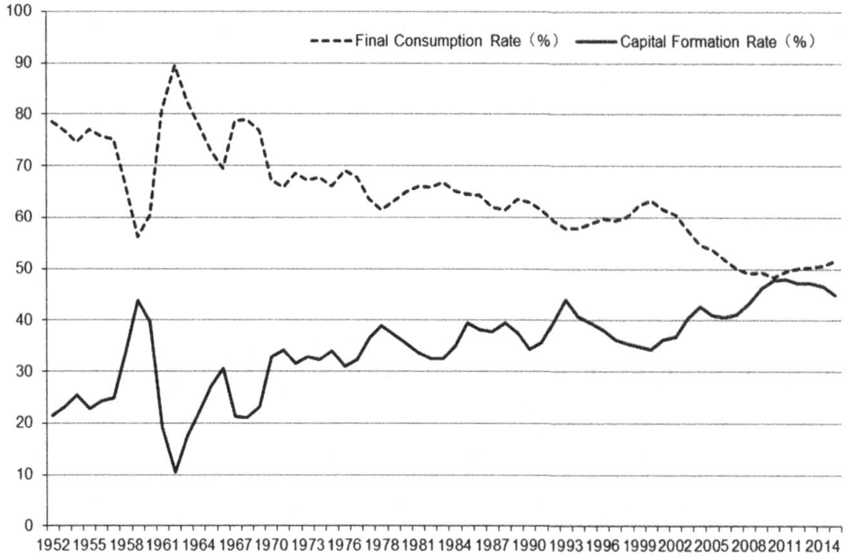

Fig. 3 Composition of GDP in China (1952–2015). Note: Before 1978, its consumption rate and accumulation rate are calculated by national income; after 1978, its final consumption rate and capital formation rate are calculated by Expenditure Approach GDP

4. Consumption Fluctuations

Consumption, another key component of aggregate demand, is actually the long-lasting engine of economic growth. Since the reform and opening-up of China, the increase of average per capita income has been giving impetus to the upgrade of China's consumption pattern. Chinese people spend more on residence, travel, and education services rather than on food, clothes, and daily articles (see Fig. 4).[2] In other words, the purpose of consumption has evolved from survival to personal development and to living a comfortable life. The upgrade of consumption patterns was a primary driver of economic growth with an optimized industry structure. In retrospect, China's consumption rate calculated by national income utilization was 78.6% in 1952 and declined to 63.5% in 1978. By expenditure approach, the rate was 61.4% in 1978 and leveled off to 51.6% by 2015. In comparison to other countries, China's current consumption rate is relatively low, staying at a level of around 50%, which is 25 percentage points lower than the world average and very far below that of high-income countries, which have a consumption level around 80%. Furthermore, the Chinese economy has long been imbalanced between investment and consumption as to impose potential risk to achieve stable and sustainable growth. With the implementation of a suite of measures such as increasing household

[2]As consumption structure series is not available, we use Engel's coefficient series (the proportion of expense on food to the consumption expense) as replacement.

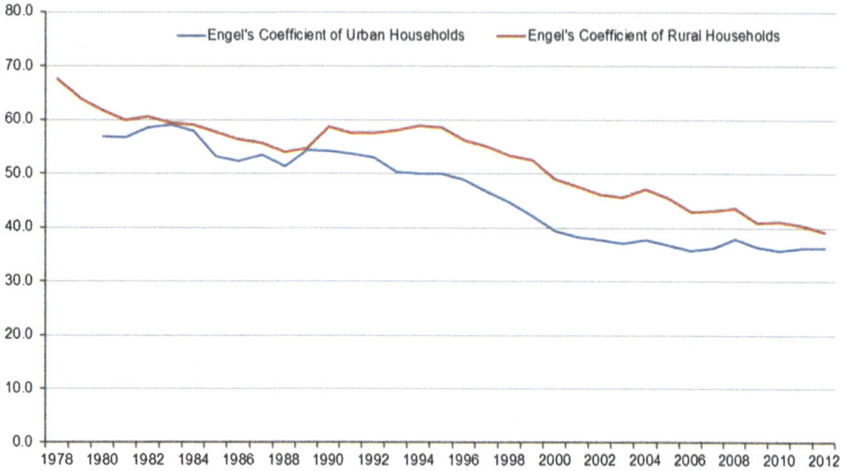

Fig. 4 Engel's coefficient of urban and rural households in China

income, stimulating consumption, and mending the social welfare system, consumption will be a larger driver and stabilizer of the economy.

5. Fluctuations of Foreign Demand

   Foreign demand, or net export, is also the key component of aggregate demand. Since the reform, especially after the 1990s, China became more open and closely integrated into the world economy (see Fig. 5).[3] Export therefore became a key driver, underpinning the fast growth of Chinese economy. However, the Chinese economy became highly influenced by global economic cycles, and the impact of foreign demand fluctuations on the fluctuations of Chinese economy gradually deepened. In 1978, the degree of dependence on foreign trade was 9.7% and then surged to 64.2% by 2006 benefiting from joining WTO in 2001; in 2009, the ratio bottomed out at 43.2% due to the 2008 financial crises but bounced back to 35.6% by 2015. In 2015–2016, developed economies such as the USA, EU, and Japan all were in economic recovery, major emerging markets face commodity prices up ahead, and Chinese foreign demand bottoms up. However, net export contributed less to the growth of the Chinese economy.

6. External Shocks

   External shocks have significant impacts on macroeconomic fluctuations. Globalization, regional integration, and the liberalization of finance and trade tie up the economies across world, and economic cycles of different countries tend to be synchronized. There is no country, including China, that is able to achieve growth despite external shocks such as world business activity cycles, industry transfer across borders, oil prices, interest rates, and US exchange rates. As for China domestically, especially since 2008 when the financial crisis created

[3]We used the ratio of value of import and export of goods to GDP as a measure of dependence on foreign trade.

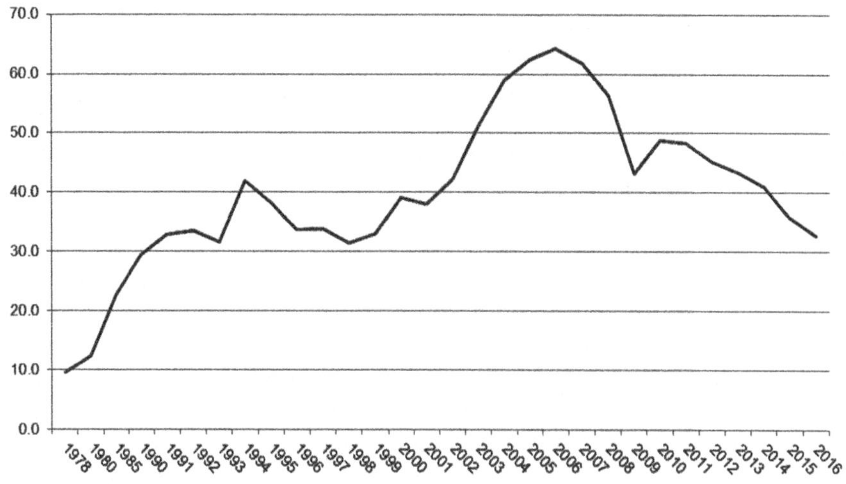

Fig. 5 Degree of dependence on foreign trade of China

chaos in the international financial market, world economic growth slowed down, and uncertainty and instability increased, which all had inevitable impacts on China's economic growth. For example, the export-led enterprises faced great pressure to reduce capacity, domestic prices fluctuated with the changes of the commodity goods prices, and the central bank issued measures to stabilize exchange rate, which left opportunities for speculators to hedge short.

7. Macroeconomic Policies

   Based on Keynesian theory, counter-cycle policies have become increasingly popular. Most countries try to use fiscal and financial measures to manage aggregate demand in order to smooth out economic cycles. However, policy intervention may deviate from forecast, which thereby causes or even exacerbates economic fluctuations. On one hand, China's economic cycles tended to be less volatile during the post-reform period, especially in the 1990s. This was partly benefited from the stability and effectiveness of policy intervention. On the other hand, as China is yet to improve its market mechanism, the Chinese financial system is also far from perfect, and polices are subject to periodicity and time lag; macro policies may not always meet the target but instead trigger economic fluctuations with volatility. Looking ahead through the latest cycle period, developed economies such as the USA, Europe, and Japan will maintain low recovery, and emerging markets will face new challenges. As China make progress in transforming its growth pattern and optimizing the industry structure through deepening reform, it will achieve an upper middle level of growth with a slower rate, thereby demanding for better regulatory measures to overcome economic cycles.

5 Conclusion

From a planned economy to a market economy, from an agriculture-based economy to a service-oriented economy, and from a poor economy to becoming the second largest economy in the world, China experienced a complex evolutional process, and the cyclical fluctuations of the Chinese economy were a result of these factors. In the early period of industrialization, investment and consumption fluctuation resulted in the fluctuation of economic cycles. At the same time, the institutional innovation and the transformation of macroeconomic policy created opportunities for continued economic growth. From an external perspective, China initially imported foreign capital to accelerate industrial accumulation and economic growth, while interruption of foreign capital input led to economic unsustainability and government debt pressure. After the reform and opening-up, China has attracted foreign direct investment and developed an export-oriented economy in the form of enterprises and played its own advantages to promote the expansion of economic scale and the enhancement of peaceful stability. Looking to the future, as China is stepping into a higher urbanization stage and the net capital flow is changing, China's economic cycle fluctuation and the characteristics of economic cycles are expected to change accordingly.

References

Huang T (2011) Analysis of China's post-reform economic cycles. Reference Material: Research Institute of National Bureau of Statistics of China (55) (in Chinese)

Liu S (2011) China's economic growth of 60 years: retrospect and outlook—discuss the new round economic cycle. Development Research Center of the State Council (in Chinese)

Wen T et al (2013) Eight crises: lesson from China 1949–2009. Orient Publishing, Beijing (in Chinese)

Xu X (2009) China's economic growth and inflation cycle after reform and opening-up. Reference material: Research Institute of National Bureau of Statistics of China (26) (in Chinese)

Yao M, Zhou C (2013) China's economic cycle fluctuations: characteristics and influential factors. Inquiry into Economic Issues (7):5–9 (in Chinese)

A Brief History of Business Cycle Measurement in South Africa

J. C. Venter

1 Introduction

South Africa has a fairly long history of business cycle measurement, especially when considering that it is a developing economy. This chapter aims to provide a concise summary of the history of business cycle measurement in South Africa, from the earliest known attempt up to the current period.

When studying the history of business cycle analysis in South Africa, three lengthy—yet distinct—periods emerge, namely, from 1806 to 1909, from 1910 to 1948 and finally from 1945 to the present. This chapter is thus organized accordingly. The distinction of these particular time periods was made for a number of logical reasons. First, different authors (or institutions) were principally responsible for studying or measuring the South African business cycle during each of the three periods. Second, the methodology employed and also the terminology used during each of these periods differed notably. Third, related to the methodology applied, the availability of statistical time series and analytical capability improved markedly with each successive period.

Despite the differences in methodology and data availability, historical reference turning points in the South African business cycle have largely been determined in terms of the "growth cycle" definition of business cycles as opposed to the "classical" definition of business cycles. Whereas classical business cycles refer to *absolute* declines in aggregate economic activity followed by *absolute* increases in aggregate economic activity, growth cycles represent the fluctuations around the long-term growth trend of aggregate economic activity, i.e. trend-adjusted business cycles (Klein and Moore 1985: 16–17). These reference turning points have always been referred to as "business cycles" in South Africa, possibly leading to some confusion.

J. C. Venter (✉)
South African Reserve Bank, Pretoria, South Africa
e-mail: iaan.venter@resbank.co.za

S. Smirnov et al. (eds.), *Business Cycles in BRICS*, Societies and Political Orders in Transition, https://doi.org/10.1007/978-3-319-90017-9_10

Nevertheless, Smit and van der Walt (1982: 50) noted that the use of the term "business cycles" to include growth cycles has generally become accepted over time in South Africa, and this is still the case.

For each of the periods mentioned above, the article will describe the methodology applied, note the statistical data and other sources used, provide a chronology of business cycle phases and turning points for the South African economy as well as briefly discuss the most important structural and economic drivers of cyclical developments. Since it is assumed to be more relevant to current readers, the most recent period's methodology and cyclical drivers will be described in more detail than that of the earlier two periods.

2 South African Business Cycles: 1806 to 1909

The first comprehensive study of business cycles in South Africa was conducted by Schumann (1938). His objective was to study and document structural changes, secular growth trends and business cycle fluctuations in the South African economy for the period 1806 to 1938. He divided his study into two separate periods: from 1806 to 1909 and from 1910 to 1936. There were two main reasons for choosing these specific time periods. The first reason was political; South Africa (at the time consisting largely of the Cape Colony) became a British colony in 1806, while in 1910, the four self-governed colonies that existed at that time were unified, and the country became known as the Union of South Africa. The second reason relates to statistical data; much more complete and unified statistical time series were available for the post-Union period than for the period before 1910 (Schumann 1938: 29).

2.1 Methodology Applied

In order to distinguish business cycle phases for the period 1806 to 1909, Schumann (1938: 59) made use of descriptive material, or "business annals" from a variety of historical sources, as well as a number of annual statistical time series that were available for different time periods. These included time series measuring population growth, foreign trade (imports and exports), government finance (revenue and expenditure), railway construction and bank deposits. Schumann noted that even though the exact demarcation of business cycle phases was not possible at certain times, there was nevertheless a fairly close correlation between the available statistical time series. Table 1 displays the South African business cycle chronology for the period 1806 to 1909, as determined by Schumann.

In order to analyse the duration of South African business cycles over this period, Schumann (1938: 113) presented his chronology in a different way, i.e. as full business cycles measured from trough to trough (revival to revival) and also from peak to peak (recession to recession). His representation is depicted in Table 2.

Table 1 Business cycles in South Africa, 1806–1909

1806 to 1814–1815	Decided prosperity
1815	Recession
1815–1816	Slight depression
1817–1818	Moderate improvement
1819	Slight recession
1820–1821	Moderate improvement
1821	Indistinct recession
1821–1826	Distinct, but moderate, depression
1826–1827	Revival
1827 to 1829–1830	Moderate prosperity
1829–1830	Recession
1830 to 1831–1832	Slight depression
1832–1833	Revival and minor prosperity
1834	Recession
1834–1835	Revival
1835–1838	Decided prosperity
1838–1839	Moderate recession
1839–1841	Depression
1841–1842	Revival
1842–1847	Prosperity
1847	Economic and banking crisis
1848–1849	Depression
1849–1850	Revival
1850–1854	Prosperity and copper boom in 1854
End 1854	Copper crisis. Financial and speculative collapse
1855	Slight depression
1855–1856	Revival
1856 to 1857–1858	Distinct prosperity
1858	Minor recession and revival
1859–1862	Strong prosperity, including a banking boom in 1861–1862
1862	Moderate recession
1862–1863	Moderate depression
1864–1865	Renewed activity, especially in Natal and Eastern Province
1865	Banking and financial crisis
1865–1866 to 1869	Severe economic depression
1869–1870	Revival
1870–1875	Marked prosperity
1876	Moderate recession
1876–1877	Moderate depression
1878	Revival
1879–1881	Prosperity and diamond boom
1881	The diamond crisis
1882–1886	Severe depression

(continued)

Table 1 (continued)

1886–1887	Revival
1887–1889	Prosperity and gold-mining boom
1889 –1890	The gold crisis. This includes an intense speculative collapse early in 1889, a severe banking and financial crisis in 1889–1890 and an economic recession towards the middle of 1890
1890–1892	Depression
1892–1893	Revival
1893–1895	Prosperity and speculative boom in 1895
1895	Speculative collapse in September, but continuing economic prosperity
1896–1897	Prosperity
1897	Economic recession
1898–1899	Depression
1899	Revival
1899–1902	War period. War destruction in Transvaal and Orange free state. Decided prosperity in cape Colony and Natal
1902–1903	After-war boom
1903	Definite recession but no sudden crisis
1903–1909	Severe depression
1909–1910	Revival

Source: Schumann (1938: 111)

Schumann (1938: 114) observed that there appeared to be no evidence of fixed periodicity in South African business cycles, consistent with international experience. Furthermore, measured from revival to revival, there are 16 business cycles during the 104-year period, with an average length of 6.5 years. Similarly, measured from peak to peak, there are 17 business cycles during the 111-year period, of which the average length was also 6.5 years.

2.2 Major Cyclical Drivers

Describing the characteristics of each cycle over the lengthy period covered by Schuman would be beyond the scope of this chapter. Instead, two important historical events that shaped the development of the South African economy over this period will briefly be mentioned.

The "Great Trek" Interestingly, Schumann (1938: 32) noted that the economic development of the Cape Colony (and the other coastal regions) progressed quite differently to that of the interior of the country. Throughout the first half of the nineteenth century, an increasing tendency existed among the pioneering farmers to trek deeper and deeper into the interior of the country, further and further away from all economic contact with the outer world. This tendency culminated in the "Great

Table 2 Business cycles measured from revival to revival and from recession to recession

Period: 1806–1909		Period: 1803–1913	
Cycles from revival to revival		Cycles from recession to recession	
Period of cycle	Length of cycle in years	Period of cycle	Length of cycle in years
1806 to 1817–1818	12	1803 to 1815	13
1817–1818 to 1820–1821	3	1815 to 1819	4
1820–1821 to 1826–1827	6	1819 to 1821	2
1826–1827 to 1832	6	1821 to 1829–1830	8
1832 to 1834–1835	3	1829–1830 to 1834	5
1834–1835 to 1841–1842	7	1834 to 1838–1839	4
1841–1842 to 1849–1850	8	1838–1839 to 1847	9
1849–1850 to 1855–1856	6	1847 to 1854	7
1855–1856 to 1858	3	1854 to 1858	4
1858 to 1864–1865	6	1858 to 1862	4
1864–1865 to 1869	5	1862 to 1865	3
1869 to 1878	9	1865 to 1876	11
1878 to 1886–1887	8	1876 to 1881	5
1886–1887 to 1892–1893	6	1881 to 1890	9
1892–1893 to 1899	6	1890 to 1897	7
1899 to 1909	10	1897 to 1903	6
		1903 to 1913–1914	10
Total	104	Total	111

Source: Schumann (1938: 113)

Trek" (in the 1830s), during which thousands of people left the border districts for the interior of the country in an effort to escape British rule. Thus, for most of the nineteenth century (at least until the discovery of minerals), a largely self-sufficient agricultural and barter economy existed in the interior of South Africa. In contrast, although the economy of the Cape Colony was also largely still based on agriculture, production of commodities such as fruit, wheat and wine occurred for the broader market. These products (later including hides, wool and ostrich feathers) were also exported. In addition, rapid banking development took place in the Cape Colony with fairly modern methods of exchange and credit provision existing, contributing to the cyclical evolution of the Cape Colony economy.

The Discovery of Minerals According to Schumann (1938: 31), the outstanding feature of the nineteenth century was the discovery of minerals (diamonds in 1870 and gold in 1886) in South Africa, leading, among others, to an influx of fortune seekers to the interior of the country as well as the rapid expansion of railway lines. This resulted in the sudden and swift transformation of the economy from a largely agricultural one to an agriculture-mineral economy in which the ultra-capitalistic mineral production became of extreme importance, with a market and credit economy suddenly introduced to the interior of the country. In addition, the transformation to a mineral economy greatly strengthened the elements of uncertainty and speculation in the business life of the country, thereby influencing business cycle developments through reinforcing the speculative element in booms and busts.

3 South African Business Cycles: 1910 to 1948

As mentioned in the previous section, apart from the 1806 to 1909 period, Schumann also determined business cycle turning points for the South African economy for the period 1910 to 1936. However, the study of du Plessis (1950) was used here as the primary source of South African business cycles between 1910 and 1948. While du Plessis used the work of Schumann as a starting point, he nevertheless extended the period covered by Schumann, had a wider variety of statistical time series at his disposal and applied a different methodology to Schumann. In addition, du Plessis made use of monthly data, whereas Schumann only had annual data at his disposal. The aim of du Plessis' (1950: 17) study was to present a statistical description of the major economic fluctuations in South Africa since 1910, with special reference to business cycles, the main purpose being to establish a pattern of "reference cycles" (as described by Burns and Mitchell 1946: 24) for the economy over the period 1910 to 1948. The starting point was chosen as 1910, since the unification of South Africa in that year marked the beginning of a new historical, political and economic phase in the development of the country (du Plessis 1950: 10).

3.1 Methodology Applied

Du Plessis made use of 16 monthly time series (not all of them available over the full period) in determining reference turning points in the South African business cycle. These included indicators such as imports, industrial share prices, railway statistics, monetary statistics, transfer duty, coal sales, retail prices, building plans passed, employment, new motor vehicle and company registrations, cement production and insolvencies. The methodology employed by du Plessis (1950: 43–47) involved seasonally adjusting each time series (where appropriate), smoothing the time series with a 31-term weighted moving average and removing the long-term trend (determined for the period 1910 to 1940) from the time series.[1] The resultant cyclical component of each time series was then standardized by dividing the smoothed cyclical fluctuation of each series by its standard deviation, thereby putting the cyclical fluctuations of the various time series on a comparable basis. Monthly averages of the standardized cyclical fluctuations of all available time series were calculated to obtain a "composite" cyclical fluctuation series, which was used,

[1]Note that du Plessis implicitly moved from the concept of *classical business cycles* to the concept of *growth cycles*. Since then, this approach became traditional for South Africa.

together with the individual indicators, to date the final reference turning points in the South African business cycle.

It should be noted that du Plessis (1950: 47) treated the period after the start of World War II, i.e. 1939 to 1948, slightly differently than the earlier period. On account of the rapid structural changes and dislocations caused by the war, he decided not to eliminate the long-term trend of the data during this period. In addition, du Plessis viewed this full 10-year period as a period of cyclical upswing, thus representing only half a cycle. He therefore calculated a separate composite cyclical fluctuation series, standardized to 1939, for the period 1939 to 1948.

Du Plessis observed a clear pattern of cyclical movement in the individual series studied and in the composite cyclical indicators, as well as a high degree of co-movement between these indicators, particularly for major cycles. In fixing the final reference turning points in the South African business cycle, du Plessis took the turning points suggested by Schumann (1938: 248) as a starting point and adjusted them where the outcome of his analysis differed from that of Schumann. Table 3 presents the final business cycle turning point dates determined by du Plessis, including the duration of each phase (in months).

3.2 *Major Cyclical Drivers*

Du Plessis (1950: 19) stated that the nature and distinguishing characteristics of economic cycles are largely determined by the socio-economic structure in which they occur. As such, when measuring and analysing business cycles, cognizance should be taken of the basic structure of an economy, as well as to changes in that structure occasioned by internal or external forces or events. In this regard, du Plessis identified a number of structural aspects of the South African economy that influenced cyclical fluctuations during the period 1910 to 1948.

Urbanization While population growth appeared to taper off somewhat during the period under review, evidence exists of an exceptionally high rate of urbanization in South Africa since 1921.

Industrialization The contribution of manufacturing to the national income rose from 6.8% in 1911–1912 to 22.4% in 1948–1949, while that of mining declined from 27.5% to 10.7% over the same period. Since gold mining in particular had a stabilizing effect on the South African economy, these developments tended to make the economy more susceptible to cyclical fluctuations (du Plessis 1950: 22). In addition, the rapid development of the manufacturing industry caused real income per capita to grow briskly during the period under review.

Income Distribution Du Plessis found evidence that the distribution of income in South Africa became marginally more equal after World War I, possibly lessening the intensity of cyclical swings somewhat.

Table 3 Business cycles in South Africa, 1910–1948

Phases		Duration (months)
1910–May 1912: Major upward swing		**29**
Jan 1910–Feb 1911	Prosperity	14
Feb 1911–May 1911	Recession	3
May 1911–May 1912	Revival	12
May 1912–Oct 1914: Major downward swing		**29**
May 1912–Jun 1913	Recession	13
Jun 1913–Sept 1913	Revival	3
Sept 1913–Oct 1914	Recession	13
Oct 1914–Jun 1920: Major upward swing		**68**
Oct 1914–Jun 1916	Revival	20
Jun 1916–May 1917	Recession	11
May 1917–Jul 1918	Revival	14
Jul 1918–Oct 1918	Recession	3
Oct 1918–Jun 1920	Revival	20
Jun 1920–Mar 1922: Major downward swing		**21**
Mar 1922–Aug 1929: Major upward swing		**89**
Mar 1922–Jan 1924	Revival	22
Jan 1924–Sept 1924	Recession	8
Sept 1924–Mar 1926	Revival	18
Mar 1926–Aug 1927	Recession	17
Aug 1927–Feb 1928	Revival	6
Feb 1928–Feb 1929	Recession	12
Feb 1929–Aug 1929	Revival	6
Aug 1929–Jul 1932: Major downward swing		**35**
Aug 1929–Mar 1931	Recession	19
Mar 1931–May 1931	Revival	2
May 1931–Jul 1932	Recession	14
Jul 1932–Apr 1937: Major upward swing		**57**
Jul 1932–Aug 1934	Revival	25
Aug 1934–Feb 1935	Recession	6
Feb 1935–Apr 1937	Revival	26
Apr 1937–Oct 1939: Major downward swing		**30**
Apr 1937–Apr 1938	Recession	12
Apr 1938–Aug 1938	Revival	4
Aug 1938–Oct 1939	Recession	14
Average major phases, 1910–Oct 1939		**44.8**
Average minor phases, 1910–Oct 1939		**12.8**
Oct 1939–Nov 1948: Upward swing		**109**
Oct 1939–Oct 1941	Revival	24
Oct 1941–Jan 1943	Recession	15
Jan 1943–Jan 1945	Revival	24
Jan 1945–May 1945	Recession	4

(continued)

Table 3 (continued)

Phases		Duration (months)
May 1945–Oct 1946	Revival	17
Oct 1946–Feb 1947	Recession	4
Feb 1947–Nov 1948	Revival	21
Average minor phases, Oct 1939–Nov 1939		**15.6**

Source: Du Plessis (1950: 50–51)

The Composition of Exports and Imports The South African economy was very open, i.e. it depended greatly on international trade in goods and services. Whereas gold exports (accounting for almost 70% of total exports between 1935 and 1939) tended to reduce cyclical fluctuations in the economy, the exportation of other products (such as diamonds and wool) coupled with increased importation of capital goods enhanced the cyclical sensitivity of the South African economy (du Plessis 1950: 25).

External Factors The period under review contained a number of external factors, in particular the two World Wars that contributed greatly to increasing the scope, intensity and amplitude of economic fluctuations in South Africa. In addition, the devaluation of the currency (the South African pound at the time) during the Great Depression of 1929–1933 greatly aided the subsequent upswing of 1933.

3.3 Business Cycle Characteristics

Du Plessis (1950: 47) noted that by inspecting graphs of his 16 smoothed time series as well as his composite series, a clear distinction could be made between major and minor cycles, with the major cycles being longer in duration and exhibiting larger amplitudes. A greater degree of concurrence in the movement of the major cycles was also visible. In analysing his results (summarized in Table 3), du Plessis noted that for the period 1910 to 1940, the average length of the completed major cycles (couples of upward and downward swings) was about 7½ years (89.6 months) and of the minor cycles (couples of revivals and recessions) slightly over 2 years (25.6 months). The average length of the upswings exceeded that of the downswings for both major and minor cycles; the average length of major upswings and minor revivals were 60.75[2] and 13.7 months, respectively, compared with 28.75 and 11.9 months for major downswings and minor recessions, respectively.

Du Plessis (1950: 55) also compared his South African business cycle turning point dates with those of Great Britain, the USA and France, as determined by the National Bureau of Economic Research (NBER). Interestingly, the South African

[2] The very long major upswing of Oct 1939 to Nov 1948 distorts the average somewhat, but this period was quite unique because of World War II.

major cycles were about twice as long as those in the other countries over the period 1910 to 1940. According to du Plessis, this either suggests that overseas influences were less strongly felt in South Africa than previously assumed or that certain overseas business cycle phases did not generate similar phases in South Africa (spillovers). Du Plessis seemed to favour the latter explanation, on account of the dominant (and stabilizing) role played by the gold-mining industry in South Africa at the time.

4 South African Business Cycles: 1945 to Present

The business cycle turning points discussed in the previous two sections were determined and published as once-off research projects by individual researchers. However, since 1970, the South African Reserve Bank (SARB) has been determining reference turning points in the South African business cycle for the post-World War II period, with the results and methodology applied described in successive articles in the SARB's *Quarterly Bulletin*. This post-war business cycle chronology of reference turning point dates is regularly published in the statistical tables segment of the *Quarterly Bulletin* (currently on page S-157).

The first set of post-war reference peaks and troughs in the business cycle was published by the SARB in 1970 (Smit and van der Walt 1970) and covered the period 1945 to 1968. Although Smit and van der Walt (1970: 21) took the well-known Burns and Mitchell definition of business cycles as their starting point, they determined reference turning points in the South African business cycle in terms of the growth cycle definition of business cycles (like Du Plessis had previously done). Their reference turning points thus represent the fluctuations around the long-term growth trend of aggregate economic activity, which was later confirmed by Venter (2005: 61) when he stated that the SARB's business cycle chronology represents reference turning point dates that distinguish between periods when aggregate economic activity increased by more than its long-term trend (the upward phases) and periods when aggregate economic activity either contracted or increased by less than its long-term growth trend (the downward phases).

4.1 Methodology Applied

In determining reference peak and trough dates for the South African economy, Smit and van der Walt (1970: 22) made use of two methods:

(a) The clustering of turning points of time series (also used by the NBER at the time)
(b) Historic diffusion indices

The clustering of turning points method involved determining the specific turning points in each of an adequately large number of time series representing as many aspects of economic activity as possible. Each time series was first seasonally adjusted and then smoothed by fitting Henderson moving averages (Smit and van der Walt 1970: 24), before the long-term trend was finally removed. The peaks and troughs in the resultant cyclical component of each time series were then identified as local maxima and minima. Concentrations of peaks and troughs at specific points in time were then used as indications of reference turning points.

To calculate a *historic* diffusion index, the specific turning points in the cyclical component of each time series are determined (similar to the clustering of turning points). A series is regarded as increasing for each period subsequent to a trough, up to and including the following peak. Conversely, a series is regarded as decreasing for each period subsequent to a peak, up to and including the following trough. The historic diffusion index value for a particular month is obtained by expressing the number of increasing time series in that month as a percentage of the total number of time series considered. An index value above 50 thus indicates that more than half of the time series considered were increasing in that month, implying that the economy is in a cyclical upswing. Turning points in the historic diffusion index therefore occur when the index passes through the 50% mark. Smit and van der Walt (1970: 26) constructed two different historic diffusion indices, namely, an unweighted diffusion index and a weighted diffusion index. In the case of the weighted historic diffusion index, a diffusion index was first calculated for each economic sector (according to the Standard Industrial Classification of All Economic Activities). The sectoral diffusion indices were then combined into an aggregated diffusion index by weighting them according to each sector's contribution to gross domestic product (GDP).

Smit and van der Walt (1970: 24) applied this methodology to a sample of just over 200 monthly and quarterly economic time series. However, not all of these time series were available for the whole period; for instance, quarterly national accounts statistics for South Africa only became available from 1960. To arrive at final reference turning points, Smit and van der Walt (1970: 28) used the results of the clustering of turning points and the two—weighted and unweighted—diffusion indices in combination with some important individual economic indicators (such as GDP) while also taking cognizance of economic events around possible reference turning point dates.

In a later study, Smit and van der Walt (1982) extended the chronology of reference turning points in the South African business cycle to include the period 1972 to 1981. In addition to extending their analysis to over 300 time series, they also made some changes to their methodology. While they still calculated a weighted historic diffusion index, they no longer used the clustering of turning points method. In addition, they added two new indicators to evaluate the cyclical stance of the economy: a composite index of coincident business cycle indicators (comprising six individual time series)[3] and a weighted *current* diffusion index. The composite coincident business cycle indicator (an indicator that had become fairly widely used internationally since their previous study) for South Africa was developed in

[3]See Chap. 26 on the SARB's composite business cycle indicators for more details.

cooperation with the Centre for International Business Cycle Research in the USA (Smit and van der Walt 1982: 51). The current diffusion index was calculated from the actual changes in a large number of individual time series, with the methodology similar to that of the composite coincident indicator.[4] The current diffusion index is basically an additional composite business cycle indicator but comprising a very large number of time series. For both the composite coincident indicator and the current diffusion index, the deviations from their respective long-term trends were used as indicators of possible reference turning points in the business cycle. In all subsequent studies where additional reference turning points were determined by the SARB, the methodology stayed largely unchanged from that employed in Smit and van der Walt (1982), barring for the number of time series used. Figure 1 depicts the SARB's composite coincident business cycle indicator for South Africa, with the business cycle phases superimposed. Since World War II, the South African economy has experienced 15 complete business cycles (trough to trough), while the upward phase of the 16th cycle has also been dated already. The SARB's post-war business cycle chronology is presented in Table 4. The average length of all the upswings was 32½ months, while the average length of the downward phases was 20½ months.

4.2 Three Subperiods: Major Cyclical and Structural Drivers

The whole post-war period may readily be divided into three fairly distinct eras of almost equal length, each with very unique cyclical and structural characteristics. Figure 2 shows South Africa's annual GDP growth since 1946, with the average growth rates during each era depicted by the solid black lines. Average annual GDP growth more than halved from 4.9% to 2.1% from the first (1946–1970) to the second (1971–1993) era, while picking up to 3.0% in the third (post 1994) era.[5]

It is interesting to note that when analysing these three eras separately, the average length of the upward phases increased during each successive era; from 1945 to 1970, the upward phases averaged 23½ months, and from 1971 to 1993, they averaged 29½ months while averaging 64 months in the post-1994 era (exaggerated somewhat by one exceptionally long 99-month upswing). The average length of the downward phases was quite short during the first (high-growth) era

[4]The words "historic" and "current" do not mean that the correspondent diffusion indices refer to different time periods or represent different vintages of the same indicator. Rather, they were traditionally used to designate two indices calculated with two different methods, as described above; the first method was initially proposed (historic index) and the second (current index) 12 years later. Both indices have consistently been used by the SARB when dating reference turning points in the South African business cycle since 1982.

[5]Somewhat worryingly, however, GDP growth in the most recent 4 years has been below this average and decelerating.

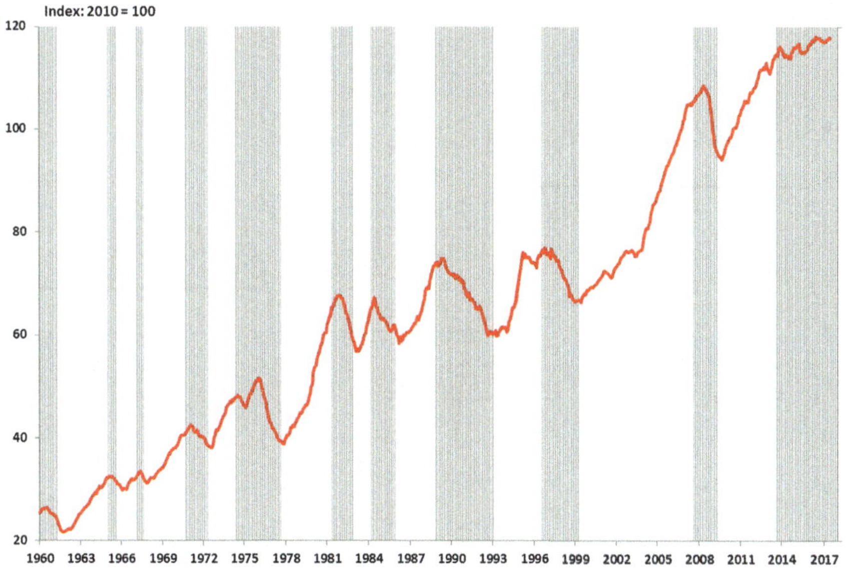

Fig. 1 Composite coincident business cycle indicator for South Africa. Note: Shaded areas indicate downward phases of the business cycle. Source: SARB

Table 4 Business cycles in South Africa: 1945 to present

Upward phase	Duration in months	Downward phase	Duration in months
Post-war–July 1946	19	Aug 1946–Apr 1947	9
May 1947–Nov 1948	19	Dec 1948–Feb 1950	15
Mar 1950–Dec 1951	22	Jan 1952–Mar 1953	15
Apr 1953–Apr 1955	25	May 1955–Sep 1956	17
Oct 1956–Jan 1958	16	Feb 1958–Mar 1959	14
Apr 1959–Apr 1960	13	May 1960–Aug 1961	16
Sep 1961–Apr 1965	44	May 1965–Dec 1965	8
Jan 1966–May 1967	17	Jun 1967–Dec 1967	7
Jan 1968–Dec 1970	36	Jan 1971–Aug 1972	20
Sep 1972–Aug 1974	24	Sep 1974–Dec 1977	40
Jan 1978–Aug 1981	44	Sep 1981–Mar 1983	19
Apr 1983–Jun 1984	15	Jul 1948–Mar 1986	21
Apr 1986–Feb 1989	35	Mar 1989–May 1993	51
Jun 1993–Nov 1996	42	Dec 1996–Aug 1999	33
Sep 1999–Nov 2007	99	Dec 2007–Aug 2009	21
Sep 2009–Nov 2013	51	Dec 2013–	
Average:	**32½**	**Average:**	**20½**
Longest upward phase	**99**	**Longest downward phase**	**51**
Shortest upward phase	**13**	**Shortest downward phase**	**7**

Source: SARB

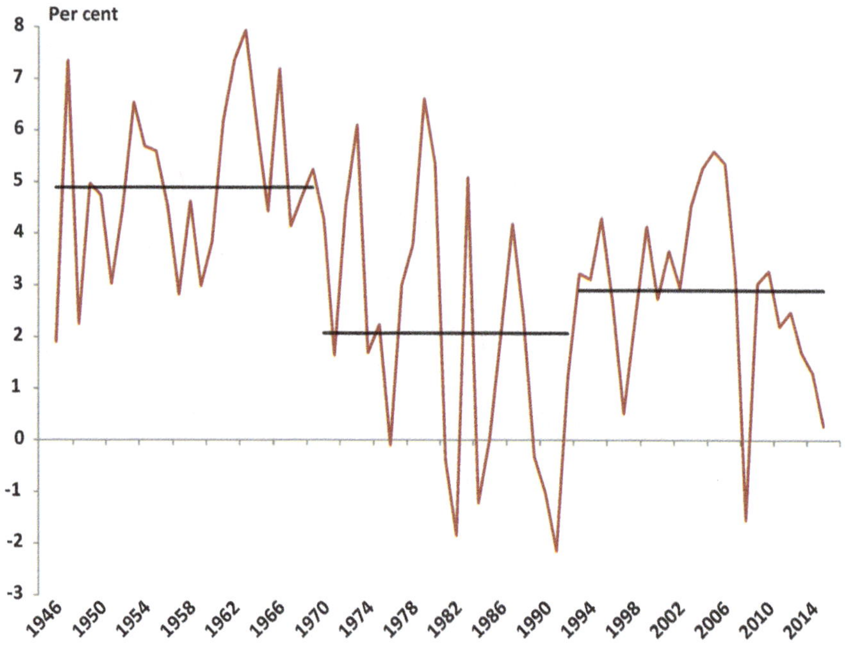

Fig. 2 Annual growth in South Africa's gross domestic product. Sources: Statistics South Africa and own calculations

from 1945 to 1970, averaging only 12½ months. However, the average length of the downward phases more than doubled to 30 months during the next (low-growth, high-inflation) era. Downswings during the subsequent era averaged 27 months, with the most recent one still in progress.

The three time periods and their distinctive features and cyclical drivers will be discussed separately below.

4.2.1 Post-War to 1970: Rapid Growth and Industrialization

The South African economy underwent significant structural change during the first 25 years after World War II, which saw the rapid development and industrialization of the economy. In fact, many of these changes were already underway before World War II. The business cycle was characterized by fairly high rates of real GDP growth being recorded throughout, interrupted only occasionally by short-lived moderations in the growth rate. The numerous strong upswings experienced during this period were frequently ended by the imposition of deliberate restrictive policy measures, often involving various forms of direct controls. Apart for attempting to curb consumer price inflation (which was not a huge problem during this era), the main objective of these controls was largely to alleviate pressure on South Africa's balance of payments, since the structure of the economy was such that virtually all capital goods required for fixed investment and most consumer goods had to be imported. Some of the most important features of this period are discussed in a little more detail below.

Changes in the Economic Structure Rapid industrial expansion was a feature of the South African economy throughout this 25-year period. Although agricultural and gold-mining output continued to expand briskly, their relative contributions to GDP declined due to the marked growth in manufacturing output. The contribution of the agriculture sector in particular fell from more than 17% in 1950 to below 10% by 1970, while that of the manufacturing sector had reached 23% by 1970. Despite being driven mostly by private initiative, government policy was also directed towards accelerating industrial development, particularly via the semipublic Industrial Development Corporation. Growth was particularly rapid in the metals and engineering, the textile and the chemical sectors over this period (Houghton and Dagut 1973: 164).

Despite the rapid industrialization of the South African economy over this period, gold mining remained an important and growing industry, likely contributing to higher economic growth rates and less cyclical volatility over this period. In particular, gold exports were the biggest foreign exchange earner over this period; the contribution of gold exports grew from around 24% of total exports in 1950 to more than 40% in the 1960s. The discovery of new gold fields and the development of deep-level mining led to a renewed mining boom (Smit and van der Walt 1970: 31). An additional fillip was the discovery of uranium in many of the gold mines, which could be recovered at a low marginal cost as a by-product of gold mining (Houghton and Dagut 1973: 164).

The urbanization trend that was established before the war gathered pace during this period. The mechanization of agricultural output reduced the number of people the rural economy could support and accelerated the exodus to the metropolitan areas, where the industrial boom offered ample employment opportunities. As such, employment in manufacturing and construction (located mainly in metropolitan areas) more than doubled (increasing by 140%) from 1945 to 1965 (Houghton and Dagut 1973: 163). The prolonged period of rapid economic expansion caused a serious scarcity of skilled labour, a constraint which was exacerbated during strong boom phases in the business cycle. Yet, an additional binding constraint was introduced in 1956, when the *Industrial Conciliation Act* included a "job reservation" clause whereby certain jobs were to be reserved for employees from specific races (Houghton and Dagut 1973: 201).

Balance of Payments and Other Financial Constraints Another recurring feature of the South African economy was the frequent appearance of deficits on the current account of the balance of payments whenever economic activity and fixed investment grew rapidly. Although exports continued to be dominated largely by gold and agricultural products, the composition of imports moved from the category of final consumer goods to machinery, industrial equipment and raw materials—as the rapid pace of industrialization required large-scale investment (Houghton and Dagut 1973: 163). It is important to note that during the period under review, South Africa followed a fixed exchange rate regime under the Bretton Woods system, with the South African pound on parity with the British pound sterling. In 1961, the

South African pound was replaced by the rand as the official currency, valued at a fixed exchange rate of two rand per pound sterling until 1967.

In order to safeguard the balance of payments during the latter part of boom phases, the fiscal and monetary authorities applied various forms of direct controls during this period (Smit and van der Walt 1970), such as:

- The curtailment of capital expenditure by state institutions
- Foreign exchange restrictions for imports from non-sterling countries
- General control of imports from the sterling area
- Controls over foreign capital
- Requests for business enterprises to reduce inventory levels
- Restrictions on credit for consumption and import purposes
- Restrictions on credit for hire purchases
- The restriction of credit for non-productive purposes
- The imposition of credit ceilings
- Increases in the cash reserve requirement at the central bank for commercial banks
- Notable increases in customs and excise duties (import tariffs)

The effect of these direct controls were usually to lower the economic growth rate, stifle domestic demand and thereby contribute to prematurely end upward phases in the business cycle.

Supply-Side Constraints The rapid pace of economic growth after World War II led to supply-side constraints in the early 1950s, such as insufficient electricity, transport and communication facilities as well as shortages of skilled and unskilled labour. In addition, the fast pace of private-sector development in preceding years resulted in the provision of public services like housing, schools, water and hospitals becoming insufficient to satisfy demand (Smit and van der Walt 1970: 32). The authorities accordingly adopted a policy of consolidation to obtain more balanced growth, such as raising or introducing a wide range of taxes in the 1952 national budget, while monetary policy was also tightened somewhat. As such, the upswing that began in April 1953 was to a large extent driven by an increase in fixed investment in an attempt to correct the supply-side imbalances that had developed.

Political Developments The first major political event that impacted the South African business cycle during this period occurred in 1948; a new coalition government favouring a policy of racial segregation—later known as *apartheid*—was narrowly elected in April 1948. The change in government resulted in increased political uncertainty, exacerbating the downswing that started in December 1948. Nevertheless, despite the government's policy of racial segregation being implemented throughout this period, the South African economy continued to expand briskly throughout the 1950s and 1960s.[6]

[6]The consequences of this policy became evidently negative only from the 1970s after international pressure and sanctions escalated increasingly.

However, as the recovery that commenced in April 1959 was still gaining momentum, political events in March 1960 gave rise to large capital outflows, causing a continuous drain on gold and foreign exchange reserves. On 21 March 1960, the police fired at a group of civilians protesting in the township of Sharpeville against the racially motivated pass laws (which restricted the movements of non-white South Africans), killing 69 people and wounding many more. This incident led to widespread instability, with the government declaring a state of emergency. Following the Sharpeville massacre, South Africa found itself increasingly isolated from the international community. Despite a number of stimulatory concessions announced by the Minister of Finance, business confidence was affected to such an extent that the economy entered another downward phase before the previous upswing had gathered momentum. Growth dipped to almost 3% in 1960, much lower than the average for the 1960s, and since trend-adjusted cycles were measured, this year was recorded as a downward phase (Smit and van der Walt 1970: 35). A general lack of confidence persisted throughout the ensuing downswing, characterized by substantial private capital outflows, declining exports and a reluctance towards capital investment. South Africa's gold and foreign exchange reserves declined notably, and even though the domestic economy required stimulation, the authorities nevertheless applied a number of restrictive measures in order to alleviate pressure on the balance of payments.

4.2.2 1971 to 1993: Political Instability, High Inflation and Low Growth

Throughout the 1970s, 1980s and early 1990s, the South African economy experienced a downward shift in the long-term trend rate of growth due to a combination of global and domestic structural changes (Smit and van der Walt 1982). Laubscher (2003: 3) mentions several authors who identified the period since the mid-1970s as representing an era of international structural change in terms of business cycle analysis. Although Laubscher chose 1973 as the start of this era for South Africa, 1971 is chosen here since the GDP growth rate had already begun trending downwards by then, and the 20-month downward phase that started in January 1971 (the longest post-war downturn at the time) heralded the start of an era of more protracted downward phases in the South African business cycle. According to Smit and Van der Walt (1982: 42), international structural changes already started to occur from 1968 and included, inter alia, the creation of a free gold market and the replacement of the Bretton Woods gold-based system of fixed exchange rates with an inconvertible dollar standard with flexible exchange rates. In addition, following the oil crisis of 1973, unusual strains had developed in international pricing and production processes, such as wages increasing without comparable rises in productivity (Smit and van der Walt 1982: 43). Van der Walt (1989: 33) later added other international developments that influenced South African cyclical developments during the 1980s, namely, the intensity of the 1981–1982 global recession, the international debt crisis of 1982 as well as the rise of protectionism from about 1981 and its impact on world trade.

In South Africa, far-reaching changes were experienced in the social, political and economic spheres over this period, with domestic events and foreign perceptions of these events impinging on the country's international financial and trade relations, affecting business and consumer confidence and propensities to spend, invest and save (van der Walt 1989:33). While output growth merely slowed down during all previous post-war downward phases of the business cycle, South Africa experienced a severe economic contraction in 1976–1977, with many economic indicators registering absolute declines (Smit and van der Walt 1982: 41). Van der Walt and Pretorius (1995: 32) reiterated that business cycle developments in South Africa during the 1980s took place against a steady erosion of the economy's growth potential, reflecting the impact of long-term structural weaknesses as well as some exogenous (non-economic) factors. Some of the most important events and structural changes that impacted cyclical developments during this period are described below.

Changes in the Economic Structure The declining trend in the agricultural sector's contribution to South African output continued over this period; agriculture's contribution almost halved from 1970 to the mid-1990s, when it amounted to roughly 5% of GDP. In addition, rapid mechanization in agriculture contributed to the ongoing trend of urbanization, as better employment opportunities were available in the metropolitan manufacturing and services sectors (Nieuwoudt 1983: 4).

South Africa remained a very open economy, and although gold mining continued to be a prominent feature of the economy throughout most of this period, mining output became increasingly diversified over time. According to Neethling (1983: 42), South Africa was the world's third largest mineral producer in 1980 and was the largest source of gold, platinum and gem diamonds and of the steel and alloy mineral commodities chrome, manganese and vanadium, as well as one of the top three suppliers of coal and uranium in the world at the time. As such, the South African business cycle became increasingly linked to the international commodity price cycle. However, gold exports remained an important foreign exchange earner during the 1970s and 1980s; gold exports as a percentage of total merchandise exports peaked at around 50% in 1980 (aided by a dramatic increase in the gold price) whereafter it declined gradually to less than 30% in the early 1990s.

The rapid pace of industrialization during the 1960s was not sustained beyond the early 1970s (Ratcliffe 1983: 124). Nevertheless, the manufacturing sector's share of GDP increased to around 26% in the early 1980s before stabilizing at roughly 23% during the second half of the 1980s. South African industrial production has tended to be skewed towards the processing of natural resources. As such, large-scale process industries dominated the industrial structure, with the chemical, paper, plastics, rubber, non-metallic minerals, basic metals, metal products and transport equipment industries comprising nearly 60% of total manufacturing output in 1980, while food, beverages and tobacco accounted for just below 20% (Ratcliffe 1983: 125).

Political Developments The South African government's policy of racial segregation had an increasingly adverse effect on the performance of the economy between

1970 and the early 1990s, eventually leading to increased international isolation, economic sanctions and disinvestment from the country by many international firms. Domestically, these events frequently had an adverse impact on business and consumer confidence. Specifically, the political disturbances in 1976[7] and developments in South West Africa (now Namibia) and Zimbabwe enhanced the atmosphere of uncertainty and led to reluctance in consumer and investment expenditure during the prolonged downswing in the mid-1970s (Smit and van der Walt 1982: 47).

The prevailing socio-political unrest and consequent proclamation of a state of emergency in many parts of the country in July 1985 contributed to widespread uncertainty and lack of confidence at the time. Foreign perception of South Africa was dented further when the president delivered his infamous *Rubicon Speech*[8] in August of that year. This was followed by the withdrawal of foreign loans and credit facilities to South Africa, coupled with economic sanctions and an intensified disinvestment campaign (van der Walt 1989: 38).

Apart from severe drought conditions and a global recession, South Africa's longest post-war business cycle downswing (from March 1989 to May 1993) was exacerbated by sporadic internal social unrest and violence in various parts of the country[9] in the run-up to political transformation. Towards the end of 1992 and early in 1993, the escalation in civil unrest and violence, coupled with uncertainties regarding the outcome of political negotiations, caused a marked deterioration in investor confidence (van der Walt and Pretorius 1995: 33).

The Rise of Labour Unions Labour market conditions in South Africa were closely connected to the political dispensation in the country. The government's policy of racial segregation resulted in a labour market that was made up of various non-competing racial groups with very little spatial and occupational mobility (Dekker 1983: 55). Skills levels, occupations and earnings were also largely divided along racial lines, while a shortage of skilled labour continued to exist.

Although White, Asian and Coloured (mixed-race) workers were allowed to organize themselves in labour unions, the government suppressed unionism among African workers throughout the 1950s and 1960s. However, African unions re-emerged in 1972, and by 1976, there were 26 African unions with membership of 120,000 workers, despite the complete rejection of these unions by employers and continued harassment from the state (Dekker 1983: 65). According to Dekker (1983: 65), the change in legislation in 1979 normalized union rights to organize and

[7]On 16 June 1976, a large number of school children protested in Soweto against the use of Afrikaans as the language of instruction in schools. Tragically, many children were shot and killed by the police, leading to further protests and disturbances in other areas of the country, as well as an international outcry.

[8]On 15 August 1985, President P.W. Botha delivered a much anticipated speech in which far-reaching reforms to the government's *apartheid* policy were expected, including the release of Nelson Mandela from prison. In the event, no reforms were announced.

[9]Following the release of Nelson Mandela from prison in February 1990, negotiations began for the political transition from a white minority government to a democratically elected government in April 1994. This period was marred by sporadic social unrest and violence in certain parts of the country, with a civil war narrowly avoided.

bargain collectively for African workers, resulting in an estimated 220,000 African workers being unionized by the end of 1981—150,000 of which were enrolled in independent African unions.

The formation of *The Congress of South African Trade Unions* (COSATU) in December 1985 was a landmark event that united 33 independent African unions under one federation that shaped the development of labour relations in South Africa in subsequent decades. Among COSATU's objectives were non-racialism and the rejection of *apartheid*, which included the participation of workers in the struggle for peace and democracy in South Africa.[10] As a result, disruptive trade union activity became increasingly widespread and aggressive from the second half of the 1980s, progressively impacting output growth and business cycle developments in the South African economy (van der Walt 1989: 33).

Balance of Payments Constraints The South African post-war balance of payment constraint also applied to this era. As stated in Gidlow (1983: 99), economic upswings fairly quickly led to a deficit on the current account of the balance of payments, largely due to a sharp rise in imports and often a levelling off in export growth. Despite net capital inflows, net foreign reserves would usually fall, forcing the authorities to adopt restrictive monetary policies (including direct controls) which would often hasten the onset of the next economic downswing. In fact, Laubscher (2016: 19) shows that swings in real exports and imports (together with fixed investment) have historically been the strongest drivers of the South African business cycle—at least since the mid-1970s. Furthermore, during this era, the gold price was often an important determinant of the extent of the current account surplus or deficit (van der Walt 1989: 37).

The political events in the second half of 1985 (described earlier) and the subsequent withdrawal of foreign loans and credit facilities to South Africa (known as the *debt standstill*), coupled with increased foreign disinvestment, led to large capital outflows and amplified the balance of payment constraint. As a result of the debt standstill agreement, the authorities were forced to suppress economic growth to a rate consistent with a current account surplus in order to meet foreign debt repayments (van der Walt and Pretorius 1995: 32). This had a significant impact on business cycle developments during the second half of the 1980s and the early 1990s, with the average length of downward phases more than doubling during this era compared to the previous era.

Persistent High Inflation Another important feature of this period in South Africa's post-war economic history is the dramatic acceleration and subsequent persistence of consumer price inflation. As shown in Fig. 3, inflation accelerated notably after 1970 and remained elevated until the mid-1990s. In fact, South African consumer price inflation averaged 12.7% between 1971 and 1993, compared to only 3.3% in the

[10]Taken from COSATU's website on 30 March 2016: http://www.cosatu.org.za/show.php?ID=925

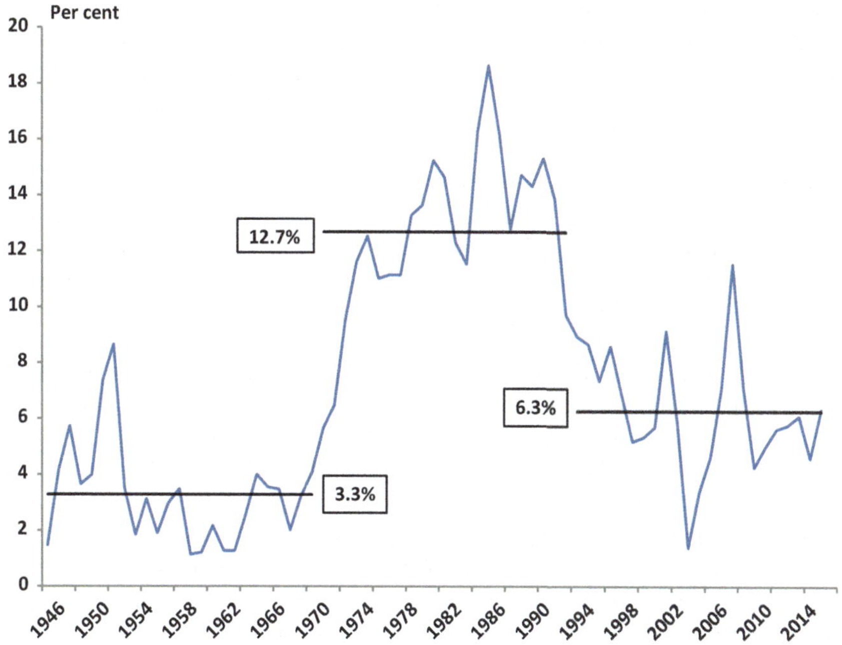

Fig. 3 Annual average consumer price inflation for South Africa. Source: Statistics South Africa and own calculations

preceding era (from 1946 to 1970) and 6.3% in the most recent era (from 1994 to 2016).

Whereas global inflation quickened throughout the 1970s largely on account of the oil price crises, before moderating during the 1980s, it took South Africa much longer to reach single-digit rates of inflation again. Apart from high international crude oil prices in the 1970s, domestic inflation resulted from increased liquidity following large foreign exchange inflows at times when the gold price was very high. In addition, inflationary pressures emanated from rapid growth in private-sector credit extension as well as marked increases in nominal unit labour cost (averaging 15% per annum between 1971 and 1993). Furthermore, following the collapse of the Bretton Woods system, depreciations in the exchange rate of the rand often resulted in additional inflationary pressures. As a result of persistently high inflation, as well as the balance of payments constraints described earlier, domestic short-term interest rates had to remain fairly elevated throughout this period, adversely affecting output growth and prolonging downward phases in the business cycle.

4.2.3 1994 to 2016: Democracy and International Reintegration

A new democratic era dawned in South Africa when the first all-inclusive elections were held on 27 April 1994. This was the most significant political event that occurred during this era, lifting the growth potential of the economy from that of the 1970s and 1980s (at least until recently), as South Africa became reintegrated into the global economy and once more gained representation in international institutions. The most important cyclical and structural drivers that impacted the economy during this period are briefly discussed below.

Structural Changes One of the most important structural changes in the South African economy during this era was the removal of international trade and financial sanctions following the advent of democracy, leading to the opening up of new export markets, improved financial stability and the gradual relaxation of exchange controls which facilitated easier cross-border movements of capital (Pretorius et al. 1999: 40).

Another important structural change was the continued diversification of South African exports, not just away from gold (the contribution of gold exports to total exports declined further from around 25% in 1994 to below 7% in 2015) but also geographically. Whereas South African exports were previously destined primarily for advanced economies, the contribution of exports to other African countries and emerging markets, in particular China and India, increased notably over this period. The contribution of exports to China, for instance, rose from less than 1% in 1994 to more than 14% in 2013. The increased contribution of exports to these countries assisted the initial export-led recovery in the South African business cycle after the global financial crisis (Venter 2011: 66).

The contribution of agriculture to GDP continued to decline throughout this period, amounting to less than 3% in 2015. Likewise, the contribution of the manufacturing sector to GDP declined gradually throughout this period, from around 20% in 1994 to less than 14% in 2015, as rapidly rising labour cost, increased global competition, supply-side constraints and barriers to entry prevented a more rapid expansion of the South African manufacturing sector. Conversely, the contribution of the tertiary sector of the economy to GDP kept rising steadily over this period, from about 60% in 1994 to 69% in 2015.

The South African mining sector's contribution to GDP initially continued to fall to below 6% in 2001, before rising to above 9% in 2008, as the sector's fortunes became increasingly linked to the international commodity price cycle. Although mining output increased initially, the South African mining sector failed to capitalize fully from the marked rise in international commodity prices between 2006 and 2008 (Venter 2009: 67). In the years following the global financial crisis, the contribution of mining output to GDP receded again, as falling international mining commodity prices and domestic supply-side constraints adversely affected the sector.

Inflation Targeting The South African Reserve Bank has applied different monetary policy frameworks over time, such as credit ceilings and credit controls in the 1960s and 1970s, money supply growth targets from the mid-1980s, money supply growth guidelines in the early 1990s and an eclectic monetary policy framework from the mid-1990s (van der Merwe 2004: 1). Although considerable progress was made in reducing inflation during the early 1990s (see Fig. 3), South Africa nevertheless officially adopted an inflation targeting framework from February 2000. The initial target variable was the annual average headline consumer price index (CPI) inflation excluding interest rates on mortgage bonds, with the target range set at between 3% and 6% for the years 2002 and 2003. The liberalization of the South African financial system in the early 1990s led to an increased decoupling of money supply and credit growth outcomes and that of inflation. At times, this created uncertainty about the monetary policy stance adopted by the central bank. Apart from greater transparency, formal inflation targeting had the added benefits of improved co-ordination between monetary and fiscal policy, improved monetary policy discipline and central bank accountability, as well as affecting inflation expectations. The target has since been changed to the monthly year-on-year change in headline CPI having to be within the 3% to 6% range. Inflation targeting has been fairly successfully implemented in South Africa, with headline CPI inflation largely remaining within the target range since its introduction, except for a few brief breaches related to international oil and food price shocks as well as exchange rate shocks. This has improved the SARB's credibility, anchored inflation expectations and aided planning and decision-making by economic agents.

Global Shocks Following South Africa's transition to democracy, the country was reintegrated with international trade and financial markets in the early 1990s and was subsequently evaluated together with other emerging market economies. This, coupled with the very open nature of the economy, has at times made the country susceptible to large currency fluctuations—often related to global economic developments and policy measures, as well as developments on international commodity markets. Large exchange rate fluctuations have often had a material impact on consumer price inflation due to South Africa's high import penetration ratio, while also affecting the international competitiveness of exporters (Venter 2009: 66). In addition, the high degree of volatility in the exchange rate of the rand increased uncertainty and complicated the planning of importers and exporters in the economy.

An example of an international event adversely impacting South African financial markets due to South Africa being grouped with other emerging markets was the Asian financial crises of the late 1990s. While it initially seemed that South Africa's economic growth prospects would not be disrupted, the second round of Asian financial market turmoil in May 1998 did transmit to domestic financial markets, resulting in large capital outflows and a marked depreciation in the exchange rate of the rand. Interest rates were increased sharply, delaying the economic recovery and prolonging the downward phase in the business cycle (Venter and Pretorius 2001: 68).

Another global shock that had a huge impact on the domestic business cycle was the global financial crisis of 2008 and its aftermath. The South African financial system held up well during the crisis, as domestic banks remained well capitalized and the domestic money market kept functioning normally without any liquidity flow disruptions, largely due to prudent banking supervision and some remaining exchange control regulations. However, as a commodity-exporting country, the global financial crisis was transmitted to the domestic real economy via plummeting export demand and commodity prices, as well as a huge loss of business and consumer confidence (Venter 2011: 65). In the aftermath of the global financial crisis, global liquidity increased notably following the prolonged period of historically low interest rates and unconventional monetary policies pursued by central banks in advanced economies. This led to increased short-term capital inflows to emerging markets, including South Africa, which resulted in rising asset prices, currency appreciation and financial volatility. However, according to Laubscher (2016: 19), these capital inflows amply financed South Africa's current account deficit, contributing to the longevity of the most recent upward phase in the business cycle.

Supply-Side Constraints Largely due to ageing infrastructure and delays in investing in new power plants, the South African economy became subject to intermittent electricity supply disruptions from the first quarter of 2008 onwards, leading to increased volatility in output growth from the electricity-intensive mining and manufacturing sectors (Venter 2011: 65). In particular, the rapidly escalating cost (to finance new generating capacity) and deteriorating reliability of electricity supply became a serious constraint during the upswing that followed the global financial crisis and contributed significantly to lowering the economy's growth potential in recent years (Venter 2016: 107).

Labour market developments also became an increasingly important supply-side constraint throughout this period. South Africa's official unemployment rate has remained quite high throughout this era, while being largely of a structural nature rather than cyclical. In fact, despite some cyclical fluctuation, the official unemployment rate has increased from 16.9% in 1995 to around 25% in 2015. Part of the reason for the high unemployment rate is the mismatch between the large supply of unskilled labour, while the economy has increasingly been demanding more skilled labour. However, despite the high level of unemployment, wage growth has often exceeded inflation without a concomitant improvement in productivity, leading to excessive increases in unit labour costs. This has contributed to inflationary pressures in the South African economy, while hampering formal-sector employment growth. The rise in labour union membership through the 1980s and 1990s, the historical connection of the labour union movement to the struggle for democracy, the highly unequal distribution of income (between the skilled and unskilled), the collective wage bargaining system and the relatively progressive nature of labour legislation in South Africa (after 1994) all contributed to this situation. In particular, the upswing that commenced in September 2009 was characterized by a notable deterioration in the labour relations environment. Increased incidents of protracted and disruptive labour strikes affected a number of sectors in the economy, in particular the mining sector, between 2011 and 2014 and led to lower output growth, increased output volatility and contributed to the demise of the upswing (Venter 2016: 109).

The Balance of Payments Due to South Africa's high propensity to import durable consumer goods and capital goods in particular, the balance on the current account of the balance of payments often reverted to a deficit during business cycle upswings, as during the previous eras. However, following the normalization of financial relations between South Africa and the rest of the world in the early 1990s, this did not restrict economic growth to the same extent as before, due to the prevalence of net capital inflows (Pretorius et al. 1999: 41). Nevertheless, the balance on the current account of the balance of payments remained highly connected to the international commodity price cycle and the domestic business cycle.

Public-Sector Expansion and Fiscal Policy Throughout the post-1994 era, fiscal policy generally remained supportive of economic growth, often in a counter-cyclical way, interrupted only by a few brief periods of fiscal consolidation to redress macroeconomic imbalances, such as during the latter half of the 1990s (Venter and Pretorius 2001: 67). A strong focus on improving the efficiency of tax collection enabled fiscal policy to gradually become more expansionary, with the aim of improving social service delivery and of dramatically extending the social safety net in the form of various grants (Venter 2009: 66). High growth rates in government consumption expenditure were maintained even during the severe downswing that accompanied the global financial crisis (Venter 2011: 65). In addition, after initially reducing employment numbers, the government increased its staff complement markedly throughout the latter part of this period, with formal public-sector employment increasing from around 1.61 million at the end of 2001 to around 2.22 million at the end of 2015.

However, the dramatic rise in social grant recipients (from around 4 million in 1994 to almost 17 million in 2015) and strong growth in the public-sector wage bill, coupled with weak output growth after the global financial crisis, forced the government to embark on a path of fiscal consolidation, leading to a less expansionary fiscal policy stance during the most recent business cycle downswing that commenced in December 2013 (Venter 2016: 109).

5 Conclusion

South Africa has a more than 200-year documented history of business cycle measurement, quite a lengthy period for a developing economy. Despite different methodologies having been applied over time, the researchers involved in business cycle measurement in South Africa all noted a high degree of correlation of cyclical movement in the respective statistical time series. From 1910 onwards, South African business cycles have been measured according to the growth cycle definition of business cycle, i.e. trend-adjusted cycles.

Throughout the 1800s, South African business cycles lasted 6.5 years on average. The average length increased somewhat to 7.5 years between 1910 and 1940. After World War II, South African business cycles were initially much shorter, lasting between 2 and 4 years until the end of the 1960s. Subsequently, the duration of business cycles increased gradually to between 5 and 10 years. Over this period, both upswings and downswings became longer.

The cyclical time path of the economy has been greatly influenced by various external and socio-political factors, while the structure of the South African economy has changed dramatically over time. In the 1800s, structural changes such as the migration of a large part of the population from the coastal areas to the interior of the country as well as the discovery of minerals had a huge impact on the development of and cyclical fluctuations in the economy. During the first half of the 1900s, the South African economy was characterized by rapid urbanization and industrialization as well as a high degree of openness, with most capital and consumer goods being imported. Industrialization accompanied by strong economic growth continued after World War II. However, some supply-side constraints and restrictive policy measures to relieve pressure on the balance of payments occasionally led to slowdowns in the rate of economic expansion.

Since the early 1970s, the South African economy experienced lower and more volatile economic growth. The pace of industrialization slowed, while the diversification of mining production and exports resulted in the South African business cycle increasingly being linked to the global commodity price cycle. Political developments led to increased international sanctions and disinvestment that exacerbated the pressure on the balance of payments (in addition to South Africa's high import penetration ratio), often retarding economic growth and causing longer downswings. Following the advent of democracy in 1994, the sanctions and financial restrictions were lifted. South Africa's exports became more diversified in terms of content as well as destination, while capital inflows allowed the negative current account balance to widen more than what was previously possible.

Historically, the South African business cycle has thus to a large extent been driven by global demand for the country's exports, coupled with the level of international commodity prices, while often being greatly influenced by South Africa's history of recurrent political and social crises. As Laubscher (2016: 17) eloquently summarized, "somewhere between these two realities—the export-driven endogenous momentum and the socio-political shocks (and structural change)—the South African business cycle has been shaped".

References

Burns AF, Mitchell WC (1946) Measuring business cycles. National Bureau of Economic Research, New York

Dekker LD (1983) Aspects of the labour market. In: Matthews J (ed) South Africa in the world economy. McGraw-Hill, Johannesburg, pp 53–95

Du Plessis JC (1950) Economic fluctuations in South Africa, 1910–1949. Bureau for Economic Research, University of Stellenbosch

Gidlow R (1983) Balance of payments trends and economic policies. In: Matthews J (ed) South Africa in the world economy. McGraw-Hill, Johannesburg, pp 97–120

Houghton DH, Dagut J (1973) Source material on the South African economy: 1860–1970, vol 3: 1920–1970. Oxford University Press, Cape Town

Klein PA, Moore GH (1985) Monitoring growth cycles in market-oriented countries: developing and using international economic indicators. Ballinger, Cambridge

Laubscher P (2003) The SA business cycle over the 1990s and current prospects. Economic research note no 3 of 2003. University of Stellenbosch, Bureau for Economic Research

Laubscher P (2016) Salient features of SA's post-2009 business cycle. Economic research note no 1 of 2016. University of Stellenbosch, Bureau for Economic Research

Neethling D (1983) Minerals and energy. In: Matthews J (ed) South Africa in the world economy. McGraw-Hill, Johannesburg, pp 25–51

Nieuwoudt L (1983) Agriculture. In: Matthews J (ed) South Africa in the world economy. McGraw-Hill, Johannesburg, pp 1–24

Pretorius WS, Venter JC, Weideman PJ (1999) Business cycles in South Africa during the period 1993 to 1997. Quarterly bulletin no 211, March 1999. South African Reserve Bank, Pretoria, pp 38–42

Ratcliffe A (1983) Industry: 1980 and beyond. In: Matthews J (ed) South Africa in the world economy. McGraw-Hill, Johannesburg, pp 121–156

Schumann CGW (1938) Structural changes and business cycles in South Africa, 1806–1938. P.S. King, London

Smit DJ, van der Walt BE (1970) Business cycles in South Africa during the post-war period, 1946 to 1968. Quarterly bulletin no 97, September 1970. South African Reserve Bank, Pretoria, pp 21–45

Smit DJ, van der Walt BE (1982) Growth trends and business cycles in the South African economy, 1972 to 1981. Quarterly bulletin no 144, June 1982. South African Reserve Bank, Pretoria, pp 41–57

van der Merwe EJ (2004) Inflation targeting in South Africa. Occasion paper no 19, July 2004. South African Reserve Bank, Pretoria

van der Walt BE (1989) Business cycles in South Africa during the period 1981 to 1987. Quarterly bulletin no 171, March 1989. South African Reserve Bank, Pretoria, pp 33–42

van der Walt BE, Pretorius WS (1995) Business cycles in South Africa during the period 1986 to 1993. Quarterly bulletin no 195, March 1995. South African Reserve Bank, Pretoria, pp 30–38

Venter JC (2005) Reference turning points in the South African business cycle: recent developments. Quarterly bulletin no 237, September 2005. South African Reserve Bank, Pretoria, pp 61–70

Venter JC (2009) Business cycles in South Africa during the period 1999 to 2007. Quarterly bulletin no 253, September 2009. South African Reserve Bank, Pretoria, pp 61–69

Venter JC (2011) Business cycles in South Africa during the period 2007 to 2009. Quarterly bulletin no 260, June 2011. South African Reserve Bank, Pretoria, pp 61–66

Venter JC (2016) Business cycles in South Africa from 2009 to 2013. Quarterly bulletin no 279, March 2016. South African Reserve Bank, Pretoria, pp 102–112

Venter JC, Pretorius WS (2001) A note on the business cycle in South Africa during the period 1997 to 1999. Quarterly bulletin no 221, September 2001. South African Reserve Bank, Pretoria, pp 63–69

Part III
Business Tendency Surveys (BTSs) in BRICS

International Tradition of Tendency Surveys

Aloisio Campelo Jr

Today Economic Tendency Surveys are considered as part of the core economic statistics for a large group of countries. Based on its conformity with growth cycles these statistics have been widely used by Central Banks and market analysts in *nowcasting* and short-term *forecasting*. They also contain information not found in other statistics, mostly related to the psychological elements that influence firms' and consumers' expectations.

In Europe, some of the pioneers in this kind of statistics are still relevant players today: the German private *Think Tank* Ifo Institute and the French National Statistical Office (INSEE). The German case reportedly grew out of the necessity for producing relatively cheap statistics to serve as guidance in an economy being restructured after World War II (Nerb 2007). Another reported reason for this endeavour was to obtain information not available elsewhere such as production and investment plans, the level of stocks of finished goods and the level of capacity utilisation for different industrial sectors (Strigel 1990).

The use of this type of statistical data in monitoring and anticipating economic trends had its relevance soon recognised in these countries and across Europe. In 1961, the European Commission launched a harmonisation programme that focused on manufacturing surveys. In 1996, this same project was multiplied by five when the Commission relaunched the programme in its 13 countries (28 today) now comprised of five harmonised surveys: manufacturing, services, trade, construction and consumer.

Meanwhile, in the USA, George Katona's research in behavioural economics at the University of Michigan during the 1940s ended up with the consideration that theoretical hypotheses would be better tested with actual data representing consumer's evaluations and expectations. The relevance of expectations had a long

A. Campelo Jr (✉)
Instituto Brasileiro de Economia, Fundação Getulio Vargas, Rio de Janeiro, Brazil
e-mail: Aloisio.Campelo@fgv.br

S. Smirnov et al. (eds.), *Business Cycles in BRICS*, Societies and Political Orders in Transition, https://doi.org/10.1007/978-3-319-90017-9_11

history in economic theory and recently had been reemphasised by Lord Keynes (Keynes 1936). But Keynes paid more attention to business expectations and its relation with investment or hiring decisions. According to Richard Curtin (1984), it was "Katona who first recognized and documented the role played by the consumer sector in determining the aggregate course of the economy" (for more on this topic, see Katona 1975).

As developed capitalist economies advanced towards the twenty-first century, academic literature aimed at understanding the drivers of consumer's spending and saving decisions increased. Acemoglu and Scott (1994) claimed that periods of economic uncertainty were usually associated with greater consumer confidence volatility and a drop in household consumption, once controlled for other potential drivers of consumption. Some years later, Bram and Ludvigson (1998) stated that the relationship between consumer confidence and household consumption expenditures had already been widely analysed in economic literature but was generally inconclusive.

Today the persistent popularity of consumer confidence as an indicator of current and short-term future economic conditions may be considered as a sign that this type of statistics might be useful in anticipating economic trends. On the academic side, it has also been a recurring theme specially since Carroll et al. (1994) showed that before the 1990–1991 US recession, consumer confidence was the only widely known economic indicator presenting a great decline. Textbooks such as Blanchard's *Macroeconomics* (2011) help sustaining this perception with discussions and evidences.

1 Economic Tendency Surveys' Uses and Characteristics

Economic Tendency Surveys (ETS) are known for producing fast-released statistics that help monitoring and anticipating economic trends. Among their recognisable qualities are:

1. Timeliness: data are published with a significant lead on quantitative data.
2. Low volatility.
3. No need for revisions.
4. Conformity with the cycle: ETS variables present a good performance in tracking the cyclical behaviour of quantitative statistics with a specially good performance at turning points.
5. Being a relevant source of historical data related to expectations, ETS provide statistical information not supplied by other economic statistics (for this last feature, see Amstad and Etter 2000).

Some sources do consider timeliness as the single most important characteristic of tendency surveys (UNSD 2014). Questionnaires are designed to be answered quickly without resourcing to accounting records or any outside references. Results are quickly computed and commonly released during the same month of data collection. Also as statistics that capture respondents' sentiment over a certain period of time, no revisions are required (or even recommended) for the original data.

Based on its conformity with growth cycles, ETS have been widely used by central banks and market analysts in *nowcasting* and *short-term forecasting* (Giannone et al. 2009). Regarding turning point detection, an empirical evidence of the efficiency of tendency survey indicators can be confirmed by its extensive inclusion as components in composite leading indicators. For instance, in March, 2016, the OECD's system of composite leading indicators (CLIs) for 39 countries included 245 component series, from which 91 (37%) originated from tendency surveys, 63 (26%) were financial indicators such as stock market indices or interest rates and the remaining 37% were other types of statistics.

The reasons behind the lower volatility generally found in tendency survey indicators when compared to quantitative economic statistics are disputable, but it might have relation with question formatting and the nature of qualitative economic information. The benefits from lower volatility are clearer and undeniable though: it makes the task of identifying turning points in the cycles much easier.

At last, tendency surveys contain information not found in other surveys because its indicators capture economic agents' expectations, a type of data that is qualitative in nature and partially subjective, therefore connected to psychological elements not found in other statistics. The nature of this kind of "additional information" might be related to Katona's findings in the 1950s: he assumed that consumer attitudes could not be explained solely by current economic events and were regularly impacted by noneconomic factors such as political crisis and wars. In fact, as Graminho (2015) proposes, the type of statistical information that is left after isolating the ETS data components that are determined by current economic conditions might be the closer we may get from "pure sentiment" or what Keynes called "animal spirits."

References

Acemoglu D, Scott A (1994) Consumer confidence and rational expectations: are agents' beliefs consistent with the theory? Econ J 104(422):1–19

Amstad M, Etter R (2000) A new approach to indicate changes in business cycles in the manufacturing industries using Markov switching models on business survey indicators. In: Economic surveys and data analysis, CIRET conference proceedings. OECD, Paris, pp 283–305

Blanchard O (2011) Chapter 3: The goods market. In: Macroeconomics, 5th edn. Pearson, Boston

Bram J, Ludvigson SC (1998) Does consumer confidence forecast household expenditure? A sentiment index horse race. Fed Reserv Bank NY Econ Policy Rev 4:59–78

Carroll C, Fuhrer J, Wilcox D (1994) Does consumer sentiment forecast household spending? If so, why? Am Econ Rev 84:1397–1408

Curtin RT (1984) Consumer attitudes for forecasting. In: Kinnear TC (ed) NA–Advances in consumer research, vol 11. Association for Consumer Research, Provo, UT

Giannone D, Reichlin L, Simonelli S (2009) Nowcasting euro area economic activity in real time: the role of confidence indicators. Natl Inst Econ Rev 210(1):90–97

Graminho FM (2015) Sentimento e Macroeconomia: uma análise dos índices de confiança no Brasil, Brazilian Central Bank, trabalhos para discussão, 408, November, 2015

Katona G (1975) Psychological economics. Elsevier Scientific, New York
Keynes JM (1936) The general theory of employment, interest and money. Macmillan Cambridge University Press, London
Nerb G (2007) The importance of representative surveys of enterprises for empirically oriented business cycle research. In: Goldrian G (ed) Handbook of survey-based business cycle analysis. Edward Elgar, Cheltenham
Strigel WH (1990) Business cycle surveys: a new quality in economic statistics. In: Moore GH (ed) Analyzing modern business cycles: essays honoring. ME Sharpe, London
UNSD (2014) Handbook on economic tendency surveys. Draft. United Nations Statistics Division, New York

Economic Tendency Surveys in Brazil: Main Features and Uses

Aloisio Campelo Jr

Business cycles, even if less of a threat, are far from conquered and still represent the most serious form of macroeconomic instability
(Zarnowitz 2004)

1 A Short History of Economic Tendency Surveys (ETS) in Brazil

The first economic tendency survey implemented in Brazil was the *Quarterly Manufacturing Survey*, (QMS), created in 1966 and maintained since then by the Getulio Vargas Foundation (FGV).[1] The April 1967 edition of *Conjuntura Econômica* magazine stated that "in October 1966, FGV launched a new survey aiming at generating indicators to monitor recent developments and expectations for the near future in the manufacturing industry". When the QMS was created, the country still lacked reliable sectoral information on a higher frequency than annual GDP.[2]

A document produced by the United Nations Economic Commission for Latin America and the Caribbean (Gallardo and Pedersen 2008) classifies FGV's QMS as the first continuous tendency survey in Latin America. The survey methodology was

The author wishes to thank Rodolpho Guedon Tobler for producing graphs and tables for this article and Ana Flavia de Paula for helping with the bibliographical references.

[1]FGV is a higher education institution in social sciences and a think tank created in 1944.

[2]The National Statistical Office launched its monthly industrial physical production statistics in 1968.

A. Campelo Jr (✉)
Instituto Brasileiro de Economia, Fundação Getulio Vargas, Rio de Janeiro, Brazil
e-mail: Aloisio.Campelo@fgv.br

S. Smirnov et al. (eds.), *Business Cycles in BRICS*, Societies and Political Orders in Transition, https://doi.org/10.1007/978-3-319-90017-9_12

inspired mainly by the French and German Surveys.[3] Perhaps for this early European connection, a document produced by the OECD (Tosseto and Gyomai 2009) mentions that 10 out of 11 regular questions from the current QMS questionnaire are comparable to the *Joint Harmonised European Union Manufacturing Survey (see also EC* 2016*).*

After an auspicious start, the hard times faced by Brazil during the 1980s and 1990s (debt crisis and hyperinflation) limited resources available for keeping up with the scope and frequency that marked the next stage of tendency surveys at the international level. In the 2000s, the convergence to the best practices that were being championed by OECD and the European Commission accelerated. In 2005, the manufacturing survey turned into monthly frequency, and the consumer monthly survey was implemented. In 2008, the services survey was created and, in 2010, the trade and construction surveys.[4]

2 Brazilian Programme of Tendency Surveys: Methodological Features[5]

FGV's Programme of Tendency Surveys (from now on the Brazilian Programme) is comprised of four business and one consumer regular monthly surveys that share among them many methodological and publishing features.

First, response options are mostly of qualitative nature with a few exceptions such as the level of capacity utilisation and the consumer's inflation expectations. Questions that focus on the present situation offer answers related to the present level of the respective variable (good/bad, strong/weak) and questions related to the future deal with comparisons (will improve/worsen, will rise/fall).

Qualitative questions are aggregated as proportions of respondents giving a specific answer or in the form of diffusion indicators. At the most disaggregated levels, these indicators are built as the proportion of respondents giving favourable answers *minus* the proportion of respondents giving unfavourable answers plus 100 (a hundred). This implies that the indicators range between 0 and 200 points.

All indicators are aggregated from their original sample stratum to higher levels of aggregation using economic weights in order to form each topic's aggregated indicator (e.g. the Services Sector Business Situation Indicator). These topic indicators are then (1) standardised and aggregated with other indicators to form confidence indices or are (2) seasonally adjusted and then standardised and aggregated with other indicators to form confidence indices.

[3]As described by Julian Chacel, Director of FGV's Brazilian Institute of Economics (IBRE) at the time (Motta 2008 and in an interview with the author).

[4]The implementation of the services, construction and trade surveys was supported by the *Brazilian Central Bank.*

[5]For more information related to FGV's ETS methodological features, please refer to the documents available at IBRE's website at http://portalibre.fgv.br/

There are three types of confidence indices:

1. Confidence index
2. Present situation index
3. Expectations index

The latter two are aggregations of the questions from the confidence index referring to each of the two time frames.

For analytical purposes, the series are seasonally adjusted using X-13 Arima-Seats methodology. Each series is pretested in order to identify the presence of seasonality and the sensibility to nonseasonal events such as moving holidays, working days and leap year. Adjustment to the sensibility to nonseasonal events is made independently from the seasonal procedure.

Results from the Brazil's Programme of Tendency Surveys are published during the same month of data collection.[6] Usually all survey results are published in the last week of the reference month. FGV also publishes separately the results for the Consumer Inflation Expectations question and an aggregation of the four business tendency confidence indicators surveys called business confidence indicator.

2.1 Brazilian Business Tendency Surveys

The *Brazilian Programme of Business Tendency Surveys* covers economic sectors with a growth pattern close to the economy's core cycle: manufacturing, trade, construction and part of the services sector. Table 1 summarises sectoral coverage and sample sizes for each sector.

Sample selection and sample size are determined by stratified random sampling technique. Samples are stratified by size and sector except in the case of the manufacturing survey, which is stratified solely by sectors. In the surveys stratified by the size of firms, data at the firm level in small and medium strata is not weighted, and microdata of large firms is weighted by the firm's total of personnel employed.[7] In manufacturing firm level, weighting scheme is determined by the total of personnel employed. Sector and size level data from all business surveys are aggregated by value added obtained from annual structural surveys produced by the National Statistical Office (IBGE).

Sampling frames are obtained from official business registers also produced by IBGE (CEMPRE) and the Ministry of Labour (RAIS). Part of the information

[6]Exceptionally survey results might be published on the first working day of the following month when a certain month contains too many holidays or a reduced number of working days. In 2015, out of 60 editions (5 surveys, 12 months), only 1 edition/survey was published on the first day of the following month.

[7]The number of employees is log-adjusted in order to limit the maximum amplitude of weighting factors following a methodology established by the Ifo Institute (see Ifo's Handbook of Survey-Based Business Cycle Analysis for more on this procedure).

Table 1 Sectoral coverage and sample sizes from Brazil's business tendency surveys

Sector	Sample Size	Number of sub-sectors	ISIC Code
Manufacturing	1200	68[a]	C
Services[b]	2000	29	H, I, J, M, N
Trade	1200	17	G
Construction	700	11	F

[a]The three-digit CNAE 2.0 stratification is aggregated into the two-digit sector aggregation that is made available for the public

[b]Subsectors not covered (with corresponding ISIC code): financial and insurance activities (K), real estate activities (L), public administration and defence, compulsory social security (O) and education (P)

Table 2 Questions found in the four regular Brazilian monthly business surveys

Item	Targeting	Reference period	Response options
Business situation	Specific products/ services	Present situation	Good, normal, bad
		Next 6 months	Improve, equal, worsen
Demand	Specific products/ services	Present situation	Strong, normal, weak
		Next 3 months	Increase, maintain, decrease
Production/ revenues	Specific products/ services	Next 3 months	Increase, maintain, decrease
People employed	Firm level	Next 3 months	Increase, maintain, decrease
Factors limiting business conditions[a]	Firm level	Present situation	Several response options
Credit	Firm level	Present situation	Easy, normal, difficult

[a]Included on a quarterly basis in the manufacturing survey

obtained from official registers is confirmed with the firms. In 2017, industry classification was based on the Brazilian equivalent to ISIC 2.0 (CNAE 2.0).

Some questions are directed towards the firms as a whole, such as the ones related to employment, capacity utilisation and credit conditions. Others are associated with specific lines of products/services offered by the firm. This procedure provides a more precise picture by identifying lines of products/services that may evolve differently along the cycle. Among this second type of questions are the ones related to demand, revenues/production and business situation.

Table 2 presents topics, time frames and response options from Brazil's business surveys.

The remaining parts of the questionnaires are specific to each sector. In the *Manufacturing* and *Trade* Surveys, there are questions related to stocks of goods.

For the *Manufacturing's* Level of Capacity Utilisation (LCU) question firms are offered 9 (nine) different intervals; the Construction Sector LCU is obtained from a quantitative question; in the services sector LCU is obtained indirectly, in two stages, following a model established in 2011 by the European countries.

2.2 Brazilian Consumer Survey

The Brazilian Consumer Survey targets the population represented by Brazilians over 18 years old living in one of the seven largest cities of the country,[8] a group responsible for 25% of Brazilian GDP and 68% of the GDP from all cities above one million inhabitants.

The survey is based on a random sample of 2100 individuals stratified by income and city of residence, considering four income classes, adding to a total of 28 strata. Stratification is aimed at ensuring an adequate representation of the Brazilian population living in large cities. The absolute sampling error at a confidence interval of 95% is equal to 22%.

Survey participants are chosen proportionally to the contribution of each stratum to total consumption as defined by IBGE's *Household Budget Survey*. The sampling list is based on public telephone registers in those cities; the sampling unit is the subscriber to the fixed or mobile telephone directory, randomly selected within the stratum. Interviews are conducted by telephone using computer-assisted telephone interviewing (CATI) technique.

Most of the questions present five qualitative response options. The only regular quantitative question refers to the consumer's inflation expectations for the next 12 months. Among the main themes are the *household financial situation, the city's economic situation, intentions of buying durables* and *perceptions about the labour market.*

Table 3 presents topics, time frames and response options from Brazil's Consumer Survey.

Inside each stratum replies are aggregated as a simple average of individual responses. The 28 strata are then aggregated at the national level using weights determined by the consumption of the stratum level as a proportion of total consumption in the seven cities.

[8]Recife, Salvador, Brasilia, Belo Horizonte, Rio de Janeiro, São Paulo and Porto Alegre.

Table 3 Selected questions from Brazil's Consumer Survey

Item	Reference period	Response options
Local economic situation	Present situation	Very good, good, normal, bad, very bad
	Next 6 months	Improve a lot, improve a little, remain the same, worsen a little, worsen a Lot
Household financial situation	Present situation	Very good, good, normal, bad, very bad
	Next 6 months	Improve a lot, improve a little, remain the same, worsen a little, worsen a Lot
Purchase of durables	Next 6 months	Increase a lot, increase a little, remain the same, decrease a little, decrease a lot
Finding a job	Present situation	Very easy, easy, normal, difficult, very difficult
	Next 6 months	A lot easier, a little easier, maintain, a little more difficult, a lot more difficult
Household budget equilibrium at the end of month	Present situation	Saving a lot, saving, balanced, getting indebted, getting a lot indebted
Inflation expectations	Next 12 months	Raise a lot, raise a little, stabilise, reduce a little, reduce a lot
	Next 12 months	Quantitative

3 Uses of Tendency Surveys in Brazil

The series obtained from Brazil's tendency surveys that are at least 10 years old have already confirmed their expected cyclical properties. Regarding overall conformity with the cycles, Mello and Figueiredo (2014) compared the predictive power of univariate autoregressive models with similar models that included confidence indices. The results showed that the Industry Confidence Index[9] (ICI) provided relevant information for both *nowcasting* and short-term *forecasting*. Moreover a technical note by the Brazilian Central Bank (2014) showed that a shock imposed to ICI in a VAR ambience had a significant impact on both inflation and the industry's output gap that lasted for several months.

Bittencourt et al. (2016) showed that FGV's consumer confidence indicator (CCI) also adds information to forecasting models of household consumption that include both AR and exogenous components. The same paper estimated well-structured VAR models and tested the dynamic impacts of a shock to confidence on household consumption, through impulse response functions. It found out that the impulse response appears to be significant until three quarters ahead but no longer significant for future periods at the 95% level.

[9]ICI is the confidence indicator related to the manufacturing tendency survey.

Campelo and Issler (2008) showed that the manufacturing survey indicators were among the best leading indicators for industrial activity in Brazil. More recently, FGV and *The Conference Board* partnered in creating coincident (CEI) and leading economic indicators (LEI) for the Brazilian business cycle. Three out of eight series selected as component indicators of the Brazilian LEI are derived from tendency surveys as described by Campelo et al. (2013). On a growth cycle approach, OECD's composite leading indicator for Brazil includes two out of six component series from FGV's manufacturing survey.

ICI shows lower volatility than quantitative indicators such as the industrial production index, a feature that helps when analysts need to identify economic cycle's turning points in real time. This can be exemplified with a measure such as the number of months for cyclical dominance (MCD)[10] from each indicator: one for the ICI and five for the physical production index considering the 20 years from 1995 to 2015. The services and construction confidence indicators show similar low volatility characteristics (MCD of 1 and 2, respectively), whereas the consumer and trade confidence indicators are not so well behaved (3).

Graminho (2015) used Kalman filters to identify a pure sentiment-based indicator extracted from FGV's consumer and manufacturing confidence indices after controlling for macro-based variables. Among some interesting properties from this *animal spirits* indicator is that it added significant information to forecasts of *total GDP* and *household consumption*, respectively, over six months ahead.

For its timeliness and cyclical conformity, there has been growing interest in tendency surveys in Brazil. Over 12 years after the manufacturing survey was turned from quarterly into monthly frequency and after the monthly Consumer Survey was launched, these indicators are among some of the most quoted by the market, press and economic policymakers.

3.1 Specific Uses of Survey Data in Brazil

Although FGV survey methodologies are comparable to the main international references, it is interesting to note some of its idiosyncrasies and specific results.

For a start empirical relations between the three main confidence indicators show a circular causality movement in which the Manufacturing Confidence (ICI) *Granger causes* the Services Index (SCI) which in turn causes the Consumer Confidence (CCI) and finally, this last one Granger causes ICI. The circular relation was described by the Brazilian Central Bank in a technical note (2014) and was reproduced by the author that found similar results. It makes sense when considering the cyclical behaviour of the different sectors: a shock impacting the manufacturing sector might influence the demand for some business-oriented services which in turn

[10]The shortest number of months for which the trend-cycle component of a series always "dominates" its irregularities.

Table 4 Causality relations between present situation and expectations' variables

	Expectations Index (3 and 6-months)	Future Business Situation Indicator (6-months)
Manufacturing	B_2	C_2
Services	C_1	C_1
Trade	B_1	B_1
Construction	C_1	C_1
Aggregated Business	B_2	C_2

Lags chosen by the Schwarz criteria; B_{lag} = Causality in both directions at the 10% level; C_{lag} = Causality from Expectations to Present Situation

can affect the labour market and then consumer confidence. Finally, a CCI rise (fall) may influence a new variation from the ICI. Extending this circular relation to the other confidence indicators (trade and construction) finds no more steps of causality but similar levels or just ambiguous causality relations.

A more consistent relation is found between the present situation and expectations variables from Brazil's tendency surveys. As Table 4 shows, when the traditional Expectations Index is considered, causality is ambiguous in the manufacturing and trade sectors. But when the more specific *Future Business Situation Indicator* is tested against the *present situation indices*, only the trade sector remains in an ambiguous situation. This might be explained by the fact that this latter question refers to a broader time span (six months ahead) than the other questions related to expectations from the questionnaire.

Tendency surveys contain questions related to different time dimensions but also related to different degrees of subjectivity. When firms are asked to evaluate the current level of demand or stocks, their answer tends to reflect some kind of objective reality such as the current level of demand when compared to the same period of the previous year or the current level of stocks when compared to some optimal level. On the other hand, questions related to the more vague concept of "business situation" should be considered as more subjective. Which kind of information is taken into account when firms analyse their business situation? It could be consensual that most firms would consider profitability or revenue growth. But there are so many variables that may affect business over time: exchange and interest rates, tax policies, political issues and so on.

FGV's Consumer Survey gathers differentiated results from questions related to the situation of the economy and household finances. The first type of question generates a more volatile time series, for being very often influenced by political events and the media. The latter appears to collect more objective evaluations throughout time. Even so, the first question presents a clear causal relation when compared to the latter.

In the same direction, although tending to be more subjective, and perhaps for that reason, business situation questions from tendency surveys turn out to be relevant indicators of investment or hiring intentions. Graph 1 shows the *Future Business Situation Indicator* from the manufacturing survey compared to a monthly measure of the gross fixed capital formation (GFCF) produced by FGV. The series are

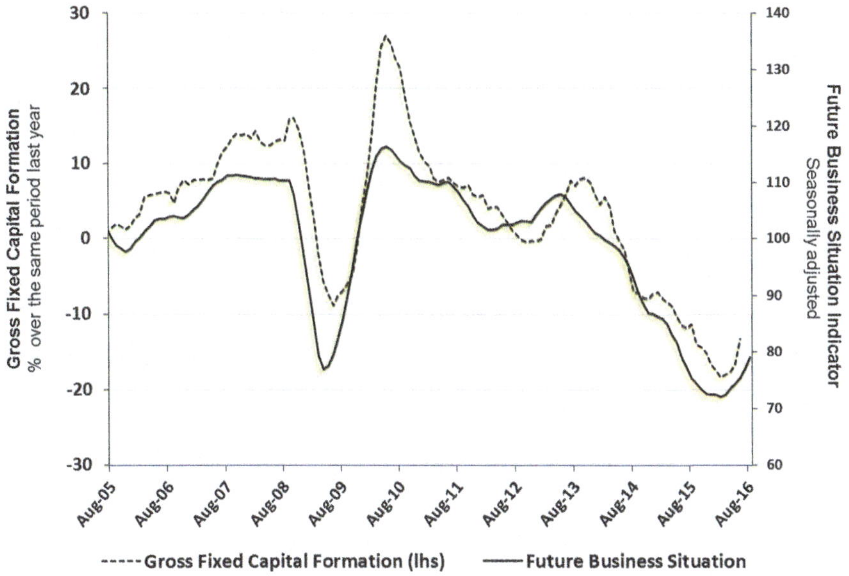

Graph 1 Manufacturing survey future business situation index and investment. Source: FGV/IBGE

expressed in traditional fashion for Tendency Surveys: the survey variable is considered to be stationary by construction and therefore appears in level terms; GDP data is presented in year on year variation form, thus reflecting a type of growth rate cycle.

Considering this set of data, the Survey variable unidirectionally *Granger causes* the quantitative investment data with optimal leads ranging from 2 (Schwarze criteria) to 4 (Akaike). When the test is produced with 3-month moving average series—aiming at reducing losses of compatibility due to the extreme volatility of the GFCF variable—the unidirectional causal relation remains strong with an optimal lead of 6 months. All tests generate P values of zero (0) which means that we reject the null hypothesis that the survey variable does not Granger cause the quantitative variable.

Despite the leading properties of the *Future Business Situation Indicator* series, the actual answers given by firms to this survey topic are far from what one could define as fully rational. The average balance of this question from 2000 to 2015 was 36 points meaning that on average there were 36% more firms saying that future situation would improve than firms stating the opposite. Before 2008, this balance did not become negative even during the two recessions dated by the *Brazilian Business Cycle Dating Committee* in 2001 and 2003. It appears as if the apparently excessive optimism of some firms is compensated by movements in the right cyclical direction, allowing the indicator to provide relevant serial information.

On the other side of the spectrum, questions related to expectations on the number of people employed by the firm returns answers that can be defined as reasonably rational on average. Graph 2 shows that the *future employment indicator* not only

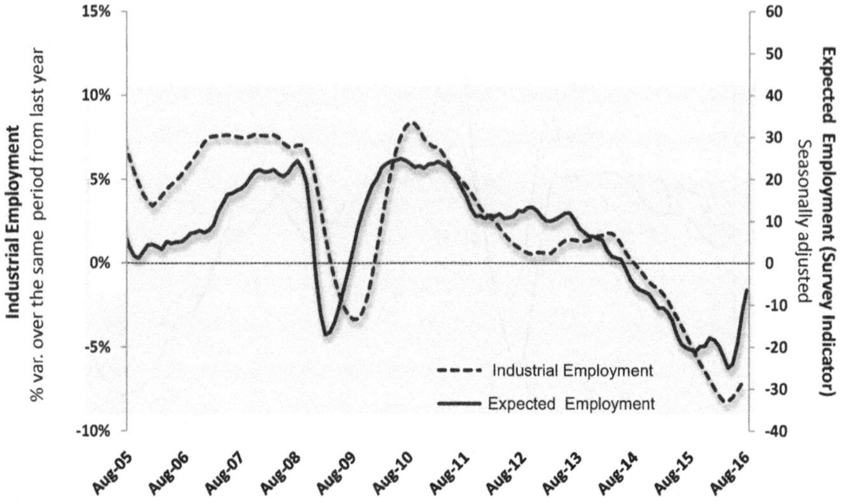

Graph 2 Manufacturing survey future employment indicator and formal employment (*3-month moving averages*). Source: FGV/Ministry of Labour

leads the *Ministry of Labour Formal Employment Indicator*, but it also signals coherently when the sector as a whole will start to dismiss workers or hire again considering the positive or negative balances. This behaviour makes sense considering that when firms answer about the prospects for hiring or firing in the short term many times the decisions about this issue have already been made for the 1–3 following months.

Granger causality tests show that the survey variable leads formal employment in manufacturing with a 2-month lead. Again, if we consider 3-month moving averages, the optimal lead rises to 6 months.

These relations are found to be lasting and stable even if sometimes expectations variables tend to depart temporarily from the quantitative growth variables and become more heavily conducted by pure sentiment or the so-called animal spirits. The graph below shows a relation of ICI and the Manufacturing Physical Production over more than 20 years. Data from 2005 backwards is here disaggregated from quarterly to monthly frequency using Kalman filters.

Without any filtering ICI *Granger causes* physical production with a 3-month lead and a *P* value of 0 (zero). Using a 3-month average as it appears in the graph, the optimal lead rises to 8 months. Thus it seems that by smoothing the highly volatile production indicator, the predictive capabilities of the survey variable increase (Graph 3).

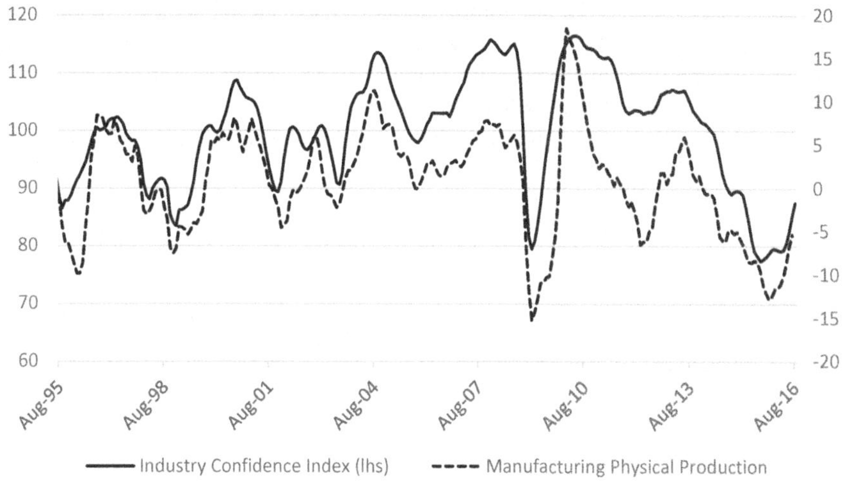

Graph 3 Manufacturing confidence index and manufacturing production *(ICI seasonally adjusted in levels (LHS), physical production, yoy, 3-month moving average)*

3.2 Other Uses of Tendency Surveys in Brazil

Some less common indicators and features from Brazil's system of tendency surveys have proven to be useful in monitoring economic cycles. Lima and Malgarini (2016) have shown that the manufacturing level of capacity utilisation indicator helps in improving prediction of Brazilian output gap in real time. Bezerra and Malgarini (2016) showed that a micro-based new measure of noninflationary rate of capacity utilisation performed well as an indicator of inflationary pressures in a Phillips curve framework. Campelo et al. (2012) have shown the leading properties of business employment expectations and the coincident properties of the consumer's labour market assessments. Finally Gaglianone et al. (2016) used bias correction techniques to show that consumer's inflation expectations combined with experts' expectations improve inflation forecasts in Brazil.

3.3 Conclusion

The results obtained from the first 39 years of quarterly tendency surveys in Brazil were useful and represented a relevant contribution for economic analysis in this country. But results obtained after 2005, when the existing manufacturing survey turned into monthly frequency and the other regular surveys were implemented are strikingly more useful. ETS have shown to be an indispensable tool for monitoring and anticipating economic trends in Brazil. Assuming that most of the time these statistics generate useful results with relatively small samples and thus run on a relatively low budget, the Brazilian experience confirms a trend and suggests that other emerging economies might also benefit from implementing similar statistics and analyses.

Appendix

Questions included in FGV's business surveys and main characteristics

	Manufacturing Industry	Services	Trade	Construction
Sales in the Past	–	–	−3M	–
Employment in the Past	–	–	−3M	–
Recent Evolution of Activity	–	–	–	−3M
Total Demand	P	P	P	–
Domestic Demand	P	–	–	–
External Demand	P	–	–	–
Current Purchasing Volume	–	–	P	–
Stock Level	P	–	–	–
Portfolio of Contracts	–	–	–	P
Current Business Situation	P	P	P	P
Level of Capacity Utilization	P	P	–	P
Current Credit	–	P	P	P
Factors Limiting the Business Expansion	–	P	P	P
Productive Capacity	–	–	–	+12M
Expected Total Demand	+3M	+3M	–	+3M
Expected Domestic Demand	+3M	–	–	–
Expected External Demand	+3M	–	–	–
Expected Production	+3M	–	–	–
Invoicing/Income Expected	–	+3M	–	–
Expected Sales	–	–	+3M	–
Purchasing Volume Expected	–	–	+3M	–
Employment	+3M	+3M	+3M	+3M
Business situation	+6M	+6M	+6M	+6M

−3M: Last 3 months, P: Present, +3M: Next 3 months, +6M: Next 6 months, +12M: Next 12 months

Questions included in FGV's Consumer Survey and main characteristics

	Consumer
Current General Economic Situation	P
Expected General Economic Situation	+6M
Household Current Financial Situation	P
Household Expected Financial Situation	+6M
Current Employment Local	P
Expected Employment Local	+6M
Savings	P
Interest Rates	+6M
Purchasing of Durable Goods	+6M
Inflation	+12M
Past Inflation Evolution	−12M
Expected Inflation Evolution	+12M

−12M: Last 12 months, P: Present, +6M: Next 6 months, +12M: Next 12 months

References

Bezerra IO, Malgarini MA (2016) New measure of the non-inflationary rate of capacity utilisation for the Brazilian economy. Revista de Economia Aplicada 20(4):441–455

Bittencourt V, Campelo A, Malgarini M (2016) Does consumer confidence help forecasting consumption spending in Brazil? Evidence from survey data, Working Paper, FGV/IBRE

Brazilian Central Bank Technical Note Índices de Confiança e Variáveis Macroeconômicas, Inflation Report (Relatório de Inflação), September, 2014

Campelo A Jr, Issler JV (2008) Leading indicators of industrial activity in Brazil. IBRE-FGV, Rio de Janeiro

Campelo A Jr, Filho FHB, Bezerra IO, Lima SPM (2012) Indicador antecedente de desemprego para o Brasil. IBRE-FGV, Rio de Janeiro

Campelo A Jr, Sima-Friedman J, Lima S, Ozyildirim A, Picchetti P (2013) Tracking business cycles in Brazil with composite indexes of coincident and leading economic indicators. IBRE-FGV, Rio de Janeiro

EC (European Commission) (2006) Directorate-general for economic and financial affairs. The Joint Harmonised EU Programme of Business and Consumer Surveys. Special Report No. 5

Gallardo AM, Pedersen M (2008) Encuestas de opinión empresarial del sector industrial en América Latina. División de Estadística y Proyecciones Económicas, ECLAC (CEPAL), p 42

Gaglianone WP, Issler JV, Matos SM (2016) Applying a microfounded-forecasting approach to predict Brazilian inflation. Brazilian Central Bank Working Paper 436

Graminho FM (2015) Sentimento e Macroeconomia: uma análise dos índices de confiança no Brasil, Brazilian Central Bank Working Paper 408, Nov 2015

Gyomai G, Tosseto E (2009) OECD, current status of business tendency survey and consumer survey harmonisation in non-EU OECD countries. OECD enhanced engagement economies and OECD accession countries

Lima S, Malgarini M (2016) Does a survey based capacity utilisation measure help predicting Brazilian output gap in real-time? J Bus Cycle Res 12(1):119–139

Mello EPG, Figueiredo FMR (2014) Assessing the short-term forecasting power of confidence indices. Brazilian Central Bank Working Paper 371

Motta M (org) (2008) Memórias do Instituto Brasileiro de Economia, Editora da FGV

Zarnowitz V (2004) Introduction – an important subject in need of much new research. J Bus Cycle Meas Anal, 1(1):7–12. OECD/CIRET

Russian Business Tendency Surveys by HSE and Rosstat

Tamara Lipkind, Liudmila Kitrar, and Georgy Ostapkovich

1 Introduction

Russian business tendency surveys provide qualitative data on the business and investment climate, main economic trends, business confidence and economic sentiment through regular collection and compilation of economic agents' opinions. Such information is complementary to quantitative statistics; it is reliable, available, user-friendly and easily interpretable. Therefore, it helps to extend the competence of decision-makers at all levels of authority and meets the information needs of expert and business communities.

In Russia, a country with a developing market, economic regulation depends on not only the change of internal structural and cyclical factors but also on external risks caused by fluctuations in raw material prices and the long-term growth in developed countries. For this reason, it is essential to create data sets that are comparable to their international counterparts, especially to the dynamics of short-term business tendency indicators in European and BRICS countries.

The paper prepared within the framework of the Basic Research Program at the National Research University Higher School of Economics (HSE) and supported within the framework of a subsidy by the Russian Academic Excellence Project '5-100'.

T. Lipkind (✉) · L. Kitrar · G. Ostapkovich
National Research University Higher School of Economics, Russian Federation, Moscow, Russia
e-mail: tlipkind@hse.ru

S. Smirnov et al. (eds.), *Business Cycles in BRICS*, Societies and Political Orders in Transition, https://doi.org/10.1007/978-3-319-90017-9_13

2 Background

The programme of business tendency surveys (BTS) in Russia was launched in the early 1990s. Methodology was designed and developed at the Centre for Economic Analyses of the Government of the Russian Federation on the basis of the Joint Harmonised EU Programme of Business and Consumer Surveys under the Tacis[1] programme 'Statistics 2, 3, 5'.[2]

Pilot surveys in various sectors have been conducted by the Centre for Economic Analysis as direct questioning since 1992; after that, the surveys were implemented in the statistical practice and included in Rosstat's Federal Program of Statistical Observation. The first regular survey in industry was carried out in 1995; then Russian BTS system was extended by covering the construction and retail trade (since 1998), wholesale trade (2000), industrial investment (2001) and services (2012). In 2009, the BTS project was relocated to the HSE Centre for Business Tendency Studies at the Institute for Statistical Studies and Economics of Knowledge.

Currently, all regular BTS are conducted by HSE in collaboration with Rosstat. The HSE area of responsibility includes methodology development (questionnaires design, requirements for sample), data treatment (seasonal adjustment, calculation of composite indicators), preparing analytical reviews (releases for mass media, information and analytical bulletins for government), scientific research and publications. Rosstat is responsible for sampling, collecting information and weighting primary data.

Although the Russian BTS programme was adapted to national specificities, its design is based on the European standards; it allows them to be considered as harmonised with the EU Programme of Business and Consumer Surveys. The Russian programme has been continuously updated using scientific and empirical resources brought to light by some of the international references in BTS such as the Ifo Institute (Germany), OFCE (France), KOF ETH (Switzerland), ISAE (Italy), CIRET, the OECD and the European Commission.

BTS by HSE and Rosstat measure regularly and quickly sectoral development paths and short-term fluctuations when traditional statistics are still unavailable, insufficient or prone to significant and frequent revisions. The main advantages of the Russian BTS system can be defined as an accumulated data set over quite a long period; coverage of a wide range of regions, sectors and economic activities; synchronisation and harmonisation of programmes that make the sectoral benchmarking possible; the unified approach to data collection and treatment; the

[1]Tacis—Technical Assistance to the Commonwealth of Independent States.

[2]Invaluable support to developing the Russian BTS system was provided by the Statistics Directorate of Organization for Economic Cooperation and Development (OECD) and Ronny Nilsson personally; Directorate-General for Economic and Financial Affairs of the European Commission; Centre for International Research on Economic Tendency Surveys (CIRET); the Ifo Institute (Germany); and the Observatoire Français des Conjonctures Économiques (OFCE, France).

Table 1 Main features of the Russian BTS system

Sectors	Starting year	Reporting units	Frequency
Industry	1995	3500	Monthly
Construction	1998	6500	Quarterly
Retail trade	1998	4000	Quarterly
Wholesale trade	2000	1000	Quarterly
Services	2012	5500	Quarterly
Investment	2001	10,000	Yearly

availability of results and their compatibility with quantitative statistics; and the compliance with international standards and classifications. Along with the strengths, a number of shortcomings should be noted: first of all, there is a lack of flexibility due to collecting information through the state statistical system and quarterly (not monthly) frequency of construction, trade and services surveys.

3 Overview of the BTS System by HSE and Rosstat

Regular business tendency surveys, conducted by HSE in collaboration with Rosstat, cover almost all regions of the Russian Federation and five sectors of the economy with the sample of about 22,500 reporting units (industrial, construction, service, retail and wholesale trade organisations). The contribution of observed economic activities to the national GDP is more than 60%. In addition, investment surveys cover about 10,000 industrial enterprises (Table 1).

4 Sample Design

Multivariate stratified sampling with random or mechanical selection of observation units in stratum is used; the fixed panel of companies and respondents is updated at regular intervals. Stratification is required due to the structural heterogeneity of the Russian economy; stratification criteria are kinds of activity, and firm size, measured by the number of employees. Target universes were obtained from official database, namely, the Statistical Business Register conducted by Rosstat.

Samples are representative at the level of sectors and aggregate kinds of economic activities for all surveys and at the level of federal districts[3]—for all surveys except industry. The results are broken down by branches according to the Russian Classification of Economic Activities (OKVED), which is compatible with the

[3]The federal districts are administrative forming, that include several regions of Russian Federation; in 2016 nine federal districts were established.

Statistical Classification of Economic Activities in the European Communities (NACE Rev. 1.1).[4]

5 Questionnaires

Sectoral BTS questionnaires include the following blocks:

- A set of harmonised questions recommended by the OECD and the European Commission (concerning demand, output, prices, employment, business situation and limiting factors)
- Additional questions related to specific trends in the Russian economy
- Pilot questions about particular events, for example, phenomena just emerging in the Russian economy

Virtually all questions are of a qualitative nature. Quantitative indicators—number of employees and daily turnover—are used for stratification and weighting.

Questions concerning recent or expected changes of indicators are exactly connected with a time frame (month, quarter, etc.). They call for an answer according to the 3-option ordinal scale: increased, improved (+), remain unchanged (=) and decreased, deteriorated (−). In some 'change questions', a 5-option scale is used. For example, there are five options in the questions about price changes: selling price over the past (next) quarter increased (will increase) at a faster pace, at the same rate, at a slower pace, remained (will remain) unchanged and decreased (will decrease).

Questions concerning assessment of current situation involve a comparison of the real situation with a 'normal' situation (usual for economic conditions and period) using the following 3-option ordinal scale: more than sufficient (+), sufficient (=) and not sufficient (−).

6 Data Collecting and Treatment

According to the federal law 'On Official Statistical Accounting and State Statistics System in the Russian Federation', the participation in statistical surveys is compulsory; respondents shall be obliged to submit free of charge the primary statistical data to compile official statistical information (Federal Law 2007). Therefore, non-response is not a considerable problem and practically depends on sample rotation, for example, liquidation of companies. The average response rate is larger than 90%.

[4]Since 2017, a new classification version compatible with the NACE Rev. 2.0 is used.

To aggregate respondent's assessments at different levels, statistical weights that characterise the unit importance are used. The weights of individual answers are determined by the size of each enterprise, which is related to the number of employees. Outcomes aggregate to a sector level as weighted average using a share of a specific segment value added (VA) in a total sector VA.

Primary survey data—weighted shares of respondents' answers—are aggregated into balances defined as a difference between 'positive' and 'negative' answers. To eliminate seasonal patterns in time series of balances, we use SPSS software with the autoregressive integrated moving average (ARIMA) module.

7 Sectoral Surveys

Regular surveys in *industry* have been carried out monthly since 1995. It covers about 3500 large and medium industrial enterprises including 600 'main' (or dominant) enterprises, i.e. organisations that produce the largest amount of production in the relevant industry. If required, the 'main' enterprises can be extracted from the total sample and analysed separately.

In contrast to the harmonised European survey, which covers manufacturing only, the Russian survey also includes information on mining and quarrying as well as gas, electricity and water supply:

- Mining
- Manufacturing:
  - Manufacture of food products, beverages and tobacco products
  - Textile and clothing manufacture
  - Manufacture of leather, related products and footwear
  - Manufacture of wood and of products of wood and cork, except furniture
  - Manufacture of cellulose and paper, publishing and printing
  - Manufacture of coke and refined petroleum products
  - Manufacture of chemicals
  - Manufacture of rubber and plastic products
  - Manufacture of other non-metallic mineral products
  - Manufacture of basic metals and fabricated metal products
  - Manufacture of machinery and equipment
  - Manufacture of electrical, electronic and optical equipment
  - Manufacture of transport equipment
  - Other manufacturing
- Gas, electricity and water supply

BTS of *services* was launched in 2012. By that time, the contribution of services to the Russian economy had increased significantly and reached almost half of the national gross value added. Therefore, we had a strong incentive for conducting this survey both to analyse the sector development and to construct an integrated indicator able to evaluate the short-term overall economic dynamics. Regular services surveys are carried out quarterly and cover about 5500 organisations providing commercial services (except micro organisations) in 14 branches:

- Maintenance and repair of motor vehicles
- Repair of housing goods
- Hotels and other accommodations
- Passenger land (excepting railway), water and air transport
- Travel agency and tour operator activities
- Public postal service, courier activities (except national postal activities) and telecommunication
- Short-term loans secured by movable property providing by pawnshops
- Insurance
- Real estate activities
- Advertising and market research activities
- Sanatoria and health resort activities
- Dental services
- Sport, amusement, cultural and recreation activities
- Personal services

Regular BTS in *construction* has been carried out quarterly since 1998 and covers about 6500 building companies, except micro organisations. The results are broken down by five groups of building activities:

- Residential buildings
- Non-residential buildings
- Civil engineering
- Capital repairs of buildings and facilities
- Maintenance of buildings and facilities

Regular BTS in *retail and wholesale trade* are carried out quarterly (retail, since 1998; wholesale, since 2000) and cover about 4000 and 3000 trade firms, respectively. The surveys cover the retail and wholesale trade sections of NACE classification except maintenance and repair of motor vehicles and repair of housing goods, which are included in the services survey. The results are divided into the following groups:

- Retail trade of food, beverages and tobacco
- Retail trade of other (non-food) products
- Wholesale trade of:
  - Motor vehicles
  - Automotive parts, components and accessories
  - Agricultural raw produce and live animals
  - Food, beverages and tobacco
  - Household electrical, radio and TV equipment
  - Perfume and cosmetic
  - Pharmaceutical and medical goods

- Household furniture and floor coverings, fuel, ores and metals
- Timber and construction materials
- Chemical products
- Machinery and equipment

Regular survey of *investment activity* has been carried out yearly since 2001 and covers about 10,000 large, medium and small industrial organisations (except micro organisations). The questionnaire includes the following questions:

- Purpose of investing in fixed assets in the current and next year
- Targets for investment in fixed assets in the current and next year
- Sources of investing in fixed assets in the current and next year
- Factors limiting investment activities
- Average age of fixed assets in the current year
- Retirement of fixed assets in the current year
- Commissioning of new and renovated fixed assets in the current and next year
- Unused fixed assets in the current year

Questionnaires for industrial, services, construction and retail surveys and time frame of questions are shown in the appendix.

The survey of *consumers* is the prerogative of Rosstat, including methodology development, fieldwork, data treatments and results publication. HSE includes the consumer confidence indicator calculated by Rosstat as a component of the economic sentiment indicator.

8 Composite BTS Indicators

The HSE Centre for Business Tendency Studies integrates the surveys' results in composite indicators that reflect the business climate in the observed sectors as well as the Russian economy as a whole. These indicators are constructed in accordance with the OECD and European Commission recommendations (European Commission 2017a, b; OECD 2003).

8.1 Confidence Indicators

Confidence indicators for industry, construction, retail and wholesale trade and services reflect entrepreneurs' perceptions and expectations at the sector level in the one-dimensional index. They are calculated as the simple arithmetic average of balances of answers (in percentage points) to selected questions.

The industrial confidence indicator (monthly seasonally adjusted balances):

- Level of order books
- Production expectation over the next 3 months
- Level of stocks of finished products (with inverted sign)

The services confidence indicator (quarterly seasonally adjusted balances):

- Present business situation, evolution over the past 3 months
- Current demand, evolution over the past 3 months
- Demand expectation over the next 3 months

The construction confidence indicator (quarterly seasonally adjusted balances):

- Current order book
- Employment expectation over the next 3 months

The retail and wholesale confidence indicators (quarterly seasonally adjusted balances):

- Present business situation, evolution over the past 3 months
- Future business situation, evolution over the next 3 months
- Level of stocks (with inverted sign)

Rosstat also constructs and publishes quarterly the consumer confidence indicator; its calculation procedure differs from the methodology recommended by the European Commission. Consumer confidence indicator is the arithmetic average of the balances of answers (not seasonally adjusted) to the following questions:

- Expectation of general economic situation in Russia over the next 12 months
- Change of general economic situation in Russia over the past 12 months
- Expectation of financial position of household over the next 12 months
- Change of financial position of household over the past 12 months
- Current environment for major purchases

8.2 *Economic Sentiment Indicator*

The economic sentiment indicator of the Higher School of Economics (HSE ESI) is a generalising indicator which summarises the main results of sectoral business and consumer surveys. HSE ESI is based on the opinions of about 20,000 economic agents including top managers of 3500 large and medium industrial enterprises, 6500 construction companies, 4000 retail organisations and 5500 services organisations, as well as 5000 consumers. Contributions of these kinds of economic activities to the national GDP are about 60%; therefore, HSE ESI is considered to be able to track the evolution of overall economic activity in Russia.

HSE ESI was constructed for the first time in 2011 with a retrospective to 1998; since then, the indicator has been calculated quarterly. It is made up from 12 components, which respond adequately and efficiently to fluctuations in the Russian economy. In fact, these are the 11 previously described components of sectoral business confidence indicators and the consumer confidence indicator as a whole.

Hence, HSE ESI and sectoral confidence indicators are based on the same set of balances of entrepreneurs and consumers opinions, but construction and interpretation of these indicators have some peculiarities. Whereas the confidence indicators are calculated as an arithmetic average of nonstandardised time series of balances, another procedure of combining the selected components is used for HSE ESI calculation. The procedure includes:

- Standardisation of individual components (balances of opinion) to make them comparable in terms of the average level and volatility before aggregation. Standardisation is computed over the frozen sample, which is extended periodically.
- Weighting of all standardised components according to sectoral weights, which have been determined according to share of these sectors in GDP (e.g. in 2016: industry 45%, construction 10%; retail trade 10%; services 25%; consumer 10%).[5]
- The sum of weighted components is scaled to have a long-term average (common mean) of 100 and a standard deviation of 10. As a result, ESI (assuming approximate normality) changes usually from 90 to 110. Values about 100 mean the normal business sentiment; notably higher than 100, the most favourable and optimistic; and markedly below 100, depressive, crisis mood.

8.3 *Economic Sentiment Tracer*

To visualise the HSE ESI cyclical development, the economic sentiment tracer is used. The tracer construction is based on the EC concept in terms of the quadrants' location and cyclic movement direction (Gayer 2008; European Commission 2017b). Additionally, according to the OECD and EC recommendations (Nilsson and Gyomai 2008; European Commission 2017b), we apply the Hodrick-Prescott filter to smooth out fluctuations in the HSE ESI time series of less than 18 months (insignificant in terms of the growth cycle visualisation). The smoothing parameter λ is given directly and calculated as follows:

$$\lambda = \left(2 \times \sin\left(\frac{\pi}{\text{cut-off frequency}}\right)\right)^{-4},$$

where 'cut-off frequency' is a parameter that characterises the period of fluctuations exclusion.

In the case of quarterly indicator and excluding fluctuations less than 18 months, $\lambda = 6.85$.

[5]The weight of services is less than their share in the total GVA, because of the survey covers some kinds of services only.

The smoothed time series are standardised to a common mean of zero and unit standard deviation. Then, the indicator levels are plotted on the Y-axis, whereas their first differences (quarterly changes) are on the X-axis. Thus, a tracer displays both the level and the dynamics of the HSE ESI. The four quadrants of tracer path correspond to the following four phases of the growth cycle:

- Quadrant I (top right): expansion phase, optimism growth for the HSE ESI; the indicator increases at an above-average level.
- Quadrant II (top left): downswing phase, optimism decline for the HSE ESI; the indicator decreases at an above-average level.
- Quadrant III (bottom left): contraction phase, pessimism growth for the HSE ESI; the indicator decreases at a below-average level.
- Quadrant IV (bottom right): upswing phase, pessimism decline for the HSE ESI; the indicator increases at a below-average level.

The tracer crosses the four quadrants counterclockwise. Cyclical maximums (peaks) are positioned in the top centre of the graph area, whereas cyclical minimums (troughs) are found at the bottom of the central region.

8.4 Business Climate Indicator

Business Climate Indicator (BCI), which generalises the results of the industrial survey at the national level, is calculated presently on a pilot basis. This indicator is built according to the principles of factor analyses (European Commission 2017a, 2000; Gayer and Genet 2006). A set of opinion balances is used as input time series. We have calculated the two versions of the BCI based on two different sets of components. The first version (BCI-1) is harmonised with European recommendations; the set of input series includes five balances:

- Level of order books
- Level of export books
- Production expectation over the next 3 months
- Production tendency in the recent month
- Level of stocks of finished products

For the second version (BCI-2), we have selected balances showing a statistically significant correlation with the dynamics of the reference indicator, namely, the Industrial Production Index (IPI). This involved a cross-correlation analysis of the balances' time series in terms of correlation with IPI and their lag/lead properties related to the reference indicator. Based on this analysis, we have selected six questions that are expected to be more important in the national context than harmonised ones:

- Changes in order books in the recent month
- Changes in export order books in the recent month

- Production tendency in the recent month
- Level of stocks of finished products
- Changes in economic conditions in the recent month
- Changes in number of employees in the recent month

Calculation of BCI-1 and BCI-2 is based on classical principles of factor analyses (principal component method); the procedure is described in the European guidelines (European Commission 2000, 2017a). Indicators obtained demonstrate different correlation with the reference series. Thus, the BCI-2 reveals a rather strong simultaneous correlation (coefficients 0.736) and leading (1 and 2 months lead) correlation with coefficients 0.739 and 0.718, respectively. The BCI-1 demonstrates less strong but also statistically significant simultaneous (0.699) and leading (0.642) correlation with respect to the dynamics of the IPI. Thus, the BCI-2, as a specific indicator for Russia, can be used as a leading indicator in the industry. The BCI-1, as a harmonised composite indicator, allows benchmarking with international counterparts.

9 Main BTS Results

The graphs below illustrate the main results of the Russian BTS for the period until Q4 2016. Figure 1 represents the economic sentiment indicator (HSE ESI) and the confidence indicators that track sectoral and overall economic activities. Looking at the HSE ESI, a gradual slowdown in economic growth since the beginning of 2012 can be observed. A sharp decrease in the second half of 2014 reflected the main economic and political events in Russia: geopolitical tensions, limited access to

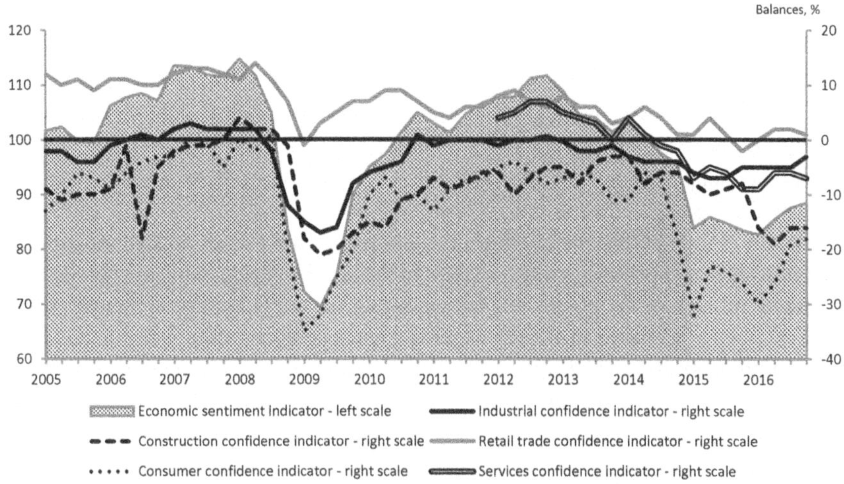

Fig. 1 Economic sentiment indicator and confidence indicators

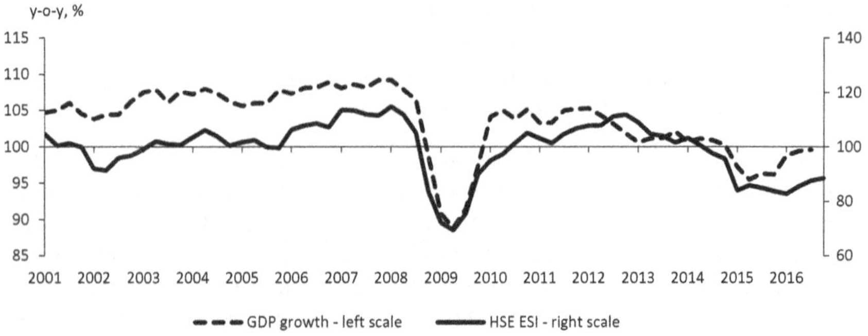

Fig. 2 Economic sentiment indicator and GDP growth

international financial markets, national currency depreciation, fall in oil prices and growing economic uncertainty. From a sectoral perspective, currency depreciation and import shrinkage gave some support to Russian manufacturing. The consumer sector has suffered the most: real disposable incomes of Russians have fallen for more than 2 years, since the end of 2014. Consumers are forced to minimise their costs as far as possible; as a result, confidence in retail trade, services and housing construction worsened notably.

The HSE ESI dynamics remained on a downward trend from the end of 2012 (the cyclical peak) until the beginning of 2016; only two short-term episodes of recovery were observed in Q1 2014 and Q2 2015. Then, there was an increase in the indicator starting from the minimum for the last 7 years value of QI 2016 until the end of 2016. Despite the compensation of the crisis values of 2015, the HSE ESI for ten consecutive quarters remained below its long-term average (100) demonstrating the unfavourable business climate in the Russian economy. However, HSE ESI was significantly lower in the previous Russian crises (economic sentiments in mid-2009 remain at absolute minimum in the retrospective of the BTS aggregate results).

Figure 2 demonstrates the joint dynamics of the HSE ESI and the GDP growth (in percentage to the previous year). These indicators reveal a stable synchronous correlation (0.85). Considering the timeliness of the HSE ESI (1.5–2 months before the first official statistics on the GDP index), it can be used as an early warning indicator of aggregated economic activity in Russia.

Finally, Fig. 3 shows the cyclical development of the economic sentiment tracer that reflects five short-term growth cycles. In the last fifth cycle, which began in 2012 (marked in black in the graph), the indicator crossed the boundary of the expansion area and began to move in the downswing phase, demonstrating a sustained slowdown until mid-2014. Then the indicator shifted sharply to the contraction phase with an intensive increase in negative economic sentiment. Since 2015, the tracer path indicated the forthcoming of a new turning point—the crises bottom. Then, transition to the upswing quadrant visualised a turn to cyclical growth.

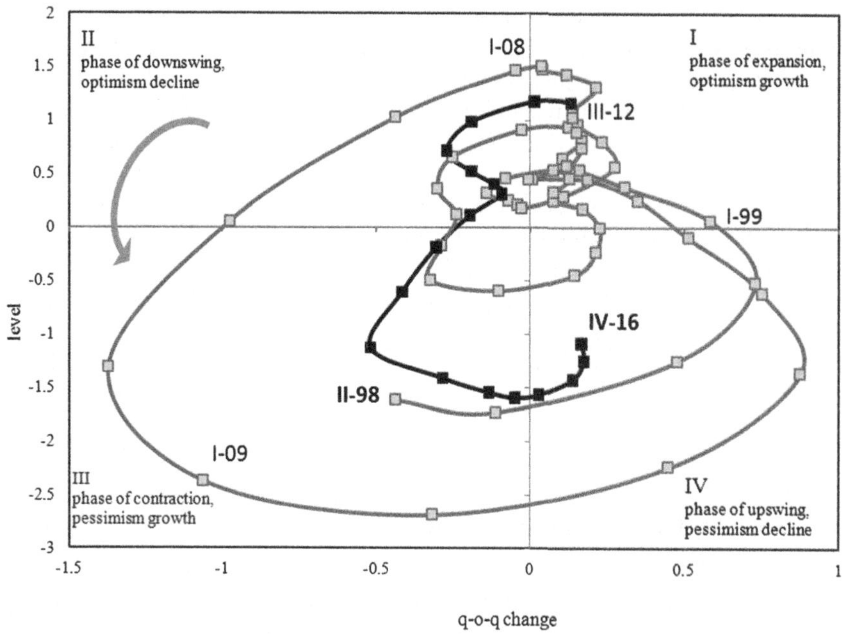

Fig. 3 Economic sentiment tracer

10 BTS Results Implementation

Based on the BTS results, the Higher School of Economics publishes regularly information and analytical materials on actual problems, including issues that cannot be described timely using traditional hard statistics. In particular, this refers to the assessment of business climate and economic situation in various economic sectors, demand for production and services, competitive position, factors limiting business activity, capacity utilisation and availability of financial resources. Press releases and analytical reports are submitted to the federal legislative and executive authorities and published in the national and regional mass media and online.

The Higher School of Economics and Rosstat maintain and update the qualitative information database that contains simple and composite BTS indicators since 1998. The main BTS results are also included in the OECD database 'business tendency and consumer opinion'.

Using the business tendency indicators together with quantitative data enhances the analysis of on-going cyclical, structural and integration changes. Long-time international research suggests that BTS time series are necessary for monitoring and forecasting business cycles (OECD 2003, 2012; European Commission 2017a). In this aspect, recent scientific research of the HSE Centre for Business Tendency Studies are focused on measuring business cycles, namely, the capability of the accumulated Russian BTS dynamics to reflect the current and expected cyclical development of aggregated economic activity. We believe that short-term indicators of business surveys should be involved in measuring the expected cyclical phases and turning points in economic dynamics (Kitrar and Ostapkovich 2013a, b, c; Kitrar et al. 2014, 2015). In this regard, we designed an algorithm built in an iterative procedure for constructing a structured set of composite indicators. The algorithm tests the indicators for cyclical sensitivity through decomposition of their dynamics. Identification of turning points in the dynamics of these indicators allows us to track the possible 'averaged' chronology of the cyclical phase's alternation. Finally, we conducted empirical tests of the cyclical profile in the dynamics of one of the composite BTS indicators—economic sentiment indicator in Russia (HSE ESI). The results have documented a high degree of compatibility of the HSE ESI and the GDP cyclical paths with the leading nature of the HSE ESI (Kitrar et al. 2014, 2015).

11 Future Development of Russian BTS

The business tendency monitoring in various sectors of the Russian economy is particularly important in the conditions of economic stagnation, loss of key macro-aggregates' potential values, external challenges and growing uncertainty of economic agents. In this regard, the forthcoming HSE research focuses on methodological support for the extended set of early response indicators based on entrepreneurial behaviour and on analysing the results. The BTS are supposed to be capable to reflect real and expected sectoral events, including risks, challenges, bottlenecks and limiting factors; they represent investment behaviour of industrial enterprises due to a programme of import substitution. Sectoral coverage of the Russian BTS system will be expanded by the surveys of IT sector and investment activity of industrial companies with a block of questions concerning the import substitution programme.

Development of information technology largely determines the country's competitiveness in the global market. Today, however, all requirements of the Russian domestic market for IT equipment are met mainly by imports. Nevertheless, the basis of an IT industry has already formed due to significant engineering and algorithmic potential as well as a growing market. Therefore, it is essential to conduct a survey on actual and prospective business trends, structural and situational features of the IT industry development.

The investment survey will be aimed at assessing the feasibility and effectiveness of various investment models. The regional structure of the sample will be able to reflect regional disparities in the investment development of the country. The special block of questions, focused on evaluating the scope and key areas of import substitution, will help to quantify the effect of the new industrial policy.

12 BTS Data Dissemination

All information and analytic materials are available on the official HSE website: http://www.hse.ru/monitoring/buscl/ (in Russian).

Database and metadata on leading indicators for economic activities are available on the official Rosstat website: http://www.gks.ru/wps/wcm/connect/rosstat_main/rosstat/ru/statistics/leading_indicators (in Russian).

The main BTS results are available on the OECD website as a part of the database 'business tendency and consumer opinion': http://stats.oecd.org/index.aspx?queryid=305.

Appendix

Questions included in business tendency surveys by Higher School of Economics and Rosstat (the harmonised questions are marked in bold)

Questions (monthly)	Level; 3-option scale	Tendency; 3-option scale	Expectation; 3-option scale
Industrial survey (monthly)			
Overall order books	Current month	Past month	Next 3 months
Export order books	Current month	Past month	Next 3 months
Production	Current month	Past month	Next 3 months
Innovative production	Current month	Past month	Next 3 months
Firm's total employment	Current month	Past month	Next 3 months
Stock of finished products	Current month	Past month	Next 3 months
Stock of raw material	Current month	Past month	Next 3 months
Selling prices	–	Past month	Next 3 months
Raw materials prices	–	Past month	Next 3 months
Capacity utilisation	Current month; percentage of full capacity	–	–
Provision of production capacity considering current order book and change in demand over the next 6 months	Current month	–	–
Availability of internal financial resources	–	Past month	Next 3 months
Availability of budgetary funds	–	Past month	Next 3 months
Availability of credit and loan resources	–	Past month	Next 3 months
Business situation	Current month	Past month	Next 3 months

(continued)

Questions (monthly)	Level; 3-option scale	Tendency; 3-option scale	Expectation; 3-option scale
Main factors currently limiting production: Insufficient demand on domestic market Insufficient demand on foreign market Competing imports High taxation level Shortage of equipment High percentage of commercial loan Financial constraints Shortage of labour force Inadequate legal and regulatory framework None	Current month	–	–
***Services survey* (quarterly)**			
Demand	Current quarter	Past quarter	Next quarter
Number of contracts (clients)	Current quarter	Past quarter	Next quarter
Volume of services	Current quarter	Past quarter	Next quarter
Prices for services	Current quarter	Past quarter	Next quarter
Investment	Current quarter	Past quarter	Next quarter
Costs	Current quarter	Past quarter	Next quarter
Profit	Current quarter	Past quarter	Next quarter
Competitive position on the market	Current quarter	Past quarter	Next quarter
Firm's total employment	Current quarter	Past quarter	Next quarter
Business situation	Current quarter	Past quarter	Next quarter
Main factors currently limiting business: Insufficient demand Shortage of space and/or equipment High taxation level Financial constraints High cost of renting premises Unfair competition from other organisations in the market Shortage of labour force High percentage of commercial loan Inadequate legal and regulatory framework Corruption of authorities	Current quarter	–	–
Construction survey (quarterly)			
Current capacity utilisation	Current quarter; percentage of full capacity	–	–
How many months of production are provided by current overall order books	Current quarter; months	–	–
How many months of production are provided by current financial resource	Current quarter; months	–	–

(continued)

Questions (monthly)	Level; 3-option scale	Tendency; 3-option scale	Expectation; 3-option scale
Overall order books	Current quarter	Past quarter	Next quarter
Production capacity considering the expected change in demand over the next 12 months	Current quarter	–	–
Amount of construction work	–	Past quarter	Next quarter
Firm's total employment	–	Past quarter	Next quarter
Competitive position	–	Past quarter	Next quarter
Prices for construction materials	–	Past quarter; 5-option scale	Next quarter; 5-option scale
Prices for construction work	–	Past quarter; 5-option scale	Next quarter; 5-option scale
Profit	–	Past quarter	Next quarter
Loss	–	Past quarter	Next quarter
Availability of internal financial resources	–	Past quarter	Next quarter
Availability of loan financial resources	–	Past quarter	Next quarter
Investment	–	Past quarter	Next quarter
Main factors currently limiting building activity: Insufficient demand Insolvency of customers High level of taxation High percentage of commercial loan Shortage of labour force High price for materials and products Shortage of building equipment High competition from other organisations Weather conditions None	Current quarter	–	–
Business situation	Current quarter	Past quarter	Next quarter
***Trade survey* (quarterly)**			
Firm's total employment	–	Past quarter	Next quarter
Turnover	–	Past quarter	Next quarter
Sales	–	Past quarter	Next quarter
Orders book (demand)	–	Past quarter	Next quarter
Volume of stock	Current quarter	Past quarter	Next quarter
Assortment of goods	–	Past quarter	Next quarter
Competitive position on the market	Current quarter	Past quarter	Next quarter
Storage space	–	Past quarter	Next quarter
Investment (only retail)	–	Past quarter	Next quarter
Availability of internal financial resources	–	Past quarter	Next quarter

(continued)

Questions (monthly)	Level; 3-option scale	Tendency; 3-option scale	Expectation; 3-option scale
Availability of credit resources (only wholesale)	–	Past quarter	Next quarter
Profit	–	Past quarter	Next quarter
Competitive position on the market	Current quarter	Past quarter	Next quarter
Selling price	–	Past quarter: 5-option scale	Next quarter; 5-option scale
Purchase price (only wholesale)	–	Past quarter: 5-option scale	Next quarter; 5-option scale
Business situation	Current quarter	Past quarter	Next quarter
Share of online sales	Percentage in turnover	–	–
Main factors currently limiting business: Insufficient effective demand Financial constraints High percentage of commercial loans Difficulties in obtaining loans (only retail) High taxation level High cost of renting premises High transport costs Insufficient assortment of goods (only retail) Shortage of storage/shopping space Shortage of equipment (only retail) High (unfair) competition on the market Shortage of labour force (only wholesale) Lack of information support (only wholesale) Inadequate legal and regulatory framework (only wholesale) None	Current quarter	–	–

References

European Commission (2000) Business climate indicators for the euro area. Presentation Paper. Brussels, November 2000. http://ec.europa.eu/economy_finance/db_indicators/surveys/documents/studies/bci_presentation_paper.pdf. Accessed Apr 2017

European Commission (2017a) The Joint Harmonised EU Programme of Business and Consumer Surveys. User guide. Directorate-General for Economic and Financial Affairs, European Commission. https://ec.europa.eu/info/sites/info/files/bcs_user_guide_en_0.pdf. Accessed Apr 2017

European Commission (2017b) European business cycle indicators. https://ec.europa.eu/info/sites/info/files/tp015_en.pdf. Accessed Apr 2017

Federal Law (2007) On official statistical accounting and state statistics system in the Russian Federation. https://rg.ru/2007/12/06/statistika-dok.html. Accessed May 2017
Gayer C (2008) Report: the economic climate tracer. A tool to visualise the cyclical stance of the economy using survey data. http://ec.europa.eu/economy_finance/db_indicators/surveys/documents/studies/economic_climate_tracer_en.pdf. Accessed Apr 2017
Gayer C, Genet J (2006) Using factor models to construct composite indicators from BCS data – a comparison with European Commission Confidence Indicators. http://ec.europa.eu/economy_finance/publications/publication856_en.pdf. Accessed Apr 2017
Kitrar L, Ostapkovich G (2013a) Issues of measuring business cycles: development of conceptual designs and basic observation parameters (in Russian). Voprosy statistiki 4:22–27
Kitrar L, Ostapkovich G (2013b) Special features and implementation of the indicator approach to cyclical monitoring of economic dynamics (in Russian). Voprosy statistiki 8:42–50
Kitrar L, Ostapkovich G (2013c) Integrated approach to construction of composite indicators with built-in algorithm for cycle evaluation in time series of the business tendencies monitoring results (in Russian). Voprosy statistiki 12:23–34
Kitrar L, Lipkind T, Ostapkovich G (2014) Decomposition and joint analysis of growth cycles in time series of the economic sentiment indicator and the gross domestic product (in Russian). Voprosy statistiki 9:41–46
Kitrar L, Lipkind T, Lola I, Ostapkovich G, Chusovlyanov D (2015) The HSE ESI and short-term cycles in the Russian economy//Papers and studies of Research Institute for Economic Development SGH, N 97. Warsaw School of Economics, Warsaw
Nilsson R, Gyomai G (2008) Cycle extraction. A comparison of the phase-average trend method, the Hodrick-Prescott and Christiano-Fitzgerald filters. OECD. http://www.oecd.org/std/leading-indicators/41520591.pdf. Accessed Apr 2017
OECD (2003) Business tendency survey. A handbook. http://www.oecd.org/std/leading-indicators/31837055.pdf. Accessed Apr 2017
OECD (2012) System of composite leading indicators. http://www.oecd.org/std/leading-indicators/41629509.pdf. Accessed Dec 2016

Business Tendency Surveys in India

George Kershoff

1 Introduction

India is fortunate, as various business tendency surveys (BTS) emerged in the post-reform period. The results of these surveys provide timeous, high-frequency qualitative data on the state of the economy to policymakers, business people and other interested parties. The central bank and finance ministry consider these findings in their policymaking. Furthermore, the results not only reveal business expectations but also probably influence them indirectly, as they are quoted widely in the news media and distributed to the members of business organisations.

Broadly speaking all the surveys reveal the same annual trends. However, the quarterly results deviate, but this is to be expected, given that all of them are based on samples (as is the international standard). All the surveys cover a few core variables, but other than this, the survey questions vary widely.

This chapter provides an overview of the different BTS in India and their survey methods, as well as shows the results for the post-reform period.

The accuracy of this overview must be qualified, as the author has no in-depth knowledge of India and BTS in India. Local experts have written the chapters on BTS for all the BRICS countries except for India. These experts carry out the surveys, publish the results or frequently use the results in their research. Despite several efforts, the authors of this book failed to secure such an expert for India. They tasked the author to compile an overview of BTS in India given his experience with them in South Africa and fluency in English. This chapter simply summarises the information on BTS in India that was publicly available, mainly on the internet, at the time of writing. Indian experts reviewed the first draft and their comments were incorporated, but all omissions and mistakes remain the responsibility of the author.

G. Kershoff (✉)
Bureau for Economic Research (BER), Stellenbosch University, Stellenbosch, South Africa
e-mail: gjkk@sun.ac.za

S. Smirnov et al. (eds.), *Business Cycles in BRICS*, Societies and Political Orders in Transition, https://doi.org/10.1007/978-3-319-90017-9_14

2 Scope

After the independence of India in 1947, the public sector assumed the lead role in industrial development. By the 1970s, a new base of heavy industries had been built, but private companies faced restrictions through licencing requirements for new units and/or expansion. Over this period, the Association of Indian Engineering Industry (AIEI) in Calcutta, which represented both larger foreign-owned companies and small- and medium-sized local companies, conducted a quarterly survey in the engineering industries (CIRET 2017; CII 2017).

In 1991, industrial licencing was abolished and other economic reforms were implemented. In the post-reform period, five institutions launched BTS in India, namely, the central bank, a research institute, two business organisations and one private business service company. The institutions are, in this order, the Reserve Bank of India (RBI), the National Council of Applied Economic Research (NCAER), the Confederation of Indian Industry (CII, the successor of the AIEI), the Federation of Indian Chambers of Commerce and Industry (FICCI) and Dun and Bradstreet. A private company, Markit Economics, also conducts a monthly manufacturing and services PMI in India, but for reasons of focus, this survey is not covered in this chapter.

Of all the providers, the CII has probably produced BTS for the longest consecutive time if one accounts for the work of its predecessor, the AIEI. In the post-reform period, the NCAER survey, which was launched in 1991, appears to be the oldest (see Table 1).

The amount of information on the different providers' survey methods and results that are publicly available vary. This is to be expected given the different *raison d'être* of providers. It is understandable that the Reserve Bank (which is publicly funded) makes so much information on the method and results freely available because it probably wishes to raise the survey's reputation and encourage its use. In contrast, a private business service company, such as Dun and Bradstreet, most likely wishes to limit the amount of information that it makes public to maintain the survey's reputation and publicity in order to protect its commercial interest and intellectual property rights. The research institute and two business organisations also would want to limit the amount of public information to protect the interest of their subscribers/financial sponsors and members, respectively.

Table 1 summarises all the information on the different providers' methods that the author could find. The main source of information was the websites of the providers. Other sources include academic literature and selected personal contact with the responsible people at the institutions. Despite an extensive search, there are gaps where no information could be obtained.

The description of the survey method is split in two. The first part deals with data collection and covers issues such as sector coverage, sampling, frequency, the data collection method and the questionnaire design. The second part considers the processing of the results and encompasses the estimation procedures, weighting,

Table 1 The survey methods of the business tendency surveys (BTS) in India

	Reserve Bank of India (RBI)	National Council of Applied Economic Research (NCAER)	Confederation of Indian Industry (CII)	Federation of Indian Chambers of Commerce and Industry (FICCI)	Dun and Bradstreet (D&B)
Commencement	1997[a]	1991	n/a	n/a	2003[b]
Data collection					
Sector coverage	Manufacturing[a]	n/a	Primary, manufacturing, services	Primary, manufacturing, services	Manufacturing, retail, building, other services
Frequency	Quarterly	Quarterly[c]	Quarterly	Quarterly	Quarterly
Sample frame	n/a	CII membership and own database	Membership database	n/a	D&B credit file
Sampling method	Deliberate sampling to maintain a representative panel, which is periodically updated to provide for firm "births" and "deaths"	Random selection and then deliberate sampling to provide for non-response	n/a	n/a	Random selection
Data collection method	Fieldwork is contracted out to a private market research company; combined postal mail and interviews	Combined postal mail (550) and interviews in five major cities (500)	Email to membership sharing the soft copy of the form and also the online link to the form	n/a	n/a
Number of responses	1250 (i.e. 45–50% of 2500)[d]	500	150–200	150–200	n/a
Questionnaire design	Since 2002 largely qualitative questions; block 3 of the questionnaire covers capacity utilisation ranges; block 4, factors constraining	Ten standard, qualitative questions on the estimated development and for some questions, expectations in 6 months' time about sales,	Like the FICCI questionnaire; estimated and expected performance of the firm, industry and the whole economy; performance of the firm in the	Like the CII questionnaire; estimated and expected performance of the firm, industry and the whole economy over the previous/upcoming	Six qualitative questions on the estimated development of the current quarter relative to the same quarter of a year ago about the volume of

(continued)

Table 1 (continued)

	Reserve Bank of India (RBI)	National Council of Applied Economic Research (NCAER)	Confederation of Indian Industry (CII)	Federation of Indian Chambers of Commerce and Industry (FICCI)	Dun and Bradstreet (D&B)
	capacity utilisation; and block 5, relative to the previous quarter, estimation for the current quarter and expectations for the next quarter regarding the business situation, the availability of finance, order books, the cost of raw materials, employment, exports, imports, selling prices, the profit margin, etc.; investment intentions and constraints questions are included annually in the 2nd quarter	production, imports, exports, profits, employment, production costs, cost of funds and the ideal level of stocks and orders; two special questions on topical issues are included every quarter	previous and current quarter i.r.o. sales, new orders, inventories, exports, imports, production costs, profits after tax, investment plans, employment, production capacity utilisation and constraints over the next 6 months	6 months; constraints; expectations about investments, sales, selling prices, profits, exports and employment in 6 months' time	business, new orders, net profits, selling prices, inventories and the number of employees
Estimation					
Data transformation	Net percentage	n/a	Per cent per answering category	Per cent per answering category	Percentage increase
Aggregation	A business expectation index (BEI) is calculated as the weighted average net percentage of nine questions, namely, the overall business situation, production, order	A business confidence index (BCI) is calculated as the weighted average of the positive responses (scaled to the base year) regarding overall economic conditions in	A current situation index (CSI) and an expected index (EI) are calculated as a weighted percentage of the firm, industry and the economy's estimated/expected performance. A	Like the CII, the FICCI calculates a current condition index, expectation index and a business conditions index; information on the calculation	A composite business optimism index is calculated as the weighted percentage of five questions (the inventory one is excluded) expressed

	books, inventory of raw materials, inventory of finished goods, profit margin, employment, exports and capacity utilisation	6 months' time, the financial position of the firm in 6 months' time, the present investment climate and the current level of operation of the firm relative to its optimal level	business confidence index (BCI) is calculated as a weighted CSI and EI	method is not publicly available	relative to the base year of 2011
Sources	RBI (2009a, 24–34, A2, A15–A18, A31), RBI (2009b, 1947–1986), RBI (2012, 1517–1520), RBI (2016, 25–28), RBI (2017a, 3, 6–7, 18), RBI (2017b)	Sinha (n.d), NCAER (2013, 4–5)	Information that the chief economist at the CII, Ms Bidisha Ganguly, provided to a joint EU-OECD Workshop in July 2012 and a copy of the questionnaire she provided to the author in June 2017	FICCI (2016, 2017)	D&B (2017)

Notes: n/a = not available

[a]Only covers firms in the formal sector of the economy and with paid-up capital of more than five million rupees (Lekshmi and Moll 2015, 2–3). The RBI also conducts a capacity utilisation, order books and inventory survey covering all economic sectors since 2007 and launched a pilot survey of the services and infrastructure sector in the fourth quarter of 2013 (RBI 2017c)

[b]Start date of historical data on Reuters

[c]Bi-annual until 2010

[d]According to Lekshmi and Mall (2015, 3), the response rate is 65–78%

data transformation and aggregation. The reliability of the results is dealt with in the last section.

3 Data Collection

Except for the Reserve Bank, all the other providers' overall results are based on all the major sectors of the Indian economy, namely, the primary, manufacturing and services sectors. At present, the Reserve Bank only makes the results of its manufacturing survey public, but it expanded the sector coverage of its survey to services and infrastructure in 2013. It will probably publish these results once the survey can be validated after more data points become available.

All the surveys in India are conducted on a quarterly basis, but the exact date when the questionnaires are sent out and have to be returned varies among the providers.

Publicly available information on the sample frame and sampling method are sketchy. Most providers select respondents partly randomly and partly deliberately from their proprietary member/client lists. Business organisations appear to contact all their members each time (i.e. they employ exhaustive sampling), the NCAER puts together a new sample each time and the Reserve Bank uses a panel. In the cases where member lists are used, it could not be established to what degree they are representative of business in India. Institutions do provide for different firm sizes.

The data collection method of only two providers could be established. Both the Reserve Bank and NCAER use a mixed mode of post/e-mail and personal interviews. It is safe to assume that the other institutions also apply a mixed mode of post and e-mail, but not personal interviews, given its high costs.

The number of responses varies between a high of 1250 in the case of the Reserve Bank to a low of 150–200 in the case of the FICCI. A response of 150+ suffices at the aggregate level (i.e. for the country as a whole and major divisions), but more responses would be required to report reliably at a disaggregated level. Only the Reserve Bank response rate could be obtained, and at 45%, it is similar to that of other non-Asian emerging economies.

There is quite a divergence in the questionnaire length of the various institutions. The Reserve Bank has the longest and Dun and Bradstreet the shortest questionnaire.

The wording of the questions and reference periods are not harmonised across the different providers. For instance, some providers refer to "business volumes" and others to "sales volumes" to pinpoint business activity. Likewise, some providers instruct respondents to compare the current period to the same period preceding it, while others ask them to compare it to the same period a year ago. The same also applies to the differentiation of the forward-looking periods. Some providers require respondents' expectations for the next 3 months, while others ask for the next 6 months. The impact (if any) of the different wording and reference periods on the survey results is unknown. If the impact is small to negligible, then one could assume that they measure the same phenomenon. This state of affairs also prevails globally, and users of BTS data across countries do not have a choice but to regard similar concepts as meaning the same thing.

Despite variations in questionnaire length and wording, all institutions cover a number of variables. They are business volumes, profits and employment. Four out of five institutions cover inventories and exports. Three out of five include orders, prices, imports, investment and special questions.

4 Processing the Results

Little information on the estimation procedure of the results is available in the public domain. For instance, it is unknown if individual responses are weighted to provide for different firm sizes and sectors or if any ex-post weight adjustment is done to provide for missing or a low number of responses in particular cells of a stratified sample. In addition, it is unknown if results—especially where respondents are asked to compare the current quarter with the one immediately preceding it—exhibit a seasonal pattern and if the published results provide for it.

Only the Reserve Bank publishes the results in the international customary format of net balances, i.e. the percentage of respondents indicating that a particular phenomenon "increased" less the percentage indicating a "decline". The other two providers that make information public release the results in "percentage increase" and "percent of the responses" format.

Every provider compiles an aggregate indicator. All of them combine a selection of data series into a single indicator. Some weight the components, while others convert the composite to an index with a base year equal to 100.

5 Reliability of the Survey Results

The discussion of the reliability of the survey results is limited to a visual inspection. This amounts to the obtainment and transformation of the historical time series of the survey (qualitative) and corresponding quantitative data and their comparison in charts.

A single, reputable data source of all India's BTS would be preferable, as it assures comparability and accuracy. However, at present no such data source exists. The only practical solution, therefore, is to use various sources, but one should take note of the obvious risk that this could result in a specific data point turning out to be incorrect.

The Organisation of Economic Co-operation and Development (OECD) includes the Reserve Bank's manufacturing survey data in its Main Economic Indicators (MEI). Bloomberg hosts no Indian BTS data, and only Dun and Bradstreet's data is available on Reuters. The website, Trading Economics, publishes the CII's data. A time series of the FICCI business condition index could be compiled from various reports on FICCI's website for the newer data and from SlideShare (the presentation and document-hosting website of LinkedIn) for the older data. Of all the surveys, the NCAER's composite index was the most challenging to put together out of public sources. At the end, the author could construct a historical time series from a combination of various reports on the NCAER's website and press coverage (A graphical story ... 2011; India's business confidence ... 2010; Business confidence in India ... 2012; Declining sentiment 2016).

Given the different transformation and aggregation methods of the various providers, all data series were standardised, which therefore made them comparable.

Obtaining long historical time series of the quantitative data also turned out surprisingly challenging. Manufacturing production and overall gross domestic product (GDP) data are available from the OECD's MEI, but not for GDP per sector. The data facility on the Reserve Bank's website only includes GDP per sector since the last base year revision in 2011/2012. Long time series of GDP per sector are also not available on Reuters and Bloomberg. The original GDP data per sector for the 1999/2000, 2004/2005 and 2011/2012 base years, therefore, had to be downloaded from India's national statistical agency's (MOSPI) website. In addition to the deflator updates, other methodological changes (such as coverage) complicated the linking of the individual time series with different base years to a single longer historical one converted to the most recent base year.

To overcome these challenges, only the year-on-year growth rates for the various base year periods were calculated. The different base years were linked together in such a manner that the growth rates always refer to the most recent base year. For instance, two sets of growth rates exist for 2011/2012, namely, one based on the 2004/2005 base year and one based on the 2011/2012. In this case, only the latter was used in the combined series. The combined series was not seasonally adjusted, but this should be less of a concern (if at all), given that all calculations are year-on-year.

The Reserve Bank's (RBI's) composite manufacturing business expectation index (BEI) and Dun and Bradstreet's (D&B's) whole economy volume of sales indicator are the longest time series available. Figure 1 shows that after moving closely together with each other and real GDP growth for many years, the RBI indicator began to "underperform" in 2013.

The relative "underperformance" of the RBI index is also evident if it is compared to the results of the other surveys, for which a shorter history is available. See Fig. 2.

Despite its relative "underperformance" vis-à-vis the other surveys and real GDP growth, Fig. 3 shows that the RBI survey data nevertheless tracks the growth in manufacturing production well.

A comparison of the growth in the quantitative series (manufacturing production and the value added in the manufacturing sector) shows that after having moved closely together for many years, they began diverging in 2013 after the GDP base year update to 2011/2012 (see Fig. 4). The GDP revision, which included an improvement in the coverage of manufacturers and a lower deflator, lifted the value added of the manufacturing sector in real terms (Bhattacharya 2015).

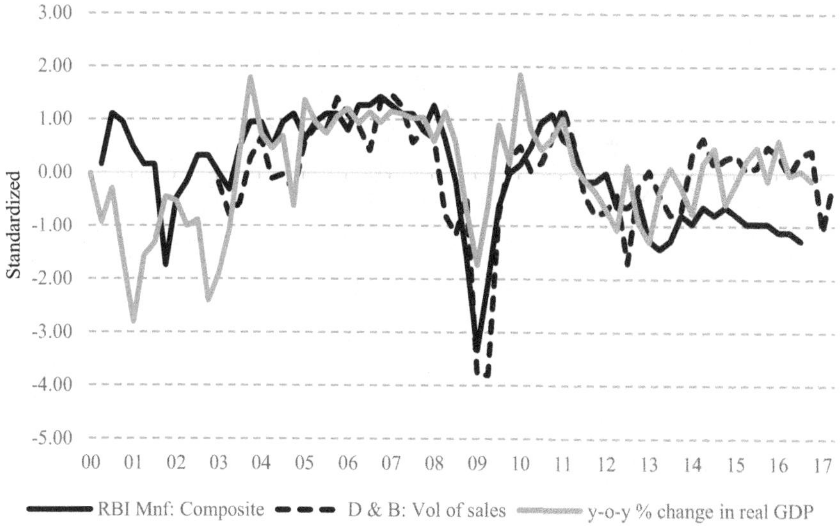

Fig. 1 Survey data vs. real GDP growth

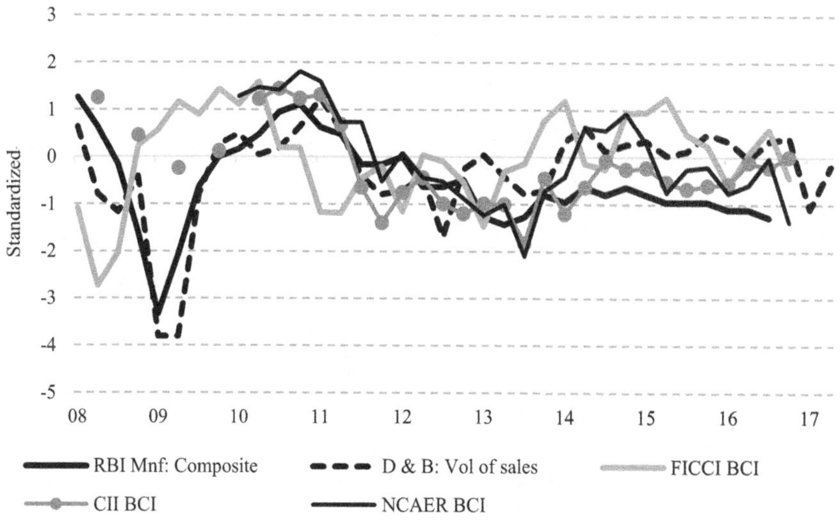

Fig. 2 The composite indices of the different BTS

A closer co-movement will be restored between the RBI index, on the one hand, and the other Indian BTS indices and the upwardly revised real GDP growth rate, on the other hand, when the bank updates the weights of the constituent series and/or starts including its services survey.

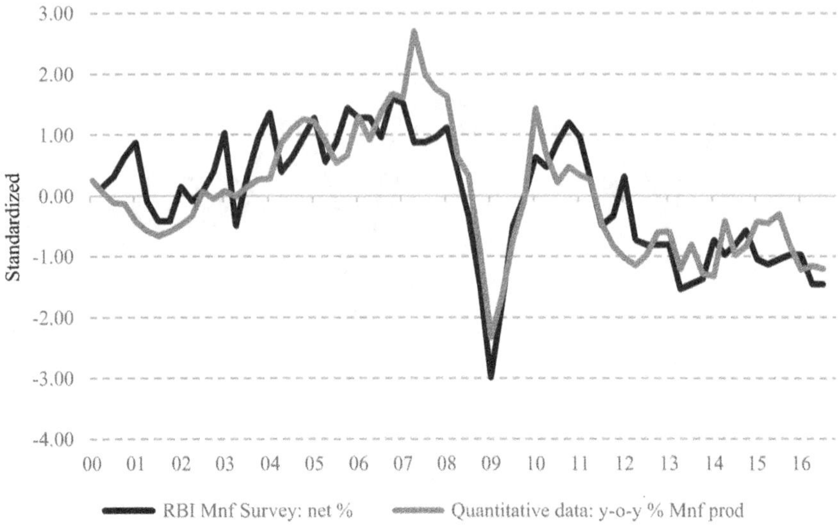

Fig. 3 Manufacturing production: the RBI survey vs. quantitative data

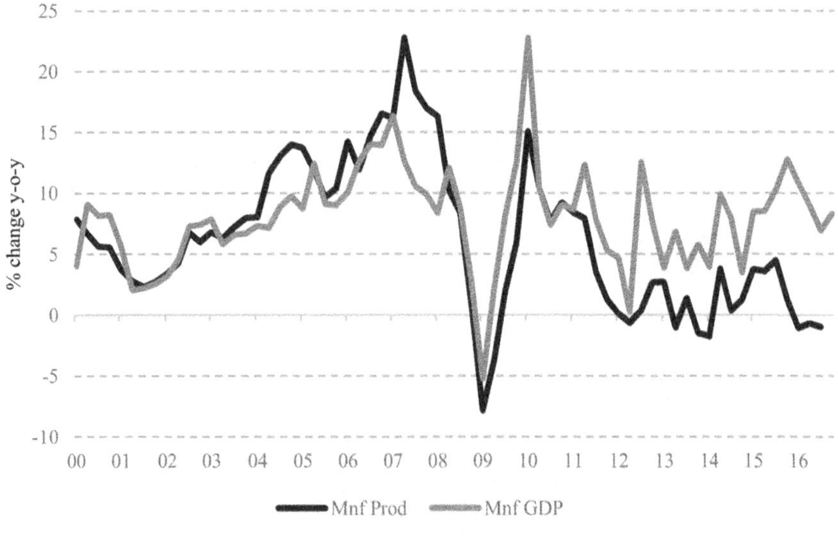

Fig. 4 Quantitative data: manufacturing production vs. manufacturing GDP

In all, the relatively tight co-movement among the results of the various surveys in general and between the survey results and real GDP growth in particular shows that they measure the same phenomenon and are by implication reliable.

6 Final Remarks

Various providers produce qualitative data in India. Although the survey methods adhere to the basics of the BTS method, there is wide variation on a detailed level. Despite these differences, the various composite indices reveal the same trend and move closely together with real GDP growth over time.

References

A graphical story of the Indian economy in 2011 (2011) Urbanomics. [Web log post]. http://gulzar05.blogspot.co.za/2011/12/graphical-story-of-indian-economy-in.html. Accessed 31 May 2017

Bhattacharya S (2015) Clearing the fog on the new GDP numbers. Ideas for India. 24 June. [Online]. http://ideasforindia.in//article.aspx?article_id=1470. Accessed 1 Jun 2017

Business confidence in India down marginally (2012) [Online]. http://www.livemint.com/r/LiveMint/Period1/2012/12/04/Photos/g-Money-business-index-(Web).jpg. Accessed 31 May 2017

CIRET (2017) [Online]. A synoptic table of inquiries, January 1998. https://www.ciret.org/idc/. Accessed 22 Aug 2017

Confederation of Indian Industry (CII) (2017) [Online]. About us. http://www.cii.in/about_us_History.aspx?enc=ns9fJzmNKJnsoQCyKqUmaQ. Accessed 30 May 2017

Declining sentiment? (2016) Business standard. 10 June. [Online]. http://www.business-standard.com/article/companies/india-inc-s-business-confidence-dips-reveals-ncaer-study-116060900989_1.html. Accessed 1 Jun 2017

Dun & Bradstreet (D&B) (2017) D&B business optimism index for India for Q2 2017. [Online]. http://www.dnb.co.in/IndiaSite/. Accessed 30 May 2017

Federation of Indian Chambers of Commerce and Industry (FICCI) (2016) Business confidence survey. February. [Online]. http://ficci.in/surveys.asp#. Accessed 1 Jun 2017

Federation of Indian Chambers of Commerce and Industry (FICCI) (2017) Business confidence survey. January. [Online]. http://ficci.in/surveys.asp#. Accessed 1 Jun 2017

India's business confidence level rises 7% to 153.8 points, says survey (2010) Moneylife News & Views. [Online]. http://www.moneylife.in/article/indias-business-confidence-level-rises-7-percentage-to-1538-points-says-survey/3677.html. Accessed 31 May 2017

Lekshmi O, Mall OP (2015) Forward looking surveys for tracking Indian economy: an evaluation. IFC Bulletin. 39. April. [Online]. http://www.bis.org/ifc/publ/ifcb39.htm. Accessed Oct 2017

National Council of Applied Economic Research (NCAER) (2013) Lower business confidence in September 2013. Macro Track. October. [Online]. http://testnew.ncaer.org/image/userfiles/file/mt-oct-2013/1391673175Macro_Track_Oct_13_4-5.pdf. Accessed 30 May 2017

Organisation for Economic Co-operation and Development (OECD) (n.d) Monthly Economic Indicators (MEI). Business Tendency Surveys. India. [Online]. http://stats.oecd.org/index.aspx?queryid=305. Accessed 30 May 2017

Reserve Bank of India (RBI) (2009a) Report of the Working Group on Surveys. August. [Online]. https://rbi.org.in/Scripts/PublicationReportDetails.aspx?UrlPage=&ID=557. Accessed 30 May 2017

Reserve Bank of India (RBI) (2009b) Quarterly industrial outlook surveys: trends since 2000–01. RBI Monthly Bulletin. October. [Online]. https://rbi.org.in/Scripts/BS_ViewBulletin.aspx?Id=10616. Accessed 30 May 2017
Reserve Bank of India (RBI) (2012) Quarterly industrial outlook survey: April–June 2012. (Round 58). RBI Monthly Bulletin. August. [Online]. https://rbi.org.in/Scripts/BS_ViewBulletin.aspx?Id=13480. Accessed 30 May 2017
Reserve Bank of India (RBI) (2016) Industrial outlook survey 2015–16. RBI Bulletin. June. [Online]. https://rbi.org.in/Scripts/BS_ViewBulletin.aspx?Id=16281. Accessed 30 May 2017
Reserve Bank of India (RBI) (2017a) Monetary Policy Report. April. [Online]. https://rbi.org.in/Scripts/PublicationsView.aspx?id=17454. Accessed 30 May 2017
Reserve Bank of India (RBI) (2017b) Industrial outlook survey (Questionnaire). April–June. [Online]. https://www.rbi.org.in/Scripts/BS_ViewForms.aspx. Accessed 30 May 2017
Reserve Bank of India (RBI) (2017c) Services and infrastructure outlook survey. April–June. [Online]. https://www.rbi.org.in/Scripts/BS_ViewForms.aspx. Accessed 30 May 2017
Sinha SK (n.d) Business expectations survey: analysing Indian data. OECD leading indicators. [Online]. http://www.oecd.org/std/leading-indicators/33653943.pdf. Accessed 30 May 2017
Slideshare (n.d) FICCI Business Confidence. [Online]. https://www.slideshare.net/search/slideshow?ft=all&lang=en&page=1&q=FICCI+CONFIDENCE&qid=432c919a-0f3a-4c4b-a931-932afcc36850&searchfrom=header&sort=&ud=any. Accessed 31 May 2017
The Ministry of Statistics and Programme Implementation (MOSPI) (n.d) National Accounts Data. Download tables. [Online]. http://mospi.gov.in/data. Accessed 31 May 2017
Trading Economics (n.d.) India Business Confidence. [Online]. https://tradingeconomics.com/india/business-confidence. Accessed 31 May 2017

Business Tendency Surveys in China

Miao Chen and Jiancheng Pan

1 Introduction

In the 1990s, the Survey and Statistics Department of the People's Bank of China and the Department of National Economy of the State Planning Commission (current National Development and Reform Commission) conducted business tendency surveys (BTS). In 1992, the Comprehensive Department of National Bureau of Statistics (NBS) started to study the feasibility of conducting business tendency surveys. In 1994, NBS conducted its first survey in some regions of China. In 1998, NBS decided to conduct the nationwide BTS, which were organized and implemented by the Enterprise Survey Organization of NBS. Business tendency surveys have been conducted by China Economic Monitoring and Analysis Center (CEMAC) of NBS since 2012. CEMAC adjusted the BTS program, including adjustment of the questionnaires and the calculating method, to highlight the forecasting capability of surveys, while the business tendency survey of the industry sector[1] is conducted by the Department of Manufacturing Statistics of NBS.

[1]The industry sector includes the manufacturing industry, the mining industry, and the electricity, heat, gas, and water production and supply industry.

M. Chen (✉) · J. Pan
China Economic Monitoring and Analysis Center, National Bureau of Statistics of the People's Republic of China, Beijing, China
e-mail: chenmiao@stats.gov.cn

S. Smirnov et al. (eds.), *Business Cycles in BRICS*, Societies and Political Orders in Transition, https://doi.org/10.1007/978-3-319-90017-9_15

2 Scope

Considering that the BTS are supposed to collect information about assessment on enterprises' business performance and plans on enterprises' production, employment, and investment, the respondents are required to be the most senior persons (e.g., the owner, store/office/production manager, the chief financial officer, the chief executive officer, the managing director) instead of other stuff such as statisticians.

BTS cover nearly 400,000 enterprises of eight sectors (the industry sector; the construction sector; the wholesale and retail sector; the transportation, storage, and postal sector; the hotel and catering sector; the information transmission, software, and information technology services sector; the real estate sector; the social services sector[2]) in the 31 provinces, autonomous regions, and municipalities directly under the central government and the Xinjiang Production and Construction Corps.

3 Data Collection

3.1 Sample Design

3.1.1 Sample Size and Sample Structure

China's BTS are sampling surveys.

In 2013, the sample size was 69,000. Considering the fact that China is in a stage of industrialization and there are tremendous differences among the subsectors of industry sector, to analyze the performance and structure of industry sector requires a large sample size. As a result, China's BTS cover 60,000 enterprises of industry sector. As to other sectors, the amounts of samples are as follows: 1500 construction contractors; 2000 wholesalers and retailers; 1000 transportation, storage, and postal services providers; 1000 hotel and catering contractors; 1000 information transmissions, software, and information technology services providers; 1500 real estate contractors; and 1000 social services providers. Some provinces willing to conduct provincial BTS are required to enlarge the amount of provincial samples to heighten the representativeness of the regional survey.

NBS enlarged the sample size of BTS in 2016 to nearly 400,000, with nearly 90,000 enterprises of industry sector. As to other sectors, the amounts of sample are as follows: nearly 36,000 construction contractors; more than 140,000 wholesalers and retailers; more than 21,000 transportation and postal services providers; more than 33,000 hotel and catering contractors; more than 5300 information

[2]The social services sector includes leasing industry; business services; professional technical services; ecological protection and environmental treatment industry; public facilities management industry; resident services and other services; radio, television, film, and television recordings services; culture and art industry; and entertainment industry.

transmission, software, and information technology services providers; more than 39,000 real estate contractors; and more than 30,000 social services providers.

3.1.2 Sampling Method and Sample Maintenance

NBS has established the database of all businesses registered for company and their details, including main business turnover, value-added tax, full-time employees, region, contact details (including address, telephone, and fax), etc.

First, all the enterprises in the pool are sorted (the enterprises of the selected sectors are sorted, respectively) according to the main business turnover or full-time employees. To make sure that the key enterprises are covered in the survey, the first 30 enterprises in the ranking are selected as samples. These 30 samples are updated according to the ranking of main business turnover once a year. Then, the other enterprises in the pool are sorted (the enterprises of the selected sectors are sorted, respectively) according to the main business turnover. From these enterprises the rest samples are selected via probability-proportionate-to-size (PPS) sampling method.

The NBS's BTS are conducted quarterly. In the survey, the same sample of participants is surveyed from the first quarter to the fourth quarter in a year. It is possible that some participant goes bankruptcy (or encounters other condition that brings about a business failure) and consequently fails to be a respondent, and then another respondent (required to be in the same sector, with the same firm size and in the same region) is recruited to replace it. Besides of this, new respondents are recruited every year to replace 20% of the sample.

3.2 The Questionnaires

NBS's questionnaires of business tendency surveys contain only qualitative questions. Respondents are required to answer the exact same questionnaire every quarter. Besides, respondents are required to fill in a basic information form in the first quarter of every year. This basic information form contains questions on information about main business, main business turnover, location, firm size, and registration type, which are used to subgroup the surveyed companies for further study.

There are eight questionnaires in NBS's business tendency surveys, including questionnaires, respectively, for the enterprises of the eight sectors.

In order to make questionnaires as simple as possible, the total amount of questions is quite limited. The principles to design the questionnaires are the following: questions are focused on the important aspects of business; answers to the questions are impossible to be collected or be collected in time through quantitative statistics; and questions are designed to collect more information about expectation. For instance, because the price statistics (including the producer price statistics and consumer price statistics) in China boasts a high efficiency and the relevant statistic data are able to be collected in time, the questionnaires of business tendency surveys don't contain questions on prices.

The BTS questionnaires cover eight types of questions in common, namely, (1) entrepreneur's assessment of the industry performance in the current quarter and entrepreneur's expectation on industry performance in the next quarter, (2) entrepreneur's assessment of the enterprise's business performance in the current quarter and entrepreneur's expectation on the enterprise's business performance in the next quarter, (3) the enterprise's overall profitability in the current quarter, (4) the labor cost in the current quarter, (5) the need of raising capital in the current quarter, (6) the number of employee to be recruit in the next quarter, (7) the plan of fixed-asset investment in the next quarter, and (8) the production in the next quarter. The wording of the questions is adopted for the unique characteristics of each sector. For instance, the production in the next quarter is referred to as the "newly signed project contract" in the construction survey; the "sales order" in the industry survey and the wholesale and retail survey; the "services ordered" in the transportation, storage, and postal survey and the social services survey; and the "rooms or tables reserved" in the hotel and catering survey.

The questionnaires of business tendency surveys also cover some questions exclusively for some sector. For instance, the "number of newly started projects" is covered in the construction survey, the "rental fee" is covered in the wholesale and retail survey, the "occupancy rate" is covered in the hotel and catering survey, and the "area of land purchased" is covered in the real estate survey.

Questionnaires of business tendency surveys are closed qualitative questionnaires. The respondent only has to choose from the given three optional answers that best fit his/her own judgment. The optional answers are usually "good/normal/poor," "optimistic/neutral/pessimistic," "up/the same/down," "above the normal level/at the normal level/below the normal level," etc.

If necessary, such as in the case of financial crisis, a small number of open-ended questions were added in the questionnaires, namely, "difficulties encountered by enterprises" and "proposals to government for policy-making" to gather more information.

During the design of questionnaires, it's necessary to take seasonal factor into consideration. When conducting BTS, many other countries in the world tend to remind the respondents to notice that if the seasonal factor is excluded in the question. For instance, "without the consideration of seasonal factor, the sales in the current quarter are above the normal level/at the normal level/below the normal level," or "taking the seasonal factor into consideration, the product inventories are above the normal level/at the normal level/below the normal level." Practice indicates that through this way, the influence of seasonal variations could be excluded to some extent but is still partially remained. The BTS conducted by INSEE (Institut National de la Statistique et des Études Économiques) took another way by proposing a question about if the respondent's answer is involved with seasonal factor at the end of the questionnaire.

In China's BTS, some indicators vulnerable to seasonal influence (such as profitability, inventory level, order level, investment plan, etc.) are excluded of seasonal variations through the question designed as a variable is "above/at/below the normal level" or a variable is "higher/the same to/lower when compared to the same period of previous year."

3.3 Collection Method, Response Rate, and Timing

According to the statistics law of the People's Republic of China, Article 3, "state organs, public organizations, enterprises, institutions, and self-employed industrialists and businessmen that are under statistical investigation shall, in accordance with the provisions of this law and state regulations, provide truthful statistical data. They may not make false entries or conceal statistical data belatedly. Falsification of or tampering with statistical data shall be prohibited" and, Article 4, "people's governments at all levels and all departments, enterprises, and institutions may, according to the needs of their statistical work, set up statistics institutions and staff them with statisticians." Protected by this law, NBS obtains the private contact details of companies' statisticians, which helps a lot in the business tendency surveys.

NBS developed a reporting system to collect almost all the data, to which a quick access is on the NBS's homepage. China's BTS are also conducted through this system.

Usually, NBS releases "A notice about launching business tendency surveys of the year 2016" (for instance) at the end of 2015, which is published on the homepage of NBS, aiming to introduce the procedure of business tendency surveys, guarantee strict confidence, and ask for respondents' cooperation.

The specific survey task is executed by the municipal statistics bureaus. They provide guidance to participants on how to complete the survey online. The guidance focuses on four aspects: vague information need to be verified with the participants; a further interpretation of the questions on the questionnaires; the importance of the requirement that the questionnaires should be completed by the most senior persons, instead of other employees such as a statistician; and alternative way to return the questionnaire in case of special circumstances, which is usually via fax or e-mail.

During the survey, respondents complete only the questionnaire applicable to their business. The municipal statistics organizations are responsible for checking the progress and calling/sending an e-mail reminder to follow-up all respondents that had not replied 2 or 3 days prior to the due date. The municipal statistics organizations are also available when participants have problems related to the survey.

The overall response rate was higher than 90% for the construction sector; the wholesale and retail sector; transportation, storage, and postal sector; the hotel and catering sector; the information transmission, the software, and information technology services sector; the real estate sector; and social services sector in 2013 (the overall response rates of other years are unavailable; the response rate of the industry sector is unavailable).

The reference period of the NBS's surveys is a calendar quarter (i.e., the first quarter refers to the 3 months: January, February, and March). Given the NBS's desire to release the results during the first month of the next quarter (i.e., April, July, October, and January), the surveys have to take place in late March, June, September, and December.

4 Processing the Results

4.1 Data Transformation

All data is converted to net balances, i.e., the unweighted percentage of respondents indicating that a particular activity is "up" less the weighted percentage indicating "down" compared to the last quarter or the same period of previous year.

4.2 Weighting and Calculation

4.2.1 Business Climate Index

Business climate index is a composite index of current business climate index and expected business climate index.

The current business climate index reflects the percentage of respondents that assessed prevailing business performance as "good" less the percentage of respondents that assessed prevailing business performance as "bad" in a particular sector. The result is multiplied by 100 and then plus 100 to convert it to an index that can vary between 0 and 200. The expected business climate index reflects the percentage of respondents that expect the business performance in the next quarter as "good" less the percentage of respondents that expect the business performance in the next quarter as "bad" in a particular sector. The result is also multiplied by 100 and then plus 100 to convert it to an index varying between 0 and 200.

To calculate the business climate index, the current business climate index is weighted by 40%, while the expected business climate index is weighted by 60%. The range of business climate index is 0–200. When business climate index is more than 100, the economic operation is prosperous, and the higher the figure is, the more prosperous the economic operation is; when business climate index is less than 100, economic operation is in recessive, and the lower the figure is, the more recessive the economic operation is.

The NBS's composite business climate index is calculated as the weighted average of the business climate indices of eight sectors, namely, that of industry sector; construction sector; wholesale and retail sector; transportation, storage, and postal sector; hotel and catering sector; information transmission, software, and information technology services sector; real estate sector; and social services sector. The composite business climate index is also in the range of 0–200.

However, the structure of sample of different sectors may vary from the sector size weights. The weight of a sector is usually based on the percentage of GDP of which its value added accounts for. The eight weights are, respectively, 40% (industry sector), 11% (construction sector), 15.4% (wholesale and retail sector), 9.6% (transportation and postal sector), 3.9% (hotel and catering sector), 4.6% (information transmission, software, and information technology services sector), 8.7% (real estate sector), and 6.8% (social services sector). The weight of each sector is approximately the same to the percentage that the sector's added value accounts for the GDP.

It may be noticed that the added value of the industry sector accounts for 40% of GDP, while the sample size of it accounts for 80% of the total sample. It's because that the industry sector boasts a crucial meaning in business tendency surveys and tremendous differences between its subsectors exist. A sample size large enough provides the possibility for further analysis of the subsectors of the industry sector. Furthermore, in order to ensure the representativeness of sample, enough respondents are necessary. Considering the large volume of China's economy, a sample of 1000 per sector is the basic requirement to meet. For instance, the sample size of both the transportation and postal sector and the hotel and catering sector is 1000, while the added value of the hotel and catering sector is less than 30% of that of the transportation and postal sector.

NBS does not apply sample weight. NBS's sample collection is based on the principle of PPS, which means that an enterprise of big size tends to be selected as a participant with a higher probability; thus the firm sizes are not taken into consideration.

4.2.2 Business Confidence Index

Business confidence index is a composite index of current business confidence index and expected business confidence index.

The current business climate index reflects the percentage of respondents that rated industrial operational situation as "optimistic" less the percentage of respondents that rated industrial operational situation as "pessimistic" in a particular sector. The result is multiplied by 100 and then plus 100 to convert it to an index that can vary between 0 and 200. The expected business confidence index reflects the percentage of respondents that expected the industrial operational situation in the next quarter as "optimistic" less the percentage of respondents that expected the industrial operational situation in the next quarter as "pessimistic" in a particular sector. The result is also multiplied by 100 and then plus 100 to convert it to an index.

The calculation method of business confidence index is similar to that of business climate index. When business confidence index is more than 100, the economic operation is prosperous, and the higher the figure is, the more prosperous the

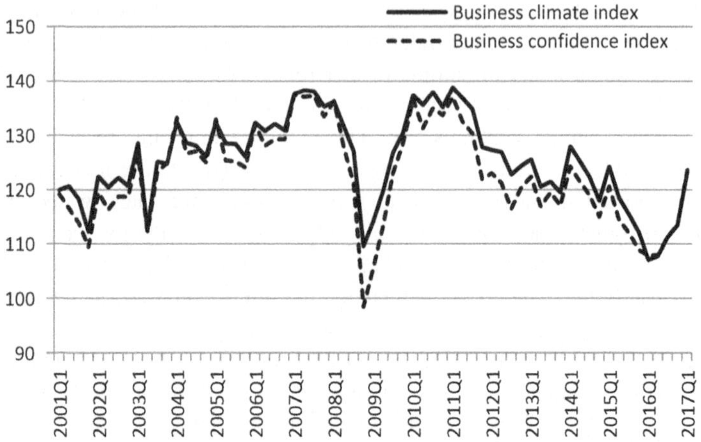

Chart 1 Business climate index and business confidence index

economic operation is; when business climate index is less than 100, economic operation is in recessive, and the lower the figure is, the more recessive the economic operation is.

The NBS's composite business confidence index is also calculated as the weighted average of the confidence indices of the eight sectors, with the same weights which are used in the calculation of business climate index. Similarly to the business climate index, no sample weight is taken into consideration.

There is a very strong correlation between business climate index and entrepreneur confidence index. They tend to change in the same direction but usually in varying degrees. The different degrees of the changes of business climate index and entrepreneur confidence index reflect whether the entrepreneur confidence index is overoptimistic or over-pessimistic (see Chart 1).

4.2.3 Other Indices

Thanks to the large amount of sample, NBS further calculate indices of industry sector according to firm sizes (large enterprises, medium-sized enterprises, small-sized enterprises), regions (eastern part, middle part, western part, and northeastern part), and registered firm types (state-owned enterprises; stock corporations; limited liability enterprises; foreign, Hong Kong, Macao, and Taiwan-invested enterprises; and private enterprises). In these cases, the weights of the eight industries are also taken into consideration during the calculation.

5 Use of the Survey Data

5.1 Business Climate Index

Business climate index is mainly used for monitoring economic cycle fluctuations. Based on the business climate index and its changes, the current economic operational situation could be illustrated, and the future economic operational situation could be forecast.

The reason why business climate index can be used to monitor economic cycle fluctuations is that it tends to change together with the macro-economy index. First, the business climate index is calculated based on the entrepreneurs' assessment on business performance, and the entrepreneurs are familiar with their own business performance and sensitive to market changes. Therefore, the business climate index complied with the surveyed entrepreneurs' assessments represents the overall economic operational situation and the future trend. Second, entrepreneurs are decision-makers of enterprises. Their judgment would directly affect their business strategy, such as increasing or decreasing production or investment. Thereby, the correlation between business climate index and macroeconomic performance is strengthened.

Business tendency surveys were originally conducted for the aim of assessing economic situation timely. It provides us with a reliable and quick overview of economic trend, especially when the economy is in fluctuations.

In Europe, the quantitative statistical data tend to be released one and a half months after they are collected. Thus, the business climate index comes to be a crucial tool for timely economic situation analysis.

While, in China, quantitative statistical data tend to be released within half a month after they are collected, economic analysis is usually based on quantitative statistical data. However, as the BTS technology matures, the business climate index makes more contribution to economic situation analysis. For instance, the figure of business climate index could tell whether the economy is in the prosperous region and which region (more prosperous or more depressed) the economy is tending toward. A series of leading indicators obtained via BTS, including orders, investment, and employment plans, can be applied to forecast the future economic situation.

5.2 Other Survey Data

Other survey data could be applied to analyze the structure and the internal impetus of economy and to assess the quantitative data.

5.2.1 Structure of Economy

The business climate indices of the eight sectors, which are processed into unified caliber and used to compile the composite business climate index, make comparative analysis among these sectors possible. The comparison among the eight sectors helps to provide an illustration of economic structure. Furthermore, considering the imperfect situation in service sector statistics in China, other BTS data could provide useful information about operational situation in service sector, including the real estate industry; the information transmission, software, and information technology services industry; the transportation, storage, and postal industry; and the social services industry.

5.2.2 Internal Impetus of Economy

The BTS questionnaires contain some questions on details of business operation. The answers to these questions help to infer the factors affecting the business operation, and then the impetus and barrier of the business operation could be concluded.

For instance, the analysis based on the answers to the question "the enterprise's access to credit is adequate/normal/inadequate" may help to assess the financing difficulties of enterprises; the analysis based on the answers to the question "the enterprise's orders in the current quarter" and the question "the enterprise's orders in the next quarter" may help to assess the market situation; the analysis based on the answers to the question "the enterprise's inventory situation" may help to assess the enterprise's operation phase (i.e., inventory replenishment period/normal production period/destocking period); and the changes of business climate indies of upstream sector and downstream sector may illustrate the interactions between them.

5.2.3 Assessment of Quantitative Data

The results of business tendency surveys can be used to assess the quality of quantitative statistic data. Despite that the quality of official quantitative statistics is improved a lot, the results are still biased due to the influence of local governments to some local statistics organizations, while the BTS collect information from enterprises, which provides a direct access for sample to report the assessment. Therefore, the influence of local governments could be avoided.

6 Limitations and Plans for the Future

6.1 Limitations

Domestic and international experience illustrates that there is a significant correlation between business climate index and economic growth indicators, such as GDP growth rate. However, sometimes they change in the same direction but in different degrees.

On the one hand, the BTS results are calculated as discrete indices. Therefore, the results are inevitably lack of some subtle information and fail to reflect the economic fluctuations accurately. The mood of the entrepreneurs exerts big influence on the results of business tendency surveys.

For instance, in the second quarter of 2003 when China was fighting the severe acute respiratory syndrome (SARS) epidemic, the business climate index of that quarter fell by 16 points to 112.6 from 128.6 of the first quarter of 2003, while the GDP growth rate fell by only 2.0 percentage points. The data typically explained the "mood" influence exerted on the business climate index (see Chart 2).

On the other hand, the GDP growth rate illustrates only the growth rate of total economic volume, without any information on the efficiency of economy or the changes in the economic structure, while the business climate index offers us with more information of market situation, profitability and future trend, etc.

Therefore, the business climate index does not necessarily change in the same direction and to the same degree with the economic growth rate. The business climate index and quantitative statistical data are not substitutable, but complementary.

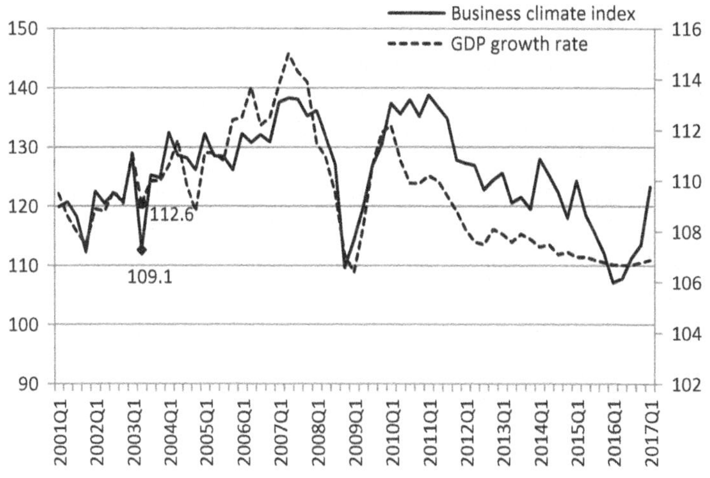

Chart 2 Business climate index and GDP growth rate

6.2 Future Plans

NBS wants to introduce some changes in the future and tries to bring the NBS's method of business tendency surveys closer in line with the international norm.

6.2.1 Seasonal Adjustment

Despite that the seasonal factors were tried to be excluded when designing the questionnaires, the time series of business tendency index from 1999 still shows a seasonal variation. Business tendency index is compiled with current business tendency index and expected business tendency index, in which the expected business tendency index shows a relatively obvious seasonal variation. Therefore, further seasonal adjustment is necessary. X12-ARIMA or factor adjustment method should be adopted to improve the validity of BTS results.

6.2.2 Frequency

Considering that during the period of economic fluctuations, the quarterly business tendency survey tends to fail to reflect the various changes of economy. When possible, it is necessary to adjust the business tendency surveys to monthly surveys.

6.2.3 Forecast

NBS has conducted BTS for over 19 years and has contained a time series of more than 70 observations. The time series could be further analyzed via mathematical statistics to find the correlation with quantitative data. Based on which the BTS results may become a useful tool for forecasting the economy.

6.2.4 International Exchanges and Cooperation

NBS should actively participate in the activities held by Centre for International Research on Economic Tendency Surveys (CIRET) and other international organizations to learn the experience of business tendency surveys from OECD, IFO, etc.

7 Release of the Survey Data

The press release of business tendency surveys was issued on the homepage of NBS, and the data was released in the publication called "China Monthly Economic Indicators." The release of the information was on a date when most of the quarterly quantitative data were published. An advance release calendar is posted on the NBS's web page at the beginning of each year. From 2014 onward the BTS results were released in the "China Monthly Economic Indicators" quarterly. The NBS's survey data is available in electronic format since 1999.

The business tendency surveys are part of NBS's official duty, so they are fully funded by NBS.

Bibliography

Campello A (2013) BRICS correlation matrices. Unpublished presentation delivered at the 2nd BRICS Working Group Meeting. October, Zurich

NBS (2011) National Statistical Programmes-2012, Beijing

NBS (2013) China's main statistical concepts: standards and methodology, 2nd edn. NBS, Beijing

NBS (2015) National Statistical Programmes-2016, Beijing

NBS (2016) National Statistical Programmes-2017, Beijing

OECD (2003) Business tendency surveys. A handbook. OECD, Paris

South Africa: The BER'S Business Tendency Surveys

George Kershoff

1 Introduction

Prof C.G.W. Schumann founded the Bureau for Economic Research (BER) at Stellenbosch University in 1944 with the objective to "(1) collect and maintain economic data to continuously assess current economic conditions in South Africa and (2) do research, especially of a statistical nature, on the Union's national income, general economic tendencies and cycles, as well as related problems of an economic or business economic nature" (Bouwer 1967: 1; own translation). This objective started taking shape when in 1950 J.C. du Plessis's research on *Economic Fluctuations in South Africa 1910–1949* appeared as the BER's second publication. In 1953 Prof Schumann launched an investigation into the feasibility of conducting quarterly business tendency surveys (BTS) in the trade and manufacturing sectors in South Africa, and in 1954 the first survey results were published. Since then the BER has been continuously conducting business tendency surveys and is therefore among the small group of institutions in the world that have done so for more than six decades. The BER has been a member of CIRET (the Centre for International Research in Economic Tendency Surveys) since the start of the association in 1960 and hosted the biannual conference in South Africa in 1993.

In 2001 Jim O'Neill, chairman of Goldman Sachs, coined the acronym BRIC in a publication titled *Building Better Global Economic BRICs* to refer to the four major emerging economies: Brazil, Russia, India and China. In 2009 these countries formed the BRIC group and, after South Africa joined in 2010, changed the name to BRICS (Wikipedia 2015).

At the 2008 CIRET conference in Santiago, Chile, closer connections between the BER and Brazilian delegates emerged, and in 2011 the BER and IBRE (the

G. Kershoff (✉)
Bureau for Economic Research (BER), Stellenbosch University, Stellenbosch, South Africa
e-mail: gjkk@sun.ac.za

S. Smirnov et al. (eds.), *Business Cycles in BRICS*, Societies and Political Orders in Transition, https://doi.org/10.1007/978-3-319-90017-9_16

Brazilian Institute of Economics) at FGV (Getulio Vargas Foundation) concluded a memorandum of understanding. The BER supported Brazil's initiative to form a BRICS working group within CIRET, which met for the first time on the side of the CIRET workshop in Moscow in 2011. The BER has participated and contributed to initiatives of this group, such as this book, from the beginning.

One could easily think that the rationale for a section on survey methods in a book about "Economic Cycles in BRICS" is only because it is spearheaded by the institutions that conduct business tendency surveys in the member countries. However, if one engages further with the topic and realises that each country has a unique method adapted to local conditions, it becomes clear that this section is indispensable for cross-country analysis and the estimation of BRICS aggregates. This, in turn, is required to facilitate studies of economic cycles in BRICS and eventually produce greater harmonisation among the countries. Furthermore, in the case of South Africa, this chapter also addresses a major shortcoming, namely, that a recent description of the survey method, the so-called metadata, is currently not publicly available.

2 Scope

As noted above, the BER conducted its first survey of the manufacturing and trade (i.e. retail, wholesale and motor trade) sectors in 1954. The sector coverage was expanded to the building sector (i.e. main contractors and sub-contractors such as electricians, plumbers and shopfitters) in 1969. The BER also took responsibility for a quantitative building cost survey in that year. In 1975 the BER started a postal survey among white consumers. In 1982 the scope of the consumer opinion survey (COS) was expanded to black consumers and the survey method changed to personal interviews (Stuart 1978: 86). In 1994, the scope of the COS was expanded to all races. The breadth of the building survey was expanded on two occasions: (1) architects and quantity surveyors were added in 1986 in order to track developments along the whole building pipeline (i.e. from the initiation to the completion of projects), and (2) civil engineering contractors were added in 1997. In 1999 a manufacturing purchasing managers' (PMI) survey modelled on the one of the ISM (Institute of Supply Management) in the USA was launched. Work on the financial sector started in the early 2000s: retail and investment banks in 2002, asset managers and life insurers in 2003 and short-term insurers in 2006. In 2005, an other services sector survey was also started.

The frequency of all the BER's surveys is quarterly, except for the PMI survey, which is monthly. Currently, the BER makes the results of all the surveys public, except for short-term insurers and the other services sector. Further work (e.g. on sector size weights) needs to be completed before the BER could start to release the other services survey results, and in contrast to the other surveys, the BER may decide to make the results available to only paying clients.

For the purpose of focus, only the BER's building, manufacturing, trade and other services surveys are discussed in this chapter. The consumer and PMI surveys are therefore not dealt with. For a detailed description of the financial sector survey, see Kershoff (2008). It is assumed that the reader is familiar with business tendency surveys. More specifically, this chapter takes the OECD (2003) and UNSD's (2014) guidelines as starting point and indicates the extent to which the BER's survey method agrees and deviates from them.

3 Data Collection

3.1 Sample Design

3.1.1 Population Universe and Survey Frame

As with all surveys, the population universe and survey frame need to be specified to establish which sectors and firms to include. The BER uses version 3.1 of the International Standard Industrial Classification of All Economic Activities (ISIC) and its previous adaptation for South Africa, the fifth edition of the South African

Table 1 Sector coverage

Sector	SIC code	ISIC code	Subsectors (with the corresponding ISIC code) not covered
Manufacturing	3	D	Petroleum (23)
Building and construction	5	F	Site preparation (451)
Wholesale trade	61	51	Petroleum (5141), precious stones (included in 5139)
Retail trade	62	52	Retail trade of second-hand goods and not in stores, repairs (524, 525 and 526)
Motor trade	63	50	Repair of motor vehicles (502), automotive fuel sale (504)
Financial services	8	J	Central banking (6511), other financial intermediation (6592), reinsurance (incl. in 6602), medical aid funding (6603), auxiliary activities to insurance and pension funding (672)
Other Services			
Catering and accommodation Transport and communication Real estate and business services Personal services	64 7 84–86, 88 94, 96, 99	H I K 90, 92, 93	Pipelines (603), air transport (62), airport and harbour operation (6303), postal services (6411), telecommunication (642), research and development (73), news agencies (922), libraries, museums and other cultural activities (924)

Standard Industrial Classification (SIC) (released in 1993 and used by the official statistical agencies until 2014), to demarcate the population universe. Table 1 shows the subsectors of each sector which the BER does not cover. It is worth noting that there are a few subsectors that the BER does cover and includes in the sector total, but for which it does not publish the results due to small samples. Examples are leather, footwear and rubber manufacturing.

Statistics South Africa (Stats SA) maintains a National Business Register, which contains the (confidential) details of all businesses registered for company and value-added tax at the South African Revenue Services (SARS). The BER does not have access to this register, as it is not an official (government) body.

The BER, therefore, has to use other sources to obtain information on the number of firms per sector, size class and region. These sources include (1) Stats SA's periodical business censuses, (2) the explanatory notes to Stats SA's various statistical releases (e.g. the manufacturing sales and production release indicates that the frame size that Stats SA used in 2011 was 51,000) and (3) SARS's Tax Statistics.

3.1.2 Sampling Method and Panel Maintenance

The BER obtains the contact details of potential participants from private address list providers, telephone directories and the Internet. In the past, the membership lists of sector associations and accreditation bodies were also used, but over the last few years, privacy concerns have just about closed this avenue, and the last time the BER had access to such a list was in 2008.

On these lists the BER selects local stores, factories/manufacturing plants and premises. In the case of large corporations with many stores or plants, the BER selects the local stores or plants and not the head office. To provide for the fact that various products or services are often produced, sold or provided at the same location, the BER asks the respondent at the time of recruitment to identify the one that represents the bulk (i.e. made up the highest percentage of total turnover during the previous year). The BER, therefore, does not survey kind-of-activity units (KAU), but local units. This makes the calculation of provincial (regional) results possible, but produces somewhat less precise subsector estimates (for instance, in the case of a retailer selling both clothing and food, all its responses are taken as indication of clothing if clothing makes up the bulk of turnover) (UNSD 2014: 30).

At these local units, the BER selects the most senior person (e.g. the owner, store/office/production manager, the chief financial officer, the chief executive officer, the managing director) that would be familiar with the performance of the business and would, therefore, not have to consult colleagues to complete the questionnaire.

The reporting units of the BER's business surveys are, therefore, the most senior people at local units. In the remainder of this chapter, these reporting units are referred to as participants or respondents.

The BER does not use random sampling, but stratified, deliberate (purposive or judgemental) sampling to put together a sample. It is stratified, as the survey frame is divided into several non-overlapping sub-frames, so-called strata (UNSD 2014: 68). In practice, these sub-frames amount to subsectors. If a large number of contact details are available per subsector, the BER applies systematic sampling. In practice, this amounts to sorting all available contact details alphabetically and selecting, say, every second one. However, if a subsector of the population universe is heterogeneous in terms of firm size (e.g. beverage manufacturing) or the number of firms is very small (e.g. vehicle manufacturers), the BER selects all available contact details (i.e. it employs exhaustive sampling). The BER's sampling method is deliberate, as the sample units are not randomly selected, and their probability of selection cannot be calculated, as the exact number of firms in the population universe is unknown to the BER.

The BER's sampling method is not fully in line with the OECD (2003) and UNSD's (2014) recommendation on how to recruit participants in the first round, but unfortunately this is the only practical option available to the BER. One, therefore, needs to be careful when one draws inferences about the population universe based on the BER's purposively selected sample. The OECD (2003: 21) notes that "there is however considerable practical experience which shows that non-random samples can give acceptable results when used for business tendency surveys".

For the recruitment process, the BER sends an introductory letter, brochure and questionnaire to the selected potential participants by post and e-mail (if available). The letter and brochure introduce the BER as a university-based research institute with a long track record in conducting surveys, describe the rationale for the survey, offer a copy of the survey results in return for completing the questionnaire, indicate that participation is voluntary and guarantee strict confidence (i.e. assure that individual responses will not be revealed).

Despite this effort, the response to these invitations is quite low. The response rate to recruitment varies among sectors and has declined over time. For instance, in 2010 the response rate ranged from 11% for building to 9% for wholesale and 8% for retail and manufacturing. In 2012/2013 the response rate declined to 7% for building, 6% for wholesale, 4.6% for motor trade and 4% for retail and manufacturing. If the recruitment does not deliver a sufficient number of responses in the first round, more invitations are sent out in a second round (wave).

At the time of recruitment, respondents have to select the sector in which the bulk of their activity falls (in recent years the BER began to use the subsector supplied by the list provider to reduce the respondent burden and boost the response rate) and their turnover range (and in the case of manufacturing, also the number of full-time employees). To not deter potential participants, the invitees are made aware that providing information about their turnover bands is voluntary and that if provided it will only be used for weighting. If no firm size weight is provided, the mode of the sector is applied. The postal code is used to determine the province (region) of the respondent.

Those that respond to the invitations are included in a panel, i.e. the same questionnaire is sent to the same sample of respondents every quarter. Panel surveys are ideal for conducting business tendency surveys, as changes in the survey results are then more likely to reflect actual changes in the variables tracked over time than changes in the sample from the one survey to the next (UNSD 2014: 72). There is also great practical advantage in using a panel, as recruiting new participants is time-consuming and costly.

However, the OECD (2003: 21) acknowledges that "once the same group of enterprises is surveyed in repeated rounds, it is no longer strictly random. This is

Table 2 Panel size

	2000	2008	2014
Building	464	668	413
Retail	670	604	445
Wholesale	384	374	454
Motor trade	258	194	149
Manufacturing	889	1129	927
Other Services	–	874	481
Total	2665	3843	2869

because the target universe will change over time as new entrants appear and as existing enterprises cease trading or change their kind of activity. The panel may have been randomly selected for the first round but, strictly speaking it cannot be described as random in subsequent rounds".

In the BER's case, the panel is partly rotating and partly fixed. It is rotating because new respondents are recruited every 2–3 years to replace the inactive ones. It is fixed between these recruitments, as the same sample of participants is surveyed from one quarter to the next. See Table 2 for the number of respondents per sector in selected years.

3.2 The Questionnaires

A key feature of the BER's questionnaires is that, similar to those of business tendency surveys all over the world, they contain only qualitative questions. In practice, respondents receive the exact same questionnaire every quarter and only have to tick if a particular variable is "up/higher/better", "the same" or "down/lower/worse" in the current quarter relative to the same period of a year ago. For some variables, respondents also have to indicate how they expect them to develop in the following quarter (relative to the same quarter of a year ago).

The selection of questions has remained largely unchanged since the inception of the BER's business tendency surveys more than half a century ago. The last time that the BER added and discontinued questions on a large scale was in 2001. In the building survey, the questions on the quarter-on-quarter change in building activity, the value of building work on hand and some of the constraints were discontinued, while questions on the number of people employed and the overall profitability of the business were added. In the retail and wholesale trade surveys, the question on the ratio of cash to credit sales was discontinued, and questions on the change in the rate of increase in selling/purchase prices and business conditions during the current quarter were added. (In the past, only expectations for the next quarter were surveyed.)

The questionnaires cover seven types of variables, namely, (1) the level of business confidence and change in business conditions, (2) the change in activity,

(3) the change in employment, (4) the change in the rate of increase in prices and costs, (5) the change in profitability, (6) an assessment of current stocks relative to expected demand and (7) an assessment of the limiting impact of selected factors (e.g. a shortage of skilled labour or an insufficient demand) on business activity. In all cases where respondents have to indicate the change in a particular variable, they are asked to report on the realised development in the current quarter and provide their expectations for the next quarter.

Not all the kinds of variables are covered in all the surveys. Only type 1 and 2 are covered in all the surveys. Type 3 is covered in all but the motor trade survey. Type 4 is not covered in the building and motor trade surveys, while type 5 is not covered in the manufacturing and motor trade surveys. Type 6 is only covered in the manufacturing, retail and wholesale surveys. Type 7, in turn, is only covered in the building, manufacturing and other services surveys.

Except for business confidence, business conditions and employment, the wording of the questions are adopted for the unique characteristics of each sector. For instance, activity is referred to as the "volume of production" in the manufacturing survey, "the volume of sales" in the wholesale and retail trade surveys, "the number of units sold" in the motor trade survey, "the volume of building activity" in the building survey and "the volume of business" in the other services survey.

Regarding the questions that are the same across the surveys, in the case of business confidence, respondents have to rate prevailing business conditions as either "satisfactory" or "unsatisfactory". This differs from the question on business conditions, where respondents have to indicate if general business conditions are "better", "the same" or "poorer" in the current quarter compared to a year ago and what they expect for the next quarter.

In the case of the manufacturing survey, additional (qualitative) questions on changes in investment and factors limiting investment and exports/imports are posed in the first and third quarter surveys.

Tosetto and Gyomai (2009: 27) assessed the harmonisation status (i.e. the extent to which the wording of the questions agree with those of the EU harmonised survey) of the BER's manufacturing survey as "good" (4 out of 5), the retail survey as "needs to be improved" (3) and the building survey as "poor" (1).

In the third quarter of 2012, the BER added questions on the extent to which "an inadequate access to credit" hampers the firm's activity and "the number of months' work accounted for by the work on hand" to, among other things, closer align the BER's selection of questions in the building sector with that of the EU. However, the latter question was discontinued in the first quarter of 2014, as the absolute variation in the provided number of months was so wide that no descriptive statistic (i.e. the average, median or mode) could summarise it satisfactorily (in effect, too many values had to be trimmed to produce an acceptable standard deviation).

The biggest difference between the wording of the BER's questionnaires and those of almost all other countries is that the BER instructs respondents to compare the current situation with that of a year ago, whereas other countries ask for a comparison with the previous period (i.e. last month/quarter). Although the international custom is to compare the survey results with the year-on-year percentage change in corresponding quantitative series, this is actually only technically correct in South Africa's case.

3.3 *Collection Method, Response Rate and Timing*

In the past, the BER exclusively used the postal service to collect information from respondents. Between 2000 and 2005, the BER also offered respondents the option to complete the survey online. Although 80% of respondents had Internet access and 28% indicated that they prefer to respond via the Internet, only 2% ended up actually responding online. The bulk (92%) continued to return the questionnaires in the pre-paid envelopes, and 6% returned it via fax (Laubscher 2005: 5, 7). As e-mail became more widely adopted in South Africa, in 2008 the BER began to also send the questionnaire as an electronic form attached to an e-mail to respondents that provided their e-mail addresses. In 2012, the BER added the option to complete the survey online to provide for those participants that have Internet access and started sending an e-mail reminder to follow up all respondents that had not replied 1 week prior to the due date. In 2014, the online survey was improved to provide for the automatic identification of respondents and for use on tablets and smart phones.

In 2014 the BER asked the respondents about their preferred communication method, i.e. do they wish to receive the questionnaire by post only, e-mail only or both. As a result, the BER today has to use a hybrid collection method—44% of respondents prefer to receive the questionnaires per post (because they have no e-mail addresses or prefer to get a hard copy per post—this is especially prevalent in the building sector where many respondents do not operate out of offices and among micro-sized firms that tend to not have computers and Internet access); 40% prefer to receive them by both post and e-mail and 16% prefer only e-mails. The BER has to allow 5 (4 until 2014) weeks for the fieldwork of the postal survey. Due to the slowness of the postal service in South Africa, it takes about 2 weeks for the respondent to receive the questionnaire from the BER and another 2 weeks for it to be returned in the pre-paid envelope. The e-mail is sent out 2 weeks before the due date.

In 2014, the combination of a deteriorating postal service, a weakening economy and a barrage of e-mails and social media notifications led to a further decline in the number of responses. Since 2015, the BER, therefore, had to start following up regular respondents by telephone to obtain a satisfactory number of completed questionnaires for some subsectors.

It has always been a challenge to get people to respond in South Africa. The overall response rate was 36% in 2000, 41% in 2008 and 39% in 2014 if one excludes the inactive respondents on the panel. (It is interesting to note that the response rate has not changed much over the years given that it was 44% in 1965–1966 (Bouwer 1967: 16–17) and 40% in 1988 (Pellissier and Smit 1988: 1)). The response rate per sector varied from 45% for the other services survey to 36% for the manufacturing survey in 2014. The overall response rate in 2014 increased to 47% if one includes the latecomers (i.e. all the questionnaires that the BER receives after the due date). The corresponding rates for the other services and manufacturing surveys are 52 and 43%, respectively. Every 2–3 years the BER has to remove slightly more than 25% of all respondents from the panel, because they became inactive. Furthermore, the percentage of latecomers has increased from 6% in 2008 (when the BER started recording them) to 16% in 2014.

Although the response rate has remained stable over time, the number of completed questionnaires has also varied with the change in the panel size: 613 in 1961–1965 from a panel of 1138 (Bouwer 1967: 17), 2323 in 1988 from a panel of 5840 (Pellissier and Smit 1988: 1), 1151 in 2000 from a panel of 2665, 1162 in 2008 from 2801 active (i.e. only taking those that have responded during the previous 2 years) respondents and 834 from a panel of 2121 active respondents in 2014.

Besides the number of completed questionnaires, the reliability of a panel (longitudinal) study is influenced by how consistently individual respondents reply. This is because if most respondents participate almost every quarter, changes in the survey results between consecutive quarters could be attributed to a greater degree of certainty to changes in the measured phenomenon than changes in the respondents, especially if no post-stratification is administered to provide for changes in the response pattern. Over the period 2005–2007, 23% of respondents replied 75% or more of the time (i.e. 6–8 times over a 2-year period), 18% replied between 50% and 75% of the time, 25% replied between 25% and 50% of the time and 34% replied less than 25% of the time. (It is interesting to note that the response pattern has not changed much over time given that the corresponding percentages over the period 1962–1965 were 33%, 25%, 19% and 23% (own calculation based on Bouwer 1967: 18.)) The response pattern shows that the number of completed questionnaires per subsector would in most cases be too low were the BER to use only those respondents that replied in two consecutive quarters.

The reference period of the BER's surveys is a calendar quarter (i.e. the first quarter refers to the 3 months, January, February and March, etc.). Given the slowness of the postal service and the BER's desire to release the results during the last month of each quarter (i.e. March, June, September and November/ December), the fieldwork for the surveys has to take place in the middle month (i.e. February, May, August and mid-October to mid-November) of each quarter. This implies that respondents either have to make forecasts for the last month of the calendar quarter in order to provide an estimate for the full 3 months or their responses only reflect the month in which the fieldwork takes place, which is then in effect taken as a proxy for (or representative of) the full quarter. The timing of the fieldwork of the survey and the manner in which respondents interpret the questions could influence the results of studies that compare the business cycle turning points and variables of the surveys with official data. For instance, should one compare the first quarter survey results to the February or the first quarter quantitative number? In the case of turning point analysis, how does one convert the official monthly figures into quarterly figures given that there is a big difference between when a new business cycle phase starts in, for instance, January compared to March even though both months fall in the first quarter.

4 Processing the Results

4.1 Estimation Procedure: Weighting and Aggregation

In line with the international best practice, all the BER's surveys, except for building, are weighted. In practice, each response is multiplied by a factor, which is calculated as the product of a firm size and a sector size weight (except for the motor trade, where there are no subsectors). The firm size of manufacturers is based on the number of full-time employees, whereas sales revenue is used in the case of the retail, wholesale and motor trade. The sector size weight is based on the composition of manufacturing production, retail sales and wholesale sales as calculated by Stats SA. In contrast to the international guidelines, the BER does not apply sample weights, because the BER does not have access to the National Business Register and can therefore not calculate the probability of selection.

The number of employees and turnover are not used directly as firm size weights. Instead a logarithmic function is used to determine weighting factors for nine turnover/employment ranges. In this respect, the BER follows the same practice as Ifo (Ruppert 2007: 29–30). Over time the BER has kept the weighting factors the same and only adjusted the turnover ranges for inflation.

The BER applies size weights in only one step. The subsector total is calculated as the sum of the weights of all respondents in that subsector. The sector total is the sum of the weights of all the respondents falling in that sector. The BER, therefore, uses the same respondent weight (namely, the product of the firm and sector size weights) at the subsector (disaggregate) and total (aggregate) level. In contrast, the OECD (2003: 44–47) recommends that only firm size weights (therefore no sector weights) be used at the subsector level and that only sector weights (therefore no firm size weights) be used at the total level.

As is customary in the case of business tendency surveys all over the world, the BER also applies the same weights to all variables (questions). No distinction is therefore made between domestic sales, export sales, employment, selling prices, etc.

Furthermore, the BER does not adjust individual weights from one survey to the next to provide for changes in the response pattern. No calibration or any other form of post-stratification to correct the estimated value (when the sample is not an accurate reflection of the population or the response pattern changes between consecutive quarters) is, therefore, carried out.

Respondents are instructed to complete only the questions applicable to their business. So, missing items (i.e. when a respondent does not answer a specific question) are not imputed. Missing responses (i.e. when a respondent does not return a completed questionnaire in a specific quarter) are also not imputed.

The results are also not revised to provide for questionnaires received after the date of return and the processing time.

When the questions on quarter-on-quarter changes were discontinued in 2001, respondents were no longer instructed on the questionnaire to exclude seasonal variations, as the instruction to compare the current situation with that of a year ago implicitly excludes seasonal variation. The BER publishes the data in an unadjusted form, but users are cautioned that some series, nevertheless, display seasonal patterns, probably because some respondents mistakenly compare the current period with the one directly preceding it.

4.2 *Data Transformations*

Except for business confidence and the constraints, all data is converted to net balances, i.e. the weighted (except for building) percentage of respondents indicating that a particular activity is "up" less the weighted percentage indicating "down" compared to the same period a year ago. The BER publishes the estimated (realised) development for the current quarter and expected development (forecast) (if applicable) for the next quarter. (At present, the BER does not maintain times series of the expected developments.)

The business confidence index reflects the weighted percentage of respondents that rated prevailing business conditions as "satisfactory" in a particular sector. The BER's composite business confidence index (BCI) is calculated as the unweighted average of the confidence indices of five sectors, namely, that of building contractors, manufacturers, retailers, wholesalers and new vehicle dealers. This estimation method differs from that of, for instance, the European Union (EU) confidence indices, which are compiled from the weighted results of three or more survey questions. (The correlation coefficient between these series and a reference series is often used as weights.)

To calculate the constraint indices, the answers of respondents rating a particular constraint as "serious" are weighted by 0.67% and those rating it as "slightly" by 0.33%, and those rating it as "not at all" are discarded. The results are then multiplied by $100/67 = 1.49$ to convert it to an index that can vary between 0 and 100. (Currently the BER does not publish the percentage rating a variable as "not at all". Users are cautioned to obtain this information from the BER and are advised to consider both to form a balanced opinion.)

5 Reliability of the Survey Results

In assessing the reliability of the results of any type of sample survey, it is customary to distinguish between sampling and non-sampling errors.

5.1 Sampling Errors

The BER's sampling errors are probably bigger than the usual ones (which arise when information is obtained from a sample instead of all the firms (units) in the entire population universe), because it does not use random sampling, employs a panel, the response rate is relatively low and, in the case of some subsectors (i.e. strata or cells), the number of (completed) responses are less than the ideal minimum number. According to the OECD (2003: 22), "a rule of thumb is that about 30 reporting units are sufficient to obtain an acceptable level of precision for each strata for which data are to be published . . . [However,] in practice this is a maximum because some kinds of activity will be dominated by a few very large enterprises so that two or three responses might suffice".

Despite these shortcomings, it is fitting to keep in mind that the representativeness of the sampling units of qualitative surveys has a significantly smaller impact on the reliability of the survey results than those of quantitative surveys. In the case of a quantitative survey, respondents have to provide an amount in rand for the activity in question so that the total (level) can be calculated. A biased selection of respondents and a high non-response rate, therefore, could have a big impact on the total. In contrast, in the case of a qualitative survey, the (weighted) view of the majority of respondents on a particular activity is taken as an indication of the direction and intensity of the trend in the activity in question. The majority view is therefore established and not the actual size (Kershoff 2008: 11).

5.2 Non-sampling Errors

A computer programme ensures that processing and estimation errors are eliminated, because it applies the same routines. Before the year 2000, the BER used the university's mainframe computer to run a programme that was specifically written to process the BER's surveys. Since 2000, the codes and command routines to process the surveys are a module in a Microsoft Access database, and the survey could be run on any desktop computer.

To prevent errors from occurring in the capturing (input) of the questionnaires, validation rules were set up in a Microsoft Access database to prevent, among other things, the capturing of duplicate responses (which sometimes happens when a participant returns the questionnaire per post, but before it reaches the BER, also responds to the e-mail reminder). Furthermore these rules also ensure that the sector in which the questionnaire is captured matches that of the respondent and automatically matches the correct sector, province and weight to the respondent.

In the BER's case, the biggest source of non-sampling error is probably the high non-response rate. Although the BER (as spelled out earlier in this chapter) takes all reasonable measures and follows all international recommendations to treat non-responses, the non-response rate remains relatively high.

However, when considering the validity of the survey results, one has to keep in mind that a high non-response rate has a much less severe adverse impact on a qualitative than a quantitative survey. Units of the target population not selected during sampling are treated differently in quantitative than in qualitative surveys. In the case of quantitative surveys, the results of respondents are weighted (multiplied by a factor so that the aggregate agrees with the total derived from a census/benchmark survey) to provide for those that were not selected or did not respond. In the case of most qualitative surveys, no provision is made for those that were not selected during sampling or were selected, but did not respond, as it is implicitly assumed that their performance corresponds with those of the participants, the so-called missing at random assumption (MAR) (EC 2006: 51). This is a reasonable assumption, given that (1) the same factors impact on firms in the same sector (the performance of firms therefore tends to reveal the same trend) and (2) the responses cannot vary infinitely (as is the case with a quantitative survey), but are limited to "up", "the same" or "down". According to the OECD (2003: 22) "business survey data are measured on an ordinal scale and the variance of ordinal-scaled data is usually significantly lower than that of metrically-scaled data". In the case of qualitative surveys, dispersions (i.e. how prevalent a tendency in these three options is) are established and not actual quantities. So, the non-participation of Mr. X and Y does not necessarily impair the validity of a qualitative survey and their future participation will not necessarily improve the validity of the survey as long as their responses do not deviate systematically from those of the participants. The reliability of a qualitative survey is enhanced if this claim can be proved. If the survey results correspond with a reference series, then one could say with a higher degree of certainty that those units of the target population that do not participate experience similar conditions than those that do participate (Kershoff 2008: 11–12).

5.3 *Sensitivity Analysis and Plans for the Future*

Practical considerations usually compel researchers to deviate from the ideal statistical method. Other detached researchers may have different views on the impact of such deviations on the validity of the survey results. What might be acceptable to one researcher might be indefensible to another. In order to be regarded as scientific work, (1) the research method has to be spelled out clearly so that users of the information are aware of its limitations and are able to use it responsibly, (2) the producers of the information have to show how sensitive (if at all) the results are to the choices they made in the research process (some of which will be deviations from the statistical norm due to practical considerations) and (3) where possible, demonstrate that the results match those of other widely accepted, independent benchmarks (in practice, this usually amounts to showing the existence of a close correlation between the business tendency survey results and corresponding quantitative data series).

The manner in which the BER conducts business tendency surveys in South Africa deviates from the statistical norm in a number of ways, and this could potentially affect the validity of the survey results. One prominent aspect is that the BER undertakes no post-stratification (i.e. adjusting individual weights) and imputation even though the non-response rate is high. Due to the latter, the firm sizes and subsectors of the respondents could vary quite a bit between consecutive quarters. Another aspect is that the BER publishes a high number of subsectors (i.e. there is a high degree of disaggregation) relative to the number of completed questionnaires. The third aspect is the BER's weighting procedure, where (1) the logarithmic transformation of the firm size weights causes the weighting factor of large firms to be many multiples of those of small firms, and (2) the same individual weight is applied at the subsector and aggregate level.

A question that may immediately come to the disinterested observer's mind is: To what extent is the high volatility of the BER's survey results the outcome of the way in which the BER currently calculates the results or is it merely a true reflection of the measured phenomenon? (Campello 2013, showed that the survey results on the current and expect business situation in manufacturing in South Africa are significantly more volatile compared to those of the other BRICS countries.) Put differently, what effect (if any) does the response (or not) of a particular large firm in an important sector (e.g. food or basic metals manufacturing) have on the results of that subsector (i.e. at the disaggregated level) and the total (i.e. at the aggregated level)?

To determine the impact of the BER's calculation method on the volatility (calculated as the standard deviation of the average absolute quarter-on-quarter difference) and tracking record (indicated by the correlation between the survey data and the corresponding quantitative series) of the survey data, alternative methods were applied to the same responses and then compared to the results that were produced by using the BER's current method. Some of the alternatives that were tested are a different allocation of firm size weights, the introduction of dynamic individual weights (post-stratification) to provide for changes in the response pattern between consecutive surveys (i.e. to handle non-responses), the application of the OECD's recommendation of a two-step weighting procedure, the inclusion of the latecomers (which, in effect, boils down to revision) to increase the number of completed responses, the employment of different sector size weights for the manufactured export variables and the combination of a number of subsectors to produce a higher level of aggregation.

The details of the design and outcome of this analysis fall beyond the scope of this chapter, and so only the key tests and the main preliminary findings are reported.

Instead of using nine logarithmically transformed firm size weights to calculate the results, four weights corresponding to the firm size groups of the Department of Trade and Industry (DTI) (i.e. micro, small, medium-sized and large-scale enterprises) were used. In the case of manufacturing, the basis for the firm size weights was changed back from the number of employees (which was applied since 1997) to turnover, as the number of employees has turned out to be an unsuitable indicator of the relative contribution to production and exports in some sectors. This stems from the fact that, for instance, a food or clothing manufacturer could have the same firm size weight than a metal manufacturer based on the number of employees, but the value of production and exports of the metal manufacturer are much higher due to its low labour intensity. Size weights were also employed for the first time to calculate the building survey results.

Dynamic individual weights were introduced to provide for changes in the response pattern between consecutive quarters. In essence, this procedure boiled down to adjusting every individual weight every quarter so that the shares of size categories continuously correspond with the censuses.

The results were revised to provide for all the responses that reached the BER after the cut-off date, and the results were processed. (The responses of these latecomers were captured since 2006.)

Given that the sector composition of manufacturing production and exports differs quite a bit, a different set of sector size weights was used to recalculate the results of all the export variables.

Currently the BER provides for 21 subsectors and publishes the results of 16 subsectors of manufacturing. Given the relatively low number of responses of some subsectors and to align the BER's subsectors with those of Stats SA, the results were recalculated for nine subsectors by raising the level of aggregation from the SIC three-digit to the SIC two-digit level. Instead of calculating and reporting the results of, for instance, the subsectors "food" and "beverages" separately (i.e. at the SIC three-digit level), they were combined to one "food and beverages" subsector (i.e. at the SIC two-digit level).

In the case of the building sector, the BER currently publishes the results for main and sub-contractors, which are each split into the residential and non-residential sectors. Given the relatively low number of responses of some subsectors and to align the BER's subsectors with those of Stats SA, the residential and non-residential subsectors of the main and sub-contractors were combined to recalculate the results for the residential and non-residential sectors, respectively. This was, in turn, combined to calculate a total for the building sector. The provincial (regional) data was also recalculated in a similar vein; the level of aggregation was raised from main and sub-contractor level to residential and non-residential building activity level.

The preliminary results show that the track record of the alternative calculation method diverges in terms of volatility and tracking record. The alternative method, therefore, does not outperform the current method across the board.

In the case of the manufacturing survey, the alternative method produced somewhat less volatility in the case of the total and significantly less volatility in the case of most subsectors compared to the current method (Kershoff 2014b: 24, 27). (See Fig. 1.)

However, the weighted building results (alternative method) turned out much more volatile than the unweighted published results (current method) (Kershoff 2014a: 14). (See Fig. 2.)

The correlation between the survey and quantitative data were higher in the case of most subsectors if the alternative method was used to calculate the manufacturing survey results instead of the current method. The correlation increased further if the data was converted to three-period moving averages (Kershoff 2014b: 32). However, in the case of the building survey, the correlation coefficients of the published and weighted results were almost identical (Kershoff 2014a: 18).

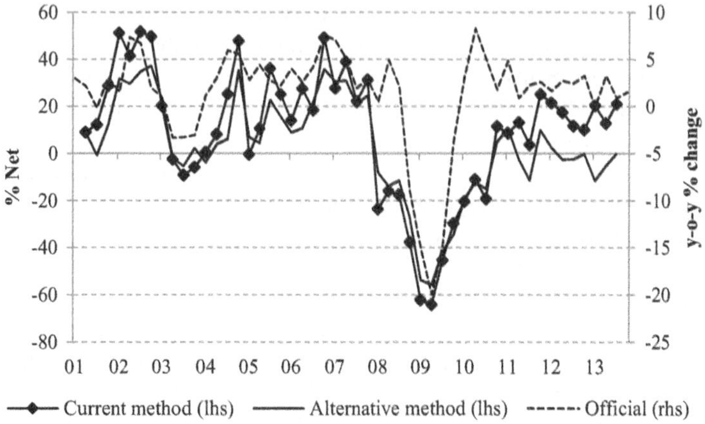

Fig. 1 Total manufacturing production

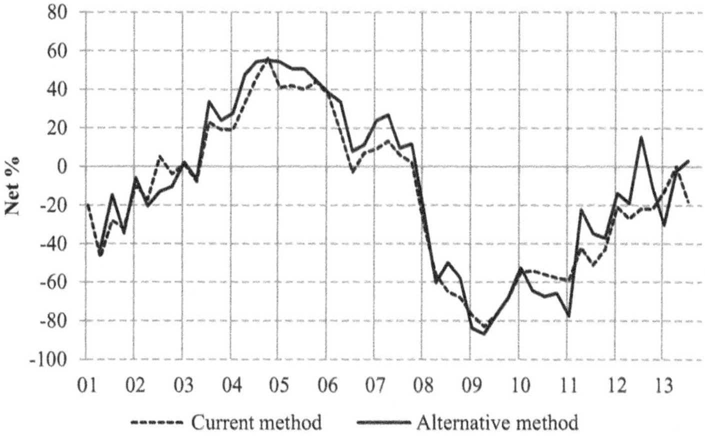

Fig. 2 Main contractors: change in building activity

The alternative method of allocating different sector weights to calculate manufactured exports produced no improvement in the tracking record relative to the current method. In the case of all but three subsectors, the correlation was low or non-existent even after converting the data to three-period moving averages (Kershoff 2014b: 34). Further research needs to be conducted to find out why there is almost no correlation. If, for instance, another quantitative series (e.g. export earnings) produces a higher correlation, then it may be that respondents confuse export volumes and earnings (where the exchange rate plays a major role).

The inclusion of the latecomers had almost no effect on the volatility and tracking record of the survey results. Although this is not entirely unexpected at the highest level of aggregation, it is surprising that it also had almost no effect at the lower levels of aggregation. In this respect, the finding supports the assumption that missing responses correspond with those that replied, i.e. the so-called missing at random (MAR) assumption holds (Kershoff 2014a: 18).

The preliminary findings of these analyses agree with the conclusions of various international (see, for instance, De Munnik 2010, and Kowalczyk and Tomczyk 2010) and own studies (see Kershoff 2010), which show that the business tendency survey technique is robust and that the results are not sensitive to the number and weights of respondents. The OECD (2003: 37) also notes that "practical experience has shown that the survey results are not very sensitive to the choice of the weighting variable".

Nevertheless, the BER may want to introduce some changes in future and recalculate the historical data going back to 2001 (when the BER started to store all individual responses electronically) given the lower volatility and improved tracking record that some elements of the alternative method produces. It may still be justified to switch to some elements of the alternative method even if they don't raise the tracking record across the board, but bring the BER's method closer in line with the international norm.

Until such changes are made and given the relatively high volatility of some of the BER's survey results, it is prudent to provide users with some practical guidance on how to responsibly use and interpret the results.

Practical experience has shown that a comparison of the survey and corresponding quantitative data helps with the interpretation of the survey data. The survey data is often used to project the (official) quantitative data given the earlier availability of the former. A comparison will prevent one from inadvertently making the wrong inference about the quantitative data from the survey results. A graphical plot of the survey and quantitative data will, for instance, show if a negative net balance signifies negative (e.g. −5%) or only slower growth (e.g. moving from 7% to 3%) in the corresponding quantitative series. The reason why one cannot just assume that a negative (positive) net balance agrees with a contraction (expansion) in the quantitative series is that the long-term average of all the survey data series is not zero. This, in turn, stems from the fact that sometimes participants respond in a more negative way (or are more conscious about declines than increases) to certain variables than others. To make the relationship between the survey (measured on the primary vertical axis) and quantitative data (measured on the secondary vertical axis) visually clearer, it may be useful to adjust the scaling of a chart's vertical axes until their zeroes align horizontally or to add the long-term average to the survey data to adjust its mean to zero.

Given the historical upward or downward bias of some survey data series (e.g. respondents typically rate current retail stocks relative to expected demand as too high), it is more enlightening to observe the fluctuations of such series around its long-term average than to merely compare the latest and the previous quarter's results.

Given the high volatility of many data series, the BER encourages users to not only examine the absolute change between consecutive quarters but also smoothed data (such as a three-period moving average end period). It is also prudent to pay more attention to the direction than the absolute size of the quarter-on-quarter change in the survey data. Furthermore, the BER regards the sector totals as more reliable than the subsectors and the provinces. Even if the international benchmark and requirement for normal distribution of a minimum number of 30 responses per subsector are satisfied, one has to bear in mind that industry concentration (i.e. the existence of a few large firms among many small firms) could introduce volatility to the results of particular subsectors.

6 Publication of the Survey Data

Until 1985, the BER's manufacturing and trade survey results were released in a publication called "Opinion Surveys". From 1986 onwards it was released in the "Manufacturing Survey" and "Trade and Commerce" (whose name changed to "Retail Survey" in 1994), respectively. The name of the publication covering the building survey results changed from "Building Survey" to "Building & Construction" in 1987.

The BER's survey data is available in hard copy format from the first survey of 1954 onwards. The time series for the main sectors is available in electronic format since 1986 and for selected variables since 1970. The length of the electronic series of some subsectors and variables are shorter due to changes in the coverage or questions. The results per respondent (the so-called microdata) are available electronically since 2001.

The time series could be obtained in electronic format from all the major global data distributors. The BER makes the microdata (with all the personal identifiable information removed) available only for academic research.

Although the BER is part of Stellenbosch University, the institute has to fully fund all its expenses (such as salaries, a university levy, office rent, travel costs, printing and postage). Until the mid-1990s, the BER financed itself out of the sale of the survey reports, donations, occasional grants and one or two positions that were funded out of the university's central fund. In the early 1990s, a steep decline in the sale of reports (primarily due to the advent of the information age) and the termination of the last university-funded position forced the BER to seek new financing sources. The BER came up with a financing model where private firms (sponsors) pay for the cost of conducting the surveys in exchange for the right to add their name to the surveys (naming rights) and have their representatives make the results public and speak to the media (media rights).

The release of the information is staggered over about 3 weeks, starting with the overall business confidence index and followed by the various sector reports. An advance release calendar is posted on the BER's web page at the beginning of each year. On the release day, subscribers can download the reports in PDF format from the BER web page and obtain the latest survey data from the data vendors. Sponsors have access to the information before the public release, but not to the individual responses and identities.

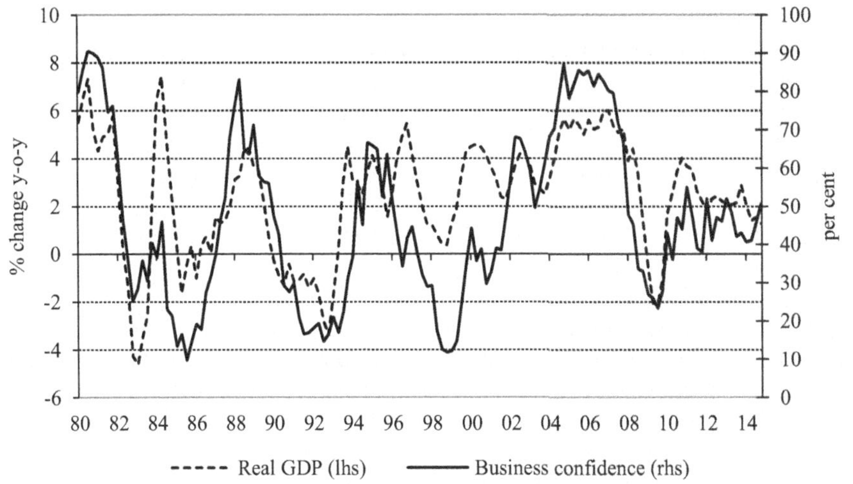

Fig. 3 Business confidence and economic growth

7 Use of the Survey Data

The BER's business survey data is not a substitute for the official quantitative data, but compliments it. Given the survey data's publication lead, the overall business confidence index and the results of the various sector surveys are mainly used to informally nowcast GDP growth (see Fig. 3), manufacturing production, retail sales and building activity.

The rate of increase in prices, employment, profitability and manufacturing investment and the assessment of stocks relative to demand and the limiting impact of various factors are also studied closely, as they reveal details about conditions in the different sectors before any other information becomes public. The BER also uses the survey results to assess the output of its macro-forecasting model over the near term.

The overall business confidence index is also a good leading business cycle indicator. Table 3 indicates that the business confidence index signals peaks and troughs on average a year in advance.

The reasons why business confidence has turned out to be a good leading indicator have not been fully explored. The index reflects the weighted percentage of respondents in the five most cyclical sectors of the economy (building, manufacturing, retail trade, wholesale trade and motor trade) rating prevailing business conditions as satisfactory. The first possible reason is that respondents apparently also take future prospects into account although the question specifically refers to current conditions. A second possibility relates to the close association between business confidence and domestic demand, which in itself is closely linked to the business cycle. (In the fourth quarter of 2000, 2001 and 2002, the BER posed a special question to find out which factor had the most, second most and third most

Table 3 Business cycle phases

Lower turning point/start of the upward phase		Upper turning point/start of the downward phase	
SARB	BER BCI	SARB	BER BCI
Jan 1978	1977Q4	Sep 1981	1980Q3
Apr 1983	1982Q4	Jul 1984	1984Q2
Apr 1986	1985Q3	Mar 1989	1988Q2
Jun 1993	1992Q3	Dec 1996	1995Q4
Sep 1999	1989Q4	Dec 2007	2006Q3
Sep 2009	2009Q3		

Source: SARB 2015: S-157

Note: In the case of the BER, the lowest (highest) level of overall business confidence during the particular upward (downward) phase of the business cycle (as identified by the Reserve Bank) is taken as the turning point. The third quarter of 2006 is taken as a turning point even though business confidence was then at 85, slightly lower than the 87 in the fourth quarter of 2004

impact on a respondent's rating of prevailing conditions. Domestic demand turned out to have the biggest impact across sectors and years.) A third possibility is that the question on which business confidence is based is the only one that does not provide a neutral/a "don't know" answering option. The fact that respondents are forced to choose between either "satisfactory" or "unsatisfactory" might have increased the question's early signalling capacity, as any relatively big improvement/deterioration in domestic demand might be sufficient to push many respondents over the threshold and make them switch from "unsatisfactory" to "satisfactory" (and vice versa) without first shifting to a neutral position.

Given the leading cyclical characteristics of the BER's survey data, the SA Reserve Bank has over the years included a number of variables in its composite leading business cycle indicator, namely, the ratio of stocks to sales in manufacturing (1980–1993), the overall business confidence index (since 1994), the volume of orders in manufacturing (since 1994), stocks in relation to demand in manufacturing and trade (1994–2007) and the average number of hours worked in manufacturing (since 2005) (Van der Walt and Pretorius 1994: 29, 31; SARB 2007: 16).

8 Final Remarks

The BER has built up a reputation and valuable experience in conducting business tendency surveys in South Africa over the past six decades. An international benchmark (or industry standard) started taking shape when the European Commission (EC) and the OECD broadened their BTS and COS harmonisation initiative to non-member countries and the OECD published a Handbook of Business Tendency Surveys in 2003. The BER's survey method agrees with most of the recommended guidelines, but deviates in a few cases. For instance, the BER does not use completely random sampling to put together the panel of participants, sample weights, a two-step weighting procedure, post-stratification and imputation. Furthermore, the frequency of the BER's surveys is quarterly; the BER instructs respondents to compare the current situation with that of a year ago, includes a specific question to measure business confidence, does not weight the building results, uses logarithmic transformed firm size weights and does not publish the other services sector survey results. The non-response rate is high in South Africa even though the BER follows all recommendations to increase the response rate. The BER's survey results are quite volatile, also compared to those of the other BRICS countries. The preliminary findings of a sensitivity analysis show that a reduction in the number of firm size categories (from 9 to 4) and the range of firm size weights, the introduction of a two-step weighting procedure and a move to a higher level of subsector aggregation in the manufacturing and building sector, will reduce the volatility of the BER's survey results. The BER will consider this and other minor changes to the survey method in the future.

References

Bouwer B (1967) 'n Statistiese Ontleding en Waardering van die Opinie-Opname-Metode soos toegepas deur die Buro vir Ekonomiese Ondersoek van die Universiteit van Stellenbosch. Unpublished doctoral dissertation. University of Stellenbosch, Stellenbosch

Campello A (2013) BRICS correlation matrices. Unpublished presentation delivered at the 2nd BRICS Working Group Meeting, October, Zurich

De Munnik D (2010) Statistical confidence intervals for the bank of Canada's business outlook survey. Bank of Canada. Discussion Paper 2010–7

EC (European Commission) (2006) Directorate-General for Economic and Financial Affairs. European Economy. The Joint Harmonised EU Programme of Business and Consumer Surveys. Special Report No. 5

Kershoff GJ (2008) Conducting financial sector surveys in South Africa. Unpublished paper delivered at the 29th CIRET conference, 8–11 Oct 2018, Santiago, Chile

Kershoff GJ (2010) The impact of weight adjustment on the accuracy of business tendency surveys. An assessment of the manufacturing survey of South Africa. Unpublished paper delivered at the 30th CIRET conference, 13–16 Oct 2010, New York

Kershoff GJ (2014a) The BER's building survey. An analysis of the impact of the response pattern and weighting on the survey results. Unpublished report, January, Stellenbosch

Kershoff GJ (2014b) The BER's manufacturing survey. An analysis of the impact of the response pattern and weighting on the survey results. Unpublished report, March, Stellenbosch

Kowalczyk B, Tomczyk E (2010) Non-response and weighting systems in business tendency surveys: are expectations influenced? Unpublished paper delivered at the 30th CIRET conference, 13–16 Oct 2010, New York

Laubscher PL (2005) Business surveys in South Africa: testing the ground for internet-based surveys keeping the impact on response rates in mind. Unpublished paper delivered at a joint EC-OECD workshop, 14–15 Nov 2005, Brussels

OECD (2003) Business tendency surveys. A handbook. OECD, Paris

Pellissier GM, Smit EVDM (1988) Ontleding van die mate van verteenwoordiging van die BEO se opinie-opname steekproewe. Unpublished report, June, Stellenbosch

Ruppert R (2007) Business survey in manufacturing. In: Goldrian G (ed) Handbook of survey-based business cycle analysis. Edward Elgar, Cheltenham

SARB (South African Reserve Bank) (2007) Quarterly bulletin. June, Pretoria

SARB (South African Reserve Bank) (2015) Quarterly bulletin. March, Pretoria

Stuart ODJ (1978) On the measurement of South African consumer sentiment. J Stud Econ Econometrics 2:82–94

Tosetto E, Gyomai G (2009) Current status of business tendency survey and consumer survey harmonisation in non-EU OECD countries, OECD enhanced engagement economies and OECD accession countries. Unpublished paper delivered at an EU-OECD workshop on Business and Consumer Surveys, November, Brussels

UNSD (2014) Handbook. Economic tendency surveys. Draft. United Nations Statistics Division, New York

Van der Walt BE, Pretorius WS (1994) Notes on the revision of the composite business cycle indicators. South African Reserve Bank Quarterly Bulletin, September, Pretoria

Wikipedia (2015) [Online]. https://en.wikipedia.org/wiki/BRICS. Accessed 20 May 2015

Part IV
Composite Cyclical Indicators for Real-Time Monitoring and Forecasting the BRICS Economies

Compiling Cyclical Composite Indexes: The Conference Board Indicators Approach

Ataman Ozyildirim

1 Introduction

Economic activity and its fluctuations are subjects of great importance in modern market economies. Strategic decision-making by individuals, private enterprises, and governmental institutions all take into account the state of the economy and its prospects vis a vis the business cycle. The difficulty rests in the fact that the state of the economy is not directly observable, but it has to be inferred from observed indicators. While there is usually general agreement about overall economic conditions during normal times when the economy is on or close to a long-term growth trend, there is generally little consensus when the economy enters a transition period from expansion to contraction or vice versa. While these transitions can appear as discrete points in time in retrospect, in real time when empirical observations are just being made and are often subject to measurement errors and revisions, the degree of uncertainty and disagreement about the state of the economy could increase significantly.[1] Thus, metrics that provide reasonable estimates of the unobserved state of the business cycle (i.e., expansion or contraction, also called cyclical phases) and its direction in the near future are very useful.

This approach to characterizing the business cycle follows the seminal works of Burns and Mitchell (1938, 1946) and later Moore (1950, 1961) and Moore and Shiskin (1967). The indicator approach has been established as one of the most

[1]For a discussion of timeliness of business cycle indicators and the importance of real-time indicators, see McGuckin et al. (2007).

A. Ozyildirim (✉)
The Conference Board Inc., New York, NY, USA
e-mail: Ataman.Ozyildirim@conference-board.org

S. Smirnov et al. (eds.), *Business Cycles in BRICS*, Societies and Political Orders in Transition, https://doi.org/10.1007/978-3-319-90017-9_17

useful approaches to business cycle analysis since the early work of Burns and Mitchell (1938). It was a major component of the National Bureau of Economic Research (NBER) business cycle program.[2]

The approach relies on a classification of economic indicators based on their business cycle timing relationships (i.e., leading, coincident, or lagging) and utilizes composite indexes of a small set of selected indicators to determine and monitor major turning points in the business cycle. It has been applied to many mature and emerging economies, and these applications have been generally successful in monitoring and predicting business and growth cycles (The Conference Board 2013). Moreover, as the GDP growth estimates are available with considerable time lag, and they are often subject to large revisions, it is essential to rely on a composite index of indicators of economic activities prior to the release of statistical data by National Statistical Offices (NSOs) to understand overall economic and business cycle developments in the short run.

This chapter presents an overview of the indicator approach introduced by researchers at the NBER in the mid-twentieth century. This approach was subsequently refined by the Bureau of Economic Analysis at the U.S. Department of Commerce and The Conference Board and is now commonly used for many countries. Section 2 briefly reviews the key ideas that have led to the use of composite indexes in the indicator approach. Section 3 discusses how the components of composite indexes are selected. Section 4 shows how the selected indicators are combined into composite indexes. Section 5 discusses the main challenges in following the indicator approach, and Sect. 6 concludes.

2 Key Ideas of the Indicator Approach

2.1 Cycles, Cyclical Phases, and Dating Turning Points

According to the indicator approach, business cycles comprise sequences of two states of economy (cyclical phases): expansion and contraction (recession). The transition from an expansion phase to a contraction phase is marked by a peak, and a trough marks the transition from a contraction or recession into an expansion. Generally speaking, there two methods for dating cyclical turning points. Firstly, it is possible to assume that the turning points of the unobserved cycle coincide with the turning points of an observable reference series which may be an aggregate or composite coincident indicator.[3] The advantage of this method is its simplicity and objectivity: it may be applied to almost any national economy with a more or less

[2]For comprehensive review of how cyclical indicators and composite indexes were developed and evolved, see Klein (1999a, b) and Zarnowitz (1992, Chaps. 10 and 11). See also Zarnowitz and Boschan (1975) and Zarnowitz (2001).

[3]See Subsect. 2.3.

mature statistical system. The disadvantage of the method is the fact that different reference series bring different estimates of turning points; they also may be revised over the time. To avoid this problem, several national experts' committees around the world have been established. These committees are considered official arbiters of reference chronologies for their respective economies. For example, the NBER business cycle dating committee for the USA, the Centre for Economic Policy Research (CEPR) for the Euro Area, CODACE for Brazil, and Russian Dating Committee (RDC) for Russia make announcements for the beginning and ending dates of recessions.

These dates are critical for being able to apply the turning point analysis.

2.2 *Timing of Indicators*

Once a reference chronology of peaks and troughs is determined either by a committee of experts or by using the (composite) coincident indicators themselves (e.g., The Conference Board or OECD approaches), the cyclical performance, consistency, and conformity of the individual economic indicators can be evaluated, and indicators can be classified into different groups based on their cyclical performance.

Along with the analysis of fluctuation in major macroeconomic time series representing current economic activity, the analyses of the fluctuations in the series which lead and lag fluctuations in these series are of paramount importance because they can help to anticipate and confirm turning points, respectively. The variables which anticipate the turning points or the turns in the reference series (i.e., series representing current economic activity or coincident indicators) are termed leading economic indicators, and the variables which react after the reference series has moved are named lagging indicators.

Classifying economic indicators in terms of their cyclical timing helps to organize economic variables with respect to their relationship with the unobserved cyclical forces or factors in the economy. Coincident indicators provide gauges of "current conditions" in economic activity. As such, they are the key to real-time determination of turning points (reference chronology) in the economic cycle. They are also important for assessing a reference chronology used in developing new indexes. Leading indicators are of particular interest in business cycle analysis because of their potential role in forecasting the future path of economic activity and specifically turning point that mark the beginning and end of recessions. Lagging indicators generally serve the purpose of confirming cyclical turning points to check for false signals.

2.3 *Composite vs. Aggregate Indicators*

A commonly used example of an indicator that is used to track the business cycle in retrospect is the GDP, the broadest measure of output and income and a good proxy for the state of the economy. Nevertheless, there are two problems with using GDP to infer the present state of the economy: first, it is only available on a quarterly basis, and with some delay, especially in emerging economies, and second, GDP data could often be substantially revised, again with some delay. For these reasons, sometimes indexes of industrial production were used as a reference series. However, industry is only one sector of national economy, and its own turning points may differ from turning points for general economic activity. That is why it has been a widespread practice to rely on the construction of composite coincident indices by combining high-frequency (usually monthly) indicators that help summarize the cyclical trajectory of economic activity on a timelier basis.

Composite indexes are often used to summarize and bring out the turning points and cyclical movements that are common to many economic indicators. Thus, they help to estimate the underlying common variable mentioned above. In order to do this, it is necessary to look beyond irregular, idiosyncratic, and seasonal movements in economic data and emphasize the common and regular cyclical fluctuations and focus on the co-movement of economic indicators.

The indicator approach to the business cycles, thus, encompasses the construction of three major composite indexes, namely, the leading, coincident, and where possible lagging. To track business cycles, a composite index of a group of economic time series that show similar characteristics (timing) at business cycle turns but represent different activities or sectors of the economy is preferred to individual series (Moore 1982). The composite indexes are used to determine the central tendency of a clustering of turning points in individual indicators and yield a more precise chronology.

The cyclical performance of the composite index is usually superior to that of any individual indicator or component because the index benefits from averaging out idiosyncratic or irregular movements of the components. While individual indicators may be correlated with business cycle and have reasonable cyclical characteristics, none of the selected indicators are ideal cyclical indicators by themselves. When combined into a composite index using a simple and transparent indexing procedure, the resulting composite index tends to perform better as a cyclical measurement tool.

Thus, when aggregated into composite indices classified by timing, the resulting composite indexes (1) bring cycles and turning points into focus, (2) are used to discern and anticipate turning points in business cycles, and (3) provide useful tools for forecasting and developing an economic outlook.

3 Selection of Individual Cyclical Indicators

Compiling cyclical indexes is a highly empirical exercise. It requires long histories of data where the changes from expansion to contraction (recession) and back to expansion phases are numerous and frequent enough.

The criteria used in the indicator approach to evaluate indicators and to select a small set of index components are:

- Economic significance—cyclical timing must have economic meaning and be logical.
- Conformity—the series must conform well to the business cycle.
- Consistent timing—the series must exhibit a consistent timing pattern as a leading, coincident, or lagging indicator.
- Smoothness—month-to-month movements must not be too erratic.
- Statistical adequacy—data must be collected and processed in a statistically reliable way.
- Currency or timeliness—series must be published on a reasonably prompt schedule, preferably within a month. "Real-time" performance, short-term outlook requires timely publication.

At the same time, the indicator approach requires a wide range of variables from different aspects of economic activity. They should reflect the conditions in:

- Money and credit markets
- Financial and commodity markets
- Real sector (manufacturing, construction, wholesale and retail trade, etc.)
- Labor markets
- Investments
- Consumer and business sentiments

Main sources of individual economic indicators may be:

- National statistical agencies—national, industry, and regional levels
- Administrative or micro-data (e.g., unemployment insurance or tax records)
- Industry associations (e.g., Mortgage Bankers Association, National Association of Realtors)
- Financial indicators (e.g., interest rates, stock and commodity prices)
- Other private or international organizations (e.g., business and consumer tendency surveys, credit rating agencies, IMF, World Bank)

Turning point analysis is applied to individual indicators chosen on the base of all these criteria to establish the regularity of the individual turning points and their correspondence to the generally accepted turning points of the business cycle. The cyclical performance and correspondence of the individual indicators to the reference cycle is crucial in selecting components of composite indexes.

4 Compilation of Composite Indexes

The candidate components are assessed based on their adherence to the selection criteria above and combined using a long-established composite index methodology.[4]

The steps of the The Conference Board methodology for calculating composite indexes are briefly described below.[5] In the notation, (t) and ($t-1$) refer to the current and prior month, respectively, and (x) and (m) refer to a particular component of the index.

In the first step, month-to-month changes are computed for each component of the index. If the component X is in percent change form or an interest rate, simple arithmetic differences are calculated:

$$x_t = X_t - X_{t-1}$$

If the component is not in percent change form, a symmetric alternative to the conventional percent change formula is used:

$$x_t = 200\frac{(X_t - X_{t-1})}{(X_t + X_{t-1})}$$

If the component X is a diffusion index[6] or an interest rate spread, the monthly level is used:

$$x_t = X_t$$

Using percent changes or log differences makes little difference to the resulting index.

In the second step, the monthly contributions of the components are adjusted to equalize the volatility of each component. Standard deviations (v_x) of the changes in each component are computed. These statistical measures of volatility are inverted $\left(w_x = \frac{1}{v_x}\right)$, their sum is calculated $\left(k = \sum_x w_x\right)$, and they are recalculated, so the index's component standardization factors sum to one $\left(r_x = \frac{1}{k} w_x\right)$. The adjusted contribution in each component is the monthly contribution multiplied by the corresponding component standardization factor ($m_{x,\,t} = r_x\, x_t$). Thus, before aggregation, the monthly changes of the components are first adjusted by multiplying them with their standardization factor. This step is called a volatility adjustment. Standardization factors determine how monthly changes in each component

[4]See The Conference Board website at https://www.conference-board.org/data/bci/index.cfm?id=2154 and The Conference Board (TCB) 2001. Business Cycle Indicators Handbook. The Conference Board: New York, pp. 47–55. See also Ozyildirim (2017).

[5]This section is adapted from The Conference Board index methodology. Please visit the website for the latest documentation: https://www.conference-board.org/data/bci.cfm

[6]If the component is a diffusion index, then it is first normalized by subtracting the sample mean and dividing by the standard deviation.

contribute to the monthly change in the associated index. These factors are designed to give each component a similar opportunity to contribute to the change in the index in any given month. This adjustment equalizes the volatility of the contributions from each component in an index. The standardization factors are based on the inverse of the standard deviation of the monthly changes in the series, and these component standardization factors are made to sum to one. This summing to one of the standardization factors is done to assure that the cyclical part of the composite index is limited to a magnitude similar to the average deviation from the mean growth rate of the components of the index.

The third step consists of adding the adjusted monthly contribution across the components for each month to obtain the growth rate of the index. This step results in the sum of the adjusted contribution $\left(i_t = \sum_x m_{x,t}\right)$ which is the monthly growth rate of the index.

In the fourth step, the sum of the adjusted contributions—the growth rates—of the composite indexes is adjusted to equate their trends to that of the coincident index. This is accomplished by adding a trend adjustment factor (a) to the growth rates of the index each month $\left(i_t' = i_t + a\right)$. For example, the trend adjustment factor for the leading index is computed by subtracting its average monthly growth rate $\left(\frac{\sum_t i_t}{T}\right)$—where T is the number of observations in the sample—from the average monthly growth rate of the coincident index.

The fifth step computes the level of the index using the symmetric percent change formula. The index is calculated recursively starting from an initial value of 100 for the first month of the sample period. The first month's value is $I_1 = 100$. The second month's value is $I_2 = I_1 \frac{\left(200 + i_2'\right)}{\left(200 - i_2'\right)}$, and this formula is used recursively to compute the index levels for each month that data are available.

In the last step, the index is rebased to average 100 in the selected base year—the history of the index is multiplied by 100 and divided by the average for the 12 months of the base year.[7] The year chosen as the base year is updated regularly, usually every 5 years or so.

5 Main Challenges

All the ideas and suggestions mentioned above seem quite straightforward, but they are very challenging, especially in emerging countries.

[7]The indexes are updated for the latest and previous 6 months of data using the predetermined factors from the sample period. Revisions in the components that fall outside of the moving 6-month window are not incorporated in the index until the entire index is recomputed.

5.1 Diversity and Heterogeneity of Statistical Sources

Working with a variety of sources creates special difficulties. While many useful economic variables may be collected and distributed by various sources, their underlying methodologies and approaches may not necessarily be harmonized. A further challenge arises if the metadata or documentation on methodologies is not readily available. As a result, the credibility of the quality of the data suffers. Comparability of the data across different sources is always an issue, but sufficiently transparent methodological information can allow researchers to assess comparability, make necessary adjustments, if possible, and use the data to advance research. At a minimum the available length of histories may be different leading to difficult choices on not being able to study the earlier history of the economy with the resulting composite indexes or at best the earlier histories covering only incomplete data.

If long histories of data are available to conduct the necessary tests and evaluation of candidate indicators, it is also crucial that the data is seasonally adjusted and adjusted for inflation where appropriate. Hence, the data should be suitable to be used in seasonal adjustment procedures (another reason for the need for long histories), and suitable measures of price indexes have to be available.

5.2 Particularities of National Statistical Systems

The statistical system of each country determines what data is collected on a consistent basis. The amount of resources allocated to data collection determines both the quantity and quantity of the data available for applications of the indicators approach.

Heterogeneity of national statistical systems may be characterized according to the following dimensions:

- Data availability: small pool of published indicators on relevant sectors, short samples, and lack of observations of turning points in the data
- Data quality: measurement errors, noise, insufficient seasonal adjustment, or lack of appropriate price indexes
- Statistical adequacy: lack of properly designed surveys, small samples, and representativeness
- Problems identifying the business cycle: lack of high-frequency and timely data on employment, wages, income, industrial production, and GDP

Even if a good selection of indicators could be achieved based on the available data sources, the indicators require ongoing maintenance updates. During their regular data collection and updating operations, statistical agencies remedy some of the shortcomings of measurement posed by these challenges (i.e., incomplete measurement, measurement biases, etc.). As a result, data can be benchmarked with more complete data sources, broader coverage, better methodologies, etc. Less frequent censuses methodological improvements can be used to benchmark and update the indicator data. Because of these improvements, indicators and composite indexes built from them should be benchmarked at regular intervals, i.e., annually (see The Conference Board 2001: 56–57).

5.3 Changing Structure of Economies

Structural changes in economies can result in changing stability or strength of economic relationships. They can also lead to shifts in the share of different sectors in overall economic activity. The lack of consistency brought on by structural changes can make the evaluation of individual indicators difficult.

Economies in different stages might have structural changes specific to their circumstances:

- Mature economies: transition from manufacturing to services and knowledge economy, rapid innovations in banking and financial sectors, and secular stagnation and/or slowing productivity leading to slowing long-term growth trends
- Emerging economies: industrialization, rapid structural change, demographic dividends, catching up/convergence, rapid productivity gains, and developing institutions
- Transition economies: institutional changes, changing industrial composition, emergence of new financial and service sectors, opening to the world economy, appearance of market laws, institutions and practices, and aging populations

Structural changes are less common and less frequent, but they also necessitate the review and updating of indicators and composite indexes created from them. Such a review that leads to changes in the underlying components of a composite index and/or its calculation methodology is called a comprehensive benchmark revision.[8] Such comprehensive revisions helps to keep the indicators and composite indexes created from them up to date with the evolving and dynamic structure of the economies they measure.

[8]See The Conference Board (2001, pp. 56–57). See also Zarnowitz and Boschan (1975), Klein (1999a, b), and McGuckin and Ozyildirim (2004).

6 Concluding Remarks

Business cycle analysis provides an understanding of the direction of the economic activity in market economies. It assists businesses as well as government policymakers by revealing the nature of the fluctuations, understanding what the current economic conditions are, and where they are headed.

It is important to note that while The Conference Board approach focuses primarily on the classical business cycles, it may be applied to analyses of growth cycles or growth rate cycles as well. Analysis of classical and growth cycles are often complementary.

The indicator approach is particularly well suited to work with the available data in emerging economies because it does not rely heavily on econometric estimation, which could be negatively influenced by finite samples and instability of estimated coefficients. Instead, the indicator approach relies on a detailed evaluation of the empirical properties of the indicators and turning point analysis. Where possible, the indicator approach utilizes supplementary empirical evidence or puts more emphasis on well-established economic theory without deviating too far from the measurement-based core of the indicator approach.

The Leading Economic Index (LEI)—when constructed from carefully selected components that have a good record at tracking and predicting turning points—can be very useful for policymakers, financial analysts, financial investors, and businesses. Together with the Coincident Economic Index (CEI), it can help better monitor an economy and provide early warning signals of future economic activity.

In the several next chapters, various cyclical composite indexes (coincident, leading, and lagging) for the BRICS countries are described.

References

Burns AF, Mitchell WC (1946) Measuring business cycles. NBER

Klein PA (1999a) The leading indicators in historical perspective. Bus Cycle Indic 4(10):3–4

Klein PA (1999b) The leading indicators in historical perspective. Bus Cycle Indic 4(11):3–4

McGuckin RH, Ozyildirim A (2004) Real-time tests of the leading economic index: do changes in index composition matter? J Bus Cycle Meas Anal 1(2):171–191

McGuckin RH, Ozyildirim A, Zarnowitz V (2007) A more timely and useful index of leading indicators. J Bus Econ Stat 25(1):110–120

Mitchell WC, Burns AF (1938) Statistical indicators of cyclical revivals, Bulletin No. 69, National Bureau of Economic Research, New York

Moore GH (1950) Statistical indicators of cyclical revivals and recessions. NBER, New York

Moore GH (ed) (1961) Business cycle indicators, vol 2. Princeton University Press published for NBER, Princeton, NJ

Moore GH (1982) Business cycles. In: Greenwald D (ed) Encyclopedia of economics. McGraw Hill, New York

Moore GH, Shiskin J (1967) Indicators of business cycle expansions and contractions. NBER, New York

Ozyildirim A (2017) Business cycle indicator approach at The Conference Board. In: Mazzi GL, Ozyildirim A, Rieser DA (eds). Handbook of cyclical composite indicators for business cycle analysis. Publications Office of the European Union, Luxembourg, pp 225–240

The Conference Board (TCB) (2001) Business cycle indicators handbook. The Conference Board, New York

The Conference Board (TCB) (2013) Understanding business cycles: the indicators approach to forecasting for agility. The Conference Board, New York

Zarnowitz V (1992) Business cycles: theory, history, indicators, and forecasting. The University of Chicago Press, Chicago, IL, pp 316–356

Zarnowitz V (2001) The record of the U.S. leading index and its components. Bus Cycle Indic 6 (9):3–4

Zarnowitz V, Boschan C (1975) Cyclical indicators: an evaluation and new leading indexes, Business Conditions Digest, May 1975

Coincident and Leading Indicators for Brazilian Cycles

Aloisio Campelo Jr, Ataman Ozyildirim, Jing Sima-Friedman, Paulo Picchetti, and Sarah Piassi Machado Lima

1 Introduction

In this chapter, we develop coincident and leading indexes of economic activity for Brazil following the approach used by The Conference Board (TCB), previously developed by researchers at the National Bureau of Economic Research (NBER). Following traditional definitions of the business cycle, our coincident indicator uses variables that synthesize the present situation of both economic activity and the labor market. Our goal was designing an index able to capture the turning points established by the Brazilian Business Cycle Dating Committee for Brazil and its implicit cycles.

The authors would like to thank Bart van Ark, Gad Levanon, and Vagner Laerte Ardeo for valuable comments and suggestions and Rodolpho Tobler for helping with calculations, tables, and graphs. The views expressed in this chapter are those of the authors and do not necessarily represent those of The Conference Board or Fundação Getulio Vargas. For more details please refer to the working paper version of this chapter at https://www.conference-board.org/publications/publicationdetail.cfm?publicationid=2610. Any remaining errors are the responsibility of the authors.

A. Campelo, Jr (✉) · S. P. M. Lima
FGV/IBRE, Rio de Janeiro, Brazil
e-mail: Aloisio.Campelo@fgv.br

A. Ozyildirim · J. Sima-Friedman
The Conference Board Inc., New York, USA

P. Picchetti
Fundação Getulio Vargas, Brazil/IBRE/São Paulo School of Economics, São Paulo, Brazil

S. Smirnov et al. (eds.), *Business Cycles in BRICS*, Societies and Political Orders in Transition, https://doi.org/10.1007/978-3-319-90017-9_18

The set of leading variables were chosen by selecting among leading indicators that precede and help predict turning points in the coincident series. The leading indicator anticipates the movements of the coincident index, with an especially good performance at turning points.

The Coincident Economic Index (CEI) and the Leading Economic Index (LEI) for Brazil were constructed by The Conference Board and the Getulio Vargas Foundation (FGV) in 2013 and have been published monthly since then. This chapter is organized as follows: Section 2 presents the Coincident Economic Index, detailing both the procedure for constructing the index and the variables of choice. Section 3 describes all the steps followed to obtain the Brazilian Leading Indicator. Section 4 concludes.

2 The Composite Coincident Indicator

2.1 The Coincident Series

Coincident variables need to present cycles that conform to the present (unobserved) state of the economy. The first challenge to overcome is to have consistent series with a cyclical coincident profile in Brazil from 1996 onward.[1] For coincident series we needed variables promptly released and reported on monthly basis. As we consider a broad concept of business cycle—that covers distinct aspects of the overall current economic conditions—we searched for national series that are closely related to them.

The TCB coincident series for the USA are industrial production, employees on nonagricultural payrolls, manufacturing and trade sales, and personal income less transfer payments. The Brazilian series chosen to represent a combination of the level of economic activity and the labor market are:

- Industrial production (Y): the index of industrial production.
- Electricity consumption in industry (E): included because the monthly industrial production index covers only manufacturing and mining in Brazil.
- Employees (N): the series considered for the number of employees is the occupied employed population, and it has been tracked by IBGE since the 1980s. Nevertheless, in 2002 there was a great methodological change in these series. Although the changes imply that the series could not be compared, as we are interested in the monthly variations of these indicators, the old series were included from 1996 to 2002 and the new one from 2002 onward.
- Income (I): the best series for income data is the average real income earned from the main activity of individuals 10 years old and over. Because of the methodological change, we decided to use the old methodology from 1996 to 2002 and the new one from 2002 onward.

[1]For building the Brazilian Coincident Economic Index, we used data from 1996 onward, avoiding the hyperinflationary period that lasted until 1994 and the adjustment phase that has taken place immediately after that.

Table 1 Coincident series

Series	Description	Type	Range	Source
Y	Industrial production	Index	Jan/1996–onward	IBGE
E	Industrial electric energy consumption	GWh	Jan/1980–onward	Eletrobras
N old	Occupied employed population (old methodology)	Number of people (thousands)	May/1982–Dec/2002	IBGE
N	Occupied employed population	Number of people (thousands)	Mar/2002–onward	IBGE
I old	Average real income of workers (old methodology)*	R$	Jul/1994–Nov/2002	IBGE
I	Average real income of workers	R$	Feb/2002–onward	IBGE
Cp	Shipments of corrugated paper	Tonnes	Jan/1980–onward	ABPO
S	Volume of sales of the retail market	Index	Jan/2003–onward	IBGE

*Deflated using the National Consumer Price Index (INPC), prices of May/2013 = 100

- Sales (S): the series that best describes sales starts in 2003. It represents the broad volume of sales of the retail market. A proxy variable recommended by Duarte et al. (2004) was the shipments of corrugated paper series provided by the ABPO—the Brazilian Corrugated Board Association—since 1980. We tested the cross correlation between these series (seasonally adjusted and in its log first difference form) from 2003 to 2012 and the significant correlation occurred contemporaneously (lag/lead zero), which strengthened the use of corrugated paper as a proxy for sales before 2003.

Coincident series are summarized in Table 1. All series are seasonally adjusted by the source agency or by FGV where necessary.

Using the TCB index methodology (see Ozyildirim 2018), we generated a composite coincident index for Brazil using the variables described above. Weighting of pre-selected variables is determined by component factors that are inversely related to the standard deviation of the month-to-month changes in each component and are normalized to sum to one. This procedure aims at equalizing the volatility of the contribution from each component. When one or more components are missing, the other factors are adjusted proportionately to ensure that the total continues to sum to one.

We built two candidate coincident indicators. The first one is constructed considering the whole set of information to represent sales, i.e., the chosen series for sales overlaps its proxy for the period before 2003: the corrugated paper series. The second one does not use any overlapping series.

For the first time, the standardization factors for the two Coincident Economic Index (CEI) candidates were calculated using 1996–2011 as the sample period for measuring volatility (see Tables 2 and 3).

As these tables show, the rate of growth of employment (N) is the series with the highest weight due to its low volatility. On the opposite side is the weight for rate of

Table 2 CEI—with overlapping series—standardization factors for each series

Period	Y	E	Cp	S	N old	N	I old	I	Sum
Feb/96–Feb/02	0.11	0.08	0.08		0.51		0.21		1
Mar/02	0.10	0.07	0.07		0.46		0.19	0.10	1
Apr/02–Nov/02	0.07	0.05	0.05		0.31	0.33	0.13	0.07	1
Dec/02	0.08	0.06	0.06		0.35	0.38		0.08	1
Jan/03	0.12	0.09	0.09			0.59		0.12	1
Feb/03–Dec/11	0.11	0.08	0.08	0.09		0.53		0.11	1

Table 3 CEI—without overlapping series—standardization factors for each series

Period	Y	E	Cp	S	N old	N	I old	I	Sum
Feb/96–Feb/02	0.11	0.08	0.08		0.51		0.22		1
Mar/02	0.13	0.09	0.09		0.57			0.12	1
Apr/02–Jan/03	0.12	0.09	0.08			0.59		0.12	1
Feb/03–Dec/11	0.11	0.08	0.08	0.09		0.53		0.11	1

growth of the shipments of corrugated paper (Cp) and the industrial electric energy consumption (E). The standardization factors and the series of the composite indexes are recalculated once a year, usually in January.[2]

To address the problem of lags in available data, those indicators that are not available at the time of publication are estimated using statistical imputation. An autoregressive model is used to estimate each unavailable component. The resulting indexes are therefore constructed using real and estimated data and will be revised as the unavailable data during the time of publication become available. Empirical research suggests that there are real gains in adopting this procedure to make all the indicator series as up-to-date as possible.[3]

2.2 *The Official Recession Chronology*

In Brazil, a respected source of reference for business cycles is the independent Brazilian Economic Cycle Dating Committee (CODACE), which was created and organized by FGV but works as an independent committee. For details about quarterly and monthly turning points dated by CODACE, see Picchetti (2018).

[2]According to the TCB methodology, in order to give stability to the indexes, the sample for measuring volatility goes until the previous year in relation to the present year. For example, if we are working with data until 2017, the sample goes until 2016. By January 2018, the standardization factors were updated by including the 2017 data.

[3]For details, see McGuckin et al. (2007) and Ozyildirim (2018).

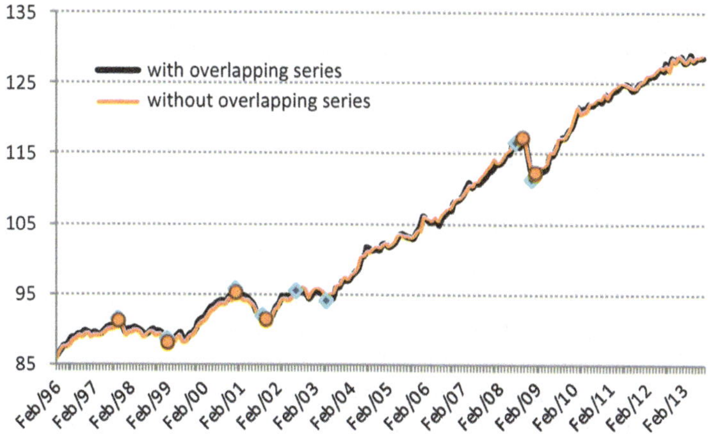

Fig. 1 Brazilian CEI—with and without overlapping series—base: 2004 = 100. Note: 1996–2013, using data available in 2013

Table 4 Recession periods

CODACE chronology		CEI—without overlapping series				CEI—with overlapping series			
		Dated by Bry-Boschan		Lead/lag (−/+), months		Dated by Bry-Boschan		Lead/lag (−/+), months	
Peaks	Troughs	Peaks	Troughs	Peaks	Troughs	Peaks	Troughs	Peaks	Troughs
(1)	(2)	(3)	(4)	(5)	(6)	(7)	(8)	(9)	(10)
Oct-97	Feb-99	Oct-97	Feb-99	0	0	Oct-97	Feb-99	0	0
Dec-00	Sep-01	Dec-00	Oct-01	0	+1	Dec-00	Sep-01	0	0
Oct-02	Jun-03	–	–	–	–	Aug-02	Jun-03	−2	0
Jul-08	Jan-09	Sep-08	Jan-09	+2	0	Jul-08	Dec-08	0	−1

Note: Columns 5–6 and 9–10 report the number of months that lead (negative numbers) or lag (positive numbers) peaks and troughs according to CODACE

2.3 *The Coincident Economic Index (CEI)*

To compare the dated coincident cycles and an official recession indicator is essential to validate the use of a better aggregated index of economic activity. Figure 1 illustrates the graph of the two coincident indexes generated with the component series previously selected (with and without overlapping).

When the CEI components were selected in 2013, it was noted that the alternative index with overlapping series captured all cycles detected by CODACE with only slightly different choice of turning points, while the CEI built without overlapping series missed the 2002–2003 recession identified by CODACE (see Table 4).

Overlapping components create some redundancy and potential double counting in a composite index; however, this might also help mitigate potential measurement errors and with offsetting errors in a larger number of series, the precision of the coincident index in identifying turning points improves. Hereinafter, we use CEI with overlapping series as our main composite coincident indicator.

3 The Leading Economic Index (LEI)

3.1 Selecting Leading Series

Using the CODACE chronology, economic indicators can be tested and classified according to their cyclical behavior. If they move in synchrony with the reference or the CEI, they are termed coincident indicators. The ones that move in advance of the reference chronology are leading indicators. Leading indicators are useful as a forecasting tool in order to anticipate turning points of the economy. Several individual variables previously qualified as leading indicators can be aggregated into diffusion and composite indexes.

Once leading indicators are identified, their performance can be evaluated relative to the whole CEI series and relative to the turning points of the reference chronology of recessions. Indicators with the best leading performance are then selected to be combined into a Leading Economic Index or LEI. In this section, we show that aggregating leading variables into a single composite index provides a better leading measure of the Brazilian business cycle than any individual component. Among the reasons for the better performance of composite indicators, we can affirm that, by including variables that represent different features of the cycles, it's easier to capture the specific driving force of any given turning point.

The first rule for selecting leading series thus is having candidates that represent different sources of cyclical changes (e.g., labor markets, residential construction, financial markets, manufacturing activity, etc.). Each component indicator often brings information about a unique aspect of economic activity. The LEI and CEI form a system of composite indexes that track the economy and are intimately linked because they share the same economic trend (i.e., the trend of the LEI is adjusted to that of the CEI). As discussed in the last section of this chapter, this system of indicators can be used to interpret major cyclical movements in an economy and analyze recession and recovery signals.

Among the major series available for the Brazilian economy on a monthly basis, 145 series on the period January 1996–December 2011 were initially selected for the tests. Where necessary, the variables were seasonally adjusted using the US Census Bureau's Census X-12 methodology,[4] and they were inflation-adjusted using the National Consumer Price Index (INPC). The time series in the dataset were analyzed and classified according to business cycle timing properties. This analysis was based on their business cycle turning points which were determined using the algorithm developed by Bry and Boschan (1971). Because turning points are relatively few in

[4]The procedure was adjusted for trading days and Carnival/Easter effects.

time series with short histories, we also relied on economic relationships between leading and coincident variables formed by economic theory as well as looking at the correlations between variables.

As the series were relatively short and there had been only four business cycle recessions (with four peaks and four troughs) at the moment of constructing Brazilian CEI and LEI, traditional turning point analysis could give incomplete results. For this reason, we supplemented this approach by a new approach developed by Levanon (2010) which uses recession probabilities developed from a Markov-switching model of the indicators being evaluated.

3.2 *Scoring Leading Indicators Using a Markov-Switching Model*

After detecting turning points for all candidate leading indicators, 30 series were pre-selected due to their capability of capturing and leading most if not all of CODACE's turning points.[5] They were tested using other methodologies among which determining the quadratic probability score (QPS) and Granger causality tests. Some of the most interesting results were obtained with scoring the leading candidate series using a Markov-switching model.

For each of the candidate series, we fit the standard Markov-switching model:

$$y_t = \begin{cases} c_1 + \varphi y_{t-1} + \epsilon_t; & s_t = 1 \\ c_2 + \varphi y_{t-1} + \epsilon_t; & s_t = 2 \end{cases}$$

$$\epsilon_t \sim N\left(0, \sigma^2\right)$$

which is basically an AR(1) model for the log changes of the series but with a potentially time-varying intercept. Each of the two possible values for the intercept is interpreted as being observed conditional on the economy being in one of two "states." These states alternate probabilistically across time according to a Markov process:

$$\Pr\left(s_t = j \middle| s_{t-1} = i\right) p_{ij}; \quad i, j = 1, 2$$

Formally, the parameters of the model are jointly estimated with these probabilities of regime changes, through an extension of the Kalman filter algorithm applied to the data. Hamilton (1989) presents the technical details of the estimation, and applies the model to the US GDP series, showing that the estimated regimes can be mapped into the dates for recessions and expansions of the US economy (independently determined by the NBER dating committee).

[5]Their list is available in Appendix 1 to this chapter.

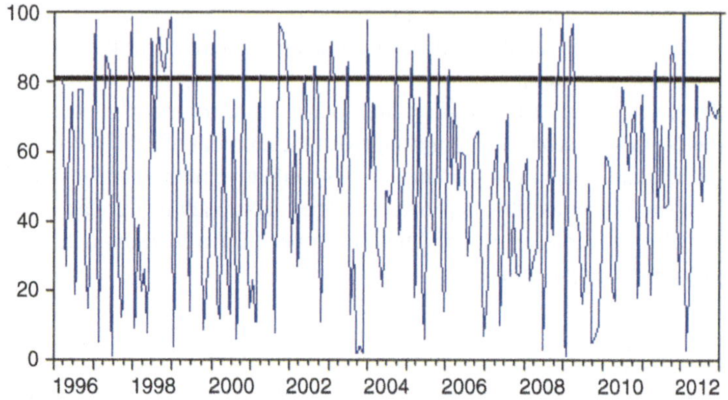

Fig. 2 Capital goods production: regime transition probabilities

The basic idea in Levanon (2010) followed here is to compare the endogenously determined regimes for each of the candidate series with the accepted business cycles chronology and evaluate which are able to anticipate the turning points better. Since it is not expected that the turning point of individual series will generally match the chronology of the aggregate cycles, we want to exploit the fact to separate series that lead the turning points from the ones which are either coincident, lagging, or even unrelated to them. After estimating the transition probabilities (from expansion to recession), the strategy is to compute the sample percentiles for these probabilities and consider the periods where these percentiles are equal or above the percentage of periods during which the economy is in recession. In this way, periods with a sufficiently high probability percentile are the natural candidates for matching the observed recession periods for the whole economy. If this match was perfect for a particular series, we would have exactly the recession months mapped into the higher probability percentiles. The fact that this match is usually not perfect creates the opportunity for the series that function as leading indicators.

As an example to illustrate the procedure, one of the candidate series was the Brazilian output of capital production goods. The percentiles for the probability of regime transitions for this series can be seen in Fig. 2.

The horizontal bar establishes the level above which the estimated probabilities (in percent) are considered as significant (81% in this case). This level is defined empirically by the share of recession months (as indicated by CODACE) in the sample (19%). Attributing a value of one for the periods where the probability percentiles would indicate a recession, and zero for the rest, we can compare the predicted regime transitions with the actual recession months (see Fig. 3).

As expected, this series seems to lag more often than lead the turning points. A very different performance can be seen, for example, in the case of the Brazilian series for output of durable consumption goods (see Fig. 4).

This series appears to have good leading and coincident performances, especially in the case of the first three recessions in the considered time period.

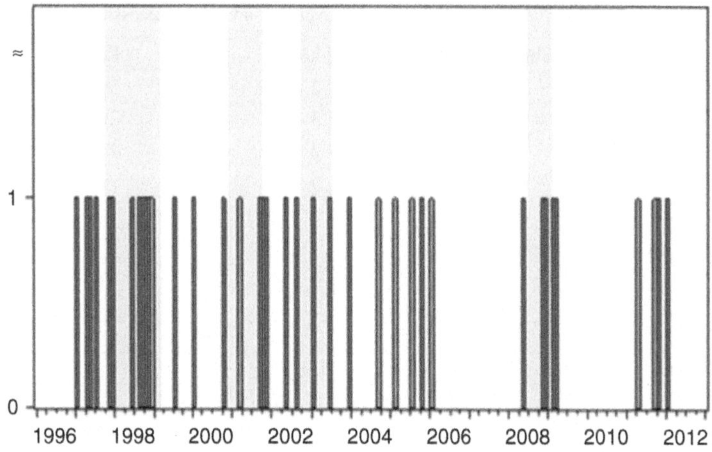

Fig. 3 Capital goods production: alarm signals for a recession. Note: Shaded areas represent recessions as established by CODACE

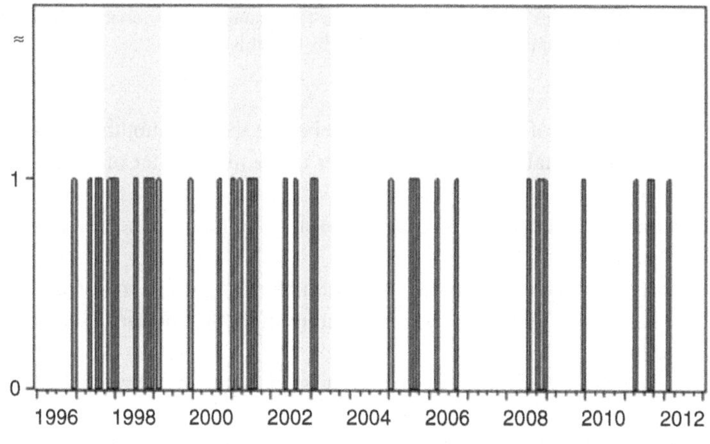

Fig. 4 Durable consumption goods production: alarm signals for a recession. Note: Shaded areas represent recessions as established by CODACE

However, we can also see a number of false positives, as, for example, between the recessions of 2002 and 2008 and after the 2008 recession. In this context, the choice of series for the leading indicator involves a compromise between leading the turning points and false positives. Again, we follow Levanon (2010) in the strategy of ranking each of the series according to a scoring procedure that attributes positive points to periods where the high probability percentiles are either leading the cycles, or coinciding with them, while penalizing series where these indications occur only at the end of the cycles, or at periods characterized as belonging to expansion phases.

More specifically, we calculated (see Table 5):

Table 5 Ranking selected leading indicators using Markov-switching recession probabilities

Series	Fa3bf	Coincident	La2fl	Other	Rank 1	Rank 2
BRAZIL_LEI10	7	19	2	12	5	9
BRAZIL_LEI8	5	22	3	11	2	9
FGV100_F_SA	6	21	2	13	4	7
BRAZIL_LEI5	4	22	5	10	−1	7
BRAZIL_LEI9	4	22	5	10	−1	7
FGV100_F_R	9	16	1	15	8	6
BRAZIL_LEI3	4	21	5	11	−1	5
BRAZIL_LEI6	4	21	5	11	−1	5
FGV100_F	9	15	1	16	8	4
PRODBCD	5	19	1	15	4	4
BRAZIL_LEI7	4	22	8	8	−4	4
SI_level_ICI	4	20	5	13	−1	1
SI_level_IE	3	20	6	12	−3	1
IBOV_M_R	7	15	1	18	6	0

Note: The numbers in the table denote the number of recession signals that occurred in the specified periods before, during, or after recessions. The 14 individual variables or composite indicators presented here are the ones with Rank 2 ≥ 0. The full names of the variables denoted by the mnemonics in the first column are shown in Appendix 2 to this chapter

Fa3bf (first month of recession and three before the first month): the number of monthly recession signals that occurred either in the first quarter of a recession or in the three quarters that preceded it.

Coincident: the number of monthly recession signals that occurred in quarters during recessions.

La2fl (last month of recession and two months after the last month): the number of monthly recession signals that occurred either in the last quarter of a recession or in the two quarters following it.

Other: the number of monthly recession signals that occurred in quarters not included in the above three categories.

Rank 1: Fa3bf category minus La2fl category. A higher number means that the indicator is more leading.

Rank 2: equal to Rank 1, plus the number of signals in other recession quarters, excluding the first, last, and one before last, minus the Other category. Rank 2 is an adjustment to Rank 1 by taking into account false and missed signals. Again, higher numbers mean a more leading indicator.

Choosing Rank 2, which penalizes more heavily the false positives, the top ranked composite leading indicator performs better not only with respect to other composite indicators but also in relation to all individual series, which justifies the approach of combining information from these individual series.

This approach, however, does not exhaust the comparison between all candidate series, since for a number of them the algorithm that estimates the regime transition probabilities fails to converge. This generally follows from the fact that some of the

Table 6 Selected leading and coincident indicators for Brazil

LEI components	CEI components
1. SWAP rate, 1 year (inverted)	1. Industrial production index
2. Stock prices, Bovespa index	2. Industrial electric energy consumption
3. Manufacturing survey: expectations index	3. Occupied employed population
4. Services sector survey: expectations index	4. Average real income of workers
5. Consumers survey: expectations index	5. Shipments of corrugated paper
6. Consumer durable goods production index	6. Volume of sales of the retail market
7. Terms of trade index	
8. Exports volume index	

series have relatively less information in the form of smaller available sample periods and also from the fact that some of them do not have well-characterized regimes. For this reason, this criterion was combined with the others outlined in Ozyildirim (2018) to arrive at the final selection of series among the candidates. Table 6 summarizes the chosen component series of both LEI and CEI.

3.3 CEI and LEI Properties

Figure 5 shows the history of the LEI and CEI going back to 1996. LEI turns down on average around 6 months before peaks and 5 months before troughs. If we exclude the deep and idiosyncratic recession of 2014–2016 due to the atypical leading behavior of the LEI in this occasion (because of political crisis, an impeachment of the president, the car wash corruption scandal, etc.),[6] still the indicator would lead on an average of 4 months before peaks and 2 months before troughs. In general, turning points ahead of troughs tend to be shorter. Improving the asymmetric nature of the leading index may be possible with special attention to the behavior of leading indicators ahead of recession troughs. This is an area we leave for further research.

4 Growth Cycles

While Brazil's economy exhibits five recessions during the period covered, as many other economies, it also exhibits growth cycles which are defined as cyclical fluctuations in the deviations from trend in overall economic activity. Figure 6 shows that the proposed LEI can also be useful in predicting growth cycle turning points. The shaded areas are growth cycle decelerations determined using deviations

[6]See Weller (2018) for details.

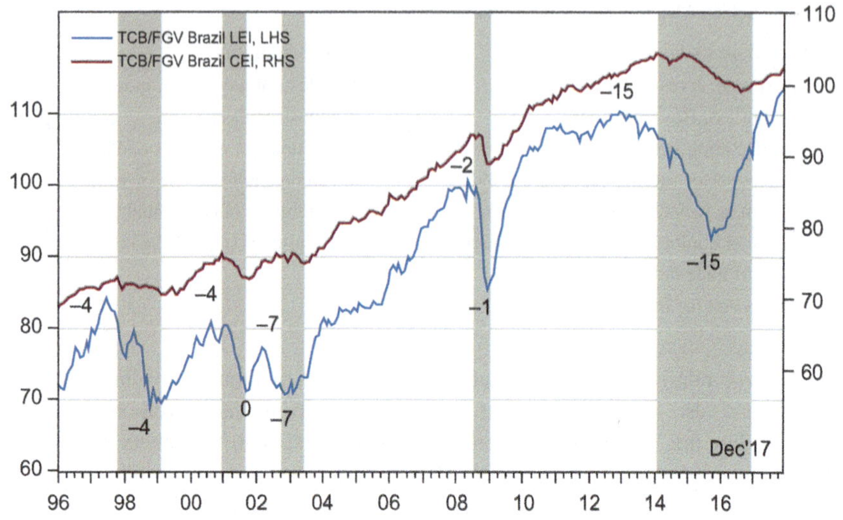

Fig. 5 Brazil CEI and LEI, 1996–2017, base 2016 = 100. Notes: Shaded areas represent recessions as established by CODACE. Negative numbers represent the lead in months to the respective CODACE peak or trough

from trend in an index of coincident indicators (CEI) and GDP. The trend estimate is based on the Hodrick-Prescott trend with sigma = 4 as suggested by Ravn and Uhlig (2001). The negative numbers in the chart denote the number of months the leading index turning points lead the growth cycle turning points.

The growth cycle chronology in the shaded areas of Fig. 6 shows that the growth cycles are more symmetric with the duration of growth cycle expansions and contractions more closely aligned in contrast to business cycles which are asymmetric, with short recessions followed by longer expansions. In the case of Brazil, the LEI leads growth cycle peaks on average by 7 months and troughs by 5 months.

5 Conclusion

In this chapter, we describe TCB/FGV's Coincident Economic Index (CEI) and Leading Economic Index (LEI) for Brazil. These monthly indicators were constructed to help monitoring and predicting short-term business cycle fluctuations in Brazil going back to 1996. This contribution adds up to the set of high-frequency indicators for the emerging markets and specifically to the BRICS countries.

We show that our selection of coincident indicators and the composite index created from them closely follow the Brazilian Business Cycle Dating Committee (CODACE) chronology. Using the coincident index as the target variable, we select a small set of leading indicators and show that the composite index of these indicators help to predict the turning points in the business cycle better than its individual components.

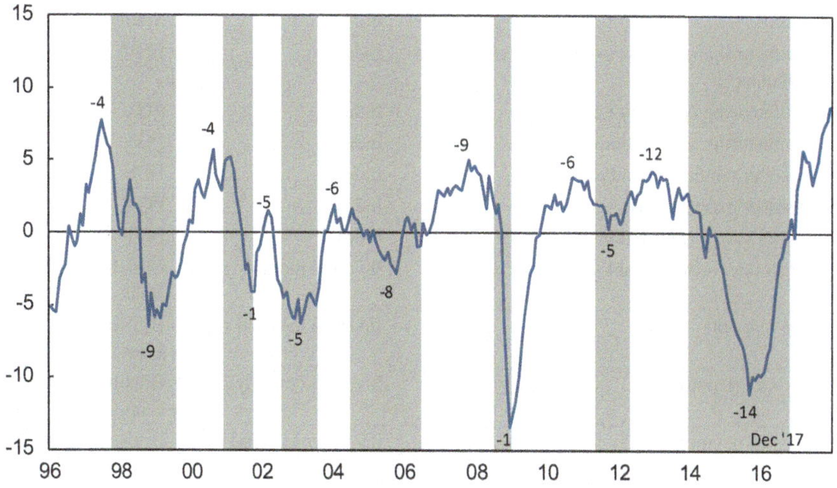

Fig. 6 HP filtered growth cycle of the Brazilian LEI, 1996–2017. Notes: Shaded areas represent periods of deceleration of the combined CEI-GDP indicator as dated by the Bry-Boschan algorithm

Appendix 1

30 Pre-selected Leading Candidate Series

Series	Format	Source
Industrial production—total manufacturing and mining	Index	IBGE
Industrial production—intermediate goods	Index	IBGE
Industrial production—consumer durable goods	Index	IBGE
Production of vehicles	Units	Anfavea
Imports—prices	Index	Funcex
Imports—quantum	Index	Funcex
Imports—(FOB)	US$ millions	Funcex
Exports—prices	Index	Funcex
Exports—quantum	Index	Funcex
Exports—(FOB)	US$ millions	Funcex
Terms of trade	Index	Funcex
Manufacturing survey—level of global demand	Index	FGV
Manufacturing survey—stock levels	Index	FGV
Manufacturing survey—production expectations	Index	FGV
Manufacturing survey—employment expectations	Index	FGV
Manufacturing survey—business situation expectations	Index	FGV
Manufacturing survey— expected level of internal demand	Index	FGV

(continued)

Series	Format	Source
Manufacturing survey— expected level of external demand	Index	FGV
Manufacturing confidence index	Index	FGV
Manufacturing expectations	Index	FGV
Consumer confidence index	Index	FGV
Consumer expectations	Index	FGV
Services sector expectations	Index	FGV
Interest rate—central bank reference (SELIC)	Inverted monthly rate	Brazilian Central Bank
Swap rate 360	Inverted monthly rate	Brazilian Central Bank
Banking discount rate	Inverted monthly rate	Brazilian Central Bank
Means of payment—M2	R$ millions—end of period	Brazilian Central Bank
Producer price index—industrial products	Index	FGV
FGV100 stock market index (later discontinued in 2014)	Index	FGV
Ibovespa stock market index	Index	Bovespa (B3)

Appendix 2

Names of Individual Variables from Table 5

IBOV_M_R	Stock market index (most traded 57 stocks)
FGV100_F_SA	Stock market index (most traded private stocks, seasonally adjusted, end of period)
FGV100_F	Stock market index (most traded private stocks, end of period)
FGV100_F_R	Stock market index (most traded private stocks, at constant prices, end of period)
PRODBCD	Production of durables
SI_LEVEL_ICI	Manufacturing confidence index
SI_LEVEL_IE	Manufacturing expectations index

Note: Indicators with the names BRAZIL_LEI3… BRAZIL_LEI10 are alternative composite leading indexes built with different combinations of the best candidate individual series

References

Bry G, Boschan C (1971) Cyclical analysis of economic time series: selected procedures and computer programs, NBER Technical Working Paper No. 20

Duarte AJM, Issler JV, Spacov A (2004) Indicadores coincidentes de atividade econômica e uma cronologia de recessões para o Brasil, Pesquisa e Planejamento Econômico 34(1):1–37. April, 2004

Hamilton J (1989) A new approach to the economic analysis of nonstationary time series and the business cycle. Econometrica, March 1989

Levanon G (2010) Evaluating and comparing leading and coincident economic indicators. Bus Econ 45(1):16–27

McGuckin RH, Ozyildirim A, Zarnowitz V (2007) A more timely and useful index of leading indicators. J Bus Econ Stat 25:110–120

Ozyildirim A (2018) Compiling cyclical composite indexes: The Conference Board indicators approach. In: Business cycles in BRICS. Springer, Cham

Picchetti P (2018) Brazilian business cycles as characterized by CODACE. In: Business cycles in BRICS. Springer, Cham

Ravn MO, Uhlig H (2001) On adjusting the HP-filter for the frequency of observations. CEPR Discussion Papers 2858, C.E.P.R. Discussion Papers

Weller L (2018) Economic cycles in Brazil. In: Business cycles in BRICS. Springer, Cham

Brazilian Business Cycles as Characterized by CODACE

Paulo Picchetti

1 Origins and Motivation

The Brazilian committee for dating business cycles (CODACE, O Comitê de Datação de Ciclos Econômicos) was created in 2008[1] by Fundação Getulio Vargas (FGV), its main objective being the determination of a reference chronology for Brazilian business cycles, characterized by alternating peaks and troughs in the level of economic activity. The main motivation behind the efforts in establishing a business cycle chronology is providing new information with relevance to the analysis of economic activity, to both public and private sectors.

2 Members

Although FGV, by means of its Brazilian Institute of Economics (IBRE), provided the initiative for creating CODACE and offers continuing operational support, the decisions of the committee are completely independent. The choice of members was entirely determined by previous public contributions on the area of business cycles, in the form of academic papers (both in journals and meetings), and also by analytical considerations on the more general press. At the moment, its members, with main affiliation between parentheses are:

[1]The first public document containing dates for cycles was released in May 2009.

P. Picchetti (✉)
Fundação Getulio Vargas, Brazil/IBRE/São Paulo School of Economics, São Paulo, Brazil
e-mail: paulo.picchetti@fgv.br

S. Smirnov et al. (eds.), *Business Cycles in BRICS*, Societies and Political Orders in Transition, https://doi.org/10.1007/978-3-319-90017-9_19

- Affonso Celso Pastore (Chairperson) (AC Pastore & Associados (private consulting firm))
- Edmar Bacha (Casa das Garças (private consulting firm))
- João Victor Issler (FGV/EPGE (Graduate School of Economics at Fundação Getulio Vargas))
- Marcelle Chauvet (University of California at Riverside—Department of Economics)
- Marco Bonomo (Insper—Department of Economics)
- Paulo Picchetti (EESP/IBRE/FGV)
- Regis Bonelli (IBRE/FGV)

3 General Methodology

The meetings of CODACE do not follow a predefined agenda. By initiative of the chairperson, the committee meets when there is a potential turning point that needs discussing, but usually at least once a year to exchange ideas and follow-ups to previous results.

Following international standards, the committee associates the downward phase of economic activity characterized by a disseminated fall across economic sectors with what is considered a recession, whereas the upward phase, between a trough and a peak, is called an expansion.

Identification of turning points in the Brazilian economy is based on a broad set of available time series for relevant variables related in different dimensions to the level of economic activity. These include the general measures of aggregate output contained in GDP and its components, but also sectoral and aggregate information of industrial production, labor market, tendency surveys, financial markets, and agricultural output, among others.

Following the standard definition of business cycles as related to movements in the "overall" economic activity, a variety of statistical procedures and econometric models are applied to the aforementioned broad set of economic variables, seeking to identify robust turning points characterizing different phases of the cycles. This method follows international practices, such as the ones employed by the dating committee of the US National Bureau of Economic Research (NBER).

4 Analysis Conditional on Data Availability

The time span considered for business cycle analysis is inevitably conditioned on the availability of historical information in the form of time series for relevant economic variables. Another key dimension is the time frequency in which information these time series is produced. Given these constraints, the choice of a period for analysis always involves a trade-off between historical time span and accuracy. Although the literature contains efforts to reconstruct Brazilian GDP figures back to the nineteenth century using auxiliary information,[2] it is only from the 1950s that official statistics following international standards became available, at the yearly frequency. Official quarterly figures for GDP in Brazil start only later in 1990. Other important series considered by CODACE, such as tendency surveys for the industrial sector, were initially produced at the quarterly frequency, and later on a monthly basis. Another issue concerns methodological breaks in series for which historical data was available, such as labor market measures.

After considering the most suitable availability of original and reconstructed data, employing methods such as backcasting and frequency interpolation based on structural models, CODACE established the year of 1980 as the starting point for business cycle analysis. The result is a chronology of turning points at the quarterly and monthly frequencies.

5 Quarterly Chronology

The quarterly chronology is summarized in Table 1, showing recessions and expansions in terms of duration in quarters and growth (as measured by GDP) both accumulated and average, between quarters identified as turning points.

At the time of this writing (November 2017), CODACE has just identified 2016Q4 as a turning point for the recession started in 2014Q2.

6 Monthly Chronology

The monthly chronology is summarized in Table 2, showing recessions and expansions in terms of duration in months. The quarter established in the quarterly dating is shown in parenthesis.

At the time of this writing (November 2017), CODACE has still not identified neither a particular month marking the beginning of the recession started in 2014Q2 nor one establishing its end at 2016Q4.

7 Conclusions

A detailed analysis of the main economic factors behind each of the identified cycles is beyond the objectives of this chapter. The periods identified here as recessions and expansions provide additional information for framing more comprehensive

[2]See, for example, Abreu (2014).

Table 1 Quarterly chronology of Brazilian business cycles

Recessions				Expansions			
Period	Duration in quarters	Accumulated growth from peak to trough, %	Quarterly average growth, % (annualized)	Period	Duration in quarters	Accumulated growth from trough to peak, %	Quarterly average growth, % (annualized)
1981Q1–1983Q1	9	−8.5	−3.9	1983Q2–1987Q2	17	30.0	6.4
1987Q3–1988Q4	6	−4.2	−2.8	1989Q1–1989Q2	2	8.5	17.7
1989Q3–1992Q1	11	−7.7	−2.9	1992Q2–1995Q1	12	19.2	6.0
1995Q2–1995Q3	2	−2.8	−5.6	1995Q4–1997Q4	9	8.0	3.5
1998Q1–1999Q1	5	−1.5	−1.2	1999Q3–2001Q1	8	7.5	3.7
2001Q2–2001Q4	3	−0.9	−1.2	2002Q1–2002Q4	4	5.3	5.3
2003Q1–2003Q2	2	−1.6	−3.1	2003Q3–2008Q3	21	30.5	5.2
2008Q4–2009Q1	2	−5.5	−10.8	2009Q2–2014Q1	20	23.0	4.2
2014Q2–2016Q4	11	−8.6	−3.2				

Table 2 Monthly chronology of the Brazilian business cycles

		Recessions	Expansions	Cycles	
		Number of months			
Peaks	Troughs	From peak to trough	From previous trough to this peak	From peak to peak	From trough to trough
Oct. 1980 (1980Q4)	Feb. 1983 (1983Q1)	28	–	–	–
Feb. 1987 (1987Q2)	Oct. 1988 (1988Q4)	20	48	88	68
June 1989 (1989Q2)	Dec. 1991 (1992Q1)	30	8	28	38
Dec. 1994 (1995Q1)	Sep. 1995 (1995Q3)	9	36	66	45
Oct. 1997 (1997Q4)	Feb. 1999 (1999Q1)	16	25	34	41
Dec. 2000 (2001Q1)	Sep. 2001 (2001Q4)	9	10	38	31
Oct. 2002 (2002Q4)	June 2003 (2003Q2)	8	13	22	33
July 2008 (2008Q3)	Jan. 2009 (2009Q1)	6	61	69	67
Average duration		15.8	28.7	49.3	46.1

accounts of the details in Brazilian economic history[3] and also for subsidizing current analysis and forecasts. In Chapter 30 of the present volume, for example, the recession dates produced by CODACE constitute the dependent variable of a model assigning monthly probabilities for recessions in Brazil.

References

Abreu M (ed) (2014) A Ordem do Progresso: dois séculos de política econômica no Brasil, 2nd edn. Elsevier, Rio de Janeiro

Baer W (2014) The Brazilian economy: growth and development, 7th edn. Lynne Rienner, Boulder

Burns F, Mitchell W (1946) Measuring business cycles, NBER Book Series Studies in Business Cycles

[3]See, for example, Abreu (2014) (in Portuguese) and Baer 2014 (in English).

A Bayesian Approach to Predicting Cycles Using Composite Indicators

Paulo Picchetti

1 Introduction

The fundamental importance behind being able to predict turning points in economic activity has produced a vast literature of applied econometric methods, as well as new indicators designed specifically for the purpose of dating and anticipating periods of recessions versus expansions. This paper combines these two dimensions, building from the newly released composite indicators for Brazil and proposing an econometric approach. This approach differs from a large set of models which could be considered to lie within the class of two-sided filters. These include the combination of Kalman and Kim filters, such as proposed by Hamilton (1989) in a Markov-switching regime context, and also decompositions based on frequencies such as the wavelet transform (Picchetti (2008) has an application to Brazilian cycles).

The problem with this class of models is that, in general, although they provide excellent descriptions of the data and characterization of cycles within sample periods, their performance is weak on the end points, which hinders "real-time" analysis of cycles. The reason is basically that two-sided filters lack information beyond the end of the sample and therefore have to rely on some form of extrapolated data to produce results. Since cycles are characterized by structural breaks in parameters, the quality of data extrapolated out of sample after one of these structural breaks is very poor and consequently so are the predictions of turning points.

The method proposed here tries to circumvent this limitation, using statistical procedures that avoid the need of data beyond the end of the sample. The methodology is related to the one proposed by Estrella and Mishkin (1996), where a probit

P. Picchetti (✉)
Fundação Getulio Vargas, Brazil/IBRE/São Paulo School of Economics, São Paulo, Brazil
e-mail: paulo.picchetti@fgv.br

S. Smirnov et al. (eds.), *Business Cycles in BRICS*, Societies and Political Orders in Transition, https://doi.org/10.1007/978-3-319-90017-9_20

model is estimated with recession dates coded as the response variable, using financial indicators such as the US yield curve as predictors. This chapter estimates a logit model for Brazilian recessions, using suitable transformations of composite leading and coincident indicators as covariates.

2 The Leading and Coincident Composite Indicators for the Brazilian Economy

The methodology proposed by The Conference Board for constructing leading and coincident economic indicators (reviewed in Ozyildirim (2018)) was considered by Rodrigues et al. (2011, 2013) for the Brazilian case, where the authors provide evidence for its robust performance in evaluating turning points in economic activity. In July 2013, a partnership between The Conference Board and Fundação Getulio Vargas resulted in the launch of monthly composite indexes for the Brazilian economy, with a historical series going back to January 1996. Detailed information on the data series utilized, the time period considered, and the methodology for choosing the series for the composite indicators are all presented in Campelo et al. (2018). The composite indicators are updated monthly and published jointly in The Conference Board's website (www.conference-board.org) in English and at the Instituto Brasileiro de Economia's website (www.fgvdados.com.br) in Portuguese. Figure 1 shows the monthly evolution of the leading indicator up to September 2017,

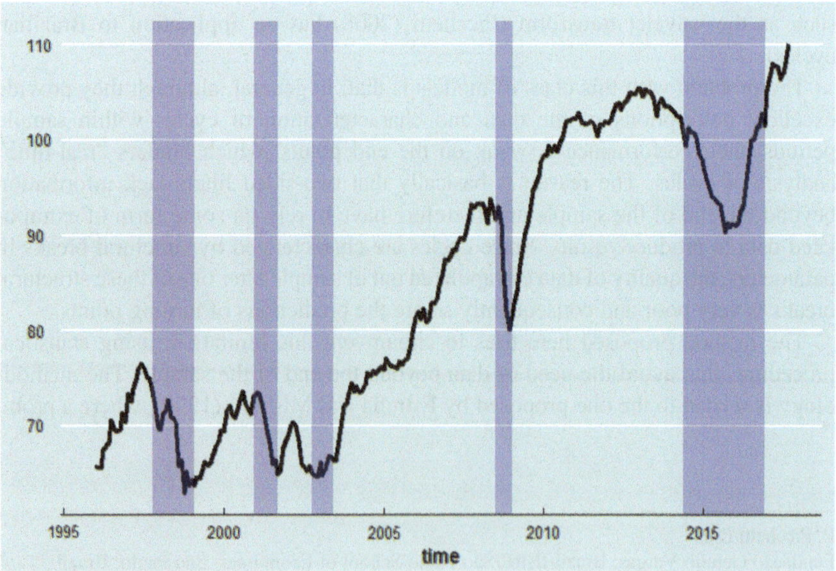

Fig. 1 Leading indicator

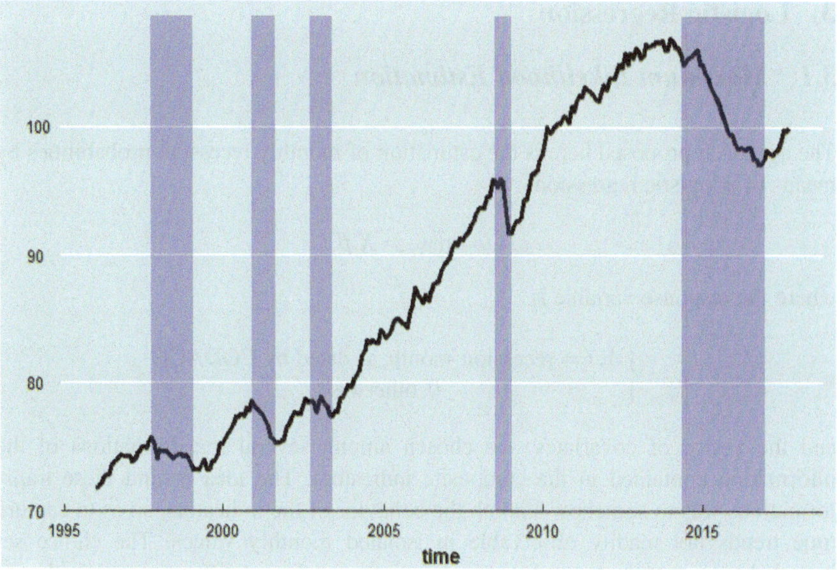

Fig. 2 Coincident indicator

along with shaded regions depicting recession dates in the Brazilian economy, as established by the Brazilian Economic Cycle Dating Committee (CODACE).

The leading indicator anticipates turning points by an average around 4 months in the case of the first three recessions in the sample and less clearly in the 2008 recession. The last and longest recession in the sample, starting in 2014, is anticipated by 8 months. Figure 2 presents the monthly evolution of the coincident indicator, again with shaded regions representing recession months.

The coincident indicator behavior seems well aligned with the starts and ends of recession periods, as desired.

Ideally, both indicators would present a smooth trajectory clearly anticipating and characterizing turning points. However, even though the noise and volatility which characterize the original series are reduced in the composite indicators by construction, they still condition the behavior of the indicators derived from them. The undesirable yet unavoidable result is a sequence of false positives or negatives, if we simply take the direction of monthly changes in the composite indicators as recession signals. This motivates the model proposed in the next section, which explicitly puts the relationship between these indicators and recession periods in a probabilistic context, allowing a much more interesting interpretation of recession signals.

3 Logistic Regression

3.1 Maximum Likelihood Estimation

The approach proposed here is the estimation of monthly recession probabilities by means of a logistic regression

$$logit(y_t) = X_t\beta$$

where the response variable is

$$y_t = \begin{cases} 1, t = \text{recession month, as dated by CODACE} \\ 0, \text{otherwise} \end{cases}$$

and the vector of covariates was chosen among several transformations of the information contained in the composite indicators. The idea behind these transformations was to somehow smooth the behavior of the indicators, so as to capture time trends not readily observable in isolated monthly values. The choice set included moving averages and standard deviations, taken at different lags but always right-aligned so as to allow for real-time assessments. Different lags were considered both to the moving statistics and to the resulting series. Additionally, year-over-year variations and interaction terms involving the constructed statistics were also considered. Based on significance of the estimated parameters and overall quality of fit of different models given by information criteria, the final set of covariates included 5-month moving statistics, yearly variations, and some interactions between these constructs:

$$X_t = \begin{cases} \text{const} \\ \text{LEI.MA5} \\ \text{CEI.MA5} \\ \text{LEI.MSD5} \\ \text{LEI.YOY}(-6) \\ \text{LEI.MA5}(-3) : \text{CEI.MA5} \\ \text{LEI.YOY} : \text{CEI.YOY} \\ \text{LEI.MA5} : \text{LEI} \end{cases}$$

All covariates above are thus transformations of the information contained in the leading and coincident indicators: the suffixes. MAn stand for moving averages of *n* months. MSDn for moving standard deviations for windows of *n* months, numbers in parentheses stand for number of lags, and interactions between variables are represented by "X:Y."

Table 1 presents estimation results for different model specifications, and the in-sample estimated probabilities for each individual month based on Model 4 of Table 1 can be seen in Fig. 3.

Although the estimated probabilities match the observed recessions generally well, the results show a number of false positives and negatives and significant

Table 1 Logistic regression for recession months

	Model1	Model2	Model3	Model4
Intercept	-1.53^{**}	-1.30^{**}	-3.57^{**}	-4.82^{**}
	(0.22)	(0.25)	(0.73)	(1.01)
LEI.MA5	-195.20^{**}	-164.70^{**}	-175.44^{**}	-985.94^{*}
	(32.63)	(35.79)	(45.72)	(429.58)
CEI.MA5		−158.66	-276.16^{*}	-399.06^{*}
		(89.47)	(119.84)	(145.74)
LEI.SD5**			217.91^{**}	337.03^{**}
			(52.58)	(75.86)
LEI.MA5(−3):CEI.MA5			-54228.04^{**}	−50395.71
			(12440.85)	(13685.48)
LEI.YOY(−6)				0.22^{*}
				(0.07)
LEI.YOY:CEI.YOY				-0.11^{*}
				(0.04)
LEI.MA5:LEI				8.89^{*}
				(4.45)
AIC	147.42	146.17	109.21	95.66
BIC	154.01	156.06	125.71	122.05
LogLikelihood	−71.71	−70.08	−49.61	−39.83
Deviance	143.42	140.17	99.21	79.66
Num.obs.	200	200	200	200

$^{***}p < 0.001$, $^{**}p < 0.01$, $^{*}p < 0.05$

volatility around turning points. One of the main reasons behind these undesirable results is probably related to biases in the MLE parameters resulting from endogeneity of the covariates. Since these covariates are derived from the composite indicators, which in turn were constructed to match the response variable closely, this endogeneity should definitely be considered explicitly. The traditional use of two-stage methods for correcting endogeneity involve the difficult task of choosing suitable instruments, which in our case also invalidates the strategy of basing estimation solely on the information contained in the composite indicators. Additionally, the performance of this class of estimators is generally not warranted in samples where the number of observations is not very big, also our case here. In what follows, we propose a different approach to address these issues.

3.2 Bayesian Estimation

The parameters of a logistic regression can be divided into the one related to the intercept and the set related to the covariates. Each of these can be interpreted in

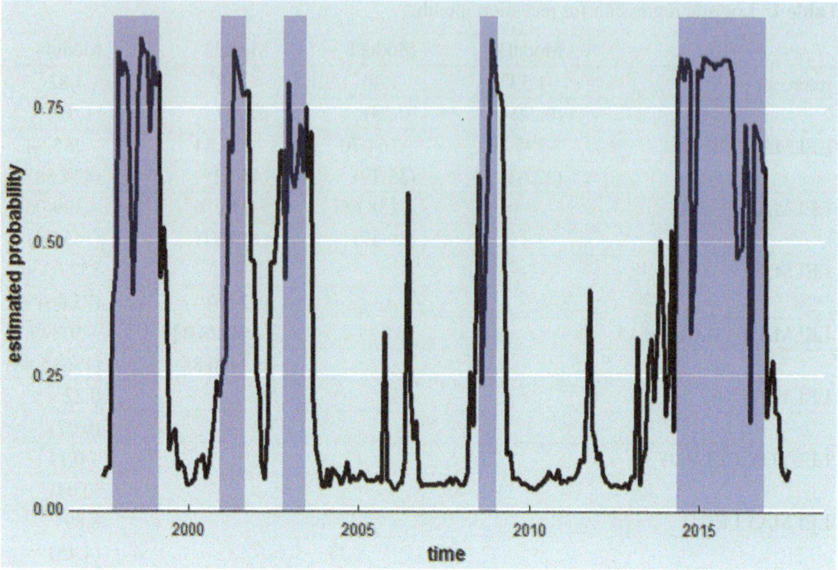

Fig. 3 Predicted recession probabilities

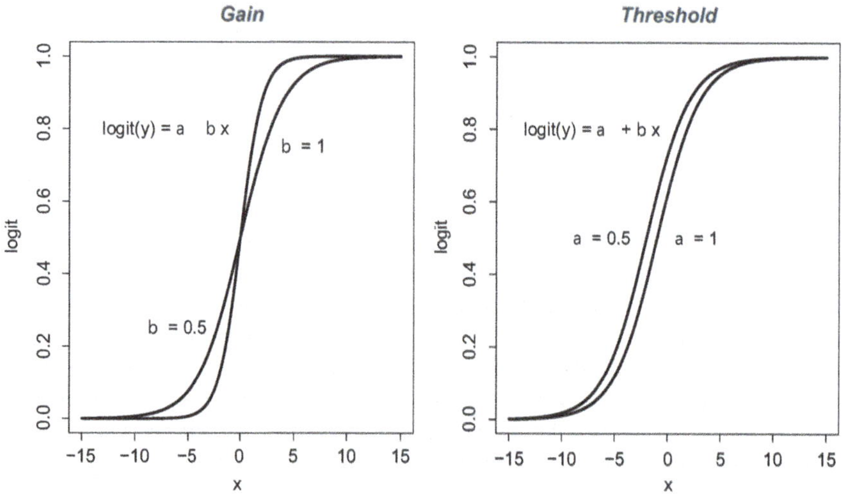

Fig. 4 Gain and threshold effects

terms of their effects on the estimated probabilities. The graphs below convey this idea in an intuitive way (Fig. 4).

As can be seen in this artificial and simple example, the estimated probabilities are sensitive in different ways to the choice of parameters. Therefore, we can alter the

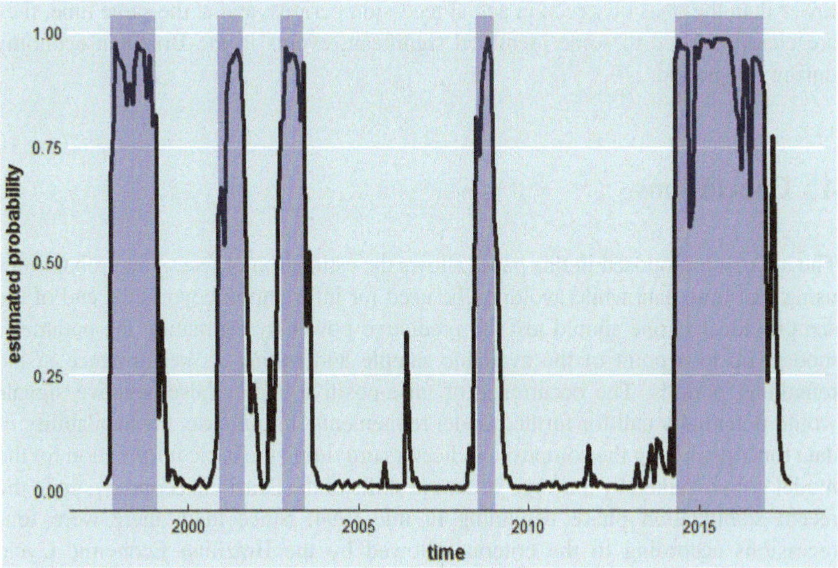

Fig. 5 Predicted recession probabilities (Bayesian model).

parameter values and check their effect on the estimated probabilities. If the in-sample estimated probabilities better match the observed data for different parameters, we take this as evidence of more robust values for these parameters. A possible strategy for estimating the model is then to consider priors for some of the parameters, based on the conditional means methodology (Bedrick et al. 1996). Basically, we impose informative priors centered on the values of the parameters for which the resulting conditional means better represent the observed data and estimate the model under the Bayesian framework.

We estimate the model using the same specification above but in a Bayesian context where informative priors are centered on the values for the parameters on the LEI.MA5 and LEI.MA5:LEI covariates (conditioning the threshold of the logistic link) and the constant (conditioning the logistic link). For the parameters of all other covariates, flat priors were imposed. The Bayesian framework also naturally allows the inclusion of a random time effect in the model. Using 10,000 iterations of a Markov chain produced by the OpenBUGS software, we obtained a predictive distribution for the monthly probabilities of recession. The monthly means of each of these predictive distributions produce the graph below (Fig. 5).

The result seems clearly superior compared to the one obtained in the MLE case, not only in the sense that turning points are much better represented in probabilistic terms but also in the sense that the estimated probabilities of recession are more compatible with actual recession and expansion periods. We still observe rises in these estimated probabilities in periods outside recessions, but the values are now lower than the ones observed in actual recession periods, and at the same time, they are clearly related to some identified significant events in the Brazilian economy during this period.

4 Conclusions

The approach proposed in this paper allows the estimation of recession probabilities using real-time data while avoiding the need for information beyond the end of the sample. Ideally, one should test the predictive power by estimating the parameter models up to a point of the available sample and testing its performance in the remaining periods. The occurrence of false-positive and/or false-negative signals would potentially call for further model refinements. In our case, the availability of data for constructing the composite indicators providing the basic information for the model is constrained by the large structural shifts of the Brazilian economy, up to the recent stabilization phase beginning in mid-1994. Since then, there were four recessions according to the criteria followed by the Brazilian Economic Cycle Dating Committee, which severely limits the above proposed exercise. This is even more true considering that the last recession, which started in the last part of 2008, was unique in terms of its severity, as can be seen in Figs. 1 and 2 depicting the behaviors of the composite indicators. Even though the estimated probabilities of recession using information for the sample prior to that period unequivocally point to the observed turning points, the subsequent inclusion of information after 2008 has a significant impact on the stability of the estimated parameters. Therefore, the robustness checking strategy of the predictions made from the approach proposed here will unravel in the future, as estimated parameters will be kept at the values obtained according to the sample information ending in 2013 and estimated probabilities from now on confronted with new turning points eventually pointed by CODACE.

References

Bedrick E, Christensen R, Johnson W (1996) A new perspective on priors for generalized linear models. J Am Stat Assoc 91:1450–1460

Brazilian Economic Cycle Dating Committee – IBRE-FGV 03 02 10 – PDF document available in www.ibre.fgv.br

Bry G, Boschan C (1971) Cyclical analysis of economic time series: selected procedures and computer programs, NBER Technical Working Paper No. 20

Campelo A, Sima-Friedman J, Lima S, Ozyildirim A, Picchetti P (2018) Coincident and leading indicators for Brazilian cycles. In: Business cycles in BRICS. Springer, Cham

Chauvet M (2002) The Brazilian business cycle and growth cycle. Rev Bras Econ 56:75–106

Crowley P (2007) A guide to wavelets for economists. J Econ Surv 21(2):207–267

Estrella A, Mishkin F (1996) The yield curve as a predictor of U.S. recessions. Curr Issue Econ Financ 2(7):1–6

Hamilton J (1989) A new approach to the economic analysis of non-stationary time-series and the business cycle. Econometrica 57:357–384

Levanon G (2010) Evaluating and comparing leading and coincident economic indicators. Bus Econ 45(1):16–27

Ozyildirim A (2018) Compiling cyclical composite indexes: The Conference Board indicators approach. In: Smirnov S, Ozyildirim A, Picchetti P (eds) Business cycles in BRICS. Springer, Cham

Percival DB, Walden AT (2000) Wavelet methods for timeseries analysis. Cambridge University Press, Cambridge

Picchetti P (2008) Wavelelet-based leading indicators of industrial activity in Brazil, CIRET Conference, Santiago

Priestley M (1996) Wavelets and time-dependent spectral analysis. J Time Ser Anal 17:85–103

Ramsey J (2000) The contribution of wavelets to the analysis of economic and financial data. In: Silverman B, Vassilicos J (eds) Wavelets: the key to intermittent information, volume wavelets: the key to intermittent information. Oxford University Press, New York

Rodrigues COF, Notini HH, Issler JV (2011) A commonfeature model for coincident index of Brazilian economic activity. In: Proceedings of the 38th Brazilian Economics Meeting 001, ANPEC – Brazilian Association of Graduate Programs in Economics

Rodrigues COF, Notini HH, Issler JV (2013) Constructing coincident and leading indices of economic activity for the Brazilian economy. OECD J Bus Cycle Meas Anal 2012(2):43–65

A Survey of Composite Leading Indices for Russia

Sergey V. Smirnov

1 Introduction

During the long period of the planned economy, there were no real-time composite indicators to trace the level of economic activity in Russia (which was a part of the USSR). Furthermore, there was an ideological dogma that cyclical fluctuations are not possible in a planned economy. In conjunction with the lack of necessary statistical information, this made any empirical research in the field absolutely impossible. Several years after the collapse of the Soviet Union, the first attempts at constructing monthly composite coincident and leading indicators were made (Davydov et al. 1993; Popov and Frenkel 1996). However, they were not very successful. In the first half of the 1990s, the Russian economy was in a prolonged contraction, and there was no opportunity to calibrate cyclical indices to give more confidence in their forecasting capabilities. After the Asian financial crisis of 1997, which seriously hit the Russian economy, a regular sequence of expansions and contractions began in Russia; it was only then that the construction of composite cyclical indicators became important for policy and business purposes. Since then, several systems of cyclical (leading, coincident, and lagging) composite indicators have been suggested. Some of them are still in use; others have disappeared and are now forgotten. In the next section, we survey all the current monthly updated composite leading indices (CLIs) for Russia and compare their components. In Sect. 3, we discuss the dating of cyclical turning points for Russia. After an examination of the real leading properties of all proposed composite leading indices (Sect. 4), we conclude.

S. V. Smirnov (✉)
National Research University Higher School of Economics, Moscow, Russia
e-mail: svsmirnov@hse.ru

S. Smirnov et al. (eds.), *Business Cycles in BRICS*, Societies and Political Orders in Transition, https://doi.org/10.1007/978-3-319-90017-9_21

2 Russian CLIs

2.1 Main Versions of Russian CLIs

Currently, three reasonably efficient sets of composite cyclical indices are available for Russia.

Indices constructed by Smirnov (2001, 2006) were the first Russian cyclical composite indices to be regularly published; they are now published every month in the survey of the Russian economy produced by the Higher School of Economics (HSE).[1] They represent an example of a traditional system of leading, coincident, and lagging indicators with corresponding aggregated (or composite) indices. These indices are designed to predict the beginning and end of recessions (cyclical peaks and troughs) where recessions are understood as periods of declining economic activity. Historically, these composite indices used year-on-year growth rates instead of month-on-month seasonally adjusted growth rates, which are more appropriate for calculating base indices; hence, turning points of the Russian business cycle estimated with these indices may be slightly displaced. Another shortcoming is that the formula for aggregating components and their weights is not published, and the current set of components is not strictly the same as that described in the latest publication (Smirnov 2014). Since September 2000 (first publication), there have been six revisions of this system (April 2005, May 2006, January 2008, August 2011, January 2013, September 2016). Half of them were caused by involuntary changes in the statistical sources; the others were initiated by a desire to refine the methodology and to increase the forecasting quality.

Several years later, the Organisation for Economic Co-operation and Development (OECD) constructed a Russian CLI, which is now part of a set of similar indices for 47 countries and areas.[2] All of these indices, including the Russian one, use the concept of growth (not business) cycles. Meanwhile, it is not clear if the Russian economy—with all its volatility and sensitivity to external shocks—really has a definite long-term economic growth trend. Generally, the methodology for all the OECD calculations and the revisions of the Russian index are well documented (see OECD 2006, 2010), but the exact time of inclusion of one component (finished good stocks) and exclusion of another (US imports from Russia) cannot be traced precisely. They happened somewhere around February 2010, when the OECD's Russian CLI was substantially revised, but we cannot be any more certain than that.

Finally, since March 2014, the Eurasian Economic Commission (EEC 2014) has calculated coincident and leading composite indices for Russia, Kazakhstan, and Belarus, which it publishes monthly.[3] Uniquely, these indices use automated selection of components for the leading indices. Revisions connected with the

[1]See https://dcenter.hse.ru/coi

[2]See https://data.oecd.org/leadind/composite-leading-indicator-cli.htm

[3]See http://www.eurasiancommission.org/ru/act/integr_i_makroec/dep_makroec_pol/economyPrognoz/Pages/Krat_prog.aspx

re-specification of the Russian composite leading index happened in April and July 2014, September 2015, May and November 2016, and March 2017.

Beside these three versions of a CLI for Russia, there are two other CLI-like aggregated indicators that may be used for understanding the current state of the Russian economy and forecasting the oncoming peaks and troughs.[4]

In 2012, a single composite index of economic activity, or some kind of a "barometer" for the Russian economy, was proposed (Frenkel et al. 2012). Several leading, coincident, and lagging indicators are mixed as components of this composite index, as the authors understand them all to be coincident. This index has been revised twice, in December 2013 and February 2014. Although this composite index can be used for monitoring the Russian economy, it is of limited use as a forecasting and dating tool for cyclical turning points. In addition, the indicator is not published monthly,[5] resulting in some inevitable additional lags in discerning cyclical turning points.

Since 2013, the Center for Macroeconomic Analysis and Short-Term Forecasting (CMASF 2013; Pestova 2013) has used a signal approach to estimate two separate risks—the risk of entrance into a recession during the 3 next months and the risk of coming out of recession (if it has already begun).[6] They calibrated their model using a panel of several dozen countries and then applied it to Russia. Hence, they also do not differentiate between leading, coincident, and lagging components but instead consider all of them as leading.

2.2 Sets of Components

All Russian composite cyclical indices mentioned above, along with their components, are given in Table 1 (we list only the most recent sets of components for all these indicators, not all historical versions of those sets). Several additional comments are needed.

Firstly, the leading indicators most frequently used as components of composite indices are crude oil prices, stock market index, and order books from (different) business tendency surveys (BTSs); on the other hand, none of the indicators are used by all authors, and no Russian cyclical composite index has the yield curve as a component.

[4]Several indicators based exclusively on surveys of enterprises (e.g., Purchasing Managers' Indices by IHS Markit) as well as some "exotic" cyclical Russian indices are not considered here; see Smirnov (2014) for a survey of these. Russian cyclical indices calculated by Economic Cycle Research Institute (ECRI) were omitted from this analysis as no public information on their methodology and components is available. Confidence indicators based on the HSE-Rosstat BTS are described in Lipkind et al. (2018) and the composite index of Regional Economic Activity (REA) in Smirnov and Kondrashov (2018).

[5]See http://www.inesnet.ru/keywords/sostavlyayushhie-kies/

[6]See http://www.forecast.ru/SOI.aspx

Table 1 Components of the available Russian composite cyclical indices

Composite cyclical indices					
Publications with descriptions of the indices	Smirnov (2001, 2006)	OECD (2006, 2010)	Frenkel et al. (2012)	CMASF (2013)	EEC (2014)
First published for (month/year)	09/2000	04/2006	08/2012	02/2013	04/2014
Components[a]					
Products and financial markets					
Crude oil price	L	L	C		L
RTS Stock market index	L	L			L
Interest rate (MIACR overnight)	L			L	
Real effective exchange rate	L			L	
Price of dwelling space in Moscow	Lg				
BTSs[b]					
Manufacturing: production tendency		L			
Manufacturing: production expectations					L
Manufacturing: order books	L	L	C		
Manufacturing: export orders books		L			
Manufacturing: finished goods stocks	L				
Manufacturing: financial self-sufficiency			C		
Industry: capacity utilization			C		
Real and household sector					
Agriculture production	C				
Industrial production			C		C
Mining production	C				
Manufacturing production	C				
Construction production	C				
Freight transportation turnover	C		C		L
Retail trade sales	C		C		C
Paid services to population	C		C		
Employment			C		
Unemployed	Lg			L	
Fixed investments			C		C

(continued)

Table 1 (continued)

Composite cyclical indices					
Publications with descriptions of the indices	Smirnov (2001, 2006)	OECD (2006, 2010)	Frenkel et al. (2012)	CMASF (2013)	EEC (2014)
First published for (month/year)	09/2000	04/2006	08/2012	02/2013	04/2014
Real disposable income			C		L
Banking sector and money supply					
Personal bank deposits			C		
Absolutely liquid bank assets				L	
Credits to real sector	Lg		C		
Consumer and enterprise loans				L	
Loans-to-credits ratio				L	
M2 Money aggregate	L				
Foreign sector					
Current account balance				L	
Foreign exchange reserves	Lg				
Foreign debt-to-foreign exchange reserves				L	
Imported autos	Lg				
Other indicators					
OECD's business confidence index for Russia				L	
OECD's composite leading index for the USA				L	

[a]The components are considered as leading (L), coincident (C), and lagging (Lg)
[b]Different authors use different Russian business tendency surveys (BTSs)

Secondly, the composite index constructed by CMASF (2013) uses the OECD's business confidence index as one of its components. Smirnov (2001, 2006) and OECD (2006, 2010) indices have several common components (crude oil price, the same stock index, the same BTS). Hence, all these indices are not strictly independent.

Thirdly, sometimes different authors use the same statistical indicators as components with different types of lags. For example, Smirnov (2006) understands freight transportation turnover as a coincident indicator, while the EEC (2014) understands it as a leading one; Smirnov (2006) considers number of unemployed as lagging while CMASF (2013) as leading.

Fourthly, there is only one full system of cyclical indicators (leading, coincident, and lagging) (Smirnov 2006). Evidently, cyclical movements of a broad range of Russian statistical time series have not been analyzed in detail.

This does not mean that the existing Russian composite leading indices are useless. In any case, their practical ability to predict recessions should be examined.

3 Dating of Cyclical Turning Points for Russia

It is important to note that there is no unanimity among Russian experts concerning the concept of business cycles. For example, the OECD investigates growth cycles, while all others analyze cycles of economic activity; CMASF (2013) identifies the beginning of a recession as the first month in which the 12-month moving average growth rate of real GDP is negative, while Smirnov et al. (2017) regards the beginning of a recession as the first month after a cyclical peak, which is the turning point between an expansion and contraction in economic activity. Meanwhile, the cyclical indicators currently used by Smirnov (2001, 2006) are more suitable for monitoring growth rate cycles, not classical business cycles; hence, some inconsistencies are evident.

Moreover, there are several leading, coincident, and (rarely) lagging composite indices proposed for Russia, but no commonly recognized set of cyclical peaks and troughs. Each leading index anticipates its unique set of turning points. Hence, there has been no way of comparing various CLIs for their leading properties in a strict way in order to choose the best one. Furthermore, recently Smirnov et al. (2017) revealed that the exact dates of turning points—if defined with formal methods only—always depend on the nuances of the procedures used (such as the choice of supposedly coincident indicators, methods of seasonal adjustment, frequency filters, etc.). As no decision may be a priori seen as flawless, there are only two options:

a) To allow each expert to estimate cyclical turning points independently. In this way, a set of peaks and troughs will change not only from one researcher to another but also when the time series is updated by the same researcher. Implicitly, the OECD has chosen this way: its set of turning points for Russia is not constant but drifts over time.
b) To establish a national dating committee comprising a number of credible experts in the field of Russian economic cycles. This committee may define—by a consensus decision—the next peak (or trough) 9–18 months after it has occurred. Thereafter, this date will never change, and any researcher should use the same set of turning points to analyze historical cyclical processes or to calibrate his own forecasting instruments. Most successfully, this option has been used in the United States where cyclical peaks and troughs dated by the NBER's Business Cycle Dating Committee are now seen as a common benchmark.[7] Among BRICS, this approach has been used in Brazil (see Picchetti 2018) and partially in South Africa, where no formal national dating committee exists, but business cycle turning points are determined by an internal committee of experts at the South African Reserve Bank (see Venter 2018).

[7]It was not always the case. In the end of the 1980s to the beginning of the 1990s, many criticized the NBER's choices. For examples, see McNees (1987); Diebold and Rudebusch (1992); Boldin (1994); Romer (1994). Later, the number of skeptics became less but not equal to zero (see Berge and Jordà 2011; Stock and Watson 2014).

Table 2 Durations of the identified Russian economic cycles and/or phases, in months

Reference dates		Contraction	Expansion	Cycle	
Peak	Trough	(Peak to trough)	(Previous trough to this peak)	(Trough from previous trough)	(Peak from previous peak)
NA	Dec. 1979[a]	NA	NA	NA	NA
Jan. 1989	Nov. 1996	94	109	203	NA
Nov. 1997	Sep. 1998	10	12	22	106
May 2008	May 2009	12	116	128	126
Dec. 2014	Jun. 2016	18	67	85	79

Sources: Smirnov et al. (2017)
[a]Rough estimate; we only know two facts: (a) 1979 was a recession year; (b) there was an expansion from January 1980 onward

In Russia, such a committee was established by the Association of Russian Economic Think Tanks (ARETT) in June 2017. It consists of eight members: Vladimir Bessonov (Higher School of Economics), Sergey Drobyshevsky (the Gaidar Institute for Economic Policy), Eugene Nadorshin (Pension Fund "Capital"), Sergey Nikolaenko (Vnesheconombank), Alexander Schirov (Institute of Economic Forecasting, Russian Academy of Sciences), Sergey Smirnov (Chairman, Development Center and Higher School of Economics), Oleg Solntsev (Center for Macroeconomic Analysis and Short-Term Forecasting), and Anton Stroutchenevski (Sberbank CIB). They work for authoritative Russian universities, independent think tanks, and financial companies; all of them have published on the topic in scientific journals and business press.

The main aim of the ARETT's Economic Cycle Dating Committee (Russian Dating Committee, RDC) is to date turning points (peaks and troughs) of the Russian business cycle, or cycle of economic activity (not growth or growth rate cycle). The main concepts and principles by which the Committee is guided in its work are outlined in a special memorandum (see Appendix 1).

According to the RDC's preliminary discussions, the latest Russian recession began in January 2015 and ended in June 2016 (December 2014 is the latest peak and June 2016 is the latest trough).[8] The RDC has not dated the turning points of preceding Russian cycles (although it is likely that it will do so in the future). Using estimates made by Smirnov et al. (2017), we may trace Russian business cycles from 1980 to the present day (see Table 2).

Note that for calibrating leading, coincident, and lagging indicators, only the turning points for the two or three latest recessions matter: there are almost no monthly time series in Russia from the beginning of the 1990s that are still in use; most of the currently available statistical indicators began at least 10–15 years later.

[8]Official press release of the RDC is not published yet.

4 Warning Signals for the Recent Russian Recession

To establish if there were timely warning signals for the recent Russian recession (in other words, for the corresponding peak and trough), we first plotted all available Russian cyclical indicators. For HSE (see Smirnov 2001, 2006), these are the year-on-year growth rates of coincident, leading, and lagging composite indices; for the OECD (2006, 2010), these are real-time vintages (editions) of the amplitude-adjusted Russian CLIs (minus 100); for the CMASF (2013), this is the probability of entering into recession; for the EEC (2014), these are coincident and leading indices (minus 100).[9]

Figure 1 shows clearly that the turning points of almost all composite leading indicators precede the cyclical turning points mentioned in Table 2. However, there are two issues that suggest that the problem of forecasting leading indicators has not been resolved. They are (a) the turning points of CLIs tend only to become evident retrospectively; because of the volatility of CLIs, there is often insufficient information to identify them in real time; (b) by construction, some CLIs do not signal a reversal in economic trends (from expansion to contraction or vice versa) but only indicate slower or faster movement in the same direction.

For this reason, we analyzed all available Russian CLIs in two additional dimensions. We considered (a) the results of applying a very simple decision rule to the CLIs real-time trajectories and (b) real-time expert judgments taken from relevant official press releases. Table 3 sets out the results of a decision rule (DR) and the appropriate expert judgments (EJ) to each composite index.

As a decision rule, we used the so-called "five-sixths" rule of thumb. This rule implies that 5 or 6 growing months (out of 6 in a row) signal an oncoming expansion, while null or 1 growing month (out of 6) signals an oncoming contraction. All other values do not give definite signals for a change in the direction of the economic trajectory.[10] "Plus" in a cell in Table 3 means that the latest available signal is positive (economic activity will grow); "minus" means that the latest signal is negative (economic activity will decline).[11]

As for expert judgments, we used the following notations for short-run outlooks of economic activity:

$<$ Definitely bad or worse (continuation of contraction or certain deterioration)
$\leq$ Slightly worse (some signs of deterioration)

[9]As time series by Frenkel et al. (2012) are never published, there is no corresponding chart.

[10]See Smirnov (2011) for a survey of such decision rules and their properties. It might appear from the results below that the "five-sixths" rule is too rigid. We tested several other decision rules, and the results were generally the same (they are available upon request).

[11]To take into account the specifics of the EEC's index, we considered zero change as growth. For all other indices, this does not matter. We also considered (1 – CLI) instead of CLI for the CMASF index: for better comparisons with other indices, we converted their estimate of probability of recession into probability of expansion. Values of Frenkel's index are not published, and so no decision rule can be applied to them.

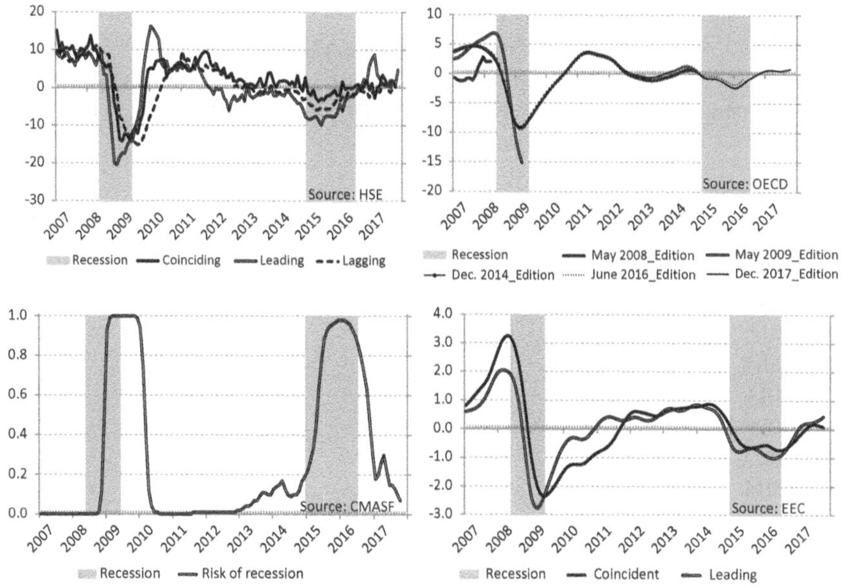

Fig. 1 Composite cyclical indicators for Russia

= Same (no definite changes)
≥ Slightly better (some signs of improvement)
> Definitely better or good (certain improvement or continuation of expansion)

As Russian authors do not use certain verbal formulas in their expert judgments, we "translated" these judgments into our own categories according to their general sense. For the OECD's news releases, we compiled a special short "glossary" (see Appendix 2).

Keeping this in mind, we should draw attention to the following:

Firstly, the beginning of the recent recession was forecasted in advance—in their expert judgments—by all experts under consideration, except the EEC: by CMASF (8 months beforehand), by Frenkel et al. (4 months), by Smirnov (3 months), and by the OECD (2 months) (the EEC's alarm signal was simultaneous with the first month of the recession, i.e., 1 month after the peak). The beginning of the recent expansion was forecasted in advance by the EEC (9 months), OECD (4 months), and CMASF (2 months). Smirnov was delayed by 1 month, while Frenkel et al. have not recognized the ending of the recession until now, more than 1 year after the trough. Evidently, the general pessimism (Frenkel et al.) or optimism (EEC) of experts matters.

Secondly, no single index gave an alarm signal for the beginning of recession in advance (several negative signals in April–July 2014 were later "compromised" with evidently positive signals; therefore, they cannot be considered as the leading alarm signals). The most impressive gap between the formal decision rule and informal expert judgment may be seen in August 2014–February 2015 when the CMASF

Table 3 Warning signals from various Russian CLIs

	Smirnov (2001, 2006)		OECD (2006, 2010)		Frenkel et al. (2012)		CMASF (2013)		EEC (2014)	
Month of release	DR	EJ	DR	EJ	DR	EJ	DR	EJ	DR	EJ
Jan. 2014		=	+	=	NA	NA		>	NA	NA
Feb. 2014		=	+	=	NA	=		>	NA	NA
Mar. 2014		<	+	=	NA	NA		>	NA	NA
Apr. 2014	–	<		<	NA	=		>	NA	NA
May 2014	–	≤	–	<	NA	NA		≤	+	=
June 2014	–	=	–	<	NA	=	–	<	+	>
July 2014		=		=	NA	=	–	<	+	=
Aug. 2014		=	+	≥	NA	NA		<	+	>
Sep. 2014		=	+	>	NA	<		<	+	>
Oct. 2014		≤	+	>	NA	<		<	+	>
Nov. 2014		<	+	≤	NA	<	+	<	+	>
Dec. 2014		<		=	**NA**	<	**+**	<	**+**	=
Jan. 2015		<		<	NA	NA		<		<
Feb. 2015		<	–	<	NA	<		<		<
Mar. 2015		<	–	<	NA	<	–	<		<
Apr. 2015		<	–	<	NA	<	–	<	–	<
May 2015		<	–	<	NA	<	–	<	–	<
June 2015		<		≥	NA	NA	–	<		<
July 2015		<		≥	NA	NA	–	<		=
Aug. 2015		<	–	>	NA	NA	–	<		=
Sep. 2015		≤	–	≤	NA	<	–	<		<
Oct. 2015		≤		<	NA	<	–	<	+	=
Nov. 2015		≤		NA	NA	<	–	<	NA	NA
Dec. 2015		=	–	<	NA	<	–	<	+	=
Jan. 2016	+	<	–	<	NA	NA	–	<	+	=
Feb. 2016		<	–	<	NA	<	–	<	+	>
Mar. 2016		<	–	<	NA	<	–	<	NA	>
Apr. 2016		<	–	<	NA	<	–	<	NA	=
May 2016		<		≥	NA	<	–	<	NA	>
June 2016	**NA**	**NA**		≥	**NA**	<		<	**NA**	>
July 2016	NA	NA	NA	NA	NA	NA		≤	NA	>
Aug. 2016	NA	NA	NA	NA	NA	NA		≤	NA	>
Sep. 2016	NA	NA	+	>	NA	<	+	>	NA	>
Oct. 2016		≤	+	>	NA	<	+	>	NA	>
Nov. 2016		>	+	>	NA	<	+	>	NA	>
Dec. 2016		>	+	>	NA	NA	+	>	NA	>
Jan. 2017	NA	NA	+	>	NA	NA	+	>	NA	>
Feb. 2017	+	≥	+	>	NA	NA	+	>	NA	>
Mar. 2017	+	≥	+	NA	NA	<	+	>	NA	>
Apr. 2017	+	≥	+	>	NA	NA	+	>	NA	>
May 2017		≥	+	>	NA	<		>	NA	>

(continued)

Table 3 (continued)

	Smirnov (2001, 2006)		OECD (2006, 2010)		Frenkel et al. (2012)		CMASF (2013)		EEC (2014)	
Month of release	DR	EJ	DR	EJ	DR	EJ	DR	EJ	DR	EJ
June 2017		≥	+	>	NA	NA		>	NA	>
July 2017		≥		≤	NA	NA		>	NA	=
Aug. 2017		≥		≤	NA	NA		>	NA	=
Sep. 2017	–	≥		≤	NA	NA	NA	NA	NA	=

Notes: NA, not available; DR, decision rule; EJ, expert judgment. Recent peak (December 2014) and trough (June 2016) are marked with bold. See text for other explanations

index showed no signs of recession but CMASF experts insisted that recession was inevitable (and they were correct!). As for the beginning of the expansion, the OECD's and CMASF's indices gave signals 2 months before the first month of growth, but their expert judgments were more perceptive, especially for the OECD.

All this means that for their judgments, experts evidently used some information not contained in the trajectories of their indices. The intuition and practical experience of experts made their verbal judgments better (more informative) than their CLIs.

5 Conclusion

Several CLIs for Russia are published on a regular monthly basis. They have different components, use different weightings and calculations, and are even based on different concepts of cycles and recessions (respectively, they use different sets of peaks and troughs).

The Russian Dating Committee (RDC), which is made up of authoritative independent experts, has been recently established. It has not yet "officially" dated cyclical turning points of the latest cycle; however, it has preliminarily identified December 2014 as the peak and June 2016 as the trough. This has provided an opportunity for meaningful comparison of the forecasting properties of various Russian CLIs.

Three CLIs were most informative: those produced by the OECD, CMASF, and Smirnov. The fact that expert judgments extracted from official news releases gave better warning signals for the beginning and the end of the recent recession than the trajectory of CLIs may mean several things: (a) the initial statistical time series compiled by Rosstat (the Russian statistical agency) or their seasonally adjusted versions are of poor quality (especially, in real time); (b) available CLIs miss some important variables, while experts implicitly use some additional information that is not contained in available CLIs. The latter may already be quite useful for monitoring the current economic situation, but additional research for more careful calibration of the broad spectrum of economic and financial indices, as well as their identification as leading, coincident, or lagging indicators for the Russian cycle, is evidently needed.

Appendix 1: Memorandum of the Russian Economic Cycle Dating Committee

Russian Economic Cycle Dating Committee (Russian Dating Committee, RDC) Under the Association of Russian Economic Think Tanks (ARETT): Key Concepts and Approaches

1. The Russian Economic Cycle Dating Committee (Russian Dating Committee, RDC) under the Association of Russian Economic Think Tanks (ARETT) uses the following concepts in its work:
   - *Cycle of economic activity* (business cycle): Fluctuations in Russian economic activity that continue through several quarters for 10–12 years or more. A full cycle in this sense comprises two phases: growth and contraction (recession), which do not adhere to strict pattern of periodicity.
   - *Phases of growth and contraction (recession):* Alternating periods of overall increase and decrease in economic activity. During the growth phase, production and sales volumes of goods and services in the entire economy, and in most sectors, grow; in the contraction (recession) phase, they fall.
   - *Turning point:* A moment in time immediately preceding the transition of the economy from one phase to the other.
   - *Peak:* A moment when economic activity is at its maximum, followed by the economy's transition from a growth phase to recession.
   - *Trough (or bottom):* A moment when economic activity is at its minimum, followed by the economy's transition from recession to growth.
2. The RDC's goal is to date turning points in Russian cycles of economic activity (business cycles) to appropriate months.
3. The RDC does not see it as its goal to date turning points of growth cycles (deviations from the long-term trend) or growth rate cycles, nor does the RDC develop or test theories that seek to explain the existence of economic cycles or identify drivers of any particular cycle or cyclical phase. Any member of the RDC may, as an individual, study these issues, but their opinion on such matters should be considered as their own personal view.
4. When offering real-time comments on the state of the Russian economy, members of the RDC may define the Russian economy as reaching or not reaching a recent turning point (peak or trough). The RDC will formulate a consolidated position of its members over time, taking as much time as is needed to conclusively analyze the situation.

5. Every RDC member uses those indicators and methods in their analysis that they feel are most useful. RDC members form a consolidated position through open and grounded discussion of the results put forward, taking into account not only the results of statistical tests but also members' qualitative analyses.
6. Although the RDC's decisions always relate to the past, rather than the current state of the economy, it would be erroneous to assume that they are "delayed." The RDC seeks to date turning points as soon as it becomes clear that the coming change in economic activity will not be a continuation of the preceding phase but will constitute a new phase of the cycle; besides, statistical data that appears should enable these turning points to be discerned with reasonable accuracy. As a rule, this takes 9–18 months, from the month of the turning point.
7. If the subsequent revision of Rosstat data radically changes the perception of the course of the Russian economic cycle, then the RDC may update the turning point dating.
8. If there are two or more months that offer almost similar grounds to be considered turning points, the RDC prefers to choose the later one.
9. Results of and grounds for dating are published by the RDC in dedicated press releases on the RDC website.
10. Dating of cyclical turning points established by the RDC can be used for further analysis of historical economic dynamics in Russia, and to predict future dynamics, in particular in developing and calibrating systems of leading, coincident, and lagging indicators.

Appendix 2: Short glossary for the OECD's news releases

Standard "diagnoses" by the OECD	Short notation
Growth below trend Weak growth momentum Growth losing momentum	$<$
Tentative signs of easing growth Growth tentatively losing momentum Signs of easing growth Signs of slowing growth momentum	$\leq$
Stable growth momentum Growth around trend	$=$
Tentative signs of positive change in growth momentum Signs of positive change in growth momentum Stabilization of growth momentum	$\geq$
Growth gaining momentum Growth picking up Stable growth momentum	$>$

References

Berge TJ, Jordà Ò (2011) Evaluating the classification of economic activity into recessions and expansions. Am Econ J Macroecon 3(2):246–277

Boldin MD (1994) Dating turning points in the business cycle. J Bus 67(1):97–131

CMASF – Center for Macroeconomic Analysis and Short-Term Forecasting (2013) A system of composite leading indicators for system financial and macroeconomic risks: sources and data descriptions (ЦМАКП – Центр макроэкономического анализа и краткосрочного прогнозирования (2013) Источники и описание данных системы сводных опережающих индикаторов системных финансовых и макроэкономических рисков). http://www.forecast.ru/SOI/Metodologja/SOI_Sources.pdf

Davydov A, Popov V, Frenkel A (1993) An index of economic activity: construction and results. World Econ Intl Rel 12:29–41 (Давыдов А, Попов В, Френкель А (1993) Индекс хозяйственной конъюнктуры в России: построение и результаты. Мировая экономика и международные отношения 12:29–41)

Diebold FX, Rudebusch GD (1992) Have postwar economic fluctuations been stabilized? Am Econ Rev 82(4):993–1005

EEC – Eurasian Economic Commission (2014) Methodological approaches to construction of leading economic indicators for state-members of the Customs Union and Single Economic Space (ЕЭК – Евразийская экономическая комиссия (2014) Методологические подходы к построению опережающих индикаторов социально-экономического развития государств – членов ТС и ЕЭП). http://www.eurasiancommission.org/ru/act/integr_i_makroec/dep_makroec_pol/investigations/Documents/LEI_meths.pdf

Frenkel A, Raiskaya N, Matveeva O, Sergienko Ya (2012) Indicator of the economy. Econ Strateg 9:2–9 (Матвеева О, Райская Н, Сергиенко Я, Френкель А (2012) Индикатор экономики. Экономические стратегии 9:2–9)

Lipkind T, Kitrar L, Ostapkovich G (2018) Russian BTSs by HSE and Rosstat. In: Business cycles in BRICS. Springer, Cham

McNees SK (1987) Forecasting cyclical turning points: the record in the past three recessions. N Engl Econ Rev 2:31–40

OECD (2006) Composite leading indicators for major OECD non-member countries: Brazil, China, India, Indonesia, Russian Federation, South Africa and recently new OECD member countries: Korea, New Zealand, Czech Republic, Hungary, Poland, Slovak Republic. OECD, Statistics Directorate, Short-term Economic Statistics Division. March 2006 http://www.oecd.org/std/leading-indicators/36414874.pdf

OECD (2010) OECD composite indicators – 5 February 2010. http://www.oecd.org/fr/std/indicateurs-avances/44556466.pdf

Pestova A (2013) Predicting turning points of the business cycle: do financial sector variables help?. Voprosy Ekonomiki 7:63–81 (Пестова А (2013) Предсказание поворотных точек бизнес-цикла: помогают ли переменные финансового сектора?. Вопросы экономики 7:63–81)

Picchetti P (2018) Brazilian business cycles as characterized by CODACE. In: Business cycles in BRICS. Springer, Cham

Popov V, Frenkel A (1996) An index of business activity for the russian economy. EKO 10:76–89 (Попов В, Френкель А (1996) Индекс деловой активности для российской экономики. ЭКО 10:76–89)

Romer CD (1994) Remeasuring business cycles. J Econ Hist 54(3):573–609

Smirnov SV (2001) A system of leading indicators for Russia. Voprosy Ekonomiki 3:23–42 (Смирнов СВ (2001) Система опережающих индикаторов для России. Вопросы экономики 3:23–42)

Smirnov SV (2006) A new system of cyclical indicators for Russia. In: 28th CIRET Conference, Rome, September 2006

Smirnov SV (2011) Discerning ‘turning points’ with cyclical indicators: a few lessons from ‘real time’ monitoring the 2008–2009 recession. NRU Higher School of Economics. Working paper WP2/2011/03

Smirnov SV (2014) Russian cyclical indicators and their usefulness in real time: an experience of the 2008–09 recession. J Bus Cycle Meas Anal 1:103–128

Smirnov SV, Kondrashov NV (2018) Indices of regional economic activity for Russia. In: Business cycles in BRICS. Springer, Cham

Smirnov SV, Kondrashov NV, Petronevich AV (2017) Dating cyclical turning points for Russia: formal methods and informal choices. J Bus Cycle Res 13(1):53–73

Stock JH, Watson MW (2014) Estimating turning points using large data sets. J Econ 178(Part 2):368–381

Venter JC (2018) The SARB’s composite business cycle indicators. In: Business cycles in BRICS. Springer, Cham

Indices of Regional Economic Activity for Russia

Sergey V. Smirnov and Nikolay V. Kondrashov

1 Introduction

In large countries, the development of national macroeconomic business cycles clearly involves regional nuances that, as a rule, fall outside scholars' fields of vision, especially when monitoring the current economic situation. As far as we are aware, it is only Brazil and the United States that regularly publish the latest statistics reflecting the current levels of economic activity in individual states and subnational regions.[1] There are no such indicators for Russia, although for a country of its size—with its diverse climate conditions, differing volumes of natural and labour resources, and particular distribution of production capacity—it is vital that regional differences are taken into account in order to achieve a sound understanding of the processes that are unfolding.

Since April 2009, Rosstat (the Russian Federal State Statistics Service) has published a monthly electronic bulletin entitled "Information for Monitoring Socio-Economic Conditions in the Constituent Entities of the Russian Federation",[2]

Support from the Basic Research Programme of the National Research University Higher School of Economics is gratefully acknowledged.

[1]See Banco Central do Brasil. Boletim Regional. http://www.bcb.gov.br/?BOLREGIONAL; The Federal Reserve Bank of Philadelphia. State Coincident Indexes. https://www.philadelphiafed.org/research-and-data/regional-economy/indexes/coincident/. For the methodologies on which these indicators are based, see Banco Central do Brasil (2009), Crone and Clayton-Matthews (2005). Of course, regional GDPs are not a rare thing for national statistical systems, but in the context of monitoring the current situation, this information is unlikely to be of much use. For example, Rosstat publishes data only on annual (not quarterly) changes in gross regional product (GRP) and does this over a year late. Other countries are not much better.

[2]http://www.gks.ru/wps/wcm/connect/rosstat_main/rosstat/ru/statistics/publications/catalog/doc_1246601078438

S. V. Smirnov (✉) · N. V. Kondrashov
National Research University Higher School of Economics, Moscow, Russia
e-mail: svsmirnov@hse.ru

S. Smirnov et al. (eds.), *Business Cycles in BRICS*, Societies and Political Orders in Transition, https://doi.org/10.1007/978-3-319-90017-9_22

which offers a regional breakdown of key socio-economic indicators. A significant volume of monthly regional information can also be found in the Unified Interagency Statistical Information System.[3] However, none of the aggregate indicators that best characterise the *current* level of regional economic activity are being estimated in Russia. Therefore, the real-time regional data amassed remains, essentially, immense and virtually useless.

In Sect. 2 we analyse the quality of official regional statistics and propose a new method for processing and aggregating data that will make it possible to easily estimate the current level of regional economic activity (REA) in every constituent entity of the Russian Federation ("oblasts"), eight federal districts, five main sectors of the economy, and Russia as a whole. In Sect. 3 we calculate composite indices of economic activity for the period from January 2005 to November 2017, the latest month for which data are available, and demonstrate how they can be used to compare regional trends and to obtain additional information regarding the current phase of the business cycle across the entire Russian economy. In conclusion, we review the experimental calculations made and outline the possible future uses of these REA indices.

2 Indices of Regional Economic Activity (REA): Data and Calculation

In Russia, one of the following two indicators is usually used to monitor the aggregate economic activity at the national level in real time:

a) Index of production for the basic economic branches; calculated by Rosstat using data for agriculture; mining; manufacturing; production and distribution of electricity, gas, and water; construction; transportation; and retail and wholesale trade.[4]
b) Index of intensity of production for the basic economic branches; calculated by the Higher School of Economics (HSE).[5] This differs from the Rosstat index as it does not include passenger transportation and also in several important methodological aspects.

The "popularity" of these two indicators is due to the fact that, for the medium term, their quarterly dynamics are close to the quarterly dynamics of GDP. Since GDP is usually considered an almost ideal indicator of national economic activity, albeit one that is published rarely (once every 3 months), and with a significant delay (up to 2 months), for real-time monitoring of economic activity, experts tend to use

[3]Its Russian acronym is "EMISS". See https://www.fedstat.ru/

[4]http://www.gks.ru/free_doc/new_site/vvp/tab45.htm

[5]See Baranov et al. (2011).

monthly indices for the basic economic branches which are supposedly close to the unobservable monthly GDP.

It would be natural to assume that assessments of regional economic activity should be based on similar indices calculated for distinct regions, but regional data on agricultural production and freight transportation is only available each quarter, not monthly. Hence, agriculture and transportation had to be excluded from further calculations, and any full analogy between national and regional aggregate indicators was impossible. Instead, we included information on paid services for the population.

Finally, for calculating REA indices, we selected Rosstat's monthly information for regional dynamics in the five key sectors of the economy: industry (the sum of mining, manufacturing, and production and distribution of electricity, gas, and water), construction, retail trade, wholesale trade, and paid services for the population. At this stage, it seemed natural to take the following four steps:

- For each region, to use monthly month-on-month (m-o-m) growth rates to calculate the chain indices for all five sectors
- For all these indices, to make seasonal adjustments using a procedure selected (e.g. X-12-ARIMA or Tramo/Seats, implemented as part of the "Demetra" package)
- For each region, to calculate a REA index as a weighted average of five seasonally adjusted chain indices (e.g. using each sector's share of gross regional product as weights)
- At last, to calculate composite REA indices for Russia as a whole, for federal districts, etc.

However it has not been possible to implement this obvious approach in practice, because using month-on-month data for assessing chain indices often leads to results that cannot be interpreted.

To back this up, we include a graph showing the chain index for industrial production in Moscow calculated by taking December 2008 as 100% and multiplying all the subsequent month-on-month growth rates (see Fig. 1). At first glance, it looks more or less acceptable (unlike, e.g. the index for Magadan Oblast, which over several years supposedly grew by 20 times and more). Stagnation in Moscow's industry over the period 2009–2013 and the sharp fall in production in 2014–2016 do not explicitly contradict common sense. However, if you look more closely, then you will notice that Fig. 1 indicates a 42% fall in the industrial index from December 2008 to December 2016. Meanwhile, according to Rosstat, this fall was only 13% when calculated using "December-on-December" indices. Of course, this is also a significant amount, but it indicates a qualitatively different picture: a serious fall, but no disaster. Intuitively, the second figure, 13%, seems more plausible than the first, 42%, and it better matches with annual statistics, which are viewed as the most accurate.

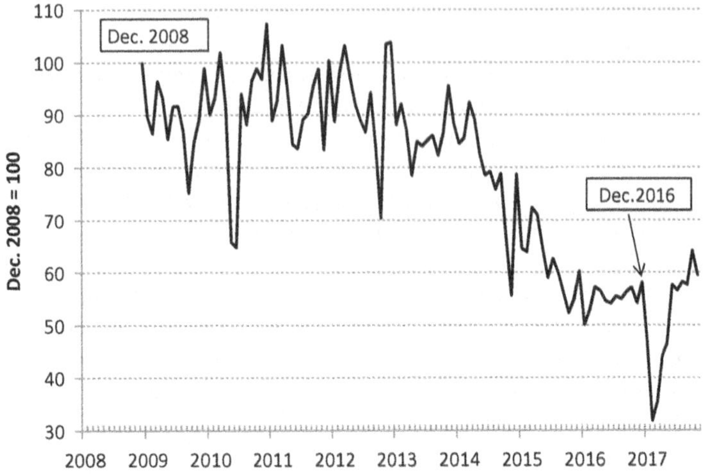

Fig. 1 Moscow, chain industrial production index (IPI)

For many other regions, the difference between indices calculated using "month-on-month" and "year-on-year" time series is even larger.[6] Figure 2 compares regional industrial production growth rates calculated from the multiplication of 12 "month-on-month" indices from January to December 2015 (the abscissa axis) and those published by Rosstat for December 2015 on "year-on-year" basis (the ordinate axis).

Of course, there is a clear correlation between these two indicators (pair correlation coefficient equals 0.74), but this is not enough to build accurate time series at regional level for at least a 5- to 7-year period. In 2015 alone, this difference exceeds 10 p.p. in either direction for 34 regions (over 40% of the total number), with the following among the leaders: Republic of Ingushetia (+65 p.p.), Chechen Republic (+39 p.p.), Bryansk Oblast (−37 p.p.), Pskov Oblast (−33 p.p.), Republic of Dagestan (−32 p.p.), and Krasnodar Oblast (−31 p.p.). In a longer perspective, the entire trajectory calculated on the basis of highly erratic "month-on-month" growth rates will be unreliable and probably misleading.

Unfortunately, "year-on-year" figures are not much better. For example, according to Rosstat, Dagestan's industrial production index (IPI) rose in November 2013 by 7.4 times compared to November 2012; Chukotka Autonomous District's IPI was 4.8 times higher in October 2008 than in October 2007; and Rostov District's IPI was 3.2 times higher in November 2015 than in November 2014. Can all this really be true? And is it worth making any kind of substantive conclusions based on these figures?

A similar situation can be found not only in industry but also in other sectors of the economy where, if anything, it might be worse. For example, according to

[6]At the Russian Federal level, they coincide. How that can be when it is not the case for individual regions is a question for Rosstat.

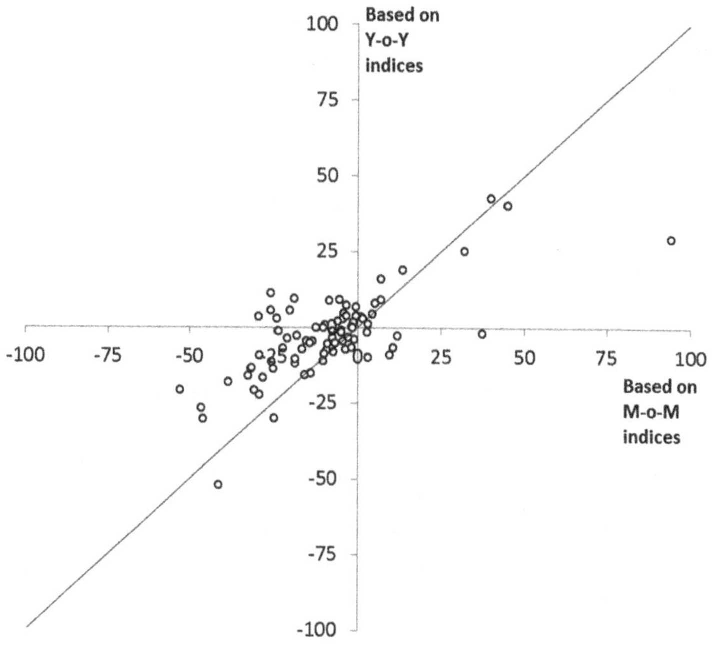

Fig. 2 Regional industrial production: growth rates, December 2015/December 2014, calculated by various methods, p.p.

Rosstat, the 2016 annual growth rate in wholesale trade was 1.4%; meanwhile, the weighted average growth rate of wholesale trade in all eight federal districts was 8.7%, quite a substantial difference. Another example shows (see Fig. 3) that monthly "year-on-year" indices do not match with "year-on-year" indices for the period from the year beginning: in Moscow, the monthly construction indices were negative for each month of 2017 except January, but "year-to-date" indices were always positive. It is clearly impossible for these statistics to be correct!

Overall, various blunders by Russian regional statistical committees combined with the inadequacy of the methodology applied by Rosstat means that the published regional data—as it is—simply cannot be used in the analysis of medium- and long-term trends.

We therefore find ourselves with the following alternatives:

- Stop using Rosstat real-time regional data, in which case, since there is no replacement, we would have to stop making any indicators for regional economic activity.
- Transform published Rosstat data so that it retains some useful information while the "white noise" is at least partly cancelled out.

We risked it and selected the second course of action.

Our first step was to create the variables, D^t_{sr}, equal to 100, if at moment t production output (work done, trade turnover, etc.) in sector s in region r is higher than 100% compared to the same month the previous year and zero otherwise. In other words, if a

Fig. 3 Moscow, indices of construction production

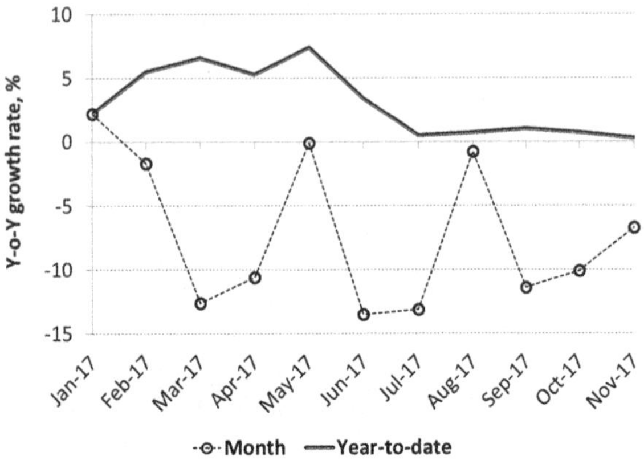

particular sector in a particular region sees growth on the previous year, then the variable is assumed to be equal to 100 and, if there was no growth, to zero. By taking the average of these dichotomous variables by region, we get nationwide indices for each of the five economic sectors (n—the total number of constituent entities of the Russian Federation, equal to 80 before 2015 and 82 from 2016):

$$S_s^t = 1/n \sum_{r=1}^{n} D_{sr}^t. \quad (1)$$

The trajectories of these indices can be easily compared with those for regular aggregate sectoral indices produced by Rosstat. If the dynamics of these indices are similar, then this would support the proposed approach as rational and effective.

In advance, we may note that the evidence cited in the next section confirms this and there would therefore be confidence in our indices of regional economic activity (REA), which can be calculated by averaging the variables D_{sr}^t for each moment t by the five key sectors in any one region:

$$R_r^t = 1/5 \sum_{s=1}^{5} D_{sr}^t. \quad (2)$$

If, in region r at moment t, we see "year-on-year" growth in all five sectors, the REA index for this constituent entity of the Russian Federation will be equal to 100%; if in none of these five areas, zero; if in one of them, 20%; and so on.[7] On the basis of R_r^t, it is easy to calculate the composite indices for REA by federal districts (m–number of regions included in a federal district):

[7]It seems that, at this stage, knowing the structure of GRP, it would have been possible to weight sectoral indices to receive more accurate indicators. However, we felt that there was no point trying to refine an inherently approximate methodology, especially since using simple arithmetic means simplifies economic interpretation.

Table 1 Statistical indicators used in calculating REA indices and their sources

Indicators (in comparable prices, in % to the corresponding period of the previous year)	Sources[a]	
	January 2005–December 2008	January 2009 and onwards
Industrial production index (IPI)	(1)	(2)
Construction, volume of work done	(3)	(2)
Retail trade turnover	(1)	(2)
Wholesale trade turnover (entities classified to a branch with code 51)	(1)	(4),(1)
Volume of paid services for the population	(1)	(2)

[a](1) Monthly bulletin "Socio-economic Conditions in Russia", Appendix "Particular Statistical Indicators of Socio-economic Conditions in Constituent Entities of the Russian Federation"; (2) "Information for Monitoring Socio-economic Conditions in the Constituent Entities of the Russian Federation"; (3) unpublished Rosstat data, provided on our request; (4) EMISS (Unified Interagency Statistical Information System), Section 1.22.1

$$R_{FD}^{t} = 1/m \sum_{r \in FD}^{m} R_{r}^{t} \tag{3}$$

as well as for the whole of Russia (n–the total number of constituent entities of the Russian Federation):

$$R^{t} = 1/n \sum_{r=1}^{n} R_{r}^{t}. \tag{4}$$

It is also possible to note that:

$$R^{t} = 1/5 \sum_{s=1}^{5} S_{s}^{t}. \tag{5}$$

In other words, the Russian national composite index of REA R^t can be calculated not only as an average of regional indices R_r^t but also as an average of sectoral indices S_s^t, meaning that it can be considered an equivalent to the regular index of production for the basic economic branches. It also turns out that a composite REA index of less than 50% means that growth is seen in less than half of the constituent entities of the Russian Federation if we understand it as "average by sector" or in less than half sectors if we understand it as "average by region" (all—in relation to the corresponding month of the previous year).

At the end of this section, we offer a more formal outline of the statistical indicators that we use and their sources (see Table 1).

3 REA Indices and Monitoring the Current Economic Situation

As was noted in the previous section, it is crucially important to establish the reliability of the composite indices calculated from specially constructed dichotomous variables. We do this by comparing the trends for the regular Rosstat indices of production (as % against the corresponding month of the previous year) and our REA composite indices for all five key sectors of the Russian economy. One can see the results of this comparison in Fig. 4, which also shows the coefficients of correlation between both time series. The results are clear: the dynamics of REA composite indices are close to those shown by "year-on-year" growth rates of regular Rosstat indices for all key sectors apart from wholesale trade.[8]

The second important result, which is completely clear from Fig. 4, is the noticeable fall in REA indices over the two most recent recessions (in some cases with a lag).[9] This means that REA indices can definitely be used to analyse economic conditions in the regions (recall that Rosstat calculates and publishes no aggregate indicators for regions in real time).

It is also possible to identify two areas for further analysis. The first is related to assessing the level and changes in economic activity of particular regions and the second, to using of a set of regional indices to outline the broader economic conditions. We will now give examples of both of these.

Regarding the first area, related to research into cyclical features of particular regions, we offer a graph of REA index for Moscow (Fig. 5). We can conclude that:

- Before the 2008–2009 recession, Moscow saw rapid economic growth (REA index usually amounted higher than 60%).
- Since the global economic crisis of 2008–2009, Moscow saw its economy shrink: first slowly and then radically from November 2008 (REA index fell to 0% or 20%).
- Moscow's postcrisis recovery took place more slowly than in the country as a whole (REA index for Moscow reached the 60% mark only in June 2010, 3–4 months later than the average for Russia).
- In 2011–2014, Moscow saw steady growth which, but for the exception of several months in 1H 2012, failed to reach precrisis levels of intensity.

[8]As for wholesale trade, the question remains as to which of these two indicators better reflects reality. For critics of regular Rosstat's data on wholesale trade, see Development Centre. Comments on the State and Business. 2016 No. 117. P. 6. https://dcenter.hse.ru/data/2016/08/03/1119859024/KGB_117.pdf?draft=1

[9]For the 2008–2009 recession, we dated May 2008 as a peak and May 2009 as a trough (see Smirnov et al. 2017). For the 2014–2016 recession, we used preliminary estimates by the Russian Economic Cycle Dating Committee (Russian Dating Committee, RDC). These are December 2014 (peak) and June 2016 (trough).

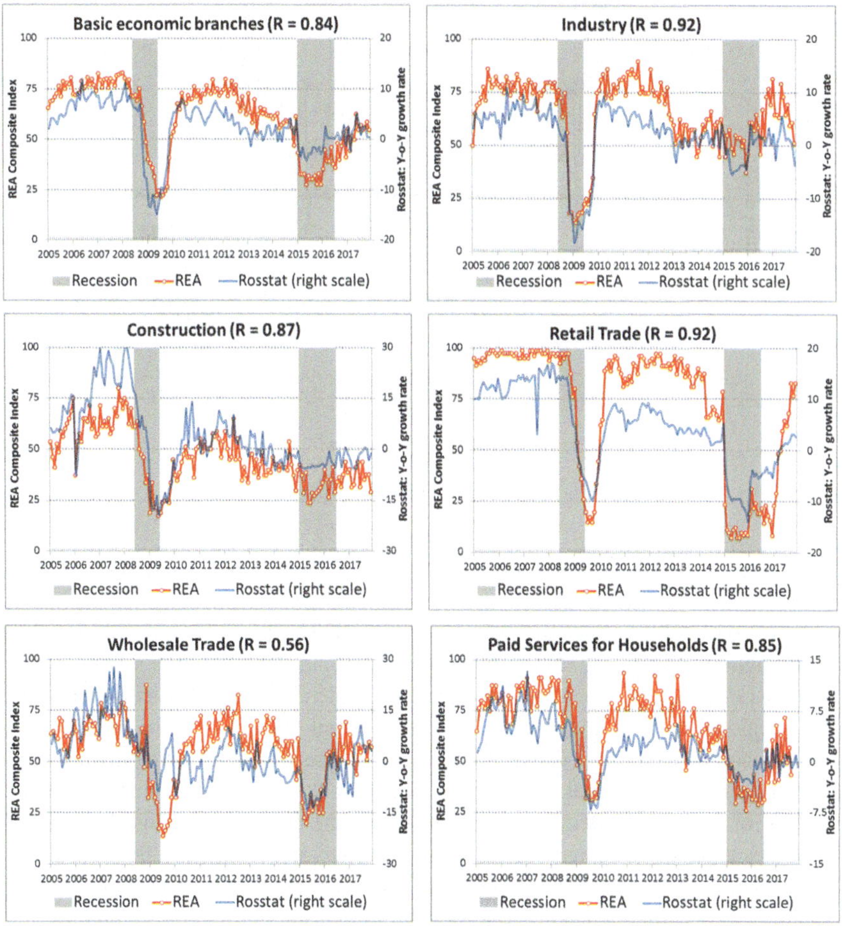

Fig. 4 Composite REA indices and Rosstat's y-o-y growth rates, by economic sector, January 2005–November 2017

- For most of 2015, Moscow's economy contracted sharply (REA index 0% or 20%). In 2016–2017, the contraction was not so deep, but a moderate recovery began only from August 2017.

On the basis of this kind of analysis of REA indices for different constituent entities of the Russian Federation, it is possible to identify groups of regions that demonstrate similar economic trends and, going forward, to identify the processes of contagion with cyclical falls and rises across Russia. Analysing individual regions, it

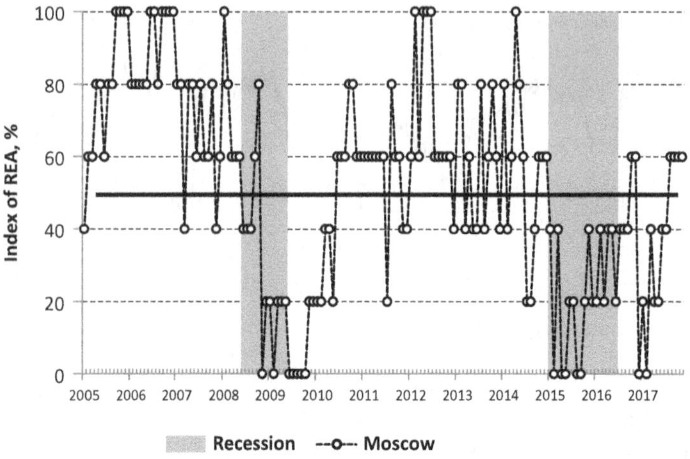

Fig. 5 REA index for Moscow, January 2005–November 2017

is possible to identify those regions that have been most successful or most depressed.[10]

It is also possible to trace the trajectories of all 82 regions of Russia and to analyse all the figures alike to Fig. 5, but here we should rather move to the second area in which REA indices can be used–describing the general economic situation in Russia using regional data. In this context, there are several tools that can be used.

First, composite indices can be compiled on five sectors of the economy and eight federal districts, which makes it easy to create a radar chart from which sectors and regions of growth or decline and stagnation can easily be localised. Figure 6 illustrates these dimensions of the Russian economy in November 2017.

Second, in order to evaluate the current level of economic activity in the Russian economy as a whole, it would be reasonable to consider a map of the country that shows the regions with the same level of economic activity in the same colour.[11] This would give a snapshot view of the level of economic activity in the country (in terms of its colour) and would also immediately draw attention to the most and least dynamic areas.

Third, one can create a histogram that shows the distribution of regions by their REA level. Aside from the fact that federal constituent entities differ significantly from each other in terms of their territory, this kind of chart presents the same information as the geographical map does but in a more aggregated manner (all REA indices are sorted to several intervals). On the other hand, it is easy to compare histograms for 2–3 sequential months and trace the changes in total economic

[10]Similar analysis and charts presented below are published each month in our overview of regional economic activity (see https://dcenter.hse.ru/rea).

[11]For similar maps for the United States, see https://www.philadelphiafed.org/research-and-data/regional-economy/indexes/coincident/maps

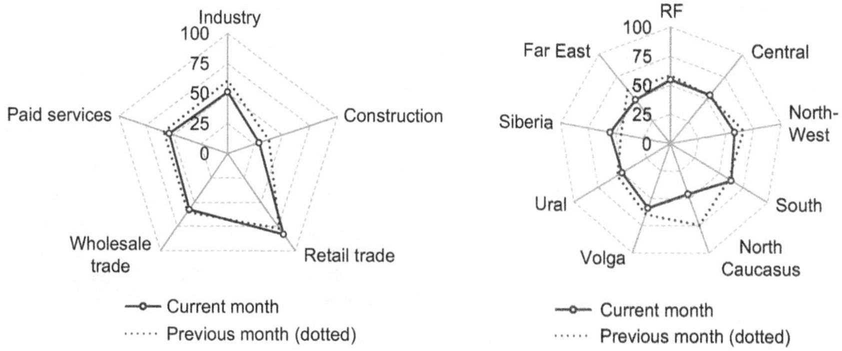

Fig. 6 Composite indices of regional economic activity by economic sector and federal district, November (current month) and October (previous month) 2017

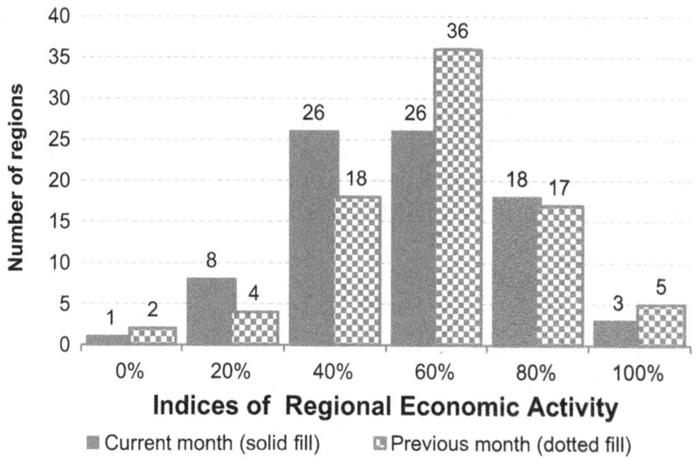

Fig. 7 Distribution of Russian regions by REA index, November (current month) and October (previous month) 2017

activity (this is completely impossible with a map). For example, from Fig. 7, it is clear that in November 2017–in comparison with the previous month–a smaller number of regions recorded moderately positive levels of economic activity (REA indices equal to 60%), and a greater number of regions recorded moderately negative levels of economic activity (REA indices equal to 40%). This supports the view that Russian growth was still sluggish at that time.

Fourth, interest could be sparked by how the distribution of regions by economic activity level (REA indices) changes over longer periods. In particular, looking solely at the histogram (Fig. 7), it is difficult to get a sense of what the "norm" is for the Russian economy in each phase of the business cycle. To answer that question, it would be advisable to use a heat map (see Fig. 8), in which each column corresponds to a histogram similar to the one above. From Fig. 8, it is clear that in

Fig. 8 Heat map: proportion of regions with different levels of economic activity (REA index), January 2005–November 2017

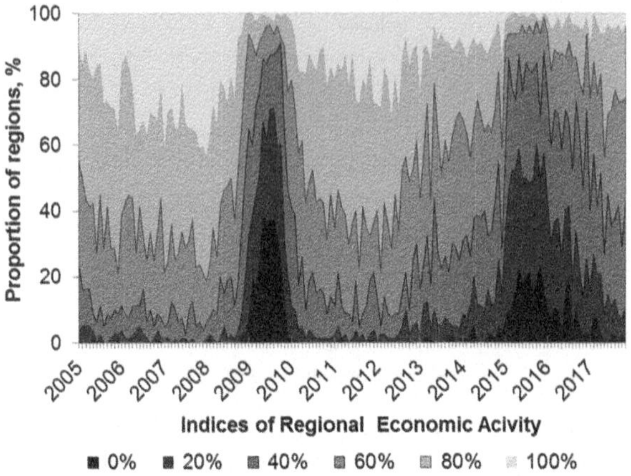

November 2017 the proportion of regions that saw contraction in all five economic sectors or which saw expansion in only one of them (coloured with shades of two most bright black) remained high. The number of regions in which all five economic sectors saw expansion (or at least four of them) was low (coloured with shades of two most light grey). Hence, the Russian economy could be described as experiencing a weak recovery which was definitely not as strong or as pronounced as it had been after the 2008–2009 recession. The scenario of a prolonged stagnation seems quite probable.

4 Conclusion

In conclusion, we can state that the easy and clear methodology we propose for handling real-time regional data from Rosstat and constructing regional economic activity (REA) indices makes it possible to use this mass of official statistical data in the macroeconomic monitoring of the Russian economy and, in particular, to identify regions that have greater and lower levels of economic activity (leaders and outsiders in terms of growth dynamics) and to describe the current phase of the Russian economic cycle. This is important, because in their initial (published) form, Rosstat's regional statistics are virtually useless due to the numerous erratic fluctuations and the radical mismatch between the "month-on-month" and "year-on-year" time series.

The regional aspect of economic monitoring acquired through REA indices makes it possible to draw a more accurate and more dimensional view of ongoing cyclical developments in the Russian economy. It is particularly important that this takes place in real time—without any significant lag regarding data for Russia as a whole.

In addition, studying the synchronisation of medium-term changes in different regions of the Russian Federation, identifying regions where trends do not match those of the country as a whole, could become a new area in research into Russian economic cycles. This will help in the development of a more well-founded macro-economic and anti-crisis policy, which takes into account the regional nuances and territorial mechanisms by which economic "shocks" are transmitted.

References

Banco Central do Brasil (2009) Índice de Atividade Econômica Regional do Rio Grande do Sul. Boletim Regional do Banco Central do Brasil 3(1):95–97

Baranov EF, Bessonov VA, Roskin AA, Ahundova TA, Beznosik VI, Ahundova OV (2011) Indices of basic branches' production. HSE Monthly Report. January 2000–November 2011. [Индексы интенсивности выпуска товаров и услуг по базовым видам экономической деятельности. Экономический доклад. Январь 2000 – ноябрь 2011.] Available at: http://www.hse.ru/data/2012/05/24/1253784638/metod.pdf (In Russian)

Crone TM, Clayton-Matthews A (2005) Consistent economic indexes for the 50 states. Rev Econ Stat 87(4):593–603

Smirnov SV, Kondrashov NV, Petronevich AV (2017) Dating cyclical turning points for Russia: formal methods and informal choices. J Bus Cycle Res 13(1):53–73

An Application of the Indicator Approach to Developing Coincident and Leading Economic Indexes for India

Atish Kumar Dash, Ataman Ozyildirim, and Jing Sima-Friedman

1 Introduction

There have been numerous attempts to understand the features of business cycles in India. Among the major studies, Chitre (1982) was the first to analyze the growth cycles in Indian economy for the period 1951–1976 using annual data on a large number of variables and observed that many key economic processes show synchronous movements around their respective long-term (deterministic) trends. Chitre (1988, 1990), further, examined the cyclical behavior of selected time series during 1951–1982 and commented on the growth cycles in India's nonagricultural income. With the liberalization of the Indian economy since 1991, studies on the business cycle for India have received renewed attention. Hatekar (1994) described individual historical path of major macroeconomic variables and their co-movements with other variables using annual data for the period 1950–1985. Gangopadhyay and Wadhwa (1997) studied the monthly data on index of industrial production for 1975–1995 for obtaining the chronology of Indian business cycles. Mall (1999) filtered output to examine cyclical behavior of the Indian economy since 1950. Six sets of turning points in industrial production, IIP manufacturing, were identified as the peaks and troughs of the economic cycle in the period.

Dua and Banerji (1999), using the NBER approach, traced fluctuations in aggregate economic activity and reported six "classical" business cycle recessions in Indian economy. Based on the Bry and Boschan (1971) procedure for determining turning points in the economy, Mohanty et al. (2003) attempted dating of business cycles in India and have identified 13 growth cycles of varying duration between the

A. K. Dash
Central University of South Bihar, Patna, India

A. Ozyildirim (✉) · J. Sima-Friedman
The Conference Board Inc., New York, NY, USA
e-mail: Ataman.Ozyildirim@conference-board.org

S. Smirnov et al. (eds.), *Business Cycles in BRICS*, Societies and Political Orders in Transition, https://doi.org/10.1007/978-3-319-90017-9_23

periods 1970–1971 and 2001–2002. The study by Patnaik and Sharma (2002) found broad agreement with the available literature on business cycles in India. Evidence suggests that the Indian economy had experienced cycles that can be tracked by changes in annual GDP.

The literature of economic cycles in India found that prior to the 1990s, fluctuations in economic activity in India were primarily related to the monsoon season which overshadowed fluctuations driven by market factors. During the 1990s there had not been an actual fall in output. Cycles which appeared could be termed more accurately as "growth cycles" that depict a periodic fluctuation in the growth rate of output or the fluctuation of economic activity around its trend, rather than outright expansions and contractions in the level of economic output or economic activity that are defined as "classical" business cycles.

Because of the emergence of India as a market-oriented economy and its increasing contribution in the world GDP a timely leading economic index (LEI) for India is needed to track its emerging business cycles. Against this backdrop, the objective of this chapter is to assess the availability of suitable indicators for India using the indicator approach and methodology followed by The Conference Board. Further we discuss the performance of the proposed set of indicators and composite indexes in describing the business and growth cycle in the Indian economy.

In this chapter we describe the development of business cycle indicators, particularly coincident and leading indicators, following The Conference Board's indicator approach which is mainly focused on classical business cycles. In the next section, we discuss how a coincident economic index (CEI) can be used to describe the historical development of the Indian business and growth cycles since 1990 by taking a broad definition of economic activity and the consensus of cyclical movements among several coincident indicators. In Sect. 3, we discuss the selection of leading indicators that help to anticipate the turning points in the business and growth cycle. In Sect. 4, we evaluate the usefulness of the constructed LEI to lead business and growth Indian cycles. Then in Sect. 5, we conclude.

2 Dating Indian Cycles with Coincident Indicators

2.1 Construction of the Coincident Economic Index (CEI)

Ever since the seminal definition of business cycles by Burns and Mitchell (1946) as common sequences of expansions and contractions in many economic variables, coincident indicators have had a central position in the indicator approach because they help to define the reference cycle relative to which leading and lagging indicators can be evaluated.

Following this definition, coincident indicators have been used as the target variables of leading indicators and indexes. Historically, employment, income, production, and sales or related series have been used as components of a composite coincident index which helps to identify the unobserved turning points in the business cycle. These indicators measure the linkages and transactions between household and business sectors in the circular flow of the economy. The composite index helps to bring out the central tendency of the many economic series that tend to turn down or up at around the same time.

In the case of India, we can use industrial production, car sales (passenger vehicles), and total imports as components of a coincident index because of a lack of availability of monthly data on employment, wages, and sales. The composite index construction methodology is summarized in Ozyildirim (2018). We believe these three variables provide a rough estimate of current business cycle conditions because they stand as a proxy of economic activity. In order to make the coincident index more comprehensive initially, exports of agricultural products were also included. However, this component was discontinued in 2014 and removed as a component from the coincident economic index published by The Conference Board in January 2015. As more high-frequency data becomes available for the Indian economy, we hope to further refine our definition of the business cycle using a coincident index.

2.2 *Determining a Reference Chronology of the Business Cycle*

We argue that for the purpose of identifying and dating business cycles, it is not possible to rely on GDP only. What is needed is a measure of economic activity, broadly defined, and a business cycle chronology that is based on a multivariate approach and separate from national income account measures such as GDP (see Zarnowitz 2001). The three coincident indicators can be combined with a monthly interpolation of quarterly GDP data to obtain another composite index that helps to determine the reference cycle turning points for India's economy by applying the computer algorithm for determining business cycle turning points developed by Bry and Boschan (1971) to this index (CEI+GDP). This approach of combining monthly coincident indicators and a monthly interpolation of GDP, when applied to US data, closely replicates the NBER Business Cycle Dating Committee decisions on the US business cycle. The Conference Board has successfully used this approach to determine business cycle chronologies in many other economies such as China, Brazil, and Euro area to name a couple of examples. A recent example of research taking this approach is Feng et al. (2008) for determining turning points for the Chinese economy and Campelo et al. (2018) for Brazil.

Following this approach, we identified two major recessions in the business cycle for India: March 1991–November 1991 and September 2008–January 2009 (see Fig. 1).

The long expansion from November 1991 to September 2008 is partly due to the higher growth trend of the economy as a result of the reforms undertaken in the early 1990s. The long expansion is interrupted by slowdowns corresponding to major growth cycles which will be discussed later. The second recession in India is not selected by the Bry-Boschan algorithm because it is too short (5 months), but given

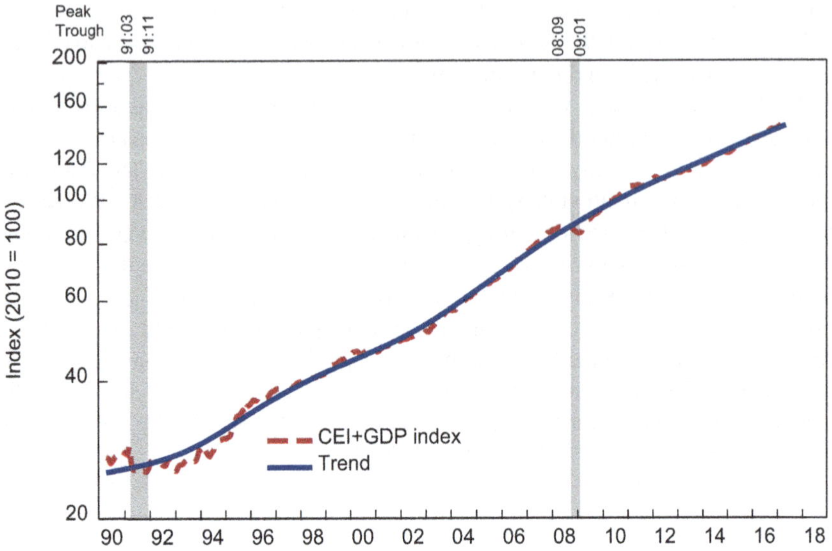

Fig. 1 Index of coincident indicators and GDP (CEI+GDP) for India, 1990–2017. Source: The Conference Board and authors' calculations. Note: The shaded areas represent *business cycles* in the Indian economy as determined by applying the Bry-Boschan algorithm to the CEI+GDP index. The long-term trend has been estimated using the Hodrick-Presscott trend (sigma = 4)

the large contraction and the state of the global economy, we believe this period qualifies as a recession, albeit a short one, for India.

While the CEI+GDP index can be used for dating the business cycle chronology, it is not appropriate for ongoing monitoring of the business cycle in *real time* because of the difficulty of using *quarterly* GDP, often released with long publication lags, as well as the potentially large revisions GDP may be subject to. Thus, for monthly monitoring, we use the composite index of three coincident indicators or CEI calculated from 1990 to present.

2.3 Determining a Reference Chronology of the Growth Cycle

Figure 2 shows Indian growth cycles—the deviations from trend in an index of the coincident indicators and monthly interpolated GDP (CEI+GDP). The deviations from trend in this index can also be used to determine the turning point dates of growth cycles. The trend shown in Fig. 1, which has been used to calculate the deviations from trend, has been estimated with the modification proposed by Ravn and Uhlig (2001) of the commonly used Hodrick and Prescott (1997) trend (see Ozyildirim and Zarnowitz (2006) and Boschan and Ebanks (1978) for a discussion of trend estimation methods suitable for growth cycle analysis). This trend is similar to the phase average trend or PAT developed by Boschan and Ebanks (1978) and used extensively by business cycle researchers. The shaded areas in Fig. 2 denote

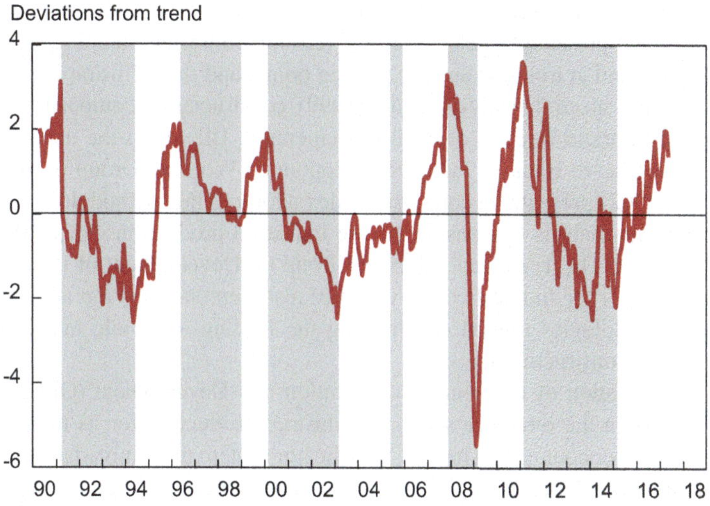

Fig. 2 Index of coincident indicators and GDP (CEI+GDP) for India, deviations from trend, 1990–2017. Source: The Conference Board and authors' calculations. Note: The shaded areas represent *growth cycles* in the Indian economy as determined by applying the Bry-Boschan algorithm to the deviations from trend in the CEI+GDP index. The long-term trend has been estimated using the Hodrick-Presscott trend (sigma = 4)

Table 1 Growth cycle peaks and troughs based on CEI+GDP

Peak	Trough
March-91	May-94
May-96	December-98
February-00	February-03
May-05	November-05
November-07	February-09
February-11	February-15

Source: The Conference Board and authors' calculations

growth cycle turning points where the index moves from above trend to below trend and vice versa. These turning points are contained also in Table 1.

3 Leading Indicators

3.1 Construction of the Leading Economic Index (LEI)

There have been a few attempts to construct leading economic index for India by researchers. Dua and Banerji (2001) identified leading indicators and constructed a composite leading index following the traditional NBER methodology with minor modifications.[1] Chitre (2001) studied the business cycles in India for the period 1951–1982 and presented a selected list of leading, coincident, and lagging indicators (at peaks and at troughs) and the turning points and the diffusion index for the indices. Using spectral analysis, Mall (1999) constructed a composite index of leading indicators to forecast cyclical movements in IIP within the manufacturing sector. The Reserve Bank of India (RBI)-appointed Working Group on Economic Indicators (2002) presented a composite index adopting the methodology of principal component analysis by considering the industrial production index, IIP, as the reference series. The Technical Advisory Group on Development of Leading Economic Indicators for Indian Economy (2006) also demonstrates the application of various methodologies toward constructing the leading economic index and sets guidelines for constructing the same.

The Organisation of Economic Co-operation and Development (OECD) tracks growth cycles in the reference series of industrial production for its members and some nonmember countries. The OECD indicator system uses univariate analysis to estimate trend and cycles individually for each component series, and then a composite leading index, CLI, is obtained by aggregation of the resulting de-trended component. Following this approach focused on growth cycles, OECD (2006) has developed a composite leading economic indicator (CLI) for India. From a set of 30 economic indicators, 8 economic indicators were identified as the leading indicators for construction of the CLI. The study by Rajeswari (2010) constructed regression-based composite index, with regression parameters as the weights for the composite index using "principal component" analysis (PCA). The regression-based leading index was constructed based on simple regression of the growth rates of reference series on other leading indicators (expressed in growth rates) that represent state of the economy.

Following The Conference Board approach and indicator selection criteria that are based on the earlier NBER approach, we have reviewed a large number of potential leading indicators, including some of those identified in previous publications.

Because there are few classical business cycle turning points in the post-1990s Indian economy, we have placed greater emphasis on the examples of other economies in The Conference Board portfolio of business cycle indicators as well as greater emphasis on economic concepts and relationships. In our analysis, we have also looked at the growth cycle behavior of the potential indicators to help with the selection of the components of a leading index. We have narrowed the selection down to eight indicators:

1. Yield spread, 10 yr–90 day
2. BSE: Index: Monthly: SENSEX: Average
3. Real effective exchange rate, REER: 36 currencies

[1]The basic steps involved transformation of each series, standardization of each transformed series using standardization factors, and combination of the standardized series into a raw index. The raw index was then adjusted for trend and finally rebased.

4. M3: bank credit to commercial sector
5. Merchandise exports
6. Cargo handled
7. IP, capital goods
8. India PMI: services business activity

The selection of these indicators is similar to others in the literature and has many common elements with other composite leading index components covered by The Conference Board. Each indicator has a leading relationship with future economic activity. The overall selection of the indicators attempts to cover economic activity as broadly as possible from monetary and credit indicators to qualitative survey data on services activity (a sector that's growing in importance for India). While about half of the components of the proposed LEI come from financial measures, the other half covers the real economy, including manufacturing and services.

3.2 Review of the Selected Leading Indicators

In this section we present a brief review and discussion of the selected leading indicators. Charts of the selected indicators are presented in Appendix. Even though there are only two recessions (two peaks and two troughs), these graphs show the good leads of the selected indicators relative to India's recessions.

Yield spread is generally considered a good leading indicator. There is a lot of empirical and theoretical evidence for interest rate spreads to anticipate future turning points (e.g., see Estrella and Mishkin 1998). It is also a good indicator of the stance of monetary policy. We looked at two alternatives: the interbank call money rate (CMR) and the rate on 91-day treasury bills (TBR). We selected the latter as a component of the LEI. Both are closely watched by the monetary authorities. However, TBR is more directly related to the long-term rate of interest, via the fortnightly auction system of treasury bills and dated government securities in operation by the monetary authority (Nachane and Ranade 2005). Further, some studies suggest that the yield on T-bills with residual maturity of 15–91 days in the secondary market is the best economic indicator to forecast the future movement in the economy. We decided to go with a more conventional approach in order to keep the selection more in line with the other countries.

The 91 TBR is a much more closely followed indicator than the long-term treasury bill, as the long-term rate is very policy driven and not as market sensitive as the short one. This is similar to China. But the spread and TBR also measure two different concepts: spread measures bank profitability while short-term rate measures the cost of borrowing. The short-term rate, while seemingly fitting the recent developments in the economy, can be much too volatile and result in incorrect signals of turning points through several cycles. A 3-month borrowing rate can also distort our view on bank credit to the real economy, as short-term borrowing/lending can often be speculative in emerging markets. Thus, we believe the spread may be a better choice in terms of measuring the health of a banking system and signaling turning points.

Monetary policy can influence the slope of the yield curve. A tightening of monetary policy usually means a rise in short-term interest rates, typically intended to lead to a reduction in inflationary pressures. When those pressures subside, it is expected that a policy easing—lower rates—will follow. Whereas short-term interest rates are relatively high as a result of the tightening, long-term rates tend to reflect longer-term expectations and rise by less than short-term rates. The monetary tightening both slows down the economy and flattens (or even inverts) the yield curve.

Changes in investor expectations can also change the slope of the yield curve. Consider that expectations of future short-term interest rates are related to future real demand for credit and to future inflation. A rise in short-term interest rates induced by monetary policy could be expected to lead to a future slowdown in real economic activity and demand for credit, putting downward pressure on future real interest rates.

At the same time, slowing activity may result in lower expected inflation, increasing the likelihood of a future easing in monetary policy. The expected declines in short-term rates would tend to reduce current long-term rates and flatten the yield curve. Clearly, this scenario is consistent with the observed correlation between the yield curve and recessions.

Stock price SENSEX average, Mumbai stock exchange, is a widely used and reliable leading indicator providing a measure of expectations of future economic conditions and business earnings. The three available stock price indexes (NIFTY, SENSEX, and BSE Dollex 30/100/200) are essentially the same in terms of cyclicality, with SENSEX having slightly longer history (by 6 months) and BSE Dollex growing at a lower rate after 2009 due to depreciation of the Indian rupee (see Fig. 3). Switching to NIFTY or BSE Dollex will not likely change the turning points of the LEI. OECD uses BSE Dollex in their CLI for India. However, BSE Dollex is calculated in US$ and is more useful to foreign investors, and in times its trend may diverge from the domestic markets (surely the case after 2009). Since the foreign exchange aspect of the economy in the LEI is already accounted for by including

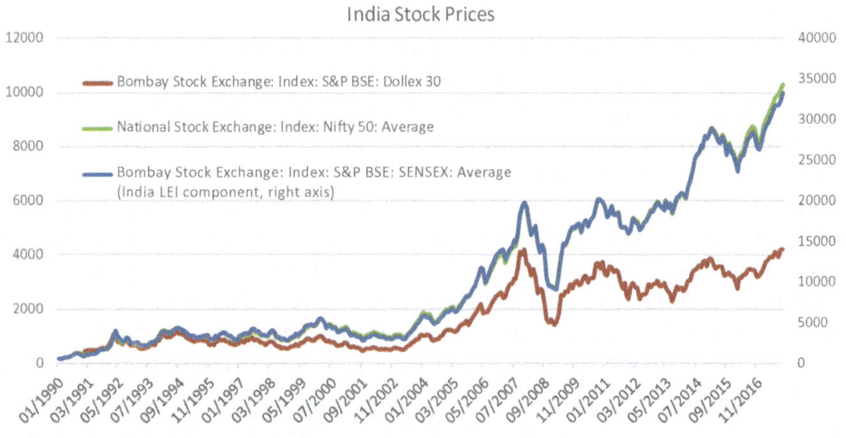

Fig. 3 Indian stock price indexes, 1990–2017

REER, it is unnecessary to also include a dollar-dominated stock price index. Although NIFTY has a broader coverage in India's stock market capitalization and is more diversified, we considered using it as a component, but because it is highly correlated with SENSEX which has been around since 1986 and has a history going back to 1979, we used the latter.

REER It measures price competitiveness of India's export sector, as well as real purchasing power for the imported goods. REER index is the weighted average of the bilateral nominal FX of rupees in terms of 36 foreign currencies, adjusted by domestic to foreign relative local prices and bilateral export weights. These 36 countries account for 70% of India's total trade. The aggregate index smooths out volatilities of a single country FX and ensures the pattern of trade is represented over a long time span (e.g., increased trade with ASEAN). When this indicator (REER) rises, it suggests that India's real purchase power of imported goods increases, while export competitiveness falls. India has been consistently running at current account deficit since the 1980s, and the deficit has become larger in recent years (imports value larger than exports), and the country has higher inflation than its trading partners. Thus, when India's currency gains strength and inflation eases, its real purchase power increases and affects India's current account balance sheet and economy positively. Therefore, REER can be used as a proxy for terms of trade for India and should be used as it is (instead of inverting it).

Bank Credit to Commercial Sector (Part of Money Supply M3) In the Indian context, money supply has a significant role in the short-run variations in output especially, in the post-reform period. The relationship between financial development as measured by M3 (broad money) and economic growth is established in the literature. There is evidence of one-way causality that runs from M3 to GDP growth (e.g., see Bhattacharya and Sivasubramanian 2003). Empirical findings also indicate that money supply (M3) Granger causes output (measured by the index of industrial production in manufacturing) in the short run (Sharma et al. 2011).

The role of credit in determining output is critical since the Indian economy is largely bank-based. One-way causality running from private sector credit to GDP ratio to real national GDP at factor cost is observed (Sahoo 2013). Among the sources of M3, bank credit to the commercial sector dominates others. Bank credit to commercial sector is the total of RBI's credit to commercial sector and other banks' credit to commercial sector. We found **bank credit to commercial sector** would be a satisfactory leading indicator. Bank credit ceiling to commercial sector is one of the first monetary policy tools used by RBI in challenging economic times. The reason not to include the entire M3 but use only the bank credit element is that M3 also includes bank credit to the government, foreign exchange assets of the banking sector, government's currency liabilities to the public, and bank credits to the agricultural sector (subsidized) which are all too smooth and noncyclical. By focusing on bank credit to commercial sector, we have a leading indicator that is more closely aligned with future market activity.

Exports measure external demand for goods produced in India. Along with exports, **cargo handled** (domestic and international) provides another measure of demand from both internal and external sources.

IP Capital Goods Capital goods accounts for 20% of IP and tends to lead production cycles. Besides its good empirical performance as a leading indicator, production of capital goods directly measures the expansion of productive assets in the economy. As such, it is a good leading indicator conceptually.

Finally, even though its history is short **PMI: services business activity** can be useful as a predictor of future economic activity because 55% of India's GDP is in the services sectors. This indicator is one of the few indicators that represent the sector. RBI started producing an indicator for exports in services, but it has an even shorter history (starts in the mid-2011), and if it proves to perform well as a leading indicator, it could be added to the LEI in the future.

Although fiscal indicators are closely followed in India by economists and analysts, their month-to-month fluctuations are so great that there is no trend or cyclicality. Thus, they are not very useful in business cycle analysis.

4 Results for CEI and LEI

Because the CEI has only three components, it tends to show a lot of short-term noise or volatility, but overall it conforms well to the history of the business cycle and the overall trend in the economy since the early 1990s as shown in Fig. 4.

Figure 4 also shows the levels of the LEI going back to 1990 as an index with base year 2010 equals 100. The composite index turns down well ahead of business cycle peaks; however, its performance in the two recession troughs observed is at

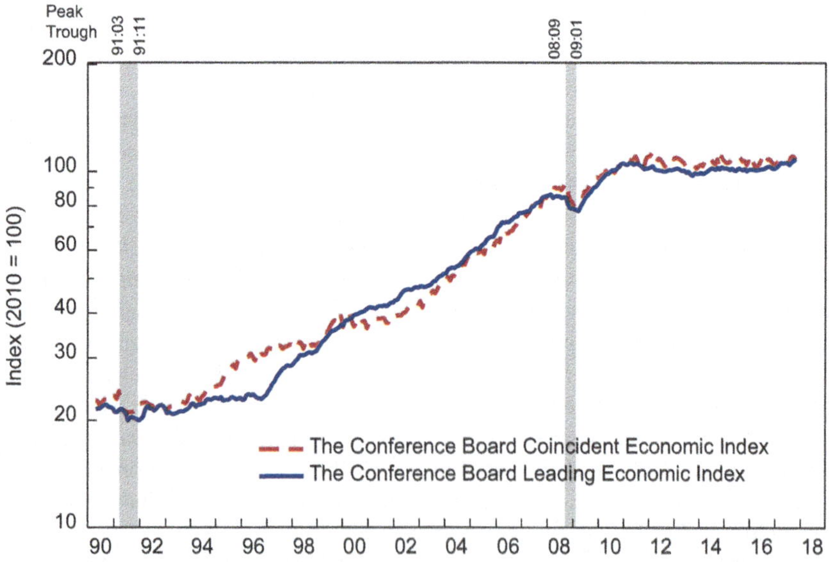

Fig. 4 Business cycles: coincident and leading economic indexes (CEI and LEI) for India, 1990–2017. Source: The Conference Board

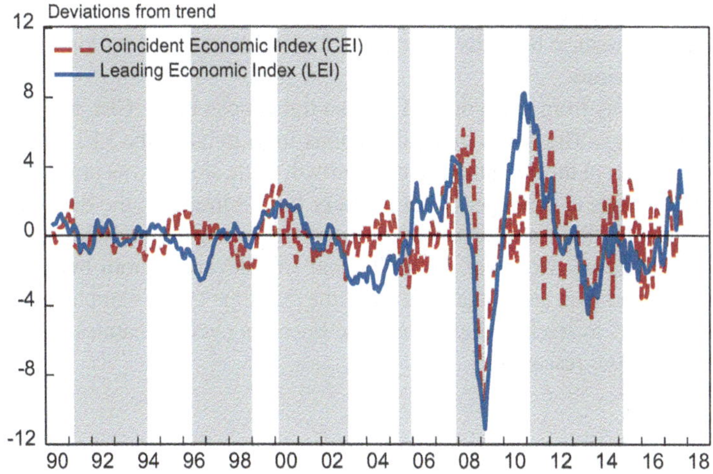

Fig. 5 Growth cycles: coincident and leading indexes (CEI and LEI) for India, 1990–2017. Source: The Conference Board and authors' calculations

best more coincident. Short lead times ahead of trough are an expected feature of such composite indexes, but perhaps because of the high growth trend in this emerging economy, the lead times are shortened even further at troughs.

After signaling the strong recovery in 2009, the trend of the LEI flattened as shown in Fig. 4. Growth rate in LEI has remained low or negative for a long time, even though GDP growth has stayed positive. But the coincident indicators also showed a flattening of the trend in current economic conditions. The rate of growth in the LEI has been decelerating for a while since 2009 signaling a growth cycle downturn after the recovery from the global recession in 2008. As long as the growth rate of the LEI remains negative, there is no sign of a trough in the growth cycle yet. While an analysis of the LEI looking at the duration, depth, and diffusion of the decline seems to border on signaling another business cycle downturn, the amplitude of the declines has not been as deep as the previous recessions. This is very much in line with what we see in India's economy since 2011: prolonged slow growth, widespread weaknesses in many sectors of the economy, and sharp deceleration in the growth rate of GDP from 7–8% to 4%. Still, no negative growth in the level of GDP so far, only long-lasting growth cycle with little improvement. The LEI has been signaling exactly that in the post-recovery period.

Looking beyond the classical business cycles, the composite indexes can also be used to track growth cycles in the Indian economy. The deviations from trend in the CEI appear to conform to the growth cycle chronology as shown in Fig. 5. There have been six growth cycle slowdowns and seven growth cycle accelerations since 1990 (Table 1 above shows the peak and trough dates in the growth cycle fluctuations of the Indian economy). The slowdowns starting in 1991 and 2007 also correspond to major business cycle contractions in the Indian economy. The long expansion since 1991 has been interrupted by five growth cycle fluctuations.

Although these fluctuations are of varying duration, they alternate more symmetrically than asymmetric business cycles which are characterized by long expansions and short recessions.

The deviations from trend in the LEI also track those in the CEI and the growth cycle chronology. The peaks in the deviations from trend in the LEI tend to occur somewhat earlier at the beginning of most growth cycle slowdowns graphed in Fig. 5 although the leads at these peaks are not very long. Moreover, the deviations from trend in the LEI don't appear to be consistently leading the growth cycle troughs shown in the figure. However, both CEI and LEI deviation from trend series are highly correlated with each other. We leave the real-time out-of-sample performance of these indexes to track and anticipate the business cycle dynamics of the Indian economy to future research.

5 Concluding Remarks

This chapter describes the application of The Conference Board's indicator approach using economic indicators for India. It focuses on classical business cycles, but it also discusses how business cycle indexes can be applied to analyze growth cycles. We describe TCB's indexes of coincident and leading indicators to examine the history of the Indian business cycle since the 1990s. The goal in the development of the LEI and CEI was to provide new tools for analysts and forecasters to track and anticipate cyclical movements in India's economy as it transitions toward a more market-based economic structure.

In our approach we take a broad multivariate definition of economic activity and the consensus of cyclical movements among several coincident indicators to define expansion and contraction (recession) periods in the business cycle. To reflect this broad perspective and approximate how the NBER Business Cycle Dating Committee determines the reference chronology in the USA, we use a composite index consisting of three coincident indicators combined with (monthly interpolation of) real GDP. This approach provides a good description of the "historical" development of the Indian business and growth cycles since 1990.

After determining a reference chronology, the coincident index can be monitored to track the real-time evolution of the business cycle. Note that the GDP data cannot be used for month-to-month monitoring of the business cycle because it is quarterly and subject to sometimes large revisions as well as not being available on a timely basis. The selection of a small set of leading indicators is aided by the reference chronology, previous literature on leading indicators, and examples of other emerging market indicators in The Conference Board's portfolio of business cycle indicators. The proposed composite index of these leading indicators is a good forecasting tool that should be helpful to anticipate the turning points in the Indian business and growth cycles. It is estimated monthly and published by The Conference Board since September 2013.

Appendix

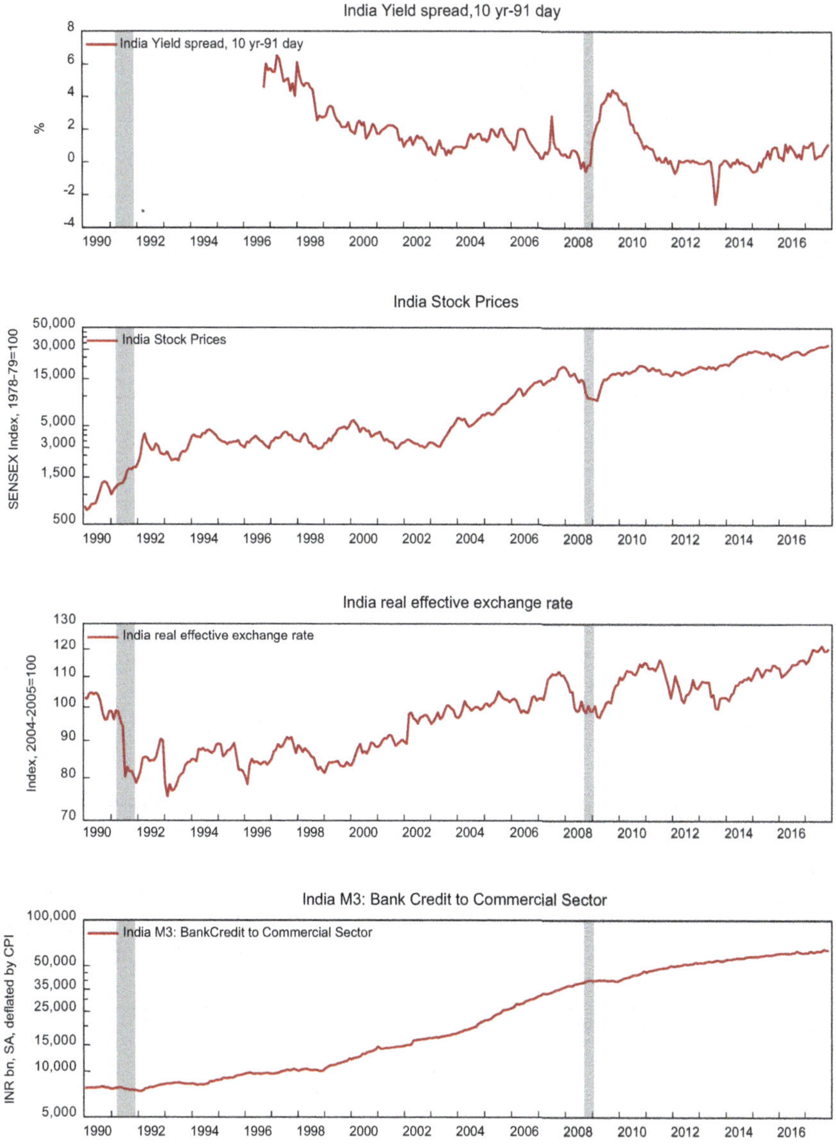

Indicators selected as components of coincident and leading indexes, 1988–2017. Source: The Conference Board Business Cycle Indicators database for India

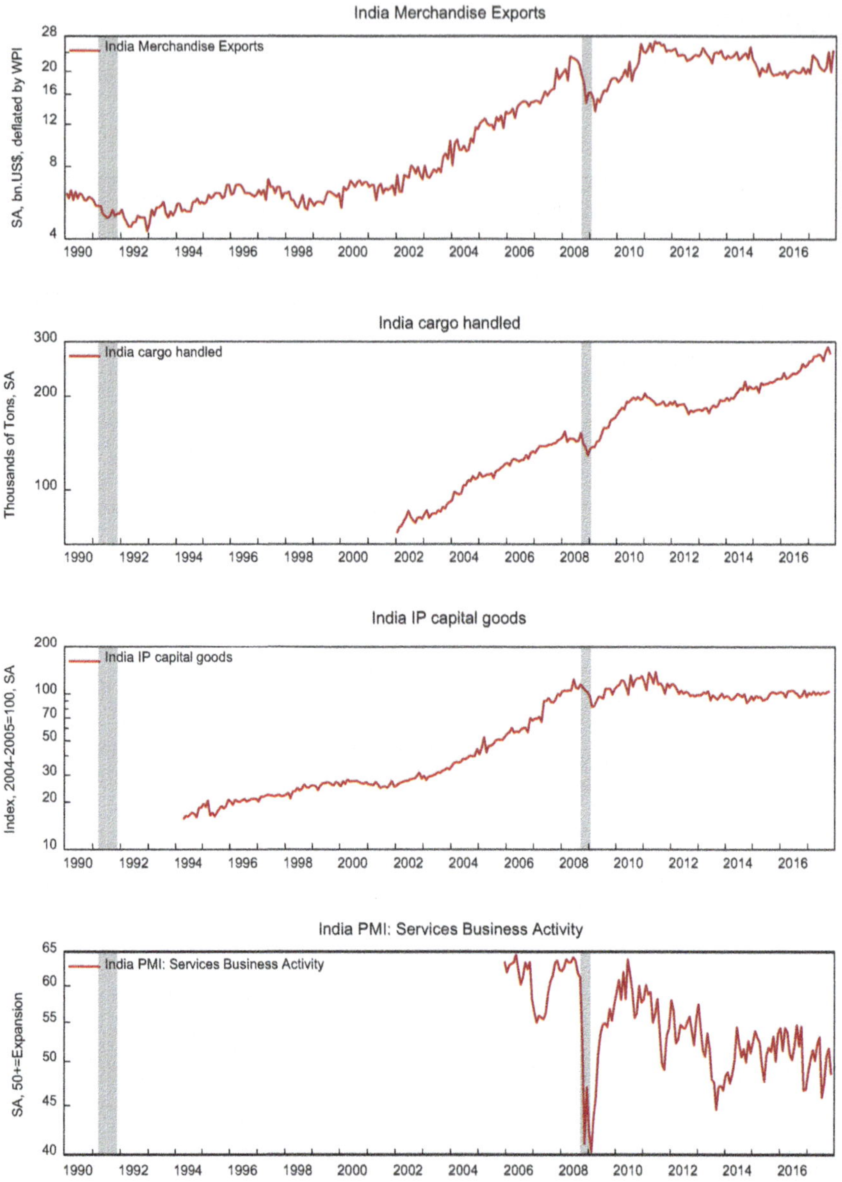
India Merchandise Exports
India Merchandise Exports
SA, bn.US$, deflated by WPI
28
20
16
12
8
4
1990
1992
1994
1996
1998
2000
2002
2004
2006
2008
2010
2012
2014
2016
India cargo handled
India cargo handled
Thousands of Tons, SA
300
200
100
India IP capital goods
India IP capital goods
Index, 2004-2005=100, SA
200
100
70
50
30
20
10
India PMI: Services Business Activity
India PMI: Services Business Activity
SA, 50+=Expansion
65
60
55
50
45
40

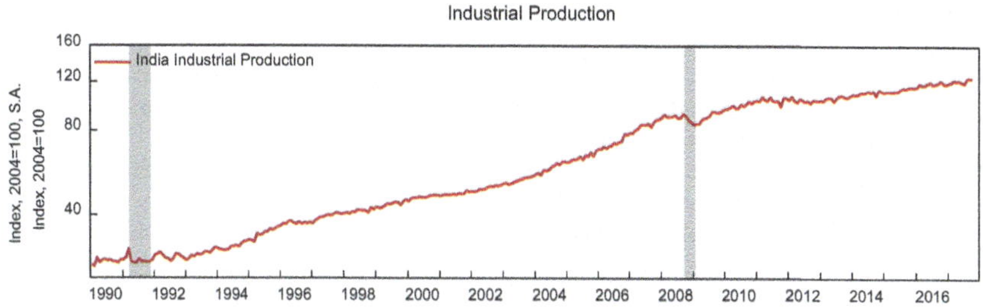

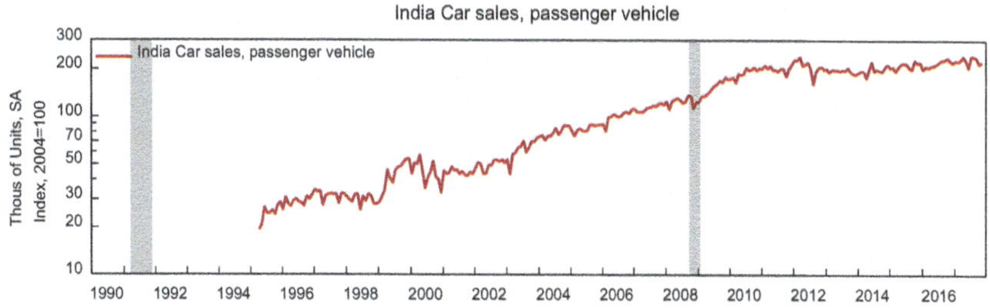

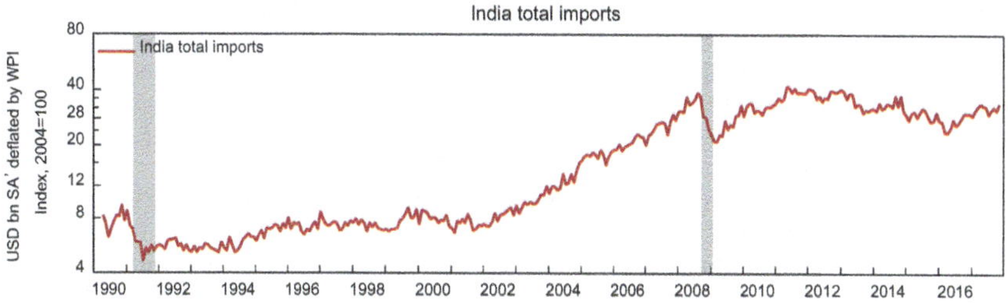

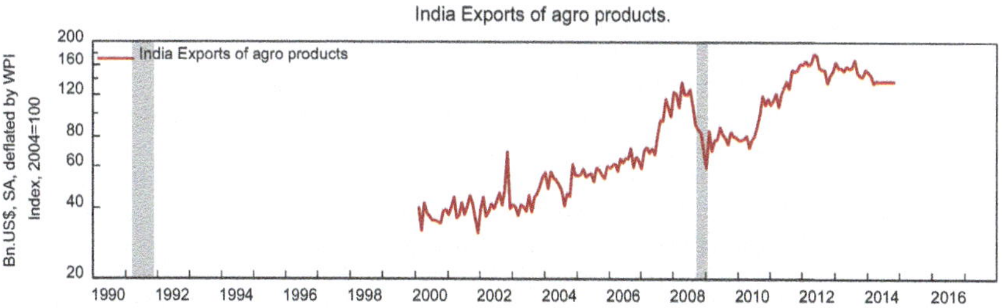

References

Bhattacharya Prabir C, Sivasubramanian MN (2003) Financial development and economic growth in India: 1970–1971 to 1998–1999. Appl Financ Econ 13(12):925–929

Boschan C, Ebanks WW (1978) The phase-average trend: a new way of measuring growth. In: Proceedings of the business and economic statistics section. American Statistical Association, Washington, DC

Bry G, Boschan C (1971) Cyclical analysis of economic time series: selected procedures and computer programs, NBER technical working paper no. 20. NBER, New York

Burns AF, Mitchell WC (1946) Measuring business cycles. National Bureau of Economic Research, New York

Campelo A Jr, Aloisio JS, Lima S, Ozyildirim A, Picchetti P (2018) Tracking business cycles in Brazil with composite indexes of coincident and leading economic indicators. In: Business cycles in BRICS. Springer, Cham

Chitre VS (1982) Growth cycles in the Indian economy. Artha Vijnana 24:293–450

Chitre VS (1988) Fluctuations in agricultural income, public sector investment, world economic activity and business cycles in India. In: Business cycles in five ASEAN countries, India and Korea. Institute of Developing Economies, Tokyo

Chitre VS (1990) Transmission of world growth cycle to the Indian economy. Artha Vijnana:281–297

Chitre VS (2001) Indicators of business recessions and revivals in India: 1951–82. Ind Econ Rev XXXVI(1)

Dua P, Banerji A (1999) An index of coincident economic indicators for the Indian economy. J Quant Econ 15:177–201

Dua P, Banerji A (2001) An indicator approach to business and growth rate cycles: the case of India. Ind Econ Rev 36(1):55–78

Estrella A, Mishkin FS (1998) Predicting U.S. Recessions: financial variables as leading indicators. Rev Econ Stat 80(1):45–61

Feng G, Ozyildirim A, Zarnowitz V (2008) On the measurement and analysis of aggregate economic activity for China: the coincident economic indicators approach, Economics program working paper #08–01. The Conference Board, New York

Gangopadhyay S, Wadhwa W (1997) Leading indicators for the Indian economy. A report for the Ministry of Finance and SERFA, New Delhi

Hatekar N (1994) Historical behaviour of the business cycles in India: some stylized facts for 1951–85. J Ind Sch Polit Econ 6(4)

Hodrick RJ, Prescott EC (1997) Postwar U.S. business cycles: an empirical investigation. J Money Credit Bank 29(1):1–16

Mall OP (1999) Composite index of leading indicators for business cycles in India. RBI Occas Pap 20(3):373–414

Mohanty J, Singh B, Jain R (2003) Business cycles and leading indicators of industrial activity in India. MPRA Paper No. 12149, Posted 13 December 2008/16:37

Nachane DM, Ranade PP (2005) 'Relationship banking' and the credit market in India: an empirical analysis. IGIDR Working Paper, No. WP-2005-010

OECD (2006) Composite leading indicators for major OECD non-members economies. OECD Statistics Working Paper, STD/DOC(2006)1

Ozyildirim A (2018) Compiling cyclical composite indexes: The Conference Board indicators approach. In: Business cycles in BRICS. Springer, Cham

Ozyildirim A, Zarnowitz V (2006) Time series decomposition and measurement of business cycles, trends and growth cycles. J Monet Econ 53(7):1717–1739

Patnaik I, Sharma R (2002) Business cycles in the Indian economy. Margin 351:71–79

Rajeswari T (2010) Construction of a composite leading indicator for India. In: Third international seminar on Early Warning and Business Cycle Indicators, 17–19 Nov 2010, Moscow, Russian Federation

Ravn MO, Uhlig H (2001) On adjusting the HP-filter for the frequency of observations. CEPR Discussion Papers 2858. C.E.P.R. Discussion Papers

Reserve Bank of India (2002) Report of the Working Group on Economic Indicators

Reserve Bank of India (2006) Report of Technical Advisory Group on Development of Leading Economic Indicators for Indian Economy

Sahoo S (2013) Financial structures and economic development in India: an empirical evaluation. RBI Working Paper No. W P S (DEPR): 02/2013

Sharma A, Kumar A, Hatekar N (2011) Causality between prices, output and money in India: an empirical investigation in the frequency domain, Working Paper of Society of Policy Modelling. http://www.econmodels.com/public/dbArticles.php

Zarnowitz V (2001) Coincident indicators and the dating of business cycles. Bus Cycle Indic 8:3–4

Business Climate Indices in China

Yuhong Liu

1 Introduction

Prior to 1978, China was in a strictly planned economic system; the question of whether there existed an economic cycle remained a sensitive one and was always avoided. However, after 1978, China began to implement reform and opening and took the path of a planned commodity economy thereafter; indeed, it was at this time that research on economic fluctuation began. The reform in 1992 transferred China from a planned economy to a market economy, from a seller's market to a buyer's market, and from a shortage economy to a surplus economy. Since then, China's economy has undergone profound changes, which has given rise to in-depth studies on China's economic growth cycle. After 20 years of development, many organizations, e.g., government departments, universities, and research institutions, are now building China's Business Climate Index (BCI). However, there is still no official BCI system in China, with every organization building a BCI according to its own preferences. For example, the National Bureau of Statistics (NBS) modified the weights of climate indicators on the basis of the composition of China's economic structure, while the Development Research Center of the State Council (DRCSC) has tended to choose climate indicators according to economic theory rather than formal statistical quality. This article uses the BCI constructed by the State Information Center (SIC) of China as an example to introduce the application of a BCI in China.

The next section details the development and application of the BCI in China, with particular focus on the SIC's BCI. The third section introduces how the SIC constructs the BCI, including the basic settings, the component indicators, the business climate composite, and diffusion index, and how the BCI can be used to

Y. Liu (✉)
Department of Economic Forecasting, State Information Center (SIC) of China, Beijing, China
e-mail: liuyh@sic.gov.cn

S. Smirnov et al. (eds.), *Business Cycles in BRICS*, Societies and Political Orders in Transition, https://doi.org/10.1007/978-3-319-90017-9_24

analyze and forecast the Chinese economy in the short term. The fourth section introduces the problems and challenges that the BCI faces in China. The final section concludes.

2 Business Climate Index (BCI) in China

2.1 BCIs in China: A Survey

In the mid-1980s, Chinese scholars Shucheng (1986) and Wenquan (1987) ventured into the topic of whether a socialist society is subject to economic cycles and made a major breakthrough both in theory and practice. In 1987, a Jilin University (JLU) research team led by Professor Dong Wenquan, in collaboration with the former State Economic and Trade Commission, pioneered the measurement, analysis, and forecasting of China's economic cycle and built the leading, coincident, and lagging composite and diffusion indices. The outcomes of the research (Dong 1987, 1995) provided a useful reference for the government's policy-making.

In the late 1990s, great progresses had been made in the analysis and forecasting of macroeconomic fluctuation, owing to the combined efforts by numerous institutions and universities, including the Survey and Statistics Department of the People's Bank of China (PBC), the National Bureau of Statistics (NBS), the Institute of Quantitative and Technical Economics at the Chinese Academy of Social Sciences (CASS), the Development Research Center of the State Council (DRCSC), the State Information Center (SIC), Jilin University (JLU), and the Dongbei University of Finance and Economics (DUFE) (see, respectively, Zheng 2011; Liu 1996; Zhang 1997, 2006, Zhu 2005; Gao 1988; Chen 1994). These studies covered practical economic forecast systems, econometric models, policy analysis models, and market survey systems.

From 2005, the analysis of the BCI in China has become routinized. A BCI analysis team was set up, composed of staff from the National Development and Reform Commission (NDRC), the National Bureau of Statistics (NBS), the State Information Center (SIC), the People's Bank of China (PBC), the Ministry of Finance (MOF), the Chinese Academy of Sciences (CAS), and the Ministry of Industry and Information Technology (MIIT). This team meets on the second month of every quarter to discuss the outcome of the last quarter and forecast the current quarter. The reports of each conference are submitted to the NDRC and in some cases also to the State Council, to provide a reference for macroeconomic policy-making.

Unlike developed countries, China's economic structure has always been changing, and the leading/lagging relationship between economic indicators changes too, thus meaning that China's BCI system must be updated continuously. This is why there now exist several BCI systems in China. From the practice perspective, the BCI system constructed by each organization has certain different indices, while the outcomes also vary. When the growth of the economy is relatively stable, different

BCI systems have similar trends, but when the economy encounters dramatic fluctuation, the differences become much bigger.

2.2 *BCI of the State Information Center (SIC)*

The State Information Center was one of the first organizations in China to calculate the BCI. In early 1988, the SIC, in cooperation with the JLU, developed and put into actual use China's first practical economic warning system. In early 1991, the warning system was integrated into the national economic information system, and by 1993, the system had covered nearly 30 provinces and cities.

Since 1996, the SIC has been tracking China's BCI and monitoring the index on a monthly basis in order to analyze China's economy. According to changing characteristics and the structures of different development stages, the SIC occasionally changes the indicators in the BCI system to reflect China's economy in a timely and accurate way. There is no fixed frequency in terms of the SIC reconsidering China's BCI; this only happens when volatile fluctuation occurs, which has only been the case six times since 1996, in 2000, 2003, 2007, 2009, 2012, and 2016, respectively. This chapter uses the latest version of the BCI, which was constructed in 2016.

3 SIC Monthly BCI System

3.1 *Basic Settings*

3.1.1 Method for Data Processing, Choosing Indicators, and Constructing the BCI

The BCI is a method used to empirically analyze an economy. The starting point of the BCI is that the fluctuation of different economic fields does not occur at the same time but is a complex process which differs from certain industries to other industries and from some areas to other areas. In addition, if only one single indicator is used to describe the economy, then irregular fluctuations in the indicator may lead to an incorrect judgment. Based on this fact, the BCI uses mathematical methods to select a group of economic indicators with the same trend in the main economic areas and combines them into a set of business climate indexes (leading, coincident, and lagging) designed to measure and judge the economy.

At this point, it is fitting to highlight the steps involved in building China's BCI (the BCI pioneered by the SIC): The first step is to determine the candidate indicators to be considered. The SIC selects the main indicators in the major areas of the economy, e.g., investment, consumption, foreign trade, price, transportation, government finance, monetary policy, etc.; these are treated as candidate indicators. The second step is a seasonal adjustment to eliminate the irregularities and seasonal elements from the candidate indicators. The SIC uses the X-12 of the US Census Bureau. The third step is to consider the indicators. Using K-L divergence (Kullback and Leibler 1951) and correlation analysis, the SIC calculates the leads or lags of the candidate indicators using the benchmark indicator.[1] In general, the indicators with K-L divergence less than 0.01 and a correlation coefficient over 0.4 can be used as the climate indicators. Those indicators whose leads or lags within 2-month period are coincident indicators, while those with leads or lags over 2 months are leading indicators, and those recording over 2 months of lags are lagging indicators. Finally, the fourth step involves constructing the index. The SIC combines the leading (coincident, lagging) indicators selected in step 3 by using the US Bureau of Economic Analysis method (BEA 1984).[2]

3.1.2 Cycle

Since the reform and opening in 1978, most economic indicators have been growing in absolute terms, although the growth rate has varied in a regular way. As such, China's researchers all use the growth rate cycle in BCI systems; simply put, all the indices in the BCI systems are in the form of year-on-year growth rates.

3.1.3 Starting Time

China began to adapt its statistical system to the United Nations' SNA system in 1992 and gradually improved the corresponding index system afterward. As a result of this, the accounting standards of many economic indicators are constantly changing. In China's statistical system, once some statistical caliber changes, the NBS can only make its growth rate comparable. This is because most indicators have a complete time series only after 1997, which was the year in which the BCI system was conceived.

3.1.4 Benchmark Indicator

The most important indicator in China is GDP, but the frequency of China's BCI is monthly, and so we need to choose a monthly indicator that can represent GDP. Prior to 2013, the secondary industry was dominant in China's economy, accounting for

[1]K-L divergence is commonly used to judge the proximity of two probability distributions. Smaller K-L divergence means higher proximity of two distributions.

[2]For current modification of this method, see Ozyildirim (2018).

Table 1 SIC climate indicators

Type	Indicators, year-on-year growth rates	Units y-o-y	Lags, months	Correlation
Leading	1. Crude steel production	%	−3	0.73
	2. Automobile production	%	−3	0.59
	3.Total loans of financial institutions (RMB)	%	−4	0.57
	4. Finished goods inventory*	%	−4	0.66
	5. Total planned fixed assets investments under construction	%	−9	0.43
Coincident	1. Value added of the secondary industry	%	0	1.00
	2. Electricity production	%	−1	0.85
	3. Urban fixed assets investments	%	−2	0.68
	4. Narrow money supply (M1)	%	0	0.62
	5. Government revenue	%	−2	0.48
	6. Exports	%	+2	0.67

Note: The value added of the secondary industry is the only benchmark indicator. In Table 1, the first five indicators under the "leading" type are the leading indicators, adding more than 2 months to the value added of the secondary industry. These five indicators are combined into the leading composite index through the use of certain mathematical methods. The same applies to the next six indicators under the "coincident" type, which are combined into the coincident composite index
Asterisk indicates reversed indicator. As finished goods inventory is a lagging indicator, reversing can make it become a leading indicator

more than 50% of the GDP; as such, the benchmark indicator in the SIC is the year-on-year growth rate of the real value added in the secondary industry.[3]

3.1.5 Components

The SIC chooses the indices based on the statistical results of K-L information and time difference correlation analysis (time difference correlation uses the correlation coefficient to calculate the leading, coincident, or lagging relationship between economic series). The calculation method involves selecting a benchmark indicator and calculating the correlation coefficient with some leading or lagging periods of selected indicators (the SIC calculates leading and lagging for 12 months each). The period with the largest correlation coefficient is the lags/leads of the selected indicator. Table 1 shows the components of the BCI; the indicators are all the year-on-year growth rates, and the finished goods inventory is the reversal indicator.

[3]Notice that the categorization of China's three industries is slightly different from that of the other countries: The primary industry is related to agriculture, forestry, animal husbandry, and fishery, while the secondary industry comprises mining, manufacturing, electricity, gas and water production, the supply, and construction industries; the tertiary industry accounts for the rest.

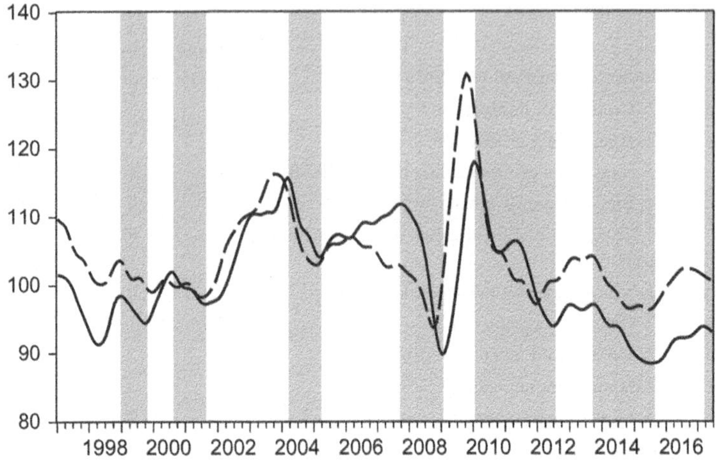

Fig. 1 Coincident composite index (solid) and leading composite index (dotted). The shaded part is the deceleration phase

3.1.6 Weights

All indicators have equal weights in the BCI system.

3.2 Composite Index

Using the climate indicators in Table 1, the SIC built the leading and coincident composite indices as follows (both indices are equal to 100 in the basic period for 2000).

As can be seen from Fig. 1, China's economy has shown a significant cyclical characteristic in growth rate. As most BCI studies in China mainly focus on the growth rate cycle, the composite indices exhibit big ups and downs. This was especially true during the period spanning January 2009–July 2012, with the combined effect of the international financial crisis and China's massive stimulus policy; indeed, during this time, the coincident composite index reached its lowest point in January 2009 but rose to a historical peak again in January 2010, just 12 months later. After 2010, China entered a new economic state, its growth began to slow down, and the fluctuation became smaller. The current cycle of China's economy began in August 2015, and although there was a minor shock in the third quarter of 2016, the upward trend has not changed. The peak of the current cycle came in March 2017, following which the coincident composite index entered a new downward stage.

As can be seen from Fig. 1, using the B-B method (Bry and Boschan 1971), the SIC estimated the turning points of China's cycle as follows (see Table 2).

Table 2 Chinese cycles measured by the SIC's BCI

	Turning points			Duration, months		
Cycle	Trough	Peak	Trough	Expansion	Contraction	Total
First	1998.4	1998.12	1999.10	8	10	18
Second	1999.10	2000.8	2001.8	10	12	22
Third	2001.8	2004.3	2005.3	31	12	43
Fourth	2005.3	2007.9	2009.1	30	16	46
Fifth	2009.1	2010.1	2012.7	12	30	42
Sixth	2012.7	2013.9	2015.8	14	23	37
Seventh	2015.8	2017.3		19	–	–

Since January 1997, China's economy has gone through six complete cycles and is currently in the falling phase of the seventh cycle. The beginning of one business cycle in the SIC is a trough, and so April 1998 was the beginning of the first cycle since 1997. China experienced two short cycles from April 1998 to August 2001, both of which lasted for a relatively short period of time, while the expansion was shorter than the contraction. The next two cycles exhibited different trends, with the duration time doubling and the expansion seeming longer than the contraction. After the breakout of the financial crisis in 2007, the duration of China's economy cycle became shorter, and the expansion was again shorter than the contraction. However, in the terms of the lasting time, the expansion has become longer and the contraction shorter since the fifth cycle, thus meaning that China's situation has gradually improved.

3.3 *Diffusion Index*

The diffusion index (DI) describes economic diffusion and is constructed based on the proportion of rising indicators in the economic indicators. A DI value of 50% indicates a balance between the upward trend and downward trend in economic activities, while the time can be considered a reference turning point. The peak date was 1 month before DI passed downward through the 50% line, and the trough date was 1 month before DI passed upward through the 50% line. The diffusion index in the SIC, as shown in Fig. 2, is composed of the same indicators as the composite index in Table 1.

The leading diffusion index went downward through the 50% line in October 2016, meaning that the peak appeared around September 2016. The peak of the composite index was only 1 month away from the peak of the diffusion index. According to the definition of the diffusion index, if the time difference of peak confirmed by the composite and diffusion indices is within 3 months, then the time of the turning point can be confirmed. Indeed, the peak of the leading composite index appeared in August 2016. In April 2017, the coincident diffusion index went through the 50% line downward, which means that the peak appeared around April

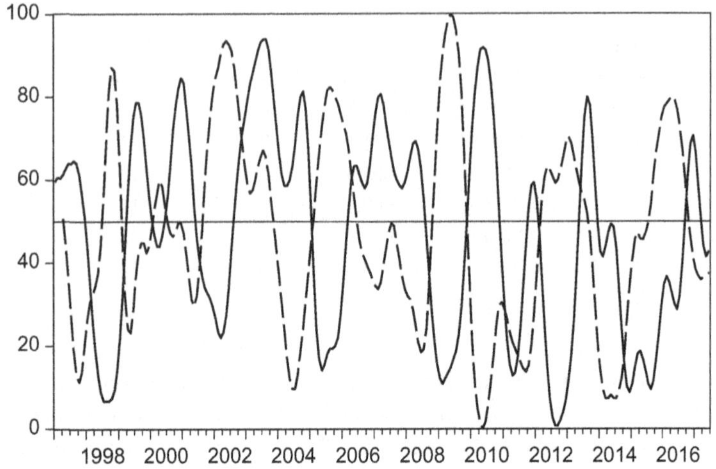

Fig. 2 Coincident diffusion index (solid) and leading diffusion index (dotted)

2017; this result is consistent with the judgment based on the coincident composite index.

3.4 Application of the BCI Composite and Diffusion Indices to the Analyses of the Current Situation

By combining the composite index and the diffusion index, we can make certain judgments on China's economy in the short or medium long run. In the short run, the turning point has appeared, and China's economy has entered the falling phase. The peak of the leading composite index appeared in August 2016, and since then the leading composite index has been falling for 10 months. As the leads of leading composite index in this round totaled 6 months and the consistent composite index was falling for only 3 months, we can expect China's economy to continue its downward trend in the second half of 2017.

As for the medium and long run, China has entered a long downward cycle, showing a W type. As illustrated in Fig. 1, 2010 is the watershed that divides China's business climate into the long rising phase and the long falling phase. The peaks of China's business climate were rising before 2010 (the peak of 2007 was lower than that of 2004 but remained at a high level) and falling after 2010. The rapid economic growth before 2010 was the result of equally fast growth in imports and exports resulting from China's access to the WTO and the release of the redundant rural labor force. After 2010, China's economy entered a new economic state, with a higher quality growth, a more complex division, and a more rational structure. The Chinese economic growth went down from "high speed" to "medium speed," and the business climate declined correspondingly after 2010. China's business climate has experienced two complete cycles, the peaks and troughs of which have been descending gradually. The trough in August 2015 was the deepest since 1997. From a long-run perspective, the cycle after 2010 can be seen as a long downward cycle, with the economy showing a "W type," and the peak and trough both falling.

4 Challenges

4.1 Trade-Offs in Constructing Indicators

After nearly 30 years of high-speed development, China has entered a new economic state, with its growth rate declining gradually and its economic structure changing to a great extent; indeed, this has given rise to more challenges for the application of the BCI in China.

As mentioned above, the SIC constantly updates the composition indicators to fit the ever-changing economic structure. As the main purpose of the BCI is to facilitate short-term analysis and forecasting, the SIC prefers indicators that can reflect the current economic structure but may not be perfect in historical phases. This highlights the fact that the present BCI can only describe the current economy accurately but may produce some errors when estimating historical economic cycles.

4.2 Choice of the Benchmark Indicator

Prior to 2014, the secondary industry was the dominant sector in China and had the highest proportion of GDP. In 2013, the proportion of the tertiary industry was higher than that of the secondary industry for the first time, and in 2015 the value added of the service industry accounted for more than 50% of GDP for the first time. Although the service industry has become the dominant sector in China, the SIC still uses the value added of the secondary industry as the benchmark indicator for two reasons: Firstly, the secondary industry still plays the most important role when it comes to the majority of matters and has done since 1997; as such, it is reasonable to use it as the benchmark indicator, because the BCI is a long-term monitoring process. Secondly, there is currently no public data on the monthly value added of the service industry in China, and so we cannot reflect on the shift between industry and service in the BCI.

5 Conclusion

Although the BCI has been used for nearly 30 years in China, its application was confined to certain institutions and never acknowledged by the government; it is for this reason that there remains no official BCI in China. The BCI originated in the United States and was applied to developed countries such as Japan and Germany; its method is suited to mature market economies. As a developing country, China has transitioned from a planned economy to a market economy, with an economic system and structure that have been constantly changing; moreover, the government has a strong control over the economy. All of this results in too much political influence on the economic indicators, which gives rise to big challenges for the application of the BCI. In practice, most institutions always choose the indicators which reflect the current business conditions when building the BCI. This approach can maximize the ability of the BCI to describe and forecast the economy but may weaken the accuracy of the description of historical business cycles and the judgment of turning points, which makes the BCI unpopular with some users. Certain institutions have noticed this problem and attempted to search for corresponding solutions, such as creating several periods when building the BCI. In addition, many institutions are debating whether the growth rate cycle is still suitable for China's BCI, given that the country has entered a new state; indeed, some of these institutions have tried to employ the growth cycle when building the new BCI. In conclusion, the BCI is still failing to play its due role in China, but with many institutions working on the problem, a BCI with Chinese characteristics is on the way.

References

Bry G, Boschan C (1971) Cyclical analysis of time series: selected procedures and computer programs. NBER Technical Paper, 20

Chen L (1994) Analysis and forecast of macroeconomic situation using Stock-Watson business climate index. J Quant Tech Econ 5:53–59 (in Chinese)

Gao T (1988) Attempt to construct China's macroeconomic monitoring and forecasting model. J Quant Tech Econ 10:33–38 (in Chinese)

Kullback S, Leibler RA (1951) On information and sufficiency. Ann Math Stat 22:79–86

Ozyildirim A (2018) Compiling cyclical composite indexes: The Conference Board indicators approach. In: Business cycles in BRICS. Springer, Cham

Shucheng L (1986) Research on fixed asset investment cycle. Econ Res 2:18–21 (in Chinese)

Shucheng L (1996) New stage of chinese business cycle. Shanghai Yuan Dong Press, Shanghai. (in Chinese)

U.S.A. Department of Commerce, Bureau of Economic Analysis (BEA) (1984) Handbook of cyclical indicators – a supplement to the business conditions digest, pp 65–70

Wenquan D (1987) Measurement, analysis and forecast of chinese business cycle. Jilin Univ J 3:1–8 (in Chinese)

Wenquan D (1995) Application of Stock-Watson business index in China. J Quant Tech Econ 12:68–74 (in Chinese)

Zhang L (1997) Research on China's business cycle. Manage World 6:34–41 (in Chinese)
Zhang X (2006) Theory and method: seasonal adjustment X-12-ARIMA. China Financial Press, Peking (in Chinese)
Zheng G (2011) Method of business climate. China Science Press, Peking (in Chinese)
Zhu B (2005) Quantitative analysis of China economy operation. China Economy Press, Peking (in Chinese)

Tracking Business and Growth Cycles in the Chinese Economy Using Composite Indexes

Ataman Ozyildirim

1 Leading Indicators for China: A Great Challenge

Internationally comparable statistics for China will become more and more valuable as the country's role in the global economy continues to grow in importance and its economy develops and matures, becoming more like a genuine market economy. Given the importance of China to global output and growth as well as the global business cycle, developing leading indicators for China to monitor and predict its emerging economic cycles has been a logical next step for business cycle researchers in and outside China. The Conference Board embarked on such a project in the 2000s and began to publish its system of business cycle indicators for China in 2010. This chapter discusses the development of The Conference Board indexes.[1]

1.1 Challenges

There is a large body of literature and ongoing debate suggesting that official China GDP growth estimates contain serious upward biases (Maddison 1998; Keidel 2001; Rawski 2001; Wu 2007). Two factors may explain the bias. First, as argued in Keidel (2001) and Wu (2007), China had a long tradition of reporting economic output by using the Soviet Material Product System (MPS), which tends to inadequately calculate the nominal output value. Despite the fact that China has switched to the System of National Accounts (SNA) in 1993, China's GDP statistics are still far from perfect, and tertiary sector statistics may be particularly problematic (Xu 2004).

[1]Adapted from Adams et al. (2010) and The Conference Board (2013).

A. Ozyildirim (✉)
The Conference Board Inc., New York, NY, USA
e-mail: Ataman.Ozyildirim@conference-board.org

S. Smirnov et al. (eds.), *Business Cycles in BRICS*, Societies and Political Orders in Transition, https://doi.org/10.1007/978-3-319-90017-9_25

Second, the existing data reporting system, established in the central planning period, tends to produce statistics skewed toward the government's economic targets. For example, Rawski (2001) argues that the official data showing 7–8% real GDP growth during 1998–2001 reflected official objectives rather than economic outcomes. Undoubtedly, if the official GDP statistics lack reliability, they will significantly affect the accuracy of assessment of business cycle chronology. Thus, we turned to the coincident indicators independent of GDP to date business cycles in China.

Unique challenges complicate the creation of composite leading indicators for China. Foremost among these is limited historical data: monthly economic data for China are largely unavailable prior to 1986, and many important indicators have histories of only 10 years or less. The very small size of our data set inevitably limits the effectiveness of traditional empirical techniques of business cycle analysis. More importantly, the structure of the Chinese economy underwent tremendous changes and reforms during the period in question, with factors of production increasingly distributed by market forces rather than economic planning, and increasing proportions of firms, employment, and value added deriving from the private sector. Idiosyncratic patterns of data reporting also affect data interpretation. For example, when this research was conducted, only the nominal year-over-year growth rate of value added of industrial production was reported, not the monthly quantity of value added. Base years for these series are estimated—a feasible but less desirable alternative to using original data. Moreover, China's statistical reporting system has undergone and continues to undergo major changes. Statistical series that originally covered only state-owned businesses have been modified or expanded to better measure private sector activity. While data released after these definitional revisions are arguably more comprehensive measures of the overall economy, the structural breaks they introduce to historical data complicate the identification and interpretation of trends (i.e., revisions of data coverage can coincide with and obscure periods of economic volatility).

1.2 The Conference Board's Response

Previous attempts at building business cycle indicators, such as those from the National Bureau of Statistics (NBS), the State Information Center (SIC) of China, and the Organisation for Economic Co-operation and Development (OECD), have concentrated on fluctuations in the growth of the industrial sector of the economy. When we set out to develop leading indicators for China, to the best of our knowledge, there were no composite indexes that explicitly focused on signaling turning points in the business cycle broadly defined (sometimes called the classical business cycle) as is done in The Conference Board indicators approach. Initial research by The Conference Board on the business cycle in China focused on defining a suitable measure of coincident activity and creating a chronology of business cycles in China since 1986, before which limited data is available. This multi-year project, summarized in the next section, served also as a point of departure for developing a complementary chronology of growth cycles and for the research on leading indicators described below. Growth cycle analysis is a natural extension of the business cycle approach. Our findings and selections of indicators remain conditional. Given the challenges faced, the decisions made regarding the composite indexes may be reviewed and changed as data quality and availability improve and China's economy continues to evolve.

Indeed, since the initial launch of **The Conference Board Leading Economic Index®** (LEI) and **The Conference Board Coincident Economic Index®** (CEI) for China in May 2010, several of the underlying indicators have undergone major methodological changes, two components have been discontinued, and some are no longer the reliable business cycle indicators they once were, due to China's unique and ongoing economic structural changes. Therefore, in May 2016, The Conference Board undertook a comprehensive benchmark revision of both the CEI and LEI for China. These revisions were intended to improve the overall performance of the LEI and CEI indexes and result in a better monitor of China's economic development and growth trends. The review of the indicators resulted in a new selection of indicators for both the LEI and CEI. This chapter discusses the development of these new indexes and the subsequent comprehensive revision of the components which resulted in the current composition of these indexes.

2 Coincident Indicators for China[2]

A composite index of coincident indicators is a necessary building block toward obtaining timely information on China's business cycle dynamics. The Coincident Economic Index or the CEI is an appropriate multivariate indicator of aggregate economic activity and helps the research on the evaluation and selection of leading indicators and indexes, LEIs.

General business cycle analysis begins with the determination of a business cycle chronology based on coincident indicators. In the United States, the National Bureau of Economic Research (NBER) business cycle dating committee determines the business cycle chronology. This reference chronology is commonly accepted as the official business cycle dates for the United States. In countries where no such committee exists, The Conference Board approximates the approach taken by the NBER committee by relying on a composite index of the components of CEI and the monthly interpolated real GDP. However, in the case of China, it is not possible to follow this approach given the questions surrounding the quality and reliability of GDP data for China. Instead, to determine a business cycle chronology for China, the CEI provides a multivariate measure of economic activity that is largely independent from national income account measures.

[2] This section is adapted and updated from Guo et al. (2008).

There are also challenges to finding appropriate coincident indicators. The available time series are still quite short and sometimes inconsistent. The more-or-less centralized control of data releases and continuing biases and measurement errors creates challenges for measuring short-term fluctuations in China's economy.[3]

2.1 *Advantages of Using the Coincident Economic Index for Business Cycle Analysis in China*

The data on coincident indicators available for China provide valuable information as raw material for business cycle dating and analysis, but they have serious deficiencies and first require substantial selection and transformation. For business cycle analysis, indicator data have to be seasonally adjusted (in the case of China, with special attention paid to the Chinese New Year holiday) and deflated with appropriate price indexes. It is easy to find fault with these simple procedures designed to convert Chinese data to a form suitable for business cycle analysis, but they are the best option available given the lack of data to develop viable alternatives. The inadequacy of China's GDP data makes it particularly important to complement them with series of monthly coincident indicators and the composite index based on these series. It is these indicators that provide the main tool for determining the business cycle chronology and tracking the monthly fluctuations in China's macroeconomic activity.

There are several advantages to relying on the CEI, rather than using only GDP in measuring economic fluctuations in China and elsewhere (Zarnowitz 2001). First, GDP is at best available quarterly, with some reporting lags; by contrast, CEI is constructed with more frequently available and timely data series, which move contemporaneously with the business cycle. Hence, CEI can be used to draw an early and more reliable picture of the evolution of the current economic activity.

The second advantage of CEI is that as a multivariate index. Real GDP is the most comprehensive measure of economic output or outlays, but CEI ideally includes elements of input as well as output, real income as well as real demand or sales. Our selected indicators for CEI for China approximate these considerations. The consensus of cyclical movements of these major coincident indicators inspires more confidence than the movement of any univariate measure, even as comprehensive as GDP. This is particularly true when the accuracy and reliability of official China's GDP statistics has come under criticism in recent years as discussed above.

The third and final advantage of CEI is a byproduct of its multivariate coverage. GDP as a complex accounting measure of economic output is often subject to long strings of sometimes large revisions.[4] CEI revisions are less prone to such

[3]Cai (2000) reports on data falsification in provincial data.

[4]According to China's National Bureau of Statistics (NBS), there are three steps of accounting procedure in releasing official figures of GDP, namely, preliminary accounting, preliminary

unexpected changes because their revisions are potentially smaller and more likely to offset each other between the index components.

2.2 Selecting Components of the Composite Index of Coincident Indicators

An indicator system is widely used to track fluctuations in real economic activity and therefore it is necessary to adjust nominal values of the chosen indicators for inflation. Some price indexes, such as CPI and retail price index (RPI), need to be converted from "previous year = 100" year-over-year percent change figures to create indexes with fixed-base periods.[5] Fixed-base CPI, PPI, and RPI going back to the 1980s need to be developed to provide deflators for the corresponding series based on current (nominal) valuations. We have made such adjustments as best as possible given the available data.

It is also important to distinguish cyclical fluctuations from seasonal movements. In order to do this, we seasonally adjust all the candidate coincident indicators discussed below, with special attention to the difficult problem of important moving holidays such as the Chinese (lunar) New Year.

The candidate components are assessed based on their adherence to the selection criteria for cyclical indicators.[6] For China, the search for the most comprehensive and representative time series with the best historical timing record in the coincident category initially yielded five choices (see Table 1, column 1). All these series start in 1986 except manufacturing employment which is only available from 2000. However, as discussed below, this list of components had to be revised in 2016.

Industrial production measures the production and supply of goods by manufacturing, mining and utility businesses. Electricity production is often considered a reliable proxy for industrial activity as it increases with increasing industrial activity as well as with increasing living standards.[7] Retail sales measures the demand for goods and services mainly for personal and household use in the economy. Total volume of passenger traffic is conceptually expected to be closely and positively related to overall economic activity and income levels, while

---

verification, and final verification. The results are released 20 days after accounting quarter, 45 days after accounting quarter, and the end of December next year when the annual final data are confirmed, respectively, for each revision step.

[5]China's National Bureau of Statistics (NBS) has published fixed-base CPI since 2000 in *China Monthly Economic Indicators* but unexpectedly ceased in 2006.

[6]See Ozyildirim (2018) in this volume and The Conference Board (TCB), 2001. Business Cycle Indicators Handbook. The Conference Board: New York.

[7]Therefore, even though the empirical performance of this indicator in China did not show marked cyclical contractions, it was included in the selected coincident indicators. This or related series on energy production are also used by several Chinese agencies as coincident indicators (e.g., SIC, NBS).

Table 1 Components of *The Conference Board Coincident Economic Index*® (CEI) for China

Initial set of coincident indicators (May 2010 to April 2016)	Current set of coincident indicators (May 2016–present)
(1)	(2)
Value added of industrial production (2005 = 100, deflated by PPI)	Value added of industrial production (2005 = 100, deflated by PPI)
Electricity production (billions of KWH)	Electricity production (Billions of KWH)
Retail sales of consumer goods (Billions of 2010 yuan, deflated by RPI)	Retail sales of consumer goods (Billions of 2010 yuan, deflated by RPI)
Total volume of passenger traffic (Millions of passenger-kilometers)	Railway freight traffic (Millions of tons)
Manufacturing employment (millions of persons)	Omitted as a component in 2016

Note: Series are seasonally adjusted by The Conference Board (including an adjustment for Chinese New Year effects) where necessary. The lists of selected components for each version of the CEI are provided on The Conference Board website; please see https://www.conference-board.org/data/bcicountry.cfm?cid=11. Also see Guo et al. (2008)
Source: The Conference Board

changing when the state of the overall economy changes whether due to unanticipated shocks.[8]

Employment measures labor input used in the manufacturing sector to produce these goods. Note that manufacturing employment receives special attention in the data available for China, even though, as a result of reforms and structural changes as well as the development process itself, manufacturing employment has undergone significant changes.

Another challenge was in finding an appropriate coincident series of personal income or wages and salaries. Unfortunately, we have not identified an appropriate coincident monthly series of personal income, although the disposable income per capita of urban household may serve as the closest available substitute. However, the time series was only available in the quarterly frequency starting in the first quarter of 2007 and the earlier monthly history of the time series only went back to 1992. Thus, the history of the series is too short and the quarterly frequency is not appropriate for this series to qualify as a satisfactory coincident indicator. While it is unorthodox to use income in the financial sector as a coincident indicator, due to a lack of more adequate series, we considered cash income of the financial sector as a CEI component, but in the end, this series was not included in the published composition of the CEI.

[8]Transportation output indexes for the US economy have been shown to have strong cyclical characteristics often corresponding to growth cycles; see Lahiri et al. (2003).

2.3 2016 Comprehensive Benchmark Revisions to the China CEI

As mentioned above, because of changes in the behavior and availability of some of the components, it was necessary to change the composition of the CEI in 2016. This comprehensive revision was undertaken after a review and evaluation of the existing components and several new candidates. As a result of this research (see Table 1, column 2):

1. The Conference Board added the "railway freight traffic" series to the China CEI. This monthly series refers to the volume of freight transported by railway within a specific period of time and reflects the service of the transport industry toward national economic activity. Since transportation plays a critical role in facilitating economic activity between sectors and across regions, this series is a useful indicator to assess the conditions in the overall economy. In addition, most heavy machinery, raw materials used in the manufacturing and industry sectors, as well as capital goods are transported by rail. Thus, this series is also an important indicator to monitor the conditions in China's other industries and is not as volatile as the total volume of passenger traffic series, nor does it seem to be as sensitive to holidays.
2. The Conference Board eliminated the total volume of passenger traffic series as a component of the CEI. This monthly series refers to the volume of transported passengers multiplied by the transport distance, using passenger-kilometers in millions as units for measurement. The series was originally included in the China CEI because of the economic importance of service sectors relative to goods sectors which has steadily increased in recent years. However, over the years, this series has not always proven to have a positive correlation with overall economic conditions. For example, when economic conditions worsen, migrant workers often have to travel longer distance from their hometown to find work. The series has also been extremely volatile and sensitive to noneconomic shocks and seasonality. The series shows a sudden and short down-and-up movement due to the SARS (severe acute respiratory syndrome) outbreak between November 2002 and July 2003 (we treated this as an outlier when indexing in the previous version of the China CEI). There was also a large drop in the series in January 2014 due to a methodology adjustment by the data source, Ministry of Transportation. However, the adjusted statistical methodology and change of the scope and coverage (if any) were not disclosed by the source. Moreover, seasonal adjustment of this series is complicated and may not be adequate as passenger transportation is very sensitive to holidays (the seasonal adjustment is further complicated by use of the lunar calendar for these holidays and external shocks, e.g., SARS in 2003). For the abovementioned reasons, we have decided to drop the series from the China CEI.
3. The Conference Board eliminated the manufacturing employment series as a component of the CEI. The manufacturing employment series covers

24 manufacturing sectors and refers to persons employed by all state-owned manufacturing enterprises as well as by non-state-owned enterprises with an annual sales income of over 5 million yuan. The National Bureau of Statistics published this series in the quarterly frequency from January 2007 through December 2010, before publishing it monthly again from January 2011 to December 2013. The series was discontinued from January 2013 through December 2014, and it became available again on a monthly basis in January 2015. Due to the lack of consistency in data availability and coverage, we have decided to eliminate the series despite historical evidence that it could serve as a good cyclical coincident indicator.

After these changes in the composition, the whole history of the composite index was recalculated and continued to be published going forward.

2.4 Dating Business Cycles in China with Composite Coincident Economic Index (CEI)

The composite indexes reviewed in this chapter were calculated using the methodology followed by The Conference Board (see Ozyildirim 2018). The indexing methodology uses an unweighted, volatility-adjusted average of the contributions of each component, and the performance of the composite index appears to be superior to that of any individual indicator. While individual indicators may be correlated with the CEI and have reasonable cyclical characteristics, none of the selected indicators are ideal cyclical indicators by themselves. When combined into a composite index using a simple and transparent indexing procedure, the resulting composite index tends to perform better as a cyclical measurement tool. The monthly change in the index is an equally weighted volatility-adjusted average of the monthly changes of its components.[9]

The CEI for China that was used in 2010 to determine business cycle turning points combined five individual indicators—which covered industrial production, electricity production, retail sales, volume of passenger traffic, manufacturing employment—into a composite index to determine the chronology of China's business cycle.[10]

The CEI that resulted from the 2016 comprehensive revision includes four components (value added of industrial production, retail sales of consumer goods, electricity production, and railway freight traffic) but gives essentially the same turning point results. This points to an advantage of the composite index approach in

---

[9]The monthly change is calculated using a symmetric percent change formula. For details see Ozyildirim (2018).

[10]We experimented with several other combinations of coincident indicators, but in all cases the dates of the recession that was identified remained the same. Details can be found in the working paper online.

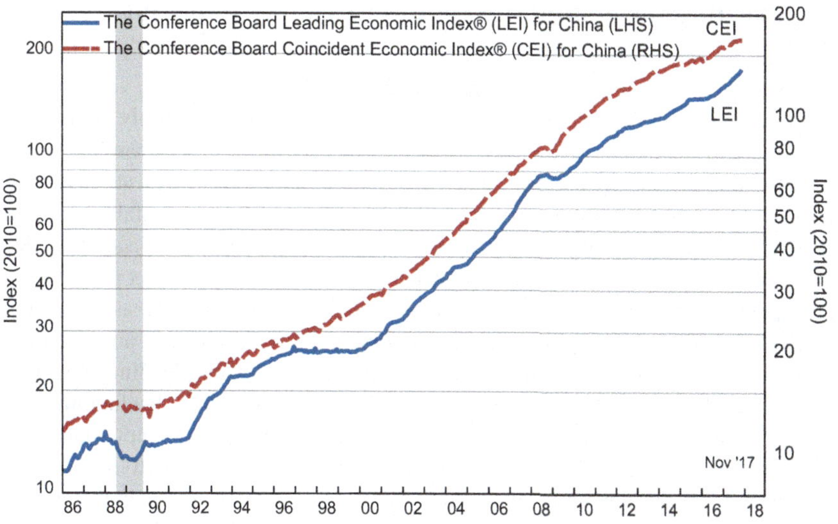

Fig. 1 *Coincident and Leading Economic Indexes* (CEI and LEI) for China: 2010 = 100. Note: Above shaded area represents China's business cycle recession using CEI, and the turning points are determined by the Bry and Boschan (1971) algorithm. CEI and LEI are graphed on different axes to make them easier to distinguish. Both indexes are 2010 = 100. Source: The Conference Board

that marginal changes in components often do not create major changes in turning points.

The dating of China's business cycle shows that China enjoyed impressively strong economic growth since 1986 with only one recession in 9/1988–2/1990 (see Fig. 1). Visual inspection indicates that the recession, while relatively long, was mild and the immediate recovery was quick. This stays roughly in line with the finding based on the expenditure accounts approach in Keidel (2001), which states that the negative growth in 1989 was due to a severe slump in rural household consumption, with the recovery in 1990 due to a strong urban and government consumption. That is, the recession, particularly in 1989, was much more serious than officially reported. The index reveals that China's economic growth was very fast in 1990–1992, a little slower but very persistent in 1993–1998, and particularly strong after accession of WTO at the end of 2001. There are no further recessions in this period. Significant slowdown in economic activity is not seen either, except perhaps briefly in 2000–2001 which correspond to a US recession and in 2008–2009 which corresponds to the Great Financial Crisis and global recession (see Fig. 1).

3 Creating the Composite Index of Leading Indicators

In China, only a few of the items approximate the well-known leading variables long used in the United States and Europe—notably the M2 money supply adjusted for inflation and the stock price index. Most represent types of investment and related data for fixed assets, real estate, and construction starts; these will at least sound familiar and not be entirely surprising. But data on investment commitments (new orders, contracts) are missing; the series on total floor space and residential floor space under construction, which may be analogous to building starts or permits, may not be reliably leading. Also lacking are labor market indicators such as the average workweek and unemployment insurance claims. So the choices are inevitably limited and tentative. After an intensive search for acceptable leading indicators, we compiled a short list of 22 potential candidates for a composite leading index for China.[11] As the structure of the Chinese economy changes and new and better statistics become available, the selection of the leading indicators will likely change to benefit from these new developments. The aim was to create a composite index with broad coverage of the economy while using indicators selected on sound economic reasoning. The composite index should be able to improve on the predictive performance of the individual components because it brings about a better estimate of the cyclical movement of leading sectors of the economy.

Averaging several components together in the index causes the noisy portions of the data to cancel one another. We focus explicitly on economic reasoning and coverage because of the scarcity and very short history of high-frequency data series in China. There is insufficient historical evidence to choose indicators based on empirical performance alone. With this goal in mind, we have identified and incorporated the best performing indicators in a composite leading index. In the initial publication of the LEI in May 2010, its composition consisted of the selected six indicators (see Table 2, column 1).[12]

We considered the sectoral coverage of the indicators we have identified to represent as broadly as possible the leading sectors of the Chinese economy. The proposed LEI gives highest weight in its composition to manufacturing (three of six indicators) largely because there are many more indicators related to manufacturing in China. Attaching a strong weight to manufacturing may be justified given its large share of GDP (approximately one-third) and strong cyclicality.

We did not include stock prices and money supply as cyclical indicators (these variables have been traditionally part of composite leading indicators in other countries). The share of the financial sector in the Chinese economy was less than 10% of GDP; furthermore, the total loan series (later, medium- to long-term loans) that we proposed to use as a component is highly correlated with money supply M2

[11]See the working paper online for more detailed information on each of these potential candidates Adams et al. (2010).

[12]See The Conference Board press release at https://www.conference-board.org/data/bciarchive.cfm?cid=11&pid=3912

Table 2 Components of *The Conference Board Leading Economic Index*® (LEI) for China

Initial set of leading indicators (May 2010 to April 2016)	Current set of leading indicators (May 2016–present)
(1)	(2)
Total loans issued by financial institutions (Billions of 2010 yuan, deflated by PPI)	Medium- to long-term loans issued by financial institutions (Billions of 2010 yuan, deflated by PPI)
NBS manufacturing PMI subindices: PMI new export orders (from 2005)/exports in billions of US$ (prior to 2005) deflated by PPI	NBS manufacturing PMI subindices: PMI new export orders (from 2005)/exports in billions of US$ (prior to 2005) deflated by PPI
NBS manufacturing PMI subindices: PMI supplier deliveries	Logistics prosperity index
People's Bank of China (PBoC) 5000 Industry Enterprises Diffusion Index: Raw Materials Supply Index (discontinued in 2013)	Omitted as a component in 2013
NBS Consumer Expectations Index	NBS Consumer Expectations Index
Total floor space started (Millions of square meters)	Total floor space started (Millions of square meters)
–	People's Bank of China (PBoC) 5000 Industry Enterprises Diffusion Index: Profitability (S.A.)
–	City labor market: demand (thousands of people, Q)
–	Imports: machinery and transport equipment (billions of US$, deflated by import price index)

Note: Series are seasonally adjusted by The Conference Board (including an adjustment for Chinese New Year effects) where necessary. The lists of selected components for each version of the LEI are provided on The Conference Board web site; please see https://www.conference-board.org/data/bcicountry.cfm?cid=11. Also see Adams et al. (2010) and The Conference Board (2013)
Source: The Conference Board

and stock prices. We believe including only the loan series (as the best financial indicator) avoided overweighting the financial sector as well as avoiding problems from the less adequate nature of money supply M2 and Shanghai Stock Index. However, this meant that the parts of money supply M2's fluctuations that are less correlated with loans (currency in circulation and foreign reserves) were not included in the LEI. The index of stock prices was also not included because of the less developed nature of the stock market considering the volume of transactions and the influence of government policy actions on stock prices.

As discussed below, the list of components had to be revised in 2016, and the current list of components is presented in column 2 of Table 2 (graphs of the current components are presented in the appendix).[13] Changes to the composition in *The Conference Board Leading Economic Index*® (LEI) for China include:

[13]In addition to the economic reasoning behind the selection of the components, we also checked the robustness of our selection by comparing the turning points of the indicators with the turning

1. Replace the total bank loans by financial institutes' series with medium- to long-term bank loans by financial institutes (after January 1999). The total bank loans by financial institutes' series are a sum of short-, medium-, and long-term loans, loans to industrial sector, loans to commercial sector, loans to construction sector, loans to agricultural sector, and other loans. Short-term bank lending since 2007 has been associated with real estate and stock market speculation and is often used to refinance existing debt. Therefore, we chose to replace the total loans series with medium- to long-term loans which represent about 55 percent of total loans and tend to be a better measure of lending that is related to real economic activity.
2. Replace the inverted PMI manufactory index: supply delivery subindex series with the logistics prosperity index series. The supplier delivery subindex asks purchasing managers about how long it takes for companies to receive shipments from their suppliers. As demand for manufacturing supplies increases, delivery times tend to slowdown. When the proportion of supplier managers reporting slower deliveries rises, this subindex rises and vice versa. However, this series tends to coincide with current economic conditions and has been highly volatile. After careful evaluation, we have chosen to replace this series with the logistics prosperity index (LPI) series, which is a monthly survey that covers over 300 logistics enterprises all over China. The data are compiled from enterprises' responses about their logistics activities and inventory situations and therefore provides a broader and earlier indication of logistics activities. The series is useful as a leading indicator of economic and business conditions in China.
3. Add the People's Bank of China (PBoC) 5000 Industry Enterprises Survey: Profitability series. This business survey is conducted quarterly and covers the profitability of state-owned large- and medium-sized industrial enterprises, collectively owned enterprises, and joint venture, foreign-funded, as well as shareholding industrial enterprises. Quarterly series are linearly interpolated to the monthly frequency. Measured in percentages, the index ranges from 0 to 100. Profitability is improving when the diffusion index ascends, and vice versa. The surveyed enterprises cover 27 industries and the outcomes of the survey reflect business profitability across the majority of China's industry.
4. Add the city labor market: demand series. This series is published on a quarterly basis, but the data is based on a monthly survey that covers about 100 of the largest cities in China, which represent more than 70% of China's economy. The survey reflects the number of monthly online job wanted ads in these cities and can provide an early signal of labor demand as well as overall expectations of economic conditions.
5. Add a new component, imports: machinery and transport equipment series. The imports series is calculated at CIF and refers to the real value of machinery and transport equipment imported across the border of China. This indicator is a

points of the CEI (both in detrended form). See Adams et al. (2010) for more on the robustness of the selection.

useful measurement of capital investment, which leads activities in the manufacturing, industry, as well as transportation sectors in the economy.
6. Eliminate the PBoC 5000 Industrial Enterprise Diffusion Index: the Raw Materials Supply subindex series which was discontinued by the publisher in 2013.

Such comprehensive benchmark revisions which change the underlying composition on the composite indexes are sometimes necessary. But, these types of extensive revisions should be done infrequently in order not to harm the continuity and consistency of the indexes. In this case, some series were discontinued and had to be replaced and some series' performance as leading indicators was not adequate. The comprehensive revisions also take into account the changing structural aspect of economies, especially emerging economies, as well.

4 Growth Cycles in the Chinese Economy

Because China has a high growth economy with a rapidly transforming economic structure, it might not be too surprising to observe only one classical business cycle recession. However, as is often the case in emerging economies, the Chinese economy exhibits growth cycles which are defined as fluctuations in deviations from a long-term trend. The CEI can facilitate the identification of such a growth cycle chronology when its trend is estimated and removed. Applying the Bry-Boschan algorithm to the resulting deviations from trend will determine the turning points of the growth cycle. Figure 2 shows the growth cycle component of the CEI graphed with shaded areas that denote the chronology of peaks and troughs of the growth cycle. Table 3 presents the growth cycle chronology for China.

The deviations from trend in the LEI series have a larger amplitude than their counterparts in the CEI series. Nevertheless, the two deviation series are highly correlated, and despite some erratic movements, the LEI series appears to track the CEI series, albeit less consistently. For the February 1988 and December 2013 growth cycle peaks in the CEI, the LEI peaks lead by 1 and 19 months, respectively. For the June 1989 and April 2014 growth cycle troughs, the LEI troughs lead by 8 and 20 months, respectively. However, the turning points in the LEI for the remaining growth cycle slowdowns are either lagging or missed despite the high correlation between the two series (correlation coefficient of 0.33 between the two deviations from trend series). The correlation between the year-over-year growth rates of the LEI and CEI is almost double the correlation between the deviation from trend series, and the smoother growth rates might be more helpful in tracking the growth cycle. More research is needed to examine the dynamic interactions between these indexes as cyclical measures and forecasting tools.

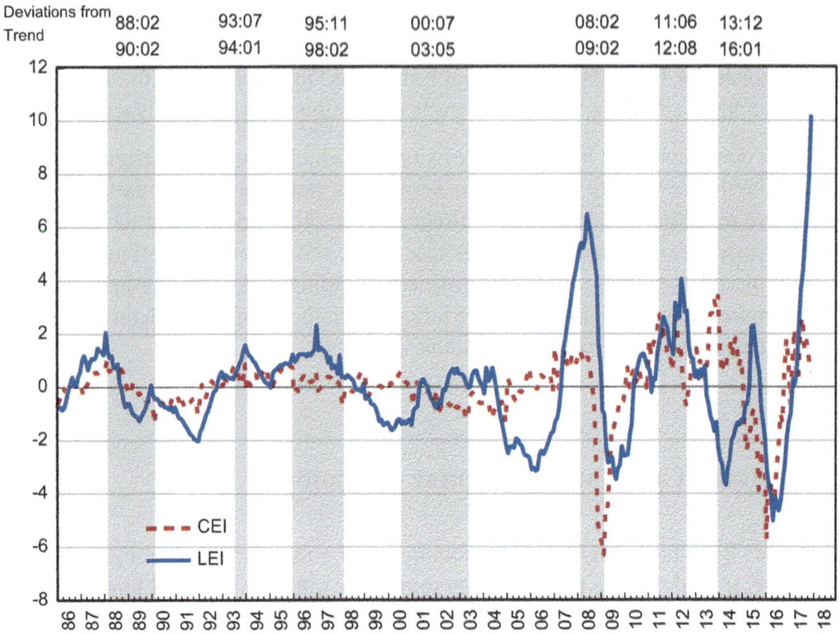

Fig. 2 Growth cycles: coincident and leading indexes for China, 1986–2017. Note: The shaded areas represent growth cycles in the Chinese economy. The growth cycle chronology of turning points was determined by applying the Bry-Boschan algorithm to the deviations from trend in the CEI. The long-term trend was estimated using the Hodrick-Presscott trend (sigma = 4). Source: The Conference Board and authors' calculations

Table 3 Growth cycle peaks and troughs based on CEI

Peak	Trough
February 1988	February 1990
July 1993	January 1994
November 1995	February 1998
July 2000	May 2003
February 2008	February 2009
June 2011	August 2012
December 2013	January 2016

Note: See note to Fig. 2
Source: The Conference Board and authors' calculations

5 Concluding Remarks

The carefully selected indicators were combined into composite indexes of coincident and leading indicators which, respectively, track and lead the economic cycles and the trend in China's evolving economy fairly well and do so somewhat more consistently than the individual indicators. The leading index leads the business cycle peak in September 1988 by 8 months and the trough of February 1990 also by

8 months. Then, it shows a rapid recovery following the recession trough that continues until 1992. Between 1992 and 1994, the growth trend in the leading economic index (LEI) slows down considerably before picking up again after 1999. Since 1999 the LEI has expanded continuously, only interrupted by fairly short-lived slowdowns. The deviations from trend in the two composite indexes, leading economic index (LEI) and coincident economic index (CEI), are correlated, and the cross-correlations suggest there might be somewhat complex feedback relationships between the coincident and leading indicators of the Chinese economy. The investigation of these relationships and the evaluation of the real-time out-of-sample performance of the LEI is the subject of future research.

While the research described in this chapter showed that the business cycle indicators' approach can be applied to a rapidly growing emerging economy such as China's, it also highlighted the major challenges in doing so. The main departure in the development of the cyclical indexes for China was to rely more heavily on economic reasoning and to consider the growth cycle chronology in the evaluation and selection of individual indicators.[14] The main areas of extension to improve the usefulness of the proposed LEI lie in better quantitative data on investment commitments (new orders, contracts) measuring demand for capital goods and for residential and commercial construction. Another area of improvement is labor market indicators such as the average workweek and unemployment insurance claims that are not currently available.

As the Chinese economy evolves and develops further, the growth of new sectors will likely change the structural relationship between data series—thus, it will be essential to periodically revisit the selection of indicators for the China LEI to ensure they continue to fulfill the criteria identified. Furthermore, China's statistical system will likely improve in the future, making further improvements in the selection of the leading indicators possible.

[14]See Adams et al. (2010).

Appendix

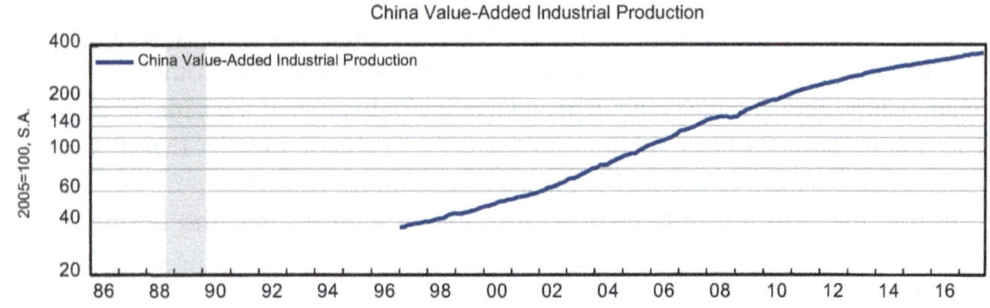

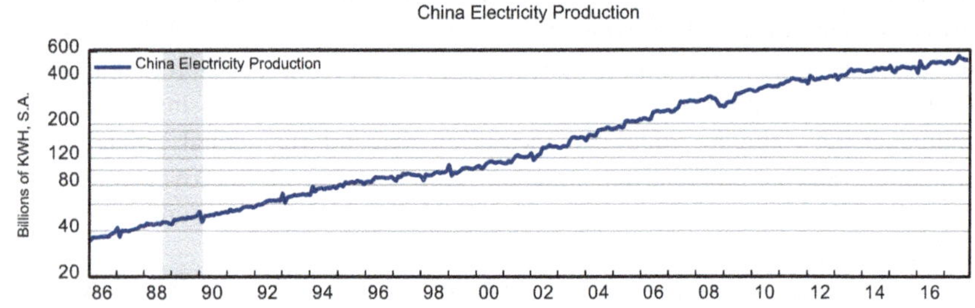

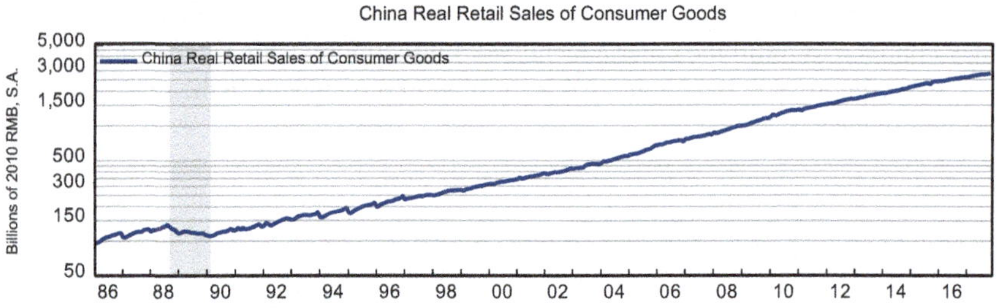

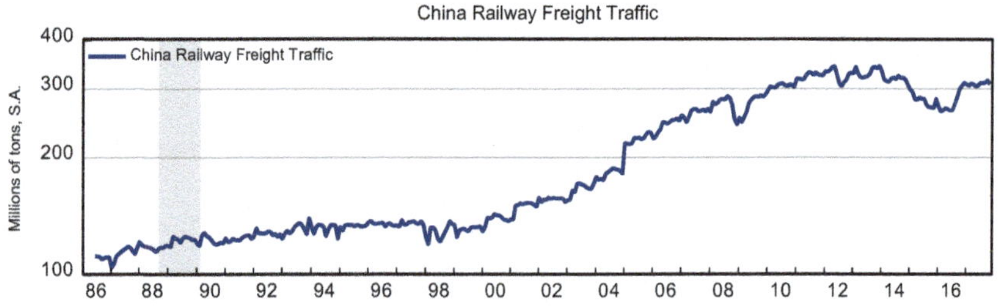

Source: The Conference Board Business Cycle Indicators' Database for China

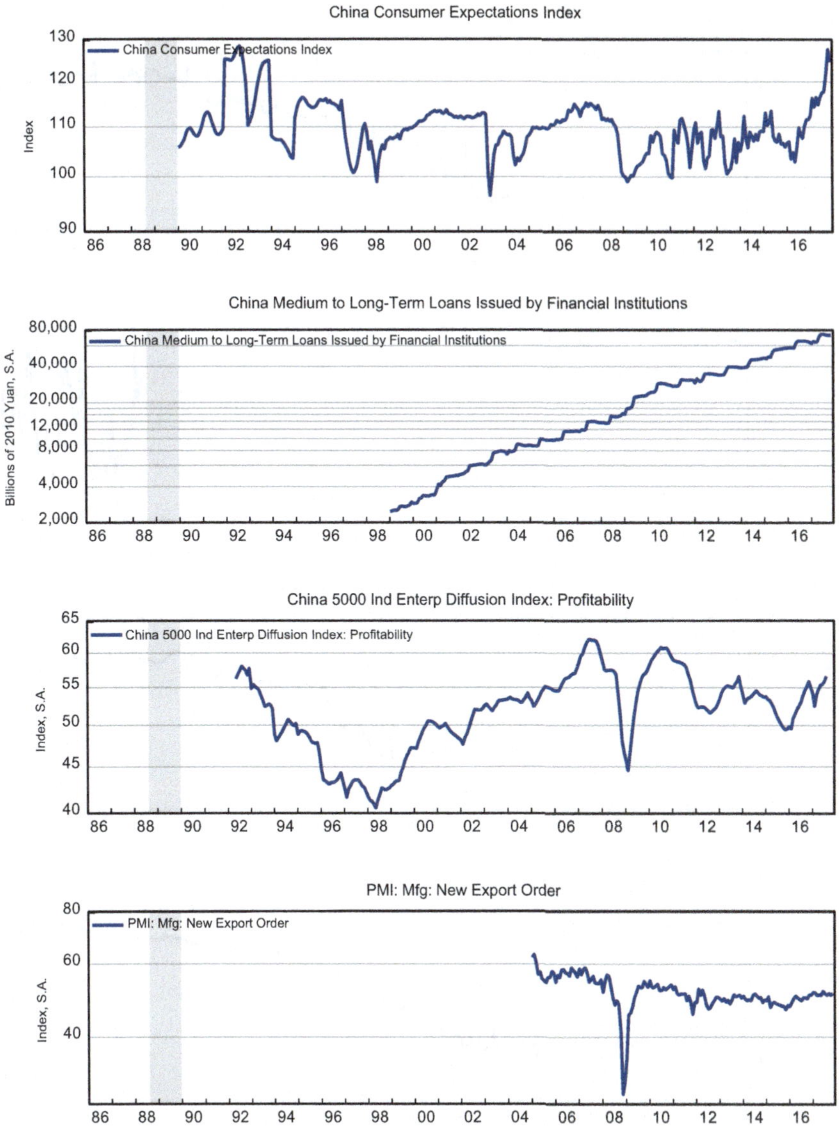

Source: The Conference Board Business Cycle Indicators' Database for China

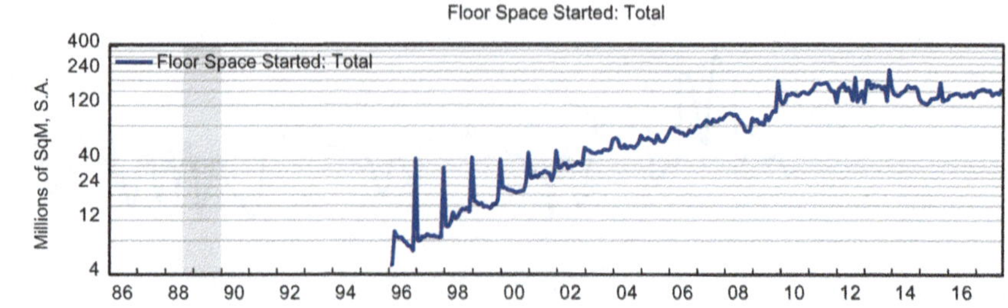

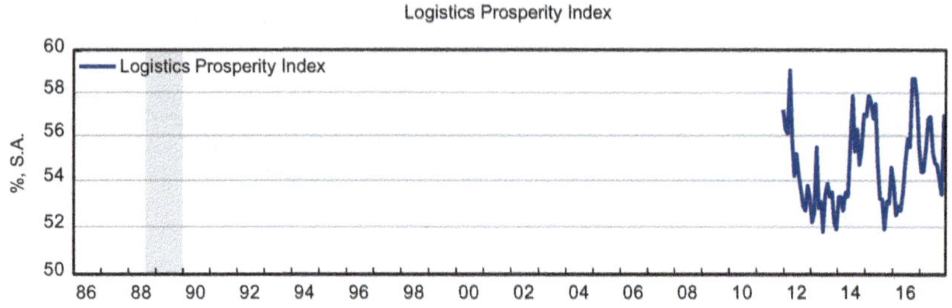

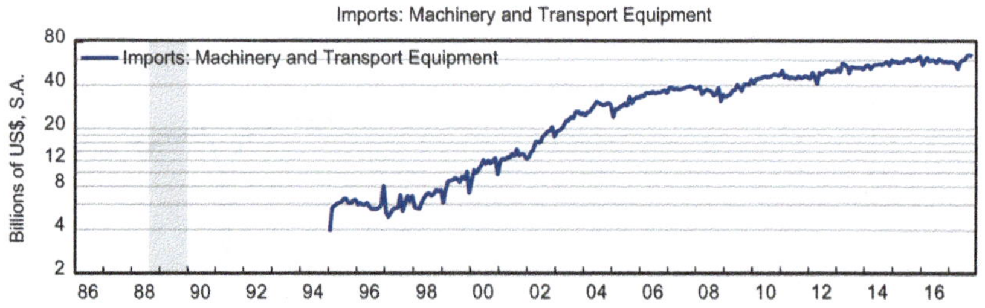

Source: The Conference Board Business Cycle Indicators' Database for China

References

Adams B, Bottelier P, Ozyildirim A, Sima-Friedman J (2010) On the selection of leading economic indicators for China. The Conference Board, Economics Program Working Paper #10-02, 2010. https://www.conference-board.org/pdf_free/workingpapers/EPWP1002.pdf

Bry G, Boschan C (1971) Cyclical analysis of economic time series: selected procedures and computer programs. NBER Technical Working Paper No. 20
Cai Y (2000) Between state and peasant: local cadres and statistical reporting in rural China. China Q 163:783–805
Guo F, Ozyildirim A, Zarnowitz V (2008) On the measurement and analysis of aggregate economic activity for China: the coincident economic indicators approach. The Conference Board, Economics Program Working Paper #08 – 01, 2008. https://www.conference-board.org/pdf_free/workingpapers/E-0027-08-WP.pdf
Keidel A (2001) China's GDP expenditure accounts. China Econ Rev 12:355–367
Lahiri K, Stekler HO, Yao VW, Young P (2003) Monthly output index for the U.S. transportation sector. J Transp Stat 6(2/3):1–28
Maddison A (1998) Chinese economic performance in the long run. Development Centre of the Organisation for Economic Co-operation and Development, Paris
Ozyildirim A (2018) Compiling cyclical composite indexes: The Conference Board indicators approach. In: Business cycles in BRICS. Springer, Cham
Rawski TG (2001) What is happening to China's GDP statistics? China Econ Rev 12:25–34
The Conference Board (TCB) (2001) Business cycle indicators handbook. The Conference Board, New York
The Conference Board (TCB) (2013) Understanding business cycles: the indicators approach to forecasting for agility. The Conference Board www.conference-board.org/data/bci.cfm
Wu HX (2007) The Chinese GDP growth rate puzzle: how fast has the Chinese economy grown? Asian Econ Pap 6(1):1–23
Xu X (2004) China's gross domestic product estimation. China Econ Rev 15(3):302–322
Zarnowitz V (2001) Coincident Indicators and the dating of business cycles. Bus Cycle Indic 8:3–4

The SARB's Composite Business Cycle Indicators

J. C. Venter

1 Introduction

There is a fairly well-established history of compiling and disseminating composite business cycle indicators in South Africa, dating back to 1977 when the first composite leading and coincident indicators were developed by J.E.M. Van Coller. This was followed by the development of composite leading, coincident and lagging business cycle indicators at the South African Reserve Bank (SARB) a few years later in 1983.

Although briefly mentioning the composite indicators developed by Van Coller as a way of providing some historical context, this chapter's main focus is to provide a comprehensive summary of the historical development of the composite business cycle indicators developed at, and still disseminated by, the SARB. The chapter is organised accordingly; after briefly discussing the composite business cycle indicators developed by Van Coller, those currently disseminated by the SARB will be analysed in greater detail. The component indicators selected by the SARB, the selection criteria used and the compilation methodology applied will be described. A historical evaluation of the usefulness of the SARB's composite business cycle indicators is then presented. Before concluding, the chapter provides information on the current dissemination of the SARB's composite business cycle indicators.

J. C. Venter (✉)
South African Reserve Bank, Pretoria, South Africa
e-mail: iaan.venter@resbank.co.za

S. Smirnov et al. (eds.), *Business Cycles in BRICS*, Societies and Political Orders in Transition, https://doi.org/10.1007/978-3-319-90017-9_26

2 Van Coller's Composite Business Cycle Indicators

The first known set of composite business cycle indicators for the South African economy, namely a composite leading and coincident indicator, was developed by J.E.M. Van Coller and was first published by the Bureau for Economic Research (BER) at Stellenbosch University in their *Trends* publication in December 1977 (Van Coller 1980: 41).

Although Van Coller (1980: 44) emphasised that the main aim of selecting component indicators for inclusion in the composite indicators was to increase the ability of the composite indices to produce reliable turning point signals, he nevertheless made use of an objective scoring system against which each individual indicator was rated. Van Coller employed a modified version of the scoring system developed by Zarnowitz and Boschan (1975). Since the availability and reliability of data were not as comprehensive in South Africa as in the United States (US) at the time, and because the South African economy was much smaller than the US economy, Van Coller made some adjustment to Zarnowitz and Boschan's scoring system, in particular to the criteria related to statistical adequacy and conformity to the historical business cycle. The criterion of statistical adequacy was dropped altogether, because of the difficulty experienced by Van Coller in locating a sufficient number of good cyclical indicators for South Africa, compared to what was available for the US economy.

Van Coller eventually selected nine leading indicators and five coincident indicators to include in his composite business cycle indicators. A departure from the methodology followed in the US was to include candidate indicators that reflected the relative openness of the South African economy, vis-à-vis the US economy. Van Coller (1980: 54) argued that this justified the inclusion of indicators such as the physical volume of mining production and the level of gold and foreign exchange reserves in the composite leading business cycle indicator, in addition to the fairly high scores that these series obtained during the evaluation process. Van Coller's component indicators are listed in Table 1.

Van Coller (1980: 63) stated that a number of potentially good cyclical indicators were expected to become more timely in future, which would make them candidates for possible inclusion in the composite indicators. Although Van Coller was never formally employed by the BER, following an arrangement with the BER, his composite business cycle indicators were published in their *Trends* publication until June 1994.[1] Subsequently, the BER reverted to publishing the composite business cycle indicators developed and disseminated by the SARB, which is discussed in the following section.

[1]The author is indebted to Messrs. Murray Pellissier and George Kershoff of the BER for providing additional information regarding the publication of Van Coller's composite business cycle indicators.

Table 1 Component indicators included in Van Coller's composite leading and coincident business cycle indicators

Leading indicators	Coincident indicators
(1) Industrial share prices	(1) Physical volume of manufacturing production
(2) Gold and foreign exchange reserves	(2) Wholesale sales (in constant 1970 prices)
(3) Car sales	(3) Retail sales (in constant 1975 prices)
(4) Money supply (M1)	(4) Imports (in constant 1970 prices)
(5) Physical volume of mining production	(5) Registered number of unemployed: Whites, Coloureds and Asians (inverse)
(6) Building plans—dwelling houses	
(7) Insolvencies (inverse)	
(8) New companies registered	
(9) Durables—unfilled orders	

3 The South African Reserve Bank's Composite Business Cycle Indicators

The SARB has determined reference turning points in the South African business cycle since 1970 (Smit and Van der Walt 1970) for the post-World War II period.[2] However, the SARB only developed and published composite business cycle indicators for the first time in 1983 (Van der Walt 1983). Following this initial study and publication, the SARB's composite business cycle indicators have undergone numerous subsequent revisions and updates, described in a number of articles, notes and text boxes published in various issues of the SARB's *Quarterly Bulletin*. The following three subsections describe the evolution of the SARB's composite business cycle indicators in terms of the selection criteria used, the component time series included and the compilation methodology employed—from the initial study by Van der Walt up to the most recent revision in 2015.

3.1 Selection Criteria and Aggregation Methodology Used

One of the main reasons why the SARB only published composite business cycle indicators from 1983 was that a large number of time series needed to be available over a fairly long uninterrupted period in order to identify reliable indicators of cyclical change in the South African economy. Notable advances in the collection of

[2]The SARB has always determined reference turning points in the South African business cycle according to the growth cycle definition of business cycles, rather than the classical definition. Thus, the SARB's upward and downward phases of the business cycle demarcate periods when aggregate economic activity has either increased or decreased relative to its long-term trend.

economic statistics were made in South Africa during the 1960s and 1970s, enabling a comprehensive investigation into the suitability of economic indicators for inclusion in a composite leading, coincident and lagging business cycle indicator.

In the original study by Van der Walt (1983: 53), the cyclical component of each individual time series was isolated and its amplitude compared to that of other time series in order to gauge its cyclical sensitivity. The cyclical component of each time series was calculated as the residual, after elimination of seasonal fluctuations, the long-term trend and random (irregular) fluctuations. The specific turning points (peaks and troughs) of the cyclical component of each time series were also analysed to determine the consistency of the indicator's timing relation with the general business cycle. In determining specific turning points, the minimum length of an upswing or downswing was set at 6 months and that of a full cycle at 15 months (Van der Walt 1983: 54).

Van der Walt chose 109 time series, representing six economic processes that were identified internationally and also used by Van Coller (1980: 50), to evaluate for possible inclusion in one of the composite business cycle indicators. These processes are:

1. Money and credit
2. Fixed capital investment
3. Production, income, consumption and trade
4. Inventories and inventory investment
5. Prices, costs and profits
6. Employment and unemployment

The selected time series were divided into three groups, namely, leading, coincident and lagging business cycle indicators. An indicator was classified as leading if the specific turning points of its cyclical component occurred ahead of both reference peaks and troughs in the business cycle by a median of 3 months or more. Likewise, an indicator was classified as coincident if the median lead/lag was not more than 2 months, while indicators with a median lag of 3 months or more were classified as lagging business cycle indicators. In order to reduce subjective judgement in the choice of component series to be included in the three composite business cycle indicators, Van der Walt (1983: 53) applied an objective scoring system with criteria similar to that used by Van Coller. In developing his scoring system (as part of his unpublished D.Com thesis), Van der Walt made use of a number of similar international studies. As the criteria of 'consistency of timing' and 'conformity to the business cycle' were regarded as the most important, they received a combined weight of 55%. The criterion of 'economic meaning' received a weight of 15%, while the criteria of 'statistical adequacy', 'smoothness' and 'timeliness' were allotted a weight of 10% each (Van der Walt 1982: 274).

The SARB's methodology for constructing composite business cycle indicators has remained broadly the same since its inception in 1983, with only two relatively minor adjustments made over time. The SARB's current compilation methodology is similar to that of The Conference Board (TCB),[3] with two minor differences.

The first difference relates to the standardisation factor used to equalise the volatility of each component time series. The SARB uses the inverse of the average of the absolute values of the monthly changes of each component series, while TCB uses the inverse of the standard deviation of the monthly changes of each component series.

Second, the SARB's three composite business cycle indicators are trend-adjusted so that they all reflect a similar long-term trend to that of the real gross value added excluding agriculture. This step enhances the visual presentation of the composite business cycle indicators while also providing their long-term trends with some economic meaning, since the inherent long-term trends displayed by the composite leading, coincident and lagging business cycle indicators all differ and are devoid of any specific economic relevance.

Over time, the following two methodological changes were affected to the SARB's composite business cycle indicators:

- Initially, the composite indicators were smoothed somewhat by using a 3-month moving average of the symmetrical month-to-month percentage changes of each component time series in the compilation methodology. Following the 1994 revision, the actual symmetrical month-to-month percentage changes were used, allowing analysts to observe the exact changes in each month (Van der Walt and Pretorius 1994: 31). An added advantage of this change was that the composite indicators were available for an additional month, improving its timeliness.
- During the 2004 revisions, the weighting structure of the composite indicators was changed, resulting in each individual component indicator being weighted equally in the respective composite indicators. Before, the weight of each individual component series was based on the score it obtained when evaluated with the objective scoring system.

3.2 Components of the SARB's Composite Business Cycle Indicators

3.2.1 The Original 1983 Version

In the original study by Van der Walt, a fairly large number of time series (23) were selected to be included in the SARB's first composite leading business cycle indicator. They are listed in Table 2. As discussed in Van der Walt (1983: 56), the selected components could be classified into three broad groups, namely, indicators related to future production and expenditure (such as new mortgage loans granted,

[3]For a detailed description of this methodology, see Ozyildirim (2018).

Table 2 Components of the SARB's composite leading business cycle indicator

Versions				
1983	1994	2004	2007	2015
– M1 money supply: percentage change over 12 months – Net gold and other foreign reserves – Value of new mortgage loans and readvances granted by building societies for the erection of buildings – Change in discounts and advances by commercial banks	– Real M1 money supply (deflated with the CPI): percentage change over 12 months – Net gold and other foreign exchange reserves – Consumer credit at constant prices	– Real M1 money supply (deflated with CPI): 6-month smoothed growth rate	– Real M1 money supply (deflated with CPI): 6-month smoothed growth rate	– Real M1 money supply (deflated with CPI): 6-month smoothed growth rate
– Value of building plans passed at constant prices: residential buildings – Net number of new companies registered – Value of real-estate transactions – Value of investments in prescribed assets by building societies	– Number of residential building plans passed – Net number of new companies registered – Number of real-estate transactions	– Number of residential building plans passed for flats, townhouses and houses larger than 80 m^2	– Number of residential building plans passed for flats, townhouses and houses larger than 80 m^2	– Number of residential building plans passed for flats, townhouses and houses larger than 80 m^2
– Ratio of inventories to sales in manufacturing	– Opinion survey of stocks in relation to demand: manufacturing and trade	– Opinion survey of stocks in relation to demand: manufacturing and trade		
– Number of new motorcars sold – Utilisation of production capacity in manufacturing: durable goods	– Number of new motor vehicles sold – Domestic manufacturing order volumes, net balance – Physical	– Domestic manufacturing order volumes, net balance – BER business confidence index: manufacturing,	– Number of new passenger vehicles sold: percentage change over 12 months – Domestic manufacturing order volumes,	– Number of new passenger vehicles sold: percentage change over 12 months – Domestic manufacturing

(continued)

Table 2 (continued)

Versions				
1983	1994	2004	2007	2015
– Physical volume of mining production, excluding gold – Physical volume of gold ore milled – Physical volume of steel exports – Value of merchandise exports at constant prices, excluding gold	volume of mining production, excluding gold – Physical volume of gold ore milled – BER business confidence index: manufacturing, construction and trade – International business cycle indicator: industrial production – Value of merchandise exports, excluding gold and agriculture	construction and trade – Composite leading business cycle indicator of South Africa's major trading partner countries: percentage change over 12 months	net balance (half weight) – BER business confidence index: manufacturing, construction and trade – Composite leading business cycle indicator of South Africa's major trading partner countries: percentage change over 12 months	order volumes, net balance (half weight) – RMB/BER business confidence index – Composite leading business cycle indicator of South Africa's major trading partner countries: percentage change over 12 months
– Company profits, after tax – Dividend yield on industrial shares – Tender Treasury bill discount rate – London gold price in rand – Prices of all classes of shares – Prices of industrial and commercial shares – Ratio of output prices to unit labour cost in manufacturing	– Company profits, after tax – Tender Treasury bill discount rate – London gold price in rand – Commodity prices in US dollars for a basket of South Africa's export commodities: percentage change over 12 months – Prices of all classes of shares – Ratio of output prices to unit labour cost in manufacturing	– Gross operating surplus as a percentage of gross domestic product – Interest rate spread: 10-year government bond less 91-day Treasury bills – Index of commodity prices in US dollar for a basket of South Africa's export commodities: 6-month smoothed growth rate – Index of prices of all classes of shares traded on the JSE: 6-month smoothed growth rate – Labour productivity in manufacturing: 6-month smoothed growth rate	– Gross operating surplus as a percentage of gross domestic product – Interest rate spread: 10-year government bond less 91-day Treasury bills – Index of commodity prices in US dollar for a basket of South Africa's export commodities – Index of prices of all classes of shares traded on the JSE	– Gross operating surplus as a percentage of gross domestic product – Interest rate spread: 10-year government bond less 91-day Treasury bills – Index of commodity prices in US dollar for a basket of South Africa's export commodities

(continued)

Table 2 (continued)

Versions				
1983	1994	2004	2007	2015
– Total employment in the mining sector	– Overtime hours as percentage of ordinary hours worked in manufacturing	– Average hours worked per factory worker in manufacturing, net balance – Job advertisement space in *The Sunday Times* newspaper: 6-month smoothed growth rate	– Average hours worked per factory worker in manufacturing, net balance (half weight) – Job advertisement space in *The Sunday Times* newspaper: percentage change over 12 months	– Average hours worked per factory worker in manufacturing, net balance (half weight) – Job advertisement space in *The Sunday Times* newspaper: percentage change over 12 months

Sources: Van der Walt BE (1983)
Van der Walt BE and Pretorius WS (1994)
Venter JC (2004)
Venter JC (2007)
SARB (2015)
Note: The rows in the table separate economic indicators into the six different economic processes mentioned in Sect. 3.1

the capacity utilisation of durable goods production, residential building plans passed), indicators reflecting the future course of the economy and the general business climate (such as share prices, dividend yields, new companies registered, company profits) and indicators related to foreign demand for South African goods (such as merchandise exports, steel exports, the gold price, foreign reserves, mining production and employment). The inclusion of indicators from the third group represented a departure from the methodology originally developed and followed at the NBER in the US, which only included leading indicators that reflected the endogenous nature of the business cycle. By including quite a number of indicators from this third group, Van der Walt followed in the footsteps of Van Coller (1980), who incorporated two such indicators in his composite leading business cycle indicator, on account of South Africa being a small, open, commodity-exporting economy.

Van der Walt included 11 component time series in the SARB's first composite coincident business cycle indicator (listed in Table 3), mostly representing comprehensive measures of production, consumption and employment. The first composite lagging business cycle indicator developed in South Africa also comprised of 11 component time series (listed in Table 4), largely representing measures of total employment, fixed investment, the building and construction industry, as well as unit labour cost.

Table 3 Components of the SARB's composite coincident business cycle indicator

Versions				
1983	1994	2004	2007	2015
– Gross domestic product at constant prices, excluding agriculture	– Gross value added at constant prices, excluding agriculture, forestry and fishing	– Gross value added at constant prices, excluding agriculture, forestry and fishing	– Gross value added at constant prices, excluding agriculture, forestry and fishing	No change
– Value of retail trade sales at constant prices – Value of wholesale, retail and motorcar sales at constant prices	– Value of wholesale, retail and new vehicle sales at constant prices	– Value of wholesale, retail and new vehicle sales at constant prices	– Value of retail and new vehicle sales at constant prices	
– Utilisation of production capacity in manufacturing	– Utilisation of production capacity in manufacturing	– Utilisation of production capacity in manufacturing	– Utilisation of production capacity in manufacturing	
– Employment in manufacturing, mining and the construction sector – Registered unemployed Whites, Coloureds and Asians	– Employment in the manufacturing, mining and construction sectors	– Total formal non-agricultural employment	– Total formal non-agricultural employment	
– Physical volume of manufacturing production: durable goods – Physical volume of manufacturing production: non-durable goods	– Physical volume of manufacturing production: durable goods – Physical volume of manufacturing production: non-durable goods	– Industrial production index	– Industrial production index	
– Value of imports at constant prices, excluding mineral products	– Value of imports at constant prices, excluding mineral products			
– Value of total building plans passed				
– Number of mortgages registered				

Sources: Van der Walt BE (1983)
Van der Walt BE and Pretorius WS (1994)
Venter JC (2004)
Venter JC (2007)
Note: The rows in the table separate economic indicators into the six different economic processes mentioned in Sect. 3.1

Table 4 Components of the SARB's composite lagging business cycle indicator

Versions				
1983	1994	2004	2007	2015
– Labour cost per unit of physical volume of manufacturing production	– Nominal labour cost per unit of production in the manufacturing sector	No change	– Nominal labour cost per unit of production in the manufacturing sector (percentage change over four quarters) – Predominant prime overdraft rate of banks	No change
– Value of fixed investment in machinery and equipment – Value of residential buildings completed – Value of all buildings completed	– Value of fixed investment in machinery and equipment – Value of non-residential buildings completed at constant prices		– Ratio of gross fixed capital formation in machinery and equipment to final consumption expenditure on goods by households – Value of non-residential buildings completed at constant prices	
– Physical volume of mining production of building materials – Value of unfilled orders as percentage of sales in manufacturing – Value of wholesale sales of metals, machinery and equipment at constant prices – Number of new commercial vehicles sold	– Physical volume of mining production of building materials – Value of unfilled orders as percentage of sales in manufacturing		– Cement sales in tons	
	– Value of industrial and commercial inventories at constant prices		– Ratio of inventories to sales in manufacturing and trade	
– Employment in non-agricultural sectors – Number of appointments per 100 production workers in manufacturing – Total number of hours worked by production workers in the construction sector	– Employment in non-agricultural sectors – Total number of hours worked by production workers in the construction sector			

(continued)

Table 4 (continued)

Versions				
1983	1994	2004	2007	2015
			– Ratio of households' use of instalment sale credit to their disposable income	

Sources: Van der Walt BE (1983)
Van der Walt BE and Pretorius WS (1994)
Venter JC (2007)
Note: The rows in the table separate economic indicators into the six different economic processes mentioned in Sect. 3.1

3.2.2 The 1994 Revision

During the first comprehensive revision to the SARB's composite business cycle indicators (Van der Walt and Pretorius 1994), the 23 component indicators originally included in the composite leading indicator were reduced to 21 (see Table 2). The revision was necessitated by a number of developments, such as a change in the size and structure of the economy, the erosion of comparability or continuity of some time series due to institutional and policy changes as well as the identification of a number of new cyclically sensitive economic indicators. All the previously included indicators and a number of newly chosen ones were subjected to the same objective scoring system that was applied in the initial study by Van der Walt.

Three of the composite leading business cycle indicator's original components were excluded due to their unstable cyclical timing relationship. They were:

- Total mining sector employment
- The utilisation of production capacity for durable manufactured goods
- The physical volume of steel exports

Another two component series were omitted because they were over-represented in the composite leading indicator, namely:

- The prices of industrial and commercial shares
- The dividend yield on industrial shares

In addition, the value of new mortgage loans granted by building societies for the erection of buildings was omitted due to non-comparability of the series over time, while another two components were omitted earlier (the value of investments in prescribed assets by building societies and the change in discounts and advances by commercial banks), with no recorded reason for their earlier omission.

Five of the original components were replaced by related series which performed better during the evaluation, namely:

- The value of real-estate transactions was replaced by the number.
- The real value of merchandise exports (excluding gold) was converted to current prices (now also excluding agriculture).

- The ratio of stocks to sales in manufacturing was replaced by an opinion survey of the ratio of stocks to demand in manufacturing and trade.
- The change in nominal M1 money supply was replaced by the change in real M1 money supply.
- The value of residential building plans passed was replaced by the number.

Six new indicators were included in the composite leading indicator for the first time, namely:

- Overtime hours worked as a percentage of ordinary hours worked in manufacturing
- Consumer credit at constant prices
- An opinion survey of manufacturing orders
- An opinion survey of business confidence in manufacturing, construction and trade
- The 12-month percentage change in an export-weighted commodity price index
- An international business cycle indicator comprising the industrial production indices of eight of South Africa's main trading partner countries (weighted to the relative size of their GDP)

During the 1994 revision, no new indicators were included in the composite coincident indicator. However, four previously included components were omitted (see Table 3), namely, the value of real retail trade sales and the total value of building plans passed (due to their irregular movements and poor timing relation with the business cycle), as well as the series measuring unemployment and the number of mortgage bonds registered (as both were no longer available).

Concerning the composite lagging business cycle indicator, the only new series included was the real value of industrial and commercial inventories, while the two series measuring buildings completed were replaced by one measuring the real value of non-residential buildings completed. Due to inconsistent timing relation with the business cycle, three previously included components were omitted altogether, namely:

- The number of appointments per 100 manufacturing production workers
- The real value of wholesale trade sales of metals, machinery and equipment
- The number of new commercial vehicles sold (see Table 4)

3.2.3 The 2004 Revision

The SARB's composite business cycle indicators underwent another fairly comprehensive evaluation 10 years later, in two separate studies. First, the composite leading and coincident business cycle indicators were reviewed (Venter and Pretorius 2004), followed by a separate review of the composite lagging business cycle indicator which also highlighted its often overlooked usefulness in business cycle analysis (Venter 2004). Following South Africa's first all-inclusive democratic election in April 1994, a number of policy changes including, inter alia, the removal of many trade restrictions between South Africa and the rest of the world and the gradual liberalisation of exchange controls, led to a number of constituent time series of the composite business cycle indicators no longer exhibiting a consistent timing relation with the business cycle.

The composite leading business cycle indicator underwent quite a dramatic revision in 2004, resulting in a marked improvement in its lead time at reference turning points in the business cycle (Venter and Pretorius 2004: 70). The number of components included in the leading indicator was reduced notably from 21 to only 13 (see Table 2). Eleven previously included component series were dropped, ten due to inconsistent timing in relation to business cycle turning points and one because it was no longer available. These were:

- The physical volume of gold ore milled
- The physical volume of mining production (excluding gold)
- The value of merchandise exports (excluding gold and agriculture)
- The ratio of output prices to unit labour cost in manufacturing
- The London gold price in rand
- Company profits after tax
- The net number of new companies registered
- The number of new motor vehicles sold
- Net gold and foreign exchange reserves
- Consumer credit at constant prices
- The number of real-estate transactions

Three new component time series were included in the composite leading indicator for the first time, namely:

- The 6-month smoothed growth rate in the number of column centimetres devoted to job advertisements in *The Sunday Times* newspaper (a nationally distributed newspaper)
- The 6-month smoothed growth rate in labour productivity in the manufacturing sector
- Gross operating surplus as a percentage of gross domestic product

Seven component series were replaced by closely related or slightly altered time series, namely:

- The number of overtime hours as a percentage of normal hours worked in manufacturing was no longer available and was replaced by an opinion survey of the average number of hours worked by factory workers.
- The indicator comprising the industrial production indices of eight of South Africa's main trading partner countries (weighted to the relative size of their GDP) was replaced by the percentage change over 12 months in a new index comprising the composite leading business cycle indicators of the same eight trading partner countries (weighted to South African export values to each country).

- The export commodity price index was now included in a 6-month smoothed growth rate format.
- The real M1 money supply was now included in a 6-month smoothed growth rate format.
- The price index of all shares traded on the Johannesburg Stock Exchange was now also included in a 6-month smoothed growth rate format.
- Building plans passed for houses smaller than 80 m^2 was now excluded from the total number of residential building plans passed (due to government constructing a large number of subsidised small houses).
- The tender Treasury bill discount rate was replaced by an interest rate spread indicator, being the difference between the yield on 10 years and longer government bonds and the yield on 91-day Treasury bills.

Three changes were made to the composite coincident business cycle indicator in 2004 (Venter and Pretorius 2004: 71); the component series measuring real imports was omitted, the employment indicator was expanded to include total formal non-agricultural employment, and the two component series measuring durable and non-durable manufacturing production were replaced by a new industrial production index comprising a weighted aggregation of total manufacturing production, total mining production and electricity generated (see Table 3).

Although the number of component series included in the composite lagging business cycle indicator was only reduced marginally, from eight to seven, during the 2004 revision (see Table 4), only one of the previous eight components was retained unaltered in the revised lagging indicator (Venter 2004: 71). Two component series were included for the first time, namely, the ratio of households' outstanding instalment sale credit to their disposable income and the prime overdraft rate charged by banks.

Three previously included components were omitted from the revised composite lagging indicator, namely:

- The value of unfilled orders as a percentage of sales in the manufacturing sector was no longer available.
- The series measuring formal non-agricultural employment was now included in the composite coincident indicator.
- The number of hours worked by production workers in the construction sector became inconsistent over time.

Four component series were replaced by related or comparable series, namely:

- The value of fixed investment in machinery and equipment was replaced by the ratio of gross fixed capital formation in machinery and equipment to final household consumption expenditure on goods.
- The real value of industrial and commercial inventories was replaced by the ratio of real inventories to real sales in the manufacturing and trade sectors.
- The level of nominal unit labour cost in the manufacturing sector was replaced by its percentage change over 12 months.

– The physical volume of mining production of building materials was replaced by cement sales in tons.

3.2.4 The 2007 Revision

In 2007, a few minor adjustments were made to the SARB's composite leading and coincident business cycle indicators, discussed in Venter (2007), while the lagging indicator was left unchanged. The composite leading business cycle indicator was revised with two specific objectives in mind. Firstly, an over-reliance on indicators measuring activity in the manufacturing sector was addressed, and secondly, the format of some component series was changed to reduce the leading indicator's sensitivity to erratic short-term changes which could possibly be interpreted as false signals. Regarding the first objective, two previously included indicators were omitted, namely, labour productivity growth in manufacturing and the opinion survey measuring stocks in relation to demand in the manufacturing and trade sectors. Furthermore, the weights of the remaining two opinion survey indicators related to the manufacturing sector were reduced to half of each of the other components' weights. In addition, the year-on-year growth rate in new passenger vehicle sales was again added as a component (after it was dropped in 2004) in order to provide an early indication of changes in consumer demand conditions. In order to achieve the second objective, the following changes were made to three of the component series:

– The format in which job advertisement space in *The Sunday Times* newspaper was included was changed from the 6-month smoothed growth rate to the percentage change over 12 months.
– The format in which the share price index was included was changed from the 6-month smoothed growth rate to the level of the index.
– The format in which the commodity price index was included was changed from the 6-month smoothed growth rate to the level of the index.

The revised composite leading business cycle indicator thus comprised of 12 component time series (compared to 13 previously) and was statistically linked to the historical leading indicator in 1999. No changes were made to the component series of the composite coincident and lagging business cycle indicators during the 2007 revisions. However, the long-term trend of the composite coincident indicator was adjusted to more accurately reflect the trend in the real gross value added, excluding agriculture.

3.2.5 The 2015 Revision

The most recent revision to the SARB's composite business cycle indicators was effected in 2015 (SARB 2015: 14). The main objective of the revisions was to redress a few minor distortions that developed as a result of domestic and international structural changes, largely related to the increased integration of South African financial markets with global financial markets and to changes in the composition of South Africa's foreign trading partners. In order to align the composite leading business cycle indicator more closely to domestic real economic developments, the following three changes were made:

- The share price index was discarded as a component of the leading indicator, since South African share price movements appeared to have disconnected from real economic activity after 2000 as a number of dual-listed companies (earning the bulk of their profits offshore) have increasingly been dominating market share on the Johannesburg Stock Exchange.
- The export-weighted index comprising the composite leading business cycle indicators of South Africa's main trading partner countries was expanded to include 12 countries instead of the previous 8, reflecting changes to South Africa's export composition (with exports to China and India in particular becoming increasingly significant).
- The weights within the commodity price index were updated to reflect the export share of each commodity in the index more accurately.

  Although the component series of the composite coincident and lagging business cycle indicators were retained during the 2015 revisions, underlying data revisions and a change in the weighting structure of the industrial production index (included in the composite coincident indicator) was incorporated.

3.3 Why the Frequent Revisions?

A criticism that is sometimes directed at composite business cycle indicators is the seemingly frequent revisions to their component time series. It is argued that the revisions are made to (ex post) improve the leading indicator's ability in particular to pre-empt business cycle turning points. However, as noted by Zarnowitz (1992: 333) in reference to the US composite indicator revisions, a close inspection of the revisions in Tables 2–4 shows that each new list of component series retained several series from the previous one and that most of the changes were substitutions or additions within the same economic process group (demarcated by the rows in Tables 2–4).

The majority of the revisions replaced some time series with other representations of similar variables. This was often due to the availability of a new time series that was viewed as either conceptually or statistically superior to the previously included series or the discontinuation of some time series. Some of the revisions also reflect changes to the structure of the South African economy, such as the declining importance of the gold mining sector since the mid-1980s and the changing composition of South African exports as well as its trading partner countries.

It is also worth noting that the number of component time series included in each composite indicator has gradually decreased with each revision, especially during the initial couple of revisions, as the quality and availability of economic statistics in South Africa have improved and stabilised over time. Furthermore, the number of opinion surveys included in the composite leading business cycle indicator has increased, as more of these indicators became available and replaced some discontinued quantitative economic indicators.

4 Evaluating the SARB's Composite Business Cycle Indicators

The usefulness of any set of composite business cycle indicators depends on the consistency of its timing relation with reference turning points in the business cycle. When the sequence of turning points in the composite business cycle indicators behaves in a consistent manner with respect to the reference turning points in the business cycle, the composite indicators can confidently be employed to develop a sequential signaling system to predict future business cycle turning points. In order to evaluate the usefulness of the SARB's composite business cycle indicators, a historical turning point analysis was done on the inverted lagging indicator, the leading indicator, the ratio of the coincident to lagging indicator, the coincident indicator and the lagging indicator. The analysis was done over the full 57-year history of the SARB's composite business cycle indicators and covered 20 reference turning points—10 peaks and 10 troughs.

The SARB's composite business cycle indicators are depicted in Fig. 1, with the reference turning points in the South African business cycle superimposed on it. Table 5 presents the results separately for leads/lags at peaks and troughs. Peaks and troughs were analysed separately because cyclical indicators typically behave differently around business cycle peaks and troughs. This is also confirmed by the results of this study; on balance, leads/lags at business cycle peaks are longer than at troughs, while the leads/lags at peaks tend to be more variable than at troughs, as evidenced by the generally larger standard deviations recorded at peaks than at troughs.

When analysing the mean and median leads/lags at both peaks and troughs, it is clear that the timing sequence among the SARB's various composite business cycle indicators has held up quite well; the inverted lagging indicators displayed the longest lead at both peaks and troughs, followed by the leading indicator and the ratio of the coincident to lagging indicator. This consistency should enable analysts to employ the SARB's composite business cycle indicators to predict future turning points in the South African business cycle with a fair degree of confidence. There were also no turning points missed and, considering the long time span covered in the analysis, not many additional turning points displayed by the SARB's composite business cycle indicators.

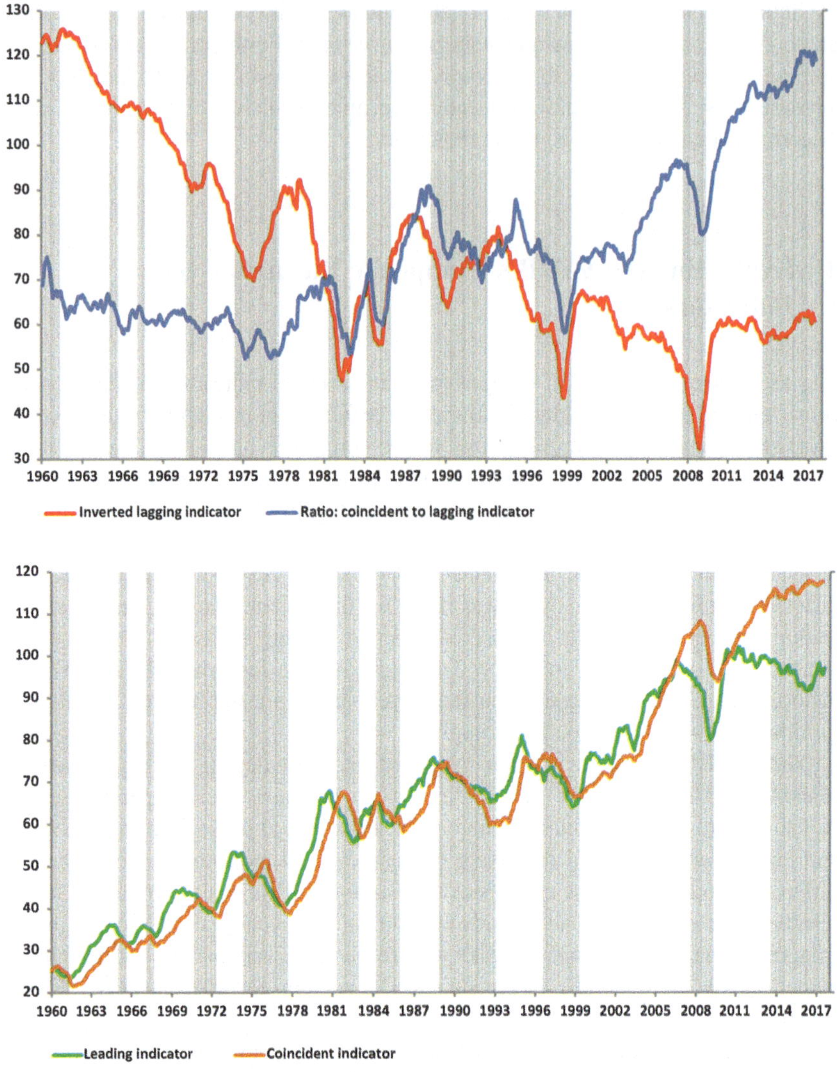

Fig. 1 The SARB's composite business cycle indicators for South Africa. Note: Shaded areas indicate downward phases of the South African business cycle

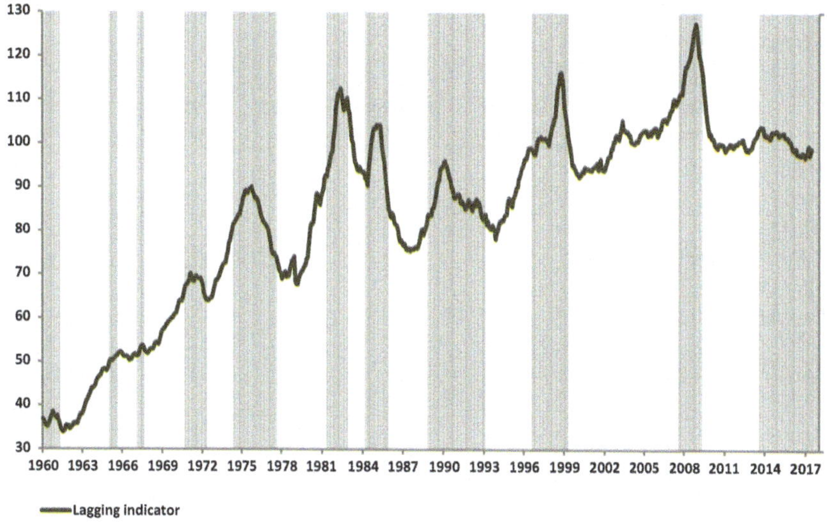

Fig. 1 (continued)

5 Current Dissemination of the SARB's Composite Business Cycle Indicators

The SARB's composite business cycle indicators are released monthly on the SARB's website, at the following hyperlink:

http://www.resbank.co.za/Research/Statistics/Pages/CompositeBusinessCycleIndicators.aspx

A PDF document highlights the latest outcome of the three composite indicators, including a graphical presentation and a data table. In addition, an MS Excel file can be downloaded that contains the historical data of the three composite business cycle indicators. A statistical advance release calendar is also available on the SARB's website, indicating future release dates of the composite business cycle indicators. The release calendar can be viewed at the following hyperlink:

http://www.resbank.co.za/SARBEvents/AdvanceReleaseCalendar/Pages/default.aspx

Apart from the monthly release on the SARB's website, the composite indicators are also regularly published in the SARB's *Quarterly Bulletin*, currently on page S-145 and S-155 in the statistical tables section.

Table 5 Cyclical timing (in months) of the SARB's composite business cycle indicators at reference peaks and troughs

	Inverted lagging indicator	Leading indicator	Ratio: coincident to lagging indicator	Coincident indicator	Lagging indicator
Timing at peaks					
Lead (−) Lag (+)					
April 1965	−45	−7	−5	−1	+7
May 1967	−10	−6	−2	0	+2
December 1970	−37	−14	−7	+2	+2
August 1974	−26	−12	−10	−1	+14
August 1981	−30	−11	−3	+4	+9
June 1984	−1	−1	−1	−1	+10
February 1989	−19	−9	−6	+4	+12
November 1996	−36	−23	−21	−1	+23
November 2007	−43	−16	−9	+5	+12
November 2013	−13	−32	−12	0	0
Additional turns	1	3	5	3	1
Missed turns	0	0	0	0	0
Mean	−26	−13.1	−7.6	+1.1	+9.1
Median	−28	−11.5	−6.5	0	+9.5
Std. deviation	14.9	8.5	5.9	2.3	6.9
Timing at troughs					
Lead (−) Lag (+)					
August 1961	−10	−2	+2	+1	−1
December 1965	−1	−3	+1	+1	+7
December 1967	−5	−3	−2	−1	−1
August 1972	−18	−10	−10	0	−2
December 1977	−26	−9	−11	−1	+14
March 1983	−10	−8	−4	−1	+14

(continued)

Table 5 (continued)

	Inverted lagging indicator	Leading indicator	Ratio: coincident to lagging indicator	Coincident indicator	Lagging indicator
March 1986	−11	−13	−11	0	+16
May 1993	−39	−9	−9	−1	+6
August 1999	−10	−10	−10	−2	+6
August 2009	−9	−7	−7	0	+12
Additional turns	1	3	5	3	1
Missed turns	0	0	0	0	0
Mean	−13.9	−7.4	−6.1	−0.4	+7.1
Median	−10	−8.5	−8	−0.5	+6.5
Std. deviation	10.6	3.4	4.7	0.9	6.4

6 Conclusion

The development, analysis and dissemination of composite business cycle indicators have a well-established history in South Africa. The initial set of indicators was developed by J.E.M. Van Coller and disseminated by the BER at Stellenbosch University. A second set of composite indicators was later developed at the SARB and has over time become widely regarded as the 'official' South African composite business cycle indicators.

While the SARB's composite indicator methodology has not changed much over time, the component time series included in the composite indicators have undergone numerous revisions. Originally, the SARB's composite indicators were comprised of a fairly large number of component series, while the earlier revisions were also more comprehensive than the latter ones. The reason for this is largely related to the initial availability and quality of economic time series in South Africa, which has gradually improved over time. The more recent revisions to the composite indicators were much smaller and related more to either structural changes in the economy or changes to the weighting structure of underlying component series. However, from the beginning—including Van Coller's composite indicators—component series related to the openness of the South African economy have been included in the composite business cycle indicators, reflecting the important role that external factors have historically played in cyclical developments in the South African economy.

A historical turning point analysis revealed that the SARB's composite business cycle indicators have been fairly reliable in measuring cyclical developments in the economy. Moreover, the sequential signaling system seems to be intact, allowing the composite business cycle indicators to be utilised in predicting business cycle turning points in the South African economy with a fair degree of confidence.

References

Ozyildirim A (2018) Compiling cyclical composite indexes: The Conference Board indicators approach. In: Business Cycles in BRICS. Springer, Cham

Smit DJ, Van der Walt BE (1970) Business cycles in South Africa during the post-war period, 1946 to 1968. Quarterly Bulletin, No 97, September 1970, South African Reserve Bank, Pretoria, pp 21–45

South African Reserve Bank, Quarterly Bulletin (2015) Box 1 – Revisions to the composite leading and coincident business cycle indicators. Text box on page 14 of Quarterly Bulletin No 276. June 2015. South African Reserve Bank, Pretoria, pp 14–17

Van Coller JEM (1980) A system of composite leading and coinciding indices of the South African business cycle. J Stud Econ Econ 8:41–73

Van der Walt BE (1982) Die identifisering en waardebepaling van ekonomiese aanwysers vir 'n studie van die konjunktuur in Suid-Afrika. Unpublished D.Com Thesis, University of Pretoria, Pretoria

Van der Walt BE (1983) Indicators of business cycle changes in South Africa. Quarterly Bulletin, No 147. March 1983. South African Reserve Bank, Pretoria, pp 53–63

Van der Walt BE, Pretorius WS (1994) Notes on revision of the composite business cycle indicators. Quarterly Bulletin, No 193. September 1994. South African Reserve Bank, Pretoria, pp 29–35

Venter JC (2004) Note on the revision and significance of the composite lagging business cycle indicator. Quarterly Bulletin, No 234. December 2004. South African Reserve Bank, Pretoria, pp 70–76

Venter JC (2007) Revisions to the composite leading and coincident business cycle indicators. Quarterly Bulletin No 244. June 2007. South African Reserve Bank, Pretoria, pp 15–17

Venter JC, Pretorius WS (2004) Note on the revision of composite leading and coincident business cycle indicators. Quarterly Bulletin, No 231. March 2004. South African Reserve Bank, Pretoria, pp 67–72

Zarnowitz V (1992) Business cycles: theory, history, indicators, and forecasting. University of Chicago Press, Chicago

Zarnowitz V, Boschan C (1975) Cyclical indicators: an evaluation and new leading indexes. Business Conditions Digest, v–xiv

Alternative Cycle Indicators for the South African Business Cycle

Willem H. Boshoff and Laurie H. Binge

1 Introduction

The South African Reserve Bank (SARB) analyses a large number of lagging, coincident and leading indicators to determine turning points in the South African business cycle. This methodology is characterised by significant time delays in the publication of turning points (Lehohla and Morudu 2011). Consequently, other institutions, including the Bureau for Economic Research (BER) at Stellenbosch University, also publish leading indicators of the South African business cycle. This chapter reviews these alternative indicators, with an emphasis on the business confidence index of the BER as a potentially useful, timely and robust leading indicator of the cycle.

The paper starts with a review of challenges facing the SARB's indicators followed by a short summary of academic research. The paper then focuses on business confidence indicators (BCIs) in South Africa, illustrating their usefulness, both as leading indicators of business cycle turning points and in forecasting real GDP growth, in comparison to the SARB's leading and coincident indicators. The final section then reviews a recession-prediction algorithm of the BER, relying on six variables (including the BER BCI), which has proven successful at dating South African business cycle recessions.

W. H. Boshoff (✉) · L. H. Binge
Department of Economics, Stellenbosch University, Stellenbosch, South Africa
e-mail: wimpie2@sun.ac.za

S. Smirnov et al. (eds.), *Business Cycles in BRICS*, Societies and Political Orders in Transition, https://doi.org/10.1007/978-3-319-90017-9_27

2 Challenges in Relying on the SARB Business Cycle Indicators

The SARB determines turning points in growth cycles, which represent fluctuations around the long-term growth trend in South African economic activity. In this chapter, we reserve the term 'business cycle' for this official SARB definition. Our analysis of the alternative indicators covers growth cycles as well as classical cycles (i.e. an analysis of turning points in the level of economic activity). As explained below, an analysis of classical cycles is partly motivated by the information conveyed by some of the leading indicators: some indicators reflect confidence relative to existing trends and can therefore be seen as detrended cyclical measures. We use the term 'downswing' to refer to growth cycle downswing phases and the term 'contraction' to refer to classical cycle contractions (recessions).

The SARB determines turning points based on an analysis of composite leading, coincident and lagging business cycle indicators (see Venter (this volume) and Venter 2005a). Composite business cycle indicators are compiled by integrating various individual economic indicators into a single time series, which mirrors the movement of, and the turning points in, the business cycle (Van der Walt and Pretorius 2004). A significant drawback of the SARB methodology is the delay involved in both publication of the indicators and determination of the official turning point dates. The SARB publishes the composite leading indicator monthly but only 6–8 weeks after the reference month. When the composite leading indicator began declining in August 2006, initial estimates became available around October 2006 and only become final around January 2007, which represents a 5-month lag. In December 2007, which turned out to be the official peak date, the SARB dating committee was still considering a very moderate decrease in the leading indicator from June to July 2007. This substantial delay limits the usefulness of the indicators in terms of business forecasting and policy formation (Lehohla and Morudu 2011).

Delays in the determination of official business cycle turning points are even more extensive. As the SARB studies fluctuations around a long-term trend in economic activity, turning points are confirmed only after a significant delay. During the extended expansion phase from September 1999 to November 2007, the composite coincident indicator exhibited two short periods of decline: during the first half of 2001 and again during the first half of 2003. As reference turning points are not subject to revision, the investigation of these two potential downswing phases was delayed until 2005, when a consistent data set became available. The official business cycle peak in December 2007 was announced in September 2009, almost 2 years after the fact.

Outside users aiming to predict cyclical conditions do not usually have access to or participate in the SARB's elaborate process of identifying turning points, which creates room for error when relying solely on the SARB's coincident or leading indicator to identify cycles. In light of these challenges, it remains important to consider alternative indicators that are timely and that may complement the official composite indicators. In South Africa, the BER has done important work in developing alternative indicators of cyclical activity based on business confidence and in developing other composite approaches to identifying turning points.

The academic literature, too, has explored the potential role that specific variables can play. The following section provides a brief review of the South African academic literature.

3 Selected Academic Results on Business Cycle Indicators in South Africa

Academic research over the past 15 years has sought to identify individual variables, often from the financial markets, that could improve on the performance of the SARB's composite leading indicator. The findings in this literature can be summarised along two lines. Firstly, the South African literature, consistent with the SARB, BER and indeed most of the international literature, finds predictive power for the yield curve in dating recessions (see Moolman 2004; Boshoff 2005; Khomo and Aziakpono 2007; Clay and Keeton 2011; Botha and Keeton 2014). Secondly, Moolman (2003) finds evidence that short-term interest rates outperform both the SARB's composite leading indicator and the yield curve, with an average lead time of 7 months. In particular, Moolman finds that the SARB's leading indicator has a consistent lead of only 4–5 months, which, given the lag in publication, renders the indicator less useful for pure forecasting purposes.

Even if other variables may outperform the leading indicator as an isolated variable for predicting cyclical turning points, academic research supports the SARB's data-rich approach to business cycle identification—where the composite leading indicator forms part of a larger assessment. Recent work by researchers at the SARB, Bosch and Ruch (2013), finds support for a data-rich approach at their institution.

4 Business Confidence as Leading Indicator in South Africa

4.1 Business Confidence Indices by BER and SACCI

Business confidence indicators have predictive power for economic growth and are often accurate leading indicators of business cycle turning points (Taylor and McNabb 2007; Gupta and Kabundi 2011). Even if the unique information content of business confidence indicators is limited, the timeliness of these survey-based indicators renders them useful for monitoring and predicting economic activity (Gayer et al. 2014; Kabundi et al. 2016).

Two indicators of business confidence are published regularly in South Africa: the BER Business Confidence Index (BER BCI) and the South African Chamber of

Commerce and Industry Business Confidence Index (SACCI BCI). The BER BCI, in particular, has proven useful both as a predictor of economic growth and as a leading indicator of turning points in the South African business cycle. Indeed, it is one of twelve leading indicator series relied on by the SARB when determining the official turning points.

The BER BCI is constructed from the BER's quarterly business tendency surveys, which are similar to surveys such as the European Commission business tendency surveys, the German Ifo Business Climate Survey and the Federal Reserve Bank of Philadelphia's Business Outlook Survey. The BER BCI is constructed from a specific question that appears in all of the sectoral surveys: 'Are prevailing business conditions: Satisfactory, Unsatisfactory?' The BCI is the weighted percentage of respondents that rated prevailing business conditions as *satisfactory*. The responses are weighted using firm size (turnover) and subsector weights. The confidence indicator reflects a rating of business conditions at a specific point in time (see Kershoff (this volume)).

The SACCI BCI is a composite monthly index of 13 quantitative subindices thought to have the greatest bearing on the prevailing 'mood' of South African business. These include the exchange rate, inflation, the prime rate, retail sales volumes, credit extension, commodity prices, import and export volumes, new vehicle sales, utility services, manufacturing production, building plans passed and the stock market index. Therefore, the SACCI BCI is an ex post measure of actual activity, based on the assumption that recent business activity is indicative of the extent of business confidence (SACCI 2011).

The BCIs enjoy some advantages over the SARB's composite indicators for the purpose of identifying and predicting turning points. The BCIs are available well in advance of official statistics, such as the leading and coincident indicators, as well as GDP. The BER BCI and the SACCI BCI are published 4 and 2 weeks, respectively, before the end of the reference quarter, which is approximately 2 months prior to the first official GDP estimates (Kershoff 2000). The composite coincident indicator, in contrast, is published 6–8 weeks after the reference month. Even if the BCIs have a coincident relationship with GDP, their early availability implies that they would still be quasi-leading indicators. The survey-based BER BCI also avoids trend and seasonality problems often encountered with composite indicators (ECB 2013). A drawback of the BER BCI is that it is only available at a quarterly frequency, whereas the coincident, leading and SACCI indicators are available at a monthly frequency.

4.2 Empirical Results

4.2.1 Correlations

Figure 1 illustrates the quarterly BER BCI, as well as the growth rates of the quarterly versions of the SACCI BCI and the SARB's leading and coincident indicators.

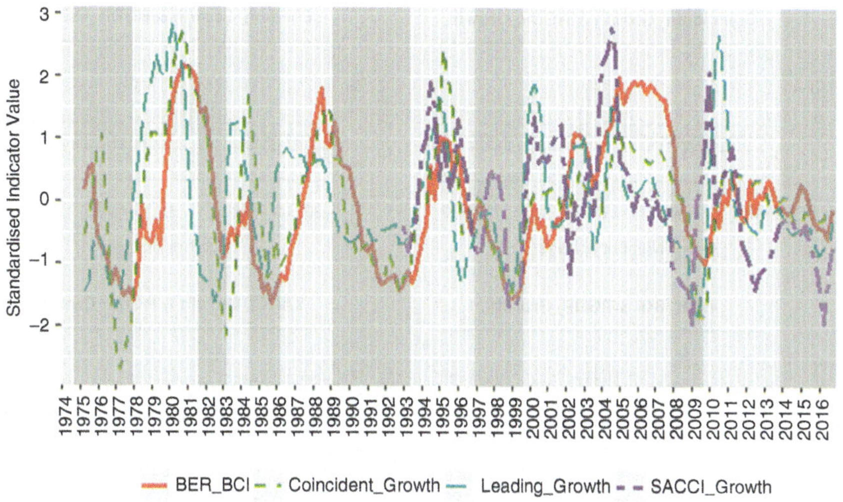

Fig. 1 BCIs and the SARB leading and coincident indicators, compared to downswing phases (shaded)

Table 1 Contemporaneous correlations between the indicators and real GDP growth

	RGDP growth	Coincident growth	Leading growth	BER BCI
Coincident growth	0.71***			
Leading growth	0.32***	0.50***		
BER BCI	0.71***	0.76***	0.31***	
SACCI growth	0.20*	0.27***	0.49***	0.29***

Note: *$*p < 0.1$; $***p < 0.01$*

Growth rates are used to remove unit roots and are calculated as annual quarter-on-quarter growth rates, e.g. 2016Q3 over 2015Q3. Downswing phases are shaded, and the indicators are standardised in order to plot them together. The SACCI BCI is only available from 1991Q4. The BCIs track the official business cycle turning points reasonably well and appear to be correlated with the two official composite indicators.

The tracking record of the indicators is measured by their correlation with the corresponding reference series. Table 1 reports the contemporaneous correlations of the annual quarter-on-quarter growth in real GDP and the growth rates in the quarterly indicators (illustrated in Fig. 1). All the indicators exhibit a significant positive correlation with real GDP growth. The correlation between real GDP growth and the coincident indicator growth rate (0.71) is the same as the correlation between real GDP growth and the BER BCI (0.71).

Figure 2 illustrates the cross-correlograms for the indicators and real GDP growth, which help to unpack the dynamic relationships. All the indicators exhibit relatively high correlations with real GDP growth. The leading indicator and the SACCI BCI exhibit the highest correlation statistics with three-quarter lagged real GDP growth. The results imply that the BER BCI, in particular, is a potentially

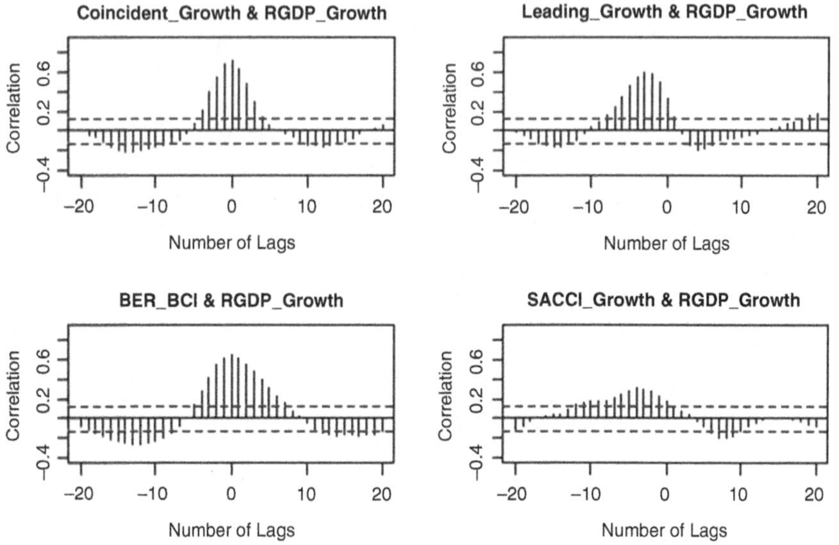

Fig. 2 Cross-correlograms of the indicators and real GDP growth

useful leading or quasi-leading indicator and may contain predictive information for real economic activity.

4.2.2 Leading Indicator Properties

While correlation statistics offer information about the general conformity of two economic series, these are of limited use when evaluating the leading indicator properties of a potential indicator. For one, unit roots in the SARB indicators require correlation calculations to be performed on growth rates, which represent a growth rate cycle compared to classical cycles in the levels of an indicator.

Furthermore, an accurate leading indicator should not only conform to economic activity in general (as reflected in high correlation statistics) but should also have turning points that match consistently with those of the reference cycle (Boshoff 2005). Therefore, an evaluation of the BCIs as leading indicators requires investigating whether turning points in the levels of BCIs consistently lead, coincide with or lag peaks and troughs of the official business cycle.

We determine turning points in the levels of (i.e. classical cycles in) the BCIs and official SARB indicators using the BBQ method, with the censoring rule suggested by Harding and Pagan (2002). The resulting phases are presented in Fig. 3. The black rectangles show contractionary phases identified for each indicator, while the grey columns indicate the official SARB downswing phases. Figure 3 therefore compares contractions in the classical cycles of the various indicators to the official SARB downswing phases based on growth cycles. There is strong support for this approach in the South African literature: Du Plessis (2006) finds significant synchronisation

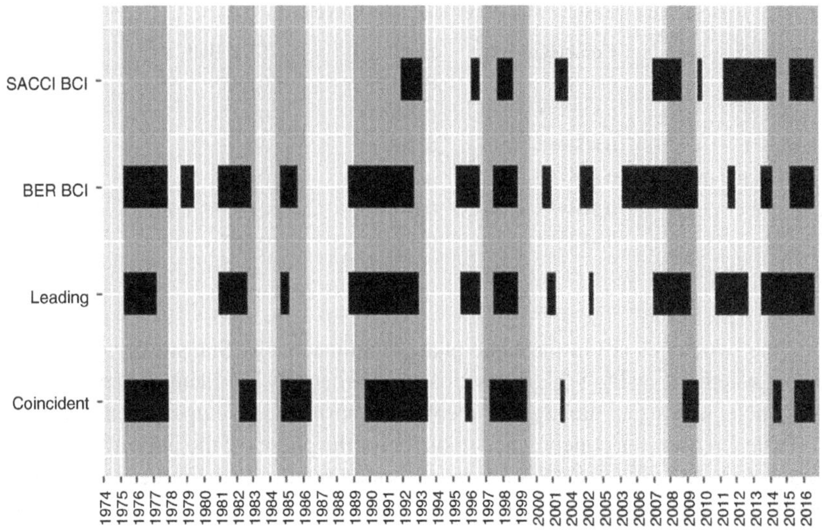

Fig. 3 Indicator turning points compared to the official SARB turning points. *Notes: Black rectangles indicate the contractionary periods for a particular indicator. Grey columns indicate the official SARB downswing periods. The SACCI BCI is only available from 1991Q4*

between the official SARB business cycle (a growth cycle) and the classical cycle in GDP, identified with the BBQ method.

The sample period (from 1975Q1 to 2016Q3) contains six official upswing phases and seven official downswing phases. All of the indicators seem to identify these phases correctly, in some cases well in advance of the official turning points. The leading indicator and the BCIs exhibit troughs before the seven official trough dates, with lead times of between zero and four quarters. The coincident indicator exhibits troughs that coincide with or lag the official trough dates by one quarter. The leading indicator and the BCIs exhibit peaks before the official peak dates, with lead times of between 0 and 11 quarters. The cycles identified with the coincident indicator range between a lead time of five quarters and a lag of three quarters.

Despite their favourable properties, the indicators are quite volatile, and the default censoring rule produces a number of short phases (two quarters), especially during the ambiguous period (2001–2004) and latter part of the sample period (2012–2015). The false positives are problematic for the use of the indicators as early warning signals.

The leading indicator and the BCIs provide advanced warning of turning points, albeit in some cases well before the official peaks. In this sense, these are leading indicators of the business cycle turning points. The coincident indicator has a relatively stable relationship with the official cycle, although in many cases it lags the official cycle.

The co-movement between these different cycle phases can be measured with the concordance statistic suggested by Harding and Pagan (2002). The concordance statistic measures the co-movement of two series, by considering the proportion of

Table 2 Concordance statistics with the official SARB cycle

	Coincident	Leading	BER BCI	SACCI BCI
Lead = 3	0.665**	0.79***	0.695***	0.74***
Lead = 2	0.731***	0.808***	0.737***	0.71***
Lead = 1	0.808***	0.778***	0.719***	0.68**
Lag/Lead = 0	0.886***	0.725***	0.689***	0.65*
Lag = 1	0.904***	0.659***	0.635**	0.377
Lag=2	0.862***	0.593	0.569	0.365

Note: $^{*}p < 0.1$; $^{**}p < 0.05$; $^{***}p < 0.01$

time the two series are in the same phase simultaneously. Statistically, this entails testing whether $I = \Pr(S_{xt} = S_{yt})$ is close to 1, where $S_{xt} = 1$ identifies an expansion in financial series $\{x_t\}$ and $S_{yt} = 1$ identifies a business cycle upswing at time t.

Table 2 reports the concordance statistics for the phases of the indicator variables, compared to the official SARB reference turning points. The significance levels are determined with heteroskedasticity and autocorrelation consistent standard errors. All of the indicators exhibit significant concordance with the official SARB cycle. For the coincident indicator, the maximum concordance statistic occurred with a lag of one quarter (i.e. one quarter after the official cycle). For the leading indicator and the BER BCI, the maximum concordance statistics occurred with a lead of two quarters before the official cycle. For the SACCI, it occurred with a lead of three quarters.

The results imply that the BCIs, and the BER BCI in particular, are potentially useful leading indicators: they appear to follow the official SARB cycle almost as closely as the official indicators and provide similar advanced warning of turning points as the leading indicator.

4.2.3 Predictive Power for GDP Growth

In addition to leading indicator properties, the BCIs may be useful in forecasting real economic activity. Granger causality tests can help to determine whether one time series is useful in forecasting another, by measuring the ability of lagged values of a time series to predict the future values of another time series. Table 3 reports the results for Granger causality tests for the growth rates in the indicators and real GDP growth. The results suggest that the lagged values of the coincident and leading indicators, as well as the BER BCI, significantly predict real GDP growth. In other words, the results suggest that these indicators contain relevant predictive information for output growth.

Standard recursive vector autoregressive models (VARs) can be used to trace out the dynamic responses of economic activity to surprise increases in business confidence (Taylor and McNabb 2007; Barsky and Sims 2012). The aim is to investigate whether the BCIs have a significant dynamic relationship with real output and whether they contain predictive information for GDP growth.

Table 3 Granger causality tests for RGDP growth and other cyclical indicators

Granger causality H0	Statistic
Coincident_Growth does not Granger-cause RGDP_Growth	2.315**
RGDP_Growth does not Granger-cause Coincident_Growth	1.02
Leading_Growth does not Granger-cause RGDP_Growth	2.581**
RGDP_Growth does not Granger-cause Leading_Growth	1.076
BER_BCI does not Granger-cause RGDP_Growth	2.823***
RGDP_Growth does not Granger-cause BER_BCI	1.154
SACCI_Growth does not Granger-cause RGDP_Growth	1.474
RGDP_Growth does not Granger-cause SACCI_Growth	1.106

Note: $^{**}p < 0.05$; $^{***}p < 0.01$

The VAR for the BER BCI is estimated on the quarterly data running from 1973Q1 to 2016Q3, while the VAR for the SACCI BCI is estimated on the quarterly data from 1991Q4 to 2016Q3. The BER BCI enters in levels, while the SACCI BCI and real GDP series enter as annual quarter-on-quarter growth rates (unit root tests confirm the stationarity of these series). The appropriate number of lags is selected by means of the Akaike information criterion (AIC), which points to nine lags, and a constant term is included.

The BCIs are ordered first in a recursive identification strategy, with the Cholesky decomposition used to identify structural shocks. With this ordering, shocks to confidence are allowed to have a contemporaneous impact on activity, but shocks to activity have no contemporaneous impact on confidence. This is the identification strategy and ordering used in the literature (Leduc and Sill 2013; Bachmann et al. 2013). It can be motivated by the timing of the BER's quarterly surveys: when the survey is completed, respondents do not know the realisations of output growth, as the response deadline is generally the second month of the quarter. The results are similar for alternative orderings.

The above identification strategy allows for the generation of impulse response functions (IRFs), which can show the dynamic impact of a shock to confidence on the system. The shock itself is an innovation to the residual in the equation of the variable of interest.

Figure 4 illustrates the IRFs of the bivariate VAR using the BER BCI. The left panel plots the responses of real GDP growth to an orthogonal shock in the BER BCI, with a 95% bootstrap confidence interval (CI). Following a positive shock to confidence, real GDP growth increases by around 0.8% on impact, with a peak at three quarters. The impact on the growth rate is transitory, dying out after approximately seven quarters.

Figure 5 illustrates the IRFs of the bivariate VAR using the SACCI BCI growth. The left panel plots the responses of real GDP growth to an orthogonal shock in the SACCI BCI, with a 95% bootstrap confidence interval (CI). Following a positive shock to confidence, the increase in real GDP growth is significant only after three quarters and smaller than is the case for the BER BCI.

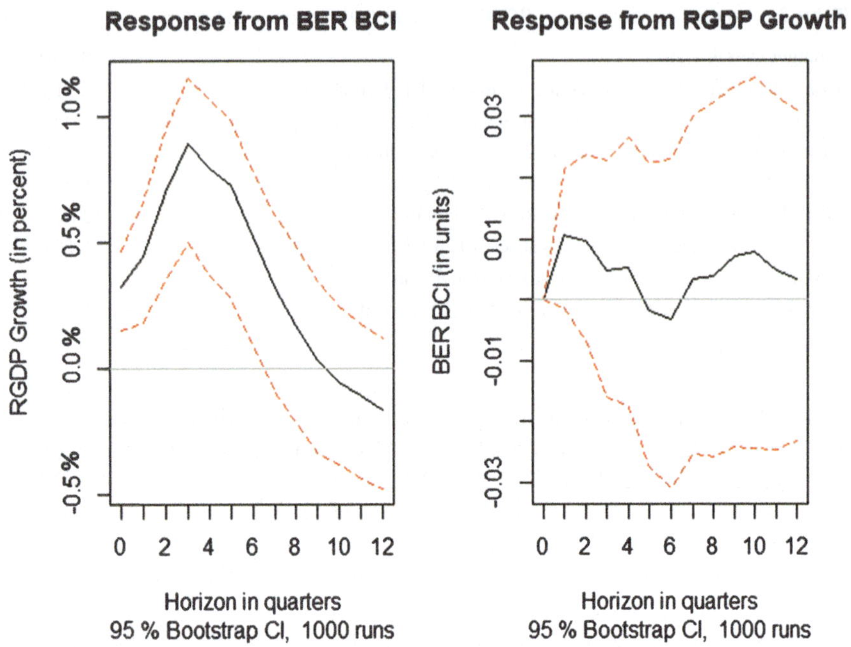

Fig. 4 IRFs of BER BCI and real GDP growth in bivariate VAR

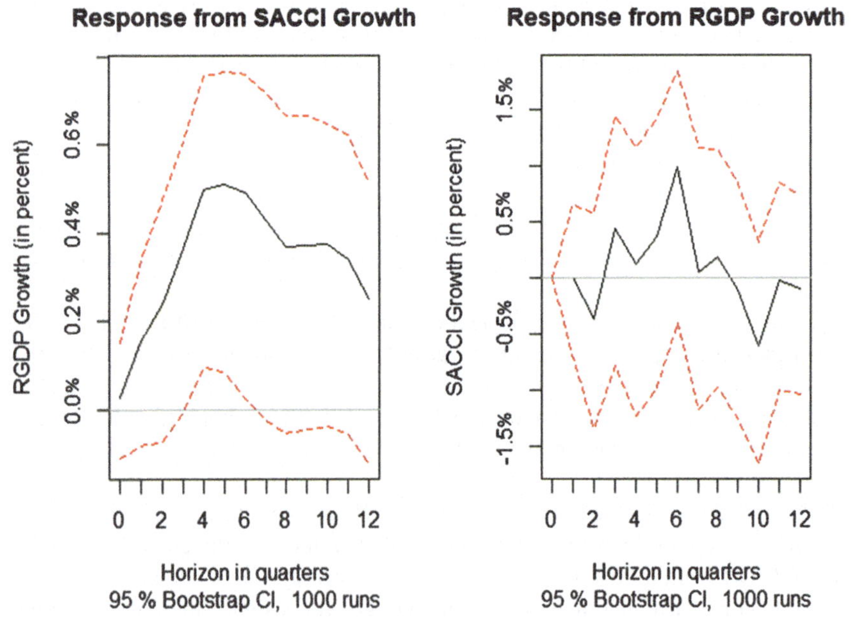

Fig. 5 IRFs of SACCI BCI growth and real GDP growth in bivariate VAR

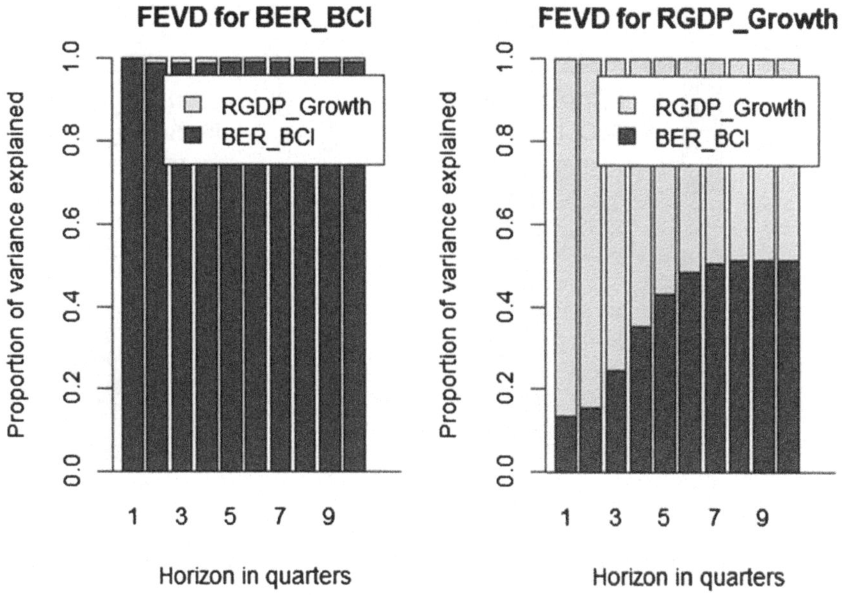

Fig. 6 FEVDs of BER BCI and real GDP growth in bivariate VAR

The system dynamics can also be examined with forecast error variance decompositions (FEVD). The FEVD shows the proportion of movements in a sequence due to its own shocks and shocks to another variable. Figure 6 illustrates the FEVDs for the BER BCI and real GDP growth. The right panel shows that up to around half (52%) of the movements in real GDP growth are explained by the BER BCI over the longer term, while the left panel shows that real GDP explains very little of the variance in the BER BCI.

Figure 7 illustrates the FEVDs for the SACCI BCI and real GDP growth. The right panel shows that up to around 35% of the movements in real GDP growth are explained by the SACCI BCI over the longer term. In terms of predictive content, the BER BCI seems to outperform the SACCI BCI.[1]

A larger VAR system allows for robustness tests. We fit extended VARs including variables commonly used in the South African literature (Leduc and Sill 2013; Redl 2015): the BER or SACCI BCI, the Johannesburg Stock Exchange (JSE) All Share Index, the yield spread (i.e. the government bond yield minus the 3-month T-Bill rate), real GDP, industrial production, investment and an employment index. The variables are ordered with the confidence indicators first, the financial variables next and the real variables last. As was the case for the previous VAR, the variables enter as real annual quarter-on-quarter growth rates, except for the BER BCI and the

[1]The results for the coincident and leading indicators are similar to those of the BER BCI and also outperform the SACCI in terms of predictive content. The results are available upon request.

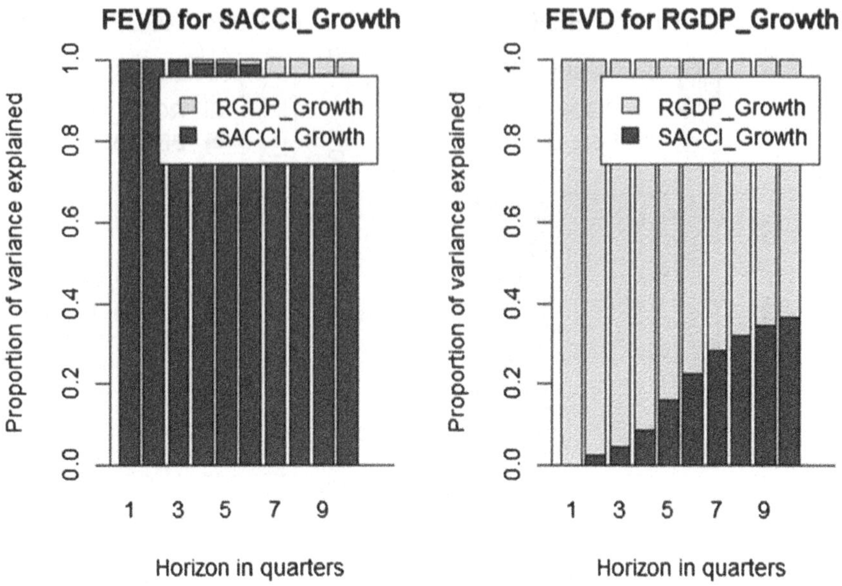

Fig. 7 FEVDs of SACCI BCI growth and real GDP growth in bivariate VAR

yield spread. The VARs are estimated on the quarterly data running from 1992Q1 to 2016Q3 and include four lags.

Figure 8 illustrates the impact of the BER BCI on the growth in real GDP, real industrial production and real investment. The larger system yields similar results to those of the bivariate VARs earlier. The impact of the shocks is larger on real production and investment growth than on real GDP growth. Figure 9 illustrates the impact of the SACCI BCI on the growth in real GDP, real industrial production and real investment. The results are similar to the larger system using the BER BCI, although impacts are slightly smaller.

According to the FEVD illustrated in Fig. 10, the BER BCI explains around 35% of the variance in real GDP growth. The numbers are similar for real production growth and real investment growth. The BER BCI therefore seems to contain useful predictive information for real activity growth. According to the FEVD illustrated in Fig. 11, the SACCI BCI explains around 30% of the variance in real GDP growth. The numbers are similar for real production growth and real investment growth.

Our empirical analysis suggests that the BCIs, and the BER's BCI in particular, are useful leading indicators of the business cycle and track the official business cycle relatively closely. The business confidence indicators perform similar to the SARB's official coincident indicator in predicting turning points. The BCIs also contain relevant information for the prediction of output growth.

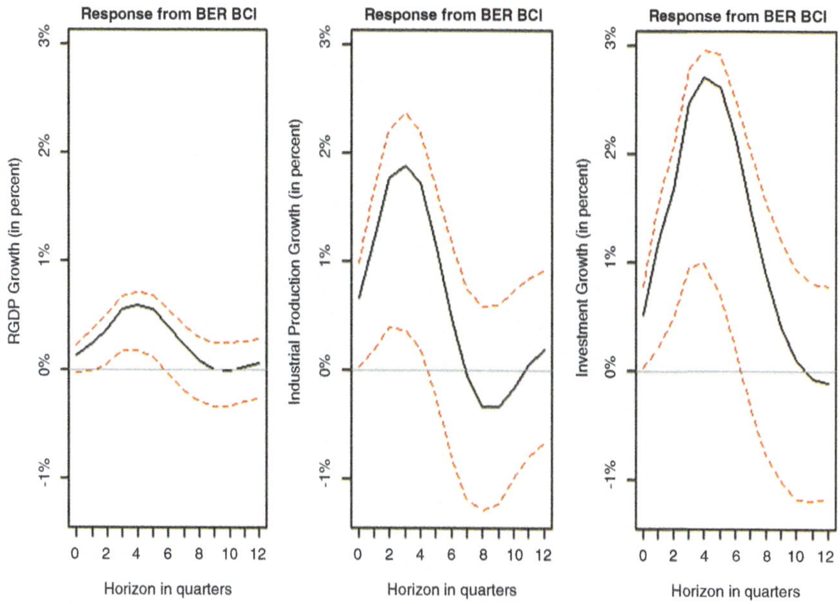

Fig. 8 IRFs of BER BCI on real GDP, industrial production and investment growth in extended VAR

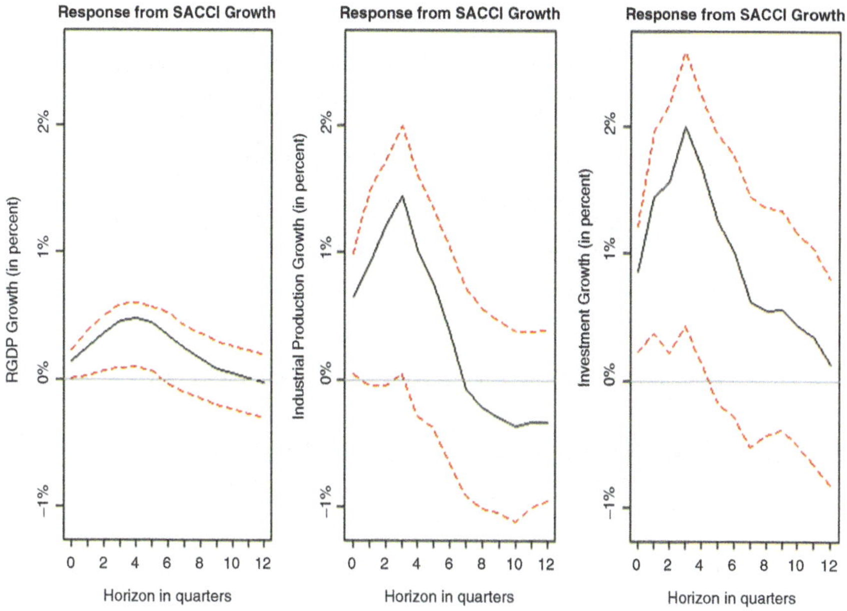

Fig. 9 IRFs of SACCI growth on real GDP, industrial production and investment growth in extended VAR

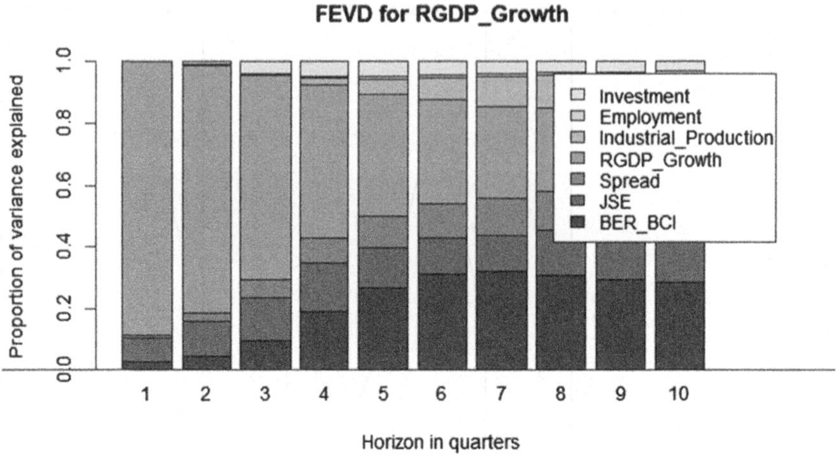

Fig. 10 FEVDs real GDP growth in the extended VAR with the BER BCI

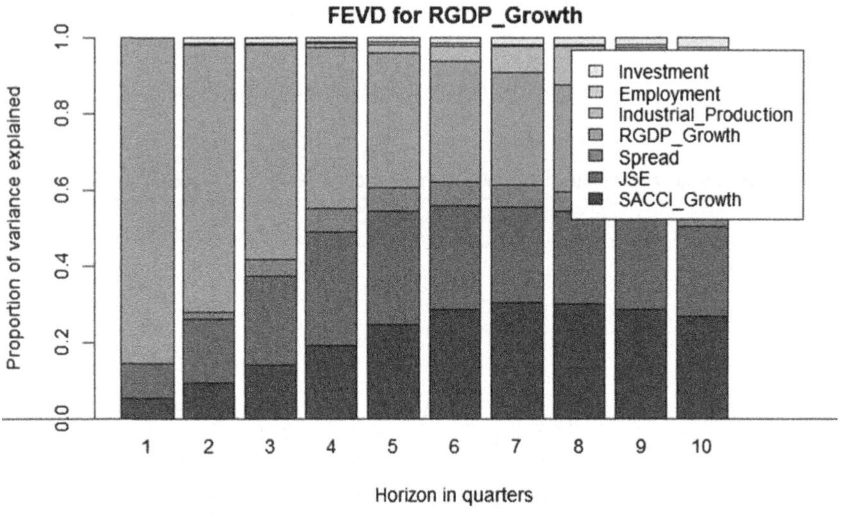

Fig. 11 FEVDs of real GDP growth in the extended VAR with the SACCI BCI

5 An Alternative Algorithm for Dating South Africa Business Cycle Recessions

Given the performance of the BER's BCI as indicator of the South African cycle, further research at the BER has explored the extent to which an alternative multi-variable approach can accurately predict cyclical turning points. In particular, the aim was to identify an approach reliant on a smaller set of economic variables than the large set currently considered by the SARB.

Laubscher (2014) identifies five time series that are close predictors of the official reference business cycle turning points identified: the BER BCI, manufacturing volume of production, manufacturing capacity utilisation, manufacturing working hours and wholesale sales volumes. Laubscher then combines these five time series with information from the yield curve to develop a two-stage algorithm for predicting cyclical turning points.

In the first stage, the algorithm relies on advance signals from the yield spread (between 10-year and 3-month government bonds). The algorithm identifies a possible business cycle peak when the 6-month advanced probability of recession, calculated from the yield spread, exceeds the 50% threshold.

In the second stage, the algorithm involves an evaluation of the five time series listed above. A probable recession is identified on the basis of predefined thresholds for each of the series. Thereafter, it is determined whether the latest reading of each of the series signal a peak (or trough), i.e. when the second derivative is maximally negative (or positive). Censoring rules are applied to take care of spurious fluctuations in specific time series. In line with Boshoff (2005), full cycles with a duration shorter than 15 months and phases shorter than 6 months are eliminated. The candidate turning point is also required to adhere to a generality requirement, by clustering with turning points in three or four other series, in order to be classified as a turning point. The candidate turning point dates suggested by the indicators are reconciled by relying on the median turning point date across the five series.

Laubscher's (2014) ex post evaluation indicates that the algorithm is successful at dating the five recessions between 1981 and 2013. While the data tends to be volatile, all spurious signals can be discarded on the basis of the censoring rules or of the generality requirement. For the best fit, Laubscher (2014) suggests that the manufacturing capacity utilisation indicator only be used for trough signals and that the wholesale sales index only be used to confirm a business cycle turning point suggested by the other indicators. The proposed algorithm achieves a high degree of accuracy, with a median 2-month lag at business cycle peaks and a 1-month lead at troughs. Laubscher (2014) converted the quarterly BER BCI to a monthly frequency, by assuming the same quarterly value for each month of the quarter and calculating a 5-month moving average. The evidence suggests that the algorithm would not only allow 'close calls' on turning points but would also be able to do this with a much shorter time delay than the SARB's official decisions. The median announcement lag was 8 months and 5 months for peak and trough signals, respectively, implying an average lead of 10 months and 19 months over SARB decisions.

We update the ex post evaluation to investigate the performance of the algorithm in predicting the most recent downswing phase in the official South African business cycle, dated as starting in November 2013. Figure 12 shows updated data elucidating the relationship between official business cycle turning points and turning points in four of the five series used by the Laubscher algorithm. The fifth series, the BER BCI, was analysed in the preceding section. The grey columns indicate the official SARB downswing phases, while the black rectangles show the downswing periods for each series. The individual series performed relatively well in predicting the most

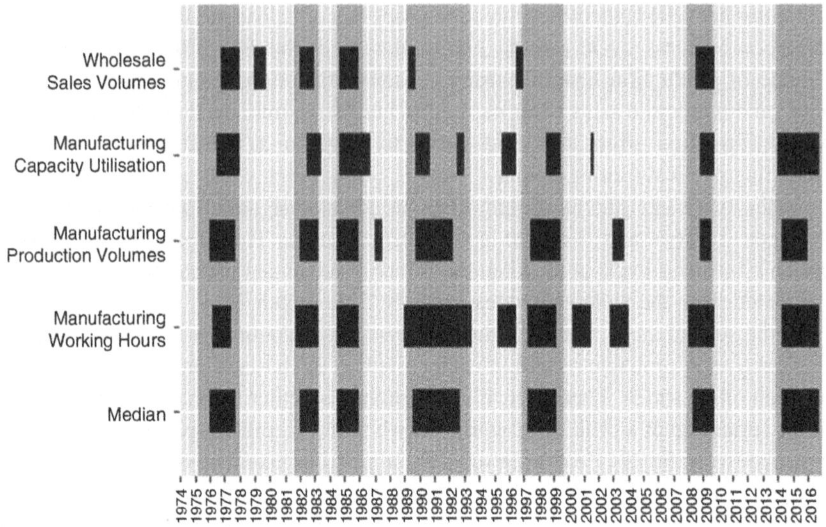

Fig. 12 Recessionary periods in the four indicators and the median (official SARB downswing phases shaded). *Notes: Black rectangles indicate the downswing periods identified for each series. Grey columns indicate the official SARB downswing phases. Source: Laubscher (*2014*), updated by Pieter Laubscher*

recent downswing phase, although all four of the series lagged the official cycle by a few months, and wholesale sales volumes did not indicate a peak.

Figure 12 also illustrates the median turning point dates, using the algorithm described above: the median of three dates for peaks (i.e. business confidence, manufacturing production and manufacturing hours) and four dates for troughs (i.e. the aforementioned three and manufacturing capacity utilisation). The results indicate that the recession-dating algorithm is relatively accurate, even in identifying the most recent growth cycle downswing phase. As there was no turning point in wholesale sales volumes, the algorithm recommends that more information should be analysed in order to confirm the turning point. Overall, the recession-dating algorithm illustrates the value of combining different leading indicators and allows a decision to be made with a shorter delay than the SARB's official determination.

6 Conclusion

This chapter has discussed the role of indicators of the official South African business cycle developed by research institutes outside of the South African Reserve Bank. The SARB identifies turning points with reference to leading, coincident and lagging indicators, as well as comprehensive historical and current diffusion indices. These indicators have tracked the official business cycle turning points reasonably well. Even so, there is a significant delay in both the publication of the SARB indicators and the determination of the official turning point dates, and these indicators are subject to revision.

As alternative indicators, we consider two business confidence indicators published in South Africa, one by the BER and one by SACCI. The two business confidence indicators, and the BER BCI in particular, are useful leading indicators: their classical business cycles track the official South African growth cycle relatively closely. They provide advanced warning of turning points, although there were a few false signals, especially over the ambiguous period of 2000–2003. Their performance is on par with the performance of the SARB's official indicators in cyclical prediction. Even so, these business confidence indicators have the benefit that they are published before the other series become available and are not subject to revision.

Apart from providing information on business cycle turning points, the BCIs also contain relevant information for the prediction of output growth. Shocks to the BCIs accounted for a sizeable fraction of variation in economic activity in our rudimentary VAR analysis. As a result, these business confidence indicators are useful for monitoring economic developments in a timely manner and for forecasting future economic activity.

Further business cycle research at the BER suggests that an alternative recession-prediction algorithm relying on classical cycles in six variables, including the yield curve, the BER's BCI and various manufacturing-related variables, is successful at predicting official growth cycle peaks and troughs in South Africa. This algorithm allows the dating of turning points with a shorter time delay than the SARB's official decisions.

References

Bachmann R, Elstner S, Sims ER (2013) Uncertainty and economic activity: evidence from business survey data. Am Econ J Macroecon 5(2):217–249

Barsky RB, Sims ER (2012) Information, animal spirits, and the meaning of innovations in consumer confidence. Am Econ Rev 102(4):1343–1377. https://doi.org/10.1257/aer.102.4.1343

Bosch A, Ruch F (2013) An alternative business cycle dating procedure for South Africa. South Afr J Econ 81(267):491–516

Boshoff WH (2005) The properties of cycles in South African financial variables and their relation to the business cycle. South Afr J Econ 73(4):694–709. https://doi.org/10.1111/j.1813-6982.2005.00047.x

Botha F, Keeton G (2014) A note on the (continued) ability of the yield curve to forecast economic downturns in South Africa. South Afr J Econ 82(3):468–473. https://doi.org/10.1111/saje.12053

Clay R, Keeton G (2011) The South African yield curve as a predictor of economic downturns: an update. Afr Rev Econ Financ 2(2):167–193

Du Plessis S (2006) Reconsidering the business cycle and stabilisation policies in South Africa. Econ Model 23(5):761–774. https://doi.org/10.1016/j.econmod.2005.10.006

ECB (2013) Confidence indicators and economic developments. ECB Mon Bull:45–58

Gayer C, Girardi A, Reuter A (2014) The role of survey data in nowcasting euro area GDP growth. European Commission Economic Papers 538. https://doi.org/10.2765/71951

Gupta R, Kabundi A (2011) A large factor model for forecasting macroeconomic variables in South Africa. Int J Forecast 27(4):1076–1088. https://doi.org/10.1016/j.ijforecast.2010.10.001

Harding D, Pagan A (2002) Dissecting the cycle: a methodological investigation. J Monet Econ 49 (2):365–381. https://doi.org/10.1016/S0304-3932(01)00108-8

Kabundi A, Nel E, Ruch F (2016) Nowcasting real GDP growth in South Africa. ERSA Working Paper. (581). Available: http://www.econrsa.org/system/files/publications/working_papers/working_paper_581.pdf

Kershoff G (2000) Measuring business and consumer confidence in South Africa. Bur Econ Res:1–11

Khomo MM, Aziakpono MJ (2007) Forecasting recession in South Africa: a comparison of the yield curve and other economic indicators. South Afr J Econ 75(2):194–212. https://doi.org/10.1111/j.1813-6982.2007.00117.x

Laubscher P (2014) A new recession-dating algorithm for South Africa. Stellenbosch Economic Working Papers: 06/14

Leduc S, Sill K (2013) Expectations and economic fluctuations: an analysis using survey data. Rev Econ Stat 95:1352–1367

Lehohla P, Morudu D (2011) Economic crises and forecasting: a review of South Africa's model. Stat South Afr:1–15

Moolman E (2003) Predicting turning points in the South African economy. South Afr J Econ Manag Sci 6(2):289–303

Moolman E (2004) A Markov switching regime model of the South African business cycle. Econ Model 21:631–646. https://doi.org/10.1016/j.econmod.2003.09.003

Redl C (2015) Macroeconomic uncertainty in South Africa. ERSA Working Paper 509

SACCI (2011) Updated and revised SACCI business confidence index. South African chamber of commerce and industry

Taylor K, McNabb R (2007) Business cycles and the role of confidence: evidence for Europe. Oxf Bull Econ Stat 69(2):185–208. https://doi.org/10.1111/j.1468-0084.2007.00472.x

Van Der Walt BE, Pretorius WS (2004) Notes on revision of the composite business cycle indicators. South Afr Reserve Bank:29–35

Venter JC (2005) A brief history of business cycle analysis in South Africa. In: Presentation to the OECD workshop on composite leading indicators for major OECD non-member economies, 2005

Forecasting Business Cycles in South Africa

P. Laubscher

1 Introduction

The two terms, *business cycle* and *forecasting*, are often used in the same vein as any attempt to measure or understand the *business cycle* invariably involves some effort in *forecasting* economic developments, or the *business cycle*. In a free enterprise economy, the evolution of economic activity does not generally follow a smooth trajectory. The recurring deviations of an economy from its underlying growth trend can be defined as the *business cycle*. In the classical sense, the business cycle is defined as recurring (but not periodic) periods of contraction and expansion in the broader economy.

Modern economic production processes are complex. The business cycle is not 'visible' and is shaped by a myriad of forces, also consisting of a range of sub-cycles (across sectors, regions and economic magnitudes). It follows that the study of business cycle developments is a tricky issue and that *forecasting the business cycle* comprises treacherous terrain, as most professional economists will agree. Yet, a great need exists in that public and private sector executives require forecasting services in order to optimise decision-making. Both analyst and economic participant, intent on rational economic decisions, need to understand the cyclical development of economic activity. For the economist, this is particularly necessary in wanting to *forecast the business cycle*.

Consultant Economist associated with the Bureau for Economic Research (BER), University of Stellenbosch. The author wishes to acknowledge the inputs and comments of Ben Smit, George Kershoff, Harri Kemp, Hugo Pienaar and Christelle Grobler. However, the author accepts full responsibility for any remaining errors or omissions.

P. Laubscher (✉)
University of Stellenbosch, Stellenbosch, South Africa
e-mail: p.laubscher@mweb.co.za

S. Smirnov et al. (eds.), *Business Cycles in BRICS*, Societies and Political Orders in Transition, https://doi.org/10.1007/978-3-319-90017-9_28

In this chapter, the topic on *forecasting the business cycle* is approached with reference to the South African (SA) experience as a developing economy and a member of the BRICS group of nations. In the *first* main section, attention focuses on *understanding* the SA business cycle. Following on from the chapter "BRICS in the Global Economy", the causes and propagation of SA business cycles are briefly investigated, considering the global influences, structural changes and some of the salient features of the SA experience. In the *second* main section, attention focuses on *forecasting* the SA business cycle. The various methods in applied work are considered, including what may be regarded as an optimum approach to economic forecasting. The Bureau for Economic Research's (BER's) forecasting experience is considered, including some history, a consideration of the forecasting process and the key forecasting lessons learnt over the years. The results of a recent accuracy analysis are also briefly discussed. Some concluding remarks follow at the end of the chapter.

2 Causes and the Propagation of South African Business Cycles

It is a simple fact that the evolution of economic activity does not follow a straight line in a market economy, it fluctuates. Periods of prosperity and rapid economic growth are followed by periods of economic contraction or slower growth in preparation again for faster growth. This cyclical movement of general economic activity embodies what is described as the *business cycle*, or more closely defined as *the fluctuation of economic activity around a growth trend.*

In each phase of the business cycle, we find the co-movement of macro-economic magnitudes (e.g. expenditure by households, the government and business; production across a range of sectors, inflation, interest rates, credit extension, money supply, etc.). It is through the study of the co-movement of various economic variables that we can get to understanding the business cycle.

The student of the business cycle is particularly interested in the drivers of the recurrent deviations of the level of economic activity from its underlying growth trend. Comprehensive statistical techniques can be applied in isolating the cyclical components of economic time series, which are then analysed in determining a reference series representing the ('invisible') business cycle [Zarnowitz (1992: 183–190) warns that it is difficult to isolate cyclicality from the trend growth elements of an economic time series; according to him they are intertwined.].

Nonetheless, both elements need to be explored in order to arrive at an understanding of the drivers of growth and the propagation of cyclical movements to improve our comprehension of business cycles. This knowledge allows the economic policy maker, the business executive and the investor (and household!) to optimise economic decisions.

One has to accept that the business cycle phenomenon in modern economies is a very complex one. Many attempts at explaining the business cycle only address partial elements, not succeeding in uncovering the essential nature of the cycle. This was particularly the case in the pre-industrial era (see Achuthan and Banerji 2004: 17–36). However, during the previous century, a vast body of literature developed on what causes business cycles. Fathered by the work of Burns and Mitchell during the 1920s, volumes of economic data were studied and a range of theories and associated economic models were built, all attempting to explain the existence of business cycles.

2.1 The Issue of Exogeneity and Endogeneity

Business cycle theories are usually differentiated in relation to a key issue (and the explanations have varied and evolved over time) on whether business cycles are caused/driven by *external shocks* (including policy errors) or are there some *endogenous 'law' of regularity* causing/driving the business cycle; or is it a combination of these two factors? The two views at the extreme ends of the spectrum can be outlined as follows[1]:

- Economists believing in the persistence of market equilibria tend to explain the business cycle as the consequence of external shocks, i.e. exogenous factors, typically that of the policy maker, causing the economy to deviate from its equilibrium growth trend. Economists favouring a classical or monetarist view of the economy usually fall into this category.
- Other economists—mainly Keynesians—believe external shocks and policy makers typically have a peripheral impact on the propagation of business cycles. Business cycles are rather an endogenous phenomenon, inherently part of any modern market economy. Rather than being inherently stable, market economies are systematically unstable—each cycle caries the seeds of its own undoing.

The father of business cycle research, Arthur Burns, believed that the 'business cycle has an unceasing round', where endogenous factors such as the evolution of economic variables (e.g. business capital spending, credit extension and levels of business and consumer confidence) interact in ways that lead to economic fluctuations. He stated that these propagation forces in a market economy are powerful and typically override economic and public policy experiments and tend to prove prophets of doom or eternal optimists wrong time and again. While Arthur Burns did not have much confidence in the impact of macro-economic policies, Keynesians

[1]A third school can be identified, namely, the structuralist—or institutionalist—school, who believes business cycles are random events dictated by structural and institutional change (see Mohr 2015: 412).

generally do see an important role for public policy to soften the edges of the business cycle.

An interesting discovery of the *Economic Cycle Research Institute (ECRI)* is the fact that their system of leading coincident indicators works across regions of the world and across time periods, with the important condition that the free market needs to prevail, not being overwhelmed by war, weather or political upheaval (Achuthan and Banerji 2004: 95). Needless to say, it does not work in centrally planned economic systems. The implication is that while each business cycle, both in its expansion and contraction phase, is unique, there is a common thread even across countries and time periods, namely, the existence of a free enterprise economy. Provided this condition, it is generally found that co-movement exists between the key economic variables employment, income, output and sales. These variables are the central drivers of the business cycle.

The implication is that when a market economy is subject to political upheaval, like South Africa during the apartheid era, that exogenous factors may distort the operation of the business cycle. Likewise in an economy where the agricultural sector contributes a large share of GDP, which exposes economic activity to the vagaries of climatic factors. Also during periods of war, the economy tends to become a planned economy, and in this way the business cycle gets suspended.

Beyond the non-market influences, the business cycle has an endogenous regularity and momentum. It does happen that during long periods of sustained growth (or subpar growth) that policy makers, analysts and business executives become convinced regarding the *death of the business cycle*. However, this has proved time and again to be a function of fantasy or illusionary expectations—in reality every period of economic expansion is followed by a period of contraction.

It is true that due to just-in-time inventory management techniques, the improved expertise in macro-managing an economy (including the operation of automatic fiscal stabilisers), the impact of technological advances (e.g. the development of the Internet), the rise of the services economy and some aspects of globalisation, the business cycle has been tamed to a large extent in the sense that the amplitude of cyclical developments was reduced. However, even in this regard, the 2008–2009 global financial crisis reminded one quite profoundly of the *unceasing round of the business cycle*.

Furthermore, Zarnowitz (1992: 387) warns the economic forecaster that '. . .the economy in motion is a complex of dynamic processes, subject not only to a variety of disturbances but also to gradual and discrete changes in structure, institutions, and policy regimes. No wonder that there are few (if any) constant quantitative rules . . . to help the macro-economic forecaster effectively and consistently over more than a few years and from one business cycle to another'.

2.2 *Characteristics of the South African Business Cycle*

South Africa has a small and open economy, being closely integrated with the rest of the world via both trade and financing channels. It follows that the domestic business cycle is likely to be closely influenced by the world economy in general and the country's trading partner economies in particular. This fact has not changed despite many structural changes, economic policy experiments and institutional changes. Although structural change and exogenous shocks (globally and in the domestic political arena) impacted the SA business cycle, particularly from the mid-1970s onwards (i.e. during the post-Bretton Woods era of flexible exchange rates), the 'typical' domestic business cycle described in the 1960s is still recognisable today (see De Vries 1994: 20):

> In the phraseology of the King James version, an increase in export earnings enjoyed by a slack economy begat an increase in industrial utilization (and better profits), which together begat an increase in investment spending, which begat excess demand and bottlenecks, begetting when they matured, price inflation and balance of payments difficulties, which begat curbs, slowdowns and slacks in the sixth and seventh generations after the increase in export earnings.

This is a somewhat poetic description of the classic SA business cycle, driven to a large extent by the evolution of the country's export earnings, in turn, a direct function of global demand for SA's exports and the level of commodity prices. Figure 1 shows the close correlation of the SA business cycle (using the year-on-year changes in the SA Reserve Bank's (SARB's) composite coincident indicator as reference series) and the G7 countries' industrial production cycle.

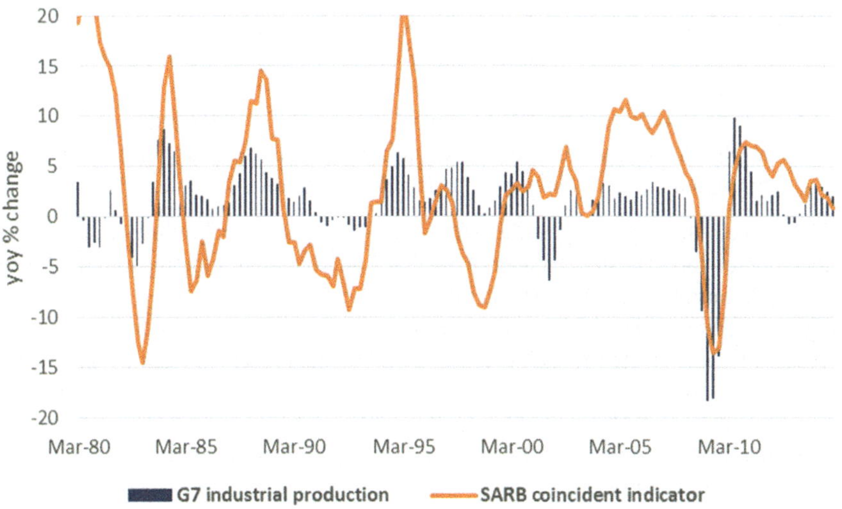

Fig. 1 The South African business cycle vs the G7 countries' industrial production cycle. Source: SARB/OECD Main Economic Indicators

Despite this qualitative continuity of the SA business cycle, the economic history of the country is one of recurrent political and social crisis. A previous governor of the SA Reserve Bank (SARB), Dr De Kock, always emphasised the qualitative continuity of the domestic business cycle, however, even he conceded, '... the course of any [business] cycle can be drastically affected by political, social and other non-economic factors' (Mohr and Rogers 1994: 298).

Somewhere between these two realities—the export-driven endogenous momentum and the domestic socio-political shocks (and structural change)—the SA business cycle has been shaped. It is useful to briefly dwell on, *firstly*, the global influences and, *secondly*, the domestic economic changes shaping the SA business cycle.

2.2.1 Global Influences

The transmission of global business cycle developments to emerging markets was considered in Part I of the current book. This section aims to provide a concise overview of both the trade and financial channels in the case of SA, which affords a deeper understanding of the SA business cycle to the forecaster. It is also important to note that the operation of these global business cycle linkages is not static, it changes over time. In this respect, the following structural changes relevant to business cycle research and economic forecasting may be noted:

- *Firstly*, the structural changes in the global economic growth environment since around 1973, i.e. the post-Bretton Woods era of flexible exchange rates, being acknowledged in business cycle literature (see Romer 1999; Basu and Taylor 1999; IMF 2002).
- *Secondly*, and related to the former point, is the impact of globalisation and particularly the closer financial linkages wrought since the 1990s (see Calvo et al. 2001).
- *Finally*, the impact of the global financial crisis of 2007–2008 and the subsequent Great Recession and the period of unconventional monetary policies (UMP) being implemented in the major advanced economies since end 2008.

As noted, the sensitivity of the SA business cycle to global influences is a well-documented fact. During calendar 2014, SA's international trade measured 64% of its GDP. Furthermore, the deficit on the current account of the SA balance of payments amounted to 5.5% of GDP, i.e. an indication of the level of foreign savings required to finance the shortfall between domestic aggregate expenditure and aggregate production (or between domestic investment and savings). Regarding the financial linkages, SA's stock of foreign financial assets and liabilities have increased dramatically following the political change in 1994 to a full democracy and SA's financial re-integration with the world economy. Despite this development, SA remains well-known for its shallow net foreign exchange reserve position juxtaposed with its deep and well-developed capital markets, both factors impacting a recipient economy's sensitivity to fluctuations in international capital flows and financial stress in developed economies (see IMF 2009: 133–134). In view of the foregoing characteristics, it becomes clear why the SA currency tends to be very volatile. Key elements of the trade and financial channels along which business cycle developments in the major advanced economies (G3 countries and China) are transmitted to SA follow below.

Trade Channel The SA business cycle has to an important degree been driven by the international commodity cycle, in turn driven by the major advanced economies' industrial production cycle (see Barr and Kantor 2002: 4–5). This suggests that the trade channel for the transmission of global business cycle influences to the domestic economy have been foremost.

Regarding the destination of SA's exports, key structural shifts occurred in recent years, with the share of exports destined for the Asian continent growing sharply at the expense of the growth in exports to the so-called G4 countries, i.e. SA's traditional trading partners—the USA, Germany, the UK and Japan. More than 60% of SA's exports are destined for Asia (36%, of which 62% are destined for China, Japan and India) and Europe (26%, of which 90% are destined for the EU countries). SA's other important trading partner region is Africa, absorbing one fifth of SA's exports (of which three quarters are destined to its southern neighbours, i.e. the SADC countries). Therefore, in terms of regions and ranked in order of importance, the EU, SADC, China, the USA, Japan, India and other Asian countries absorb the bulk of SA's exports (i.e. 82%).

Regarding the composition of SA's exports, two thirds of the basket consists of basic commodities (i.e. agricultural and mineral products, as well as heavy manufactures such as chemicals and basic metals). The demand for bulky heavy manufactures and commodities typically has a lower income elasticity. The demand for fully manufactured machinery and built-up vehicles and components may be more income and price elastic, but this comprise only one quarter of the SA export basket. Whereas the share of fully manufactured products in exports has increased during the 1980s and 1990s, this trend reversed again over the past 20 years due to manufacturing's reduced contribution to the country's GDP (see McCarthy 2015: 9).[2]

The overall income elasticity of SA exports (in response to the major advanced economies' real GDP) ranges between 1% and 1.5% over the long term, while the price elasticity is very low at between 0.2% and 0.4% (BER 2015b). This suggests the volume growth in SA exports is driven stronger by advanced economy growth than commodity price (or exchange rate) changes.

Financial Channel Regarding the financial channel, a key change occurred on SA's balance of payments as SA was financially re-integrated with the rest of the world following the first full democratic elections in 1994 (see the improvement in

[2]This is mirrored in the fact that during 1993–1995 minerals contributed 17.5% of merchandise exports, increasing to 26.9% during 2011–2013 (McCarthy 2015: 9).

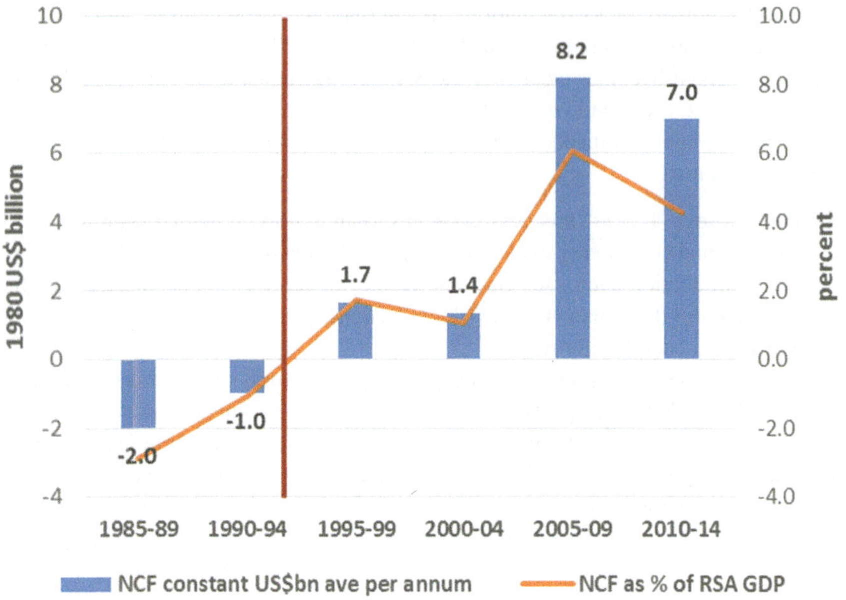

Fig. 2 Total net capital flows on the SA balance of payments: 1974–2014. Source: SA Reserve Bank; own calculations

capital inflows, Fig. 2). Coincidentally this occurred at a time when the transmission of global financial influences on emerging market economies intensified (Calvo et al. 2001: 3). The key financial channels in the case of SA are the exchange rate, the bond and other asset markets (e.g. the JSE) and prices (i.e. particularly the second round effects of currency-induced inflation). The period since the 1990s was characterised by substantial financial volatility (e.g. the Mexican financial crises of 1994–1995, the abolition of SA's financial rand mechanism in March 1995, the East Asian financial crisis of 1997–1998 and the September 2001 World Trade Center event).

One also has to distinguish between the period before November 2008 and thereafter when the major advanced economies began implementing unconventional monetary policies (UMP)—see Laubscher (2015). Key amongst the 'spillover effects' after 2008 has been the increase in global liquidity due to the expansion of the advanced economy central bank balance sheets and the increased (short-term) capital flow into emerging economy bonds and equities, which caused asset prices to increase in these economies and currencies to appreciate, in turn, leading to potential asset price distortions and financial volatility (see Chen et al. 2014: 3). According to the IMF, the financial stress levels in emerging market economies, being transmitted from the major advanced economies experiencing financial stress during and in the wake of the 2008–2009 global financial crisis, rose to levels last experienced with the East Asian economic crisis in 1997–1998 (IMF 2009: 134).

In sum, while SA's international indebtedness is low by international standards, its deep and well-developed capital markets, combined with its trade openness and export commodity intensity, seem to make the country vulnerable on both fronts. The potential volatility (of particularly financial variables) challenges economic forecasters, who tend not to anticipate the spikes—see Sect. 3.2.3.

2.2.2 The South African Economy

At the time of writing, SA was in its 16th (trough-to-trough) business cycle of the post-war period.[3] It is interesting to note the changed characteristics of SA business cycles before and after the mid-1970s (see De Vries 1994: 18–21; Mohr and Rogers 1994: 294; Du Plessis and Smit 2002). During the first structural period from 1946 to 1973, a clear upward trajectory in the secular growth trend was observable. In this period SA witnessed nine complete business cycles averaging 36.1 months in length with upswing phases lasting an average 23 months and downswing phases 13.4 months. In none of the calendar years, over this period was negative real GDP growth registered.

However, since the mid-1970s this changed. This change is captured in the following quote by a SA historian, Charles Feinstein (quoted in McCarthy 2015: 17):

> From the 1920s to the 1970s an expanding industrial sector was supported by a combination of high profits and abundant foreign exchange derived from unlimited international demand for gold. There was then a dramatic structural break and the economy switched from apparently triumphant progress to distressing decline.

Over the 1973–1993 period, 4 calendar years of negative growth were registered, the length of the business cycle increased to 62.5 months, mainly due to much longer downswing phases, which lengthened from 13.4 months on average to 33 months. In fact, the growth trend turned downwards over this period. The onset of the cyclical downturn in September 1974 has been regarded as the turning point (De Vries 1994). Not only did the downswing phases of the business cycle lengthen, but the amplitude of fluctuations increased (see Table 1), implying greater economic instability.

As noted, the key measure of distinction regarding the international structural periods is the changeover from the Bretton Woods period of fixed exchange rates (1972/1973) to the subsequent floating exchange rate regime. SA only moved to a system of floating exchange rates in 1979 and a unified currency in 1995 (with the final scrapping of the financial rand). However, the oil shocks of 1973/1974 and the conflict in Angola following that country's independence had major implications for the domestic economy. There has been an important debate regarding the instability

[3]Since 1970, the South African Reserve Bank regularly determines the upper and lower turning points of the domestic business cycle using extensive statistical and econometric techniques (see Venter 2018).

Table 1 South African business cycle phases: September 1974–December 2013

	Downswing phases	Length (months)	Depth (peak-to-trough)[a] (%)	Upswing phases	Length (months)	Height (trough-to-peak)[a] (%)
1.	Sept 1974–Dec 1977	40	+2.4	Jan 1978–Aug 1981	44	+22.6
2.	Sept 1981–Mar 1983	19	−5.3	Apr 1983–Jun 1984	15	+8.1
3.	Jul 1984–Mar 1986	21	−3.2	Apr 1986–Feb 1989	35	+10.1
4.	Mar 1989–May 1993	51	−5.1	Jun 1993–Nov 1996	42	+16.0
5.	Dec 1996–Aug 1999	33	+3.2	Sep 1999–Nov 2007	99	+46.1
6.	Dec 2007–Aug 2009	21	−2.5	Sep 2009–Nov 2013	51	+13.8

[a]Percentage change in the level of GDP at constant 2010 prices. The change is measured from peak-to-trough and trough-to-peak in the level of GDP and not over the business cycle phase dating period

Source: SA Reserve Bank *Quarterly Bulletin*, March (2015)

of the 1970s and 1980s with some economists emphasising adverse structural factors explaining the fluctuations in economic activity and others arguing that—despite these exogenous shocks—the SA business cycle still possessed an underlying regularity (see Mohr and Rogers 1994: 298).

Apart from the major structural break in the mid-1970s, other structural changes on the domestic front include the international debt moratorium and the collapse of the rand in 1985, the political change in 1994 and SA's financial re-entry into the world economy and, finally, the impact of the Great Recession in 2009 and its aftermath. (Other exogenous developments, which often impacted, include large fluctuations in the gold price, domestic political unrest and instability, e.g. June 1976, July 1985 and June 1986 and 1992–1993, protracted agricultural droughts in the 1980s and early 1990s—see De Vries 1994: 21.)

The problem since the mid-1970s was that both monetary and fiscal policies were often subject to non-economic factors and may have contributed to economic fluctuations. Fiscal policy tended to be expansive due to the demands of defence spending and the reigning view at the time of Keynesian demand management to stimulate economic growth. The fiscal expansion was often accommodated by monetary policy, which contributed to excessive growth in bank credit utilisation and real domestic expenditure and imports. This, in turn, led to both inflation and balance of payments bottlenecks and consequent sharp adjustments in monetary policy and the attendant 'stop-go' business cycles. The balance of payments constraint was the domestic economy's Achilles' heel.

While these exogenous shocks did influence the business cycle, its characteristic regularity also persisted. It is interesting to note that SA's peak-to-peak business cycle (end 1989 to end 1996) at the time of the tumultuous political change and the country's financial re-integration continued to share this 'stop-go' pattern as monetary policy had to be tightened during 1995–1996 due to a serious, albeit somewhat relieved, balance of payments constraint. Exports were still the driver of the general economic recovery and a revival of fixed investment spending accelerated growth (see Fig. 1).

SA's financial re-entry to the world economy was a 'baptism of fire', and the growth improvement was slow to get off the ground. Capital flows on the balance of payments reversed from heavy net outflows during the period in the run-up to 1994 to net inflows subsequently (Fig. 2). The fact of the matter is that this domestic change coincided with the global trend change discussed above, i.e. the onset of greater financial volatility related to increased financial integration of the global economy during the 1990s. SA had to be patient as the capital flows were volatile at first (second half of the 1990s and early 2000s), but they became more substantial particularly in the wake of the loosening of monetary policies in the major advanced economies during the 2000s and the strong growth globally (2003–2008), also being boosted by the growth of China and other emerging economies.

The relieving of the balance of payments constraint had a major impact; however, structural reform policies introduced in February 1996 (which contributed to the 1997–1999 'growth recession') prepared the economy for a longer-lasting upswing. In both the monetary policy and fiscal policy fields, huge strides were made to stabilise the macro-economic conditions (Du Plessis 2004; Du Plessis and Smit 2005; Smit 2006; Laubscher 2004). The improvement in the domestic economy was embodied in a more stable macro-economic environment enhancing steady growth in after-tax real disposable incomes and affording the fiscus to embark on a more expansionary route (circa 2002). Fixed investment responded strongly to the improved demand conditions, and the economy registered its longest post-war economic expansion (September 1999–November 2007). While some structural improvements were evident in the economy, the growth acceleration was slow off the mark and not great by SA's own and international peer-group standards (Du Plessis and Smit 2005: 39). It was also overtaken by the onset of the Great Recession impact in 2009.

The economy rebounded after the 2009 recession, with real GDP growth reaching 3% in 2010–2011 (in line with its post-apartheid performance during the first decade). However, the revival of business confidence fell flat, fixed investment remained lacklustre (even when compared to business cycle expansions from the mid-1970s) and growth tapered to an 1.6% annual tempo (2012–2016).

While the impact of structural change and exogenous shocks has been quite evident in influencing the SA business cycle, a closer inspection of the business cycle characteristics reveals its underlying regularity.

Tables 2 and 3 provide an indication of the amplitude of the SA business cycle over the 1974–2013 period across the various expenditure components of GDP, i.e. the depth of economic recessions and the height of expansions, respectively. Figure 3 provides an indication of the speed of adjustment, i.e. the average rates of contraction or expansion across the expenditure components.

From the tables and chart, it is clear what important role swings in real exports (and imports) and fixed investment play in the SA business cycle. On average,

Table 2 The depth of SA recessions in the post-Bretton Woods era: 1974–2013[a]

	HCE	GC	GDFI	GDE	Exports	Imports	GDP
Recessions							
07Q4-09Q3	–3.5	7.6	–14.8	–2.9	–20.0	–23.3	–2.5
96Q4-99Q3	5.0	–3.8	–11.2	–3.6	–8.6	–11.6	3.2
89Q1-93Q2	–3.4	4.6	–19.1	–7.2	–11.2	–14.1	–5.1
84Q2-86Q1	–8.0	4.9	–30.3	–7.7	–1.1	–27.7	–3.2
81Q3-83Q1	–1.7	3.5	–10.3	–11.8	–14.7	–36.8	–5.3
74Q3-77Q4	–3.9	22.8	–16.8	–7.6	11.6	–37.3	2.4
Averages	–4.1	6.6	–17.1	–6.8	–11.1	–25.1	–4.0
lead(–)/lag(+)	2.0	na	3.5	0.0	2.0	1.0	1.5

[a]Percentage change calculated from peak-to-trough in respect of each expenditure component of GDP

Source: SA Reserve Bank, *Quarterly Bulletin,* March (2015); own calculations

Table 3 The height of SA expansions in the post-Bretton Woods era: 1974–2013[a]

	HCE	GC	GDFI	GDE	Exports	Imports	GDP
Expansions							
09Q3-13Q4	15.7	14.3	14.1	21.8	21.0	36.3	13.8
99Q3-07Q4	52.4	46.9	134.5	62.9	63.5	114.7	46.1
93Q2-96Q4	19.3	2.7	51.5	22.0	67.3	94.0	16.0
86Q1-89Q1	18.3	16.7	26.4	13.4	31.5	53.2	10.1
83Q2-84Q2	13.1	17.3	2.7	12.3	4.0	29.3	8.1
78Q1-81Q3	26.0	13.1	41.4	31.2	3.5	50.5	22.6
Averages	24.2	18.5	45.1	27.3	31.8	63.0	19.4
lead(–)/lag(+)	–0.5	0.0	2.5	0.0	0.0	0.5	0.0

[a]Percentage change calculated from trough-to-peak in respect of each expenditure component of GDP

Source: SA Reserve Bank, *Quarterly Bulletin,* March (2015); own calculations

exports contracted by 11% during economic recessions and expanded by 32% during economic recoveries over the 1974–2013 period. The rate at which exports contracted averaged 6.5% per annum during recessions and expanded at 5.3% per annum on average during economic recoveries (Fig. 3). The corresponding numbers in respect of real fixed investment spending are –17% and –8.3% per annum (during recessions) and +45% and 9.0% per annum (during expansions), i.e. a clear driver of the general business cycle momentum. The current text does not permit a fuller exposition of the cyclical process.

Considering the recessionary phases of the business cycle, the sharp export contractions during the early 1980s (15%), early 1990s (11%) and the 2008–2009 recession (20%) are evident, indicating that these recessions were externally induced. While the contractions in exports permeated throughout the economy, also impacting fixed investment spending, monetary policy tightening invariably aimed at rebalancing the current account of the balance of payments (witness the

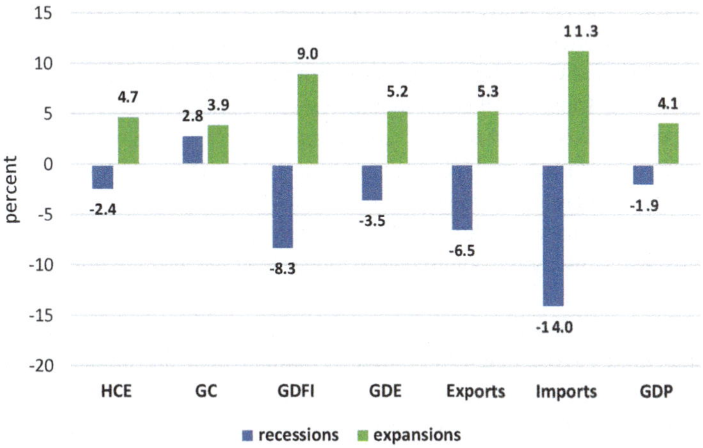

Fig. 3 Average annualised growth rates during SA recessions and expansions: 1974–2014. Annualised growth rate calculated from peak-to-trough (recessions) and trough-to-peak (expansions) in respect of each expenditure component of GDP. Source: SA Reserve Bank *Quarterly Bulletin*, March (2015); own calculations

sharp contractions in imports), and attending to inflation pressures, caused real domestic expenditure also to contract. Recessions with strong domestic components include those of the 1980s and early 1990s. In the former period, the 1981–1983 and 1984–1986 recessions were deep, characterised by sharp contractions in fixed and inventory investment. Strong declines in the gold price and the domestic housing market were also key features. The early 1990s recession was externally induced, but possessed a strong adverse domestic component in the form of a serious drought in agriculture as well as intense socio-political instability in the run-up to the country's first full democratic elections in 1994. This recession is on record as being the longest post-war one, i.e. 51 months.

Considering the expansionary phases of the business cycle, Table 3 shows that fixed investment spending (expanding by 45% on average during economic recoveries over the 1974–2013 period) and export growth (32%) are the typical drivers. The fixed investment spending momentum during the first two post-apartheid economic recoveries (1993–1996 and 2000–2007) was quite strong; however, it failed to materialise during the current economic recovery following the global financial crisis. The 2009–2013 upswing has been consumption led, with both strong procyclical fiscal policy and growth in real household consumption expenditure being key elements. The upturn in fixed investment spending has been weak (also accompanied by poor business confidence levels) and the growth in exports comparatively weak in a historical context. As such, the growth in real household expenditure was unsustainable. The economy entered a downturn in November 2013, which developed into an outright recession towards the end of 2016. Refer to the chapter "A Brief History of Business Cycle Measurement in South Africa", Part II.

Notable from Table 1 is the fact that the two post-apartheid recessions have been relatively mild affairs, with real GDP continuing to rise by 3.2% over the 1997–1999 period (i.e. a so-called growth recession) and only contracting by 2.5% during 2008–2009. Furthermore, Table 1 shows that the two expansion phases of the post-apartheid business cycles lengthened quite dramatically to 99 months and 51 months, respectively, i.e. significantly longer than the average post-war business cycle upswing of 26 months.[4]

The discrete structural changes (and exogenous shocks) on the SA economic landscape—mid-1970s, mid-1980s, mid-1990s and then the impact of the Great Recession—are evident, which make it very difficult for the economic forecaster to navigate the SA business cycle. However, this does not mean the underlying regularity of the cyclical development of the economy has been suspended, which, in turn, renders economic forecasting of the business cycle a rewarding exercise.

3 Forecasting the Business Cycle

As noted in the introduction, business cycle analysis invariably involves some interest in generating forward-looking information. Economists are often the subject of jokes when it comes to forecasting. John K. Galbraith remarked a long time ago that 'the only function of economic forecasting is to make astrology look respectable'. Clements and Hendry (2002: 11) quote the quip regarding economic forecasting: 'those who could, did; those who couldn't, forecast'. Economists themselves often state that it is impossible to forecast. In fact, economic forecasters' track record in terms of accuracy is not great. In a recent article in the *International Journal of Forecasting*, it was reported that the accuracy of economic forecasting did not improve in the major G7 industrial countries over the past 50 years!

The question therefore arises, why do economists continue with the discipline of forecasting and why does an insatiable demand for economic forecasting services exist? The short and simple answer is that economic forecasting meets a great need amongst business executives, policy makers, investment officers and other users of economic information. Our inability to know the future must not be confused with the idea that forward-looking economic information is dispensable in the modern economy. Experience shows that economic forecasting adds value to decision-making. The role of the economic forecaster may have changed over time. In today's world of rapid change, technological innovation and ever-closer financial and real economic linkages across geographical borders, the role of the forecaster becomes

[4]This is the average duration of 14 post-WWII economic expansion phases up to the end of 1996, i.e. excluding the 1999–2007 and 2009 to date expansion phases.

that of *interpreter*, i.e. making sense of the current economic conditions, i.e. knowing where we are and then to proceed in attempting to chart the future.

Economists have little choice but to persist in applying their trade as forecasters. A good economist, or economics team, typically has the qualifications and tools to do this. In this section, some of the basic economic forecasting techniques are outlined (first section); and, thereafter, the forecasting exercise of one of the oldest economic research institutes in SA, i.e. the Bureau for Economic Research (BER), comes under closer inspection (second section). The BER has been studying the SA business cycle from 1944 and adopted economic forecasting from the onset.

3.1 Basic Economic Forecasting Techniques

Economic forecasting ranges from the projection of relatively stable macroeconomic magnitudes, such as GDP growth and its major expenditure components, unemployment, inflation and interest rates, with strong trend and cyclical components, to the more volatile time series such as bond yields, share prices and exchange rates, which often follow a random walk, making forecasting hazardous.

While the primary objective of economic forecasts is to inform and improve public and private sector decision making, specific needs for economic forecasts vary from client to client. As Zarnowitz summarises: '... economic and business forecasters serve many different masters' (1992: 388). Accuracy analysis of competing forecasting methods, interestingly enough, does not produce a superior method with any degree of confidence, albeit that in terms of choice, outside econometric models, leading indicators and anticipation surveys rank relatively more favourable (Zarnowitz 1992: 404). These survey findings generally point to a high degree of eclecticism in the choice of forecasting method.[5] They also suggest that applying a combination of methods ensures the better forecasting results. In the section below, this theme is developed further.

Some of the key techniques are discussed, commencing with *indicator analyses* and ending with a brief consideration of what may point to the proverbial 'state-of-the-art' in the economic forecasting trade. The idea is not to explain the technicalities of the various forecasting methods, but rather the advantages and disadvantages of

---

[5]In a US survey of forecasting methods applied by forecasters conducted in the early 1980s, the American Statistical Association (ASA), working in conjunction with the National Bureau for Economic Research (NBER), found that an informal GNP model served as the most popular technique (74% of the respondents using this method, with 56% rating it as the most useful); second in line was econometric models (53% and 13%, respectively); third was leading indicators (49% and 12%) and fourth, anticipation surveys (42% and 1%)—see Zarnowitz (1992: 402). This usage pattern may have changed as computing technology developed over the years. In a 1987 survey by the National Association of Business Economists (NABE), it was found that on average the contribution of econometric models to the forecasting outcome was 60%, judgement around 30% and time series methods, current data analysis and interaction with others around 15% (Zarnowitz 1992: 405).

each, and to reach some formulation of what may be seen as an 'optimal' forecasting process. The one department of business cycle forecasting, namely, the estimation and forecasting of business cycle turning points using composite business cycle indicators and other parametric and non-parametric methods, is covered elsewhere in the book and is not repeated here. The origins and broad content of indicator analysis are only highlighted in order to show how it may be used to complement time series and structural econometric modelling in order to arrive at what may be described as an optimal approach to economic forecasting.

3.1.1 Indicator Analysis

The so-called indicator approach to forecasting has a long history. One of the key 'discoveries' in early dedicated business cycle research has been the observation that turning points in different economic time series tended to cluster and that the sequence of developments during these *clustered turning point* periods tended to be durable from the one business cycle to the next even though individual business cycles differed in many respects. This approach to the study and forecasting of the business cycle, through the collection and close observation of many time series and other economic data in a so-called 'bottom-up' manner, is known as the *indicator approach*. Its method contrasts with 'top-down' theorising and econometric modelling aimed at understanding and forecasting the business cycle.

The intellectual fathers of the *indicator approach* to business cycle analysis and forecasting are Arthur Burns and Wesley Mitchell, at the time employed by the NBER, and who published their *magnum opus* just after the end of WWII (*Measuring Business Cycles* 1946). This work and approach came under attack from the mainstream economics fraternity, led by Tjalling Koopmans' (1947) critique at the time, titled: *Measurement Without Theory.* He postulated that any attempt to observe cyclical patterns from extensive data collection as being 'unscientific'.[6] Achuthan and Banerji counter in their recent book '... "scientific" methods have repeatedly failed to predict cyclical turning points' (2004: 25).[7] This is probably the key weakness of structural econometric and time series models, which provides an

[6]Koopmans' critique (1947) had its origins in the ideas of the celebrated philosopher, Sir Karl Popper, who published his *The Logic of Scientific Discovery* in 1934. He stated that science can only advance through *apriori* theories capable of being rejected through empirical testing. Whereas theories had to be falsifiable, Achuthan and Banerji point out that the Burns and Mitchell approach to understanding economic turning points relied on descriptive observations that were not 'falsifiable' like mathematical equations (2004: 25–26) and hence Koopmans' and others' (notably Paul Samuelson's) critique of the 'indicator approach'.

[7]Achuthan and Banerji currently lead the *Economic Cycle Research Institute (ECRI)* in the USA having continued the work of Geoffrey Moore, originally employed by the NBER, but leaving that institute when it became clear that it moved away from its *dedicated business cycle research* origins in the 1970s. Moore is well-known for the development of composite leading, coinciding and lagging business cycle indicators for the USA and many other countries. Even the American scientific community acknowledged his work during the 1970s (see Achuthan and Banerji 2004: 33).

opening for indicator analyses in augmenting the economic forecasting process. Time series models are also a form of a so-called 'theory-free' approach to economic forecasting.

Whereas a structural econometric model attempts to capture the complexity of the economy, it does this by the adoption of simplifying assumptions, which—according to Achuthan and Banerji—causes it to break down when needed most. Models, which tend to mimic the past, for instance, fail in capturing the complexity of the economy at turning points in the economic cycle (2004: 116). The reality is that many cycles and sub-cycles exist which all shape the underlying business cycle.

It is key to observe all these 'sub-cycles', be it the key drivers of the business cycle such as output, employment, income and sales, or other (secondary) driving factors such as inflation, profits, inventories and the money supply, or even at the sectoral level (construction, manufacturing and services), etc. By observing all these tendencies, cyclical indicators can be combined into composite leading, coincident and lagging indices that reveal the various cycles, be it in economic activity, inflation or employment, etc. In this way the complexity of fluctuations in economic activity, which changes from one business cycle to the next, is navigated in a way that new economic relationships are uncovered, inter alia, timely indicating turning points and empowering the user to conduct economic forecasts. According to Achuthan and Banerji, it is exactly when economic variables begin operating out of synch or non-standard that econometric models break down. This is when the indicator approach can deliver superior results, particularly in terms of predicting turning points.

Turning points may be identified when any shift in economic activity meets predetermined criteria in respect of three aspects. *Firstly*, the analyst needs to look for turning points or shifts in the economy by assessing how *pronounced* a shift is (by comparing to previous cycles, for instance); *secondly*, how *pervasive* it is (in other words, how many indicators share the movement); and, *thirdly*, how *persistent* it is (it should last for at least 4–5 months). Applying these principles in the construction and maintenance of composite indices will uncover the various cycles.

While the evolution of the four variables—employment, income, sales and output—*coincides* with business cycle turning points, other indicators exist, also reflecting drivers of the business cycle (such as profits, inventories and money supply), on which the focus fall in designing leading economic indicators. The key in designing composite indicators is to focus on the drivers of the business cycle, which then tend to reliably track the business cycle across time and across countries. The original ECRI leading economic indicators were sensitive commodity prices, length of the workweek, non-residential building contracts, start-ups, housing starts, stock price indices and business failure liabilities (see Achuthan and Banerji 2004: 82 and 94).

In terms of the construction of composite indicators, Zarnowitz emphasises the importance of including the indicators that are systematically related to the business cycle:

- Leading indicators have to consist of price and flow variables that are highly sensitive to overall cyclical influences; these time series tend to show high volatility and lead cyclical developments.

- Coincident indicators are smoother and correspond with the turning points in the reference business cycle; they are less responsive to cyclical influences.
- Lagging indicators include massive stock variables and respond slowly to cyclical developments; they are usually very smooth.

A rich literature on composite indicators has developed (see the foregoing chapters, Part IV of this book). There is a whole body of knowledge regarding lead and lag structures and how these changed over time in respect of individual countries and due to structural change, on how composite indices have to be constructed and which criteria they should comply with, etc. The SARB's method in the construction and use of composite business cycle indicators, including diffusion indices, is discussed in detail in the chapter "The SARB's Composite Business Cycle Indicators", Part IV, and is not repeated here. As noted, other attempts, employing parametric and non-parametric (data-intensive) methods aimed at indicating and predicting turning points in the SA business cycle, exist in the academic literature (see Du Plessis 2006; Moolman 2003). Finally, Part III discusses the role of business tendency surveys (BTS) in business cycle analysis. BTS may be regarded as part and parcel of the indicator approach to economic forecasting. This is an extremely valuable approach to economic analysis, also as a complementary activity in the economic forecasting process.

3.1.2 Extrapolative Techniques/Time Series Models

Forecasting with econometric models requires prior theoretical knowledge and the structural specification of the model, which is not always the forte of the forecast practitioner. Even academic economists lost interest in forecasting due to the debates and controversies regarding economic theory. This reduced complexity and lower costs presumably explain the growth of interest in statistical methods of univariate and multivariate time series prediction (Zarnowitz 1992: 406).

Time series extrapolative forecasting techniques consist of the simple univariate autoregressive (AR) and autoregressive integrated moving average (ARIMA) models and their generalised multivariate versions ranging from the basic vector autoregressive (VAR) model to its variants, such as the Bayesian vector autoregressive (BVAR) model, structural vector autoregressive (SVAR) and cointegrated vector autoregressive moving average (VARMA) models. With some qualification, the common factor in these models is that the economic variables they contain are specified as some lagged function of their past values, not requiring a theoretical specification.

As such, the VAR models provide a theory-free method in estimating economic relationships, and applied in forecasting, these models were regarded as either being better, particularly regarding some variables, time horizons and periods, or could improve econometric modelling results if used in conjunction. The latter—even simple averaging—has proved to improve forecasting accuracy. The VAR models can typically also be produced much less costly compared to the complex and comprehensive multi-equation econometric models. According to Clements and Hendry, the multivariate models (i.e. VAR, VECM, BVAR and other variants) are competitive in accurate forecasting and are the 'work horses of the forecasting industry' (2002: 4).

Proponents of time series models tend to argue that more efficient use of the available information is achieved, inter alia, by combining econometric model forecasts with time series forecasts. Various statistical techniques are available to construct the combined forecast. Furthermore, the benefit of time series models is that they teach forecasters important lessons on how to decompose, de-trend, de-seasonalise and use the stochastic properties of time series for forecasting purposes. Time series models often provide good projections of recent trends. However, this brings one to the Achilles' heel of time series models.

Critics argue that they tend to lag behind actual developments in the economy and therefore fail to provide timeous indications of turning points in the broader economy, e.g. turning points in growth rates and levels of income, output and prices (Zarnowitz 1992: 401). This is precisely the need of economic forecast users. Econometricians also argue that any econometric model which does not encompass the information contained in a time series model is simply miss-specified. Furthermore, time series modelling results (also when in combination with econometric modelling) often contain internal inconsistencies (e.g. the sum of the individual forecasted expenditure components of GDP not adding up to aggregate GDP).

The interesting theoretical issue is whether the forecasting process should be made more efficient (read: smaller forecast error) by pooling the information contained in the various modelling outcomes, or should the information be pooled earlier with the specification of the modelling structure. This question has led to a more comprehensive mining of the available information going into the forecast (e.g. econometric modelling of the micro-economic foundations of decision-making) and expanded indicator analyses (e.g. 'back-casting' and 'now-casting'), which has become doable due to the availability of higher frequency economic data and the required computing power.

3.1.3 Econometric Models

Econometric models—or econometric systems of equations—are the main tool in economic forecasting (Clements and Hendry 2002: 5). Econometric models have different uses and a range of model types exist; however, they all consist of systems of equations which seek to 'model' the economy by adopting simplifying assumptions of the reality. An econometric model consolidates existing empirical and theoretical knowledge of how economies function and provides a coherent analytical framework for conducting, amongst other, policy analysis and economic forecasting.

The use of econometric models dates back to the 1950s and 1960s and these models have undergone major development and refinement over the years. Forecasting modelling really took off during the 1970s. The original so-called first-generation models, based on the Keynesian IS/LM framework, were followed by the second-generation models, which added a supply-side component and dynamic features (through the use of error-correction specifications) and the contemporary third- and fourth-generation *dynamic stochastic general equilibrium* (DSGE) models.

The latter-mentioned models have micro-economic foundations where behaviour at the level of the micro-economic decisions of consumers and firms is dissembled and aggregated to yield estimable relationships (for a detailed discussion, see Fukač and Pagan 2009). A key distinction between the semi-structural macro-models (second generation) and the DSGE models is that the former rely on backward-looking expectations whereas the latter models incorporate forward-looking (rational) expectations (Hjelm et al. 2015: 21–22). The famous Lucas critique—that structural macro-econometric models fail in modelling structural changes or breaks in the economy—spawned the development of third- and fourth-generation DSGE models. However, DSGE models are, according to the experts, better suited for policy analysis and rather impractical (and costly) as forecasting tools (Hjelm et al. 2015: 18). The modelling of monetary policy transmission in the economy is key in these models and these models are therefore popular at central banks with substantial resources.

So-called (conventional) semi-structural macro-models contain a large number of behavioural equations and identities defining the structure of the model. They can be regarded as Keynesian in the short term, with neoclassical elements in the longer term. These models are large and detailed and generally of the second-generation type noted above, better suited for economic forecasting, particularly if the user's need is for a wide range of forecast economic variables. The advantage of semi-structural econometric models in forecasting is that a comprehensive macro-economic forecast is obtained simultaneously. Furthermore, depending on a particular institution's need, elements such as monetary and financial policy can be treated endogenously or exogenously in the model.

A disadvantage of econometric modelling in general is the inbuilt neoclassical notion that the economy reverts to a steady state over the longer term. As a result, econometric models tend not to project large deviations from the long-run equilibrium tendency, they tend to revert to the modelled steady state too easily. Furthermore, whereas judgement can be applied to overcome this shortcoming, forecasters also tend not to deviate too far from the consensus. In other words, both model and forecaster suffer from the same malaise when it comes to economic forecasting.

While the answer to the question of which forecasting method is superior may remain elusive, it may be useful to formulate what approach to forecasting can be regarded as being optimal.

3.1.4 State-of-the-Art

From detailed surveys on model usage and preference and accuracy analysis, there does not seem to be a superior forecasting method and/or modelling structure in any systematic way.[8] Various combinations of methods and models are used depending on the needs of the user. Regarding econometric models, a key consensus is that even though they represent a simplification of reality, models do facilitate a *consistent interpretation* of economic development. In the hazardous exercise of economic forecasting, this consistency is of immense value. Furthermore, where models do fall short, judgement, indicators and even 'gut feel' (or guesses) can plug the gap.

Zarnowitz concludes after a comprehensive forecast accuracy analysis of US forecasters that while the quality of forecasts has not deteriorated, forecast errors during the second half of the 1970s and during the 1980s were relatively big due to major shocks at the time. He also picked up an inability to identify economic slowdowns or contractions and suggested at the time that econometric and time series modelling should be complemented by indicator analysis in order to reduce the length and the variability of the lags in recognising recessions (Zarnowitz 1992: 413/534).

Judgement has always remained a key requirement (and preference) in economic forecasting, even amongst those users of large-scale econometric models. Accuracy analysis of forecasting in the USA also proves that model results having been adjusted through judgemental intervention are superior to those produced mechanistically. However, note that the size of the improvement in the forecasting error is bigger the shorter the forecasting horizon and it became smaller in time as the specification of econometric models improved (Zarnowitz 1992: 404–410).

In terms of econometric modelling forecasting practice, the recent comprehensive survey by the Swedish National Institute of Economic Research (NIER) of model usage across the globe finds two key contemporary trends. *Firstly*, most central banks have over the past 10 years moved to DSGE modelling frameworks, but not all; some retained their conventional macro-econometric models alongside the development of DSGE models (e.g. the central banks of Denmark, the Netherlands, Spain and the USA). It needs to be pointed out that central banks prefer DSGE models due to their basic design centring on cyclicality and the modelling of monetary policy, in turn, being the core business of central banks. The *second trend* is that independent research institutes and finance ministries tend to take a different route by sticking to their conventional macro-econometric models (Hjelm et al. 2015: 9).

The tendency seems to be that institutions (including central banks, international organisations and independent institutes) are moving towards a suite of model approach, employing both DSGE and conventional econometric models, as well as purely statistical models, such as the time series models discussed above (Grobler and Smit 2013b: 2). The combination of forecasts generated may provide an

[8]For a comprehensive treatment of this topic, i.e. surveys on forecasting methods and accuracy in the 1970s and 1980s, see Zarnowitz (1992: 389–413). These findings tend to agree with the results of a global survey of model usage conducted recently by the Swedish National Institute of Economic Research (NIER) (Hjelm et al. 2015). Institutions adopt different models and methods depending on their respective needs, and it is difficult to conclude that one particular method/model is superior all the time.

outcome being closer to an optimal forecast. Either the range of model outcomes are pooled or judgement can be applied as to how the secondary model outcomes may dictate adjustments in the core forecasting model outcome.

The question on which is the preferred core forecasting modelling approach continues to evolve. It appears that the shift away from conventional econometric models is far from complete. Even if we come to this point, it is unlikely to exclusively be DSGE models. The IMF is currently developing what is known as a hybrid option, consisting both of a DSGE component and retaining a conventional macro-econometric equation block per country/region being modelled (see Andrle et al. 2015).[9]

According to Clements and Hendry (2002: 4), of the available range of economic forecasting techniques today, econometric models and time series models seem to be the primary methods applied in the trade. In terms of process, it would appear as if a dual forecasting process, 'top-down' econometric analysis and 'bottom-up' indicator analysis (including anticipation surveys discussed in Part III), provides a clue to what may be deemed an optimal approach to economic forecasting.

In all, there seems to be consensus on adopting a suite of model approach to economic forecasting being the 'binding element', with indicator analysis, (theory-free) time series modelling and pure judgement being essential complementary activities.

3.2 *Economic Forecasting at the BER*

The BER is one of the oldest economic forecasting units in SA. The institute owes its origins to the conducting of business opinion surveys of the SA economy and analysis of the cyclical development of the economy, being part and parcel of the institutes' work from the start in 1944.[10] Dedicated business cycle research remains one of the BER's core departments to this day. Formal forecasting of the economy took longer to germinate, but had developed into the BER's other core department. Below a brief historical overview of economic forecasting at the BER is provided, as well as an outline of the forecasting process and the main lessons drawn over the years.

[9]The IMF is developing a global modelling structure, called the *Flexible System of Global Models (FSGM)*. The model consists of three core modules, each containing 24 blocks for countries and regions. Household consumption and business fixed investment decisions are modelled from micro-economic foundations similar to that in DSGE modelling, but elements such as trade, labour supply and inflation have reduced form representations. The IMF describes each FSGM module as 'an annual, multi-region, general equilibrium model of the global economy combining both micro-founded and reduced-form formulations of various economic sectors' (Andrle et al. 2015: 5).

[10]Prof CGW Schumann, who helped in establishing the BER, published a remarkable book in 1938 on business cycles in South Africa over the period 1806–1936, titled: *Structural Changes and Business Cycles in South Africa, 1806–1936*.

3.2.1 Historical Overview

During the early years of the BER's existence, economic forecasting was an informal process. The aim was to generate useful forward-looking economic information for policy makers and business executives. From the 1960s to 1970s, the forecasting process involved leading minds on the SA economy coming together to discuss, analyse and forecast developments over a 12–18-month time horizon—the results were captured in the BER's publication, *Economic Prospects*. While this approach to economic forecasting may these days be frowned upon, this was pioneering work in the field of forecasting in SA at the time. It should be borne in mind that, internationally, judgement was rated higher as a forecasting method compared to any modelling effort (see Zarnowitz 1992: 402). Furthermore, the BER's suite of business tendency surveys provided valuable forward-looking information, which assisted in informing the participants in this forecasting exercise.

Nonetheless, this 'soft' approach to forecasting to an extent also stimulated econometric modelling work. At more or less the same time, three modelling efforts got underway in SA during the mid- to late 1970s.[11] PDF Strydom and FJ du Plessis developed a macro-econometric model of the SA economy, which was never published (Strydom, PDF 2017); at the central bank of the country, the SA Reserve Bank, De Wet and De Jager developed their version in 1976 (see De Wet and Dreyer 1978), and at one of SA's leading commercial banks, Standard Bank, Shostak also developed an econometric model for the purposes of forecasting the SA economy (see Shostak 1978).

The BER followed suit and in 1977 Frank Briggs was commissioned to visit *Wharton Econometrics* in Philadelphia, USA, with the specific task to develop an econometric forecasting model for the BER. At the time *Wharton Econometrics* possessed a model of the world economy, including a SA block. The intellectual father of Wharton's econometric work was Lawrence Klein. The development of this model also coincided with the BER's appointment of Ben Smit, a previous Director of the BER (from 1998). His academic interest was in the field of econometrics, and he assisted Frank Biggs with the development of the BER's first full quarterly econometric model of the SA economy. Smit also completed a study visit to *Wharton Econometrics* in 1980 (on a study stipendium from the SA *Human Sciences Research Council, HSRC*). The first model forecast was produced in 1981, consisting of both an annual and a quarterly forecast; Smit was involved with the building of the quarterly model, and Briggs originally developed the annual model (1980).

[11]These developments occurred at a time when econometric modelling and a so-called scientific approach to economics came into vogue. For instance, at more or less the same time, Achuthan and Banerji describe in their book (2004: 32–34) how the US National Bureau for Economic Research (NBER) 'veered off its sixty-year path of dedicated business cycle research' labelled by some as 'measurement without theory' by shifting the institutes' focus to a more 'scientific' approach. The roots of this shift lie further back (end of the WWII), with the attack by the mainstream economics community on dedicated business cycle research as being 'unscientific'.

This model was regularly expanded and maintained by BER employees. The next definitive moment in the development of forecasting at the BER was the re-estimation of both the annual and quarterly models using cointegration techniques (see Smit and Pellissier 1997).[12] The model was also adjusted in the late 1990s to calibrate it for the modelling of the impact on the SA economy of the HIV/AIDS epidemic—the BER simulated the effects of the epidemic in its forecasts from the year 2000 onwards (see Smit et al. 2003).

The most recent development in the forecasting approach of the BER has been the expansion of the number of econometric forecasting models. It is the BER's aim to continue developing the suite of models approach. Its current range of models include:

- The full annual and quarterly (structural) econometric models (of the second-generation type in the foregoing discussion) containing around 26 behavioural equations (and more than a hundred identities) defining the structure of each. The model can best be described as a Keynesian expenditure-based model featuring a specific supply-side constraint in the form of a potential output estimate and resultant capacity utilisation measure which serves as a supply constraint impacting on trade (imports), investment, prices and wages (Grobler and Smit 2013a). The BER is currently extending its modelling capabilities into DSGE-type models. However, as noted, one advantage of conventional structural models is that they are usually smaller and can provide a consistent set of forecasts for a broad range of variables, meeting the needs of the BER's clients. DSGE models cannot, with current technology, match the size of structural models. Although a shift away from the conventional semi-structural model as the core tool is not imminent, results from these more micro-founded models will be used in practice to guide adjustments to the standard model.
- The former models are then complemented with attempts at 'now-casting' and 'bottom-up' informal models for projecting inflation and sectoral GDP. Now-casting is defined as the prediction of the present, the near future and/or the recent past. The basic principle is the use of statistical techniques in the exploitation of information published at an earlier date, or at higher frequencies, than the target variable (say GDP) in order to obtain an 'early estimate' before the official figure becomes available (Banbura et al. 2013). The BER has developed such a now-casting framework for the SA economy based on work by Matheson (2011) and Banbura et al. (2013). The model is used to track economic activity in real time and serves as input into internal discussions on the current state of the economy, as well as informing the forecasting process. The now-cast in effect provides a 'starting point' for the forecast, after which the standard forecasting models are used to forecast the medium term.

[12]The application of cointegration techniques was initially done using a two-step Engle-Granger method, but later refined by Linette Ellis and Ben Smit (after the publication of the Bank of England's Macro-econometric Model in 1999) using one-step, or so-called autoregressive distributed lag (ARDL) cointegration techniques.

The BER is constantly developing its forecasting armature in synch with international best practice. According to Prof Smit, leading this process, the future of macro-econometric model based forecasting is probably linked to the so-called DSGE (dynamic stochastic general equilibrium) models and the forward-looking semi-structural models—see the modelling approaches of the Swedish Riksbank, the Fed's Sigma model of the USA, the Fed's FRB/US model and the Bank of Canada's LENS model (BER 2015a).

3.2.2 The Forecasting Process

The foregoing provides some background on the historical development of the BER's econometric modelling experience. However, the actual forecasting process involves a wider range of activities. The BER is known for the energy that is puts into its forecasting process. The following activities form part of the BER's economic forecasting process:

- First and foremost is the BER's suite of business opinion surveys (discussed in the chapter "South Africa: The BER's Business Tendency Surveys", Part III). This information provides a comprehensive overview of the current sectoral real economic conditions, expectations of the respondents regarding the quarter and year ahead and some sentiment and constraint indicators. The business opinion data is in itself of a forward looking nature and an invaluable input into the forecasting process. The survey results are typically compiled 3 weeks ahead of the quarterly forecasting exercise.
- During the preparation phase, which are critically important in the whole forecasting process, the BER economists conduct thorough desk research and interview key policy makers (at the National Treasury and the SARB, for instance) as well as key business executives and other analysts when possible. Furthermore, the BER economists gain good insight into the prevailing economic conditions from close contact with their clients in the public and private sectors. It is important that the forecast team members interact closely with the economic data in order to gain a good 'feel' for the data itself, the interrelationships, etc.
- The forecasting process commences with a comprehensive discussion—by all economists involved—of the exogenous assumptions feeding into the econometric models. An important part of this exercise is also to revisit previous views on the economy and in what way they remain relevant. The use of a 'now-casting' model is also beneficial in order to see what impact the most recent economic data changes have on the forecast. The activities during the preparation phase and the assumptions' meeting form part of the so-called 'bottom-up' process with the aim of anchoring the forecast in realism.
- Following the 2008–2009 global financial crisis and subsequent Great Recession, the range of assumptions feeding into the models was expanded, allowing for more comprehensive modelling of the transmission of global business cycle influences to the SA economy via both the trade and financial channels. This

entailed a more detailed set of assumptions regarding the commodity sector as well as the financial sector. Other important assumptions feeding into the econometric models include additional international assumptions (on growth, inflation, interest rates and exchange rates), net capital flows, public sector fixed investment, fiscal assumptions (government consumption, tax rates and ratios as well as government social transfers to households), employment, domestic interest rates, the rand exchange rates, etc.

- The responsible economist motivates his or her assumptions, and the rest of the team has to agree before they are accepted into the econometric models. Once the assumptions have been finalised, i.e. the projected values for the exogenous variables in the models, they are then fed into the model and a first model run is simulated, including the application of add factors (i.e. statistical error terms that are used to incorporate expert judgement into the forecasting process). Some of the assumptions can also be treated as endogenous variables in the model, i.e. they have specified equations and can form part of the model output. The BER uses this feature to test the coherency of key assumptions such as the rand exchange rate, domestic interest rates and employment.
- Various out-of-model single-equation simulations are also conducted in order to evaluate the model output. The BER also conducts a comprehensive and detailed 'bottom-up' forecast of the inflation rates (CPI, PPI and core inflation), which are used to corroborate and/or adjust the modelling outcomes. A sectoral 'bottom-up' exercise is also done for GDP growth and compared with the demand-side outcome of the econometric model. Once the first model run is complete, an iterative process follows where the forecasting team assesses the model run and makes adjustments where necessary. Usually two to three iterations are necessary before the forecast is finalised.
- The BER has a quarterly forecasting exercise—in January, April, July and October of each year during which the quarterly model is used to generate a 2-year quarter-by-quarter forecast, as well as a 6-year forecast. Generally, particularly the financial variables such as the interest and the exchange rate forecasts are updated on a monthly and ongoing basis.

Forecast Accuracy The BER conducts accuracy analysis of its forecast from time to time (see Laubscher 1992; Van Walbeeck and Sessions 2007; Van der Wath 2013). These analyses confirm a general finding with forecasting, namely, that accuracy is greatest over the near term, say one or two quarters or a year ahead. In the most recent forecast accuracy analysis referred to above, the BER performed well in comparison with a local consensus forecast over the first 2 years of the forecasting horizon (Van der Wath 2013: 13). However, the analysis shows that of all the forecasters considered (BER, SA National Treasury, IMF and Sake24 consensus of 20 local economists), the 'big' changes in direction (e.g. the Great Recession in 2009 and currency-induced spikes in inflation and interest rates in 2002 and 2009) were generally not anticipated more than 1 year in advance.

As discussed, the indicator approach provides fertile ground in addressing the weakness in econometric modelling (including time series modelling) in the prediction of business cycle turning points. As noted in the chapter "Alternative Cycle Indicators for the South African Business Cycle", Part IV, in 2014, the BER designed a recession-dating algorithm, which performed well in accurately indicating business cycle turning points over the period 1980–2013 before they were officially announced by the SARB (Laubscher 2014). Given its wealth of business opinion survey indicators, the BER is well-positioned to develop its indicator approach.

3.2.3 Key Economic Forecasting Lessons

The question on what is a good or successful forecast is not entirely straightforward. Issues of bias, rationality, variance and how well the available information is used are all at stake. However, refraining from becoming too technical on the subject, it is worthwhile to consider some basic lessons drawn from experience with economic forecasting at the BER.

- *Firstly*, while most analyses of the accuracy (or efficiency) of economic forecasting focus on the comparison of point estimates with actual outcomes, there is another dimension often omitted from these analyses. This dimension is best captured in the quote by John Maynard Keynes: '... it is better to be broadly right, than to be precisely wrong'. The implication is that one should remain very humble in how accurate one can be with point forecast estimates. In the same vein, users of economic forecasts should not overestimate economists' abilities in this regard; they are bound to be disappointed. Clements and Hendry suggest: '... forecasters are squeezed between wanting accurate and precise forecasts, yet not claiming so much precision that they regularly fail' (2002: 5). *However, getting the broad picture right is doable.* It is really in getting the bigger picture right that companies, policy makers and other users find value in forecasting.
- *Secondly*, sound interaction between science and evidence is a sure recipe for greater success. The combination of *top-down economic analysis and econometric modelling* and *bottom-up (empirical) research and forecasting methods* appears to be an optimum approach to forecasting. This combination ensures both theoretical rigour and realism. At the BER this approach consists—on the one hand—of the maintenance and simulation of more than one forecasting model, complementing—on the other hand—the dedicated business cycle and other economic research conducted by the BER economists, including the BER's suite of business opinion surveys.
- *Thirdly*, sound judgement, combined with the internal consistency gained with econometric modelling, is a tested formula of good practice in economic forecasting. Econometric techniques and modelling provide the forecaster with the discipline of remaining consistent and the ability to distil huge volumes of data. The use of econometric models ensures consistency and internal cohesion of forecasts and as such tends to eliminate unnecessary mistakes. Judgemental reasoning, or more bluntly so-called gut feel, which really only develops with

experience, is critical in finalising any forecast given the structural changes, out-of-model developments and other influences. It is not a matter of choosing between judgemental reasoning and econometric modelling. The latter may fit the historical reality perfectly; however, due to exogenous factors, the assumptions, on which the projection is based, may change. In these circumstances, an experienced individual may fare better in forecasting (Smit, Director of the BER, quoted in Bisseker 2013: 42).
- *Fourthly*, these days it is almost impossible to present a forecast without outlining the *risks contained in the outlook* and—better even—by presenting *alternative scenarios*. In a world where the exogenous assumptions (reflecting the policy environment, for instance) are often subject to short-term change, more than one picture has to be offered in order to allow companies, policy makers and other users in having a plan B should the conditions for plan A fail to materialise. Here again, the econometric model as an economic forecasting tool is invaluable.
- *Finally, a team works better than a one-man show*. As in most life matters, the old adage, *two (or more!) heads are better than one*, is very applicable in the practice of economic forecasting. Views get challenged in a team environment and ultimately more rigour is generated. Furthermore, the more dedication, energy and experience put into a forecast, the better the result is likely to be.

4 Concluding Remarks

The SA economy seems to be a case study of a country whose business cycle has been shaped by both discrete structural change (and exogenous shocks) and its inherent regularity (i.e. endogenous cyclical forces). Being a small and open economy, the SA business cycle is sensitive to global influences, via both the trade and financial channels. Often non-economic factors gave rise to the so-called 'stop-go' business cycles of the 1970s and 1980s (and first half of the 1990s). However, through all these tumultuous times a certain export and fixed investment-centred business cycle momentum persisted, exerting itself more fully during the 1990s in response to the political change and macro-economic policy improvements.

Unfortunately, SA's longest post-war business cycle expansion was aborted due to the impact of the Great Recession in 2009 and its aftermath. This latter-mentioned period of unconventional monetary policies in the major advanced economies has witnessed heightened financial volatility, lacklustre export growth (with SA faring worse than its peers), poor business confidence and a flat fixed investment trend, producing real economic growth around an 1.6% annual tempo (2012–2016). Suffice to note that the two post-apartheid recessions (1997–1999 and 2009) have been relatively mild affairs and the two expansion phases (1999–2007 and 2009–2013) exceptionally long in a historical context.

While the discrete structural changes and exogenous shocks render economic forecasting hazardous, this does not imply the endogenous regularity of the business cycle has been suspended. Economic forecasters have little option, but to continue applying their trade. According to Clements and Hendry, pondering the future of economic forecasting, econometric models 'provide the best long-run hope for successful forecasting'; however, they do add the proviso that suitable methods need to be developed in order to improve models' robustness to unanticipated structural breaks (2002: 11). Forecasters need to continuously think about structural changes in the economy and their influence on the forecast. This may be even more so in SA. In this regard, the indicator approach to economic forecasting can compensate for the weakness in econometric modelling (and time series models) in predicting business cycle turning points. While the economic forecaster needs to tread carefully beyond a forecast horizon of more than 1 year, sound interaction between science and evidence in the forecasting process, good judgement combined with sound econometric modelling, teamwork and the contemplation of alternative scenarios are all elements of value addition in economic forecasting. Provided these elements, the demand for economic forecasting services is likely to continue to grow.

References

Achuthan L, Banerji A (2004) Beating the business cycle: how to predict and profit from turning points in the economy. Currency Doubleday, New York

Andrle M, Blagrave P, Espaillat P, Honjo K, Hunt B, Kortelainen M, Lalonde R, Laxton D, Mavroeidi E, Muir D, Marsula S, Snudden S (2015) The flexible system of global models – FSGM. IMF working paper, WP/15/64, March 2015

Banbura M, Giannone D, Modugno M, Reichlin L (2013) Now-casting and the real-time data flow. ECB working paper series no. 1564

Barr G, Kantor B (2002) The South African economy and its asset markets – an integrated approach. University of Cape Town, Rondebosch

Basu S, Taylor AM (1999) Business cycles in international historical perspective. J Econ Perspect 13(2):45–68

Bisseker C (2013) The fine art of forecasting. Financial Mail, 17 May

Bureau for Economic Research (BER) (2015a) Personal interview with Ben Smit (Director), 9 June

Bureau for Economic Research (BER) (2015b) Personal interview with Christelle Grobler (Senior Economist), 18 June

Burns AF, Mitchell WC (1946) Measuring business cycles. National Bureau of Economic Research (NBER), New York

Calvo G, Arias EF, Reinhart C, Talvi E (2001) The growth-interest-rate cycle in the United States and its consequences for emerging markets. In: Paper delivered at the annual meetings of the board of governors, Inter-American Development Bank and Inter-American Investment Corporation, Santiago de Chile, 18 Mar 2001

Chen J, Mancini-Griffoli T, Sahay R (2014) Spillovers form United States monetary policy on emerging markets: different this time? IMF Working Paper, WP/14/240

Clements MP, Hendry DF (2002) A companion to economic forecasting. Blackwell, Oxford

De Vries AJM (1994) The South African economy, 1944–1994, Memorial volume of the bureau for economic research. US Printers, Stellenbosch

De Wet G, Dreyer J (1978) A quarterly econometric model of the South African economy (and a simulation exercise on the price effect of the 1975 devaluation). J Stud Econ Econ 2:19–51

Du Plessis S (2004) Reconsidering the business cycle and stabilization policies in South Africa. Stellenbosch economic working paper no 10, Department of Economics, University of Stellenbosch

Du Plessis SA (2006) Business cycles in emerging market economies: a new view of the stylised facts. Stellenbosch working papers 2/2006. Bureau for Economic Research and Department of Economics, University of Stellenbosch

Du Plessis S, Smit BW (2002) Stretching the South-African business cycle. Paper delivered at the 7th annual conference on econometric modelling for Africa, Kruger National Park, July 2002

Du Plessis S, Smit BW (2005) Economic growth in South Africa since 1994. Paper delivered at the conference, economic policy under democracy: a ten year review, Stellenbosch, 28–29 October

Fukač M, Pagan A (2009) Structural macro-econometric modelling in a policy environment, Reserve Bank of New Zealand discussion paper DP2009/16

Grobler C, Smit BW (2013a) The BER annual macro-econometric model of the South African economy. Bureau for Economic Research, unpublished paper

Grobler C, Smit BW (2013b) The BER's annual macroeconometric model: a non-technical description and a practical application illustrating the impact of a sudden halving of foreign capital flows. BER research note 13/No 1, University of Stellenbosch

Hjelm G, Bornevall H, Fromlet P, Nillson J, Stockhammer P, Wiberg M (2015) Appropriate macroeconomic model support for the Ministry of Finance and the National Institute of Economic Research: a pilot study. National Institute of Economic Research, Mar 2015

International Monetary Fund (IMF) (2002) Recessions and recoveries. Chapter 3 in World economic outlook April 2002, Washington, DC

International Monetary Fund (IMF) (2009) How linkages fuel the fire: the transmission of financial stress from advanced to emerging economies. Chapter 4 in world economic outlook April 2009, Washington, DC

Koopmans TC (1947) Measurement without theory. Rev Econ Stat 29(3):161–172

Laubscher, P (1992): The BER's quarterly forecasts: an analysis of its accuracy, 1982–1991, Stud Econ Econ 16(1)

Laubscher, P (2004): The SA business cycle over the 1990s and current prospects. Stud Econ Econ 28(1)

Laubscher P (2014) A new recession-dating algorithm for South Africa. Stellenbosch economic working papers 06/14, June 2014

Laubscher P (2015) A brief history of the US interest rate cycle and international capital flows to SA: any guide to the short to medium-term future? BER research note 15/No 1, University of Stellenbosch, May 2015

Matheson T (2011) New indicators for tracking growth in real time. IMF working paper no. 11/43

McCarthy CL (2015) South African trade policy: what can it achieve given supply-side stumbling blocks. Tralac, Stellenbosch

Mohr PJ (2015) Economics for South African students. Van Schaik Publishers, Pretoria

Mohr P, Rogers C (1994) Macro economics, 3rd edn. Lexicon Publishers, Isando

Moolman E (2003) Predicting turning points in the South African economy. S Afr J Econ Manag Sci 6(2):289–303

Romer C (1999) Changes in business cycles: evidence and explanations. J Econ Perspect 13 (2):23–44

SA Reserve Bank (2015) Quarterly bulletin. http://www.resbank.co.za, Mar 2015

Schumann CGW (1938) Structural changes and business cycles in South Africa, 1806–1936. Wiley, New York

Shostak E (1978) The monetary block of the Standard Bank econometric model: an application of the portfolio approach to monetary analysis in South Africa. J Stud Econ Econ 4:20–50

Smit BW (2006) The South African current account in the context of SA macro-economic policy challenges. Paper delivered at the SA Reserve Bank conference on macro-economic policy challenges for South Africa, Pretoria, 22–24 Oct

Smit BW, Pellissier GM (1997) The BER annual econometric model of the South African economy: a cointegration approach. J Stud Econ Econ 21(1):1–35
Smit BW, Ellis LL, Laubscher P (2003) The macro-economic impact of HIV/Aids in South Africa. Stud Econ Econ 27(2):1–28
Strydom PDF (2017) Personal interview, 21 May
Van der Wath N (2013) Comparing the BER's forecasts. Stellenbosch economic working papers, 23/13, Nov 2013
Van Walbeeck C, Sessions M (2007) A directional analysis of the Bureau for economic research's quarterly forecasts. J Stud Econ Econ 31(3):119–138
Venter JC (2018) A brief history of business cycle measurement in South Africa. In: Smirnov S, Ozyildirim A, Picchetti P (eds) Business cycles in BRICS. Springer, Cham
Zarnowitz V (1992) Business cycles: theory, history, indicators, and forecasting. University of Chicago Press, Chicago

Part V
Concluding Remarks

Measurement, Monitoring, and Forecasting Economic Cycles: BRICS Lessons

Sergey V. Smirnov, Ataman Ozyildirim, and George Kershoff

1 Introduction

Investors and experts currently show less interest in BRICS countries than they did 10–15 years ago when they were considered locomotives of the world economy. Brazil, Russia, and South Africa are struggling to escape from recessions and to overcome stagnation; the trend growth rate of the Chinese economy is declining, and only India has clearly far from exhausted its potential to push up the rate of global growth. Today the steady long-run expansion of the world economy is not as dependent on the outlook for BRICS as on other populous emerging countries in Asia and Africa. However, as all BRICS are strong regional leaders (and some of them are evidently global ones) cyclical movements in both the global economy and regional economies—with all their medium-term fluctuations—are still interdependent to a high degree on dynamics in BRICS countries. For this reason, monitoring business cycles and their economic and socio-political consequences in BRICS is an important and timely issue. Hence, it is important to understand the special features of BRICS economies and to use appropriate analytical tools to track and forecast the trajectory of economic activity.

There are two common approaches to these issues: (a) conducting Business Tendency Surveys (BTS) and (b) constructing composite cyclical indices (CCI). Both instruments were initially created in the USA and some Western European

Support from the Basic Research Program of the National Research University Higher School of Economics is gratefully acknowledged by Sergey Smirnov.

S. V. Smirnov (✉)
National Research University Higher School of Economics, Moscow, Russia
e-mail: svsmirnov@hse.ru

A. Ozyildirim
The Conference Board Inc., New York, NY, USA

G. Kershoff
Bureau for Economic Research (BER), Stellenbosch University, Stellenbosch, South Africa

S. Smirnov et al. (eds.), *Business Cycles in BRICS*, Societies and Political Orders in Transition, https://doi.org/10.1007/978-3-319-90017-9_29

nations. In recent years, they have also been used—or may be used—in emerging or developing economies. In this regard, the practical experience of BRICS countries is highly important because they have had to solve many problems, which are quite difficult for emerging economies but easily solvable or simply non-existing in mature economies.

In this chapter, we summarize what we now know about economic cycles, their measurement, monitoring, and forecasting that we have not known before. In the next section, we discuss some of the most general features specific to emerging economies or economies in transition. In two subsequent sections, we describe some traits of BTSs and CCIs in BRICS countries as their experience may be useful in conducting business surveys or constructing cyclical indicators for other economies. Then we give some concluding remarks.

2 Cyclicality and Other Driving Forces of Economic Activity

One may find a short historical survey of the main theories of economic cycles in Mazzi and Ozyildirim (2017). Several observations are relevant: (a) various concepts of cycles consider a moderate expansion as a normal state of the economy and a recession as a consequence of excessive growth or overheating; (b) from this point of view, cycles may be managed to some extent (e.g., via more efficient inventory control), but perfect foresight is impossible; and (c) hence, some cyclicality or irregularity is an inherent nature of any market economy.

History of BRICS economies demonstrates that in reality many other determinants also matter.[1] Revolutions, wars, and political and social turmoil, onsets of new technologies and stages of industrialization, external trade shocks and foreign debt crises, and market reforms and counterreforms—all these circumstances have changed the patterns of national economic dynamics in BRICS to a great extent. They affected trend, but they also interacted with cyclicality as well. It is difficult to imagine an economic theory which incorporates all these factors. It is also difficult to imagine a statistical base and statistical method which allow us to separate cyclicality per se from the aftermaths of different, multiple, and long-lasting shocks.

Fortunately, insulating the pure cyclicality is not very important in the context of tracking current economic activity and its prediction for several months and quarters ahead. For whatever reasons the activity will change, it is highly intriguing in what direction it will change, and if a recession—with all its problems—is unfolding. Two traditional instruments for dealing with this task successfully applied to BRICS economies are Business Tendency Surveys (BTSs) and composite cyclical indices (CCI).

[1]See "national" chapters in Part II of this book.

3 Business Tendency Surveys and Their Applications

BTS are not standardized/harmonized in BRICS, but they differ due to different legacies and the unique requirements of local conditions. To better track and observe the economic performance and business cycle of BRICS countries in a comparative sense, one has to either harmonize the BTS or select/focus on all the questions and sectors covered in all the countries.

The section on BTS in BRICS shows that there are similarities and differences among the countries.

- Major political changes took place in all the BRICS countries in the beginning and mid-1990s.
- Since the mid-1990s, all the BRICS countries conducted BTS, although South Africa and Brazil started much earlier (in the 1950s and 1960s, respectively, but with a disruption in the 1980s and early 1990s in Brazil).
- Except for India, all the countries cover the manufacturing, retail, wholesale, building, and other services sectors separately. India only covers the manufacturing sector separately but provide for the primary and services sector (i.e., retail, wholesale, and other services) in its whole country survey. South Africa currently does not make the results of its other services survey public.
- Excluding South Africa, the historical time series for the different sectors vary greatly in length. For instance, long series of 22 years are available for manufacturing in Russia (since 1997) but shorter series of only 7 years for trade and building in Brazil (since 2010) and of a mere 5 years for other services in Russia (since 2012).
- The frequency of all surveys is quarterly, except for the manufacturing sector in Russia and of all sectors in Brazil, which are conducted on a monthly basis. South Africa conducts a monthly survey of manufacturing purchasing managers, but this survey differs slightly from the standard BTS surveys.
- Except for India, all countries use partly fixed, partly rotating panels. In India, some producers include all members, while others put together new samples each time.[2] While India and South Africa use stratified, deliberate sampling, Brazil, Russia, and China use stratified, random sampling to put together panels and partially replace some after a number of surveys.
- The sample sizes vary from 2500 to 2800 in India and South Africa, respectively, to 22,500 and 400,000 in Russia and China, respectively.
- The response rate exceeds 90% in the countries where the official statistical agency conducts the survey, and participation is compulsory, such as Russia and China. It is below 50% in India and South Africa, where non-official bodies conduct the surveys, and participation is voluntary.
- Brazil, Russia, and South Africa apply firm and sector weights to individual responses when aggregating the results. China weights responses indirectly

[2]See Kershoff (2018) for details.

through the sampling method to ensure that a higher number of larger firms are selected. No information is publicly available on weighting in India, but it is reasonable to assume that no weights are applied.

- If the selection and wording of questions are compared to the EU's harmonized surveys, then the Brazilian, Russian, and Chinese surveys agree closely. In contrast, there are relatively large differences between the selection and wording of many of the questions in India and South Africa vis-à-vis the EU's harmonized surveys.
- All countries apply the standard transformation of BTS data, namely, calculating net balances, but Brazil and China rescale their data so that it varies between 0 and 200 instead of −100 and +100. Brazil and Russia also produce seasonally adjusted series. South Africa is an exception insofar as its surveys instruct respondents to refer to the same period a year ago, which in effect removes seasonal variations. The surveys of all the other countries refer to the change relative to the period directly preceding the reference period.
- All countries calculate a composite indicator. In Russia, China, and India, the results of selected questions are combined into a single confidence and/or climate indicator. In Brazil, present situations and expectation index are merged into a confidence indicator. In contrast, in South Africa the result of a specific question is used as a confidence indicator.

This analysis shows that the BTSs are far from standardized within the BRICS countries, and they are not harmonized with the EU programme. At present, the long-term potential benefits of harmonization between BRICS are probably outweighed by the costs. Unlike the EU, the BRICS group currently does not have a permanent institution with wide-ranging powers and funding that could spearhead and finance standardized questions additional to country-specific ones, as well as prescribe certain standardized frequency and other methodological requirements. However, overtime harmonization is likely to improve as more countries converge to the "state of the art" spelled out in the handbooks (manuals) on BTS of both the OECD (2003) and UNSD (2015).[3]

In all countries, the results of BTS are regarded as important for the monitoring and forecasting of cyclical developments. Comparisons across countries and regions have become easier, given that with the publication of this book, a single, comprehensive overview of the various BTS approaches and methodologies is now available.

[3]In fact, UNSD and Eurostat with the cooperation of Statistics Canada, the CBS (Statistics Netherlands) and Rosstat organized a series of seminars (held in 2009 and 2010) to discuss these and related issues and initiated projects to document the state of the art.

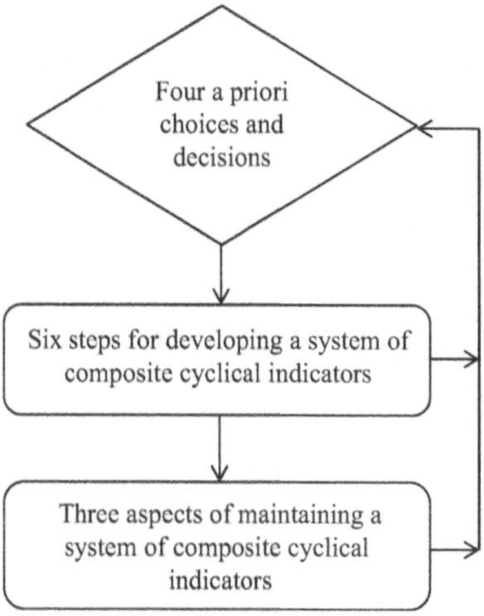

Fig. 1 Challenges in developing a system of cyclical indicators

4 Creating Composite Cyclical Indices

Besides BTSs, another conventional tool for monitoring and forecasting fluctuations in the level of economic activity is composite cyclical indices. In broad strokes, the process of their development was described in Mazzi and Cannata (2017). However, this description focuses only on the experiences of highly developed countries and does not contain sufficient recommendations for emerging countries. BRICS experience allows us to delineate the procedure and to clarify some important details specific to emerging economies and economies in transition.

In general, the entire path to regularly published composite cyclical indices consists of three groups of challenges (see Box 1). The first group comprises of four decisions that ought to be made in the very beginning, even before any practical actions. The second group consists of six practical steps which are inevitable for any attempt to develop a new system of cyclical indicators. The third group includes three exercises related to updating and maintaining an existing system. From time to time, any system of cyclical indicators has to be considerably revised; in such cases, a revision of a priori choices is necessary (see Fig. 1).

4.1 A Priori Choices

The choices are genre setting, producer designation, cycle definition, and approach to dating cyclical turning points. In other words, it should be clarified if the aim of research is a single scientific exercise or a regular public news release. Then it should be decided who (personally) and at whose expense will the job be done. BRICS experience reveals clearly that, typically, a deal begins from a private initiative. Only later, in the case of at least relative success (which means some level of awareness in the media), a government ministry, central bank, large university, or analytical think-tank may take on the responsibility for regular and timely dissemination of updated cyclical indices. As private initiatives are usually plural, the whole process could hardly be centralized. The barriers to entry in the field do exist but they are not insurmountable. Actually, there are several independent sources for composite cyclical indices in every BRICS country.[4]

Box 1. Step by Step Development of a System of Composite Cyclical Indicators

Four a priori choices and decisions

1. Genre setting
   - Single analytical study
   - Regular updating and (public) dissemination of results
2. Producer (and financial resources) designation
   - National statistical office or other government entity
   - Think-tank (university, analytical company, etc.)
   - Single expert
3. Choice of a concept of economic cycles
   - Business cycles (ups and downs in economic activity)
   - Growth cycles (deviations from the long-run trend)
   - Acceleration cycles (ups and downs in growth rates of economic activity)
4. Approach to defining a set of cyclical turning points
   - Usage of estimates produced by national dating committee
   - Setting a single reference series
   - Setting a composite reference series

Six steps to develop a system of cyclical indicators

1. Pre-selection of indicators
   - Developing a (monthly) data base with available statistical indicators
   - Outlier detection
   - Seasonal adjustment
2. Dating of cyclical turning points of the selected cycle concept

(continued)

[4]See "national" chapters in Part IV for details.

Box 1 (continued)

- Adoption of the set of cyclical turning points developed by dating committee (if any)
- Calculation of composite coincident index (if needed)
- Dating of cyclical turning points

3. Timing of indicators
   - Elimination of cyclically insensitive time series
   - Detection of turning points for each indicator considered
4. Sorting cyclically sensitive indicators into coincident, leading, and lagging
5. Calculation of composite indices (this is an iterative step where many alternatives can be tested)
   - Selection of components
   - Weighting of components
6. Description of methodology

Three aspects of maintaining a system of cyclical indicators

1. Presentation and dissemination
   - Set of standard tables and charts
   - Template for expert's judgment
   - Channels for dissemination
2. Monthly updating
   - Data updating and recalculation of composite indices
   - Forecasting with a decision rule or other formal method
   - Final expert's judgment
3. Maintaining and updating
   - (Preliminary) dating of successive turning points
   - Methodological revisions, including new compositions of components
   - Transparency of revisions in methodology

As can be expected, if a researcher decides to construct a system of cyclical indicators he should accurately fix a type of cycles to be investigated: business cycles, growth cycles, or growth rate (i.e., acceleration) cycles. Paradoxically, this simple hypothesis is not confirmed for BRICS. Quite often, the national designation of cycles do not coincide with their conventional definition; or method of calculation of an empirically used composite index do not strictly correspond to the declared type of cycles; or the concept of recession is filled with an unusual content, etc. One may hope that in the future, experts from emerging countries and countries in transition would be more thoughtful in using one or another empirical concept of economic cycles.

Choosing between business cycles (ups and downs in economic activity) and growth cycles (deviations from the trend), experts should firstly ascertain if there is a positive long-run trend in economic activity of their country. They should also grasp what kind of recession (which means a "retreat" in Latin) disturbs national economic agents (public officials, businessmen, households, expert community). If a deceleration of economic growth is enough to cause serious anxiety, then growth or growth rate cycles should be the focus; if only contraction of economy is considered as a trouble, then the concept of classical business cycle should be in the foreground. Different concepts of cycles may also be used in parallel if their distinction is communicated clearly to the users (composite cyclical indices for Brazil, India, and China calculated by The Conference Board illustrates this opportunity).

Finally, an approach to dating cyclical turning points should be pre-decided. If an authoritative dating committee, which consists of competent independent experts, already exists, it is logical to use its set of turning points. In recent years, such dating committees have been established in Brazil and Russia, but they are still absent in other BRICS countries.[5] Establishing such a committee is always an outcome of collective efforts by several experts and organizations; it can never be the first step in developing a system of cyclical indicators. Hence, in most cases, a researcher should pre-decide if he or she wants to use a single reference series (usually, an index of industrial production) or a composite one (having several components). The evident flaw of this approach is that we have to identify an indicator as coincident without any possibility to prove this (as there are no cyclical turning points to compare with, this becomes a major assumption underlying the approach). Anyway, if a dating committee does not exist, the usage of a coincident index is likely the only alternative. BRICS experience shows that a composite index (with several components) is definitely preferred to a single indicator.

4.2 Composite Cyclical Indices: Step by Step Construction

At *the first step*, a database with a possibly broad spectrum of statistical indicators should be developed. The included time series should be:

- Monthly (this frequency is commonly considered as the most appropriate for analyzing cycles)
- Long enough
- Free of omissions and outliers
- Seasonally adjusted (if necessary)
- Deflated (if necessary)

[5]See Picchetti (2018b) and Smirnov (2018).

This step is not an easy task in emerging, and especially in transition economies, because their statistical systems are still in adjustment: methodologies used by national statistical offices are not very stable; regular statistical information produced by private companies is small; and statistical culture and traditions are often poor. Especially in countries in transition, statisticians rarely think in terms of long comparable time series; year-on-year annual indicators are often the focus, while monthly data is considered as rather technical, interim, and then non-interesting. Respectively, official seasonally adjusted time series are quite rare for these countries, and a researcher should do seasonal adjustments himself. In BRICS countries, X-12 ARIMA or Tramo/Seats methods are usually used for this purpose, but some modifications are often needed to deal with carnivals in Brazil, Christmas according to Julian calendar in Russia, Lunar New Year in China, etc. Probably, in other emerging countries, there would be some other uncommon seasonal effects based on national or religious holidays, which have to be controlled.

In practice, developing a database, which is suitable for analyzing economic cycles in emerging economies, is full of compromises. For these countries, it is quite common that outliers or omissions (i.e., missing data) occur too often; seasonal adjustments are evidently not very precise or even fully possible (because of evident discrepancy between monthly year-on-year and chain month-on-month growth rates); some indicators should be extrapolated or interpolated using instrumental variables, etc. In all these cases, an alternative is usually tough: one may include an imperfect indicator with all its imperfect information in their database or may not include and therefore lose all useful information contained in the imperfect indicator. Evidently, the first option is commonly preferred. In BRICS countries, the initial database usually contained more than 100–150 time series to begin an analysis of cyclical fluctuations.

At *the second step*, a set of cyclical turning points should be accepted (if a dating committee produces it) or otherwise estimated on the base of a specifically composed coincident index. The components of such an index are often selected (from the developed database) as analogues to the components of the US monthly composite coincident index calculated by The Conference Board.[6] Indices of output in some main sectors of national economy are broadly used in Russia and South Africa. Sometimes the choice is unconventional: for example, in Brazil, shipments of corrugated paper are used as one of the components.

One way or another, national composite coincident indicator is calculated as a weighted average of previously selected seasonally adjusted components (in most cases, using the weighting scheme designed by The Conference Board or its slight modification).[7] Then the cyclical turning points may easily be defined by the

[6]See https://www.conference-board.org/data/bci/index.cfm?id=2160

[7]See Ozyildirim (2018) for details.

standard Bry-Boschan procedure.[8] Using this internationally accepted procedure delivers credibility, but there may be some pitfalls which may distort precision of the calculations. Therefore, the output of the Bry-Boschan procedure should be always reviewed, and adjusted if necessary, by researchers. The set of components of a composite coincident index, as well as outlier detections and seasonal adjustments may all be inaccurate to an unknown extent.

The core of *the third step* is dating of cyclical turning points for all time series included in the initial base. Preliminary, it is reasonably to eliminate all time series which have no pronounced cyclicality (there is no opportunity to do this before, using seasonal unadjusted time series); graphical analyses are very helpful on this stage. Then the Bry-Boschan procedure may be applied to define sets of turning points for each indicator under investigation.

At *the fourth step*, all indicators are classified as coincident (if their turning points are mostly concurrent with the turning points of a national cycle), leading (if an indicator leads national cycle at its turning points), or lagging (if an indicator lags national cycle). BRICS experience proves that this is not a plain task because many indicators have missed or extra cycles. The leading-lagging structure is also not very stable (an indicator which is leading at one turning point may be coincident or even lagging at the other and vice versa). Special attention should be paid to situations when a central bank tries to prevent a devaluation of the national currency but after a period finds this to be unsuccessful. Deferred devaluation and inflation shocks may distort cyclical pattern and shift estimations of turning points for "real" (inflation-free) indicators. For these reasons, classification of indicators to leading-coincident-lagging groups is a sphere of compromises. In this context, theoretical concepts of interrelations between economic indicators in a national economy are as critical as their estimated leading-lagging structure.

At *the fifth step*, composite leading and lagging indices are aggregated; if the turning points defined by a dating committee are used, then a composite coincident index also may be estimated (otherwise, it has to be estimated at the second step and then used for timing all other indicators). Selection of components for all composite indices is a creative process; some formal procedures may be applied, but they are hardly enough, and some informal considerations are also necessary.[9] In BRICS, the most commonly used leading components are new orders and inventories (often taken from BTSs), various measures of money supply, national stock market indices, interest rates and interest rate spreads, prices and volumes of some kind of export, and real effective exchange rates. There is no "universal" leading component; even the national stock market index (Johannesburg Stock Exchange index) was *excluded* from the SARB's composite leading index during the latest revision in 2015.

At *the sixth step*, a description of the methodology is prepared and published (usually, as a manuscript on the author's personal website or as a working paper of producing organization). Without such documentation of the metadata—which

[8]See Bry and Boschan (1971).

[9]See Campelo et al. (2018).

presents estimates of cyclical turning points, lists of components, and weighting schemes—the methodology behind the indexes remains opaque, and their credibility suffers. Unfortunately, those descriptions of national cyclical indices are not always in English; therefore, they are not always accessible to international users.

4.3 Maintaining a System of Cyclical Composite Indices

If construction of cyclical composite indices is not only an academic exercise but their regular monthly presentation and dissemination are undertaken, then a standard form (set of tables, charts, and expert's comments) should be generated and channels for dissemination defined. Each month all components (time series) should be updated (seasonal adjustments may reiterate annually), composite indices recalculated, and news release—including an analysts' interpretation—revisited. BRICS experience shows that all this becomes feasible if calculations of cyclical indices cease to be an individual project, and some government or private think-tank takes responsibility for it.

Over time, any system of cyclical indicators wears out because of structural and institutional changes in national economy, incomparability of statistical methodologies, and discontinuation of time series used as components. In BRICS, comprehensive revisions of composite cyclical indices usually have taken place each 5–10 years. It is clear that personal initiative is not sufficient for this, and some kind of institutional support is definitely needed. And even in the latter case, comprehensive revisions are usually not well-documented (at least, in BRICS), and actually used indices differ to some extent from those which have been described in the latest versions of published documentation.[10]

5 Concluding Remarks

The beginning and the first half of the 1990s was a milestone for all BRICS countries: after a long period of hyperinflation, the Brazilian economy was stabilized by introducing the real plan; Russia, on the ruins of the USSR, passed through the painful transformation from an isolated planned economy to an open market one; India implemented deep market reforms; China started on a course to pursuing an aggressive export-oriented policy; and South Africa removed the system of apartheid and gained from the lifting of the international sanctions. All the economies became more market oriented, more open, and integrated into the global economy. Their fluctuations begun to be more dependent on market forces, and an interest in

[10]"National" chapters from Part IV of this volume distinctly fill this gap.

statistical and analytical tools for tracing and forecasting the dynamics of economic activity grew significantly.

Business Tendency Surveys (BTSs) have been conducted in all BRICS countries since the mid-1990s. They differ in terms of questionnaires, periodicity, sampling methods, etc. While there are organizational costs discourage the harmonization of BTS in BRICS, the potential benefits of harmonization are not very evident. It is likely that the evident costs will continue to outweigh the non-evident benefits, and national BTSs in BRICS will remain not fully comparable. Even in this case, BTS can aid in monitoring and forecasting regional cyclical developments as long as producers and users of such surveys are aware of the various approaches and methodologies when making comparisons across countries or regions.

As for composite cyclical indices (CCI), it is noteworthy that in several BRICS countries (Russia, India, China), experimental systems of cyclical indicators had appeared before two or three full cycles passed; in some cases only one recession with two bordering expansions had occurred (hence, only two turning points—one peak and one trough—had been available).[11] Strictly speaking, such short histories are not sufficient to establish a reliable system of cyclical indicators but the necessity to have an indicator for tracking economic activity in real-time outweighs (quarterly GDP with its several months publishing lag is usually too late to make adequate policy decisions). Good reputation of composite cyclical indices for the USA and other developed countries prompted researchers to construct them early for emerging countries and countries in transition. Ordinarily it is justified, especially because one way or another, a comprehensive revision always happens. Such systems of cyclical indicators are dynamic: they develop and evolve over time.

In BRICS countries, national systems of cyclical indicators (leading, coincident, and lagging) are all derived from the ideas memorialized in Burns and Mitchell (1946), but owing to their different economic structures, levels of vulnerability to external shocks, roles of the government sector, availability of statistical information, etc. are unique. Moreover, it is worth noting that there is no consensus over the concepts of economic cycles in BRICS. For the most part, Russia uses the concept of business cycles (ups and downs); India and South Africa use the concept of growth cycles (positive and negative deviations from the trend); Brazil uses both of these concepts; and China prefers the concept of growth rate cycles (accelerations and decelerations). This is not only a tribute to national traditions. For example, there is not much sense in analyzing classical business cycles in China as the Chinese economy has been growing continuously for 40 years (but at different rates). Similarly, there is no sense in using the concept of growth or growth rate cycles for Russia, as the Russian economy has no definite positive long-run trend. On the other hand, concern over a slowdown in output in China is comparable to concerns over a fall in output in Russia. This means that unlike system of national accounts

[11]Mazzi and Cannata (2017: 542) advised to use time series covering "at least two or three cycles, i.e., 15–18 years." Developers from emerging and transition countries are often more impatient and narrow this period by a decade to 5–8 years (approximately one cycle and a half).

(SNA), full harmonization of cyclical concepts and indicators between BRICS countries (as well as between other emerging countries) may be impractical and unnecessary.

Furthermore, it is apparent that in BRICS countries, composite cyclical indices are usually estimated, not by National Statistical Offices (NSOs) or other government's agencies but rather by independent national or international think-tanks, universities, or analytical companies. Of course, there are some opposite examples (the composite leading index by Eurasian Economic Commission for Russia, the Business Climate Index by State Information Center in China, the Reserve Bank's leading index in South Africa, and some others), but they are exceptions. This is not by chance. First, in countries in transition (as in Russia or China), a lot of politicians and bureaucrats simply do not believe in the cyclicality of their national economy (this is a remnant of the planning ideology). For this reason, they have no interest in any special cyclical indicators and no desire to spend money on their construction. However, this is not the main reason. The main reason is the NSO's usual lack of responsibility for analyses and forecasting. They have to gather and aggregate statistical information but are not required to analyze the data or draw economic or political conclusions. This is perhaps not surprising, because analyses and forecasting ordinarily include significant components of a subjective or even a political nature, and initial statistical data must be free of such things. As composite leading indices are specifically designed for forecasting cyclical turning points, then they clearly cannot be the NSO's focus. One may also add that NSO definitely prefer to work with standard and fixed methodologies, and there is no such methodology for estimating composite cyclical indices.

Thus, on the one hand, NSOs rarely have forecasting of economic activity among their aims and competencies. On the other hand, construction of composite cyclical indices and especially their regular dissemination, updating and revisions, is a time- and resource-intensive task. Therefore, neither single experts nor governmental agencies seem to be the most probable potential developers of monthly cyclical indices for emerging countries but rather non-governmental think-tanks (probably in cooperation with NSOs). BRICS countries experiences summarized in this book should definitely help them.

As for forecasting economic activity (and especially for predicting turning points) using formal statistical methods, it is necessary to emphasize that this issue is still rather an academic exercise. Picchetti (2018a) and Laubscher (2018) gave good examples for Brazil and South Africa; and other publications on the subject in BRICS may be found in the literature, mostly in national languages. However, in BRICS countries, no producer of composite cyclical indices practices such sophisticated procedures monthly (possibly, because they have to be understandable to all users, most of which are not statisticians). Instead of strict forecasting methods, verbal expert's judgments based on informal "rules of thumb" are widespread. For example, The Conference Board (2001) recommends the so called 3-D (duration—depth—diffusion) rule to recognize a recession. For the USA, it requires (a) the 6-month growth rate (annualized) of the composite leading index to fall below a preselected threshold value (usually depending on some average value of the past negative growth rates of the index) and (b) the 6-month diffusion index (a ratio of growing components) to be lower than 50%. Nonetheless, even though the rule of thumb is widely applicable, all the figures: a preselected threshold (depth), 50% (diffusion), and 6 months (duration) are derived from historical dynamics for the USA and cannot be mechanically applied to any other country. Other "rules of thumb" have also been suggested in economic literature for detecting changes in direction of economic tendencies in real time,[12] but in practice they are rarely used for predictions.

At the same time, almost all regularly published composite cyclical indices are accompanied with an expert's verbal comments that contain a summarizing judgment, which concerns the near term future of the national economy. Perhaps, at least in some countries, those judgments are based not strictly on trajectories of estimated composite cyclical indices but also on some additional information known to an expert and even on his general "pessimism" or "optimism," or his psychological propensity to predict recessions (see Smirnov 2011, 2018). In BRICS and other emerging countries, this effect is almost inevitable, simply because of the deficient statistical data bases (inaccurate information, short time series, etc.). In some cases, publication of the next value of a composite index is only another occasion to highlight some important features of the current economic situation. To use more sophisticated methods, we should do nothing and wait for a sufficiently long-time series. However, there is no serious reason to go this way. The significance of an expert's qualitative judgment concerning future economic trajectory (based on composite cyclical indices) should be fully recognized.

Nevertheless, despite limited theoretical foundations and some methodological complexities and challenges, Business Tendency Surveys (BTS) and composite cyclical indices (CCI) are definitely proven tools for real-time monitoring and predicting changes in national economic activity. These approaches have been used and tested for decades in various countries. And they work!

References

Bry G, Boschan C (1971) Cyclical analysis of economic time series: selected procedures and computer programs, NBER technical working paper no. 20

Burns AF, Mitchell WC (1946) Measuring business cycles. NBER

Campelo A Jr, Ozyildirim A, Sima-Friedman J, Picchetti P, Lima SPM (2018) Coincident and leading indicators for brazilian cycles. In: Smirnov S, Ozyildirim A, Picchetti P (eds) Business cycles in BRICS. Springer, Cham

Kershoff G (2018) Business tendency surveys in India. In: Smirnov S, Ozyildirim A, Picchetti P (eds) Business cycles in BRICS. Springer, Cham

Laubscher P (2018) Forecasting business cycles in South Africa. In: Smirnov S, Ozyildirim A, Picchetti P (eds) Business cycles in BRICS. Springer, Cham

[12]See Smirnov (2011: 10–13) for their survey.

Mazzi GL, Cannata RR (2017) Guidelines for the construction of composite cyclical indicators. In: Mazzi GL, Ozyildirim A (eds) Handbook on cyclical composite indicators for business cycle analysis. Publications Office of the European Union, Luxembourg, pp 533–560

Mazzi GL, Ozyildirim A (2017) Business cycles theories: an historical overview. In: Mazzi GL, Ozyildirim A (eds) Handbook on cyclical composite indicators for business cycle analysis. Publications Office of the European Union, Luxembourg, pp 27–71

OECD (2003) Business tendency surveys: a handbook. http://www.oecd.org/std/leading-indicators/31837055.pdf

Ozyildirim A (2018) Compiling cyclical composite indexes: The Conference Board indicators approach. In: Smirnov S, Ozyildirim A, Picchetti P (eds) Business cycles in BRICS. Springer, Cham

Picchetti P (2018a) A Bayesian approach to predicting cycles using composite indicators. In: Smirnov S, Ozyildirim A, Picchetti P (eds) Business cycles in BRICS. Springer, Cham

Picchetti P (2018b) Brazilian business cycles as characterized by CODACE. In: Smirnov S, Ozyildirim A, Picchetti P (eds) Business cycles in BRICS. Springer, Cham

Smirnov SV (2011) Discerning 'turning points' with cyclical indicators: a few lessons from 'real time' monitoring the 2008–2009 recession. National Research University "Higher School of Economics". Working paper WP2/2011/03

Smirnov SV (2018) A survey of composite leading indices for Russia. In: Smirnov S, Ozyildirim A, Picchetti P (eds) Business cycles in BRICS. Springer, Cham

The Conference Board (2001) Business cycle indicators handbook. New York

UNSD (2015) Handbook on economic tendency surveys. https://unstats.un.org/unsd/nationalaccount/docs/ETS_Handbook_wCover.pdf

The manufacturer's authorised representative in the EU is Springer Nature Customer Service Centre GmbH, Europaplatz 3, 69115 Heidelberg, Germany. If you have any concerns regarding our products, please contact ProductSafety@springernature.com

Printed and bound by CPI Group (UK) Ltd, Croydon, CR0 4YY
30/09/2026
02225235-0012